Lee

*Books on the Confederacy*
*by* CLIFFORD DOWDEY

BUGLES BLOW NO MORE

EXPERIMENT IN REBELLION

THE LAND THEY FOUGHT FOR

DEATH OF A NATION

LEE'S LAST CAMPAIGN

THE SEVEN DAYS

LEE

*Editor with Louis H. Manarin*

THE WARTIME PAPERS OF R. E. LEE

# LEE

## A BIOGRAPHY

BY CLIFFORD DOWDEY

*with photographs and maps*

Skyhorse Publishing

*For my wife, Frances;*
*and to my daughters, Frances Blount and Sarah Bowis,*
*and to the memory of their great-grandfathers,*
*James Monroe Bowis and Michael O'Dowda,*
*who served with Lee*

# Foreword

D R. William Gleason Bean, professor emeritus at Washington and Lee University, was the first academic historian to stress to me the need for a one-volume Lee which would use the extensive new material uncovered in the past twenty-five years in a fresh interpretation. Fundamentally, a fresh interpretation would remove Lee from the delimiting frame of the Civil War and, by placing him in the context of the total history of the Republic, reveal both his "eternal relevance" and the nature of his involvement in the evolutionary stage of nationalism which is still in the process of change. In his reluctant involvement Lee, who was — as one of his chief opponents said — "essentially a peacemaker," became a tragic national figure on a scale far to transcend the four years of actual warfare.

In addition to the new material that has come to light on Lee, since World War II considerable specialized research has been made available on the period from 1850 to 1876. This has been used, or drawn upon, in contemporary studies on the relation of this total period to our times. When *Experiment in Rebellion*, a narrative of the Confederacy's civil leaders, was published in 1946, the late Randolph Adams wrote that the book proved his point that history should be rewritten every twenty-five years. Attitudes change and the writer of history views the past from new perspectives.

Today, for example, Americans have lost their illusions about war as a political resolution and no longer believe a permanent pattern of good will result from mass killings and destruction, spreading ruin and misery. From this current attitude, Lee's contemporaneity can be found in his unchanging disbelief in the efficacy of war and his conviction that civilization would not advance until "reason" and "humanity" were the bases for the settlement of disputes. When sections of the United States showed an inclination to resolve their differences by arms, he wrote, "I shall mourn for my country . . . and for the future of mankind."

Yet, with the perspective of changed attitudes and the availability of new material, I was awed at the prospect of trying to offer any supplement to Douglas Southall Freeman's definitive biography. Having begun work as a reporter on the Richmond *News Leader* when Dr. Freeman very personally combined the jobs of editor and managing editor, I wrote my first signed words for publication (book reviews) under his tutelage, began my first research in history under his guidance, continued with his encouragement and support, and long used his *R. E. Lee* and *Lee's Lieutenants* as guides as well as sources for bibliographical references. And yet, a less comprehensive, less military, less detailed biography *was* needed to present the fresh interpretation. I was decided, finally, by the proportions the new material reached when the George Bolling Lee Collection of more than two hundred personal letters — mostly unseen previously — was acquired by the Virginia Historical Society and made available to me specifically for a Lee biography.

The bulk of these letters were written before the war, many between Lee's thirty-fourth and forty-ninth years (he was fifty-four when war embraced him). In one of Lee's letters from Mexico, he stated that General Scott had requested his services on the commanding general's staff — thus disposing of the long-held belief that it was a myth that Lee was the only junior officer whom Scott personally asked for. The letters to older women of his family, to whom he revealed his most intimate thoughts, contained fresh insights into Lee during periods in his life when no shadow of a divisive war, or any controlling external events, lay in his consciousness.

Prior to this windfall, when I edited *The Wartime Papers of R. E. Lee* with Mr. Louis H. Manarin in 1960, we discovered that on the war period alone available Lee correspondence had grown to more than six thousand items, and new material — prewar as well as war period — was being collected yearly in various repositories. Since then, the Virginia Historical Society has acquired one collection of 557 items of correspondence restricted to a single period in 1861.

Of the prewar and very few postwar letters that are continually appearing, significant personal letters have been published in the *Huntington Library Quarterly* and by the Missouri Historical Society. The Huntington letters, written to his wife during the first years of marriage, show Lee as a young lieutenant outraged at the long absences of his lady from her husband. The Missouri Historical Society letters were written to a confidant, Henry Kayser (who had been Lee's assistant engineer during his work on the Mississippi River at St. Louis), and they reveal some of his personal attitudes with a frankness seldom found in Lee's correspondence.

The importance of all the recently uncovered personal and mostly prewar letters, in juxtaposition to the considerable volume of personal letters already available, has been to emphasize the human aspects of — as they said — "a Christian gentleman" whose fate it was to personify not only a society that was destroyed but an Old America of "the federated republic" that was doomed. Of this Old America as reflected through his Virginia environment, Lee towered above all others as the single most perfected product. Indeed, it was the suggestion of a total perfection that has tended to dim Lee with a certain remoteness. Even the die-hard "Unionists" who renounce Lee as a "traitor" tend to place his villainy in the abstract.

But with contemporary perspectives, sharpened by clinical psychology and philosophical theology, Lee's appearance of "perfection" can be understood in very modern terms. E. R. Keyes, a fellow cadet at West Point and, later, a Federal general who opposed Lee, explained the young Lee's "completeness" in terms of his lack of any feelings of "inferiority" (Keyes's word) — or, as we would say, the absence of unresolved inner conflicts. He grew in organic wholeness, as a work of art is whole. As if he were a work of art, Lee created himself — in an image implanted by his mother and on a monumental design of moral concepts. Nothing of his life-potentialities was wasted or negated. He acted in accordance with his belief that in God all good would be affirmed in God's time. With this eternal view of life, Lee also met the modern precept of being "ultimately concerned," though he would have said that to do God's will was his constant concern.

Once Lee is viewed as a simple man, whose character grew in proportion to his commitment to the life-task he felt God had assigned him, he becomes explainable and very human. He assumes heroic stature because he was a product of an age in which men and women held heroic concepts of life and its meaning. To that extent, he is a product of the past, but a past which is available as an American heritage. Belonging to his own day, embodying the chivalric attitudes of his age and place, Lee's timeless view of timeless values — sustained through all the grief and anxiety and traumatic dislocation endured by him and his people — gives him a particular relevance today.

Though this nondefinitive biography is presented without footnotes, I do not consider that it is presented without — what is called — "documentation." Footnotes largely serve scholars seeking sources for their own use. No reader, while reading a thousand-page book, is going to stop to go digging into the *Official Records* to behold the reproduction of the form from the Adjutant General's office which ordered a certain brigade to move on a certain date, nor to old almanacs to confirm the minute the sun rose nor to old newspapers to read the weather report. Any general reader interested in discovering background sources he would like to pursue in a particular area should experience no difficulty in locating the references in the bibliography. These references should also provide any knowledgeable scholar with the sources that substantiate the context.

In the bibliography, no remote attempt has been made to list every book, article, pamphlet, letter, diary and so on that has been read over the past thirty-odd years. The references are restricted to those that were drawn upon for the subject of this particular book and not its general background. The references list other books of mine, whose bibliographies relate to other aspects — some more specialized, some more generalized — of the period here covered. Countless books on subjects that were useful in writing this book would be inappropriate in its bibliography. These subjects would include social and political history, psychology and theology, memoirs and biographies, along with dialetical books and essays. But everything specifically relating to R. E. Lee that was used has been listed.

The material most used, always used when possible, was his correspondence, personal and official. In the text it is usually stated when Lee's decisions or attitudes of mind were drawn from correspondence and the name of the recipient is given. Thus, in the bibliography, a single reference to a collection of letters could contain "documentation" for fifteen years of Lee's life. In summary, the bibliography has been kept as brief as possible, but I believe it serves the purpose of providing readers with the basic sources.

# Contents

# List of Maps

# Illustrations

# PART ONE

# The Son

CHAPTER 1

## "An Event that Promises the Most Auspicious
## Fortune to the Wedded Pair"

THE CARRIAGES had been coming all week, turning off the shadowed river road into the driveway leading to the manor house of
Shirley plantation. The carriages rolled slowly over the drive that
wound between the fields where hands worked, wearing bright-colored
bandannas against the hot June sun. There was nothing of the landscaped
park of the English models on the flat plantation land, stretching to the
horizon on east and west. Stands of field pines grew on acres worn out by
tobacco, and primal forests, the trees draped by vines and creepers of
vivid green, skirted meadows where beef cattle and riding horses grazed.
Outbuildings were scattered in groups, like villages, bustling with the
movement of artisans.

After a final tilting turn, beyond the last of the countless fences, the
carriages approached the formal area of Shirley. High two-story red-brick
buildings formed an avenue of dependencies — kitchen, schoolhouse,
laundry, quarters of house servants and such — at the head of which rose
the graceful red-brick Georgian manor house against the background
of the James River. The broad tidal river, close to the house, formed
part of the pattern of shaded lawns, of old trees and shrubs and rose garden,
and lacy white clematis on the vines bordering the shore.

The passengers, hot and tired and dusty, climbed stiffly from the carriages in front of the stone portico of Charles Carter's house. There were
no formalities about being received. Guests already in residence swarmed
about, carrying cold toddies, and every new arrival had known everyone
else there all his life and was kin to half of them. By the end of the week,
the guests were sleeping five or six in a room, including the guestrooms on
the second floors of the dependencies. Nobody minded the crowding.
They had all grown up on Virginia plantations where two dozen house-
guests were no novelty. Besides, the wedding at Charles Carter's Shirley in
1793 was the nearest to a royal occasion that could be provided in the
nation newly formed from the thirteen colonies.

The bridegroom, thirty-seven-year-old Henry Lee, was governor of the largest, most powerful state in the four-year-old republic, and Ann Hill Carter the daughter of the richest planter. The Carters and the Lees had held dominant positions in Virginia's ruling class since the 1640's, and this June wedding was the first time the two great families had joined in marriage.

Shirley plantation, built on land patented in 1610, was one of the dynastic baronies occupied by the children and grandchildren of the magnificent Robert Carter, the one called "King." In this ordered, regulated domain, timeless and unchanging, twenty-year-old Ann Hill Carter had never encountered anything quite so romantic as "Light-Horse Harry" Lee, and one look into her eyes showed that she loved him totally.

He was, as they said, a "gallant figure." Famous during the Revolution as chief of cavalry in the Southern campaigns and (as was said by a non-admirer) "a man of splendid talents," the young governor reflected vitality in every move and in the boldness of his gaze. His eyes were clear blue, prominent in an oval-shaped face of high coloring, and, though grown a little fleshy, he was a handsome man. His light brown hair, worn fashionably long, was queued at the back of a strong neck. He stood above middle height and had a flair for bright colors and styles that set off his finely proportioned build. Possibly the vital force he suggested had been an element in attracting the heiress.

Ann Hill Carter was a contrast to Light-Horse Harry Lee in every way. She was most often called "lovely." She was a slight girl of medium height and quite dark in hair and coloring, with fine brown eyes. Her soft face, rather intense, was characterized by a gentleness of expression. All her life people were drawn to her by her happy heart and a sweetness of nature which suggested a quiet inner strength. There was a serenity about Ann Hill reflecting the tranquillity of Shirley, which, of all the river plantations, most held a quality of warm and intimate repose.

As the hour for her wedding approached, the guests began to gather in the great hall. At Shirley, instead of the wide central hall typical of Georgian houses, the hall was a magnificently paneled great room featuring a famous "flying staircase" — it ascended without visible supports. From the great hall the guests flowed back and forth into the dining room, where punch was served from a sideboard and the table was spread with a variety of dishes.

At the wedding hour the guests — resplendent in white brocade and tulle, silk and satin, crepe and lace — gathered in the large, oblong parlor and in the doorways leading into it from dining room and great hall. In the paneled parlor, an altar was decorated with flowers. From the raised windows, looking across the lawn to the river, fragrant movements of air stirred through the room. The rector read the ceremony from the Book of Common Prayer, the Church of England Prayer Book revised for the Episcopal Church which succeeded the Mother Church after the Revolution. When Ann Hill Carter, of "beauty and fortune," as a friend described her, and "Virginia's favorite young soldier," as a newspaper described the bridegroom, were pronounced man and wife, nearly everyone at the ceremony would have agreed with the correspondent of the Richmond newspaper who wrote that the wedding of the heiress and the hero "must give the highest satisfaction to their numerous . . . relatives."

The one person at the wedding who did not agree was the bride's sixty-year-old father, grandson of King Carter.

## 2

To Charles Carter, plantation master of vast holdings, the manor house at Shirley was one of the seats of empire of Virginia's ruling oligarchy. For the rule of the planter elite was not changed by the shift of Virginia's political status from a British colony first to an independent commonwealth and then to a commonwealth in the new federated republic. The aristocratic principle on which the colony had operated extended into the state structure, and the society became in no sense democratic. As Carters and Lees had sat on the august King's Council when the planter oligarchy was forming in the 1640's, so had Carters and Lees a century later led in the General Assembly during the action that built to the break with England; and so after the Revolution Carters and Lees gathered with uncles and cousins and in-laws, lifelong friends and personal enemies, to share in the shaping of a new nation — with their brothers and in-laws and friends in positions of power.

There seemed to be no clear reason why the Carters and the Lees had not intermarried before the wedding at Shirley. Typical of the custom among dynastic plantation families, Carters had married among Carters and Lees among Lees; they had married neighbors and family friends, brothers of stepmothers and sisters of in-laws, until each family tree was entangled with cross-kin and crosslines. As every person who was kin by marriage was called "Uncle" or "Sister" or "Cousin," just as if blood kin, it would have been difficult for the Carters and Lees to know precisely who was a Carter or a Lee — except for a certainty no Carter was part Lee and no Lee part Carter.

This separateness of the families had begun in the early days when two of the titans had locked horns over property, the most common cause of clashes in Virginia. In a society founded upon land, property was the source of wealth as well as representing the idea of the "estate" of the landed gentry in the English pattern which Virginia adopted, and by the early eighteenth century no holdings in Virginia could seriously rival those of King Carter. Though the Lees possessed extensive holdings, King Carter was perhaps the richest man on the Continent, and financed his sons and daughters in the building of great plantation manor houses on a scale unapproached by any other family.

The Carters originally settled in Northern Neck, the strip of land between the Potomac and the Rappahannock, and in that region the sons of King Carter were established at Nomoni Hall, Sabine Hall and Corotoman. In Gloucester, on the northern bank of the York River, his daughter Judith and her husband Mann Page erected Rosewell, the most magnificent house until that time in English-speaking America, with masonry that was never surpassed. (This was the only Carter branch that ever ran out of money: the grandeur of Rosewell impoverished later generations of Pages.) But it was on the James River that the plantation mansions of the King's descendants formed a private Carter domain in the region of the original settlement at Jamestown.

Shirley had been built by son John and his wife Elizabeth Hill, whose family had originally owned the property. Their son Charles also owned Corotoman, and had moved to Shirley shortly after the birth of Ann Hill Carter in 1773.

Next to Shirley was Berkeley, built by King Carter's daughter Anne and her husband, Benjamin Harrison V, on land settled in 1619. Benjamin Harrison, Charles Carter's uncle by marriage, had been a political power before and during the Revolution (a signer of the Declaration of Independence) and served as governor of the independent commonwealth after the Revolution. The manor houses at Berkeley and Shirley had both been built around 1725.

Next to Berkeley was the classically beautiful Georgian mansion of Westover. This was built by the elegant and learned grandee William Byrd, whose son, William Byrd III, married Charles Carter's sister Elizabeth. Farther east, on the other side of the ruins of Jamestown, Carter's Grove was owned by the King's grandson Carter Burwell, first cousin of Charles Carter.

From this Carter demesne, and similar Tidewater strongholds, had come the conservatives who opposed the break with England. They had nothing to gain by severing ties with the mother country and many lost irreparably. However, once Virginia was committed by her revolutionaries to independence, the Old Line served as leaders and gave everything they had to give — time, brains, energy, money and, for some, life itself. Some of these families never recovered from the drain of the Revolution, when plantation masters were absent as long as eight years.

Then again, at the formation of the Republic, the Tidewater grandees opposed Virginia's ratification of the Constitution. Their fears were expressed by Benjamin Harrison when he was governor: he wrote his intimate friend George Washington that "the seeds of civil discord" were planted in the Constitution and he foresaw a time when the states south of the Potomac would become "mere appendages" to the commercial-minded Northern states.

On both stands, the Lees were among the pro-Revolution and pro-Constitution leaders. Harry Lee had been too young for the political action that preceded the war. During that phase the family was represented in the General Assembly by "harmonious" Richard Henry Lee, and in England by Arthur and William Lee, two of the Colonies' most successful revolutionary agents. Richard Henry Lee, a friend and co-worker of John Adams, was a power in the Colonies' confederated revolutionary movement and in the Continental Congress.

It was after the war — from which he emerged a Continental hero with the sobriquet of Light-Horse Harry — that the younger Lee assumed his place in the General Assembly as an advocate of ratification of the Constitution. Intimately connected through friendship with President George Washington and many of the state's political leaders, by the time the General Assembly elected him governor Lee was regarded by his friends as a presidential possibility.

The different political attitude of the revolutionary Lees and the conservative Carters seemed not in itself a significant factor in previously keeping the families from intermarrying. The fact was that the Lee men were very good marriers as a rule and frequently improved their estates through wives. As the Carter men could scarcely improve their estates by marriage, they held an uncanny record in marrying women who were in themselves superior, while the Carter girls were not encouraged to make marriages with men who would find the family fortunes helpful. Charles Carter's sisters and aunts had married into families of substance in the Harrisons, Byrds, Pages and Burwells, and such was his plan for his own daughters — particularly Ann Hill, the pet of his later years.

It happened that the English tobacco market fell off drastically after the Revolution, and planters whose money crop was tobacco were hard hit. On the James River wood was rotting in the planters' wharves where tobacco had been shipped to and luxuries imported from London. Shipping centers were becoming ghost towns. Many of the younger princelings, such as Charles Carter's Byrd and Harrison kinsmen, went under. Having known in their lifetimes only imperious ease, to them the tales of the harsh adaptiveness required to carve private baronies out of the wilderness belonged with the folklore of another era. Charles Carter was not among them. He turned successfully to wheat. But Light-Horse Harry Lee was very much a representative of the generation of the squanderers, and he had already gone through the fortune of one wife.

Thus it was when the two great families were at last joined, the bride's father looked with disfavor on her choice as financially unsound. Indeed, as Charles Carter viewed the hero-governor, he could well have seemed — with all his colorful talents and promising future — an unsound man.

### 3

All the Lees in Virginia derived from the great Richard Lee I, called "The Emigrant," who planted in the Northern Neck in 1641. He was entitled to the generic arms of Lee of Shropshire, a line descended from a twelfth-century Norman, Reyner de Lega, or de Le'. The first Richard apparently had some training in law before coming to Virginia, as he became clerk of the Quarter Court at twenty-seven, and three years later was appointed attorney general of the colony. At the age of thirty-six, Richard Lee rose to the powerful post of secretary of state and was intimately associated with the British royal governor, the worldly dilettante Sir William Berkeley.

This first Lee was truly an empire builder. Landowner and planter, shipowner and merchant, he managed vast enterprises with great capabilities, and was one of the founders of the Virginia colony on an aristocratic structure. Beginning with him, when a family triumphantly emerged from the struggle with the Indian-infested wilderness, the plantation master himself served in the General Assembly. This was the oldest legislative body of representative government in the New World, formed in 1619, and through it the planters formed a habit of assuming personal responsibility for the colony's operation. On the bases of county courts and Church of England vestries, interlocking planter families formed a political oligarchy that continued unbroken from generation to generation.

With Richard Lee's grandchildren, the family branched into two major lines — the Lees of Stratford Hall and the Lees of Leesylvania. For two generations the Stratford Hall line, sired by the dynamic Thomas Lee, was the more distinguished. From this branch came the famous statesmen of the Revolution, including two signers of the Declaration of Independence.

Light-Horse Harry Lee, born in 1756, descended from the Leesylvania line, which had been more prosaic until vitalized by Harry Lee's mother, Lucy Grymes. The celebrated "lowland beauty" of her day, she had, according to legend, at the age of fifteen turned down the proposal of a lovesick George Washington. Harry's father, like his grandfather, was a capable manager of his inherited estate, but the best his friends could say about the rather dull man was that he was pleasant-featured and agreeable. With Lucy Grymes's spark, the Leesylvania branch suddenly blossomed.

Among Harry's brothers, Charles Lee became an outstanding lawyer and was soon to be appointed to Washington's Cabinet as attorney general;

Richard Bland Lee, a successful planter and prominent Federalist politician, completed the behind-the-scenes maneuver that was to place the nation's capital on the Potomac. The brightest star was Light-Horse Harry, who had displayed a fine gift for life even before the war gave him the opportunity for fame.

He entered Princeton before he was fifteen and, while cutting a figure socially, the precocious young man showed a facile taste for scholarship. Never losing a love of learning, Harry Lee retained his familiarity with Latin poets and historians and was himself a talented phrasemaker. At Princeton he formed a lasting friendship with a fellow Virginian, James Madison, whose agile mind would advance him politically while Lee was winning glory in the field.

It had been his intention to study for the law in London, but the tension between the Colonies and England caused him to remain at home. For a couple of years on his father's Leesylvania plantation, the handsomely developed young man, still under twenty, passed the days pleasantly as a Colonial version of an English gallant. For the first time he experienced the lavish bounty of a Carter household at Robert Carter's Nomoni Hall. Philip Fithian, a Princeton acquaintance, was ensconced there as tutor, and he noted the good impression young Harry made on Mr. and Mrs. Carter. While decorating plantation parties all over the countryside, young Lee developed his already strong body with riding and hunting, acquiring — between the dancing and the outdoor exercise — a supple grace of movement.

With the war, Harry Lee found his métier: he was a natural soldier. He enlisted in a regiment of Virginia Light Dragoons raised by his kinsman Theoderick Bland, and contributed substantially (or his father's estate did) to outfitting a troop which he captained. Everything up to that moment seemed to have prepared him for the reconnaissance action performed by the regiment of light-horse cavalry — the men armed only with short sword and horse pistol.

Very brave, vain and showy, his somewhat gaudy uniform topped by a leather helmet with a horsehair plume, Lee gloried in the quick dashes, the danger of tempting the enemy, and the excitement of hand-to-hand combat. He was as skillful as he was colorful, and his recommendation for promotion came personally from the commander in chief. As a friend of his parents, General Washington had known young Lee since he was born and had offered him a post on his own staff.

After successful exploits in the Eastern theater as lieutenant colonel, especially in the bitter months at Valley Forge, Harry Lee realized his full potential when he was transferred to Nathanael Greene's army in the Southern theater. Commanding a superbly mounted force called the Lee Legion, he showed a gift for high strategy as well as hard fighting. Gen-

eral Greene himself attributed to his cavalry chief the strategic plan behind the successful Southern campaign.

For six years of his early manhood Harry Lee knew the completion of
self-expression in a field which won him the applause his nature required.
Suddenly, at the age of twenty-five, it was all over. Peace came, bringing
the tedium of routine army life and no glory.

Against the advice of his staunch friend Greene, Lee resigned from the
army just before his twenty-sixth birthday in 1782. He wanted, he wrote
General Greene, "to make my way easy and comfortable." Harry Lee
found the comfortable way by marrying his cousin, Matilda Lee, the nineteen-year-old mistress of Stratford Hall in Westmoreland County. A
beauty like his mother, she was called "the divine Matilda," and the hero
seemed genuinely to have loved the cousin he had known all her life. With
their marriage the divergent lines from the great Richard Lee I rejoined in
a romantic union, and the son of the Leesylvania line found himself master
of a private empire.

Yet, though his home life was certainly happy, the ex-soldier could not
content himself as the operator of a large plantation. By the time of Harry
Lee's generation, the baronies on which the young princelings had grown
up could appear to be self-operating (except where tobacco had been the
money crop). At Stratford overseers directed the slave labor in field
crops; distant tracts were more or less sublet in a loose approximation of a
tenant-farmer operation, and skilled artisans worked mills and fisheries.

From the rolling fields at Stratford, from the grazing meadows, the pig-
sties and the smokehouses, as if by magic beef and mutton and ham, flour
and cornmeal appeared in the ivy-covered kitchen building with the seven-
foot-high fireplace. From there house servants served the elaborate meals
in the dining room. These house servants, owned outright as a result of
the enterprise of earlier Lees, kept linens changed and fresh, silver polished, portraits dusted, and fires burning in all the rooms.

It was not that Harry Lee exactly assumed all this would last forever
without attention from the master. The nature of the attention required
bored him. After briefly piddling around as something of a gentleman-
farmer, he began to conceive of financial speculations in land that appealed to him more than speculating on what fields to fallow and which
corn to store in the crib for next winter's sale. As nothing in his nature
suggested acquisitiveness and the Stratford Hall estate stood in no need of
increased revenues, Lee would appear to have turned restlessly to land
speculation, then the equivalent of stock-market speculation, for the excitement, and perhaps to make a spectacular coup as a civilian.

However, he lacked the remotest talent for finance. As a speculator he
was all "Light-Horse Harry," dashing in to the attack. The accumulated
cash at Stratford disappeared and distant tracts of land were sold off as

Lee began to act like a desperate gambler trying to recover his losses. Then, in 1788, he conceived of the one big killing that would make up everything. On paper his greatest project did look good.

George Washington had long been interested in connecting tidewater Virginia with the mountain country by canals, one extending navigation on the James River west from Richmond and one extending navigation on the Potomac (Virginia's border with Maryland) west from Great Falls. An engineer believed the Potomac project feasible, George Washington supported it, and James Madison was interested. But only Harry Lee put up money to buy the land around Great Falls. There he envisioned houses and inns, mills and warehouses emerging from the wilderness to form a city. Had the canal been built then, Lee would have been a rich man. Characteristically he charged in before it was certain that a canal could be built, and it could not at that time.

To complicate the affair, the title was not clear to the five hundred riverside acres, which belonged in the vast Fairfax estate. Lee was enjoined against selling any of the sites — which would have brought him needed cash — until thousands of dollars in back quitrents were paid to the Fairfax estate. Carried along by his desperate dream, he planned to pay off these debts to the Fairfax estate by selling off parts of his wife's property, including twelve hundred valuable acres called Sugar Lands in Loudoun County. This was in 1790, when Matilda Lee lay grievously ill. Fearing for the future of her children after her death, she took the step which could only have been an humiliation to the displaced soldier.

With Harry's brother, Richard Bland Lee, and her sister's husband, Ludwell Lee, Matilda drew up a paper for her husband to sign which placed Stratford Hall and the Sugar Lands in trust to her children. He was then given the rights of occupancy until the oldest son reached his majority, when the property would come to him outright. As only two years before, his own father had named his younger sons as executors of the Leesylvania estate, Harry Lee stood labeled as an incompetent in handling money.

Short of dishonor, nothing could be more damning in the eyes of any Carter, and that was not the worst to the father of Ann Hill.

4

In Charles Carter's eighteenth-century world the ruling elite were supposed to excel in the Aristotelian "virtue," in which character balanced the skills of accomplishment. George Washington, "the good as well as the great," was the model.

A hugely successful planter, a man of great wealth before the Revolution, Washington had shouldered community responsibilities at every stage of his career, from county level to national. When he left his estates for the army, he became a capable soldier, with powers of leadership that enabled him to carry the Revolution by his courage, indomitability and the awesome might of his presence. During the postwar period of the loose confederation of commonwealths, he produced a vision of the republic. Though his self-trained, realistic mind may have lacked subtleties and profundities of pure intellectuality, he possessed the disciplined intelligence, pertinacity and persuasiveness to implement the vision. All this was what he *did*. Supporting all his acts and beyond all his achievements was the man of honor. It was his embodiment of the Aristotelian "virtue," his immalleable principles, that caused Washington's contemporaries to regard him as the arch of the ideal of his time.

No one believed more wholeheartedly in this ideal than Charles Carter. From his grandfather on, the Carters had been characterized by deep religious devotion and community responsibility, and of Charles Carter's widely known generosity it was said, "From the mansion of hospitality his immense wealth flowed like silent streams." By the standards he subscribed to, Light-Horse Harry appeared unstable in those traits required in the complete man of the ruling elite.

Lee's increasing popularity, after his war career, seemed to be caused partly by his vital and colorful personality. He was brilliant socially and wrote charming, literate letters. Then, though no one could question Harry Lee's principles in politics (he was one of the men who would literally die for his convictions), there was something of the dilettante about him rather than the aristocrat seriously assuming community responsibilities. Lee confirmed this impression, to Charles Carter, by revealing a most harebrained impulse.

More or less by hereditary position, Lee had first entered the General Assembly as his county's representative at the age of twenty-nine. He was so well liked by his fellow delegates that they sent him three times to the Confederation Congress in New York and in 1791 elected him to the first of three one-year terms as governor. This was the year following Matilda's death, and in Richmond, Lee's oldest son died. His personal losses seemed to occupy him more than his public post, and he wrote his friend Alexander Hamilton that the two events "removed me far from the happy enjoyment of life."

In all truth, the governor's plain house was a bleak enough place for an undomesticated widower with a five-year-old son and a six-year-old daughter. Richmond itself, a longtime tobacco trading post and frontier outpost, had been the capital only since 1780 and was a city in little more than name. Lacking any of the comforts and pleasures of urban life, the governor's place of residence was a dreary contrast with the splendors of Stratford. The cramped life depressed Lee and the governor's job bored him.

He wrote Madison that he was "never so serene and happy as when I am most uninformed of political objects and measures." Soon he began to look for means of escape.

Harry Lee looked in two directions — a new adventure and wife-hunting. For the first he wrote Lafayette, his friend of Revolutionary days. France was then undergoing its own revolution and embroiled in European wars, and Lee asked what rank would be given him if he went to Paris to offer his services to the French Army. He also wrote Francesco de Miranda, a man influentially connected with the French war department. After a long delay, he heard from Lafayette: the marquis had run afoul of the Jacobins, who had removed him from command and made him a prisoner. From de Miranda he received an oblique assurance that he would be offered a commission as major general when he appeared in person to accept it.

Though power was constantly changing in revolutionary France (as he could see from Lafayette), Lee was inclined to leave Virginia to take the tenuous offer. Before committing himself completely, though he had made preliminary plans, he started for Mount Vernon to ask Washington's advice. Learning on the way that the President had left his plantation for Philadelphia, Lee then wrote the family friend and put the question to him. He gave a simple reason for wishing to go. "Bred to arms, I have always since my domestic calamity wished for a return to my profession as the best resort for my mind in its affliction."

Washington's guarded reply made it clear he was writing personally and not officially. As a friend he pointed out the dangers of serving the army of a country "in the highest paroxysms of disorder . . . those in whose hands the government is entrusted are ready to tear each other to pieces and will more than probably prove the worst foes the country has." Then, typically, he referred to the factor of responsibility to office. If he were in Lee's place, he wrote, "I should ponder well before I resolved, not only for private considerations but on public grounds. The latter because, being the first magistrate of a respectable state, much speculation would be excited by such a measure."

Concurrent with developing his foreign service dream and before he received Washington's letter, Lee had been escaping the tedium of office in the city by attending parties at the James River plantations, including Shirley and Westover. He always rode down the river on one of the handsome horses he kept. During this period he wrote Hamilton that he was "in love with every sweet nymph" he saw. Although he said he was not ready for matrimony, he asked his friend to discover if a certain Philadelphia belle was still unattached. At the same time he began paying court to nineteen-year-old Maria Farley, at Westover.

Maria Farley was the granddaughter of Charles Carter's sister and, as he was close in affection to his great-niece, Maria was often at Shirley in companionship with her friend and cousin Ann Hill Carter. While the thirty-seven-year-old governor was courting Maria, Ann fell in love with him. Not a love she tried to hide, she watched the romantic figure with her heart in her eyes. When Maria told her that she intended to refuse Governor Lee's proposal, guileless Ann said, "You don't know what you are throwing away." It was after Maria Farley had refused him that Harry Lee, aware of Ann's infatuation, proposed to her. Nancy, as she was called by her family, was only too happy to become Lee's wife.

For any father this would have been a painful circumstance. Charles Carter's Shirley family was a particularly close-knit unit. When he had moved from Corotoman to Shirley, Charles Carter had only recently married his second wife, Ann Butler Moore (a descendant of Governor Spotswood), and newly born Ann Hill was the first child of his second family. Shirley became the homeplace of the family of his later years, and Nancy was the favorite among her six surviving full brothers and sisters. Enclosed in the sheltering center of her family, she had grown up in innocence of the world beyond the James River plantations of her kinspeople.

However, the only objection her father made to her marriage was the governor's proposal to serve in France — presumably taking Nancy with him. With Ann's respect for and dependence upon her father, it was most unlikely she would have married against his opposition. When Lee's adventurous dream was raised as an obstacle to his marriage to Ann Hill Carter, he also received Washington's dampening letter. Taking the two together — Washington's disapproval and Mr. Carter's objection — Light-Horse Harry relinquished the proposition.

On May 15, 1793, he wrote Washington thanking him for his letter and saying he felt himself "yielding to its weight of reason." Then he sought an audience with Charles Carter at Shirley. Presumably without mentioning the exchange with Washington, he told the plantation master he would abandon his plan to fight with the French. Once Carter was assured that his daughter would remain nearby, he withdrew his one stated opposition.

Three days later he wrote the governor, "The only objection we ever had to your connection with our daughter is now entirely done away with. You have declared upon your honor that you have given over all thoughts of going to France, and we rest satisfied with that assurance."

He tried to put as good a face as possible on this acceptance of the inevitable, but his last lines, very sad for a father to have to write, revealed his concern. "Mrs. Carter and I are perfectly satisfied that our dear girl will make you a dutiful and loving wife, and we flatter ourselves that you will be to her a most affectionate and tender husband, in full confidence of which I beg leave to subscribe myself. Your very affectionate, Chas. Carter." The words "and tender," an afterthought, had been inserted between the lines.

## 5

Apparently Charles Carter indicated nothing of his reservations about Governor Lee to his daughter, as she seemed to feel that his abandonment of the French venture cleared the only obstacle to her happiness. Certainly no doubts disturbed her own dreams. After the wedding party, a radiant Nancy left the plantation in a coach with her husband and jostled over the sandy road to Richmond.

Approaching the state capital, the road curved down from the plateau of a long hill to run close to the river, not as wide as at Shirley, and browner. The dense green of the countryside, scented with wildflowers, fell behind, and the coach lurched through the bogs of what was grandly called Main Street. The mostly frame buildings were crude affairs.

Close to the center of town, where Main Street climbed, to Ann's right a bare hill rose abruptly to a commanding crest upon which spread a columned neo-classical building. This was the new state Capitol, which Thomas Jefferson had suggested be built on the model of the Maison Carrée, a Roman temple at Nîmes, France. East of the imposing building, goats grazed in the muddy ravines slicing through the rough terrain of the hillside. Across from one of these gullies perched a thin, rickety-looking frame house. This was the Governor's Mansion, Ann's new home.

Alighting from the coach, she entered the plain house which consisted of only four rooms, two on each of its two stories. And in these cramped quarters were two children to become acquainted with. Six-year-old Henry was an amiable boy, who grew up to be a man of charm, but his older sister was a different proposition. Named for the beautiful grandmother who had ignited the Leesylvania line, Lucy Grymes Lee was at seven a self-willed, clannish princess, whose future — as it could have been predicted — was to follow an imperious, highly individualistic course.

No love was lost between her and the gentle, naive stepmother. Later Lucy Grymes married Ann's brother Bernard — to spite her stepmother, the story went. Judging by one of her letters, in which she complained of "what a fool" she found Bernard in comparison with the colorful men of her own family, there might be truth in the story. She formed an early love for urban life and hated the country so intensely that, while married to the patient Bernard, Lucy Grymes threatened to burn their house down if he didn't move her back to Philadelphia. When the house did burn, such was her reputation that many thought her capable of having done it.

The boy, the fourth Henry Lee — who, following a scandal, was to be distinguished from his father by the uncomplimentary sobriquet of "Black-Horse Harry" — was much like Light-Horse Harry in character and personality. Though no deep bonds of intimacy were established between Henry and the second Mrs. Lee, their relationship was pleasant as far as it went. Ann Hill seems not to have made any effort to replace his mother, and nothing suggests that he came under her guidance.

It required all she could give to try to adjust to her volatile husband, under conditions so foreign to the material abundance and wealth of love she had known for her first twenty years. What Harry Lee came to feel for his second wife was never known with any certainty. In later years his references to her, and to them as "two humble lovers" on their wedding day, might have indicated little more than the sentiments considered proper. As he had behaved with noticeable infatuation toward Maria Farley so shortly before he proposed to Ann, it seems hardly possible that he was in love with her when they married. During their years together he probably developed an affection and certainly a deep respect, for she became one of the most highly spoken of women in the history of Virginia.

Fundamentally Light-Horse Harry was self-indulgent, spoiled by too many gifts. Having won early with little effort everything his world had to offer, he could not become a man of application. This inability extended specifically into his role as head of a family. Though he was a devoted father, and warmly remembered by his children, he could not bring himself to do those things that would provide for them nor for his wife's security — financially or emotionally.

His second marriage changed nothing in the impractical pursuit of some undefined dream that beckoned him away from, beyond, a reality that in itself was more than most men would dare aspire to. He needed only to stand still and be blessed of fortune. But even where his deepest political convictions were concerned, he acted rashly and most imprudently. Ann Hill Carter had come into his life actually at the point where his star was about to begin its descent.

## 6

To Ann, "Mr. Lee" (as she always addressed him) ceased to be a glamorous figure, though nothing indicates the exact stage in their life when she lost her romantic concept of him. When Ann began to have her own children she made long visits to Shirley, and to her then aging father turned again for the protectiveness her husband failed to provide. Her first trip home, however, a year after the wedding, was caused by outside circumstances and in itself suggested no change in her feelings. In that summer of 1794, when she was pregnant, Governor Lee had to go to the Alleghenies on a mission of his office.

While Ann spent the early stages of her pregnancy in late summer and early fall with her family at Shirley, her husband was engaged in an action which became one of those turning points in a destiny from which everything else led downward. To some extent the consequences of the so-called "Whiskey Rebellion" derived from Lee's unthoughtful political course.

During the formation of the republic, Harry Lee, by virtue of having gone to college out of his state and his years with cosmopolitan associates in the army, had been less provincial in attitude than the average Virginian or New Englander. He was, of course, first a Virginian, and he made this unequivocal when he said, "Virginia is my country; her I will obey, however lamentable the fate to which it may subject me." But he was not among those who had believed that a state's liberties would be lost by allocating powers to a central government.

All the separate commonwealths had been concerned over the representation of their states as sovereign entities. The men of property who dominated all the state Constitutional conventions feared a rule of numbers in a central government, as distrust of mob rule was by no means restricted to Virginia's planter-based oligarchy. The Constitutional compromise designed to safeguard the states' sovereignty against numerical majorities placed only the election of congressmen, from districts, in the votes of the people. Each state was to be represented *as a state* by two senators to be elected by their state's General Assembly. These senators were to represent their states in the republic, under specific instructions from the states' legislative bodies, just as the political entities had been represented in the Confederation. The United States meant united sovereignties.

Even with this compromise and many others, the big states of Virginia, New York and Massachusetts were slow to be brought around. In the Richmond 1788 convention for ratification of the Constitution, Harry Lee added the force of his conviction to the support of James Madison and young Governor Edmund Randolph. Madison, an adroit maneuverer, made skillful use of Washington's prestige to gain the votes needed for ratification.

These activities associated Lee politically with the Federalists in the new national government. His conviction more significantly coincided with Washington's. Though President Washington remained aloof from political party alignments, and the reverence in which he was held personally kept both the Federalists and the Anti-Federalists from including him in their maneuverings, by sentiment he drifted steadily toward the strong national government advocated by Alexander Hamilton's Federalists.

When the republic was formed in 1789 the primary purpose of the compact, as generally understood, was to insure safety in foreign relations by establishing a single policy for and by pooling the resources of the thirteen former colonies. The separate states had also feared that in a federated republic preferment might be given one group of interests over another, but the prevailing opinion — brilliantly advocated by Madison — pointed out that checks and balances would prevent any single group of interests from dominating. Essentially, in an age when reason was much revered, the Constitution drafters believed that leaders would act from rational motives in an understanding that the good of the whole depended upon the good of its parts. It was also a time of deism, when Washington and others believed that a Providence regulated affairs in an all-powerful control.

Early in this "more perfect union" Harry Lee's Federalist loyalties grew confused by the policies of his wartime friend Hamilton, then Washington's Secretary of the Treasury. Hamilton had soon showed a favoritism for the commercial interests that aroused alarm and resentment in the agricultural communities such as Virginia. Lee became personally involved in Hamilton's refunding plan, which called for the national government to pay off the debts separately contracted by the states during the Revolution. As Virginia had already paid off her own debts (and private citizens, such as Benjamin Harrison of Berkeley, and communities such as Richmond, had absorbed severe losses from the ravages of British armies), this was naturally offensive to all Virginians. Particularly offensive to Lee was the plan to redeem at face value the certificates given to soldiers during the Revolution.

Since most of these veterans had long ago sold their certificates for as little as one-twentieth of their face value, one of the central government's first acts was to reward financial speculators at the expense of the taxpayer and veterans. Light-Horse Harry held long loyalties to the men who had fought with him, and from his own pocket had generously helped many of them get on their feet. When Lee observed the policy of what he called "the insolent North," Patrick Henry's dire prophecies about the national government no longer seemed unfounded.

Still believing it possible for Virginia's interests to be served in a federated republic, Lee recommended fundamental changes in which the Northern money powers would deny their self-interest in the welfare of the whole. It was his impassioned words on being aroused to Virginia's danger that led to his being elected governor. Introducing the note of "secession" within three years of the compact, he said the changes must be made or the people south of the Potomac would "be forced to cut the Gordian knot."

Once in the Governor's Mansion, however, in his general indifference Lee did nothing to implement his eloquence. His inaction came at a time when the tide in Virginia was running strongly against the centralized power represented by Federalism. Along with his inaction, the impulsive man made the mistake of gaining the enmity of Thomas Jefferson. In jealousy, he repeated to Washington something someone had told him Jefferson said at his dinner table. Jefferson's leadership in relation to the Anti-Federalist organization in Virginia might be something like the chicken and the egg question of which came first — whether he formed the organization or the organization found him. The fact was that in time Jefferson became the undisputed leader of a powerful organization, and the thin-skinned, long-remembering Democrat had Harry Lee in his black book.

With this background, Light-Horse Harry became indelibly identified with the other side, the Federalists, when George Washington commissioned him major general to lead a Federal army in 1794 against defiers of the new government. Bored with his chief executive's office, Lee doubtless gave no thought to the political consequences in the relief of leading armed forces again.

The rather shabby affair, the "Whiskey Rebellion," was caused by the government's placing a tax on the whiskey made by Westerners from their home-grown corn. To the isolated families west of the Alleghenies whiskey was their "money crop," like tobacco in the Tidewater, and the people's sole source of cash. When taxes were imposed, the mountaineers refused to pay and chased off or frightened away the Federal officers sent to arrest them. President Washington regarded the Westerners' intransigence as a threat against the inviolability of the Federal laws and ordered out the states' militia to disperse the insurrectionists. Fifteen thousand troops gathered under Harry Lee. Back in his element, he organized units and devised uniforms, recapturing the glory of the Revolution by bedecking the cavalry in the green jackets and white leather breeches of Lee's old legion.

Two months in preparation and one month in marching west to Pittsburgh, the expedition appeared ridiculous when the small armed bands dispersed at its approach and representatives of the whiskey-makers sent in agreements to abide by the national laws. As a matter of fact, Washington had acted wisely in sending a force that made resistance impractical and ended the rebellion without bloodshed.

To the Anti-Federalists in Virginia the suppression was tainted by Lee's force remaining in the Pittsburgh area while Federalist authorities harassed, tracked down and brought to trial various former leaders of the insurrection already peaceably ended. By the time Harry Lee was ready to come home from the less than glorious adventure, his term of office had expired (November 26) and his enemies in the state capital were out for his head.

As his successor took office before Lee returned, Major General Lee relinquished the Governor's Mansion without fanfare or regrets. During his period with the army, he had revealed no interest whatsoever in the administrative affairs of the state and went from the Alleghenies directly to Shirley. Ann evidently suffered from sickness during her pregnancy and showed no desire to leave her family's home for another strange place, this time Stratford Hall. Lee seems to have spent the winter with her at Shirley, where her first baby was born in April, 1795. After the birth of the boy (christened Algernon Sidney), Ann remained on at Shirley into the summer. Then she left her father's house again, this time for the hundred-mile journey to the Northern Neck and the home of her husband's first wife, for whom he was building a mausoleum.

## 7

The countryside approaching Stratford Hall was subtly different from Ann's familiar Tidewater. The lowlands of Tidewater always seemed enclosed, with the draping vines suggesting a quality of privacy and intimacy. Though Westmoreland County was not high ground, and its green woods were densely entangled and the carriage wheels brushed past roadside wildflowers and fragrant honeysuckle, the country gave the impression of being more open. When the carriage turned into the plantation driveway, she looked upon stretches of flatland baking under the sun, with little of the activity that was part of the scene at Shirley. Then the carriage turned again and she saw, rising above the flat ground, a massive pale brick structure as coldly forbidding as a fortress.

Not only dissimilar from anything in Tidewater, Stratford Hall was unlike any house she had ever seen in Virginia. While the Georgian houses she had known were indigenously adapted to the country, this institution-like building belonged among the castles of England. Even its grounds, though showing neglect, were formally landscaped, and the four dependencies formed the corners of a huge square with the manor house in the exact center.

The main house was H-shaped. The wings contained four large rooms on each of two floors and — in themselves good-sized houses — were connected by a great hall. This hall was on the second floor, which, approached by a broad flight of steps in the center, was actually the main floor of the house. Above the sloped roof of each wing towered columns of four banked chimneys, a unique architectural feature which managed to deepen the oppressiveness of the first impression.

In addition to the balustraded stone steps that rose to the doorway in the great hall, off the end of each wing entrance steps enclosed by brick walls led to both floors. Ann entered her new home by one of the side doorways. Inside, the house lost much of its cold formality, though compared to Shirley it was scarcely cozy. The high-ceilinged second-floor rooms in the wings, with paneled walls, were finely proportioned, and the southeast corner bedroom — with attached nursery forming something like a separate suite — was charming. All the rooms, however, reflected the lack of care since Matilda Lee's day, and this was particularly apparent in the great hall, thirty feet square.

Probably the most monumental in design then in America, the symmetrical room was magnificently paneled. Corinthian pilasters, flanking the openings of windows and doors, reached to a full entablature that bordered the eighteen-foot-high ceiling. A dozen portraits of earlier Lees hung from the walls without dominating the great hall. To Ann it probably suggested a place "for Feasts and other Jollities," according to the recommendation of Sir Henry Wotton for such center halls. The jollities would have to run to raucous gatherings of red-faced men in from shooting who, between swings from tankards, would throw raw meat to huge hounds circling and growling around the muddy boots. But the room did not suggest to Ann a place where *she* would like to entertain.

With a three-month-old baby and not having recovered her own health, Ann Carter Lee began her life in the huge house with no interest in entertaining at all. There was much to get used to. Cash was tight for running the establishment and servants comparatively few for the scale of living demanded. In the atmosphere of slow decay, Ann watched the formal parks of the distant grounds change into small wildernesses of untended brush and vines tangling in scrub trees. Most of all she missed the river. Where at Shirley the broad James had run so close as to seem an extension of the rooms, here she must climb to the roof above the enclosed attic for a glimpse of the Potomac.

Adjustment was made simple for her by the frequent visits of some of their numerous kinspeople. Two families of Carter kin were not far distant at Sabine Hall and Nomoni Hall. Not having to feel apologetic with her family for the fading grandeur, she welcomed all intimates whether they dropped in or came to tarry awhile. Ann quickly developed a close friendship wih her sister-in-law, Mrs. Richard Bland Lee, and she won friends throughout the new neighborhood. Men and women alike became devoted to the lovely, fragile young woman who was beginning to demonstrate the inner strength that was to characterize her mature years.

Unless relatives or neighbors were visiting, she and Mr. Lee passed quiet evenings together. Sometimes they played chess. Whether or not her husband was at home, Ann was also disinclined to go about socially. This was readily explainable. During her second summer at Stratford, her first child died at the age of fifteen months, and this grief sapped the energy that had run low since she had become pregnant. Then, two years later, in 1798, Ann began having children every other year for the next four years. By the time she was thirty, Ann had two boys, Charles Carter and Sydney Smith, and a girl, Ann.

She lavished a good deal of attention on the children, and the oldest boy was a delight to her. She wrote her sister-in-law that Charles Carter Lee had inherited none of the "superlative beauty of his Father and Mother," but "He is a little black eye's, Brown boy; very healthy, lively and (his Mother thinks) very sweet." Yet, with all the gratification her children gave her, Ann Carter Lee wanted to bear no more offspring by Mr. Lee. This she wrote very candidly to her sister-in-law.

During the time Ann Carter Lee was building her own family, her husband's fortunes started the decline that accelerated ever faster until the ex-hero seemed to hurry to his own ruin. As was customary, after his terms as governor were over he returned to the General Assembly. At this time, while Lee's identification with the Federalists made him persona non grata with the dominant faction at Richmond, the Federalists had been given doubt of his loyalties by his impassioned speeches on the protection of Virginia and the agricultural interests. Lee seemed insensitive to the shifts in balance.

His friend James Madison, who originally believed the Federalists offered the means of achieving the desired end, had shifted away from the party's practices. He turned toward the Democratic means and the rising star, Thomas Jefferson, for the protection of liberties that was his chief concern. Lee, with no mind for practicalities, remained steadfast in his attachment to George Washington. He came out strongly for the Federalist positions on issues the Federalists lost.

Despite moving against the current, Lee stood for election as United States congressman from his district in April, 1799. George Washington personally rode to the polls to cast a ballot for his younger friend. With timely assistance from his political ally John Marshall, Lee squeaked to a narrow victory and took his wife and children to the temporary capital at Philadelphia. Life in a new city was one of the pleasanter interludes for Ann Carter Lee. In apologizing to Mrs. Richard Bland Lee for not corresponding while in Philadelphia, Nancy wrote in a gay vein that she had been "immersed in the pleasures of a City life."

In Philadelphia, however, Light-Horse Harry saw the burial of his political life when he was only forty-four. December, 1799, brought the death of his hero, George Washington, and Lee's last brush with the fame of the great years came in his writing of the funeral oration. In this eulogy he included the now famous words, "First in war, first in peace, first in the hearts of his countrymen."

In the resolutions Lee wrote on Washington's death, he could not garner the support even for a monument to the giant who, in all simple truth, had been the father of the new country. Washington was dead. Adams, the Federalist President, was going out of office, and the minds of the politicians were intent on getting their party into power. Thomas Jefferson and Aaron Burr were deadlocked in the 1800 race for President, and congressmen balloted to decide the issue. True to his convictions, Harry Lee doggedly cast his vote for Burr and signed his own political death warrant. When Jefferson was elected, Lee's political life ended.

At the same time his shaky financial structure collapsed. Lee had become reinfected with the fever of land speculation when — with his gubernatorial duties behind — he established his family at Stratford in 1795. Having learned nothing from his involvement with the lands of the Fairfax estate around Great Falls, he invested in another tract of land also involved in the Fairfax estate. In an effort to bring in large money powers, he interested Robert Morris of Philadelphia, who had helped finance the Revolution. Morris was then old, with his own affairs entangled, and he was short of the ready cash to support his interest. It ended up with Lee lending *him* $40,000, not a penny of which Morris was ever able to repay.

This senseless act, involving the sale of productive lands, was the beginning of the end for Harry Lee's dream of the easy way. By then a financial genius would have been required to bring order to the muddle he had made. Before Washington's death Lee had made a payment on a $27,000 personal debt to him partially with bank shares. Light-Horse Harry had wistfully counted the shares at par value when they were worth far less. Washington, whose fortune had been seriously hurt by his twenty years away from Mount Vernon in his country's service, was a careful man with a dollar and did not take kindly to this at all. Lee became caught in the closing circle of robbing Peter to pay Paul. At the same time he continued to take mortgages on new lands.

By the time he returned to Stratford in 1800 from his term in the United States Congress, for bare living expenses he was forced to begin selling off the last property of the Stratford estate. By 1802 nothing was left of the once great holdings except the land attached to the manor house, left in trust to his son Henry.

The following year Lee was sued by Alexander Spotswood, at Spotsylvania Court House, for $15,000 owed on a mortgage for land he had acquired. He had to lose this land, along with the equity he had put in, for want of cash.

By then, with his credit known to be worthless, creditors began to badger the master of Stratford, bringing deep humiliation to Ann Carter Lee. Colonel McCleery wanted $14,000. Lee's neighbor Sheriff Willoughby Newton demanded $5,000, John Potter $425, William Franklin $100, and Lawrence Muse wanted the payment on "one fine hat, rope, powder, shot, gunflints and 2½ quires of paper" bought on credit from his store. Friends wrote asking for the repayment of loans and tradesmen sent the sheriff up the long driveway of Stratford Hall with court orders for the recent congressman from their district.

Also in 1803, unknown to Ann at that time, her father rewrote his will to protect from her husband the property he would leave her. It was the document of a father totally without faith in his son-in-law. Doubtless aware that Lee had sold off Stratford properties Matilda Lee had intended for her children, Charles Carter's new will was designed to place Nancy's inheritance beyond the reach of Lee or his creditors.

Near Shirley, back from the river, one of his plantations was on the plateau of Malvern Hill, then worked by a farmer. Originally this plantation was to go outright to Ann Hill. In the new will, Charles Carter left the property to four executors — two friends, his oldest son Robert, and his son-in-law Dr. Carter Berkeley. They were to secure the property "for the use and benefit of my said daughter in such a way that she solely during her natural life may enjoy the rents, issues [children of the slaves on the Malvern Hill plantation], profits, emoluments, interests and advantages of the said property . . . free from the claim, demand, let, hindrance or molestation of her husband, General Lee, or his creditors directly or indirectly."

While Ann Carter Lee lacked this proof of her father's attitude to her husband, she could not have been unmindful of his feelings, for the reputation of "Mr. Lee" was a shame to every value she herself held dear. Concurrent with his disgrace, Nancy developed a series of debilitating ailments. As the Lees were too poor to call in doctors, little can be known about the specific nature of her illnesses. At times she was subject to fainting spells and once mentioned that she suffered from "dropsy." Mostly in her letters, to sister-in-law or brother, Nancy began before her thirtieth year to refer to herself as "a chronic invalid," without going into details.

Since she was not a strong woman (she mentioned being fatigued by a horseback ride) and was known for the selfless care she devoted to her children, it is unlikely that Ann Hill was afflicted with those hypochondriac "miasmas" that plagued the minds of gentlewomen. With some evidence suggesting that she had a difficult time in childbearing, it appears probable that Ann was a victim of primitive medical science, the lack of strength-restoring diets, and — with the possibility of a weak heart as suggested by the reference to dropsy — suffered from one or more of the chronic maladies to which many of her contemporaries more or less resigned themselves.

The visits with her family were the tonics that sustained her. Her father became the strong man in her life, and her younger brothers and sisters, as their increasing ages diminished the disparities between them, became more meaningful to her. Nancy grew aware of this when she suffered the loss of her oldest brother, Robert, in December, 1805. Her family and her intimate friends, especially Mrs. Richard Bland Lee, filled the empty places in life left by a man who could give only a little of the tenderness which Charles Carter had, hopefully, asked for his daughter.

By then the ruined man probably loved her in his way, within the limitations of his emotional capacities. But any wife represented an adult responsibility he was incapable of assuming.

No one can ever know what Harry Lee expected from her father. Though it is not unreasonable to assume that he hoped for some of the famed Carter bounty, none of the "silent streams" of wealth flowed his way. Instead, Lee fell into unfavorable comparison with the master of Shirley. Even the assets of Lee's colorful presence, his personal force, his joy in learning and his exciting phrasemaking (which his children never forgot) became vain ornaments in the absence of the virtues inculcated in Nancy by her father.

Probably the emotionally durable young woman, who did mature under the acceptance of bitterly harsh realities, came to realize what her father had recognized from the beginning — she had married a shell of a man. There is little doubt that she recognized his irresponsibility when, after more than a decade of sordid insecurity and deepening shame, the fullness of tragedy struck her.

In the summer of 1806, Ann, pregnant with a child she did not want, left Stratford with her own children for a renewing visit home. She arrived at Shirley to find that her father had just died.

8

It had been a brutally tiring journey through a hot country seared by drought, bumping along in their last carriage, so broken down as to barely deliver Nancy and her three children to the driveway leading to the familiar red brick buildings of the Shirley forecourt. Then, as she wrote her husband, "the arms which had ever received me in so much delight were folded in death! the eyes that used to beam with so much affection on me were veiled for ever! and the cold grave was closed on my too *dear* and ever lamented father! It would be vain to attempt to describe the grief his loss has occasioned me. It is greater than I can express, and will only cease with my existence!"

Then the stricken woman wrote these revealing lines: "Shirley, so lately the scene of happiness and gayety, is now literally the House of mourning! We all feel that our best hopes are buried in the grave of our blessed and dearly beloved friend. Oh! my dearest Mr. Lee, remember that your poor, afflicted *Fatherless* wife can now only look to you, to smooth her rugged path through life."

Mentioning that both her boys, Charles Carter and Smith, were sick, she returned to the theme of her need of protection: "Forget not, my dearest Mr. Lee, to guard your health with more care than for several years past. Your life is more important to your poor wife and children now than ever it was: their other protector is taken from them, for ever and ever."

Then, telling him that her mother, bowed down with sorrow, was "in very low health" and planned to leave for a different climate by the end of the month, she wrote, "I trust, my dear Mr. Lee, you will certainly bring a conveyance for me by that time. Do not disappoint me, I conjure you."

Despite this appeal in early June, Harry Lee neither sent a carriage nor came to Shirley during the whole summer. Growing heavy with the child she did not want, Ann Carter Lee remained in the house of mourning after her mother had left until the end of October. By then, she had obtained the use of an open carriage for herself and the three children (none of whom seemed to be sick) to make the long journey back. The countryside was turning bleak at the approach of winter and damp winds blew off the rivers — the James, which they rode near for twenty-odd miles to Richmond, the Chickahominy and Rappahannock, which they crossed, and the Potomac, which the carriage approached on the last barren stretch in early November. On arriving, Nancy found that the chills in the open carriage had brought on a cold that settled in her chest.

Waiting for her was a defeated man, old at fifty. Harry Lee had taken up a fugitive existence, dodging his creditors and going off on wan trips to Philadelphia and the new capital city of Washington. During the winter the once vigorous man was brought down with a tenacious cold that half invalided him. In the total despair of ill health climaxing the failure of his life and the waste of his gifts, Light-Horse Harry dreamed of a complete escape. He wanted to go to a warm, dry climate like Brazil.

He could not afford to replace any of the carriages that had worn out, and he was literally hiding from the sheriff's deputies, bearing a *capias* from the merchant Muse, who had grown incensed at being unpaid for the "fine hat" and quires of paper. Yet Lee hoped through friends to settle himself and his family in a foreign country where he would regain his health, and incidentally be free of the harassments of creditors.

While this vaporous dream was in the air, Ann Carter Lee approached her next confinement with dread. It was a bitter cold day in January, with wind off the Potomac blowing against the house, when she went to bed in the warm southeast chamber where chunks of logs burned in the fireplace. This restful bedroom, with the nursery attached, was something like a delivery room at Stratford Hall. There Hannah Ludwell Lee, wife of the Thomas who built the mansion in 1725, had borne the sons who were to be signers of the Declaration of Independence, and Elizabeth Steptoe Lee, wife of Philip Ludwell Lee, had borne the "divine Matilda." There, on January 19, 1807, Ann Carter Lee gave birth to another of her little dark-eyed boys, healthy and amiable, whom she named for her two brothers, Robert Edward Lee.

# CHAPTER II

## "I Have Kept the Faith"

THE EVIL DAYS had fallen upon Stratford in the year when Ann Carter Lee's fourth child was placed in the nursery adjoining the Mothers' Room. Only in these rooms were the fires kept up. The great hall, heated by charcoal braziers, was an icy passageway connecting the two wings. Behind its door, opening on the broad outer steps, chains were strung across to guard the entrance against the approach of the sheriff's deputies or bill collectors. Except for the loyal brother, Richard Bland Lee, and the periodic arrival of Carter kin in coach-and-fours, few visitors besides the dunners approached the paneled doors that had swung wide in hospitality in the days when the Lees were the most distinguished family in Virginia.

Outside the house, the dependencies were in a state of decay, one having collapsed altogether. Beyond the center unit, the remaining acres under cultivation barely produced a sufficiency for the relatively small family and the people working the fields. The overseer, for want of wages, moved away with his family that winter, leaving unsupervised such work as was done. Wild vines crept up to the outbuildings and engulfed the vacant carriage house.

To the children the very existence of a near-jungle encroaching on the outbuildings was like a wonderland spreading, illimitable and unhorizoned, to the distant Potomac. Unaware of any comparisons with the great days, they viewed the untended fields only as open meadows and hillsides for their play. The vine-entangled scrub woods were places of secret glens and shadowed ravines, and the bushes that overran lawns were projects for berry picking. Robert, growing to extend his exploring operations from the vastness of the main house to the outdoors, sturdily tagged along behind his older sister and two brothers.

Though he never forgot the idyllic quality of those first years, Robert did not record any details of his impressions. The chronicler of their childhood at Stratford Hall was his oldest brother, Carter, nine when Robert was born. In later life Carter Lee wrote a collection of Georgian elegiacs, recalling the world of "green boughs" that was the children's domain. In one verse he captured the essense of their joyousness with a charming picture of picking berries with Ann, who was closest to him in age.

> Yet even now, methinks I see
> My sister, busy as a bee
> In picking from the wild vine, berries;
> Her cheeks in color, like the cherries,
> Her bonnet fixed with many a pin
> Lest the warm sun should tinge her skin,
> Which glowed as alabaster white,
> More lovely for her black eyes' light . . .
> Happy, Happy then were we!
> Our father's and our mother's joys,
> Their daughter fair, and sunburnt boys. . . .

Protected from the cares that burdened the parents, the children grew up with the sense of completeness, of fulfillment, that plantation life could yield to the happy-hearted. All their lives Robert and his sister and brothers showed the effects of a happy childhood. Light-Horse Harry, even in the darkest times that came to his spirit, took pleasure in his children and communicated to them a sense of his warmth and color. It might be said that his last acts of gallantry came in the performances he gave to this uncritical, admiring audience. If he could not live by his own precepts, Harry Lee was most convincing in stating the ideals drawn from the wisdoms of the past (with Latin quotations) and the models of great contemporaries.

Carter wrote, " 'Honor thy father and thy mother' were not then mere words to be idly repeated in the Catechism every Sunday, but the fifth in the commandments of God, and the next in sanctity, as the next in order to those immediately concerning Himself. Is it then so wonderful that our Revolutionary worthies, being thus brought up, with Washington at their head, should have been so wonderfully good as well as great?"

The "good as well as great" was an expression of the ideal which had been embodied in their grandfather, Charles Carter, and which their mother constantly held before them. A quality of goodness flowed from Ann Carter Lee, "playing angel to me as mother," as Carter later wrote. The religious devotion which had characterized her father and her great-grandfather, King Carter, was a natural part of her life, though she was never overly pious or other-worldly. Like all the Carters, she was high-mindedly realistic about man's relationship to his environment. Her precepts were those her family had prospered by for generations, and the Carter convictions were to her as life itself. In inculcating these principles into her children, she showed them the untouched sweetness of her nature and the unlost innocence of pleasure in simple things.

Carter remembered always the henhouse she built and stocked as the "joint possession" for him and "a dear, bright, blackeyed, rosy-cheeked little sister, eighteen months younger than myself." And one of Robert Edward Lee's earliest memories was of a chestnut tree he helped her plant in the driveway.

When Robert began exploring the world beyond the house, Ann Carter Lee's were the only children at Stratford, and this may have been an element in the close attachment formed early between him and his mother. The house was free of high-spirited Lucy Grymes, then married to Robert's Uncle Bernard, and Henry Lee IV was at William and Mary in Williamsburg. Lucy Grymes apparently had little to no connection with Ann Hill's children at any time. While at Stratford Hall, Henry was close to Carter, eleven years his junior, and Carter wrote that Henry had shown him all the affection that a full brother would extend. As Henry was away at college when Robert was born, those two were never close. They shared the loyalties of a clannishness that characterized all Lees, but Robert seldom referred to the half-brother who was twenty years older.

While Henry was a younger version of Light-Horse Harry, Robert showed scarcely any influences of character or temperament from his father. Physically he was fortunate to inherit his father's strong and well-proportioned body, with the incalculable legacy of vital energy. The father's physical courage, which appeared in all the boys as virtually fearlessness (literally, without fear), was a standard virtue of their class. In some triumph of environmental conditioning, courage seemed implanted in a large proportion of their contemporaries. Beyond this, and generalized attitudes typical of the Lee family, Robert was his mother's child. His mental cast was formed totally by her. He had, as did all her children, Ann Carter Lee's dark brown hair and dark eyes, though his were a subtly colored brown.

Robert's older sister and full brothers, though predominantly influenced by their mother, reflected aspects of Light-Horse Harry's personality. Carter had a strain of easygoing self-indulgence, and both Carter and Smith possessed the charm for which the old hero had been famous. Smith, five years Robert's senior, was the most dear to his heart. Between them (and later Ann's last child, Mildred, born when Robert was four) was established the bond that existed between Carter and Ann. Where Robert was sweet-natured like his mother and very contained, Smith was warmly outgoing and developed a personal appeal that made him a social favorite.

With the visible gradations between the children from Henry at one end to Robert at the other, these two could have been born of different ancestors and formed by different environments. Actually, in terms of the dominant parent and the condition of the estate, their environmental influences were significantly dissimilar. To Robert the heroic days of Stratford were only tales, belonging with the stories of the great Lees of the past and of his father's glory in another time — all parts of an oral history of heroes as told to a child. These tales of his family's golden age were his heritage, and they exerted a powerful influence in his formative years.

But Henry's heritage was tangible, Stratford Hall, where Ann's children lived only on his sufferance after Robert was one year old. Born in his own right to be a plantation master, formed by his mother's era of boundless luxury, Henry was to be like his father in marrying an heiress to maintain the estate — only Henry was to marry a girl whose money was her own.

Thus, while it was natural for Harry Lee's oldest son to follow his father's course, it was equally natural for the youngest son to follow the guidance of his mother. For, from Robert's second year, it was his mother who held the family together and became the dominant figure in his world. Ann Carter Lee, herself having grown up in a happy childhood with affectionate respect for her father, tried to train all her own children in the values by which she had been raised, and was most successful in imparting this training to the child who came immediately and intimately under her dominion.

It happened that most of the values emphasized were, except for Harry Lee's integrity in matters of his convictions, antithetical to the values reflected in her husband's squandered gifts. As the consequences of Lee's irresponsibility overtook him, his wife may have unconsciously borne down harder in stressing those traits that were, in effect, the opposite of his. For instance, Robert was the antithesis of his father and half-brother Henry in money matters: never forgetting the value of a dollar, he was always patient in working out the details of the smallest economies and very prudent (almost tight) in handling money.

Robert was just two years old when the ultimate disaster happened to his father. In April, 1809, General Lee was imprisoned in the jail of the county he had represented (by right of birth) in the state assembly. Being jailed for debts was not as disgraceful as criminal imprisonment; poor Robert Morris, the financier of the Revolution, had at the end of his useful life in Philadelphia suffered imprisonment for debt. Nor was failure in money matters as disgraceful as affairs involving one's personal honor in more abstract values. However, it was undeniably a blot on the reputation, and a personal shame to one trained to be as scrupulous about money matters as the daughter of Charles Carter.

Whatever the moral effect on General Lee, he suffered his misfortune at least outwardly with grace, and used the confinement in a cell for the discipline he was unable to impose himself. He finally put to use those two and one-half quires of paper he had bought on credit from the relentless Lawrence Muse, and began to write his long-planned memoirs of the Southern campaign with Nathanael Greene. General Greene was then dead, and Lee, with the loyalty he always displayed to his heroes, wanted to glorify his reputation along with his own. From the Westmoreland County jail he was moved to the jail at Spotsylvania Court House (named for his wife's ancestor Governor Spotswood) and was confined about one year altogether.

The effect on Robert was that from the age of twenty-seven months to about forty months his father was not at home and, as the head of the house, was never to be again. When Harry Lee returned to Stratford in the spring of 1810, Henry, then twenty-three years old and finished at William and Mary, was waiting for his father's family to move out so that he could claim his inheritance from his mother.

By some unrecorded means General Lee's various creditors had been satisfied while he was in jail — perhaps, as has been suggested, by members of his family. (As early as 1807, Richard Bland Lee had offered help directly to Ann Hill, which she courteously refused.) Freed of the obligations that had grown to absorb his days, Lee lost himself in the continued writing of his *Memoirs*. Having found for the time an outlet for his energy, and a focus for his days, he was engaged in correspondence with Revolutionary veterans all over the country, gathering facts for his book. Possibly, with a flare-up of his optimistic dreams, the old soldier hoped for an oblique recapture of fame.

While her husband was thus immersed in re-creating a time of lost glory, Ann Carter Lee was preparing her own family for leaving her stepson's home. There was little enough property to take along, with her four children ranging from three to twelve, and another child due after the first of the year. She would move into the city, Alexandria, that served as the hub of the community where she had spent the thirteen years of her married life, and where she would be near the friends of her adult years. In a rented city house the family would at last be beyond the need of pretense of acting as plantation masters. In the new life, the little family would be frankly supported by the income from the trust left by her father and a smaller trust from her sister Mildred, who had died three months after Robert was born.

A reason for Robert's becoming the center of his mother's life was that his birth came in the sixteen-month period of emotional upheaval during which first her closest brother had died, then her father, then her closest sister. In her emotional displacement then, and during the successive agitations of her husband's imprisonment and the move from Stratford, the new child was a rewarding and renewing focus of her energies. Though the exact date of the move is unknown, it is assumed that Ann Carter Lee moved her family sometime after the first of the year 1811, at about the time of Robert's fourth birthday.

2

If Robert Edward Lee could be said to have had a home town, it would be Alexandria. There he first went to church and recited his catechism to the Episcopal rector, William Meade (later bishop), there he attended school, and from there he left for college. Yet, the usual meaning of a home town would not obtain, for Robert was essentially the child of plantations. Though he formed an attachment to Alexandria, he never developed a taste for urban life, never forgot that he had been born at Stratford Hall, and from an early age held the ambition to reclaim his birthplace.

Nothing would seem to have been a more abrupt transition than moving from the boundless private world of a plantation to the cramped quarters of a narrow-fronted two-story house built flush on a city street. For Ann Lee, however, the pleasant red-brick house on Cameron Street might well have been a welcome change. In the run-down condition of the last years, with insufficient servants, the vast spaces of Stratford Hall must have grown bleak in the winter. Then, judging from her stay in Philadelphia, Ann liked the city.

Alexandria, with a population of approximately 7000, was no metropolis like Philadelphia, but it definitely was a city, and thriving. It boasted a theater, a school, a fire department, a large and imposing modern apothecary shop, and endless features of pleasure and convenience unimagined in the country. At the same time, compared to an industrial community, Alexandria could scarcely have been called urban. It was a planter's city.

The center of its life was at the wharves and docks on the Potomac, six miles from the new city of Washington on the other side of the river. Alexandria was one of the port cities that flourished while many of the smaller ports were abandoned. This was partly because the plantations whose shipping was handled in Alexandria had not been as dependent on tobacco as those in Tidewater and southern Virginia. All around the city, and in it, there was considerable solid wealth in prudently managed estates. Many planter families had homes in Alexandria, fine brick houses set in shady lawns bordered with boxwood. Totally new to Robert's eyes were rows of red-brick houses with paneled doors placed, as was his house, flush on the sidewalk. The breaks provided by the larger houses with gardens prevented any monotony of impression and, with the bustle restricted to the riverfront, the shady streets of mostly red-brick sidewalks held a charming quality of quiet, ordered, well-to-do city life.

Once the Lee family adjusted to the physical change of living in a small
house, exposed to street noises and the unfamiliarity of next-door neighbors, they found that Alexandria came as close as a city could to approximating the customs and manners, the tone, of plantation life. Along with
the surrounding plantations and the planters' town houses, many planter
families — as Harry Lee's brother and sister and cousins — had moved
into the city after the dislocations of the Revolution, bringing the country
with them. Between the families in town and those on nearby plantations
visiting back and forth was continual, and the social life interflowing between Alexandria and the manor houses was composed of the same
groups, sharing the same interests. Unless General and Mrs. Lee and their
children wished to make new acquaintances from backgrounds previously
unfamiliar to them, they were not required to — and from the prevalence
of Lees and Carters in Northern Virginia, doubtless none of them ever
sought friends outside their known background.

Most importantly for Ann Lee, the house on Cameron Street brought
her close to a powerful friend, William Fitzhugh, of Ravensworth plantation. Fitzhugh was also a great-grandchild of King Carter and by blood
Ann Lee's third cousin. He took over the counseling of the administration
of the estate left by her father and sister, and Ann did not feel so alone in
handling affairs for which she had not been trained. (Evidently her husband took no part at all in the modest maneuvering by which she paid living expenses.) Also nearby, at Arlington plantation, was Fitzhugh's sister,
Mrs. George Washington Parke Custis. Washington Custis, the grandson
of Martha Washington and the adopted son of the late President, having
grown up at Mount Vernon, was the official custodian of Washingtoniana
in Alexandria.

The sense of George Washington, then dead only twelve years, was
very pervasive in Alexandria and did much to fix in Robert's mind the
model of this giant who was "good as well as great." Because of his
father's personal friendship and his family's intimate association with
Washington, Robert's hero was never a remote historic figure to him.
Washington was a man of Robert's own time who, like his other model, his
grandfather Charles Carter, he had happened not to know. Washington was
a family figure to the child. When Robert went to nearby Christ Church,
he was shown the pew in which Washington had worshipped and where
his horse had been tethered in the brick-walled churchyard. In this atmosphere of George Washington, with the stability of the gentle society surrounding him, the boy's ideals began to take shape in his Alexandria years.

3

When the Lees settled in Alexandria, from which they could see the new buildings of the national capital, a new note in the nation's politics was disturbing their neighbors. There was talk of war with England over the impressment of American merchant seamen, some of whom were natives of Alexandria. Harry Lee's enemy Thomas Jefferson had then retired to Monticello, where he remained head of the party organization, and Lee's former Princeton classmate James Madison was nearing the end of his first term as President. Around Madison, new young men from the South were making their voices heard in Congress, calling for war. In the Lee home were now heard the names of John C. Calhoun, a twenty-nine-year-old Yale graduate from South Carolina, and Henry Clay, a thirty-four-year-old Virginia native representing Kentucky. When Harry Lee was governor, gangling young Clay from Hanover County had been reading law near the Capitol in Richmond.

When the war came closer the following year, Light-Horse Harry was reactivated as major general by President Madison. At this turn in his career bad luck, and again bad judgment, prevented Lee from returning to usefulness as a commanding general.

By purest chance he happened to be in Baltimore when a casual friend of his, Alexander Hanson, got in trouble with a Democratic mob over antiwar editorials published in his Federalist newspaper. It was really no fight of Lee's. Hanson's plight over "freedom of speech" appealed to Lee's sense of Constitutional rights and, perhaps like the Irishman, "it was a poor fight but better than none at all." It ended with the old soldier, young Hanson, and a handful of cohorts barricading themselves in the jail, where they were swarmed over by a vicious and bloodthirsty mob. Tortured and beaten, Lee and Hanson's friends were left for dead, and only saved by doctors who dragged them out on the pretense of burying them.

Weeks in recovering from the immediate effects, General Lee returned to the Alexandria house physically broken, his once handsome face permanently disfigured, and the active period of his life ended. His son Henry went off to war, while Lee at last fulfilled his dream of going to foreign lands for his health. With the help of his friends, Madison and Secretary of State Monroe (the youngest member of the Virginia dynasty in Washington), he boarded ship in 1813 for the British possession of Barbados, from which he began a melancholy round of the islands seeking to recover his health.

What supported him is unknown. He was desperately poor and lonely, attempting with little purpose to work on his proposed biographies of Washington and Greene. Before he left Virginia, his *Memoirs* had been published in a two-volume edition, and won him neither the fame nor fortune for which he had wistfully hoped. With the new biographies, he evidently never progressed beyond the stage of collecting material. Instead of working without hope, he kept a diary and wrote to Carter, his favorite child. They were pitiful letters, of a proud man begging for news of his loved ones and trying to achieve parental immortality by imparting the wisdoms of life which he had learned and, except in the integrity of his principles, had never been able to live by. Affable, self-indulgent Carter, who entered Harvard in 1816, seldom answered his father's letters.

Ann Carter Lee seldom had time to write him. The family had then moved into a larger house on Orinoko Street, owned by William Fitzhugh, and she was more than fully occupied with trying to make ends meet and "keep up appearances." On about $1200 a year she was supporting a son at Harvard and three children in school — one of whom, Ann, was very sickly — and had Mildred, the baby of the family, underfoot. Living in the strain of pinched gentility, making every penny count and with nothing to spare for luxuries, "Mrs. Genel Lee" (as Nancy was called in Alexandria) ran her home with more ease and comfort than she had known in the great rooms of the decaying mansion at Stratford. Somehow she squeezed out enough to purchase a carriage, which was driven by old Nat, her personal servant.

Though the work and the care of her brood were taxing to Ann Hill's frail health, her spirit was equal to the stress, and she never surrendered even when the recurrent attacks of illness ("my old troubles," she wrote in a letter) half invalided her. Somewhere in those years Robert began to give his mother physical support in running the house as well as the emotional support that came of the strong communication between them.

In one of his letters to Carter, General Lee summarized the course the boy was taking and would continue to take. "Robert was always good," he wrote, "and will be confirmed in his happy turn of mind by his ever-watchful and affectionate mother. Does he strengthen his native tendency?"

Though the father was never to know the answer to that question, the son ever did strengthen his tendency of native sweetness of character and thoughtfulness. Alone of all the children he combined the happy heart of his mother with an instinctive sense of responsibility. He enjoyed the outdoors as naturally as all boys of his time and place, developing his body and a sensitive appreciation for nature. But the happy heart was not expressed by him, any more than by his mother, in play. A serious-minded boy, he responded as unthinkingly to the duties inherent in his position as Ann Carter Lee had responded to hers, and as his grandfather Charles Carter had before him.

In 1816, when Robert was nine years old, his world was widened by two events, both of which — one positively and one negatively — confirmed him in his natural tendency. With the War of 1812 over, his half-brother Henry returned to reopen Stratford Hall, and his cousin Hill Carter returned from the navy to take possession of Shirley. Within one year, Henry Lee began the restoration of Stratford to its days of glory by marrying his rich neighbor Anne McCarty, whom he had known all her life. Hill Carter, just turned twenty, came from New York to a plantation at Shirley nearly as run-down as Stratford. Hill's father, Nancy's beloved brother Robert, had died when Hill was only nine years old. As Hill had been at school in England before his naval service, Shirley had been in the indifferent hands of overseers since the death of Charles Carter in 1806. To restore the plantation, both in productiveness and in physical repair, Hill Carter undertook to do the job himself.

Training himself day by day in the practicalities of farming, this young man became one of Virginia's most successful antebellum planters. While it was impossible to acquire wealth on the scale of his grandfather's (which had been divided among many children), Ann Lee's nephew slowly restored Shirley as a manor seat in the tradition of the great plantations of the eighteenth century. Hill Carter, cast in the likeness of the men of Ann Carter Lee's family, became Robert's closest kinsman outside his immediate family. Hill was eleven years older than Robert, a man when he was a boy, and a man to be looked up to — a model in the great tradition. Later, as Robert grew older, he and Cousin Hill established an intimacy that lasted to the end of their days, growing ever closer as they became old men.

These two manor houses, then, Shirley and Stratford, joined the plantations which Robert visited as a boy. Shirley became his second home, enduringly a place of familiar comforts, as it was to his mother. Stratford held a different meaning for him. The felicitous hospitality of his half-brother and new sister-in-law extended only briefly, from his ninth to thirteenth years. Yet these were impressionable years, and the impressions of Stratford fortified the memories of early childhood before they had entirely faded. There was the chestnut tree he had planted with his mother in the driveway. Stratford Hall and, more significantly, its traditions became deeply imbedded in his consciousness.

With the grandeur restored by Anne McCarty's money, it was easy to imagine its heroic history, as represented by the portraits in the great hall and in the partly mythical tales, though there was nothing mythical about the Lee signers of the Declaration of Independence having been born in the room where he had been born. In a typical Carter trait, the boy developed then a custodial sense of obligation to the heritage of his forebears — at Stratford, to the name of Lee.

From his own words, then or later, it would be difficult to approximate the position of Robert Edward Lee's father in his feelings and attitudes. During the brief period of Stratford's recaptured grandeur, when Robert was eleven, his father died on the way home. With the long distances to be covered by coach-delivered mail and the uncertainty of the postal system, news of death reached the family long after the father was in his grave.

Later details revealed that, having despaired of regaining his health and homesick beyond endure, the sixty-two-year-old man had started home on a boat bound for Savannah. Becoming miserably ill as the ship neared Georgia, he asked to be put off at Cumberland Island, where the daughter of his old hero, Nathanael Greene, lived at Dungeness. In her home he died, on the 25th of March, 1818, and was buried with a military funeral in the Greene family's cemetery.

The effect of his death on Robert could only have been the end of a myth rather than of a man. Since his father had left when Robert was six, and for much of the time before had been more of a visitor in Ann Carter Lee's Alexandria home than the head of the house, the boy scarcely could have remembered him. He was unquestionably acutely aware of his father's career, in both its brilliance and its decline. With his strongly implanted filial feeling, Robert's later actions in relation to his father's memory looked as if he regarded him with pride and defensiveness, or a defensive pride.

Harry Lee had been a man of consequence, almost a great man and certainly a great soldier, but the new generation had not been kind to his memory. Robert was aware of that. He was also aware that in his father's direst poverty, when he constantly fought for pensions for his soldiers, Light-Horse Harry never asked nor received any recompense for his years of service or for the companies he outfitted. Then, Robert's mother, with her family pride, would have done everything possible to concentrate his attention on those qualities of his father that had been admirable.

The traits that characterized Robert, and which his father had remarked on by the time he was seven, were instilled by his mother long before his awareness of his father's bad habits about money or fall from high estate. What Robert Edward Lee felt about his father's reputation increased as he grew older. When the family received the delayed news of the father's death, it could have made no practical difference to the family in the red-brick house in Alexandria.

4

What affected Robert profoundly in relation to the Lee name happened when he was thirteen, in 1820. On Anne McCarty's fortune, half-brother Henry displayed agreeable talents as a host and, with a good mind, became renowned as a gifted and engaging conversationalist. As had his father, he impressed observers with his promise for high place. Yet, at thirty-three, Harry Lee the younger had not applied himself seriously to anything beyond playing the social role of master of Stratford. In that year, the course of life was suddenly removed from his decision.

The change began with a tragic accident. His two-year-old daughter Margaret, playing in the great hall, darted through the front door and, unable to check herself, fell to her death down the high flight of stone steps. Anne McCarty Lee became inconsolable and her grief, on the borderline of derangement, could be assuaged only by morphine. In a short time, the mistress of Stratford Hall became a drug addict.

While the mother became temporarily incompetent, Henry Lee sought his own solace in the arms of his wife's nineteen-year-old sister Elizabeth. Lee's sister-in-law, owning a sizable estate in her own right, was also his ward. With their parents dead, the wealthy McCarty girls had been under the guardianship of Richard Stuart before Anne's marriage. When Anne left their home, Elizabeth had decided to go along with her to Stratford, and Henry Lee had replaced Stuart as her legal guardian.

Harry Lee's betrayal of his trust became public knowledge when his ward gave birth to a stillborn child. The scandal, giving Lee the sobriquet of "Black-Horse Harry," was spread from Westmoreland County throughout Virginia by the court action of Richard Stuart. Taking Elizabeth back to her own home, he successfully petitioned the court to return her to his legal guardianship. As an ugly refrain from the past, it became revealed that Henry Lee owed money to Elizabeth McCarty's estate. While this debt was being discussed, the unwed mother cut off her hair and went into mourning, thus making a public spectacle of her shame.

In Black-Horse Harry Lee's time, with the Church of England having become in America the Episcopal Church, a Protestant evangelicalism swept through Virginia and replaced the bland tolerance of the Anglican Church with strictest moral rectitude. As Virginians had broken their social ties with England in the same period, nothing of the Regency's love of pleasure nor the cult of Byronic romanticism reached the rural plantation society. The family dominated every other consideration, and inherent in the matrix of the family was its honor. Whatever analyses might explain the motivations, male members of the ruling class of families regarded "taking advantage" of a virginal lady as the most heinous of moral and social offenses. Thus to "dishonor" a lady was the ultimate violation of a code of honor in which even to speak a lady's name in a public place provided grounds for a duel. There was nothing empty in this gentlemen's code of honor: they would and did die for it. In this moral background, the master of Stratford was ruined.

His wife left him, he sold the remains of his Stratford estate for $25,000, and left Westmoreland County. After a time he left Virginia and went to Tennessee. There Andrew Jackson, sympathetic to scandal, employed him as what today would be regarded as a member of his personal staff.

Robert Edward Lee was just entering his first formal school when his brother's disgrace became public knowledge. To a boy with a custodial sense of his family's traditions, the scandal must have served as a goad, reaffirming his ingrained course of rectitude. While his father and half-brother served as vivid examples of the consequences of departing from the values in which he had been trained, in turn he would exemplify the Biblical axiom of "Train a child in the way he shall go and when he is old he shall not depart from it." Only with Robert it went further: he never seemed to experience the impulse to depart from his training. An Alexandria neighbor said of him then that he learned from his mother to "practrice self-denial and self-control, as well as the strictest economy in all financial concerns."

It was during this period, when he entered school in Alexandria, that neighbors observed the young boy was "the man of the family." Carter, then graduated from Harvard, was practicing law in Washington; eighteen-year-old Smith had been appointed midshipman in the navy and was beginning his career at sea; Ann was sickly, and nine-year-old Mildred was still the baby. But it was more than this chance circumstance that caused Robert to be the one to assume the support of his mother's house. Carter and Smith had never shown a strong urge to look after their mother. As the center of her life, Robert had drifted into his duties gradually and naturally. In doing this he matured early and soberly. With all his sweetness of nature and capacity for affection, he never possessed Carter's unreserved affability nor Smith's gay charm.

Yet, in serving as his mother's support in childhood, Robert knew an inner security, a completeness of himself in relation to his environment, which he was never to lose. With an indivisible oneness, he was at home in his world.

In the house, he did the shopping and apportioned the food for the meals. When his mother was sick, he waited on her. If she was well enough to go abroad in the afternoons, he took her for a drive in the carriage when he came home from school, carrying her in his arms and arranging the cushions for her comfort. None of this seemed to interfere either with his studies or outdoor pleasures. For want of a saddle horse he indulged in the strenuous exercise of following fox hunts on foot. It seemed that, in absorbing his mother's precepts on self-discipline and purposefulness, by following her practices, he formed a ritualistic sense of order in which everything that should be done was done — and done without waste motion or time lost in deciding what to do.

In Ann Carter Lee's frailty and ill health, she was sustained by the simple absoluteness of her belief in the will of a merciful God in setting goals for her sons. Her unquestioning faith as transmitted to her son implanted in him that total acceptance, inherent in his inner security, of working the best he could within the design of God. Whatever action duty assigned him, implicit in the duty was the *need* to do it the best he could. Nothing he wrote or any recorded word indicated that he ever presumed on any course of action, large or small, which did not assume its accordance with God's will. If his aim fell outside the divine design, then "God's will be done." Without articulating his attitude, it was as unreflectively assumed as breathing.

It was inevitable that, with his strongly developed motivation, Robert applied himself diligently in school. Before attending a regular school he had, after the custom where no plantation tutors were available, learned reading and spelling, writing and basic grammar at home. In Alexandria, for some undetermined period he went to a tutor's plantation school at Eastern View, the estate of his aunt, his mother's sister Elizabeth Carter Randolph. Whatever was taught among his cousins at the Randolph family school, Robert was well prepared when he entered the regular curriculum at the new Alexandria Academy. William B. Leary, a learned Irishman and a good teacher, gave him a glowing recommendation when he applied for entrance into West Point three years later.

Vouching for his "correct and gentlemanly deportment," Leary wrote: "In the various branches, to which his attention has been applied, I flatter myself that his information will be found adequate to the most sanguine expectations of his friends. With me he has read all the minor classics, in addition to Homer and Longinus, Tacitus and Cicero. He is well versed in arithmetic, Algebra and Euclid."

During the three or so years Robert was under the tutelage of Mr. Leary, there is nothing to suggest why he decided on the army as a career. As with most Virginians of a plantation background, the land held an appeal for him, but to be a planter in early life one had to be lucky in one's father. Then, by the time Robert was sixteen, his mother's income suffered from lowered bank dividends, and manifestly Carter was the last son who could be supported through college. As Ann Hill wanted her sons to enter a profession, the choice was fairly well reduced to the army or the navy. It is possible, though entirely conjecture, that the army might have drawn Robert because the military was associated with the proud phases of his father's career. After all, he was the son of a major general, and every letter written by supporters of his application for appointment mentioned the fact that he was the son of Light-Horse Harry Lee.

The Military Academy, founded in 1802, had experienced a spurt in growth after the War of 1812, and more than forty Virginians had applied for appointments in 1823. Among Robert's fellow applicants in 1824 was

Joseph E. Johnston, whose father had served as major under Light-Horse Harry in Lee's Legion. West Point as a source of education was in the air. Nothing indicated that the widow's son dreamed of feats of glory in the field, or had ever manifested any prior interest in arms.

In making his application to West Point, Lee significantly did not give Alexandria as his residence. He listed Westmoreland County, the site of Stratford, indicating his identification with his birthplace and showing that the family regarded town residence as only an interlude. Once the application went in, Ann Carter Lee saw to it that congressmen and other dignitaries wrote in support, including William Fitzhugh, who continued to act as counsel for her estate. In his letter, Fitzhugh, with the usual reference to General Lee, wrote more lengthily on Lee's mother, whom he referred to as "one of the finest women the state of Virginia has ever produced."

In March, 1824, shortly after his seventeenth birthday, Robert received by mail his appointment from Secretary of War John C. Calhoun. In the same batch of appointments, Calhoun also mailed one to an applicant from Mississippi, Jefferson Davis. Because of the large number of successful applicants from Virginia, Robert — and his future friend Joe Johnston — were appointed with the class to enter the following year, the summer of 1825.

Characteristically, Robert used the period of waiting for preparation. A Quaker, James Hallowell, had opened a private school next door to the house occupied by the Lee family, and Robert was among the first of his few pupils. Mr. Hallowell wrote the most revealing summation of Robert Edward Lee at the age of eighteen:

"His specialty was *finishing up*. He imparted a finish and a neatness, as he proceeded, to everything he undertook. One of the branches of mathematics he studied was Conic Sections, in which some of the diagrams are very complicated. He drew the diagrams on a slate; and although he well knew that the one he was drawing would have to be removed to make room for another, he drew each one with as much accuracy and finish, lettering and all, as if it were to be engraved and printed."

Mr. Hallowell, in writing about his former pupil years later, said, "A feeling of mutual kindness and respect continued between us to the close of his life." The Irishman, Mr. Leary, also knew Robert when each was an old man. Both teachers found his character fully developed beyond change before he left for West Point, the traits that were to endure all in evidence.

His appointment came at the end of James Monroe's second term as President, ending the twenty-four years' reign of the Virginia dynasty in Washington. These years of Virginia's post-Revolutionary giants, extending from Washington, comprised the period of Robert Edward Lee's formation. He was a man out of those times, a product of eighteenth-century Virginia's "golden age" extended into the first quarter of the new century. When he left his mother's house for the institution on the Hudson, the mold was cast.

## 5

After he left the Alexandria home, his mother said, "How can I live without Robert? He is both son and daughter to me."

With her diminished family, and her diminishing income, Ann Carter Lee moved into Georgetown and made a home for Carter. This genial lawyer, fond of books and good living, assumed no more responsibility for the family affairs than he had when his mother was warning him at Harvard to stretch the little money she was able to send. Two years later she wrote in a letter to son Smith that Carter "is driving at law and if he makes any money he must be laying it up, for we see little at home."

Fifty-two years old when Robert left home, she was sinking steadily in health and hanging on to a frail thread of life by will until she could see her children successfully launched. (Ann would be married the following year to William Louis Marshall, of Baltimore.) Ann Carter Lee was cheered by frequent visits from members of her vast clan, all of which she dutifully reported to her absent sons. Evidently she kept none of their letters (none has as yet been found), though she was kept abreast of Robert's life at the Military Academy and was obviously proud of his record.

As Mr. Leary had predicted, Robert's progress fulfilled his friends' most sanguine expectations. He showed nothing of the quality called genius, nor was he anything of the grind. He showed application of a superior intelligence, and in his studies this placed his name on the list of "Distinguished Cadets," the top five students of each class. Where he was outstanding was in his adaptability to the total routine and in a uniform excellence in the performance of all his duties. For this he was awarded at the end of his first year the highest honor that could come to a cadet of his class. At that time were appointed the fourth classmen (freshmen) who would serve as noncommissioned officers — corporals and sergeants — for the following (third class) year. The highest noncommissioned rank was staff sergeant, and this went to Cadet Lee.

The curriculum and the severity of the routine had made no demands which the young Lee was unaccustomed to meeting in his own habits. At that time the superintendent of the Academy was Lieutenant Colonel Sylvanus Thayer, a forty-year-old engineer. An able administrator determined to raise the standards at West Point, Thayer was intellectually narrow, a cold and harsh disciplinarian, and won a hard name among cadets. He was, however, quick to recognize and encourage merit. The commandant of cadets, Major William J. Worth, another engineer, was cut from the same cloth and more vigilant about the minutest details of discipline than broadening mental horizons. Between the two of them, the rigidly enforced regulations that encompassed all waking hours of the boys made for a hard, dull life.

Some of the boys broke under the oppressive regimentation and some revolted against it, going out of bounds. Bounds consisted of a bleak area of four buildings — two stone dormitories, the Academy building and a mess hall — around the parade grounds. "Outside" consisted of the unsavory settlement at the ships' landing, where the boys could find a drink or a woman, a fight or a frolic. Some restless souls went along purposelessly, receptive to any high-jinks that might break the monotony. These were by no means the only regulations broken. Demerits were given for countless little lapses resulting from no more than boredom or fatigue, momentary carelessness or inattention. As Cadet Lee had no memory of life without its ordered routine of duties, and it was natural to his habits to do everything the best he could, he became the first cadet at West Point to receive no demerits at all.

He did a good deal of outside reading and, in his second year, was given the assignment of acting assistant professor of mathematics. This consisted of little more than working with some of the struggling fourth classmen. For this he received $10 a month besides his regular allowance, which his mother pridefully noted in a letter to Smith. At the end of his second year he would leave in June for the Georgetown home on a summer vacation, and his mother, in the letter to Smith, wrote, "Robert will then have been absent two years."

When Robert arrived at home, he found his mother an invalid. Nothing is known of the illness that proved terminal. She wrote, "My disease is an unconquerable one, but the symptoms at present do not threaten a speedy death." Her heart was cheered by the presence of the gray-uniformed young man who at twenty had filled out into a magnificent physical image.

It was the period of his life when contemporaries began to refer to his "manly beauty" and superb carriage. With a classically handsome face and the symmetrical proportions of his figure, he gave even then the impression of having been cast in a design rather than of growing. The look of the perfected product, the full flowering of his civilization, was completed by the composure of his expression. Neither warm nor austere, it was simply composed as a work of art is composed.

For the perfectly adjusted cadet it was a summer of return, after the first absence in his life, to a world of cousins. To the mother watching him, in his gracefully contained movements, he was the realization of all her training, the fulfillment of the efforts she continued to make on his twenty-five-year-old brother Smith. As Light-Horse Harry had begged Carter for letters, so she wrote her son at sea.

"Exclusive of my desire to hear from you, I lament your dislike of writing because it will be such a disadvantage to you through life. A man that cannot write a good letter on business or on the subject of familiar letters will make an awkward figure in every situation and will find himself greatly at a loss on any occasion. Indeed I cannot imagine how he will pass through life with satisfaction and respectability; should you arrive at any eminence in your profession, my dear Smith, it will be essential to your reputation to write a good letter, the knowledge of which cannot be acquired in later life . . ."

Aware that time would not permit her many more long letters to Smith and, anxious about his welfare, she ended with a plea. "Oh, that I could impart to you the knowledge gained from the experience of fifty-four years, then would you be convinced of the vanity of every pursuit not under the control of most inflexible virtue. I wish the powers of my mind were equal to the affections of my heart, then could I give you such precepts as would influence your conduct through life, but as the advantage has been denied me I just entreat you, my dear son, to reflect upon your poor Mother's solicitude for you, let it stimulate you to require the best habits and indulge not one that you could not remember on your deathbed with satisfaction."

Light-hearted Smith was not guilty of the bad habits nor the lack of virtue that his mother's letter might suggest. He was a different type from Robert, and the unworldly mother could not comprehend that in Robert she possessed that rarity of a son who lived completely in his mother's ideal for him. For the ultimate fruit of the communication between the widow and her son was that her ideal was transmitted in total to the boy, to become his self-image.

When Robert returned for his last two years at the Military Academy, he entered work that interested him more in terms of his future than the fundamentals of his first two years. Along with military studies that advanced from the school of the soldier into the science of war (including field and permanent fortifications), he concentrated on the scientific courses that led to engineering. Engineering was the goal of all ambitious cadets and to Lee specifically it offered a profession within the profession of arms. In building for his future, the end toward which he worked was unrelated to success in combat. The possibility of war appeared only as an incidence to his career.

In entering on his last year as an engineering student and first classman, he became, by his performance and by his presence, the outstanding cadet of his time at West Point. The ultimate honor was his appointment to corps adjutant, the highest rank a cadet could attain, and only one cadet could have it. He won this honor not as the first student in his class. Always near the top in any subject, he was never at the top in any. The honor was awarded him on the general excellence of his standing in all phases of Academy life and his position of natural leadership among his fellows.

Joe Johnston, his fellow Virginian with whom a long friendship was established, later wrote of the impression Cadet Lee made at West Point. "We had the same intimate associates, who thought as I did, that no other youth or man so united the qualities that win warm friendship and command high respect. For he was full of sympathy and kindness, genial and fond of gay conversation, even fun, while his correctness of demeanor and attention to all duties, personal and official, and a dignity as much a part of himself as the elegance of his person, gave him a superiority that every one acknowledged in his heart."

Johnston was the first of many who commented on the natural superiority of Lee. Many mentioned that the naturalness of his superiority placed him beyond the envy of others. Erasmus D. Keyes, a fourth classman when Lee was corps adjutant and later a Federal general, wrote, "I doubt if he ever excited envy in any man." Writing much later, with a long perspective, Keyes came the closest of anyone to reaching the cause of Lee's position among his fellows. "All his accomplishments and alluring virtues appeared natural to him, and he was free from the anxiety, distrust and awkwardness that attend a sense of inferiority."

Keyes's modern diagnosis went to the heart of the Lee image. The inner security that grew in his childhood relationship with his mother, freeing him from disharmonious self-doubts and unresolved conflicts, permitted an organic growth of every positive gift for life. In a total flowering, nothing was wasted and nothing warped. Born with a good mind, good health and good looks, but not evincing the exceptional in any single aspect, by an orderly cultivation of the whole man he developed into the exceptional by becoming a whole man. Years later Alexander Stephens referred to him as "the most [manly and] *entire* gentleman I ever saw."

This wholeness was the single key to the "mystery" that some have found Lee to be. The wholeness only appeared mysterious because so seldom encountered — even in his day when the model was the hero as man of virtue. Lee surpassed the models in becoming a perfectly symmetrical whole, complete as a finished work of art is complete. It was this rarity which his contemporaries observed, or sensed, and which placed him beyond the envy of his fellow cadets.

### 6

When all the counts were in for the four years' work — including tactics and artillery, which were given no yearly grades — Lee graduated as second in his class, as the top cadet, and as the first to complete the course without receiving a single demerit. However, there was no proud homecoming. His mother was in the last stages of her terminal illness. With no Robert at the little house in Georgetown, she had moved for the end into the Fitzhughs' large house at Ravensworth. There Robert found her in bed.

The newly graduated honor student became her full-time nurse. With no pull toward the pleasures of celebrating with companions of his own age, he gravitated naturally to his mother's bedside. What else could mean as much to him? The product of her stifled dreams, he was what he was because of her. Each intuitively understood the other, and he understood that a part of himself lay dying.

It was told that her dark eyes followed him whenever he left the room, and her gaze remained on the door until he came back in. In those last hours he was to Ann Carter Lee the hum of her days on earth.

He was beside her when her eyes closed in death. The vision remained vividly with him the rest of his life. When he was himself an old man, at Ravensworth for another funeral, he lingered at the doorway of the room where she had died and said, "Forty years ago I stood in this room by my mother's deathbed. It seems now but yesterday."

When Ann Carter Lee was buried at Ravensworth, her son Robert was soon to be without a home. At the Georgetown house, her children gathered to follow her will in disposing of her pitiful belongings, symbols of the unrelenting struggle of the former Shirley heiress to maintain her family in sparse gentility.

To married daughter Ann went the widow's maid, along with the Negress's child, and legalization of the ownership of the three slaves Ann had taken with her when she married. She also received the wardrobe, the white tea china, half the napkins and half the tablecloths — only two. (At Shirley in Ann Hill's childhood, a tablecloth was removed after each course of a meal.) Mildred, then a young bookish woman of eighteen, received the other two tablecloths, half the napkins, the piano, the carriage and horses, and old Nat, the coachman and general handyman. Mrs. Lee's clothes were divided among the two daughters, each of whom also received $10,000 of the bank stock that comprised the trust fund.

The other furniture evidently contained nothing of especial value or sentimental interest (the Lee furniture had been left at Stratford Hall). Ann Hill's will directed that this be sold, the cash to be added to the cash value of the bank stock after the $20,000 was deducted for the girls. Reasoning that the boys had been provided for by their education, the widow divided the residue of the cash between them. Robert, with his brothers, received perhaps as much as $3000. This remnant of Carter money was the only estate ever received by the legatee of the great Lee heritage: he was the first generation of Lees in Virginia who would be dependent on what he could earn away from the plantations. But the plantation dream was in him, and Stratford remained his spiritual home, and a goal became that of reclaiming it.

Shortly after his mother's death, further repercussions of Henry Lee's stewardship of Stratford came to public knowledge. When he had sold Stratford in 1821 for $25,000 to William C. Somerville, $3000 of the payment had been withheld for Somerville to apply on the claims of Elizabeth McCarty against the estate. The claims of Henry's former ward actually came to $9,647.92 more than the $3000, and this amount was owed by Black-Horse Harry to Somerville. Then Somerville died intestate, and the county put Stratford up for bids in 1827. The estate went for $11,000 to Henry D. Storke, along with the release of Harry Lee from his $9,647.92 obligation. Not at all by chance, the highest bidder, Henry D. Storke, was the new husband of Elizabeth McCarty. After six years in mourning for her shame, Henry Lee's plump sister-in-law married the man who was to return her to Stratford Hall as its mistress — with much of the McCarty fortune.

In 1828, when the complicated transactions were completed and the dishonored ward returned in triumph to the Lee's dynastic seat, Henry Lee was in Nashville, working for presidential candidate Andrew Jackson. Probably the last Lee master of Stratford would have remained out of the news following this local event except that Jackson, after he was inaugurated as President, rewarded his services with a consulship at Algiers. Lee's wife had by then returned to him, and the couple were already established in Algiers when, in February, 1830, the Senate surprisingly rejected the confirmation of his appointment.

The vote of twenty-one senators against General Lee's son, with not one voice raised in his behalf, was not a small affair. Raising the question of Jackson's popularity, it also aired the unexplainable vindictiveness of men from Virginia and Tennessee whom Lee had regarded as his friends. In the decade since the scandal, Henry Lee had led an exemplary life — honorably employed, winning back his wife and living modestly in order to pay off his debts. Accepting his social ostracism with the same grace with which his father had accepted the consequences of his own folly, he had won many supporters in building a new life. His former neighbor Richard T. Brown prepared a statement with a group of Westmoreland County men and delivered it to President Jackson:

"Educated in as strict a moral code as his most vindictive persecutors, we equally condemn one circumstance of his life, but we do not consider it a generous policy or a Christian virtue to pursue forever with unrelenting ferocity the unfortunate victim of a *single* act of passion." Voicing what was in the minds of many, the Westmoreland group stated, "What circumstances unknown to the public have influenced the decision of that honorable body we are unable to say, but we cannot help believing that their virtuous indignation has been grossly abused by the most exaggerated statements and malicious invectives."

This last was in reference to the action of John Tyler, Lee's classmate at William and Mary and supposed friend. Tyler circulated some letters that misrepresented Henry Lee, making it appear that his affair with Elizabeth McCarty had been motivated by mercenary interest. Nothing could have been more false. Careless about money as he was, Black-Horse Harry, like his father, was always generous with what he had — or didn't have. It was believed that the slander was accepted, or at least acted upon, because of jealousy of Henry Lee's intimacy with the President. Certainly the self-righteous persecution seemed too unrelenting to have been motivated only by moral outrage of an act ten years in the past.

Henry Lee, with all prospects ruined and stranded penniless in Europe with his wife, hurt his own cause by writing in bitter intemperateness about his persecutors, particularly John Tyler. Following the outlines of his father's course to the end, Major Henry Lee turned to writing and eked out a squalid livelihood in Paris until his death in 1837.

At the time of the Senate rejection, when the previously Virginia family scandal became known to the nation, Henry Lee's half-brother Robert had recently been commissioned second lieutenant in the engineering corps of the U. S. Army. It must have seemed that he would never be done with the ghosts of Stratford. Though the new lieutenant needed nothing to strengthen his purpose of living in his mother's ideal, the venom cast on his family's name intensified the reality of her concepts as he began his adult life.

When Ann Carter Lee died, the *National Intelligencer* wrote, "Her death is such as might have been expected from her life — exhibiting the resignation and composure of a practical Christian, conscious of having faithfully discharged her duties to God and her fellow creatures."

In lasting as long as she was needed, Nancy could have said with Paul, "I have finished my course, I have kept the faith."

Her son would do no less.

# PART TWO

# Career Soldier

## CHAPTER III

## "I Wish I Was Back in Virginia"

LIEUTENANT LEE experienced only two years between the death of the mother he took care of and marriage to a young lady who liked to be taken care of. Mary Anne Randolph Custis was not typical of Southern-raised girls in her attitude to gentlemen: instead of looking to their comfort, she expected them to look to hers. Nor was she any beauty. She was frail, bony of figure, and her patrician face was thin, sharp-featured and imperious. She had brown hair and eyes, like Lee's mother, but, careless of her appearance, her hair was the despair of the maids who helped her dress. At that age, twenty-two, Mary Custis had developed no habits of trying to please anyone or of making herself attractive for others.

Born to vast privilege at Arlington, a showplace of the Washington-Alexandria area of the Potomac, she was the only child of George Washington Parke Custis and the former Mary Fitzhugh, whose brother had been such a staunch friend to Lee's mother. Powerfully connected to many of Virginia's ruling families, including the Lees, Mary Custis was a distant cousin of Robert's and had known him all her life.

Her eccentric father, Washington Custis, fancied himself as "the child of Mount Vernon," and at Arlington acted as something of a one-man guide service to the memorabilia of the great Washington. Heir to 15,000 acres and 250 slaves, Washington's adopted son had built the Arlington manor house on the model of a Greek temple. On a hill overlooking the Potomac and the capital across the river, the house and its array of outbuildings had been built at great cost over a period of years and was the pride of its owner. The house was approached by a landscaped hillside, like a park, and set against a background of woodland. Inside, its many rooms were stocked with heirlooms from Mount Vernon, and Custis delighted in showing visitors the four-poster Washington had slept in, the punch bowl he had served guests from and even clothes the general had worn.

Balding and undistinguished in appearance, with some wan pretensions to learning, Martha Washington's fifty-year-old grandson was a garrulous dilettante. He indifferently administered his inherited properties, was slovenly in his housekeeping and in his personal habits, and did nothing to discourage his daughter's self-indulgence.

Yet, the lines of beaux who rode up the hill to the impressive-looking mansion crowning the crest did not come courting only because of the Custis wealth and position. By all accounts Mary Custis was an attractive girl despite her lack of beauty. Her dark eyes were bright and alive, lighting her expression, she was spirited, had a sense of humor and was a good conversationalist. How long she had decided on Robert Lee, a visitor to her home all through their childhood, cannot be known. It is known that she took none of her other suitors seriously, and that when he was a cadet and then a newly commissioned lieutenant he came riding to Arlington alone, and not with his mother on a family visit. However, he did not actually propose until he had been in the army for two years and was transferred to a post, at Fort Monroe, Virginia, which provided adequate quarters for officers' families.

Prior to his proposal, Robert Lee had never shown serious attention to any other girl. As with most woman-raised children, he was much at ease in female society and admittedly receptive to the charms of good-looking women. Except for a single known flirtatious romance in the stylized gallantry of nonpurposeful attentions, there is nothing to indicate that he was ever involved with a woman of any kind before his marriage. The attentions he paid Eliza Mackay, of Savannah, seemed no more than the results of propinquity on a lonely young man who had recently lost his mother.

Lieutenant Lee's first assignment had been as assistant to the engineering officer in charge of constructing a fort on bleak Cockspur Island, on the mud flats in the roads at the mouth of the Savannah River. Along with the sorrow that accompanied him to the work in the desolate isolation, Lee had brought along old Nat, the ancient coachman and factotum his mother had willed to Sister Mildred. Nat was too sick to work anymore and the young lieutenant, whom he had helped raise, took him to the warmer climate for his health. It was no good. The family retainer died, deepening Lee's division with his past. During this period, Lee's younger sister Mildred married Edward Vernon Childe and soon moved to Paris. The family which Ann Carter Lee had held together was scattered beyond the possibility ever of meeting even for a reunion.

At his post, Robert Lee was, as always, lucky in finding or making friends in a new place. At nearby Savannah he found his West Point classmate and intimate Jack Mackay, and Lee's social ease, his courtesy and consideration soon won him a warm place in the Mackay family. It was after Jack went off on his army assignment that Lee began squiring around his sister Eliza and, characteristic of Lee's associations, his friendship with Eliza and her family endured throughout life.

The Savannah period was only an interlude before life began for him as a married man comfortably garrisoned at the pleasant site of Fort Monroe, in his home state and not too far from Shirley. At the age of twenty-four (a little less than two years older than Mary) he was married at Arlington on June 30, 1831, with Lee's brother Smith coming in from sea to act as best man. As at his own father's wedding to Ann Hill Carter, Lieutenant Lee did not have the approval of his new father-in-law.

In the case of Washington Custis, aware of the ruin of the Lee fortunes, he did not think a lieutenant's pay could provide his daughter with her accustomed luxuries. This particular lieutenant, however, had the support of the bride's mother, his distant kinswoman, was personally well regarded in the community, and had one element strongly in his favor. In the custom of plantation families of marrying one of their own, it would be difficult to find another son-in-law as intimately connected, through blood and marriage, with the ruling families of the society. By Custis's standards, he was simply poor, and the father had only reluctantly permitted himself to be overruled.

As for Robert Lee himself, it would never have occurred to him to marry outside — if, indeed, he knew anyone outside his world of cousins. Unlike his father and half-brother, he did intend that the heiress of Arlington should live entirely on his army pay. Mary would of course bring along her personal maid and any house servants required, but the only Custis luxury she would know would come in visits home. As it turned out, the visits home became very frequent.

2

Fort Monroe was the site of the oldest fortified position in the United States, dating back to Fort Algernourn, which served as an outpost for Jamestown in 1609. Situated on the sandy tip of the Virginia Peninsula between the York and the James, where the rivers emptied into Hampton Roads, the position guarded the sea approaches to the port of Norfolk and the James River approach to Richmond. Outside the fort, the wharves, an 1802 lighthouse and the new Hygeia Hotel — including a strip of beach — formed the post office address of Old Point Comfort, near the charming seventeenth-century small city of Hampton.

The new fort was begun in 1819 and, under the supervision of Simon Bernard, an engineer on Napoleon's staff, work continued during the administration of President Monroe. The outer works were constructed in a stone heptagonal, three of the seven sides directly facing Hampton Roads. These ramparts, of gun embrasures and casemates, enclosed about eighty acres of flat ground, on which the barracks and officers' quarters were built. By the time Lee came in May, 1831, most of the major work had been completed, Bernard was gone, and the finishing up work was in the charge of Captain Andrew Talcott, of the U. S. Army engineering corps.

Typically Lee made a fast friend of his immediate superior, Talcott, a Connecticut native of the West Point class of 1818. The engineering corps was no favorite with the Regular Establishment, but the engineers regarded themselves as a superior group, partly because of their visible accomplishments — even though much of their work, as on rivers and harbors, was nonmilitary and done on government civilian projects. At Fort Monroe the engineers naturally regarded themselves as the accomplishers and the large contingent of artillery officers as drones. Friction was constant between Captain Talcott and the post commander, Brevet Colonel Eustis, but in spite of the jealousies Talcott managed to garrison Lee in the fine accommodations of Building No. 17.

This was a handsome, airy, yellow-painted brick building of two stories, high basement and dormered attic. On the second floor of these preferred quarters, Lieutenant Lee settled with his bride. Building No. 17 opened a happy period in Lee's life. Brevet Second Lieutenant Lee kept his friends through punctilious correspondence, and his spirit was reflected in the light vein of his letters, touching nearly all subjects with a turn of humor.

The one grimly serious subject that came to the life at the post was the Negro uprising in the so-called Nat Turner's Rebellion on August 23, 1831. In Southhampton County, about forty miles from Norfolk across the James River, Nat Turner was one of the few slaves of a kindly coachmaker who operated a small farm in adjunct to his trade. Conceiving himself to be divinely appointed to act as an avenger for the oppressed, Turner and a few of his followers killed the coachmaker's family in their sleep and then started on a march of terror through the isolated farms and plantations of the agricultural community. Gathering force as it went, the band killed fifty-six men, women and children before it was dispersed by a hastily gathered company of militia and a stand by the family of Dr. Simon Blunt, whose slaves remained loyal.

From Fort Monroe three companies of artillery had been sent by steamer to the danger zone and the post was alerted for what the area feared might be a general slave uprising. As far as investigation discovered, Nat Turner was the sole instigator of the insurrection, but this was not known at the time. It happened that abolitionist publications had been urging the slaves to rise up (the *Liberator*, praising the murderers, exhorted other slaves to do more of the same). People throughout Virginia, as well as the soldiers at Fort Monroe, believed outside agents had provoked and were provoking the slaves. The reaction in the state caused the General Assembly to meet to examine the whole institution of slavery and the place of the Negroes.

Judging by Lee's later expressions, at the time of Virginia's 1831 convention he shared the views of a growing proportion of Virginians who believed in emancipation (an emancipation society had been founded in 1801) but could find no practical solution for the freed Negroes. Most national emancipationists — as distinguished from abolitionists, who had no concern about either the freed Negro or the white society — leaned toward deportation as a solution. James Madison was national president of the American Colonization Society, founded in 1816 for the purpose of transporting freed Negroes to Liberia, and John Marshall was president of the active Virginia branch. It was over the problem of the freed Negro that the 1831-1832 convention split.

The emancipationists showed organized strength in the convention — a bloc of 58 out of 132, with only 60 of the majority solidly pro-slavery. Their spokesmen advanced powerful arguments. They attributed to slavery Virginia's decline in population, from first to third and falling, as the self-reliant farmers (whom Jefferson had envisioned as the foundation of a democracy) steadily migrated from the state. James McDowell of Rockbridge County, himself the owner of four taxable slaves, warned that "the slaveholding interests of the country will and can coalesce with no other interest and must, as a consequence, be separate and hostile to all others." With prophetic vision he pointed out the possibility of disunion with slavery becoming a crusade in which, "in the name of liberty but with the purpose of plunder . . ." interests in the North would hold up the South ". . . as the enemies of men whom it will be a duty to overcome and a justice to despoil."

The emancipationists might well have won except for some cross-politicking. At that period the western counties in and beyond the Alleghenies, growing in population, were challenging the rule of the Tidewater oligarchy, whose power was maintained by restricting the vote to property owners. The oligarchy had been forced in 1829 to yield some concessions, satisfactory to nobody, and on emancipation several voted from class loyalties. Only eight votes out of twelve fence-sitters — uncommitted either to slavery or emancipation — would have exerted a most profound effect on American history.

At that, the issue came down to the problem, including cost, of deporting the freed Negroes. No one, not the most zealous emancipationists, advocated freeing the slaves and leaving the freedmen in Virginia. The purpose, forced by Nat Turner's insurrection, was to remove all Negroes, and the emancipationists ultimately failed for want of a practical solution to this.

They had come so close that emancipationists all over the state, including Lee, were encouraged to hope for the passage of the bill. Lee, referring later to the close vote on the ordinance of emancipation, was quoted as saying, "Every one fully expected at the next convention it would have been carried." This was a practical expectation, because in the convention the emancipation bloc had managed to get a vote, 65 to 58, favoring a preamble to the committee's report which admitted slavery to be an evil. The preamble stated that, while action was "inexpedient for the present legislature . . . a further action for the removal of slaves should await a more definite development of public opinion."

Two factors caused public opinion to shift against the emancipationists. Following Nat Turner's insurrection, the abolitionists became more bloodthirsty in their distant incitements to murder and extended their attacks from the institution of slavery to abusive condemnations of the morals, customs and character of the white Southerners. As all Virginians became antagonized by this hostility, the emancipationists could only be hurt by being associated in people's minds with such fanatics, and their movement lost its momentum. This left the field to the large slaveholders. Aroused by the threat to their property, representing to some individuals as much as half a million dollars (as much as several million to some families), the slavery bloc became active and vocal in defending the institution.

Individual families continued to free their own slaves, though depriving their children of wealth accumulated across generations. Some slaveowners, such as childless John Randolph, were financially able to write off the property loss and still pay for the deportation of five hundred freedmen to the Liberian colony. But as an organized movement, emancipation drifted to an end in Virginia.

Just when the last of the cosmopolitan-minded humanists from the eighteenth century's "golden age" were disappearing from the Virginia political scene, slavery became fixed as an institution and the state began to go on the defensive in attitude. Since such a subtly fundamental change was not readily apparent, Lieutenant Lee evidently was unaware of the climax reached in the 1831-1832 convention and of the shifts in balance that followed. It can be observed, however, that when the slave issue began to grow national Lee expressed the deepest aversion for extremists of both sides, pro-slavery and abolitionist. He always believed the emancipationist movement in Virginia had been halted by the abolitionists.

At the time of Nat Turner's insurrection, the repercussions that concerned Lee were immediate and practical. In the continuing alarms, the garrison was strengthened at Fort Monroe, and Colonel Eustis grew reluctant to bring inside the stone walls the Negroes employed by the engineers. To Lee this meant that lack of labor interfered with his work. Then and all his life, no matter what was happening around him, Lee was compelled to concentrate on the task that had been assigned him. Having absorbed his mother's patient practicality in details, he was drawn to the concrete job which would yield results to his efforts. Whatever the job, *he had to get things done.*

Lee's job was primarily to construct the moat around the outer works and to build the outer escarpments to the fort. As the marshy-banked Mill Creek separated the ramparts from the landslide, this part of his work consisted chiefly of drainage and masonry. Secondarily, Lieutenant Lee worked on building up the stone base for a small fort at Rip Raps, a mile out in the Roads from the main fort. As Talcott was much away, Lee was given final responsibility for ordering all supplies and equipment for the works in progress. Here for the first time in his adult life he showed the effects of having shared his mother's stringent economies in disbursing cash and making do. As if each penny spent came from his own pocket, Lee showed an imaginative prudence in the purchase and use of supplies, and an abhorrence of waste he was never to lose.

During the two years he worked on completing the moat, building the base at Rip Raps and in finishing up many of the details in the ramparts, the conflict between the post commander and the engineers did not affect Lee's relationship with the younger artillery officers. The comradeship continued after he moved into the favored quarters of Building No. 17, though the line officers were sharply aware of Talcott's care for his own. When Mrs. Lee was away on visits to Arlington, the lieutenant joined in the nightly frivolities in the unmarried officers' barracks. Genial Joe Johnston had come to Fort Monroe then, in the garrison, and the two non-drinkers made the rounds together.

Not then, or ever, did Lee show any disapproval of brother officers who did drink. He was baffled, somewhat disturbed, by heavy, chronic drinkers and developed an uneasiness about men who drank themselves out of self-control. But where the evening was convivial, the young lieutenant showed himself to be as at home among those drinking as among those who chewed tobacco or smoked cigars. It was just something he did not want to do himself. Since he never expressed himself on the subject, his aversion might well have been associated with his own ingrained ideal of maintaining possession of himself on all occasions. In other aspects of life, as in guarding his temper and in hiding his feelings in the presence of non-intimates, he showed such a steadfast purpose of retaining his self-composure that others could assume he had no strong feelings.

Where his feelings were the strongest, he showed the most composure, and this concerned his wife. The heiress of Arlington revealed the effects of having been spoiled by her father and early in marriage displayed a reluctance to be deprived of the luxuries of her home. On their first Christmas at the fort, the young couple went to Arlington for the holidays, and when the lieutenant came back to his post, Mrs. Lee remained at home.

Weeks passed into months for the healthy young man unwillingly returned to bachelorhood, and then on April 17 he wrote, ". . . from your
last letter I suppose I can not expect you until the *last* of May! What am I
to do in all that time! I hope your reasons are *very* good for this long
delay and that you will be better reconciled to this interminable separation better than I shall be . . ."

After this plaint from her new husband, Molly — as he then called her
— delayed returning until the next month, and on June 6 the lieutenant
wrote that he would prepare to meet her boat on June 12. When Molly,
with her maid and her luggage, came ashore at the Old Point Comfort
wharf, she was six months pregnant.

Perhaps she had been sick during the early months of her pregnancy
and then, like Lee's mother with her first child, had been reluctant to leave
her familiar comforts. By the time she returned to Fort Monroe, instead
of bringing herself to her husband, she would need, in the heat that comes
to the Virginia Peninsula, comfort from him for her last stages of pregnancy.

Their first child was born on the second floor of Building No. 17 on
September 16, 1832, and named George Washington Custis Lee. Lieutenant Lee was a natural father and became the same kind of doting parent his
mother had been to him. The child opened areas of affection and response,
a new sense of wonder Lee had never imagined.

Then, two months after Custis was born, Molly was gone again, taking
the little boy to the home of his grandparents. On November 27 Lee was
again writing his wife at Arlington. "My sweet little Boy, what would I
give to see him! The house is a perfect desert without him and his Mother
and there is no comfort in it. Take good care of him, Molly, and don't let
him be spoiled; direct him in *every* thing and leave *nothing* to the guidance of his Nurse. I am waking all night to hear his sweet little voice and if
in the morning I could only feel his little arms around my neck and his
dear little heart fluttering against my breast, I should be too happy."

He wrote that he had suffered a slight cold and that a long-troublesome
tooth was giving him acute pain. "I would have had it drawn . . . but
they seem to be so wedged in together and of such long root, that I should
like an experienced hand to operate, for I have no ambition of having my
jaw fractured." *

Then he made a reference to what may have been an altercation arising
between his meticulousness and her carelessness, especially her indifference to time schedules. "I don't know that I shall ever overcome my pro-
pensity for order and method," he wrote, "but I will try." Saying that he

---

* Spelling and usually punctuation of Lee's letters have been modernized, and am-
persands have been written as "and."

did not feel this was a small matter, the perfectionist promised to try to mend his ways as a means of avoiding friction.

After Christmas, Molly and little Custis were back at Fort Monroe, and remained until the following July, 1833. Then she went home again, and again in November. On those occasions, there was no excuse of pregnancy nor of allowing her parents to see their grandchild. Molly's tolerance for garrison life was very low, and Lee submitted to his spoiled wife's need of the luxuries of Arlington.

At that, Mary Custis Lee's visits home may have been an element in winning her father over to her husband. Washington Custis soon forgot that he had disapproved of his son-in-law, and the older and younger man established a friendly relationship. With Mrs. Custis, Lee became very close. He called her "Mother," and wrote her with the intimacy of a son.

With his love of family, and his own immediate family dispersed, Mary's family became meaningful to him and Arlington a surrogate home. This fulfilling sense of kinship with the family into which he married, and to which he was distantly related, might have contributed to his acceptance of his wife's trips home. But there is no reason to assume the strongly built soldier liked being returned to a celibate life.

By 1834, the good days were gone at Fort Monroe. The conflict between the post commander and the engineers had been resolved, at personal loss to Lee, by the transfer of good friend Talcott. With the main fort then completed, Lee was placed in charge of the uninspiring assignment of piling stones in the waters at Rip Raps. To this tedium was added the depressing sense of the lack of advancement in the engineering corps. Not until 1832 had he passed from his brevet status to become a second lieutenant of regular rank, and after five years in the army he was still a second lieutenant. At this stage of affairs, General Gratiot, chief of engineers, interceded in Lee's career and brought him to the engineering department in Washington.

3

For the next twelve years, from his twenty-seventh into his thirty-ninth year, Lee learned the treadmill of army routine. He experienced a tedium that grew literally insupportable, the stultification of dull tasks and the frustration of the slow advancement in the engineers. In 1836, he was promoted to first lieutenant, and two years later, nine years out of the Military Academy, he finally made captain. There he hung. At one point only the illness of his wife prevented him from following the course of his friend Talcott, who left the service. The creeping advance in rank worried him in the practical aspects of meeting his obligations on his pay, for by 1846 the Lees had seven children.

After Custis came Mary in the summer of 1835, then in June of 1837 Fitzhugh, called "Rooney" to distinguish him from brother Smith's son called Fitz. Rooney was followed by two girls — Annie in June, 1839, and Agnes early in 1841. Another boy came in October, 1843, and, against the father's preference, was named by his mother Robert Edward Lee, Jr. (The second Robert Edward signed himself Robert E. Lee, Jr., but the father never signed himself Robert E. Lee. Called Robert, he signed himself and was officially R. E. Lee.) The last child, Mildred, was born around the first of the year, 1846. Each child took his own niche in the limitless parental affections of the father (the first-born son was "Boo" and the first-born daughter was "Daughter"). But the responsibilities began to weigh on him from 1835, when he worked in the engineering offices in Washington.

Mary Custis Lee never recovered fully from the effects of an infection following the birth of her second child in that summer. An abscess, which she called a tumor and Lee called an inflammation, was probably one of the complications of what was then called "child-bed fever." Before antisepsis was discovered, doctors knew little to nothing about the dangers of infection. An infection that began in the lining of the uterus, or womb, spread into the lymph glands of the groin, the lymph glands of the pelvis and into the veins, and a clot in the large vein leading back from the foot, leg and thigh caused swelling and pain near the hip.

With Mrs. Lee, then at Arlington, the doctors called in advanced various diagnoses as they treated her symptoms. Leeches on the abscess caused her, she wrote, "the most exquisite pain." The doctors' treatments did no harm, the abscess finally came to a head and broke, and the mother began a slow, very slow, recovery during the early months of 1836. She had been in bed nearly four months, much of the time under "constant and corroding pain," as Lee wrote Talcott, "and is dreadfully reduced."

When she first began to sit up in bed, devouring partridges and buckwheat muffins for breakfast, Mary Lee became so irritated with a snarl in her hair that she cut it all off. As her hair grew back rapidly and she was bored at the problem of brushing it out, she threatened to shave her head. The patient husband wrote Talcott that he expected to come home and find her bald.

It was during those months, from the birth of Mary in the summer of 1835 to the mother's relative recovery in May of 1836, that Lee struggled with the temptation to resign from the service. With spring his spirits revived. "The country looks very sweet now," he wrote Talcott from Arlington, ". . . and perfumed by the blossoms of the trees, the flowers of the garden, Honeysuckles, Yellow Jasmine, etc., is more to my taste than at any other season of the year. But the brightest flower there blooming is my daughter, O, she is a rare one . . . I must confess she has, as yet, some little ways about her that do not altogether suit a man of my *nervous temperament*."

The role of father gradually claimed him during the following decade. From the sparkling-eyed lieutenant for whom life had opened at Fort Monroe, Lee became a family man following a routine profession without surprises. The dashing black sidelocks of the young lieutenant's days were gone, replaced by a sedate black mustache. Gone too was the gloss from the dark hair, now brushed across his scalp from a low part and worn long on the sides. Yet, with the maturity he looked even more impressive, for the stifling of the inner ebullience was not reflected outwardly in his attitude to others.

As seen late in this period by a young artillery lieutenant, Henry J. Hunt, "He was then about 35 years of age, as fine looking a man as one would wish to see, of perfect figure and strikingly handsome. Quiet and dignified in manner, of cheerful disposition, always pleasant and considerate, he seemed to me the perfect type of a *gentleman*."

### 4

Lee began this stretch of twelve years by working as assistant to General Gratiot at engineering headquarters in Washington. For his home life and social life, the situation was almost ideal. The Lees lived at Arlington, from which the lieutenant rode six miles to his offices. In the city, where friend Joe Johnston was then stationed, Lee joined a congenial officers' mess. He enjoyed the comings and goings of family visitors at Arlington, the parties in Washington, and he liked seeing the pretty girls. But all the pleasant aspects of living were undermined by his detestation of office work.

Headquarters of the engineering corps operated in association with the government in its projects on public works, and to this extent took on the atmosphere of a bureau. There Lee encountered the pettiness, the obstructions and the inaction involved in the bureaucratic maneuverings of politicians, all of which profoundly depressed him. To a man who had to be using the best of himself, the frustrating waste agitated him more than anything in life and bore the hardest on his self-control.

In the summer and early fall of 1835 — while his first daughter was a baby and his wife ill — Lee received a brief release from the stagnation, by making a trip to settle the boundary dispute between Ohio and Michigan. While he was there, his wife, sicker than Lee realized, evidently wrote urging him to come back to Arlington. Lee sent, for him, a very strong answer.

"Why do you urge my *immediate* return, and tempt me in the *strongest* manner, to endeavor to get excused from the performance of a duty, imposed on me by my profession, for the pure gratification of my private feelings? Do you not think these feelings are not enough of themselves to contend with, without other aggravation; and that I would rather be strengthened and encouraged to the *full* performance of what I am called on to execute, rather than be excited to a dereliction, which even our affection could not palliate, or our judgment excuse?"

After this statement on his feelings about duty, Molly apparently left him in peace. In early September he wrote her, "I am always longing for the hour that shall unite us . . . I shall then see again that *Boo*, and the little one, and Mother, and all of you . . . We are encamped on the verge of the Lake, in a wilderness of Land, with nothing around us but dwarf Wild Poplar and pine . . . There are no inhabitants near us, and even the Indians that live in the country back of us are all at Chicago, on the west side of the Lake, waiting to receive their annual annuities."

When the renewal from this interlude had passed, the cooped-up office life became less endurable, and in 1836 only his wife's condition prevented him from resigning his commission. To escape from work that had become intolerable he asked for the assignment of changing the course of the Mississippi River at St. Louis. Lee's training for this sort of work was rudimentary, and he was wholly inexperienced with rivers. But someone had to go, no one else volunteered, and First Lieutenant (soon to be Captain) Lee left the East Coast in 1837 at the age of thirty.

St. Louis was a boom city — very costly and very dirty, Lee found it on his arrival in August — dependent on boat traffic on the Mississippi. The current of the river was gradually bearing to the eastern bank, wearing away the shoreline on the Illinois side. One island rose in the river directly in front of the city, and the alluvial mud carried along by the water was forming a second island. Between the islands and the changing current, St. Louis was threatened with being stranded and transformed into an inland city.

The city government had appropriated some money, long petitioned Washington, and the problem had been studied by General Gratiot personally and by that remarkable riverman, Captain Henry Shreve. A former bargeman and innovator of steamboats on the Mississippi, Shreve had given up his own profitable shipping to work at a sacrifice for the government in clearing the Mississippi, the Missouri and the Red Rivers of driftwood. In Western eyes, Captain Shreve, with his personally invented "snagboat," was the master of the Mississippi. But Shreve had his hands more than full with keeping the waters clear for shipping, and he had time for no more than a suggested plan for saving St. Louis as a river port.

When Lee arrived alone, leaving his family at Arlington (in charge, he wrote a friend, of five-year-old Custis), he began a careful study from the very beginning, as if no preliminary surveys and suggested plans had been made by Shreve or Gratiot. The St. Louis citizens, frantic for action, resented the slow thoroughness, and what they regarded as the imperious independence, of the young lieutenant from Virginia. The local newspaper voiced the general dissatisfaction, and the city government withdrew its appropriations.

Outwardly Lee remained unmoved by the criticism. A young Georgian, Lieutenant Meigs, who worked with him as assistant the first year, said, "He was one with whom nobody ever wished or ventured to take a liberty, though kind and generous to his subordinates, admired by all women, and respected by all men." Publicly Lee only said, referring to the withdrawn appropriation, "They have a right to do as they wish with their own; I do not own the city. The Government has sent me here as an officer of the army to do a certain work. I shall do it."

Though Lee privately resented the way the army was treated (writing John Mackay he wished the job was done and "I was back in Virginia"), his feelings did not interfere with his work. He went out with the civilian workers every morning about sunrise and worked beside them during the heat of the day. A steamboat moored to the bank was used as headquarters, and there the patrician lieutenant (as some of the townpeople had found him) shared the men's rations and sometimes ate at the same table in the cabin — though an observer pointed out that he never became familiar. Mayor John F. Darby remembered that "he maintained and preserved under all circumstances his dignity and gentlemanly bearing, winning and commanding the esteem, regard and respect of every man under him."

Lee showed there his capacity for leading men by sharing with them without being one of them. As had his fellow cadets, the men accepted his natural superiority and were drawn to the courtesy and thoughtfulness in a nature free of any need for self-assertion.

A close working relationship developed between Lee and Henry Kayser, a twenty-six-year-old German-born engineer appointed as civilian assistant. The young German took over his work with the same painstaking thoroughness as did Lee, and night after night the two of them worked together in the steamboat cabin, on drawings, plans and estimates, until eleven o'clock. To be ready for work at sunrise the next morning, Lee frequently slept on the old boat. Out of their working together, a rather formal friendship slowly grew between Lee and Kayser. Kayser was disturbed by the rise of anti-foreign sentiment in the new country, and Lee, only a few years the senior, acted as paternalistic adviser.

During the winters, work had to be halted on the river, and Lee went to Arlington. During his second and third years at St. Louis, he brought his family with him — or part of it. Dark-eyed Mary ("Daughter") seems to have remained at Arlington, at least some of the time, for she became extremely spoiled by her Custis grandparents. A separateness from her parents, that developed noticeably as Mary grew older, evidently began with that period of independence from them. Unlike her brothers and sisters, she became emotionally independent of the family.

In St. Louis the Lees rented quarters in a house owned by a Mr. and Mrs. Beaumont and acquired random furniture for their temporary residence. This came to an end in October, 1840, when Lee was recalled from the job. It was not completed but, basically adapting Shreve's and Gratiot's plans (after satisfying himself they were the most practical), he had broken the back of the work and won the lasting respect of riverman Shreve. St. Louis was saved as a port. Henry Kayser, appointed city engineer, carried on the work according to Lee's plans, writing Lee frequently after he returned East.

On April 10, 1841, Captain Lee entered the last phase of his long peacetime routine. After doing a repair job on a fort on the North Carolina coast, he was assigned to his engineering specialty, fortifications, at Fort Hamilton in New York Harbor. While he was in New York State again, near the site of his studies, the forces began to gather in the nation's course that were to control his future.

5

From Lee's graduation in the first year of Andrew Jackson's administration, the expanding nation began to undergo a fundamental change beneath the apparently unchanging surface of an agricultural and trading community. Where previously workshops of craftsmen had grown into small factories, owned and operated by a master workman as entrepreneur, the new and larger factories became owned by capitalists who, divorced from the workmen, began to exploit labor. With a rapid rise in speculation, the stockholder–proprietor emerged as a power in the nation.

These entrepreneurs tended toward the Whig Party, the legatee of the old Federalists and composed of men of property. As Whigs, the Northern powers were the natural allies of big planters in the South. The lines, however, were by no means clearly drawn. Many planters, under the Jeffersonian heritage, were Democrats in principle and others in distrust of the Northern Whigs. Many Northern men of property were Democrats for a variety of reasons, including the desire to stay with the party in power. These entangled alignments, formed of conviction, habit and expediency, obscured the more basic conflict developing between the actually unchanging South and the North in a process of dynamic change.

Lee was a regular reader of the daily newspaper and liked to read history, but neither knowledge of the past nor current information could have provided much understanding of the subsurface forces that, undirected, began to move the new nation toward division.

The divergent interests in the federated republic — which the contemporaries of Lee's father had believed would be controlled by natural checks and balances — began to coalesce in the Northern states into a single sectional interest combining the new finance with industry and commerce. The course of this single interest led inevitably toward domination of the compact of states. This placed the agricultural Southern states, built upon a fixed plantation system with a static labor force, in a position of defense against being dominated in the central government. Many Southerners recognized the danger, but there was no agreement on courses of action by the leaders in the separate states — which themselves differed widely in their economic interests and cultural affiliations.

Virginia, predominantly agricultural, tended toward some balance in its economy. During the Colonial period Great Britain had suppressed its manufacturing (which had begun with the glassworks at Jamestown). In the 1840's, however, small-scale manufacturing was scattered through the state and industry was developing steadily if modestly in comparison with the North. Its agriculture was more diversified than in the Cotton States and, through shipping, railroads and turnpikes, its commerce was healthy. With this economy Virginia maintained an interflow with the East and, culturally, since London ceased to be their capital, any ties Virginians formed (including marriage) outside their social self-sufficiency were in the East.

However, while nothing approached unity of attitude in the Southern states, and no general sense of threat existed among the people, there was an inchoate, unarticulated drift toward coalescence against a common danger. In early fulfillment of James McDowell's warning in the 1831-1832 convention, Virginia could coalesce only with other slave states.

By the 1840's, even without legislation, through the natural laws of economics and general sentiment the ownership of slaves was declining in Virginia, along with the decreases of the great plantations of Charles Carter's day, as estates were broken up to be divided among heirs. Yet, in defense against the Northern financial-industrial domination of the central government, Virginia's drift loosely aligned her with those new Southern states where slave-operated plantations were just beginning to flourish. These states of the Lower South were emerging from the frontier when Lee was stationed at Fort Hamilton. With new fortunes creating new Bourbons on the money crop of cotton (scarcely grown in Virginia), their interests were less similar to Virginia's than Virginia's with the East. In fact, Virginia was actually caught between. This reality was largely concealed by the state's slave bloc, which, since 1832, had become a strongly unified and powerful minority.

Nothing indicated that Lee was particularly aware of this drift. He may have been, despite the absence of reference in his correspondence. It was a time when politics were beginning to serve special interests rather than subordinate the interests to the good of the whole, according to the vision of lofty rationality held by the Constitution drafters. This would have confirmed Lee's abiding distrust of politicians and limited his interest in their works. Perhaps regarding politics as contributing to his father's downfall, at all times he stayed as far away as possible from political action. Then, he witnessed the introduction of presidential "campaigns," where principles were replaced by slogans, at least one of which — that referring to Harrison's humble birth — he knew to be a ridiculous representation. Whatever the extent of Lee's awareness, the undeclared power struggle for domination of the central government became so confused by slavery as a political issue that it is doubtful if anyone, then or since, understood precisely what was happening.

On the surface, the struggle centered on new territories and on the new states west of the Alleghenies and north of the Ohio River. For an amalgam of reasons the North was winning in bringing the Middle Western states into its orbit. First of all, the northern tiers of the states had been settled by emigrants pushing west from the Northeast. Where Southerners settled the southern tiers in Ohio, Indiana and Illinois, they carried only their customs, and not ties with the plantation society. Many possibly held resentments from having been outside the ruling class. Then, the whole section was connected with the East by the railroads that began stretching across the country during the thirties, and the Eastern banks and financial interests drew the Westerners to the North through the interchange of money. With all else, the Middle Westerners (including emigrants from the South) disliked slavery for essentially practical reasons. They did not wish the competition of slave labor nor the presence of Negroes in their communities.

At the same time that practicalities were allying the Middle West with the East, the abolitionists (as distinguished from emancipationists) were growing louder and more skillful in propaganda — as in the fantastic exaggerations of the number of slaves they helped flee to the North. (The true heroes of the slaves' flights north were the Southerners who aided their escape and who, for practical reasons not obtaining in New England, were forced to remain silent.)

It was a period when all sorts of anti- movements, anti-Catholic and anti-foreign among others, were springing up all over the Northeast side by side with Utopias. Since demands for abolition were directed through hatred of white Southerners, anti-slavery combined all appeals by permitting the expression of hostility within a socially approved ideal. No knowledge of the total conditions was required, no plans for the future of freed Negroes in white communities and, of all things, no efforts were to be made to work in cooperation with fellow citizens in the Southern states — 75 per cent of whom had no association with slavery. The direct appeal to faraway slaves, unburdened by any responsibility for consequences, offered a purified passion that transcended all puritanical frustrations with the moral narcissism of the zealot possessed.

While the only practical result of this highly vocal zeal had been to halt the emancipationist movement in Virginia, the abolitionists did produce another and more subtle effect. They gave an issue to political outs in the North and they gave ammunition to those large planters in the South who opposed emancipation under any conditions. When the sociological problem became a political issue, used on both sides of the Potomac, the fundamental conflicts between the sections became distorted, and an intelligent, humanistic approach to the abolishment of slavery became difficult.

From the beginning, the republic had avoided facing the institution of slavery as a national problem. During the period when England and Mexico were preparing a practical emancipation, which neither worked a hardship on nor stigmatized those planters to whom chattel labor had been economic, the Southern leaders made the irremediable strategic mistake of permitting their institution to become involved with regional politics. This was in 1820, when the country was divided into eleven so-called free and eleven so-called slave states.

To block the increase of Southern representation in Washington, the Northern legislators opposed the admission of Missouri as a "slave state." In a tit for tat, the Southern legislators then blocked the admission of Maine as a state. The deadlock was broken, in the Missouri Compromise, by the Southerners agreeing to restrict further slavery to the parallel of the southern Missouri border.

Physically the country west of Missouri was not feasible for slave labor in any case, and Jefferson, aging on his mountaintop, warned the Southerners against establishing the precedent that slavery could be restricted. Disregarding Jefferson, the shortsighted Southerners permitted the precedent to be established, with the result that the institution was shifted from the area of national interest into sectional politics.

Once the sectional power struggle was joined over such an issue, dividing the nation into slave and free states, the union was literally a "house divided" — and divided into unnatural alignments with unclear differences. It was not, as the simile suggests, a static structure. To extend the simile, it was a house under construction expanding without plan in all directions.

In 1836 the power struggle was again focussed on the admission of a single state when Texas won its "freedom" from Mexico. The area of Texas had been only sparsely settled by Mexicans, mostly in the southern part, and Americans had taken up residences in the vast spaces with hardly a by-your-leave to the Mexican government. Most of the settlers were

Southerners, many slaveholders, and as their settlement grew, a clash with Mexico was inevitable. There were enough Texans, and enough guns sent from the United States, to insure the defeat of the inept Santa Anna and, by right of self-determination, the great territory became a republic. Naturally the South wanted Texas admitted as a state, and the North, trying to gain control of the central government, naturally did not. The annexation of Texas was resolved in 1840 as a result of the strangest of American elections.

The Whigs saw their chance to break the Democrats' hold with a homey hero who, to disassociate their party from entrenched privilege, would appeal to the plain people. The people's hero they selected, William Henry Harrison, had in point of fact grown up at Berkeley plantation next door to Shirley, where he had been a companion of Ann Hill Carter. As the youngest son of the Signer, this grandson of King Carter had been given a military appointment by his father's friend, President Washington, and gone west to make his fortune. In the course of winning a place for himself in Ohio, he defeated some Indians at the Battle of Tippecanoe, and "Tippecanoe" Harrison could not be anything except a folk hero. In America's first presidential campaign (in a representation which Lee knew to be grotesque), the descendant of the James River grandees was palmed off as a son of the soil, who had grown up in a log cabin and was addicted to coon hunting and hard cider.

To insure Harrison's acceptance in the South (where, outside of Charles City County, his native heath was unknown), the Whigs selected John Tyler, a Democrat, from the same county where "Tippecanoe" had originated. With party lines blurred, Whig Harrison and Democrat Tyler represented a cross-sectional ticket rather than any party merger. Anyway, Tyler was supposed only to be a figurehead as vice president.

Then old Harrison caught a cold from exposure to the weather during his inauguration, dying within a month of taking office, and the Whigs' imaginatively won victory resulted in their putting a Southern Democrat in the White House. Tyler had no loyalties to the Whigs nor was he a return to the Jeffersonian democracy of the Virginia dynasty. He was a slave-holding Southerner who could be counted on to maneuver for the annexation of the Republic of Texas.

John Tyler took office at the same time Captain Lee took up residence in a house the government provided his family at run-down Fort Hamilton. Turning to his new duties, Lee certainly felt no involvement with — if, indeed, he had an awareness of — the confused, subsurface power struggle symbolized by the freak chance of the presence of his half-brother's enemy in the White House.

6

Except for the raw, booming Western community of St. Louis, itself a center of farming and trade, Lee had encountered no environment outside the isolated army posts that suggested any change from his first impressions of life at Stratford. At Cockspur Island and Fort Monroe, he had lived in plantation country, and in Washington in the paternalistic feudalism of Custis's Arlington. Like other nineteenth-century planters with a guilty conscience about owning human chattels, Washington Custis operated on a philosophy of comfort in his own time: indulging his lightly worked and lazy slaves, he had a will providing for their manumission after his death.

Then, as far as possible from the world where stockholder proprietorships of labor forces were forming power combines, on his visits to Cousin Hill Carter at Shirley, Lee shared the intimate life of one of the great personal entrepreneurs of an eighteenth-century style of agricultural establishment.

Hill Carter was one of the planters who demonstrated there was nothing anachronistic or uneconomic in the labor system where adaptive enterprise was employed. The anachronism was in those planters who, like the two Harry Lees, wanted the lordship of the plantation without applying themselves to maintain it. Also the new planters of the Lower South were anachronistic in their concentration on one big money crop of cotton or rice. But in Alabama and Mississippi they were planting in virgin soil, from which the big money rewards came suddenly, like gold strikes, and the successful planters understandably were more interested in building white-columned symbols of the master-class than in developing a broad sufficiency in agriculture.

Hill Carter was working land that had been farmed for more than two hundred years, with soil long since exhausted by Virginia's old money crop of tobacco. Wheat became his big crop. Not bringing in the fluctuating fortune of the golden leaf, it was sold directly to the flour mills in Richmond, their schooners loading at his wharf, and by the end of the thirties Hill Carter was getting nearly $7000 cash a year from his wheat. He developed the growth of corn from a few hundred barrels sold a year, when he took over the plantation, to more than two thousand barrels. In a self-sustaining operation, he grew fruit, oats and clover, peas, turnips and potatoes, with strawberries in May; he raised beef, hogs and sheep, weaving several hundred yards of wool. In 1837, in addition to feeding all the people on his property, he earned a cash income of $13,000.

Overseers came and went; Carter could not get a good man. By the same painstaking attention to every detail with which his aunt, Ann Carter Lee, had managed to educate her children, Hill Carter made of his vast, complex operation a one-man enterprise. Day in and day out he directed his workers to the unending jobs on something that needed repair — shingles for the porticoes, shingles for the granaries, post-and-rail fences, carpenters repairing the ferryboat, buying and fixing equipment, buying and fixing mill machinery, painting the house, cutting and hauling timber. Season in and season out men worked at fertilizing the land: wagonloads of manure were hauled from the stableyard, tons of guano spread, experiments were made with "plaister" and oyster shells, and then in one year twenty thousand bushels of the new marl invented by Edmund Ruffin.

There was nothing of the lordliness associated with the image of the slothful, arrogant, vice-ridden plantation grandee becoming current in abolitionist publications. Hill Carter's simplicity was more akin to the men of the soil, with his constant watch on the weather and recording every shift in the wind. Detached as his Cousin Robert from the forces gathering around his static world, he recorded such items as gelding "the lame mare's colt, as a consequence of which he died," the vaccination of the slaves' children, and "the little roan horse died."

To Captain Lee, nothing in the continuity of this life known by his mother suggested elements gathering force to change the world in which he had been born. With his cousin he talked of homey things of the land, for Lee held a strong interest in the practical aspects of farming, along with his dream of reclaiming Stratford. They talked of horses and men, of marriages and births, of the familiar cycles of life on the land they loved. From his visits in the stable society, where time seemed held in thrall, Lee drifted without disruption into the quiet tempo of the days at Fort Hamilton.

## 7

The fort, only ten years old, was built on the western tip of Long Island, where the curving land formed one shore of "The Narrows" between the Upper Bay and Lower Bay of New York Harbor. Adjoining Fort Hamilton was the village of New Utrecht, about six miles south of Brooklyn (now a part of Brooklyn). For a man who had grown up on the banks of the Potomac, the situation was physically ideal. From the porch of the white-framed two-story house, Lee watched the ocean ships passing through The Narrows to the Lower Bay and on into the Atlantic or, incoming, into the Upper Bay — the inner bay. (The passage of The Narrows was like the handle of a dumbell.) Steamships were then replacing sail, but there were always high-masted schooners sailing by in front of Lee's house and the fort.

Fort Hamilton was the strongest of four fortified positions that formed a chain of defense against an enemy's seapower. Offshore from Fort Hamilton was the smaller Fort Lafayette, and across The Narrows two harbor batteries were on the Staten Island side. The four forts were under Lee's supervision, and his task was to renovate the whole system, bringing the fortifications to a condition of preparedness for defensive action. The assignment, somewhat anticlimactic after his struggle with the Mississippi River, was little more than an exercise in his trained skills.

First, there were seawalls and leaky casemates to repair, gun positions to be strengthened and modernized, and a variety of improvements to bring the forts into effective operating condition. Beyond this rehabilitation, he was to make such changes and advance such suggestions — especially on the number, caliber and positions of new guns — as he believed would make the chain of forts impregnable against warships. To an extent the work was a repetition of Fort Monroe, with the difference that in New York he was in complete authority. Though the work was routine, at least he could use his own initiative and make his own plans in redesigning a defensive network.

The dull part was the detail work necessitated by the low appropriations with which the engineering corps operated. He had only one clerk, a superintendent at each fort where civilian labor was employed, and not until he had been at Fort Hamilton six months did a garrison of soldiers move in. Yet, perhaps because he was older and because he was not confined to office work, Lee seemed better adjusted than he had been in Washington before going to St. Louis. His five years at Fort Hamilton, from the age of thirty-four to thirty-nine, appeared to be a placid period for Lee. Settling down to the gratifications of family life, he left behind him the unrest of his twenties, when he had chafed for advancement and work that demanded the full play of his faculties. Judging by at least one letter, he began to regard himself as an older man.

His correspondence with Henry Kayser, which continued over the work in the Mississippi River, had grown more personal within the formalities of address, and Lee wrote him on the subject of women. Evidently in reply to some observation of Kayser's, Lee wrote, "You are right in my interest in pretty women. It is strange that I do not lose it with age. But I perceive no diminution. Young men, however, ought not to lead them into indiscretions, and fighting duels and shooting each other can't remedy it."

Along with referring to his middle thirties as "age," Lee's (for him) unguarded letter suggested that his interest in ladies was not — as sometimes assumed — entirely social. His quickened response to the presence of "pretty women" was obvious all his life, and his wife said, in later years, he was never so happy as when the house was filled with ladies. On this basis, with his natural physical energy and the superb condition in which he kept himself, it would seem likely that Lee practiced conscious suppression of urges that violated both the principles by which he lived and the code of honor to which he subscribed. To "lead them into indiscretions" was, of course, an attitude of his time that placed responsibility solely on man, the aggressor. But it also placed man in the role of protector — of ladies and of honor. Though self-restraint would have, in any case, been imposed on Lee by his marriage vows, he wrote Kayser from a different aspect of control, and probably one that obtained before he was married.

This was Lee's only reference to his interest in pretty women. Mostly he wrote Kayser about his more active interest in money matters. Lee and Kayser had developed an exchange of favors. Kayser had his troubles with the political authorities at St. Louis, and Lee, along with avuncular advice, tried to help advance the career of his younger friend. For his part, Kayser acted as something of an unofficial agent in collecting the interests on some investments Lee had made in St. Louis.

Lee wrote candidly to Kayser about his concern over getting proper returns on the investments of his savings — not speculation, he wrote, "but safe investment." The money in St. Louis, not including City of St. Louis bonds he had bought, represented only a small part of Lee's investments. It is reasonably certain that Lee had not spent a penny of the $3000 he inherited, through his mother, from his grandfather Charles Carter, and to the accumulated interests his "savings" undoubtedly were growing from money he managed to put aside from his army pay. The long visits of his wife and children to Arlington (which continued from Fort Hamilton) offered means for frugal Lee to save on such basic items as food, and he knew where every dollar went. After he left St. Louis, Kayser helped the former landlady, Mrs. Beaumont, to sell at auction the furniture Lee had acquired for the temporary residence.

Lee never stinted his family. But, with seven children to educate for a place in a highly privileged society, he worked carefully at the management of expenditures, stressing the avoidance of extravagance, waste and indulgence. His only personal indulgences were in fine uniforms, as he was meticulous about his appearance, and he always rode good horses. Horseback riding was his favorite outdoor pastime.

Though Lee sought the aspects of his job that kept him outdoors and on his feet, and the work entailed considerable physical movement, he always looked forward to getting on a horse. Expressing no interest in jumping or advanced equitation, he simply liked the act of riding, aimlessly, without objective. After his youthful pleasures in following fox hunts on foot, his life in the army was never in fox-hunting country, and he expressed no regret at not riding in the hunting field. Nor did he ever express interest in shooting. If he owned any weapons in addition to his regulation sidearms, he never referred to them. For a certainty he never kept any hounds.

Like any family of country background, the Lees always had a cat or cats around, but Lee was known to have shown attachment for only one dog — a mutt that came into his life at Fort Hamilton. The children picked up a female stray, and one of a litter she bore was a black-and-tan terrier, called "Spec," of most engaging disposition. Spec, however, was a family dog, who attended church with the children and adapted himself to the dignified ways suitable to the family of a vestryman.

Church offered an abiding source of interest to Lee as well as a place to worship. Lieutenant Henry Hunt, one of the commanding officer's younger army friends, observed later that Lee's family "formed a charming portion of our little society," and Lee, Hunt wrote, "was a vestryman of the little parish church of Fort Hamilton, of which the post-chaplain was the rector, and as thorough in the discharge of church as of other duties."

Hunt reported a controversy in the church which revealed a characteristic and significant instance of Lee's aversion to factions. The parish was divided between the traditional "Low Church" and the "High Church" movement that began in England in 1834. When feelings grew warm, Lee, though himself of a Low Church diocese, kept aloof from the quarrel. As he was an important member of the church, each faction tried to draw his support. The efforts were, Hunt said, "without success, for he always contrived in some pleasant way to avoid any expression of opinion which would commit him to either faction."

Hunt also revealed a turn of Lee's sense of humor during this controversy. One night the captain came into the quarters of one of the younger officers, where some of the officers who were members of the church were entertaining a couple of civilian parishioners. The usual topic was being discussed, with the argument centered around "Puseyism," as the High Church movement was called, after its chief advocate, the Reverend E. B. Pusey.

After a while Lee grew amused at the efforts of the younger men to draw him out. In a serious tone, Lee told them he was pleased they remained aloof from the dispute that disturbed "our little parish," and that they must continue to support each other in remaining uninvolved with both factions. "But," he said, "I must give you some advice in order that we may understand each other." Then deliberately mispronouncing Puseyism, he said, *"Beware of Pussyism! Pussyism* is always bad, and may lead to unchristian feelings; therefore, beware of *Pussyism."*

The elegant captain had created a garrison joke, as well as indirectly revealing his position in the controversy. Regardless of his own convictions, the point for Lee was that when sides were chosen over a controversy, he felt that factionalism promoted wrong in both sides.

Of such small affairs were his days composed. In the fall of 1842, the excessive paperwork brought eyestrain, and he wrote his mother-in-law that after a day's work he could scarcely read the newspaper. As the nights grew longer, he wrote, the lack of reading was "a great deprivation to me, as well as a loss my small store of knowledge can ill afford." From his letters to Mrs. Custis, "Mother," his family was the absorbing center of his thoughts.

In April of 1844, his wife — whom he then sometimes referred to as "Mana," a contraction of Mary Anne — was ill with an inflammation of the jaw, and he experienced a shaking episode with son Rooney. The most sanguine natured of all the Lee children, Rooney, then approaching his seventh birthday, was the least interested in books. From the time he could walk, he loved the care and handling of horses. Evidently he had developed a trick of complaining of pains when there was something he did not want to do, and his father paid no attention when the boy complained of pains in his legs.

A day came when Captain Lee needed to go into New York, to buy supplies for the fort and do some shopping for books, and Rooney wanted to go along. Lee told him, in mock solicitude, that he could not go because of the pain in his legs. As Lee expected, the boy immediately protested that his pain was not too bad to prevent a trip, and they set off together. They rode from their house to the ferry, left their horses, and walked from the ferry to the stores Lee visited in New York. From the beginning he was aware that his sturdy son was clinging to his hand as they walked, and Lee soon saw that Rooney was making an heroic effort against real and not play pain. By the time Lee finished his shopping (deciding the books were too dear), it was clear that the little boy was in agony, and thrifty Lee indulged in a carriage ride back to the ferry.

At home, Lee carried his son into the house and began a series of old-fashioned remedies. As with plantation people, it did not occur to Lee to call in a doctor at once. After he discovered that scalding hot baths brought relief, the captain daily administered to the little boy just as he had to his mother and did for his wife. With his gentleness, he was a natural healer, and within a week or so Rooney was all right again. Lee wrote Mrs. Custis that, with Mana sick, he did everything for Rooney himself, as "his father's touch hurt him less than any one."

The following year, just before Christmas of 1845, Rooney gave his father a bigger scare. Lee had been in New York at a meeting of the Board of Engineers and returned after dark to find his house in a hub-bub and his eight-year-old son in the post hospital. The doctor and several army officers met the captain. They told him Rooney, while in the Public Stables, had cut off the tips of the middle and forefingers on his left hand in trying to operate some new patent straw-cutters worked by a crank. While Lee hurried to his son, the doctor and officers described to him how Rooney had quietly held up his bleeding fingers until they arrived and tried to quiet *their* anxiety. They could scarcely believe a boy that young could have such powers of self-possession.

When Lee entered the room, where his wife was sitting with the boy, as Lee wrote Kayser, "He was sitting up waiting for me; received me with his usual cheerfulness, made light of the accident, and it was only after his mother left the room, from whom they had thought it prudent to conceal the extent of the injury, that he told me the whole evil." Lee was obviously proud of his son's courage, though he seemed to expect it from the boy of whom he wrote, "He is a large, heavy fellow and requires a tight rein."

Lee and Mrs. Lee spent some anxious days until they learned the use of his hand would not be impaired, though the fingers would be permanently disfigured. With passing time even the disfigurement became scarcely noticeable.

Before Rooney's accident, Lee enjoyed a brief vacation from the fort that would profoundly affect his future. In June, 1844, he was one of a special commission of officers selected to attend the final examinations at West Point, and there Lee was thrown into daily association with the general in chief of the army, Winfield Scott.

Then fifty-eight years old, Lee's fellow Virginian still carried his huge body with impressive vigor, and his outsize vanity was supported by a forceful, confident military mind. General Scott had been one of the ornaments of Washington society when Lee worked in Gratiot's office, but the two weeks at West Point gave Lee his first opportunity to become personally acquainted with the general in chief. Unassertive though equally self-confident, Lee made a lasting impression on the older man.

In less than three years Scott was to call personally for Lee in the field, and the engineering officer would be presented with the opportunity he had come to despair of in the nearly twenty years since his graduation from West Point. Those subsurface forces of which Lee was unaware had gathered momentum, and in 1846 the sweep of events brought him into the United States war with Mexico.

## CHAPTER IV

## "A Hero Was Born"

THE WAR WITH MEXICO was fought for the same reason the Indians had been fought — to possess the land they occupied. In 1844, in the fifty-five years since the thirteen colonies formed their federated republic, the western sweep of empire had been carried from the Alleghenies to the Rockies, accompanied by a strain of assertiveness in the expanding nation. A new generation had risen without awareness of the formative days of the Union, when the former colonies had looked eastward, across the Atlantic to the Mother Country of England. The new generation — fructified by Irish, German and Swedish immigrants without even memories of ties with England — looked to the west, toward expansion to the Pacific. But California, though thinly populated around the few presidios from the old Spanish push northward, was Mexican territory. Then in 1845 a Democratic editor loosed the phrase "Manifest Destiny," and this concept obliterated the impediment of Mexican claims to the manifest destiny of a continental United States.

The movement toward California and New Mexico began with the 1844 presidential campaign. The Whigs had a good man in colorful, wanton Henry Clay. The divided Democrats, knowing they could not win with Tyler, settled on the country's first "dark horse" in the colorless person of James Polk, a regular party politician from Tennessee. Narrow-minded, obstinate and suspicious, Polk withal was a man of his convictions, and his single strongest conviction was on the annexation of Texas. Since Tyler had failed to get the support in Congress to annex Texas, the subject had become one of those issues on which a presidential campaign hangs. Clay, trying to appraise the country's sentiments, first opposed annexation; Polk, following his own convictions, came out strongly for annexation and was elected. In March, 1845, before Tyler left office, he was able to sign the bill of annexation, and the Republic of Texas became a state in the Southern part of the United States.

When Polk assumed office, he took the step beyond the annexation of Texas to the acquisition of California. Outside of New England, where the possibility of adding any new territory to the South met with a grim resistance, the country's prevailing mood encouraged Polk in his execution of "Manifest Destiny." In the South, where any move that added territory south of the 36°30′ parallel was generally viewed with enthusiasm, the new planter Bourbons dreamed of a vast empire expanding to the Caribbean. Thus supported, Polk opened his maneuvers to gain California by sending John Slidell as a special envoy to Mexico.

Slidell, a Columbia College New Yorker who had risen to power and prominence in the Eldorado of Louisiana, was to offer $25 million for California and New Mexico. To no one's surprise, Slidell was not received. Indeed, at the time, Mexico claimed a state of war existed between itself and the United States over the annexation of Texas. With the legal appearances attended to, an "incident" was then created.

Historically, the southern boundary of Texas had been the Nueces River. When Texas won its independence, the treaty signed by Santa Anna, while a prisoner, fixed the new boundary farther south at the Rio Grande. Once Santa Anna was safely back in Mexico, he repudiated the treaty, and the stretch between the Nueces and the Rio Grande became disputed territory. There the matter stood until Polk used the disputed area for an incident in 1846.

Polk sent a force under General Zachary Taylor south of the Nueces to establish possession of the territory north of the Rio Grande. Predictably, an American reconnaissance party was wiped out by Mexicans, and in response to this invasion of "American soil" Congress declared war on Mexico in May. General Taylor gathered his army at the Rio Grande, crossed the river at Matamoros to advance southward into Mexico and, with no more ado, the war was on.

The war was three months old before Captain Lee received orders, on August 19, transferring him to the scene of action. Leaving his family at Arlington (which, to all intents, was then the Robert Lee family home), he reported to Brigadier General John E. Wool at San Antonio on September 21. Since a fast trip of one man from New York to Southern Texas required slightly more than one month, obviously the logistical problems of moving bodies of men, supplies and equipment were making Taylor's southward advance something less than a flying column.

When Captain Lee arrived at San Antonio, General Taylor had moved his main force from the river port of Matamoros westward along the Rio Grande to an assault center at Camargo. North and west at San Antonio, Lee joined Wool's secondary force as it was completing preparations to mount a joint assault — Taylor striking for Monterrey and Wool for Chihuahua. At the same time another column was moving through New Mexico toward the Pacific, with naval support on the way to the coast of California.

Engineer officer Lee, approaching his fortieth birthday, exchanged the routine of garrison life for the chores in camp and on march. Though he was not much closer to fighting than he had been at Fort Hamilton, at least he was with an armed force campaigning in enemy country.

The engineers operated out of general headquarters, performing assignments of reconnaissance, road building and bridge building. Captain Lee was no sooner adjusted to the bustle of the army camp at San Antonio than Wool's columns moved out, making a good march of 165 miles to the Rio Grande. There the army paused, while the engineers built protective bridgeheads of earthworks at the river, and the news came that the main force had defeated the Mexicans and captured Monterrey. On October 12, Wool's force advanced southward two hundred miles to the city of Monclova, and there, on October 30, halted again. After exchanges back and forth between Wool and Taylor, the objective of Chihauhau was tentatively abandoned and, on November 24, Wool's force moved another 165 miles to Parras. There they halted again, with Lee and the engineers fortifying a defensive position.

Captain Lee kept busy practicing the rudimentary skills of his profession in the field and, for the first time since he entered West Point, got the feel of a force in movement preparing for battle. The Mexicans continued to make themselves scarce. Though alarums came in at intervals, the Mexican forces were mostly concentrated in front of Taylor.

Then, on December 17, an urgent call came to march to make juncture with another detached column, under General William J. Worth, one hundred miles to the east at Saltillo. Worth was about to be attacked. Under rough conditions, sixty-one-year-old Wool held his well-disciplined troops to a forced march, and four days later arrived to support Worth. It was another false alarm.

When the force went into camp at Saltillo, disillusionment began to descend on the worn troops far away from home at Christmas. Lee wrote his wife, "It is the first time we have been entirely separated at this holy time since our marriage. I hope it does not interfere with your happiness, surrounded as you are by father, mother, children, and dear friends. I therefore trust that you are well and happy, and that this is the last time I shall be absent from you during my life."

After the first of the year, everything suddenly changed for Lee. Since November, General in Chief Scott had been preparing an armada to land at Vera Cruz, for an inland move across country to Mexico City, and he began to draw troops, including Worth's division, from Taylor's forces. On January 6, 1847, from his base at Brazos, he wrote Taylor, "Of the officers of engineers, topographical engineers, and ordnance, with you, or under your command, I propose to take only Captain R. Lee, of the first named corps."

Thus, of the troops from Taylor's army which Scott was drawing to him, Captain Lee was the only junior officer the general in chief specifically asked for. Scott wrote Taylor that Colonel Totten, who had replaced General Gratiot as chief of engineers and was then on Scott's staff, desired Lee. "I shall write [Wool] to have him sent down from Saltillo."

On January 17 Captain Lee wrote his wife, "Last night . . . I received another summons to report to General Headquarters, when he [Wool] showed me a letter from General Scott requiring me to report to him as soon as possible at the Brazos . . . I regret very much to leave General Wool on many accounts. He has been exceedingly kind to me in every way, and his letter on my being relieved today is kind and flattering in the extreme . . ."

Nothing in his letter indicated his pride or excitement in being transferred, at the order of Scott himself, to the headquarters of the general in chief. He could not have been unaware of the opportunity offered him. With Wool's small force he operated out of headquarters on the same kind of chores he had been performing for the past five years. With Scott, he would be operating *at* army headquarters, truly on the general staff. His five months with Wool had been a rehearsal. For Captain Lee the war without combat was over.

2

Talent in reconnaissance could scarcely be listed as an inherited trait. Yet, it was a spectacular performance in this field of his father's gifts that brought Captain Lee into overnight fame. With his first opportunity at important strategic reconnaissance the peacetime engineer became the most celebrated junior officer in Scott's army.

Scott's engineering corps contained some of the army's most promising younger officers. First Lieutenant P. G. T. Beauregard, of Louisiana, was eleven years Lee's junior, and George B. McClellan, of Pennsylvania, a brilliant graduate of the class of 1846, was a brevet second lieutenant at twenty. With the topographical engineers were Lee's old friend Joe Johnston, thirty-one-year-old Lieutenant George Gordon Meade, of Pennsylvania, and a twenty-six-year-old Kentuckian, Gustavus W. Smith, a handsome young man who had made an imposing record in the class of 1842. All these younger officers, hungry for glory, were established with Scott's army when Lee, just turned forty, joined the headquarters staff at the port of Brazos, where the Rio Grande emptied into the Gulf.

Colonel Joseph C. Totten, chief of engineers, had a reputation for looking after his own and, with Scott favorably impressed with Lee, the newly arrived captain was assigned a place in the commanding general's "little cabinet." Ranking immediately below Major John L. Smith, Captain Lee was third in importance in the engineers on Scott's personal staff. Politically ambitious Scott, a "mountain of vanity," in his own drive for the big glory made an intelligent employment of his staff engineers. As his strategy and tactics were to be based upon their personal reconnaissance, he placed a responsibility upon the individuals that could either become burdensome or promote their initiative.

Lee was at general headquarters only a few weeks when the part of the armada formed at Brazos sailed, February 15, by way of Tampico, for Lobos Island, where the fleet rendezvoused. At Lobos Island, two hundred miles north of Vera Cruz, the amphibious force tarried while Scott fretted at the delayed appearance of additional troops and animals for the inland transportation. The army was racing against the coming of April to the low, hot country around Vera Cruz, *tierra caliente*, where the warm weather brought yellow fever. On March 3 Scott sailed with what he had, and on March 5 the ships came within sight of Vera Cruz, where United States men-of-war patrolled outside the harbor in a blockade.

The port city of Vera Cruz, with its protecting coastal forts, was situated on a shallow jut of land, with sandy, densely brushed country open to the north and south. Scott proposed to land on both sides of the city and, fighting off opposing ground troops, establish a siege of the city and its forts from the inland side. After several days of maneuvering outside the range of the forts' heavy guns, on March 10 the transports were brought close to shore under protection of gunboats, and foot soldiers were loaded in surfboats. Late in the afternoon the 6th Regular Infantry led the landing on the beach and up onto the high dunes where it was assumed the enemy's soldiers were waiting.

Unknown to Scott, the Mexican General Santa Anna had attacked Taylor outside Monterrey, on February 22-23, and was roughly repulsed at the Battle of Buena Vista. Santa Anna's soldiers, especially his cavalry, had charged with great gallantry, but the commanding officers revealed a primitive sense of the firepower of massed artillery. Conspicuous among the defenders was a West Point–trained congressman from Mississippi, Jefferson Davis, colonel of a regiment of volunteers.

After his repulse, which he called a "victory," General Antonio Lopez de Santa Anna retired southward to San Luis Potosi. There he rested his army for four days and plotted his own future. This fantastic adventurer, then fifty-two years old with a seventeen-year-old bride, had twice been president-dictator of Mexico and twice driven out of office. In March his immediate problem was another revolution in Mexico City, out of which he expected to be returned to power once again. Thus it was that, except for a detachment of cavalry which acted as distant spectators, the Mexicans had no soldiers available to contest Scott's landing.

Captain Lee, after watching the landing from Scott's ship, waded ashore at the end of the day with Colonel Totten and Major Smith, each carrying his overcoat and haversack. Lee wrote his wife that the flea-infested area of their camp consisted of "mountain ranges of sand, the valleys of which are impenetrable thickets of chapparal, through which roads had to be cut."

Lee was immediately assigned the task of selecting and preparing gun positions in a semi-circle around the city. He was delighted to encounter his older brother, Smith, in command of a battery from the ships. On March 24 the bombardment opened. Captain Lee, personally directing a battery of the guns he had placed, that day for the first time in his life came under direct shellfire from the enemy. His reactions can only be suggested from his letters home written in the nights between the three-day bombardment.

Saying nothing whatsoever of his own exposure to shell bursts, he wrote his wife, "I am now about establishing 18 new mortars, which will make 28 in all, and 12 guns; 6 of the guns are manned by sailors from the different ships. Yesterday I was in field battery with my dear Smith . . ." In another letter, Lee indicated that his thoughts had been entirely on his brother. "No matter where I turned, my eyes reverted to him, and I stood by his guns whenever I was not wanted elsewhere. Oh! I felt awfully and am at a loss what I should have done had he been cut down before me. I thank God that he was saved. He preserved his usual cheerfulness, and I could see his white teeth through all the smoke and din of fire."

It was characteristic of Lee that he appeared unaware of his own danger when under fire. This was not the bravery of overcoming fear: he seemed simply unafraid. Though this obtained with other men, different types, in Lee's case it was probably at least in part a reflection of his implicit belief in the will of God. Always doing what was at hand, he never imagined the disaster that might be visited upon him. In the sense of the active imagination that conjured up phantoms, of delight or of evil, the engineering officer would have to be called unimaginative. Objective-minded, he concentrated always on the knowns, the tangibles, and, according to the view of life he accepted, the reality of God as a ruler of men's destinies would be among the certainties.

After the three-day bombardment of Vera Cruz, the surrounded defenders surrendered. As soon as the garrison had been paroled and the city occupied, General Scott hurried to prepare his force to move inland before April brought the dreaded yellow fever to the thirty mile stretch of *tierra caliente* inland to the foothills. His army then totaled about thirteen thousand troops of all arms. One division of regulars was commanded by General D. E. Twiggs and another by Lee's old commandant of cadets at West Point, now General Worth. General Robert Patterson commanded the division of volunteers. The artillery, like the engineers, was commanded directly from general headquarters. Before the army moved out Lee spent a night with Smith on his brother's ship, the *Mississippi*.

On April 8 and 9, Twiggs and Patterson put their columns in motion, accompanied by three batteries of artillery. For want of horses and mules for transportation, Worth's division and part of Patterson's command remained with General Scott at Vera Cruz. Twiggs's and Patterson's laden troops, advancing over the sandy road between the brush, found the going hard in the intense heat. Thirty miles inland, the men began the ascent toward Jalapa, about seventy miles from Vera Cruz. The weather grew better with *tierra caliente* behind and below, and the road climbed among "natural gardens," many of which belonged to Santa Anna's large estates. Suddenly, on April 11, the advance found its way blocked by the enemy.

General Santa Anna had composed the differences in Mexico City, been restored to power, and, with the National Guard and segments of his veterans of Buena Vista, marched east of Jalapa to a strong position on the road from Vera Cruz. About twenty miles east of Jalapa, near the ranch of Cerro Gordo (Fat Hill), a formidable terrain of mountain ridges, flanked by conically shaped hills, formed a barrier across a stretch of level meadowland called Plan del Rio. The road from Vera Cruz, after crossing the narrow stream of the Rio del Plan, wound its way between three projecting ridges to the south and the conically shaped hills, Atalaya and Cerro Gordo, to the north. The tops of both hills and the crests of the three ridges were lined with artillery, and Mexican soldiers had erected lines after forming an abatis of felled trees in their firing front.

"Old Davy" Twiggs was all for attacking the position right away. One postponement and another withheld any action, beyond reconnaissance, until General Scott arrived with his staff on April 14. Worth was following with his division. Scott was told that the engineers with Twiggs, including Lieutenant Beauregard, had found what they believed might be a practical line of advance to the north of the road. The next morning, the 15th, Scott sent out his own staff engineer, Captain Lee, to extend the reconnaissance.

This was the opportunity through which Lee won his first prominence since leaving West Point eighteen years before. Going with one guide, the middle-aged captain clambered and slid through the matted brush up and down ravine walls. He worked his way slowly around the Mexicans' left until he reached a point where he appraised the entire area of the flank and rear of the enemy's position. What Lee did was *appraise*, within a concept of strategy.

Beyond absorbing the lay of terrain he could see, he calculated the effects of moves there on the enemy's position beyond his vision, and envisioned a total strategic maneuver that would nullify the enemy's entrenched works. Of his feel for ground as revealed that day, Captain Raphael Semmes said in his report, "His talent for topography was peculiar, and he seemed to receive impressions intuitively, which it cost other men much labor to acquire."

Lee extended his reconnaissance so far that he almost became among those listed as "missing." Pushing through a clump of thickets he came suddenly upon a spring used by Mexican soldiers. Lee glimpsed the Mexicans before they spied him. With no heroics he crawled beneath a fallen tree near the spring. There he crouched during the long afternoon, while enemy soldiers even sat on the tree, engaged in careless conversation. Not until night came could he slip away. Then he made his way back to his own lines with his report and recommendation.

Scott acted immediately upon Lee's strategic reconnaissance. The next day, the 16th, Lee retraced his steps with a small party of pioneers. As quietly as possible, the working party hacked out a passage for troops that would turn the conical hills of Atalaya and Cerro Gordo and, if successful, reach the Jalapa Road behind the enemy's camp.

On April 17, Lee led Twiggs's division on the rugged march where the ravine walls were so sheer that the animals could not haul the guns. The pieces had to be lowered and pulled up by rope. Late in the afternoon Twiggs's troops carried home an attack on Atalaya. There, with Worth's division coming up, the troops had reached the position to complete the execution of Lee's suggested maneuver the next day.

When in the first light of April 18, Lee directed the line of march, through ravines and around boulders, he came under the heaviest fire he had yet experienced. Shell fragments and bullets were ricocheting off the rocks. His thoughts turned to his fifteen-year-old son Custis, and Lee wondered where the boy would be safe if he were along. Then, his thoughts turned to the business of placing gun batteries. As Cerro Gordo was overrun, he directed fire on the enemy camp while the wider flanking movement carried to the Jalapa Road. With their line of retreat cut off, the Mexican force dissolved on all fronts. Disintegrating as a unit, the army fled the field. General Santa Anna barely escaped in the debacle, riding off on a mule.

In the elation at the decisive victory, opening the road to Mexico City, the commanding officers whose troops Lee had directed to their positions were generous in their praise, and "Fuss and Feathers" Scott singled him out in his report. "I am impelled to make special mention of the services of Captain R. E. Lee, Engineers. This officer, greatly distinguished at the siege of Vera Cruz, was again indefatigable, during these operations, in reconnaissance as daring as laborious, and of the utmost value. Nor was he less conspicuous in planting batteries, and in conducting columns to their stations under the heavy fire of the enemy."

A hero had been born. When he was brevetted major a few months later, the date of rank would read April 18 — Cerro Gordo. When Lee wrote to his wife on the night of the 18th, mentioning that he was in "comfortable quarters, beautifully furnished," at the Haciendo Encero, he told nothing of his own adventures. He wrote, "My poor Joe Johnston [was] severely but not critically wounded . . . picket fire — ball in arm [and] above hip."

### 3

By May 15, after a stay in Jalapa, the advance of Scott's army moved to Puebla, Mexico's second largest city. A couple of weeks later Scott came on with his staff, and established a base in the city of seventy-five thousand. With proper support from Washington, Scott should have continued his march on to Mexico City. Santa Anna was having trouble raising a new army around the nucleus of his veterans who drifted back from Cerro Gordo in groups. However, to Scott's disgust, expected reinforcements were diverted to Taylor, just at the time his own one-year volunteers were clamoring to go home at the expiration of their term. With hundreds of sick, his force dropped below six thousand effectives.

Also, President Polk suggested that Scott victual his army by levying on the country. The general was trying to conciliate the population. As it was, guerrillas bothered his troops and the Mexican government had issued a strong proclamation demanding resistance to the end. The result was that Scott waited three months in Puebla until some reinforcements arrived, while he victualed his army by purchases from the countryside. To maintain morale and conditioning during the wait, the men were drilled hard.

During this period in the pleasant city, Captain Lee was kept busy mapping the country on the way to and in the great valley in which Mexico City was situated. Then on August 7, Lee rode out with the army when Scott took the risk — "like Cortes," he wrote — of abandoning his base and striking for the enemy's heartland. Leaving his sick behind, Scott advanced toward the city of two hundred thousand with something less than eleven thousand effectives, then including some cavalry.

Four days later the van breasted the rise of the ten-thousand-foot-high range, and the men gazed down at the wondrous sight of the high valley of Mexico. With all its physical beauty, the valley offered only hazards to an army advancing to the capital city spread twenty miles to the south. The land was covered by large lakes or the marshes of dried lakes, and men and animals could move only along the roads built on causeways. During the halt of the advance, while the other columns struggled to the crest of the range, Captain Lee was sent out with the engineers to find the most promising direction for an assault upon the city.

By August 14 the engineers' reports convinced headquarters that no feasible route existed for an approach from the north and east against the batteries girding the city. The obvious course, devoid of strategy, was a marching campaign. The army would follow a route that first turned the eastern boundaries of Lake Texcoco, to the north and east of the city, then turned the east and the southern boundaries of Lake Chalco to the south and east. Finally, skirting the south of Lake Xochimilco, a little east of south of Mexico City, the route led back northward to the west of Xochimilco. Striking upward from the south, the attacking columns would have the advantage of operating on firm ground and away from the massed guns facing to the east.

Scott's columns had the disadvantage of marching on the periphery against a compact enemy with shorter distances to cover. Scott took the chance on the grounds that Santa Anna's rebuilt army would, except for the cavalry, remain on the defensive, and these horsemen — after Buena Vista — had grown very shy of artillery fire.

The circular march worked as Scott planned. The enemy cavalry was easily driven off and the well-conditioned soldiers concentrated, August 18, at the assault area of San Agustín, nine miles south of Mexico City. The difficulties, which could not have been anticipated, appeared on the terrain west of Lake Xochimilco around San Agustín. There the old highway from Acapulco to the capital ran between the marshes of the lake and the *pedregal* — a lava bed formed in grotesque rocky shapes that, as a naval officer observed, looked like a stormy sea turned to stone. Since both the lava bed and Lake Xochimilco were impassable for troops and guns, the columns would be forced to advance along the causeway road directly into the artillery fire at the fortified hacienda of San Antonio, two and one half miles north from San Agustín.

At this stage, Lee was called on for his specialty of reconnaissance. He was sent to discover if some passage could be found across the jagged boulders and crevasses of the *pedregal*. Accompanied by a detachment of infantry and cavalry, along with his big new reputation, Lee started across the rocky waves. By mid-morning he discovered a trace, a rough pathway. This followed a course westward on which men and mounted horses could move slowly and with care. Lee believed pioneers could clear the trace of lava sufficiently to make the way negotiable for guns.

When Lee and the detachment had followed the unmarked pathway westward about three miles, their party came under sudden rifle fire. The American troops began to shoot back, and the Mexican patrol retired in good order, masking the desolate *pedregal* to the west. The western edge of the lava bed was estimated to be about two miles farther on, and Lee reasoned that, since the Mexicans had crossed from the west, the trace must extend all the way across. With the detachment, Lee returned to San Agustín and made his report to Scott.

The commanding general was very sanguine. West of the *pedregal* a road led north to San Angel, from which in turn a road to the southeast approached the rear of the fortified hacienda at San Antonio on the main highway. For the next day, August 19, Scott ordered parts of two divisions into the *pedregal* to build a road across to the San Angel road, at the same time ordering Worth's division to approach San Antonio directly up the causeway. While Worth was occupying Santa Anna, who had done nothing right since the army left Jalapa, the forces directed by Lee would complete an arduous turning movement.

It happened that just west of the *pedregal*, General Valencia, in disobedience to President-General Santa Anna, had taken a strong position with his Army of the North near the Padierna Ranch. Supported by twenty-two heavy guns, his troops were placed on the slope of an impassable ravine directly west of Lee's line of march through the stony convolutions. Before one o'clock on the 19th, the heavy guns opened on Lee's advance working parties.

Though only captain, Lee was responsible for the road building. He ordered the working parties back and guns brought forward. Two light field batteries moved up over the recently cleared trace, one commanded by Captain John Bankhead Magruder, a fellow Virginian who had been one year behind Lee at West Point. In Magruder's battery was another West Point–trained Virginian, twenty-three-year-old Lieutenant Thomas J. Jackson. Brevet Second Lieutenant McClellan, the good-looking young engineer, helped the artillerists place the guns.

When the two light batteries proved ineffective against the heavier pieces, the commanding officers in the area — General Pillow, General Smith, Colonel Riley — decided between them to continue the artillery fire as a demonstration and send some of the infantry on a circuitous flanking movement west of the *pedregal*, across the San Angel road to the village of San Geronimo. There, north of Valencia's forces, they would be potentially on his rear.

The troops completed the tortuous flanking movement, only to discover a force (sent by Santa Anna) approaching from San Angel to the north. At the end of the day the detached Americans, not more than 3500, found themselves caught between Valencia's army at the Padierna Ranch and Santa Anna's reinforcements. Like Scott, the commanding officers had formed a low opinion of Mexican military leadership. Instead of trying to escape the trap, they decided to attack Valencia through a covered ravine at three o'clock the following morning.

Lee joined the council held by the generals around San Geronimo after dark, and vounteered to take the battle plans back to Scott's headquarters. It was this act of Lee, already prominent in Scott's attention, that placed him lastingly at the very top of soldiers in the commanding general's estimation.

Before Lee started from west of the San Angel road to recross the *pedregal* by night, a heavy rainstorm broke. In her chartless waste of stone shapes, the driving rain obscured any night light and any formations that might have been familiar from his earlier trip. Occasionally a flash of lightning briefly illuminated the rocky pile called Zacatepec, where Scott had established his advance headquarters. Stumbling on foot over lava fragments, feeling his way through the rain, Lee held the direction of Zacatepec in his mind and unerringly made his way to it. When Lee arrived, Scott had returned to his headquarters at San Agustín. On Lee went in the blackness. He reached the commanding general at eleven o'clock, having completed the exhausting, climbing walk in three hours.

When the rain-soaked engineering officer appeared like an apparition in the snug headquarters, Scott was particularly impressed by — what he called — "the greatest feat of physical and moral courage performed by any individual, to my knowledge," because during that night he had previously sent out seven engineering officers to negotiate the *pedregal* and not one had made it.

Lee was not unaware of the superiority of his performance. Later, in writing his wife about their children's diets, he made a reference to his often mentioned "indefatigability." Saying that he had been a "dainty feeder" in his youth, he wrote, "There were but few things I would eat. I do not recollect, however, that anything special was provided for me, but I had to share with the other children. Nor do I know that abstemiousness has been any the worse for me. There are few men more healthy or more able to bear exposure and fatigue, nor do I know of any of my present associates that have undergone as much of either in this campaign."

This simple statement of fact does not equate with the impression of self-depreciative modesty that grows from the many observations on Lee's unassertiveness. But self-depreciation should not be inferred by the absence of assertiveness. While Lee's freedom from insecurity removed him from the need of boastfulness and self-assertion, he placed no "modest" value either on himself as a man or on his gifts. Knowing with his total inner security *what* he was, his ambition sought only the opportunity of displaying what he *had* in the action of duty.

Of all the engineers, the field officers and line officers present, Lee had been the one to volunteer. It was not that he wanted victory more than those who were itching for night to pass to risk their lives in combat the next morning. He perceived the valuable feat that could be performed, and his self-confidence supported his ambition to perform it. Once committed to a task, unlike the other seven engineers sent by Scott, nothing would stop him until it was completed.

The day following Lee's crossing of the *pedregal*, the American assault was delivered as planned. The Mexicans, divided by dissension between Valencia and Santa Anna, broke and fled the field. Valencia's Army of the North was dissolved. The fighting that swirled around the village of San Geronimo and the Padierna Ranch, through and around other hamlets and ranches, was generally called the Battle of Contreras — the one locality where no action occurred.

Scott's forces, flushed with victory, and "Fuss and Feathers" himself, in a state of elation, made the mistake of overconfidence in the pursuit. While the Mexicans were being routed west of the *pedregal*, the garrison on the main highway at San Antonio fell back before Worth's division, attacking from the south. The retreat saved the garrison from being cut off by Twiggs's division, hurrying eastward from north of the *pedregal*. Two miles to the north of San Antonio, the retreating garrison joined forces with other Mexican troops to make a rearguard stand at the Churubusco River.

A strong bridgehead was erected, manned by guns, and to the west the San Mateo Convent was fortified. The American troops came rushing forward from the south and from the west with more impetuosity than plan, and little understanding of the ground. The Mexican defenders delivered their first sharp repulse of the campaign. For three hours they held the river crossing, inflicting upwards of a thousand casualties, and what should have entered reports as a rearguard action became the Battle of Churubusco.

Late in the afternoon, Captain Lee directed forward the new brigade of volunteer General Franklin Pierce. Though the engineering officer had no more familiarity with the ground along the Churubusco River than the infantry, General Pierce reported, "As my command arrived, I established the right upon a point selected by Captain Lee of the Engineers, in whose skill and judgment I had the utmost confidence."

When the Mexicans finally retired at the end of the day to the gates, *garitas*, of the city, the way was open for Scott's army to the enemy's capital, and literally "indefatigable" Lee came in for more praise from the generals with whom he had served. General Persifor Smith reported, "In adverting to the conduct of the staff, I wish to record particularly my admiration of [Lee's] conduct . . . His reconnaissances, though carried far beyond the bounds of prudence, were conducted with so much skill that their fruits were of the utmost value, the soundness of his judgment and his personal daring being equally conspicuous."

For Contreras and Churubusco, Lee was brevetted lieutenant colonel, giving him the nominal rank — with its title in address — while retaining his regular rank of captain. In eight months with Scott, the engineer had moved fast in winning the honors of recognition, and one more opportunity awaited him in the final move on the capital.

4

After Santa Anna had played for time through an armistice, presumably designed to lead to peace, on September 7 Scott resumed preparations for taking the city with plans that offered little scope for Lee's specialty of strategic reconnaissance. Instead, Scott transformed the engineer into something like an aide-de-camp and acting chief of artillery. By then, General Erasmus D. Keyes said that Scott had an "almost idolatrous fancy for Lee, whose military ability he estimated far beyond that of any other officer of the army." Scott later bore this out when he wrote that Lee was "the very best soldier I ever saw in the field."

Through his favored position with the commanding general, Lee's experience gave him an intimate study of the science of war at the top — a sort of practical, advanced school of staff and command. As Scott talked out his decisions, the engineering officer actually could observe the workings of his mind. Then, by observing how Scott acted upon the reconnaissance provided him, and by his own transmission of Scott's orders and the direction he himself gave the subordinate generals, Lee experienced at firsthand the operational procedures of Scott's methods of command.

The deep and lasting impression made upon Lee was the general's practice of planning his battle and leaving the execution to the initiative of the field generals. Each of his strategic successes, Cerro Gordo and Contreras, had been achieved by the opportunistic exploitation of opportunities made by the generals in combat. In turn, Scott's strategy had been evolved, through Lee's own reconnaissance, solely in terms of the terrain and the relation of the enemy's position to it. Making no detailed plans in advance, Scott, for all his love of pomp, based his strategy on self-confident boldness.

He was particularly bold in view of his political ambitions, which caused him to maintain an ill-advised bickering with Washington. His audacious abandonment of the base at Puebla was criticized adversely, and he would have been ruined had his campaign failed. With his small force, failure to succeed would have exposed his army to destruction. What impressed Lee was the assurance with which the enormous man played only to win. He left no line for retreats.

While admittedly Scott was not facing first-rate opposition, the very audacity that kept him advancing deep in hostile country — where one mistake means disaster — crowded the enemy into losing all his poise. The bravery of the patient Mexican soldiers, suffering long on little, was constantly negated by frantic Santa Anna's collapses before the necessity of making sound military judgments. Having retired into the guarded city, the President-General, with his tenuous hold on office, simply turned over the last defenses to his subordinate generals.

Faced with the primary objective of overcoming the last physical obstacle, Scott dismissed approaches by maneuver and made his opening assault a soldiers' battle. On the hill at Chapultepec, the national military college occupied a huge stone structure, a former palace that looked part castle and part fort. Its extensive grounds were enclosed by a high wall. At the western end of the enclosure, about three-quarters of a mile from the guns in Chapultepec, was the stone building of Molino del Rio, a former foundry. This was flanked by the stoutly built fort of Casa Mata, the two buildings covering about a five-hundred-yard front. Ostensibly because of a rumor that the foundry at Molino del Rio was active, and powder stored in Casa Mata, Scott ordered a frontal assault by Worth's division on these two buildings. The September 8 attack was successful, in that the Mexican defenders were driven out. However, the indifferently designed assault came at a cost of 25 per cent casualties and was nothing to magnify a commanding general's reputation.

Scott was in the position where attrition in his dwindling army forced him to quick action, but where its small size could not afford any more "victories" like Molino del Rio. For the next three days, Lee and the other engineers were kept busy studying the approaches to the city. On the 11th, Scott decided to go directly at Chapultepec, while making a feint at the southern gates of the city. During these hurried actions Lee, in his dual role of engineering officer and aide-de-camp, worked under the most intense, prolonged pressure of any period in Mexico.

On Saturday the 11th, he was charged with laying out the batteries that were to open on the former palace of Chapultepec from the south and southwest. The guns were placed by patrician Captain Benjamin Huger, an ordnance officer from South Carolina who had graduated from West Point before his twentieth birthday the year Lee entered. On September 12 the guns opened and continued a day-long bombardment. The light force of defenders within Chapultepec were somewhat shaken by the considerable damage done by Lee's cannon fire. More importantly, four thousand infantry coming up as reinforcements were discouraged from hurrying, and a large body of cavalry to the west of the enclosure was frozen into immobility.

Through the night of Saturday–Sunday Lee worked, rearranging the batteries between trips back and forth to Scott's headquarters. Counting on his powers of endurance, he did not go to bed at all. Early in the morning of the 13th the cannonade was resumed. It continued until after eight o'clock, when the gunners ceased firing to allow the infantry to pass forward. Lee then turned from supervising the bombardment to directing the advance of the assault troops of Pillow's division.

Pillow's troops, who had occupied the buildings at Molino del Rio and Casa Mata during the night, rushed forward within the enclosure, crossing the boggy ground of a cypress grove. Parts of Worth's and of Quitman's divisions moved against the ten-foot walls of the enclosure from the north and south sides. By the time Pillow's infantry had advanced to the deep ditch at the foot of the two-hundred-foot cliff on which the main building perched, segments of Worth's and Quitman's divisions had breeched the enclosure. Bodies of troops from the three units mingled for the final assault. At this stage battle tactics reverted to the medieval warfare of storming castles, with scaling ladders and small parties selected to climb the rocky heights.

Though the defending numbers were not heavy, the men — and boys from the military college — were firing through apertures with determination and accuracy. Casualties were sharp. Lieutenant Lewis Armistead, son of a general, was the first man in the ditch, where he fell wounded. A big, burly twenty-six-year-old lieutenant, James Longstreet, also went down in leading his men across the ditch. Lieutenant Longstreet was carrying a battle-flag, and it was taken from his hand by a young Virginian, George Pickett, who had graduated from West Point only the year before. Longstreet had grown very fond of his colorful looking junior officer. Lying in the ditch, he watched in admiration as the graceful figure of the younger man went up the heights of Chapultepec, carrying the colors.

It was all over in an hour, except for disposing of the Mexican reinforcements which had been slow to move up. This force had been contained by two regiments and the grim-faced young artillery lieutenant Thomas J. Jackson. With one gun of his section knocked out of action, horses and men down, Jackson stood to his one remaining gun and personally kept it firing steadily. When Scott's reinforcements moved up in support, the Mexican troops gave way and the advance was open to the two fortified causeways leading into the city.

The commanding general and his staff rode up on the terrace at Chapultepec. No one observed that Lee was groggily holding to his saddle by an effort of will. Somewhere in all his riding back and forth since he had first directed Pillow's advance into the cypress grove, Lee had taken a flesh wound. He paid no attention to it. But the loss of blood, following two nights of little to no sleep, was beginning to tell.

Scott was excited at the quick victory and determined upon following the demoralized Mexican troops into the city. Taking no notice of the ruddy captain's pallor, he sent Lee forward to survey a line of march for

Worth to one of the defended gates into the city. After seeing Worth on his way, Lee returned and started riding ahead with Scott. Suddenly, without warning, he toppled from his saddle. The "indefatigable" had fainted.

Fortunately Scott had no immediate need of his all-purpose staff officer. Worth and Quitman fought their way through the gates of the city. During the night Santa Anna, resigning the presidency, left the capital with about fifteen hundred cavalrymen and a few guns. He went seeking some detached American unit which, as general, he could defeat. His adventures had run out. The next day the new government sent him an order to relinquish his command and hold himself for court-martial. (Santa Anna finished out his days in poverty-ridden obscurity, dying in 1876.) Before daylight on the morning of September 14, a delegation from the city rode to Scott's headquarters to announce that Santa Anna had decamped and the capital was open to the conquerors.

Lee was recovered the next morning. With the other members of the staff and commanding general, he turned himself out in full-dress uniform for the official entrance into the city. This was the sort of pageantry dear to the heart of "Fuss and Feathers." With a mounted escort, the general's group filed along one side of the Grand Plaza, turned and halted, where arms were presented, the colors lowered and the drums rolled. Removing his hat, the massive man led the way into the patio of the National Palace, mounted the stairway to an apartment overlooking the plaza and had the order announcing the victory read to those gathered around him.

With Scott's little personal drama, the war ended for Brevet Colonel Lee: he was brevetted full colonel for Chapultepec. After street fighting died off in a few days, when the interminable peace negotiations commenced between the two countries, Lee began work on a series of maps of the terrain around Mexico City.

The months dragged on to another Christmas away from home, and then another spring, 1848, before the negotiations were completed. In the settlement, Mexico ceded all claims to Texas, New Mexico and California, and was awarded $15 million, ten million less than was offered before the war. The United States also assumed the claims of American citizens amounting to about $3 million against the Mexican government.

5

For Brevet Colonel Lee the eight peaceful months in Mexico were like being stranded between journeys. In the letdown following the campaigns, Lee's routine duties did nothing to relieve the tedium of waiting to go home. In his sense of kinship with his wife's family, Lee had formed an affection for Martha Custis Williams, one of her young cousins, and for

"Markie" he performed a melancholy duty. He sent her a letter of commiseration along with the bloodstained swordbelt her father had worn when he was killed at Monterrey. Also during this period Lee's feelings became involved when he was drawn into the edge of an ugly army controversy between Scott and two of his major generals, Worth and Pillow.

William J. Worth, who had been commandant of cadets when Lee was at West Point, was a career soldier protective of his reputation. At odds with the commanding general during most of the campaign, his charges against Scott — and Scott's countercharges — were more or less typical of clashes over glory-credit. But Gideon Pillow was something else. A Tennessee politician, he had been a law partner of James Polk, and as President, Polk had appointed Pillow brigadier general of volunteers and then promoted him to major general. Scott's egotism betrayed his judgment when he brought charges against Pillow. He had really done no more than grab some laurels for furtherance of his career back home, and Polk was already annoyed by Scott's complaints and innuendoes. In support of his friend Pillow, the President relieved the commanding general of command and ordered him to attend the court of inquiry at which all charges would be heard.

Though Lee recognized Scott's high-handed harshness with his subordinates, he felt the government's action was unfair and unwise, and he was disturbed at the disharmony created in the army by the rise of factions. Henry Hunt, his younger friend from Fort Hamilton, was then stationed with his gun battery in a suburban hacienda, where Lee often stopped to chat on his way back from surveying the western valley. In the flowering gardens where orange groves were in blossom, Lee, extremely responsive to natural beauty, liked to enjoy the scene before returning to the city. As he relaxed, invariably his conversation turned to means that might "heal the differences between General Scott and some of his subordinate officers . . ." Hunt, later the great cannoneer of the Federal Army opposing Lee, said, "He was a peacemaker by nature."

Lee's testimony at the court of inquiry, while deepening Scott's personal regard for him, could accomplish nothing in saving Scott from the consequences of his egotism. All charges were dropped — Worth's against Scott and his against Worth and Pillow. The President went so far as to say that Pillow had been "persecuted." The result was the death of Scott's presidential aspirations. When Polk refused to serve a second term, the Whigs nominated Scott's fellow Virginian Zachary Taylor. This general, Jefferson Davis's father-in-law, had been completely overshadowed in Mexico by Scott, but Taylor's geniality kept him from making political enemies, and he was elected in 1848.

The political involvement in the army controversy made a deep impression on Lee. He wrote about it at length, especially to his brother Smith.

However, soon after the court of inquiry was over in April, his thoughts turned again to home, for the army would soon be leaving Mexico. On May 27, 1848, Lee began the return trip to the Coast over and down from the mountains, whose spectacular beauty he would never forget. From Vera Cruz he went by boat to New Orleans, then up the Mississippi and on to Wheeling, Virginia. For the last stage he "rode the cars," arriving in Washington on June 29.

Once again Lee made the ride across the bridge over the Potomac to the road to Arlington, which he had left twenty-two months before. He turned into the drive up the long hill, shaded by the trees his wife so dearly loved. In contrast to the vivid colors on Mexico's high plateau and mountains, the grounds at Arlington were a restful, familiar green, of shrubs and vines, thick grass and old trees, brightened by summer flowers and fragrant with that indefinable aroma of heat and foliage associated with his earliest memories. Riding up the hill he saw the great Romanesque columns of the house on the crest, toward which he had ridden long ago in a carriage with his mother and then when he had come courting alone, nearly twenty years before this June.

Since those days of his young dreams he had become the most famous soldier under general rank in the army. Yet, it was an army reputation, giving him no aura of the public hero. It was entirely as family man that he returned to his "flock" — as he once referred to his wife and children in a letter, in which he said he felt "like a patriarch of old" when they were all gathered around him.

Then he came up on the crest where he saw them gathered between columns on the wide portico. Spec, the black and tan terrier, was the first to run to greet him. The older children — Custis, Mary, Rooney, Annie and Agnes — who remembered their father, converged on him as they moved into the large central hall. He greeted them in order of their ages, kissing each one.

Robert E. Lee, Jr., the child next to seven-year-old Agnes, had been not quite three when his father left and did not remember him clearly. For what he recognized as a great occasion, Rob turned himself out in his favorite blouse, a blue ground dotted with white diamond figures, and Eliza, his mammy, had freshly curled his hair in long golden ringlets. He stood shyly, waiting his turn. To his intense mortification his father, saying, "Where is my little boy?" grabbed up a friend of Rob's who happened to be visiting there. Holding the startled young visitor in his arms, the mustached army colonel had planted a kiss on the boy's cheek before he was directed to his own son.

The youngest child, Mildred, had been only eight months old when her father left, and she stared silently at him as at a stranger she had never before seen. After Mildred, the plainest of the children, grew to understand who the man in uniform was, she became the brightest and gayest of any of them when with him. From his homecoming, Lee began to call her "Precious Life," and she became her father's pet from then on.

Lee noticed, as he wrote Smith, that the older children gazed "with wonder and astonishment" at him and "seem to devote themselves to staring at the furrows in my face and the white hairs in my head . . . and seem at a loss to reconcile what they see and what was pictured in their imaginations." He was still, as Lieutenant Cadmus Wilcox saw him, "the handsomest man in the army," and the few white hairs were not evident (except under close inspection) in the thick dark hair brushed sidewise from a part above a fluffiness at the temples. But the marks of the hard campaigning showed in the gentleness which the children remembered, a more forceful resolution in the habitual composure. Knowing nothing of the exploits that had brought great praise to "Colonel Lee," the boys and girls were simply concerned with rediscovering "Papa."

In a very short time, to all of them it was as if he had never been away.

## CHAPTER V

## "As the Twig Is Bent"

AFTER BEING AWAY from all the comforts and gratifications of life with his family for nearly two years, Brevet Colonel Lee accepted cheerfully enough those humdrum chores of peacetime defenses that had agitated him to the borderline of resignation when he was younger. His first assignment, beginning in September, 1848, and lasting until April, 1852, took the Lee family to Baltimore. In his work the colonel supervised the construction of the foundation for a new harbor fort, Fort Carroll, to be built at Sollers' Point. Socially he found a circle ready-made by his sister Ann and her husband, William Louis Marshall, and in the Baltimore years Lee enjoyed the pleasures of a general society with a fullness not possible before in the army. Leaving the red-brick house on Madison Avenue in the mornings for his engineering job and returning at the end of the day, Lee followed a routine almost like a civilian's.

Mary Custis Lee, twenty years and seven children beyond the spoiled heiress of Arlington who had gone with her husband to Fort Monroe, had long since shifted her center to her family and become an indulgent mother. Mrs. Lee was not the most systematic manager of a household, and the rooms in the three-story house were small — at first giving a cramped sensation after Arlington — but she loved her home and loved to entertain in it. During the Baltimore years she was not plagued with ailments, nor shocked by such minor calamities as had befallen Rooney at Fort Hamilton. Her robust husband was the one who came down sick, though not seriously.

In July of their first summer in Baltimore, Lee began to suffer from a debilitating fever, which was not diagnosed. When the fever continued, he went for recovery to his mother's haven at Ravensworth.

The mistress of Ravensworth, Mrs. Anne Maria Fitzhugh, was the widow of Mary Lee's uncle (her mother's brother), William Henry Fitzhugh, who had been the supportive friend of Lee's mother. Fitzhugh had died shortly after Lee's mother, and Mrs. Fitzhugh, who had made Ravensworth always open to Ann Carter Lee's family, continued her affectionate interest in the Lee children as they grew up and developed their own families. Thus, Anne Maria Fitzhugh, though no blood kin either to Lee or his wife, had been close to each of them since their childhood and her home a familiar place as long as they could remember. Colonel Lee, as well as Mary Lee, called her "Aunt Maria," as did their children. Since Aunt Maria had no children of her own, she gradually adopted the whole Lee family and they adopted her.

As Lee grew older and his parents' generation died off, his attachment for Anne Maria Fitzhugh was as deep as any in his life. Very devout and very generous, with her hospitality and her wealth, Mrs. Fitzhugh combined a warm-hearted goodness with great elegance of person. In a portrait painted when she was younger, Anne Maria Fitzhugh had the worldly-looking regality of a duchess in London's regency period. At the time of Lee's recuperation at her plantation, this great lady was taking a place in his life as a kinswoman of his mother's generation, though Mrs. Fitzhugh was considerably younger than Lee's mother would have been.

The long fever that beset Lee was his first illness to be recorded and gave an impression that he had never been sick before. However, in March, 1841, he had written Henry Kayser, "I have been quite sick from the effects of the grippe that is very prevalent. It has attacked my head and I am now under the operation of mustard plasters and blisters. Tomorrow I am going to have 20 leeches and the next day God knows what. Some periods of the day the pain is almost intolerable." From the matter-of-factness of Lee's letter, he would not seem to be encountering illness for the first time. Though he retained in his forties an undiminished vitality, reflected in the beautiful carriage of his massive upper body, it is probable that occasional sieges of sickness were — as with the grippe — simply not recorded in any records that became official.

After he returned, recovered, to Baltimore, nothing appeared to change the pleasant, if unexciting, pattern of Lee's life. He and Mrs. Lee often went out in the evening, and Rob vividly recalled the impression of seeing them go off. His father was always in full uniform and always ready, waiting for Mrs. Lee. She was generally late. "He would chide her gently, in a playful way and with a bright smile. He would then bid us goodbye, and I would go to sleep with this beautiful picture in my mind, the golden epaulets and all — chiefly the epaulets."

In the close warmth of this family, the children were reaching ages in which they would be more interesting to the father, each according to his level. With the younger children, he liked to romp and play, joke with them, and tell them stories. He loved to have the bottoms of his feet tickled, and he removed his house slippers, placed his feet in one of the children's laps, and told stories as long as the child would tickle his feet. He showed an intense interest in their studies, their failures and their triumphs, and gave them, his youngest son recalled, "kind, sensible, useful" guidance. As he had been taught by his mother, so he taught his children the virtues of application, to do the best they could. With each of his daughters he was a doting parent, and clearly he wanted the boys to excel.

2

The first break in the family circle came in 1850 when Custis went off to West Point. When first at the Military Academy, Custis ("Boo" or "Mr. Boo") did not seem to have absorbed his father's precepts on application. Well enough endowed, the serious-minded oldest son lacked the dynamic energies that often characterized the Lees (as brother Rooney), and disappointed Lee by making a sluggish start as a student.

Then, in 1852 the family followed Custis when Lee was given a change from engineering work and appointed superintendent of the Military Academy. There he was to remain nearly three years, until April, 1855, continuing the placid period of life as a career soldier.

Lee returned to West Point to an enlarged and greatly changed institution from that of his cadet days. The changes in his own life were indicated by the presence in the cadet corps of his son, and then nephew Fitz, the frolicsome son of brother Smith. Custis had settled down to apply himself before his father came. During his last two years and Lee's first two, Custis was a good student and worked up to his capacities.

Graduating in 1854, he followed his father into the Regular Army, and always followed his father's examples in his conduct. An intuitive closeness developed between Custis and his father that gave their relationship a slightly different tone, more one of peers, than that between Lee and his other children.

The year Custis graduated, gigantic Rooney, the horse-lover, made the unwise choice of Harvard College. Rooney's high spirits and zest for physical things, which gave him a special place in his father's affections, made him appear an imperious non-intellectual to classmate Henry Adams. As viewed by a scholarly New Englander, he probably was. The inherited privilege and the privilege assumed by plantation sons frequently gave the impression of imperiousness. Of Rooney, who had never taken to the books available in his own home, his mother said he possessed "a warm and affectionate heart, but too careless and reckless a disposition." Though there were other non-intellectual students at Harvard, it was Rooney's hearty lordliness that made Henry Adams draw conclusions about the society from which he came.

When Lee's family moved into the large and roomy stone house at West Point, nine-year-old Rob succeeded Custis and then Rooney as his father's companion. In the afternoons, as soon as the superintendent was, as his son said, "released from his office," he made for the stables. With

Lee mounted on his old mare, "Grace Darling," and Robert on the pony, "Santa Anna," his father had brought him from Mexico, the two of them went for a trot of from five to ten miles. Lee would not let his son post, but forced him to learn the "dragoon-seat" — telling him that the hammering he suffered until he mastered the seat was good for him.

With all of Lee's casual intimacy with his children, he demanded the strictest obedience. Robert said, "I always knew it was impossible to disobey my father. I felt it in me, I never thought why, but was perfectly sure when he gave an order that it had to be obeyed." It had to be obeyed because Lee expected obedience, and not only because he was a soldier. Having been raised in the security of a loving but firm discipline, this was in his nature.

His wife was the one person who remained unaffected by his order of things. He had not been able to keep the promise, made at Fort Monroe, about becoming less of a perfectionist, especially in matters of punctuality, and Mary Lee had not felt urged to mend her ways. By dawdling, she continued to be late for any and all occasions. Even when guests came she was not ready. Usually for church, Lee, after rallying his wife about not forgetting something at the last minute, marched off alone, or followed by any of the children who were ready.

In church, sitting very straight, "well up the middle aisle," Lee invariably became overcome by drowsiness during the sermon. With all his devotion, the minister's words served as a soporific as he sat stiffly in the enforced inactivity. Sometimes, to his son's horror, the peerless father did the "inexplicable" thing of dozing off into a nap.

During his tour at West Point, Lee gave himself to the formality of receiving confirmation in the Episcopal Church — Christ Church, which he had attended as a child in Alexandria. This act has been grossly misunderstood, even confused with some religious emotionality leading him "to join the church." Lee had always thought of himself as belonging to the church, as shown by serving on the vestry at Fort Hamilton.

The fact was that when he was growing up, young confirmations were not common practice in Virginia. This was a vestige of Colonial days when the Church of England did not maintain bishops in the colony. Since only bishops performed the "laying on of hands," the communicants came to regard confirmation as unimportant and Holy Communion was served to "baptized persons." Lee had been baptized as a child and had learned the Catechism (which actually prepared him to receive confirmation) from Reverend William Meade, later bishop, when he was rector at Christ Church.

When Lee's children were growing, the old custom began to change. Then it happened that on a family visit to Arlington, Agnes and Annie were confirmed at Christ Church, and it occurred either to Lee or his wife that he had never performed this ceremony. As a bishop was available, he joined his daughters at the chancel, and the bishop, laying his hands upon Lee's head, said, "Defend, O Lord, this thy Child with thy heavenly grace; that he may continue thine for ever; and daily increase in thy Holy Spirit more and more, until he come into thy everlasting kingdom." Nothing was changed for Lee, but perhaps his children felt better about him as a fellow communicant.

In the regular order of his days, Lee enjoyed every aspect of his life except the confinement to an office. In that office, however, he showed himself to be a highly able administrator. This was Lee's third type of work since he had been a cadet. As in engineering he had changed the course of the Mississippi and in combat had performed more conspicuously than any soldier under general rank, he demonstrated a capacity to get inside every task he undertook. Though he performed nothing spectacular in his relatively brief tour of duty at West Point, he did, as in everything he touched, make improvements.

Discipline was at a high level during his superintendency. He quickly won the respect and regard of the cadets by an understanding tolerance of human inadequacies that, never undermining his authority, added the dimension of humanity to his standards as a disciplinarian. He also worked in harmony with the Secretary of War, his former fellow cadet, Jefferson Davis, who was not always an easy man to get along with.

The even flow of the family's days was broken in the spring of 1853 by the death of Mary Lee's mother. Since Lee's mother's death twenty-four years before, they had not lost anyone in their immediate families. Mrs. Custis was a greatly admired woman, of, as Bishop Meade said, "benevolence . . . deep humanity and retiring modesty." Lee was almost as shaken as his wife. While she was at Arlington with her father, he wrote of Mrs. Custis, "She was to me all that a mother could be . . ."

As his wife's mother had come into his life shortly after his own mother died, and as Mrs. Custis's place was to some extent taken by "Aunt Maria" Fitzhugh, it seems that Lee needed an older woman of the family to sustain his inner sense of security. While he continually formed enduring friendships with men who were his contemporaries or younger, and his love and admiration for colorful Smith went very deep, these three women — so remarkably similar — represented his continuity with the past and personalized the matrix of family as center on earth. Some of his personally most revealing letters were written to Aunt Maria. Not by detail or length, these letters often revealed by some sudden phrase an illumination of the heart.

Two years after the death of Mrs. Custis, the quiet period of domestic life came to an end. While Lee could have felt no premonition that this was the end of family life as he had known it since childhood, he was reluctant at the age of forty-eight to leave his wife and children. It was a time when his daughters particularly needed the presence of their father. He was given no choice. In April, 1855, he received orders to leave for the West to take his first field command.

Because of Indian fighting on the plains War Secretary Davis had been able to get the support from President Pierce's administration to raise two new regiments. Lee was to join the new 2nd Cavalry as lieutenant colonel, regular rank. The assignment of superintendent at West Point had carried with it the temporary rank of colonel of engineers. Transfer from the engineering corps for the field had the bright aspect of removing him from a branch in which promotions were discouragingly slow and the way to the top at regular rank was blocked by older men with seniority. But Lee did not seem to look on this aspect when he wrote his wife's cousin, Markie Williams.

"The change from my present confined and sedentary life, to one more free and active, will certainly be more agreeable to my feelings and serviceable to my health. But my happiness can never be advanced by my separation from my wife, children and friends."

In this humor he escorted his wife, the four girls and young Rob back to Arlington, where the grounds were bright and green and sweet with spring. Leaving his family at this home of his mature life, Lee started the lonely journey for Louisville, Kentucky, and his first experience with combat troops.

### 3

When, in the summer of 1855, Lee went with the new regiment to Jefferson Barracks at St. Louis, the forces that had gathered momentum during the Mexican War were no longer subsurface. In 1850 the power struggle had come into the open with forthright and irrational sectional alignments. The stands once taken by Light-Horse Harry Lee on the need of national interests controlling the central government were all but forgotten in the rapidly changing nation. Sides were being chosen in a frank struggle for the rule of the new Continental United States.

The admission of California as a state was the occasion for the conflict in 1850. Though the southern part of the state belonged south of the boundary agreed upon in the Missouri Compromise, the new inhabitants of the territory voted to come into the union as a single state in which slavery was prohibited. The gold rush was on in California, and the last interest of the mobs rushing West was in building plantations with slave labor. This was a bitter pill for the aggressive leaders among the big slaveholders, and they made the same talk of secession the New Englanders had made over the War of 1812.

Veteran compromiser Henry Clay came up with a new compromise in 1850, which gave the unrealistic slave powers nothing except sops to their pride. Utah and New Mexico were to be created as territories without restrictions as to slavery, and teeth were to be put in the Fugitive Slave Laws. This last item was worse than useless, as it served chiefly to exacerbate an anti-slavery element in the North and to provide ammunition for the abolitionists.

In practical terms not enough fugitives escaped to make it a national issue, and for those runaways who did make their way North the Northerners could not be forced to obey laws to which they were sentimentally opposed. The new slave powers, heady at their aggrandized status in the world, were incapable of realism. Defending an institution regarded as anachronistic even by the conservative slaveholders in their own region, this small minority — assertive, vocal and powerful — met the demands of Northern zealots by going on the offensive with irrational counterdemands of their own.

While the mass segments of population in both regions went about their business, the two extremes promoted a sectionalism in which the political parties were losing their direction, and the compromising Whigs even their identity. The Whigs were still the conservative party of capital, North and South. They drew the allegiance of old-line planters, especially in Virginia, where the enlightened slaveholders were still actively interested in discovering practical means of emancipation. The more successful and less respectable Democrats attracted the new slave powers in the Lower South because, though containing Northern anti-slavery men, this party stood fast for permitting each state to decide its own policy on slavery. The fact was that neither party wished to grapple with the tangled economics in a practical solution of the problem that had become a political powder keg.

While the power struggle for national control went on unrelated to slavery, this publicized issue aggravated awareness of inherent conflicts between the sections. From South Carolina to the south and the new southwest the tendency toward secession, which manifested itself during the 1850 Compromise, began to gain support among representatives of the slave interests.

A distrust of the value of a union had existed among some South Carolinians since the nullification fight in 1832. When Andrew Jackson threatened an armed invasion to enforce the tariff laws which the state had nullified, South Carolinians — like the man convinced against his will — felt that the threat of force had decided no principles. Even though the discriminatory tariff laws were changed, the threat of the use of force from a majority continued to rankle, and the idea grew of avoiding a repetition of the circumstance by withdrawing from the compact of union.

There was nothing in the Constitution to prevent an abrogation of the compact, but the advanced secessionists — the "fire-eaters" — confused the whole thing by their dream of a slave empire. The conservative Southerners were only trying to prevent being dominated in the central government of a changing nation, where mathematics were against them ("look at the census returns," a Northern sectionalist said with cold cynicism). But the neo-Bourbons trumpeted for an expansion of slavery that offended everyone else in the United States. Yet, by the undirected drift to defensiveness, Southern Whigs were thrown into an alliance with Democratic slave powers, with only the "fire-eaters" knowing what they wanted. They wanted a separate nation.

The lines in the North were no clearer nor more logical, except time and arithmetic were on the side of the dominating financial-industrial interests. The revolutionary abolitionists wielded no power comparable to the Lower South slaveholders. They were not economically involved and their careers in moral indignation, unrelated to the practicalities of emancipation, gave them none of the position of a responsible force. But in 1854 the abolitionists were welcomed in a non-exclusive new party formed of refugees from the dissolving Whigs and an assortment of "outs," such as the Free Soilers and Know Nothings.

This Republican Party, containing a hard core of shrewd and ambitious politicians, cared nothing about abolition. It did commit itself to the containment of slavery where it then existed, as did most everyone else North and South, except those taking extreme positions on the issue. On its founding, the new party was given a rallying point and a push by the Kansas-Nebraska Bill, the most stupidly and needlessly inflammatory move made in the amorphous struggle.

The author of the provocative bill was Stephen A. Douglas, senator from Illinois. A small, magnetic man, Douglas had succeeded to the eminence in Washington formerly enjoyed by the great trio of Clay, Calhoun and Webster, themselves successors of the Virginia dynasty. Douglas proposed to create new territories in the flat stretches west of Missouri and Iowa, slicing off squares of land to form the future states of Kansas and Nebraska. Since California had been admitted into the union by the citizens voting on the legal status of slavery, Kansas and Nebraska would be admitted on the same principle. However, as both states were north of the 36°30′ parallel, this was a violation of the Missouri Compromise. It was not that a violation of a former agreement was so heinous; California had already gotten around that. But this particular violation ran counter to the will of the national majority and against the tide of the containment of slavery where it existed.

Douglas's motives are obscure. To the young Democrat of soaring ambitions, the bill might have seemed a means of cementing a political alliance with the proslavery Southern Democrats, whose leader, Jefferson Davis, was his friend. Davis, as Secretary of War, was the power in the cabinet of Franklin Pierce, a pro-Southern Democrat from New Hampshire. As Pierce was a strict observer of the Sabbath, on a Sunday morning Douglas took his bill to friend Davis.

The Mississippi spokesman for the slave powers was anything except an astute politician. A high-minded theoretician, who lived on a plantation provided by a successful older brother, Davis actually scorned the connivings of politics' back rooms. Though he was a spokesman for the Lower South, Jefferson Davis had come to believe that the South's future should lie within the Union. Obviously at that stage, in the Union the South's interests would be best served by avoiding agitation over the slave issue and by seeking friends in the North. Davis, remote from the hearts of men and lacking a *feel* for the political climate, saw only that the Kansas-Nebraska Bill offered a concession to the slave interests. With Douglas, he violated the President's Sabbath privacy, and obtained Pierce's support for the Kansas-Nebraska Bill.

What Davis unthinkingly had done was to bring on a miniature civil war. The slave powers and the abolitionists vied with one another in sending families into Kansas, along with arms and gunmen, and the long conflict between the extremists of both sides flared into the open in bloody, personal fighting. Still unrelated to the underlying power struggle for control of the industrializing nation, the guerrilla war in Kansas took the surface conflict between factionalists from the academic question of the spread of slavery to the tangible problem of the spread of the fighting.

The faraway and apparently local outbreaks of violence did not arouse the national public to the implications. Times were good, a new continental empire was opening illimitable opportunity for every man, and the slave issue was largely regarded as a peripheral conflict between the more aggressive slave interests and the fanatics. This general attitude was reflected in Lieutenant Colonel R. E. Lee and in the soldiers who comprised his total world in the boundless wastes of West Texas's plains. As a matter of fact, when the Kansas fighting was first carried in distorted news coverage, Lee was parching in the heat of Comanche country. His sole contacts beyond his isolated post were visits back and forth with an unimposing, polygamous chief named Catumseh.

4

The period at Camp Cooper in West Texas was the bleakest, loneliest time in Lee's life. Uprooted from seven years of family life in dignified if unexciting aspects of his career, he went — following a dreary round of attending court-martials at army posts — to his Siberia on an almost uninhabited prairie on the edge of the wild country called "the Staked Plains." Lee went to Camp Cooper with only a detachment of two squadrons. One hundred seventy miles to the south the rest of the regiment was temporarily posted at Fort Mason, itself one hundred miles north and a little west of San Antonio.

With the major part of the regiment was the colonel, Albert Sidney Johnston, and a roster of distinguished officers, mostly Southerners. Johnston himself, a year ahead of Lee at West Point, was a magnificent-looking soldier and a man whose character was much admired — particularly by his former classmate, War Secretary Jefferson Davis. Behind second-in-command Lee was another Virginian, Major George Thomas. The captains in the 2nd Cavalry were Earl van Dorn, a romantic-looking Mississippian, and Kirby Smith, a Floridian who had commanded troops among those directed by Lee at Cerro Gordo and Contreras. Among the lieutenants were Charles Field, a stockily built, good-humored Kentuckian, and later Fitz Lee, who joined the regiment at Fort Mason immediately after his graduation from West Point in 1856.

At Camp Cooper, Lee did not get to see his nephew, nor most of the imposing military talent around Colonel Johnston. With his two squadrons Lee had as his only companion Lieutenant John B. Hood, a Kentucky native who had graduated from West Point in Lee's first year as superintendent. A big, powerfully built young man, who was to adopt Texas as his state, Hood was very cheerful and alert about soldiering, but scarcely a stimulating mental type.

When Lee first arrived at Camp Cooper, on April 9, 1856, not a building had been erected on the barren stretches where the blinding glitter of the sun seemed to be cooking the earth. Lee's new home would be in a tent, in which the heat passed 100 degrees during the long months of the summer. For his seven chickens, which he had brought along in a coop, he built a henhouse above the ground to protect the hens and eggs from the serpents that infested the region. Tarantulas were also plentiful, making their sudden hops with hideous hairy black bodies. Lee tried to get a cat, preferably one of the yellow spotted variety familiar at home, but could get none of any kind.

After five months in the isolation, Lee welcomed the break of attending a routine court-martial at Ringgold Barracks. Then, in early November, a court-martial at Fort Brown, at Brownsville, gave him a complete and needed change. Across from Matamoros on the Rio Grande, Brownsville was a picturesque border town and seemed a hub of civilization to Lee after the months on the barrens among the rattlesnakes. He shared a room in the officers' quarters at the fort. He was there at Christmas, when among his presents came a packet of Alexandria newspapers, the latest as recent as three weeks.

In the newspapers, Lee read of President Pierce's admonitions to the radical abolitionists. "Extremes beget extremes. Violent attack from the North finds its inevitable consequence in the growth of a spirit of angry defiance in the South."

Speaking of indirect aggression, the President said, "The second step in this path of evil consisted of acts by the people of the Northern states . . . to facilitate the escape of persons held to service in the Southern states and to prevent their extradition when reclaimed according to law and in virtue by express provision of the Constitution."

Lee wrote immediately to his wife. In expressing his own sentiments, he managed here to summarize the attitude of the humanistic, conservative Southerner who had been associated with the institution of slavery.

"The views of the President: of the Systematic and progressive efforts of certain people of the North, to interfere with and change the domestic institutions of the South, are truthfully and faithfully expressed. The Consequences of their plans and purposes are also clearly set forth and they must also be aware that their object is both unlawful and entirely foreign to them and their duty; for which they are irresponsible and unaccountable; and [abolition] can only be accomplished by *them* through the agency of a Civil and Servile war.

"In this enlightened age, there are few I believe, but what will acknowledge, that slavery as an institution, is a moral and political evil in any Country. It is useless to expatiate on its disadvantages. I think it however a greater evil to the white than to the black race, and while my feelings are strongly enlisted in behalf of the latter, my sympathies are more strong for the former. The blacks are immeasurably better off here than in Africa, morally, socially and physically. The painful discipline they are undergoing, is necessary for their instruction as a race, and I hope will prepare and lead them to better things. How long their subjugation may be necessary is known and ordered by a wise Merciful Providence. Their emancipation will sooner result from the mild and melting influence of Christianity, than the storms and tempests of fiery' Controversy. This influence though slow, is sure.

"The doctrines and miracles of our Savior have required nearly two thousand years, to Convert but a small part of the human race, and even among Christian nations, what gross errors still exist! While we see the

Course of the final abolition of human Slavery is onward, and we give it the aid of our prayers and all justifiable means in our power, we must leave the progress as well as the result in his hands who sees the end; who Chooses to work by slow influence; and with whom two thousand years are but as a Single day.

"Although the Abolitionist must know this, and must see that he has neither the right or power of operating except by moral means and suasion, and if he means well to the slave, he must not create angry feelings in the Master . . . although he may not approve the mode by which it pleases Providence to accomplish its purposes, the result will nevertheless be the same . . . The abolitionist must see that the reasons he gives for interference, in what he has no Concern, holds good for every kind of interference with our neighbours when we disapprove their Conduct; still I fear he will persevere in his evil Course."

Lee's underlying faith in the workings of Providence was similar to the beliefs the Constitution makers held in an All Powerful Force which controlled orderly development. While Washington and some of the others were probably Deists (Jefferson certainly was), Lee's religious faith, neither emotional nor evangelical, also essentially submitted to what he conceived as a divine will, or order.

On this foundation, Lee's view was typical of his class, whether in Virginia, or in the border states of North Carolina, Tennessee, Kentucky and Arkansas. He did not presume to speak of conditions of which he knew nothing, and recognized he had little more knowledge of the slave plantations in the Lower South than the Northern abolitionists had — which was none at all.

Lee's experiences were at Arlington and Shirley, where an Englishman described the working population as better cared for than in any country he had ever visited. Lee had seen nothing of the absentee-owned plantations where slaves labored in fields on the money crop of cotton or rice. From his distance, Lee fundamentally disapproved of the secessionist attitude of the slave interests as disruptive.

At the same time he found disruptive the abolitionist's premise that interference with other states, in matters in which "he has no Concern," was permissible whenever "we disapprove their Conduct." Lee was not referring to the moral element in the abolition of slavery when he said the distant abolitionist interfered in matters in which he had no concern. While no more than 10 per cent of the population employed slave labor in the Lower South, the institution was so inextricably involved with the social-economic structure that every man, woman and child in the region would be affected by sudden abolition. The abolitionist had no concern, because he assumed no responsibility for the consequences of his interferences with this society. Obviously the union would become chaotic if any group of states could impose its will on any other without regard to the social stability and economic health of the region which happened to be disapproved of.

While Lee characteristically disapproved of both factions, he also resented the abolitionists for a fanaticism that set race against race under revolutionary conditions, instead of appealing to national reason. This violated all his convictions about a rational approach to the common good as held by the Constitution makers. Along with Lee's personal beliefs in the workings of Providence was the environmental influence of a stable society. In this society, change came by orderly processes, as American liberty had grown from deep roots in his father's generation.

This son of a man who risked his life for liberty, this kinsman of leaders of the libertarian ideal, was also the child of those Carters who perpetuated, generation after generation, the regulated society out of which liberty grew. By orderly, controlled change that did not disturb the society — by "suasion" and by avoiding the incitement of the slave that created "angry feelings in the master" — slavery would pass in natural progress. This, to Lee, represented the positive good. To force things, by fomenting racial hatreds and sectional conflict, was to him the evil, for this threatened the stability of the republican structure.

Though he seldom expressed himself on the subject, or on any subject outside his own experiences, his December 27 letter to Mrs. Lee placed him where he always stood. It represented no change and from it he never changed. His position represented a conviction rather than a rationality. With his own duties defined by the U. S. Army, it is not likely that he brooded overmuch on the future when orders returned him to the God-forsaken spot between the Brazos and the Colorado rivers, Camp Cooper.

He got back to his two squadrons and the reptiles in April, in time to begin another tropical summer in his tent. He was fifty years old then, the gray in his hair multiplying, and for once in his life there was nothing at which he could do his best. He endured.

In late July, 1857, he was reprieved by the chance of Albert Sidney Johnston being called to Washington. For a few months he enjoyed the comparatively cosmopolitan world of San Antonio as acting commander of the 2nd Cavalry regiment. From this pleasant relief from the wilds he was called, on October 21, to Arlington. Washington Custis had died. Lee needed to join his wife, and the children who'd had no father for two years.

5

Lee rode again up the long hill at Arlington, where the trees on the hillside park and in the forest blazed in fall colors, to a far different homecoming than on his return from Mexico. Dismounting in front of the columns across the wide portico, he found no "flock" waiting to receive him.

Along with the two gentle people of the older generation who were gone, Lee's oldest sons — boys on his earlier return — were away in the army. Rooney had resigned from Harvard and been commissioned directly into the infantry. The middle girls, Annie and Agnes, were off at school, and very homesick. Twenty-two-year-old Mary, more independent-minded than ever, was concerned with her own affairs, which did not seem to include interest in marriage. From a later remark of her mother's, Mary could find no one to please her; for a certainty she tried to please no one else. Yet, in her separate way, she was enjoying that period of her life, with many friends and frequent visits back and forth. Of the seven young Lees who had welcomed their father before, only two children were left — Rob, a sturdy fourteen, and eleven-year-old Mildred of the gay heart and bubbling spirits.

All this Lee had expected. The shock came when he passed through the wide hall of the house and saw his wife in the family sitting room. She was partially crippled by arthritis, her right arm hanging uselessly. In bearing his startled inspection, her face showed by a sharpening of the features the effects of pain that racked her.

Expecting to comfort his wife over the death of her father, Lee was totally unprepared for her appearance. In the maturing that had come to Mary Custis Lee since she had urged her husband to come home when she was sick after Mary was born, she had spared him her afflictions when answering his lonely letters written from Camp Cooper. Knowing he would be shocked, Mrs. Lee had written a friend, "I almost dread his seeing my crippled state."

What Lee felt he never revealed. Within the imposing façade of control, it would be improbable that he never speculated on the circumstances that returned him to the duties of nurse he had known through his youth with his mother. Beginning with the day he first saw his crippled wife, all Lee ever showed was the same patient attention and care he had given his mother.

Though a circle was curiously complete, Lee never placed his wife in any aspect of a mother's role. He never called her "Mama" or any of the names the children used. At different periods of their marriage, he called her by variations of her own name, just as he gave private names to his children and called brother Smith "Rose." But fundamentally she was Mary, the woman he protected and cherished as his mother had cherished him.

With the saddening effect of his wife's semi-invalidism — and his awareness of it was deepened by sharing her wakefulness when the agony of the pain broke her sleep — Lee was profoundly depressed by the burden of administrating his father-in-law's entangled estate. As he was the only executor to qualify, and as bringing order to Custis's estate represented a full-time job, Lee was forced to ask for a year's leave from the army. This leave was extended, and more than two years passed before he returned to his regiment.

At the basis of the disorder in which indulgent and indulging Custis had left the estate, entrusted to him by George and Martha Washington, was an attitude not unique with him. Washington Custis epitomized those planters born in the eighteenth century who wanted to lead a baronial life of ease while salving their consciences about keeping human chattels. Knowing no way to maintain the operation of his lands without the labor of slaves, Custis rented out distant tracts of land to farmers, and coddled the Negroes who kept Arlington more or less as a park. In his will he showed the desire to play at baronial largesse by leaving plantations to his grandsons and cash settlements of $10,000 to each of his four granddaughters. At the same time he instructed his executors to free his 196 slaves within five years. In his grandiose thinking, while neglecting his properties, Custis left no cash to be bequeathed — and that was not the worst. The estate was $10,000 in debt and non-self-sustaining Arlington was physically much run down.

To complicate matters, Custis's will provided that cash bequests for the granddaughters be raised if necessary by selling off lands from the plantations bequeathed to the grandsons — Arlington to Custis, the White House plantation on the Pamunkey River to Rooney, and Romancoke, also on the Pamunkey, to young Rob. Lee was not sentimental about selling off land but, since the plantations were going to his sons, he preferred to hand them on intact. The problem was how to pay off creditors from operations that were then losing money and raise the $40,000 cash for his daughters' legacies *within the five years* allotted by Custis's will for the emancipation of the slaves. The practicalities in emancipation can be illustrated by the fact that the slaves — representing the investments of hardworking George Washington — could have sold for five times the amount needed by Lee.

Lee went at the complex problem in the only way he knew how to work: within a master plan, he gave infinite attention to each of a multitude of details, one detail at a time, proceeding one day at a time. Never considering any quick way, any spectacular stroke, at the age of fifty he became a planter. As a planter, he applied the efficient technical methods of an army engineer. In doing this Lee showed that, with all his gentleness of nature, he was not a soft man. While his sense of honor required him to fulfill the letter of Custis's will with scrupulous exactitude, nothing required him to follow his father-in-law's sentimental indulgence of field workers. To Lee they were the same as any troops under his command.

Lee's operation at Arlington was his first practical experience with slaves as a plantation labor force. Previously he had known Negroes only as house people. In 1847 Lee had himself been taxed as the legal owner of four slaves, though no records reveal how they came into his ownership or whatever happened to them. The likeliest assumption seems that Washington Custis gave him title to four Negroes who were among the White House slaves. The Negro woman, Nancy, and her three children (who were over sixteen and taxable in 1847) seem not to have left the White House during Lee's unknown period of ownership, since neither he nor anyone in his family ever referred to them. In fact, it is known that he held legal title to them only by their listing in the Alexandria County Property Tax Book of 1847.

Some time after that listing they evidently were freed, according to provisions in the will Lee wrote August 31, 1846, before leaving for Mexico. In this will he provided: "Nancy and her children at the White House, New Kent [County], all of whom I wish liberated as soon as can be done to their advantage and that of others." Since Nancy and her three children never appeared again as taxable property, it can be assumed these slaves were emancipated around the period of the Mexican War.

The Reverend John Leyburn, who enjoyed a candid interview with Lee in Baltimore in 1869, said Lee freed his slaves before the war and sent to Liberia those who wished to go. While Lee was known to believe in deporting the freed slaves who wished to go to Africa, no record of any kind substantiates Dr. Leyburn's memory. In any event, according to all evidence, Lee had never personally employed those Negroes at any of his established residences before and after he went to Mexico (he did not even know their names). By the nature of his career he had never managed slave labor at all on a plantation.

At Arlington, he soon perceived that Custis's Negroes had neither the habit nor the expectation of working. He resolved this with cold pragmatism: the prime field hands were hired out for cash to small planters and to the railroads. After one day three of the first eleven out returned to Arlington with plaints that the work was too hard. Lee sent them back. From his experience at Arlington Lee developed a conviction, which he never lost, that plantations could not be operated at top efficiency by Negro labor, slave or free.

For the less demanding work of rehabilitating Arlington, Lee used the younger and the older slaves. They helped him in rebuilding roads and fences, repairing leaks in the manor house roof and the stable roof, and making general repairs on the manor house and outbuildings. The overseer's house, in such disrepair that no respectable family would occupy it, was rebuilt, as was the mill. Feeling that milling was not in his line, Lee rented the new mill to a neighboring miller. He disposed of most of Custis's decorative horses and cattle, and planted heavily in wheat and corn.

At the same time that Lee was bringing in cash on the labor of the former deadwood at Arlington, on former weedy fields and abandoned mills, as well as increasing the value of the property by improvements, he was also supervising the planting operations at distant Romancoke and the White House. The White House was giving a good yield from its fertilized land when Lee took over, but he had to bring in a cargo of shell lime for Romancoke, upriver from the White House on the other side of the Pamunkey. Evidently he hired out from Romancoke and the White House those slaves he considered superfluous for the planting jobs.

After coming in at the end of the day from his work in the fields and on the buildings, Lee had before him hours of figuring at night. At one corner in the south wing, enclosed by the formal dining room and a conservatory, was a small office or study, and perhaps Lee worked in there on his interminable figuring. Handling accounts and making disbursements were all too familiar to him, going back to the stringent economizing he had learned in his mother's home. Often he wrote his oldest son, as it was in this period that Custis and his father established an adult relationship.

Custis had generously offered to sign his rights to Arlington over to Lee, in order to simplify his task with the estate. When Lee would not hear of this, Custis proposed the possibility of his resigning from the army, in order that he might help at Arlington and Colonel Lee could return to his regiment. Lee answered "the confirmed bachelor" — as Mrs. Lee called Custis — with the practical and traditional suggestion that he could help Arlington best by marrying a rich lady. Also in a letter to Custis, Lee gave an idea of himself in business transactions. "You must be aware of one thing, that those you deal with will consider their advantage and not yours. So, while being fair and just, you must not neglect your interests."

Most of all it was to Custis that Lee unburdened himself about the dreary, depressing nature of his salvage work on the estate. "I have no enjoyment in my life now but what I derive from my children." While Lee was then practicing his inclination toward farming — and showing himself highly equipped for it and advanced in it — the rewards of his accomplishments were negated by the somber conditions. Arlington had then become the home of his own family, and he loved it as no other place (except the memory of Stratford Hall). But the immense spaces, the handsomely furnished family rooms and the formal rooms, seemed a most unfitting background for a return to the penny-pinching of the days of "poor gentility" in his mother's modest rooms in Alexandria.

The center block of the house, divided by the wide hall, was of two stories with basement, and the flanking wings, of three rooms each, were one story. Excluding the bisecting hall, there were ten rooms on the ground floor, of which the formal parlor was enormous. It was impossible not to miss the voices of the children, the comfortable presences of Mr. and Mrs. Custis — constantly brought to mind by her flowers in the conservatory and by his Mount Vernon heirlooms which had constituted the "career" of the generous-hearted drone. There was never an occasion to entertain in the formal parlor or dine in the formal dining room, both on the south side of the high-ceilinged central hall. With the few children around, they used only the side of the house containing the family sitting room and family dining room. Mrs. Lee went to the south wing only in personal attention to the silver and china and other heirlooms from her great-grandmother, Martha Washington, and the general.

Gradually Lee brought order to the estate. First the debts were paid. Though no cash was then accumulated for his daughters' inheritance, two of the plantations were operating at a cash profit, and Arlington was at least self-sustaining. Most gratifying to Lee was the restoration of the grounds, always Arlington's pride. It was as if Washington Custis, in building the showplace, had run out of cash and inspiration when he progressed to the interior decoration. The well-proportioned, high-ceilinged rooms contained good, conventional paneling but lacked the grace of Shirley and the splendor of Stratford. The grandeur was outside — in the gardens, which Mrs. Lee had taken over from her mother, the woodland, which must have reminded Lee of Stratford, and the magnificent vistas, including the view of Washington City.

Yet, with all his progress, Lee's spirits seemed never to lift. From various references he made, it seems probable that Lee disliked working slaves in the fields. This would not be only because of the failings of his father-in-law's pampered people in the eyes of the army disciplinarian. Lee was not disturbed by the domestic work done by the house people. Having known them long and intimately, this association was familiar and personal. In manumitting Custis's slaves during the five-year period of the will, Lee tried to place all of the Negroes in positions to their benefit, but with the house people — personal maids and waiters in the dining room and the like — he took particular care in seeing to their future, even when he himself was at war. Perhaps his distaste for working the slaves in the field was exacerbated by the personal tone of accusations in Northern publications which he could not, in any dignity, answer. One of these called him by name in a lying charge.

Colonel Lee himself was not a nationally known figure. Reference to him was newsworthy only because the prominence of his family and his wife's family would cause his name to be recognized in the East as a distinguished Virginian. The New York *Tribune* published an anonymous letter accusing him of physically beating "his" Negroes. The colonel smoldered at that one, and revealed how the whole thing agitated him by a letter to Custis. Mentioning that the paper "has attacked me for my treatment of your grandfather's slaves" — here disassociating himself from ownership — he said, "but I shall not reply. He has left me an unpleasant legacy."

The assumption must be that had the estate been left in financial condition to fulfill the terms of Custis's will, Lee would have manumitted the slaves as quickly as he could place them advantageously to themselves. Besides satisfying creditors, his only concern had been to place the properties in condition to yield the profits, by paid (free) labor, which would in time fulfill the terms of Custis's will. To this end he employed Custis's slaves for the allotted five years, when the last were freed and most — despite the upheavals of war — established in a new life.

In his second spring as a planter, 1859, an event occurred which brightened him, though it had not started that way. Before Rooney was twenty-one, he had begun to pester his father and mother about marrying his Carter cousin, Charlotte Wickham. Had the horseman been in the cavalry instead of the infantry, he might have been less headstrong. But he was determined to resign from the army and, with a bride, to take up planting at his White House heritage. His parents succeeded in postponing the events until Rooney was nearly twenty-two.

Charlotte Wickham, kin to the Carters of Shirley, was a delicate, patrician girl, of whom both Colonel Lee and Mrs. Lee were very fond. Lee doubtless enjoyed the first wedding among his children when, with his daughters, he attended the elaborate wedding given by Cousin Hill Carter at Shirley. He stood in the room where his own mother had been married and where he had spent so many happy hours in his childhood. Charlotte became as close in Lee's affections as his own daughters.

Then, in the fall of that year, Lee became personally involved with the first racial warfare that spread from the guerrilla fighting in Kansas. It was also the first armed invasion inspired by abolitionists, and it placed Lee in the position of defending the existing order and his own land. Unquestionably, this event, into which he was drawn by the chance of settling the Custis estate, influenced his later choice.

6

On a Monday morning in October, 1859, Lee was working at figures in the study when a caller was announced. Dressed in the dark civilian suit he wore about the house, Lee went into the central hall to meet the visitor. He recognized the stocky young lieutenant in cavalry uniform as J. E. B. Stuart, who had been a favorite cadet during Lee's superintendency at

West Point. The blue-eyed first lieutenant, also in the Washington area by chance, was to play a most important role in Lee's life.

"Beauty" Stuart, as he had been called at the Point, was also a Virginian. He came from one of the southwestern counties, where his father, a lawyer, had been famous as a bon vivant and drinking companion. Not planters, his father's family and his mother's family were substantial people, or had been before Alex Stuart's conviviality. Similarly to Lee, Stuart had come strongly under his mother's influence and was a teetotaler and devout Episcopalian. The lieutenant was married to the daughter of an army colonel from Virginia, Philip St. George Cooke, and she and Stuart had each inherited one slave as a personal servant. Each freed the slave.

Stuart had been stationed in Kansas territory, where he had fought Cheyennes (taking a wound) and helped suppress a massacre led by John Brown, a paranoid gunman operating with the abolitionists in the guerrilla wars. Like Lee, Stuart was on leave from the army. He and his wife had brought their first child back to Virginia to visit his grandparents. While on leave he attended the General Convention of the Episcopal Church in Richmond, as a lay delegate, and then came up to Washington. On that Monday morning Lieutenant Stuart had been waiting in the outer offices of the War Department, where he was trying to sell a patent to a new device he had invented for attaching the cavalryman's saber to his belt. Instead of getting the interview, he was asked to hurry across the river to Arlington and deliver an urgent message to Brevet Colonel Lee. Lee was to come at once to the War Department.

Without changing from his civilian clothes, Lee left immediately with Stuart. In Washington he was told by War Secretary Floyd and President Buchanan that somebody named Smith, with "Kansas Border Ruffians," was leading a slave insurrection at Harper's Ferry. The government arsenal had already been seized.

"Slave insurrection" were the most dread words that could be heard by a Virginian, and War Secretary Floyd had been governor during Nat Turner's uprising. Before Lee reached Washington, the governors of Virginia and Maryland were sending units of militia, Fort Monroe was preparing to send three companies, and a detachment of ninety marines from the Navy Yard had taken the cars west. Colonel Lee was to proceed at once to Harper's Ferry and assume command of the force. Lee happily accepted Stuart's offer to go along as volunteer aide. In this way two Virginia emancipationists went to suppress a slave insurrection attempted by outsiders with no responsibility to the community.

The cavalrymen left by a special train on the B&O at five o'clock in the afternoon. Taking the roundabout train ride, they arrived on the Maryland side of the Potomac, across from Harper's Ferry, at ten o'clock that night. The town of Harper's Ferry was situated at the bottom of a cup of mountains, where the Shenandoah River converged with the Potomac. Lee learned that a band of about twenty white insurrectionists had been driven by the militia out of the arsenal and had retired into a stone fire engine house. They had with them as hostages elegant old Colonel Lewis Washington, grandnephew of the President, a farmer and half a dozen of his slaves, along with the arsenal workers, who had been grabbed as they appeared for work.

Before retiring in the engine house, the band had shot and killed two men — Hayward Shepherd, a freed Negro who worked as a station baggage-master, and Thomas Boerly, on his way to work. The band had lost a couple of men captured and two killed, and several in the engine house were known to be badly wounded. The engine house was a stout affair about thirty-five feet wide, with stone buttressed double doors of oak. Behind the doors sat the fire engine. Barricaded in there, the marauders were pinned down by the rifles and shotgun of militia and farmers. But this makeshift force showed no disposition to storm the small fort.

Lee soon appraised the violence as being contained. He found nothing of the slave uprising they had feared from the wild messages. The mountains around Harper's Ferry supported no plantations, and there were few slaves in the region. None of these had turned on their masters nor joined the leader "Smith," or whatever his name was. On the scene, the natives told Lee that a fiercely bearded old man calling himself Andrews or Anderson had established a group at a farmhouse on the Maryland side several days before. The band was armed with Sharp's carbines, pistols, pikes and cutlasses.

Lee, Stuart and the marines under Lieutenant Israel Green walked across the railroad bridge in the dark to the cleared armory grounds. There Lee decided to wait until daylight before rushing the engine house. In the chilly first light of October 18, he sent forward his volunteer aid under a flag of truce to read a message to the bearded leader. One of the double doors edged back a crack, and a pair of fierce, pale eyes stared at Stuart over a carbine. "Osawatomie!" Stuart shouted. He had recognized John Brown, and gave him the name the gunman had been called in the Kansas guerrilla wars.

Then, in the stillness, Stuart's golden voice rang out with the message. If the insurrectionists would surrender, they would be turned over to the civilian authorities. If Colonel Lee was compelled to use force, he could not answer for their safety. Brown wanted to make a deal. He wanted to be allowed to pass through their lines with his wagons and prisoners until he reached the Maryland side. There he would release the hostages. Lee had instructed Stuart not to parley, but some of the captured workmen called out to Stuart not to use force on Brown. He would kill them, the men said. Colonel Washington shouted, "Never mind us, fire!"

Mounted on a horse on the lawn about forty feet back from the engine house, Lee said, "The old Revolutionary blood does tell."

Stuart tried to explain that no bargain would be made. Then, following his instructions, he jumped to one side and flashed his hat down in the agreed-upon signal. A dozen marines, in dark blue frocks and light blue breeches, ran forward with heavy hammers and battered at the double doors. Carbines crackled inside and powder smoke drifted out through the cracks. Marine Lieutenant Green, observing that the hammers made little impression, ordered the marines to run forward a heavy ladder lying nearby. On the second lunge, one side of the doors splintered inward. Lieutenant Green, armed with a dress sword, crawled through.

In the smoky gloom inside he stumbled past John Brown, evidently reloading his carbine at the moment. The first two marines following Green inside were shot, one in the face and one mortally in the body. Colonel Washington then pointed out the leader to Green and he lunged at the bearded man with his dress sword. After the blade bent, he beat Brown into unconsciousness with the hilt. The following marines scrambled through with bayoneted rifles, under orders not to fire because of the hostages. The marauder nearest Brown was pinned to the wall by a bayonet thrust. Another one crawling under the engine was stuck. Both died. With Brown down and the marines pouring into the smoky building, the fighting was suddenly over.

Brown and his followers were brought outside to the grass, where the wounded were looked after. Fiercely bearded Brown soon recovered consciousness. When Virginia's Governor Wise and other visitors came to question Brown, from his answers Lee regarded the harebrained scheme for a mass freeing of slaves as the "attempt of a fanatic or a madman." In his report he played down the serious aspects of slave insurrection and dismissed Brown's gang as "rioters."

Since Brown's fantastic plan had been unsuccessful, Virginians were at first not seriously disturbed. Then, during his trial in Charlestown, Virginia, zealots in the North began praising his attempt at inciting servile insurrection. They regarded the murders he committed as incidents in a noble cause. He was called "Saint John the Just" whose hanging would make the gallows holy like the Cross. No halos were suggested for the eight abolitionists who, from a safe distance, had backed Brown's mob. However, the fanatics' irresponsibility was illustrated by the plotters' refusal to face the consequences. They went into protective hiding — one leader, Gerrit Smith of Peterboro, New York, finding refuge in a lunatic asylum.

It grew upon the South that some Northerners actually regarded mass murder as a desirable means of achieving abolition. As Northern publications expressed the hope that the monomaniacal Brown would serve as a precursor of worse to come, the amalgam of long-repressed conflicts assumed an emotional basis. A feeling of bitter resentment, unrelated to any of the extreme doctrines advocated by the slave interests, hardened in the whole Southern population.

To the Southerners unassociated with slavery in any way, the Negro, as distinguished from the slave, existed as a permanent proletariat in a static caste society. What the nonslaveholding majority of Southerners feared, aside from being murdered in their beds, was a revolution in their social system. When Northerners supported violent upheaval, with indiscriminate pillage and killing, the average Southerner became, in simplest terms, against the Northerner.

Whatever may have been the immediate goal in Brown's raid, the Bible-quoting gunman had made it forever impossible to disassociate slavery from the power struggle between the sections or to approach the practicalities of emancipation with rationality. When John Brown was hanged on December 2, 1859, passion replaced even the expedient reasoning of politicians. The element of hatred entered the national schism which had existed since Colonel Lee's father battled his fellow Virginians to win votes of ratification for the Constitution of a republic.

### 7

Before Lieutenant Colonel Lee left to rejoin his regiment in February, 1860, he obtained for Custis a Washington assignment, in order to have a man at Arlington. On his return to San Antonio, he encountered the repercussions of John Brown's apotheosis in franker and more frequent talk about separation. Before the John Brown affair, the secessionist spokesmen had found small audiences for their talk of disunion, and their position could be taken little more seriously than that of the abolitionists of the North. Afterwards, such men as Yancey of Alabama and Rhett of South Carolina began to draw attention, and in the Lower South secession came to be spoken of as a reality.

In San Antonio, as temporary commander of the department of Texas, Lee was very much opposed to these developments in Texas and the states of the Lower South. "I am not pleased with the course of the 'Cotton States,' as they term themselves," he wrote in a letter home. As his father had, R. E. Lee believed the differences could and should be resolved within the republic. "Secession is nothing but revolution," he wrote.

Yet, if the secession movement was opposed by force, "a Union that can only be maintained by swords and bayonets, and in which strife and civil war are to take the place of brotherly love and kindness, has no charm for me. I shall mourn for my country and for the welfare and progress of mankind. If the Union is dissolved, and the Government disrupted, I shall return to my native State, and share the miseries of my people, and save in defense will draw my sword on none."

These unguarded statements written in private letters revealed Lee as the same neutral, disavowing both factions, he had shown himself to be in the parish controversy at Fort Hamilton. This attitude reflected, by count, the majority of Virginians and probably the majority of Americans outside the Lower South. The one proviso that separated Lee from other Americans was the contingency over Virginia's being drawn in. Never fearing that Virginia would assume an aggressive position with either faction, he stipulated what he would do if Virginia needed to be defended. The conviction that he would come to the defense of his own state was as innate as instinct. It was nothing he thought about at all.

Nor was there anything he personally could do to change the course of events that finally was catching him up in its sweep. His hopes and his prayers all turned toward the possibility of the forces changing to a direction that would save the nation, that "wisdom and patriotism" would prevail. But the signs indicated that the eighteenth-century ideal of "the dictates of reason" was being abandoned, along with the commonality of welfare.

"Economic egotism," as it was called by R. H. Tawney, had developed interests "untrammeled by subordination to any common center of allegiance." Concurrently the aggressive minorities in the two regions were inciting passions that blinded the population to the fundamental division in the nature of the republic as it was conceived. What distressed Lee, in his detachment from hostilities, was the failure of responsible men to recognize the threat to the existence of the republic itself.

Politicians spoke as intemperately as the factionalists or, in party interest, ambiguously. No counterforce checked the appeals to the primal passion of hatred that were nudging everyone toward a point of ultimatum where the average American would not knowingly choose to go.

Lee's anxiety over the deepening divisiveness in the republic was accompanied by a personal sense of failure about his own career. Lee had just turned fifty-three when he took lodgings with the landlady, Mrs. Phillips, on the Plaza in San Antonio. He no longer referred to the "white hairs among the black." He was turning gray. He was entering a different phase of physical appearance, when the word "majestic" was more often applied. There was no austerity in his face but, with maturity under gathering stress, observers began to refer to the composure in the classic features as casting him in a different mold from his fellows.

Evidently he did not feel what his looks suggested when, as acting department commander for General Twiggs, he began another uninspiring assignment. Lee administered a territory from west of Camp Cooper — where Comanches were stealing the stock of isolated ranchers — to a 135-mile stretch along the Rio Grande from Brownsville to the west. This was the territory where Juan Cortinas, the Mexican bandit, operated against little restriction. After trying various long-range methods against Cortinas, Lee made one active "campaign" to break up his band. This ended in dickering with Mexican authorities over the support and sanctuary given the raider from south of the border. Though Cortinas's unchallenged reign was over, and the Comanches were brought to mend their ways, it was all rather discouraging to the lonely man in his cheerless quarters.

At his time of life, Lee would have found it depressing to be away from his family under any conditions where his work neither used his gifts nor advanced his career. But the special condition of his wife's growing invalidism, while giving a sense of futility to his isolation, turned his thoughts homeward in anxiety.

Previously when he was away, Mary Lee had enjoyed visiting among her friends and innumerable kinspeople in the Arlington area. Now her trips were largely confined to the healing baths in the springs of the Virginia mountains, though she managed a visit to Shirley and to Romancoke. Lee's removal from active support of his wife and all he held dear, unmitigated by a sense of accomplishment, promoted the gloomy foreboding that time was passing him by in the army.

Having been the outstanding cadet of his day at the Military Academy, he had performed capably at every assignment given him in the preferred corps of engineers; in the one war during his career, he performed, at great hazard and with feats of endurance, as the most brilliant soldier in the field; he ranked at the very top in the esteem of the commanding general and was generally regarded as the coming soldier in the army. Yet, it was twenty-two years ago that he had been commissioned captain, and his total allotment — for quarters, rations, travel and his salary of $1205 — had risen only to $4060. Young George B. McClellan, graduating from West Point at the outbreak of the Mexican War, had resigned to go with a railroad and was already earning $10,000 a year. Staying in the army Lee had stood at an absolute deadfall, while others advanced by politicking.

Lee expressed himself on this when in July, 1860, his former companion Joe Johnston was appointed quartermaster general, to rank as brigadier general, staff. Though Lee had frequently written in the past several years of the poor rewards the army gave for the application a man could put into it, he revealed a strain of real bitterness in the letter he wrote Custis.

Since the Mexican War, Lee had observed Johnston's maneuverings for promotion, and the two men, though still friendly, were no longer intimates. Johnston had been promoted to lieutenant colonel the same time

Lee was, and sent as second in command to the 1st Cavalry, the other new regiment raised in 1855. Since then Johnston had been posted in Washington, where his cousin by marriage, John B. Floyd, was Secretary of War. When the quartermaster general died, Floyd asked General Scott to recommend a successor. Scott sent several names — including, with Joe Johnston, Lee and Albert Sidney Johnston, the latter a full colonel regular rank and brevet brigadier. Floyd chose Joe Johnston and the Senate confirmed the appointment.

Referring to Johnston in his letter to Custis, Lee wrote, "I think it must be evident to him that it never was the intention of Congress to advance him to such a position assigned him by the Secretary. It was not so recognized before, and in proportion to his services he has advanced beyond anyone in the army and has thrown more discredit than ever on the system of favoritism and making brevets."

Lee himself could not maneuver for promotions and had never encouraged supporters who wanted to lobby for his advancement. At the same time he felt a normal resentment at being passed over by favoritism to another. As for Johnston personally, Lee wrote him — "My dear General" — a gracious note of congratulation.

Along with the sense of failure Lee carried the continuing burden of straightening out the Custis estate. He was still faced with desperate juggling to hold the plantations intact and realize the cash to fulfill Custis's will. Also, he was continually trying to steady Rooney, farming the White House plantation. It was Rooney who presented Lee with his first grandson. On June 2, 1860, Lee wrote of his "gratification . . . at the compliment paid me, in your intention to call my first grandchild after me," and suggested it would have been better to name him after his great-grandfather, as his own name was "not a good example."

On Rooney's marriage to Charlotte, the Shirley Carters made a generous settlement, and Lee was anxious that his sanguine son make his own way. On marriage, he wrote him to "realize . . . the full satisfaction of the performance of all your duties to God and man." On economizing, he wrote, "As you have commenced, I hope you will continue, *never to exceed your means*. It will save you much anxiety and mortification and enable you to maintain your independence of character and feeling. It is easier to make our wishes conform to our means than to make our means conform to our wishes."

In urging Rooney to finish his administration of the White House part of the estate, Lee revealed his somber state of mind. "Life with me is very uncertain and I am anxious to accomplish what has devolved upon me. After that I shall feel free to consult my own wishes and to devote my few remaining years to your poor mother, whom I am afraid will never be relieved from her malady, and as life advances to its close will require more attention. You children will be independent to pursue your own inclinations and she and I can go where it may be best for her."

On the tightening conflict, he wrote Rooney, "Things look very alarming from this point of view . . . As an American citizen, I prize the Union very highly and know of no personal sacrifice I would not make to preserve it, save that of honor."

"Honor" meant the position of Virginia, and by the end of the year, 1860, her neutrality was placed in peril. The secession movement had begun, in South Carolina, on December 20.

8

Lieutenant Colonel Lee was riding to assume command of the regiment at Fort Mason, one hundred miles north of San Antonio, when the news of South Carolina's secession reached Texas. Before leaving San Antonio, Lee wrote in simple pride on the condition of the department he was returning to the command of General Twiggs, a seventy-year-old veteran of the Mexican War. "I have just received an order from Gen. [Twiggs] assuming command of the Department . . . I suppose he thought the Department was going to pieces and he must endeavor to save the fragments. I shall be happy to turn it over to him in perfect peace and quiet in all its wide borders, whereas when he relinquished it, or at least when I took it, there was war and Indian aggressions on all of the frontiers from the mouth of the Rio Grande to the Red River."

In those unhappy years, his accomplishments seemed taken for granted by others, and he at last assumed command of the regiment at a time when no accomplishments were possible. Lee arrived at Fort Mason, December 22, to find that the minds of his officers were not on soldiering. Everyone was talking of the dissolution of the Union. Lee recognized that this was no academic question to the troops of the 2nd U. S. Cavalry. Texas showed a strong tendency to follow South Carolina's lead. Governor Sam Houston, twice president of the Republic and the state's strong man, stood almost lone in trying to hold back the tide sweeping through the Lower South.

In less than three weeks after Lee took command, other states began to follow South Carolina out of the Union. From January 9, 1861, to January 26, Mississippi, Florida, Alabama, Georgia and Louisiana seceded. The reason given was the election of Abraham Lincoln, bringing the "Black Republicans" into office. To a conservative Southerner such as Lee, the election of a Republican seemed more of an excuse than a cause. Actually the Southern extremists had split the Democratic Party and willfully done all possible to assure their own defeat on a sectional vote.

As for Lincoln himself, a regular party man of the Illinois state machine, he was manifestly a compromise candidate, chosen to please the hodge-podge of elements in the new Republican Party. Personally he was nothing of an abolitionist. It was true that, as a skillful politician, he was given to poetical ambiguities that could mean everything to everybody, and his words out of context were quoted for and against him on both sides. But, though believing in eventual emancipation, he repeatedly and firmly committed himself to a policy of non-interference with slavery where it existed. Reduced to its fundamentals, Lincoln's stand did not differ essentially from Lee's, including belief in deportation as a solution for the freed Negroes.

The slave powers chose not to trust him, or at least his sectional party. This contained the radical abolitionists among its diverse factions, and Lincoln had not disavowed them. With passions aroused, only an accelerated operation of the slave interests' political organizations had been necessary to stampede a majority in the six state conventions to vote for secession.

Then, on February 1, little more than one month after Lee took command at Fort Mason, the Texas convention overrode Sam Houston to become the seventh state to secede. A solid bloc of South Atlantic and Gulf states was formed. Three days later delegates from those states met in Montgomery, Alabama, to form a provisional government for a new nation on the continent. On the same day, Virginia sent a commission to Washington to act as emissaries for a peaceful settlement. And on the same day, February 4, orders were sent relieving Lee of duty and instructing him to report to Washington.

The orders reached Lee on Februray 13, and he prepared to leave immediately. Personally, he was relieved of anxieties for his family by the order that returned him to Arlington. To his wife's cousin "Markie" he had written in late January, "My own troubles, anxieties and sorrows sink into insignificance when I contemplate the sufferings present and prospective of the nation. Yet, I am very desirous to be near those who claim my protection, and who may need my assistance."

In hurriedly packing his accumulated belongings, he gave presents to friends. Even in the brief period Lee had been actively associated with the regimental officers and their families, he had as usual drawn people to him by the cheerfulness and consideration innate in his imposing presence. A captain of the 2nd Cavalry, calling him "as courteous as a knight," said that "he was universally beloved by all the officers of his regiment."

His inner disturbances never changed the self-image he presented to the world. A Texas lady seeing him at that period, standing upon the gallery of a government building as he watched troops, was so impressed that she frankly stood gazing at him in admiration. "There was a remarkable repose about him, singularly in contrast with the group of officers about him. He seemed a column of antique marble, a pillar of state — so calm, so serene, so thoughtful, so commanding."

When the colonel arrived at San Antonio, riding with his luggage in an ambulance-wagon, his famed composure was all on the outside. On the way from Fort Mason Lee stopped overnight at an inn, where he had an unsettling conversation with one of his younger officers. Captain George B. Cosby brought close to home the possibility that Lee might soon be forced to make a painful decision. Captain Cosby remarked that he believed Lee was being ordered to Washington because General Scott was preparing a campaign against the South in the event that war came. Lee glumly agreed.

Then, changing from dinner-table conversation to a searching of his own heart, Lee said that if events forced Virginia to secede, he would offer her his services. He had been taught that his first allegiance belonged to his Mother State. While he devoutly hoped that some agreement could be reached to avert a decision by arms, as for himself he had no choice: under no circumstances would he fight against "Virginia's sons." As he spoke of this possibility, his control broke and he turned away to hide his emotions.

He was still suffering this inner agitation when the ambulance in which he was riding entered San Antonio around two o'clock in the afternoon. Pulling up at the Read house on the plaza, he was shaken to see an armed mob apparently in command of the city. The hundreds of armed men were hard-faced, rough-looking fellows, many without coats, and some wearing shawls or blankets. On their shoulders the men wore a strip of red cloth. As Lee climbed down from the ambulance he saw Mrs. Caroline Darrow, the wife of a Unionist friend of his. He asked her who the strangers were.

"They are McCulloch's," she said. Ben McCulloch was a tough leader of Texas Rangers. "General Twiggs surrendered everything to the State this morning, and we are all prisoners of war."

Lee could not hide his shock, and tears filled his eyes. "Has it come so soon as this?" he murmured.

On his way to his hotel room, Lee learned that old Twiggs, a Georgian, would not fire on Southerners. He had advised the War Department previously of this position, but Washington was late in action and the orders relieving him of command were slow to reach him. Before the orders came, Twiggs had been negotiating with the Texas state authorities over relinquishing Federal property — mules and horses, wagons and harness, commissary and ordnance supplies, and the public buildings. When the order finally came for him to turn over his command to Colonel White, a Unionist New Yorker of the 1st Infantry, Twiggs instead surrendered the properties to a show of Texas force. The few United States soldiers in San Antonio marched out of town, on their way out of Texas.

After changing into civilian clothes in his hotel room, Lee crossed the plaza to his former headquarters office. He found this occupied by three civilians — Samuel A. Maverick, Thomas Devine, and Phillip N. Luckett — forming a Committee of Public Safety. The three men received Lee without warmth. They told him that, as Texas was out of the Union, he must declare himself for the Confederacy. If he refused, he would not be allowed transportation for his belongings.

This was not the way to come at Lee. He reacted instantly to the threat, with sudden anger giving an outlet to the pent-up sadness and agitation. He told the men in outrage that he was an officer of the United States Army and a Virginian, not a Texan. Then he stormed from the room.

Lee was still seething when he encountered another Unionist friend, Charles Anderson, of Kentucky. Anderson was the brother of the Major Robert Anderson then besieged in Fort Sumter, where he had retired his Charleston garrison to prevent surrendering to South Carolina militia as Twigg had to Texans. Lee told Charles Anderson the happenings and Anderson offered to take charge of his luggage. Later he could ship it to Lee.

Before Lee entrusted the chore to Anderson (who himself encountered trouble with the local authorities), Lee recalled to his friend an earlier conversation in which he had stated his convictions. "I still think," he said . . . "that my loyalty to Virginia ought to take precedence over what is due the Federal government. And I shall so report myself at Washington. If Virginia stands by the old Union, so will I. But if she secedes (though I do not believe in secession as a constitutional right, nor is there sufficient cause for revolution), then I will still follow my native state with my sword, and if need be with my life. I know you think and feel very differently, but I can't help it. These are my principles, and I must follow them."

Anderson probably dressed up the speech in his recollections in accord with his own Unionist sentiments and those which he wished to attribute to Lee. There was nothing fundamentally different from the convictions Lee had expressed in his letters, and the statement on following his principles could have been an echo of "Light-Horse Harry" proclaiming his primary allegiance to Virginia.

## 9

Lee returned to Arlington on March 1. He was relieved to find that his family, like himself, determined to cross no bridges before reaching them. Mrs. Lee's arthritis had advanced to a crippling stage where she was forced to use a wheelchair, and the threat of being uprooted from her home was particularly alarming to her. While clinging to the hope that reason would prevail, none of the Lees held any illusion about the fate of Arlington if Virginia was drawn into the struggle. It lay directly in the path of any invading forces. But, though the atmosphere was tense, family life reflected Lee's outward composure. Each morning, Mrs. Lee and the girls gathered at breakfast (Rob was away at the University of Virginia), after which they went into the informal sitting room where the father read the family prayers from their *Book of Common Prayer*.

A few days after Lee came home, the family anxiously read the report of Lincoln's inaugural address in the Alexandria newspaper. Looking for reassurances, they found the tone to be generally conciliatory, with appeals directly to the Southern people.

"We are not enemies, but friends . . . Though passion may have strained, it must not break the bonds of affection. The mystic chords of memory, stretching from every battle field and patriot grave, to every living hearth and hearthstone . . . will yet swell the chorus of the Union, when again touched, as surely they will be, by the better angels of our nature. . . . The government will not assail you. You can have no conflict without being yourselves the aggressors." He promised he had no intention of interfering with slavery where it existed. "I believe I have no right to do so."

And yet, stating that he considered the Union unbroken, "I shall take care, as the Constitution itself expressly enjoins upon me, that the laws of the Union be faithfully executed in all the states . . . In doing this there needs to be no bloodshed or violence; and there shall be none unless it be forced upon the national authority." Then, after the sentimental expressions, Lincoln came to the heart of the message. "The power confided to me will be used to hold, occupy, and possess the property and places belonging to the government, and to collect the duties and imposts; but beyond what may be necessary for these objects, there will be no invasion — no using of force against or among people anywhere."

The contradictions within the friendly approach were obvious to Lee. It would not be possible "to hold, occupy and possess" the properties of the government, nor collect duties and imposts, without the use of force. If the Southern authorities resisted the force, they could be termed aggressors and bring civil war upon their heads. Since Lincoln could scarcely expect the people in the newly formed nation to relinquish properties claimed by the United States within their borders, he evidently was maneuvering for events to determine the course of action.

If this course led to armed coercion by the central government, then Lee's hope would be reduced to the slim possibility that Virginia could remain neutral. For the General Assembly had gone on record with one unequivocal stand: a resolution was adopted, in the House by a vote of 112 to 5 and in the Senate by 39 to 0, that Virginia was in opposition to the use of arms as a means to "reunion or submission" and would resist force "by all the means in our power."

At the same time, the state showed a two-to-one sentiment against secession. The people had voted for delegates for a convention, formed to consider the state's course. In this special election the people also voted on a "reference" provision which would require the convention to refer to a poll of the electorate any action it took in connection with withdrawal from the Union. Since the secessionists opposed this reference, a Unionist attitude was reflected when the people voted for it (in round figures) one hundred thousand to forty-five thousand. In the convention, which met in Richmond on February 13, Unionist sentiment dominated, though its strength was diminished by the implied threats in Lincoln's inaugural. What the convention would do seemed pretty well up to how Lincoln acted on the "to secure domestic tranquillity" clause in the Constitution he had sworn to uphold.

Lincoln had inherited from President Buchanan the unresolved status of Fort Sumter, which had come to symbolize — as a sort of test case — the issue over Federal property. As soon as South Carolina seceded, Major Anderson had acted quickly to avoid what happened later in Texas. He secretly moved the whole garrison, with such supplies as were portable, into Fort Sumter rising on its made island in the Charleston harbor. Although the South Carolinians were infuriated, the militia units were restrained by the Confederate authorities. Recent U. S. Army Captain Beauregard, appointed brigadier general in the Confederate forces, took command at Charleston and negotiated amiably with Major Anderson. The mail went out daily to the Federals in the fort, who shopped for fresh vegetables in town. With Anderson refusing to evacuate the fort and the Confederates applying no force, the test case was a stalemate except for the element of time.

Time became a factor in the dwindling provisions of the garrison. Without reprovisioning, the men would be starved out, and if reprovisioning were attempted South Carolina made it clear that this would be resisted by force. The conflict that had taken forty years to come to a head then hung on the single issue of the rations for one fort.

During this period of mounting tension, Colonel Lee outwardly tried to conduct himself in what could appear to be his normal course. General in Chief Scott went to some pains to hold him to it. On March 16 Scott appointed Lee full colonel, to assume command of the 1st U. S. Cavalry, and on March 28 the commission came through signed by President Lincoln. Earlier the old Virginian held an interview with his younger friend. Though neither of them ever revealed what passed between them, it has been assumed that Scott sounded Lee out on the possibility of leading an army against the South. Mrs. Lee wrote, "My husband was summoned to

Washington, where every motive and argument was used to induce him to accept the command of the army destined to invade the South."

It was known that Scott was finagling to hold a number of Southern officers in the army, that Lee was his favorite soldier, and that he himself would be unable to take the field. Then seventy-five years old, the general had physically deteriorated since the days in Mexico. His huge body, once the monument of his pride, was cumbersome and racked with the infirmities of age. At the interview Lee evidently stated the position he had articulated in Texas: if Virginia was drawn in, he would offer his services to his home state.

Scott may or may not have told Lee of his preference to field an army of a size and strength to make it impossible for the South to resist. His plan was in principle the same George Washington had used when he appointed General Henry Lee to lead an irresistible force against the mountaineers in the "Whiskey Rebellion." Scott knew that the South would fight if invaded. Unless the states in secession were overwhelmed at once, a civil war would wear on into a destructive struggle in which inevitable defeat would come slowly and painfully to the South, with a deep divisiveness in the nation. Southerners simply lacked too much of the material for a war — men, money, arms, factories, ships, everything except the people's willingness to die in defense of their land.

To avert a long struggle and to bring in the seceded states as quickly as possible, Scott and many of Lincoln's advisers were anxious to sustain the neutrality of Virginia, North Carolina, Tennessee, and Arkansas. The first three of these were more industrialized than the states which had established the Confederacy and more thickly populated. Virginia, with the largest population in the South, had the fifth largest in the country. To this extent, Lee's hopes for Virginia's neutral position were buttressed by the interests of powerful figures in Washington.

On March 27, thanking Rooney for some hams he had sent from the White House, Lee wrote, "The Administration is trying to work out their policy, which is said to be peaceful, but they are no doubt surrounded by embarrassments caused as much by the extremists in their own party as by their opponents." No other analysis, then or since, ever defined the Washington dilemma more simply or more free of involvement with any bias of hostility.

Whatever the new administration did, Lee would not in any case participate in the invasion of the Southern states. On that point he shared completely the conviction of his state's General Assembly about coercion. Beyond the environmental influences that conditioned him to believe in the inviolability of any state, as a soldier Lee had seen the corruption of war at first hand. He was convinced that the ravage of invasion was not the way to restore the republic his father helped bring into being.

As Lee had been born during the Napoleonic Wars, his studies of Napoleon and the French Revolution were not to him remote history. Combined with his personal experiences, these studies (and studies of other wars) gave him a deep, and very advanced, disbelief in war as a permanent solution to anything. For his personal course, if war did become the means of trying to remedy a rift that had grown in peace, and if Virginia was not drawn into it, he planned to resign from the army and resume farming at Arlington.

While Lee was enduring the wait, in April the Virginia Convention, in a desperate effort to prevent an irrevocable action, appointed a committee of three to wait on President Lincoln in Washington. The three men were carefully selected. George W. Randolph, Jefferson's grandson, was a secessionist from Richmond; Alexander H. H. Stuart, a cousin of Jeb Stuart, was a Unionist from the Shenandoah Valley; William Ballard Preston was a moderate who introduced the resolution for the committee. The committee was to inform Lincoln of Virginia's opposition to armed coercion and to "ask him to communicate to this convention the policy which the federal authorities intended to pursue in regard to the seceded states."

The three gentlemen left Richmond on April 9. A heavy storm washed out the railroad and they did not arrive in Washington until Friday afternoon, the 12th. President Lincoln made an appointment with the committee for the next morning at nine o'clock. When they were ushered into the President's presence on the morning of Saturday, April 13, Lincoln was said to have greeted them with the words, "You're too late." At that moment the flag of the United States at Fort Sumter was being fired upon by Confederate guns on the Charleston Battery.

Lincoln had forced the issue on the test case. Against the advice of Scott and some of his Cabinet, he had dispatched a ship with the provisions which South Carolinians had assured Washington would be resisted by force. Most probably Lincoln could not have obtained the support of the nation for sending troops into the seceded states to repossess obsolete forts, customs houses and scatterings of government supplies of no great value. So, he didn't try. Instead, he did something that would cause the secessionists to fire on the United States flag. Then he could say to the Virginia committee, "An unprovoked assault has been made upon Fort Sumter [and] I shall hold myself to repossess, if I can, like places which had been seized before" he became President. ". . . In any event I shall to the extent of my ability repel force with force."

This position was officially stated in a written memorandum, which called attention to the part of the inaugural address that referred to his intention to occupy government property in the seceded states. But the memorandum also included the part of the address which stated "there will be no invasion, no using of force against or among the people" beyond what was necessary for the repossession of government property. After Lincoln gave the three Virginians the memorandum, he conversed with them at some length. Both from his talk and the written memorandum, the committee received the impression that Lincoln — as Alexander Stuart later told the convention — intended "nothing like a general war, nothing in the shape of a general system of hostilities."

The three gentlemen left the White House totally unsatisfied with the interview, but at least feeling assured there would be no war. On the next day, while they broodingly rode the cars back to Richmond, Fort Sumter surrendered without casualties. Major Anderson, having upheld the honor of the flag in a bloodless exchange of artillery fire, marched his garrison out to steamers with bands playing in the full pageantry of knightly war.

The following day, Monday, April 15, the three committeemen back in Richmond were thunderstruck to learn that Lincoln had called for seventy-five thousand volunteers to "suppress the combination" too powerful for ordinary proceedings. Alexander Stuart could not believe it. Thinking it was a story planted by the secessionists to stampede the convention, he wired Washington. The news got worse. Virginia — along with North Carolina, Tennessee, and Arkansas — was called upon to furnish her quota of troops for the "suppression" of sister states.

Two of the committeemen, Preston and Randolph, felt betrayed by Lincoln. The next day William Ballard Preston, the moderate, offered an ordinance of secession to the convention. In the torrent of debates that followed, moderates began to shift away from the Unionists toward secession. Lincoln had acted as if their committee might as well have not made its appeal. He dismissed Virginia's opposition to coercion as of no consequence and ignored her government's avowed intention to resist the use of force. The state was to have no voice in his government, not even recognition of its historic position.

Then moderates recalled Lincoln's earlier refusal to entertain any compromise settlement. Before he was inaugurated, when Virginia's peace commission in Washington gathered support for a compromise between the sections, Lincoln at home remained aloof from the effort at peace. The majority in the convention concluded that the new President's purpose was to wage a general war upon sovereign states. The moderates, holding the balance of power, determined that Lincoln's war would not have Virginia's help. They would secede before they would be coerced into making war on sister states.

Alexander Stuart did not give up the fight to hold the state in the Union. A bloc of Unionists rallied to his support. They urged the convention at least to wait. Lincoln's sending troops to Charleston and the Gulf of Mexico need not bring on a general war, they argued. Virginia, however, by seceding, would offer a battleground. Stuart predicted that Northern Virginia would become another Flanders.

The debates raged into the second day as the convention went into secret session. No Virginia of Lee's background held any doubts about the outcome. Lincoln had touched a nerve with coercion. Lee could only cling to the hopeless hope that did not die until the finality of the end. On April 17, the second day of the debates, Lee received a letter to come to General Scott's office the next day. To Arlington came also a message asking him to call on Mr. Francis P. Blair, Sr., an intimate of the administration. With spring returning in full blossom to Arlington, where wild flowers were appearing in the great woodland, the hour of decision had come for Lee.

10

With or without premonitions, Lee rode across the bridge into Washington for the last time in his life on April 18. He dismounted at the Pennsylvania Avenue home of old Blair, a power in Washington politics since 1832. As editor of the pamphleteering Washington *Globe,* he had been a member of Jackson's "Kitchen Cabinet" and his influence was still great. He was a frail-looking man of seventy when he received Lee alone. The doors were carefully closed and Blair came right to the point. He was authorized by Lincoln to offer him command of the new army then being called into being.

After the long years at regular rank of captain and after the sense of failure at being passed over while a lieutenant colonel, here in one minute he was offered the top rank — and under conditions he could not possibly accept. Lee answered promptly and candidly. Thanking Mr. Blair for his consideration, he told him (as Lee recounted later) . . . "though opposed to secession and deprecating war, I could take no part in an invasion of the Southern states."

From Blair's house, Lee went also for the last time to Scott's office in the War Department building. There he told his old supporter of the conversation.

"Lee, you have made the greatest mistake of your life," Scott said. "But, I feared it would be so."

Then, sadly, he told Lee they had come upon a time when every officer must determine upon a course and declare it. "No one should remain in government employ without being actively employed."

In other words, there was no place for neutrals. If Lee could not accept an offer to lead a United States Army, he should resign his commission.

Lee took the familiar ride back across the Potomac to Arlington in a depression compared to which all his recent feelings of futility faded into insignificance. With all his grievances at slow advances and hard use, the army had been his home. Since the age of eighteen he had known no other life. Nor, from a practical viewpoint, did he have any other source of income for the support of his family. It was not that the anguished man had any choice. The decision was made with his birth. The problem was that the act of severance was so unthinkable.

The next day, the 19th, this act of resignation became inevitable. Lee went to Alexandria, the city from where he had left his mother's house to go to West Point, and returned home with the Alexandria *Gazette*. He silently gave the copy to Mrs. Lee. She read the words they had prayed never to see: the Virginia Convention had voted two to one to secede. Ratification by popular vote would be a mere formality.

After that, there could be no further delay. Lee spent the rest of the day and worked into the night upstairs in his room composing a letter of resignation in his mind. Downstairs in her wheelchair, his wife heard him pacing on the floor above. After midnight, he came downstairs. Without speaking, he handed her the letter he had written General Scott.

General:

Since my interview with you on the 18th instant I have felt that I ought not longer to retain my commission in the Army. I therefore render my resignation, which I request you will recommend for acceptance.

It would have been presented at once, but for the struggle it has cost me to separate myself from a service to which I have devoted all the best years of my life and all the ability I possessed.

During the whole of that time, more than 30 years, I have experienced nothing but kindness from my superiors, and a most cordial friendship from my companions. To no one Genl have I been as much indebted as to yourself for uniform kindness and consideration, and it has always been my ardent desire to meet your approbation.

I shall carry with me to the grave the most grateful recollections of your kind consideration, and your name and fame will always be dear to me. Save in defence of my native State, I never desire again to draw my sword.

Be pleased to accept my most earnest wishes for the continuance of your happiness and prosperity and believe me most truly yours

R. E. LEE.

There was nothing Mrs. Lee could say to him. To a friend she wrote, "My husband has wept tears of blood over this terrible war, but as a man of honor and as a Virginian, he must follow the destiny of his State." To Mildred, then away at school in Winchester, she wrote, "With a sad and heavy heart, my dear child, I write, for the prospects before us are sad indeed, and as I think both parties are wrong in this fratricidal war there is nothing comforting even in the hope that God may prosper the right, for I see no *right* in the matter."

Her husband was in full agreement with her. He had sacrificed his career and their future for a war which he believed to be unnecessary and in which he felt no cause. On the day of his resignation, a Saturday, he wrote his sister in Baltimore to tell her of his action:

"The whole South is in a state of revolution, into which Virginia, after a long struggle, has been drawn; and though I recognize no necessity for this state of things, and would have forborne and pleaded to the end for a redress of grievances, real or supposed, yet in my own person I had to meet the question whether I should take part against my native state. With all my devotion to the Union and the feeling of loyalty and duty as an American citizen, I have not been able to make up my mind to raise my hand against my relatives, my children, my home."

This was the crux of everything. There were homes from the Potomac to the James in which his kinspeople lived and where his family had visited; there were Stratford, where he had been born, and Shirley where his mother had grown up, and the White House, where his grandson played; and there were the graves of his ancestors in the yards of little churches and in evergreen groves on plantations. It was not possible to lead the tramping boots of an invading army over the land that was sacred to him. If defending his own was revolution, after all, he *was* the son of a Revolutionary, Light-Horse Harry Lee. And the greatest hero of his childhood, George Washington, had been the greatest revolutionary of them all. As his mother had trained him, had given him to know the faith, he kept the faith.

# PART THREE

# The Virginian as Confederate

## CHAPTER VI

# "The Times Are Indeed Calamitous"

IN RESPONSE TO a request from the governor of Virginia, ex-Colonel Lee arrived by train in Richmond on Monday, April 22, just two days after submitting his resignation to the Secretary of War and his personal letter to General Scott. Lee had few associations with his state's capital, though his mother had come there as a bride when his father was governor. Since the days when his parents had occupied the cramped house above the gullies in Capitol Square the city had grown into an urban center of 38,000 inhabitants.

In the older Lees' time Richmond had progressed little beyond its frontier days as a trading post at the Falls, the head of navigation in the James River. When their son arrived in 1861, the handsomely built city, picturesquely spread over seven hills rising above the river, was advanced in the South for a sound economic structure that combined commerce and manufacturing, finance and transportation. Four railroads served the city, a canal west and a network of turnpikes. At its wharves flags were seen from nations all over the globe. Tobacco was the core of its trading and industry, and its rankly sweet aroma hung over the business district and the older residential sections in the eastern part of the city. Among diversified manufacturing, Richmond's flour mills were the largest in the world, and the progressive Tredegar Iron Works was the biggest plant in a thriving iron industry.

Yet, though cosmopolitan in its economic outlook — with British importers among its residents and a strain of intellectualized Germans — culturally Richmond was a family city, a place of homes. The outstanding characteristic of the homogeneous population was its proud civic attachment. Three days before Lee's arrival, the usually staid citizens had given in to the excitement of a spontaneous "Secession Night" parade. The overtones of that wild night were still evident when Lee climbed down the steps of the train coach in the open depot at the foot of Broad Street hill.

Coming from Arlington, Lee had first ridden the Orange and Alexandria Railroad southwestward to Gordonsville, in the Piedmont country.

There he changed to the Virginia Central for a trip eastward, and a little south, to Richmond. Approaching the city the tracks ran due south along Shockoe Valley, between the two major hills that divided the city. In the seventeenth and early eighteenth centuries frontiersmen had floated their products on bateaux on Shockoe Creek to warehouses on the James River, and the first houses in Richmond had been built on the eastern slope above Seventeenth Street.

By 1861, these early structures had all gone. Lee saw a few late eighteenth-century houses from the period his parents had lived in Richmond, but down in the valley and on both hills nearly all the houses had been built since 1800. They were predominantly red brick of the misty flame color of Tidewater clay, and the newer houses featured the small, columned porches of the Greek Revival period of the eighteen-forties. Typical of Richmond houses, most of the houses were built close to the red-brick sidewalks, with their gardens in the back. The houses in the Valley were substantial, unpretentious and, spread among the old trees then coming into full leaf, usually gave an impression of tranquilly stable urban life.

As Lee glanced about him, the usual impression was changed by the fluttering of bright color in new flags flying from windows and porches. Many were the single-starred Bonnie Blue Flag of South Carolina. Though Virginia was not then in the Confederacy, there were all sorts of variations — some clearly homemade — of the new Stars and Bars. (These did not include the starred cross on the red field which later became the battle flag of Confederate regiments and, while commonly used as the Confederate flag, was never the official flag of the new nation.) In the distance bands were playing, and he heard the catchy air of an old minstrel song that was new to him, "Dixie."

On wide Broad Street, climbing the two hills, there was a sense of unusual bustle, and flags fluttered near the crests. On the plateau of Church Hill, around white-framed St. John's Church (where Patrick Henry had delivered his fiery address on liberty) were large and imposing houses, called "villas" by Dickens. By the flags displayed as far as Lee could see, it was evident that many families had prepared for secession before the convention voted.

Most of the city mansions were in the newer, more fashionable sections north and west of Capitol Square, beyond Lee's vision from the depot, but the atmosphere of excitement obviously spread over the whole city. Largely this was stirred by the relief from the long tension, the release in reaching a decision. Nothing indicated that Lee shared this excitement.

No welcoming committee was there to greet him. Lee had not informed the governor when he was coming, and other officers from the "Old

Army," as it came to be called, were arriving at every depot at all hours. Lee, wearing a black civilian suit, climbed into a public hack. Avoiding the steepness of Broad Street, the hackman drove across town three blocks to parallel Main Street. There the climb was more gradual.

Cobblestoned since Lee's mother, as a bride, had been driven lurchingly through the bogs, the busy street was solidly lined with brick buildings. Two story and dormer, three story and dormer, and four stories, all had peak roofs and from many fronts wooden awnings slanted out across the sidewalk. Main Street was the business street, of stores and banks, hotels and coffee houses, Pizzinni's famous confectionery, and dry-goods houses displaying bolts of cadet-gray cloth for uniforms. Traffic was heavy with carts, wagons and carriages, and horseback riders who seemed in a hurry.

At Eighth Street, near the crest of the hill, Lee left the carriage at the Spotswood Hotel, the newest and grandest hotel in the city. Entering, he passed the telegraph office and the paneled barroom, where planters and businessmen stood talking in groups. After he registered, Lee walked down Main Street to Ninth, and turned up the very steep rise to Capitol Square. Now a lovely park, and surrounded by buildings, the Square — as when his mother first saw it — was still dominated by the great columned capitol on the crest.

Enclosed by a fence, the fresh green of rolling lawns and shade trees covered an area of about ten city blocks. Southward the park extended from Capitol Street, half a block south of Broad, to Bank Street, half a block north of Main. Bank and Capitol streets ran only the three blocks bordering the Square, from Ninth to Twelfth streets. On Bank Street, at the foot of the Square, sat a heavy building which had been, when Lee saw it last, the U. S. Customs House. Now the flag of Virginia rippled in the spring breeze. On Capitol Street was the graceful City Hall, and nearby a bay-windowed gray house where Edgar Allan Poe had lived while editor of the *Southern Literary Messenger*.

Climbing the steep hill of Ninth Street, Lee passed the Mechanics' Hall Building and East Franklin Street, which debouched into Ninth where the slender red-brick Bell Tower rose just inside Capitol Square. The Bell Tower was the gunroom of the city militia, and its bell was designed to sound the tocsin for slave uprisings or other insurrections. This general area, around where fashionable East Franklin entered Ninth across from the Square, was the neighborhood where Lee would spend the next months of his life, much of the next year and — as incredible as it would have seemed to him — where his home would be in years to come.

Climbing another block Lee reached East Grace, also a residential street of fashion, which entered Ninth across from the main entrance into Capitol Square. On one side of Grace Street sprawled the St. Clair Hotel, with verandas across the front, and on the other side was imposing St. Paul's Church, with its Roman columns not unlike Arlington. There Lee would worship.

Walking alongside the driveway into the Square, Lee passed the equestrian statue of George Washington, surrounded by figures of other great Virginians. Beyond, he entered a side door into the Capitol and climbed the stairs to the office once occupied by his father. Governor John Letcher received him without ceremony and immediately got down to business.

"Honest John" was a plain-looking man, bald and red-faced, characterized by a glint in a straightforward gaze of steely determination. Letcher was a "hill" man, from Rockbridge County at the foot of the Shenandoah Valley, and he had not been among the secessionists. When the first Southern states began to go out, he had advocated a convention of all the states to discuss measures of preventing a sectional withdrawal. When that failed, he had promoted the Peace Commission led by former President John Tyler. But when Lincoln called on him for volunteers to invade sister states, he instantly wired, "You have chosen to inaugurate civil war."

Letcher briefly told Lee that immediately after the state's secession an ordinance had been passed calling for a commander of Virginia's military and naval forces, with the rank of major general, to serve under the governor's authority. An advisory committee had recommended Lee to the governor.

This probably came as no surprise to Lee, and he did not beat about the bush in accepting. He did ask that when the governor submitted his name to the convention for confirmation, it be specified that he had resolved on resigning from the U. S. Army before the Virginia post had been created. There was talk, as he had realistically anticipated, to the effect that he had traitorously accepted command of the Virginia forces while still a U. S. Army officer — or, at best, that he had resigned in order to accept the state command. He had known nothing about the state command until April 22.

On the next day, Tuesday the 23rd, Lee was officially appointed to his new post in a ceremony at the Capitol which he would have preferred to avoid. On the arm of Marmaduke Johnson, Lee was led into the packed chambers, where the members of the convention rose on his entrance. After Johnson presented Lee to John Janney, the convention president, the members took their seats and Janney made the most of the occasion with a sonorous address.

"Major General Lee, in the name of the people of your native state, here represented, I bid you a cordial and heartfelt welcome to this Hall, in which we may almost hear the echo of the voices of the statesmen, the soldiers and sages of bygone days, who have borne your name and whose blood now flows in your veins."

Lee stood gravely, "his manly bearing" the center of all eyes, as Janney eulogized Westmoreland County, the birthplace of Washington, Richard Henry Lee, Monroe and Lee himself. After paying Lee some embarrassing compliments, he said, "Sir, we have, by this unanimous vote, expressed our conviction that you are at this day, among the living citizens of Virginia, 'first in war.' We pray God most fervently that you may so conduct the operations committed to your charge, that it will soon be said of you, that you are 'first in peace,' and when that time comes you will have earned the still prouder distinction of being 'first in the hearts of your countrymen.' . . .

"Yesterday, your mother, Virginia, placed her sword in your hand upon the implied condition that we know you will keep to the letter and in spirit, that you will draw it only in her defense, and that you will fall with it in your hand rather than that the object for which it was placed there shall fail."

Lee was no speechmaker. As uncomfortable as he must have been, he made an appropriate answer all the more impressive for its sincerity and obvious lack of preparation. "Mr. President and Gentlemen of the Convention, profoundly impressed with the solemnity of the occasion, for which I must say I was not prepared, I accept the position assigned me by your partiality. I would have much preferred had your choice fallen on an abler man. Trusting in Almighty God, an approving conscience, and the aid of my fellow-citizens, I devote myself to the service of my native State, in whose behalf alone will I ever again draw my sword."

2

In beginning his new life, Lee's first act was a talk with Alexander Stephens, Vice President of the Confederacy, in Richmond to establish a military alliance with Virginia. Lee walked east through Capitol Square, passing the charming, gray-painted "Governor's Mansion" which had replaced the mean frame house his parents had occupied.

East of the Square the continuation of Franklin Street was of quite a different character from the fashionable residential section west of the Square. Here saloons and variety theaters catered to the "sporting" element, and off Franklin Street ran Locust Alley, the one-block "high class" red-light district. In the heart of the section was the Exchange Hotel, Richmond's finest before the Spotswood, and still a favorite for planters. Its dining room held on to a fine clientele, and its parlors were a meeting place for young ladies and dandies. Across the street from the Exchange was the Ballard House, never as fashionable as the Exchange, and somewhat raffish surroundings for unworldly Vice President Stephens.

In one of its parlors, Lee met the tiny man, little bigger than a dwarf, with huge eyes staring out of a wrinkled face like a prematurely aged child's. Though Stephens did not reveal it to Lee, he was a confused person who understood nothing of the power struggle which had reached its climax in secession.

A Georgian of humble background, as he rose in life he attached himself to the prevailing power in his state, the slave interests. In their behalf he prepared himself as a constitutionalist and was totally a theoretician. To "Little Aleck" the formation of the seceded states into a separate nation was essentially an answer to Northern aggression. He never comprehended that this separate nation was in a war to the death. What Stephens actually wanted was a position in the Union free of Northern domination of the central government. To this end, in the political maneuver of *Constitutional* secession, the Confederacy would counter force with force in order to establish a good bargaining position.

In his talk with Lee, Stephens was not required to discuss any general aspects of Virginia entering into a military alliance with the Confederacy — or, in effect, becoming a state in the new nation. ("Confederate" was a carefully selected emphasis — con-*federated* — on the return to the nature of the federated republic of *states* as originally formed.) Lee assumed Virginia would act in common cause with the other Southern states. Whatever he thought of secession, once Virginia seceded the only possible course was a united resistance against the use of force. With this cleared, Stephens turned to a petty consideration that would never have occurred to Lee.

All volunteers who received commissions from Virginia held their rank only in the state forces, and Stephens was worried that Lee might object to receiving orders from Confederate officers whose rank was lower than his. Lee was a major general in Virginia State Forces, while at that stage the Confederacy gave no rank higher than brigadier general. Lee immediately dismissed any such consideration. He had not resigned from the U. S. Army to worry about his personal advancement. As Stephens recorded, Lee told him "that he did not wish anything connected with himself individually, or his official rank or *personal* position, to interfere in the slightest degree with the immediate consummation" of Virginia's alliance with the other Southern states.

Judging from his first letter to his wife, written three days after his interview with Stephens, he did not think again of what problems might arise for himself in terms of Virginia's future absorption into the Confederacy. Personally, all his anxieties were centered in his family. "War is inevitable, and there is no telling when it will burst around you . . . You have to move and make arrangements to go to some point of safety which you must select. The Mount Vernon plate and pictures ought to be secured. Keep quiet while you remain, and in your preparations . . . May God keep and preserve you and have mercy on all our people."

### 3

By the time Lee wrote his wife, he was already facing a job that combined the worst features of all the less interesting chores he had performed in the U. S. Army. Before Lee came to Richmond, Governor Letcher had acted with promptness and common sense on the unprecedented task of hurrying preparations for a state to defend itself against invasion. The Secession Convention had appointed an advisory commission of three, later five, which included Colonel Francis Smith, superintendent of the Virginia Military Institute, and Matthew Fontaine Maury, the famed oceanographer, who had left the Naval Observatory in Washington to offer his services to his home state. On his own, Letcher, appointing no committees, quickly dispatched qualified men who happened to be available to the obvious spots of danger.

To take charge of the Potomac, Philip St. George Cocke, a distinguished and wealthy planter from near Richmond, was sent to the area south and west of Washington. Stately Cocke, who had been at West Point with Lee, had served two years in the army before resigning to attend to his estates.

The stretch of the Potomac southeast from Mount Vernon to the mouth of the Rappahannock went to Daniel Ruggles, brevet lieutenant colonel of the U. S. Army. Ruggles was stationed at Fredericksburg, at the head of navigation of the Rappahannock River, and midway between Richmond and Washington. Ruggles, native of Massachusetts, had married into a Fredericksburg family, and for the two previous years had been living in the charming small city while on a leave of absence because of health. In Fredericksburg, Ruggles had been active with the county militia, and he seemed a natural selection for the area defense once he decided to go with his wife's state.

Another New Englander who adopted his wife's state was Andrew Talcott, Lee's old friend from Fort Monroe days, who had resigned from the army a quarter of a century before. Engineer Talcott was sent first to the York River, to begin preparations for river forts at Gloucester Point and Yorktown. After selecting the sites and starting the work under civilian engineers, Talcott hurried to the port city of Norfolk to erect defenses for this key spot and to build river forts on the James River.

The James, navigable to Richmond, the York and the Rappahannock, along with the Potomac, all led to Virginia's fertile plantation country, where isolated families and small communities were exposed to Federal warships. Landing parties might incite slave insurrections, or at least run off the Negroes, halting work in the fields as well as damaging property. From the day of secession, an unidentified boat or a loitering stranger would cause alarms through the whole Tidewater region.

A few days after Lee's commission, Letcher directed him to order Colonel Thomas J. Jackson to command at Harper's Ferry, at the northern tip of the state and on the way from the North into the Shenandoah Valley. Stony-faced Jackson, whom Lee remembered as the indomitable artillerist at Chapultepec, had been a professor at V.M.I. in Letcher's home county, where he was known mostly for his eccentricities.

A convert to the Presbyterian faith the Scotch-Irish brought to the Shenandoah Valley, Jackson's devotions appeared excessive even for a deacon, though his faith in Providence did not save him from acute hypochondria. His experiments with weird diets and strange disciplines caused him to be called "Fool Tom," and some neighbors wondered if he were actually "crazy." Nor did his religion cause him to temper justice with mercy. Totally indifferent to his impression on students, as a letter-of-the-law disciplinarian Jackson provoked one cadet to the point of challenging him to a duel.

Fundamentally, Jackson was noticeable in a small, close-knit rural community because he did nothing to conform. He acted as if he were not aware of people, and he probably was not. That was the basis of Jackson. Saying once, "I have no talent for seeming," he was inflexibly committed to being what he was. What he was inside the plain exterior could scarcely have been suspected.

Beginning life as a poor mountain boy, illy prepared for West Point, and never losing his rustic manners, Jackson was an intensely ambitious man, all of whose energies were gathered to preparing himself for advancement. He showed only two interests: his wife and his church, including a Sunday school for colored children. Inside his home, after his evening meal he went into a dark room. There he sat on a high stool, so that he would be awakened by falling off if he dozed, and practiced concentration by projecting military problems.

Governor Letcher knew nothing of this habit, but he was one of the very few to recognize in the pale-eyed Jackson a tremendous force to be tapped. A non-secessionist, once he committed his singular singlemindedness to a cause, Jackson would be as fierce a zealot as Cromwell.

As events developed, the little-known Jackson was the only officer importantly placed in Virginia's early defense system who would distinguish himself, although at the time the governor seemed to have made sound enough choices for Lee to work with. At least, all of Letcher's choices were his own: he resisted both the importunities of politicians and the easy way of committees. Also, the points he selected for defense were soundly chosen. Bringing great energy to the mobilization of volunteers, Letcher wisely turned over to Lee the gritty chores of transferring volunteers and militia into armed forces at the selected points of defense.

Militia had a long history in the state, beginning with the pre-Revolutionary 1st Virginia Regiment, originally commanded by George Washington. After John Brown's attempted insurrection, militia units proliferated throughout the state and there were about thirty in Richmond alone by the time of or shortly after Virginia seceded. All of these units had outfitted themselves in a variety of — mostly impractical — uniforms, some of which were strikingly beautiful on the parade ground. As volunteers came in, the individuals could draw on state allotments for material from which their families or tailors could make uniforms out of the cadet-gray cloth prescribed by somewhat informal regulations. As had Lee's father in the Revolution, many men of means outfitted whole companies and, of course, became captain.

While the volunteer units were forming, the militia outfits were rushed to the various points of concentration. Each unit carried a flag — often personally stitched by sisters and sweethearts — but usually not much else. It was Lee's task to provide the gathering militia with such mundane items as rifles, powder and balls, percussion caps, horses and limbers and caissons for guns, tents, utensils, wagons, harness and animals. Above all, Lee needed officers capable of forming regiments of the militia companies commanded by the locality's leading or most popular citizen.

There were no government arsenals from which rifles and cannon could be ordered. Aside from the state's collection of flintlocks, many dating back to the War of 1812, two main sources existed, both the former property of the United States. Virginia authorities had acted immediately on secession to seize the government's rifle-producing arsenal at Harper's Ferry and the navy yard at Norfolk. The navy yard was the big windfall. It yielded more than a thousand big guns, many of them rifled Dahlgrens, with vast quantities of powder, and the hulls of burned and abandoned ships on which salvage work was begun. U. S. Naval officers, who had been commissioned by Letcher, worked heroically to move and mount the guns at the river forts being erected from the Potomac to the James.

Harper's Ferry was peculiarly exposed to attack, from three sides, and was well-nigh indefensible. In time its machinery would have to be transferred to Richmond and set up in the state armory. However, rather than interrupt its production of rifles, Lee preferred to risk capture of the arsenal. Finding Jackson to be of like mind, Lee directed a gradual removal of the machinery, which would allow work to continue until the last installation was dismounted. Jackson, bringing harsh and unwelcome discipline to the training camp that served as outpost, showed immediately his boldness and an intuitive comprehension of Lee's purposes.

Lee's fundamental purpose, as he advised Jackson, Cocke and Ruggles, was to remain on the defensive as long as possible. They must do nothing to invite attack on the poorly armed, undisciplined and unbrigaded uniformed civilians who were garrisoned in church basements, schools or any building in which they could sleep indoors until the men were inured to camp life.

4

While the officers in charge understood Lee's purpose, civilians did not. Defense was antithetical to the aggressive delusions of those Southerners who believed the first show of force would send the Yankees hurrying back to their money counters. In Richmond, the Virginia Convention refused to be persuaded by Lee's arguments to make enlistments for the duration of the war. Lee had observed in Mexico the difficulties caused by one-year enlistees returning home in the midst of a campaign. Also he had studied George Washington's troubles from the same cause. The politicians, with other interests, voted for one-year enlistments. Even this represented a compromise with those who thought one year was unnecessarily long.

The representatives of the extremists among the slave interests were still more sanguine. These men had lived in their unreal world for so long that, like Vice President Stephens, they held no conception of the magnitude of the forces involved. They were deaf to Lee's prediction that the war would be hard and long, maybe ten years. One of the representatives in Richmond declared that Lee was out of sympathy with the Confederacy when he dismissed their demands for instant action.

On April 24 Virginia entered a military alliance with the Confederacy, which led to its formal incorporation into the new nation. Shortly after the military alliance, D. G. Duncan, representing War Secretary Leroy Walker, wired from Richmond that he was convinced that Lee "wishes to repress enthusiasm of our people." Civilian Duncan was impressed by all the appearances of military might as Richmond was turned into a training camp, and the first troops from the South — Maxcy Gregg's South Carolina regiment — paraded gallantly down East Franklin Street with its band playing "The Bonnie Blue Flag." By May 7 Duncan went so far as to report, "I believe there is treachery here." Only the presence of President Davis, he advised, could rally the people and save the state from returning to the Union.

Giving no outward recognition of the criticisms, Lee wrote his wife, "I agree with you in thinking that the inflammatory articles in the papers do us much harm. I object particularly to those in the Southern papers, as I wish them to take a firm, dignified course, free of bravado and boasting. The times are indeed calamitous. The brightness of God's countenance seems turned from us, and its mercy stopped in its blissful current . . . Tell Custis he must consult his own judgment, reason and conscience as to the course he may take. I do not wish him to be guided by my wishes or example. If I have done wrong, let him do better."

On May 2, twenty-nine-year-old Custis resigned his first lieutenant's commission in the engineers and was commissioned captain in the Confederate engineers. Rooney joined the cavalry, and was commissioned captain. Lee's brother Smith had come with the Confederate Navy; and his son Fitzhugh with the cavalry. Lee's seventeen-year-old son Rob remained at the University of Virginia, persuaded by his father not to enlist for the present. Mildred, the youngest child, was still at school in Winchester. The other girls, with their mother, were preparing to leave their home in Arlington. After shipping off the Washington portraits and the silver, the four ladies would take only their clothes with them to the temporary shelter of "Aunt Maria" Fitzhugh at Ravensworth.

With these disturbing happenings in Lee's mind, it must indeed have been a calamitous time to endure the importunities of unqualified advisers while drudging at the endless chores and problems brought by each new day. The "fire-eaters" were unaccustomed to such mild words as those spoken in a deep bass voice by the gentleman dressed in a plain gray uniform without insignia of rank. Lee's office, on the top floor of the Mechanics' Hall building across from Capitol Square, was simply furnished with office desks and chairs, without even a sentry at the door. There were two or three clerks and a small staff, as courteously unassertive as their superior.

The ranking officer, Virginia's adjutant general, was forty-one-year-old Robert Garnett, a major in the Old Army who had served as Lee's adjutant at West Point. Among the younger officers, the only one who was to be permanent was Captain Walter Taylor. An extremely good-looking young businessman from Norfolk, Taylor had studied at the Virginia Military Institute, and been introduced to Lee by a distant kinsman of each of them. They were all hard workers, and Lee set them an example with his rapid, orderly dispatch of business. In making appointments, he was a quick and sound judge of character. He never showed impatience with petitioners for what they regarded as safe and pleasant staff posts, and they came by the hundreds.

Perhaps his example exerted a broader influence when the Confederate authorities in Montgomery made it clear that the officers of Virginia's forces were acting on a temporary basis. Their ranks might not be respected in the Provisional (permanent) Confederate armed forces. At the same time the Virginia Convention, after commendable quietude, felt the need for action. This body required the governor to submit to it all ranks above that of lieutenant colonel for confirmation and, to have something to do, reduced everyone except Lee by one grade.

Protests naturally followed. Most outraged was Daniel Ruggles, reduced to colonel, who claimed he had been promised the rank of brigadier when he, a Massachusetts native, offered his services to the state. As such protests gained nothing, Joe Johnston took more direct action. On Lee's recommendation Johnston had been appointed major general and placed by Lee in charge of Richmond's defenses. When his state reduced him to brigadier, Johnston silently left Virginia and appeared in Montgomery, on May 15. There he was commissioned Confederate Regular Army brigadier, with the tacit understanding that he would be in time made general. Johnston was the only prominent Virginian to enlist directly with the Confederate forces.

The example of Lee's attention to the job at hand, in Virginia, was followed by the younger officers coming home — J. E. B. Stuart, A. P. Hill, Richard S. Ewell, Henry Heth, George Pickett among others — and by Lee's contemporary, John Bankhead Magruder. Resplendent Magruder, whose seignorial manner of living had won him the sobriquet of "Prince John" in the Old Army, brought his usual enthusiasm to the camp of artillery instruction at Richmond College, where militia batteries were being prepared for battle.

None of the men who knew war wanted, any more than Lee, to be hurried into action. They were all waiting on the enemy's move. That came on May 24, the day after the voters of Virginia ratified the ordinance of secession.

## 5

Led by forty-three-year-old Brigadier General Irvin McDowell, the first armed force undertaking to "suppress the combination" of seceded states crossed the Potomac into Virginia and occupied Lee's hometown of Alexandria. From there contingents spread over the grounds of Arlington and around the house. Mrs. Lee, from her temporary haven at Ravensworth, wrote General Scott and McDowell to point out that Arlington was the home of the grandson of Martha Washington and adopted son of George Washington. She asked that it be protected and that the servants, who were left behind, be looked after. In a courteous exchange, McDowell assured her that no harm would come to the historic mansion — a promise he was unable to keep. The house was looted and Mrs. Lee's cherished heirlooms from Mount Vernon carried off. The two-year efforts of Lee as a planter became as nothing.

While his home was being occupied by invading troops, General Lee went by train to Manassas Junction, near the familiar neighborhood. With enemy troops — United States forces had become so soon "the enemy" — in Alexandria, Lee needed to make a personal inspection of the area around the vital junction of the Orange and Alexandria and the Manassas Gap railroads. The whole defense system of the state would be shaken by the loss of Manassas Junction, from which railroads ran west to the northern Valley and southwest to Gordonsville, and from there by the Virginia Central to Richmond.

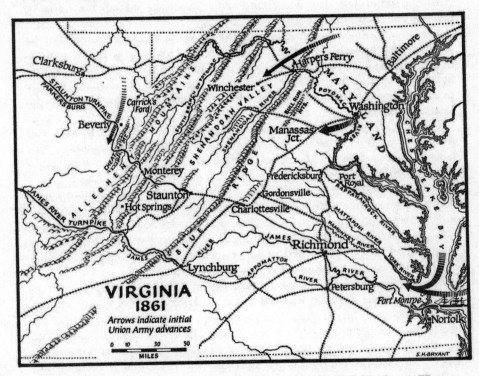

VIRGINIA
1861
Arrows indicate initial
Union Army advances

0  10    30    50
MILES

When Lee went on May 29 to the advance lines at Fairfax Court House, he occupied an anomalous and uncomfortable position of command. For the past month Confederate troops from other states had been coming into Virginia along with Confederate commanders, and little coordination existed between Governor Letcher and the Confederate authorities. Lee was left hanging somewhere between state and Confederate authority. On May 10 President Davis had given him command of all troops in Virginia. This authorized him to send troops to points of his selection, provide for their transportation, subsistence and arms, and assume responsibility for the preparation for battle — but only the preparations. For the battles,

Lee was charged with transferring Virginia troops into Confederate commands.

These thankless chores, removing Lee from consideration for field command, returned him to the detested confinement of office work. He may have felt some consolation by recognizing that, actually, he was the only person in Virginia who could have performed the task of creating an armed force approaching forty thousand in seven weeks. He combined his military knowledge, administrative gifts and tact in handling individuals with his habits of working in the infinite details of a master plan — all within a selflessness that was found with surprising infrequency among patriots (of both sides) committed to a cause.

Lee never seemed to consider that the faster he worked the quicker he would work himself out of his command. For his task as major general in command of Virginia's forces would be finished when the organization he built was absorbed in the Confederate forces. As it was, the change over to Confederate command had brought personality problems to the Manassas line.

Philip St. George Cocke was dissatisfied with his reduction in rank and nebulous status after being superseded by a Confederate brigadier, Milledge Bonham. Lee could scarcely blame the trained soldier. Bonham, a South Carolina lawyer and politician, had received his commission as a "prominent citizen" rather than for a military background limited to inconspicuous service with volunteers in the Mexican War and in the Seminole uprising in Florida in 1836. The press acclaimed him, but Bonham was manifestly unqualified for command of the area where the main test seemed likely to come. Whatever was done about Cocke, Lee decided Bonham would have to be removed as soon as practical.

For the present, Lee formed an observation force of cavalry and infantry placed under Colonel Richard S. Ewell. Dick Ewell, a recent captain of a company of border dragoons, had grown up in the neighborhood. He was advanced beyond Fairfax Court House. Other units were established on the flanks of the growing force at Manassas and, under continuing orders to remain strictly on the defense, Lee presented a front which would appear as formidable as possible. The Manassas line was interrelated, in Lee's mind, with the advance force at Harper's Ferry.

Jackson had also been superseded by a Confederate brigadier, Joe Johnston. On his reappearance in Virginia, this rank-conscious career soldier immediately took a position contrary to Lee's plans and demonstrated a military character that he was to impose on the war in Virginia. Johnston was well known as a student of strategy and much admired by friends as a "picture soldier." With a slight, compact build he made a fine appearance in his carefully tailored uniforms. His florid, well-modeled features were given a piquance by a pointed gray chin beard, and his intelligent eyes were brightened by humor. He was very charming when he felt unthreatened by a rival or superior and was a superb conversationalist, especially on the science of war.

At Harper's Ferry, Johnston ignored Lee's considerations of continuing rifle production at the arsenal and the morale effect of a withdrawal. Taking one look at the risky position, he advocated retirement and lectured Lee on the dangers to which the occupation of Harper's Ferry exposed his force. By implication, Jackson, instead of having audaciously taken the risk, had remained there because he and Lee knew no better.

From Manassas, Lee wrote his former classmate that Ewell's observation force would protect him from any attack from his rear. In the event of such a movement, Lee suggested that Johnston combine with Bonham for an attack on the enemy at Manassas. In this unimportant message, which made no impression on Johnston, Lee revealed the aggressive military cast of his mind. His first thought on a threatening enemy was not how to avoid but how to get at him.

Johnston's next message to Lee revealed *his* cast of mind. He was worried about the Federal force gathering to his north at Chambersburg, Pennsylvania, under old General Robert Patterson, relic of the War of 1812. Patterson's army was obviously aiming at a move into the Valley, and Johnston foresaw that the enemy's advance would cause his force to "be lost here." Lee, then back in Richmond, wrote Johnston that "the difficulties which surround it [Harper's Ferry] have been felt from the beginning of its occupation, and I am aware of the obstacles to its maintenance with your present force." Nonetheless Johnston could move out, Lee suggested, when the enemy actually approached. To make his columns more mobile, agents had been sent east and west of the Blue Ridge to impress wagons for him. Johnston had no intention of remaining at Harper's Ferry.

Lee had no authority, and soon he would not be able even to advise.

## 6

When Lee returned to Richmond on May 31, President Davis had arrived with the vanguard of Confederate authorities. Virginia's state capital had become the capital of the new nation. Its capitol was to be shared with the Confederate Congress; the former United States customs building became the main government office building, Mechanics' Hall became the War Department Building, and various bureaus were scattered among buildings in the area adjacent to Ninth and Main streets. Tobacco warehouses were turned into government warehouses for military supplies. A

gray-stuccoed brick mansion on Clay Street was to become the Confederate White House, though on arrival Jefferson Davis took rooms at the
Spotswood, unofficial Confederate headquarters.

Lee had been acquainted with Davis, never intimately, since their days
at West Point. Their closest association came when Lee was superintendent and Davis War Secretary, and he respected the Mississippian. Davis, of
course, was aware of the high regard in which Lee had been held in the
Old Army, and of his eminence in and knowledge of Virginia. Except for
his cadet-hero, Albert Sidney Johnston, who was to command in the
West, Davis evidently evaluated no one above Lee. Yet, the nature of
their relationship would depend on Lee's considerable gifts for getting
along with people. The President could be a very difficult person.

Davis was a linear type, standing very erectly above middle height, and
his nervous system had a thin covering against the shocks of human contact. The antithesis of Lee, he was a "made" article as contrasted with the
natural, and he suffered a neurotic's anxiety over insecurity.

Not born into the ruling class of which he became a leader, he subscribed rigidly to all its codes, especially of personal honor, and had an
inviolable sense of his own dignity. Unfortunately for his relationships, his
protective self-awareness made him insensitive to the dignity of others.
His obtuseness to human nuances was particularly unfortunate in a leader
of proud, assertive individualists because his insecurity made it necessary
for him always to be right. When a person differed from him, over even
the slightest matter, Davis took this as a personal affront. If the difference
concerned military policy, and the other person could not be convinced
of his wrongheadedness, he became an enemy. It was not in Davis's inflexible character to try to win someone over.

Since the need to be infallible placed him under intense strain, he
suffered physically from neuralgic facial spasms and upset stomach. He
had lost one eye, probably from glaucoma, and frequently his other eye
gave him excruciating pain. These physical effects of his tension exacerbated his temper, and occasionally an irritated sharpness caused men to
turn against him.

Lee, with his judgment of character, understood the touchy areas in the
thin-skinned man and admired Davis for the good qualities he brought to
his enormous, complex job. Though his mind was derivative and he was
somewhat overimpressed with his own mental powers, Davis's intelligence was superior and his principles unshakable. Perhaps his very lack of
political adroitness was a favorable point to Lee. He trusted Davis and
believed, correctly, that no man ever gave himself more whole-souled to a
cause.

In this dedication Davis suffered the neurotic's need to be omnipotent.
He retained all military authority under his personal control and made

himself a one-man general staff. Leaning hard on the literal interpretation of the "commander in chief" title and identifying himself with the military since his West Point education, the tactless man antagonized many by his authoritarianism. But Lee, accustomed to authority, was himself too secure to be antagonized by the seemingly egotistical manner with which Davis sometimes exerted it.

He did, however, move carefully to avoid conflict. With no need to assert, it was always simple for Lee to subordinate himself toward an end, and his native courtesy turned aside the slights delivered by a less complete man. Because his own gentle diplomacy brought out the best in Davis's personality, he saw the best of Davis. The President — like Lee, a devoted family man — could be very agreeable when not crossed.

In their first consultation, Lee suggested that Bonham be replaced at Manassas with Beauregard, who had just arrived at the Spotswood. Then the "Hero of the South," Pierre Gustave Toutant Beauregard was actually a specious hero, in that any militia artillery captain could have commanded the futile bombardment on Fort Sumter. But he was associated with the epic event, a dramatic declaration of independence, and he looked the part of a military hero.

A French Creole from New Orleans, "Old Bory" had romantically Latin looks, with olive skin, slumbrous eyes, and a smart mustache. Though only a captain of regular rank in the Old Army, he had seen service with Lee as an engineer of Scott's staff, and was highly educated in the principles of warfare. Most of all he had self-belief and found it perfectly natural that he should be the "Hero of the South." When Beauregard went off to the Manassas line in early June, Lee was nearing the end of his command both of Virginia's forces and the forces in Virginia.

That came on June 8, when the last of the Virginia troops was mustered into the Confederate armed forces. Davis, personally directing Beauregard and Johnston, assumed command of the important sectors where the Federals' "On to Richmond" drives were headed.

7

Lee had hoped for a field command when Virginia's defenses were absorbed by the Confederate leaders. Commander in Chief Davis, with his insensitivity to the feelings of others, left the man who had created the defenses in a vacuum.

"I do not know what my position will be," Lee wrote his wife on June 9. "I should like to retire to private life, so that I could be with you and the children, but if I can be of service to the State or her cause, I must continue."

Two days later, in answering a letter of Mrs. Lee's on her anxieties, the

General without command expressed his own feelings. "In this time of great suffering to the State and the country, our private distresses we must bear with resignation, and not aggravate them by repining, trusting to a kind and merciful God to overrule them for our own good."

When the Confederates took over command of the major threatened areas in northern Virginia, this only indirectly included Daniel Ruggles's defensive line on the Rappahannock, with its strongpoint the terminus of the Richmond, Fredericksburg and Potomac Railroad at Aquia Creek. Ruggles was superseded by Theophilus Holmes, a deaf North Carolinian pushing sixty, all of whose fire had burnt out in the Old Army. Without any definition of his duties, Lee continued in an advisory capacity with Holmes on his secondary front and, more or less by default, maintained an active supervision of defenses in Virginia's Tidewater and in the western mountains.

At Norfolk he had placed his contemporary, Benjamin Huger, the South Carolina patrician who had helped Lee mount the guns at Chapultepec. Huger had thickened since the days in Mexico, grown slow and somewhat pompous, but his preparations against attack called for thoroughness rather than initiative.

On the lower Peninsula, east of Williamsburg, was energetic "Prince John" Magruder. Magruder won the glory of halting a Federal advance in the first armed clash, June 10, between government forces and those called "Rebels." Later the meeting would be regarded as no more than a skirmish, but the Battle of Big Bethel — a place on the road between Fort Monroe and Yorktown — was a fine morale builder for the Southerners.

Fort Monroe, whose outer escarpments had been completed by the young Lieutenant Lee, was the one Federal installation in Virginia that remained safely in Union hands. It was known to be so impregnable that no attempt was made to take the fort. Without one of its guns being fired during the war, Fort Monroe provided a base for invading forces on Virginia's watery flank. From camps located outside the fort, an unsavory Boston politician, Benjamin Butler, had sought some quick laurels by advancing up the Peninsula with a force supported by U. S. Regular artillery batteries.

It happened that before the war, Jackson, then at V.M.I., had advised a state commission to buy a dozen or so new model rifled Parrott guns. Some of these had gone to the militia artillery battalion of the Richmond Howitzers, commanded by Jefferson's grandson, George W. Randolph. When Joe Johnston had served briefly on Richmond's defenses, he had countermanded Magruder's order for placing these new-styled Parrott rifles with the Howitzers but, after he went South, artillerist Magruder retained them. The result was that the Richmond artillery militia broke up the Regular U. S. Army batteries and the government force quit the field under the inept command of the politically appointed General Butler.

Having turned back the enemy, high-living Magruder indulged himself by bringing pageantry to his command of an area. But he also showed initiative, along with almost childlike dependence on reporting in detail to Lee. Between Magruder and the experienced Huger — standing steady against the menace of the U. S. Navy — Lee's defensive structure had passed its first test in the area to the east of Richmond. In the counties west of the Alleghenies (later the state of West Virginia) it was a different story.

In the first hurry of fortifying the state, Lee had been forced to neglect distant northwest Virginia. Then, though it was nowhere stated in writing, Virginia's authorities acted as if they did not actually expect to hold the extreme northwest portion of the state bordering on the Ohio River. It is also possible they underestimated the strength of the Unionist, or anti-Virginian, sentiment throughout the western counties. For generations this area, bound by trade and custom with western Pennsylvania and Ohio, had been out of sympathy with the original sections of the state dominated by the Tidewater grandees.

When the defense pattern was first drawn the few western Virginia volunteer forces were centered at Grafton, about 100 miles southeast of Wheeling and 175 miles west of Harper's Ferry on the Baltimore and Ohio Railroad. As early as May 10 Major Boykin, an officer in the Virginia volunteers sent to Grafton, wrote Lee, "The feeling in nearly all the counties is very bitter . . . organizations exist in most of the counties pledged to the support of what they term the Union. We have various rumors about forces being sent from Ohio and Pennsylvania for the purpose of holding the B.&O. at Grafton. I have no doubt from the confidence and bearing of the Union men in and around here that they are expecting aid from some quarter."

Lee, whose associations in Virginia were entirely east of the Blue Ridge, was long out of touch with the state's internal mutations. Evidently accepting the prevailing Richmond attitude, he assumed Boykin was an alarmist and wrote him that he hoped the difficulties in obtaining volunteers would be overcome. Boykin had described the situation very accurately. Not only did no enlistments come in but there was growing evidence of disaffection and Unionist activities.

In late May a Federal force advanced south of the Ohio under major general of volunteers George B. McClellan, who at thirty-five had returned to the military glory. McClellan's march was uncontested all the way to the Grafton area as his troops moved through obviously friendly country. Then, near Grafton, McClellan's advance came at early morning of June 3, after a rainy night, upon a sleeping Confederate camp. Colonel Porterfield, one of the few locally prominent citizens to whom Letcher had given command, had thought to spare his recruits the rigors of standing sentry in the dark rain. Abandoning the camp, the startled Confederates fled for their lives in an affair known as "the Philippi Races."

The path was opened for ambitious McClellan to the counties west of the Shenandoah Valley. He would encounter stronger Virginia loyalties there, but if no force could be gathered to impede his progress, he could make Virginia's granary his goal. Occupying Grafton, at Philippi McClellan was only 120 miles from Staunton, in the heart of the fertile Valley.

With this state of affairs, Lee could only send out a few regiments along with his adjutant general, Robert Garnett, to assume command of the scattered companies in northwestern Virginia. After Garnett left, June 8, Lee was prevented from giving his attention to the salvage expedition by demands from President Davis that were to become dishearteningly habitual. Davis began to call on Lee for consultations about the physical conditions of the state and the dispositions of the troops. Having transferred Virginia's forces to the Confederacy, Lee continued to supervise the mundane details relating to arms, subsistence and transportation.

Only the lonely stretch on the Texas plains had comprised a bleaker period, and then at least his family had had security and he a future. As the damp heat came to Richmond in June and July, the former favorite of General in Chief Scott became the misused soldier in his hotel room at the Spotswood.

8

Lee could do nothing to prevent the quick collapse that came to Garnett's Western Virginia campaign. Garnett could muster scarcely five thousand poorly trained and inadequately armed troops, and he made the mistake of dividing this small force. McClellan, showing great administrative gifts in organizing the well-armed and comparatively large force under his command, also displayed sharp strategy in turning the position at Rich Mountain (July 11) held by Lieutenant Colonel John Pegram, a Regular Army soldier from Richmond. When Pegram's force was gobbled up, and the handsome thirty-year-old Richmonder was captured, Garnett's flank was turned and he was forced into a hurried retreat. Trying to rally his green and shaken troops at Carrick's Ford (July 13), Garnett was shot dead by a sharpshooter, to become the first general officer casualty of the war.

For the second time the mountain force disintegrated. But this time Virginia's northwest was irretrievably gone and McClellan was in striking distance of Staunton. Within less than three months after secession, Virginia had lost a slice of territory sufficient to form a new (Unionist) state, the defensive periphery had alarmingly shrunk, and the "breadbasket" of

the Valley was threatened from the west as well as north. McClellan naturally made the most of his victory. He placed no emphasis either on the
friendly reception given by the native population nor the indifferent quality of the small Confederate force opposing him. Overnight he became
the Union's hero, the Federals' answer to Beauregard. Even though his
achievements were inflated, his reputation had at least a sounder basis than
the Hero of Fort Sumter.

While Lee and other Virginians grew anxious about the west of their
state, the eyes of the Confederacy centered on their hero, "Old Bory." He
was about to get the big chance at fame on the plains south of Washington. Near Manassas McDowell showed by a tentative advance, on July 18,
that he was ready to begin large-scale operations in the "On to Richmond"
drive.

Trained soldier McDowell did not personally believe his volunteer
forces, built around a nucleus of regulars, was ready to assume an offensive. But Lincoln, under pressures from newspapers and politicians, had
ordered the movement. In Richmond, Lee, with the decisive action approaching, was held to the chores of rushing troops and supplies to Manassas Junction. At the defensive line behind the sluggish stream called Bull
Run, Beauregard spun grand strategy for a counteroffensive against Mc-
Dowell.

Davis in consultation with Lee had already rejected one of Beauregard's
fanciful offensives. However, as Lee had suggested earlier, Johnston could
use the Manassas Gap Railroad to make juncture with Beauregard for a
less grandiose counteroffensive on McDowell. Johnston had retired a
month before from Harper's Ferry, and at Winchester was in ready
marching distance of the railroad. On his front, where the over-aged Patterson was dormant, Johnston's movement away from Winchester would
be screened by the cavalry of Jeb Stuart. In his first actions Stuart's native
gifts and enterprise, along with his high spirits, had already won him the
respect and affection of then Confederate Brigadier General Jackson.

On a mildly warm Sunday, July 21, the telegraph service in the War
Department in Richmond brought the information of the opening of the
battle regarded as the test between government coercion and state resistance. The news spread fast throughout the city. Cabinet members left
their homes and joined Secretary of War Walker in his office on the first
floor of Mechanics' Hall. President Davis commandeered an engine and
rode off on a special train to Manassas Junction. With total unawareness
of the desperate urge of Lee to be at the scene where he had laid the
foundation of defenses, the President ignored the soldier. As acting aide-
de-camp, he took along his nephew, Joseph R. Davis, a lawyer.

In this act of purblindness, the President revealed the way in which he
had come to take Lee for granted as an all-purpose unfeeling executive

assistant. By his subordination of the superior soldier, Davis also revealed his belief in his own fitness for high command, despite an undistinguished military career. After a mediocre record at West Point he had served only a briefly uneventful stint in the army and enjoyed a moment of minor heroics with a volunteer regiment with Taylor at Buena Vista. However, infatuated with everything about the military establishment (except peace-time service), he equated his accomplishments as Secretary of War in Pierce's administration with qualifications for wartime leadership.

Repeating the methods he had used successfully in peacetime Washington, Davis arranged Confederate operations in bureaucratic departments. In this fashion, Lee was then departmentalized in organization of peripheral sectors. Though there was considerable doubt in Richmond that there would be any sectors at all after the clash at Manassas, the top soldier from the U. S. Army then available in Virginia was left at his desk — under orders to organize a new campaign in the western mountains.

What Lee did with himself in Richmond during that long Sunday is not known. The Cabinet members, getting gloomier as the day wore on to dusk, made no mention of seeing him in the War Department. Mrs. Davis and the other anxious wives waiting with her at the Spotswood evidently did not see him in his hotel. Part of the time at least he spent in his own deserted office, to which no one came. He dated July 21 two letters he wrote to General W. W. Loring, the new commander of the forces in the northwest.

During the afternoon Adjutant General Samuel Cooper received a wire from Davis saying that a terrible battle was raging. Aging Samuel Cooper, Hudson River descendant of a Revolutionary line and former adjutant general of the U. S. Army, had adopted the state of his wife. She was the sister of James Mason, recently United States senator from Virginia and then Confederate commissioner to England. Then, after dark the wire they had all been waiting for came to Cooper. "We have won a glorious though dear-bought victory. Night closed on the enemy in full flight and closely pursued."

Maybe somebody thought to tell Lee, or maybe he was attracted by the shouts of joyous relief of the lower floor. Anyway, Davis also wired his wife at the hotel, and within an hour everybody in downtown Richmond knew that the attempt at coercion by force had failed. Lee would never have admitted to feeling slighted, but there could be little doubt that he felt disappointed and embarrassed to have spent the day uselessly among civilians.

"I wished to partake in the . . . struggle, and am mortified at my absence," he wrote his wife. Then, trying to put a good face on his neglect, he added, "But the President thought it more important that I should be here. I could not have done as well as has been done, but I could have helped, and taken part in the struggle for my home and neighborhood. So the work is done I care not by whom it is done."

In relation to his own ambitions, the last sentence was probably a totally true statement. He wrote warmly spontaneous notes of his "joy" at the victory to Beauregard and to Johnston, who overnight supplanted Lee as Virginia's preeminent soldier. But, for his own employment, he could only accept as God's will the place assigned himself. From his unofficial and generalized direction of the peripheral actions, Lee was to be shunted off to distant operations far removed from the main theater in Virginia.

### 9

The "glorious victory" had been essentially a lucky victory. It was largely determined by two little-known Confederate brigadiers of Old Army background — a cold-eyed, hard-drinking South Carolinian named "Shanks" Evans and the stern-faced eccentric who that day became "Stonewall" Jackson. Beauregard had been saved from the disaster of an offensive by McDowell's beating him to it. Beauregard had known so little of what was going on that while he was trying to mount his offensive on his right, his own left was being rolled up by McDowell. That his left was not routed was due entirely to the undirected initiative and stout fighting first of Evans and then of Jackson. Jackson's troops, the first from Johnston's Valley army to come on the field, went to Evans's support.

Then Johnston arrived. Seeing the point of danger, he threw in his reinforcements on the bent-back Confederate left flank. By the late afternoon the brigade of Kirby Smith (one of Lee's officers in the old 2nd Cavalry) went in on the Federal flank, the men giving a high-pitched eerie scream which became known as "the Rebel yell." McDowell's people, worn out from the daylong fighting and demoralized at having had victory snatched from their hands, fell back. Being mostly raw recruits, the men reverted to civilian status and sought safety in flight. Panic spread among the spectators who had driven out to watch the rebellion crushed. As their carriages blocked the roads, McDowell's battle ended in a stampede all the way back to Washington.

McDowell's fugitives were not "closely pursued," as Davis's wire stated. In fact, they were not pursued at all. The relief at turning back the invaders went as deeply through Davis, Johnston and Beauregard as through the leaders waiting in Richmond, and no one at Manassas assumed authority for a pursuit. The three men talked about pursuit in the afterglow of victory, and later they recriminated with one another, but when the sun went down on the disordered field, the leaders did not look beyond the incredible magnitude of the victory over the forces sent to "suppress" them.

In the days, the weeks and then the months following the repulse of the armed coercers, this lassitude of relief persisted in Davis and Johnston. Beauregard, forced to share the hero's role with Johnston, did press for one of his fanciful offensives. This only resulted in antagonizing Davis, and he sent "Old Bory" to the West to become second-in-command to Albert Sidney Johnston. Afterwards Joe Johnston claimed he also had proposed offensives. However, he was naturally a defensive fighter, and most of his aggression was vented against Davis over the matter of his rank.

When the Confederate government published the list of full confederate generals on August 31, Joe Johnston was outraged to find himself fourth down on the list, ranking only Beauregard. After leaving Virginia to maneuver in Montgomery, he found himself outranked by Adjutant General Cooper, the Davis hero Albert Sidney Johnston, and then Lee. It had been understood that Confederate rank would follow the order held in the U. S. Army, and next to old Cooper, Johnston had ranked first as quartermaster general with rank of brigadier general, staff. Davis used the specious argument that Johnston's staff rank did not apply to field rank. Both Lee and Albert Sidney Johnston had been full colonels with field commands, Johnston having seniority.

In his bitterness at the listing — which "transfers me from the position of first rank to that of fourth" — Johnston lost his perspective. Approaching the President as something like a fellow club member who had been temporarily elected to fill an office among equals, he wrote an intemperate letter accusing Davis of singling him out for a "studied indignity." He so forgot appropriateness as to say Davis's act was "degrading one who had served laboriously from the commencement of the war on this frontier and borne a prominent part in the one great event of that war, for the benefit of persons neither of whom has yet struck a blow for the Confederacy."

This uncalled-for slap at Lee and Albert Sidney Johnston was too much for Davis. In point of fact, Johnston "had served laboriously" in Montgomery for Confederate rank while Lee was building the defensive forces and line of defense which made possible the victory for which Johnston received the credit. Davis would never let it be said that anyone could denounce him for being wrong and go unchallenged. He sent Johnston a curt note that put him in his place — a subordinate to the commander in chief, and one no longer in favor. The grievance settled in Johnston like an infection. From then on, his hatred of Davis became a crack in the Confederacy's defensive structure.

Lee was outside all this, as he was outside all policy and decisions during the lull that Davis allowed to descend over the Confederacy. On July 28, the soldier who had refused command of the U. S. Army was sent to the western mountains to salvage a hopeless command situation, but even now he was not sent as a general to take field command. Reaching the very bottom of his fortunes, as Jefferson Davis's executive assistant he left the city, unnoticed, to act as something of an expediter without authority.

## CHAPTER VII

## "I Do Not See Either Advantage or Pleasure
## in My Duties"

THE ROAD ran west from Staunton across the rolling Valley floor, contoured by the geometric patterns of wheat fields and meadows enclosed in stone fences. The limestone base of the grass was good for stock, and workhorses and beef cattle grazed in the bright green meadows. Lee, accompanied by Captain Walter Taylor and Colonel John Washington, had left the Virginia Central cars at Staunton and rode west at a leisurely pace in the late July sun. From the Valley, the road climbed in continuous curves into the Shenandoah Mountains. Up in the hills the three soldiers, with Lee's cook and personal servant, pitched camp the first night.

Resuming his twisting ride, Lee looked down onto the isolated cabins in the shallow side valleys and into the shadowed coves where mountaineers made their moonshine. About forty-five miles from Staunton, he reached the town of Monterey in the lushly beautiful valley that, east of the Alleghenies, ran south to Warm Springs. The Warm Springs baths, where Jefferson used to "take the waters," was in the area of the spas where Lee's wife went seeking relief from the encroachments of arthritis. She was close in his thoughts when he rode through the spectacular scenery, for Lee was depressed by the contrast between the tranquil grandeur of nature and the armed strife that destroyed the regulated order of the world he knew.

"The views were magnificent," he wrote Mary Lee. "The valleys so beautiful, the scenery so peaceful. What a glorious world Almighty God has given us. How thankless and ungrateful we are, and how we labour to mar His gifts."

The attempted resolution by force was then developing into the full-scale war feared by Lee. The hotheads who had deprecated his defensive preparations and the foolish politicians who believed a one year's enlistment was unnecessarily long had promoted the illusion that the test of force would be decided in a single clash. Volunteers who arrived at

Manassas after the fighting felt ashamed to go home without having fired a shot in the struggle. Now, while the Southerners settled down into an anticlimactic waiting period, Lincoln was preparing an army as if to engage a powerful foreign enemy.

McClellan, hailed as the "Young Napoleon," had been called to Washington to organize and lead a mighty machine that would exploit the superior manpower and resources of the United States. The Unionist states outnumbered the white population in the seceded states by four to one, and this did not take into account the volunteers in the Federal armies from Southern states. Some officers from the North volunteered with the Confederate armies, but these were usually men married into Southern families or who had lived for some while in a Southern state.

In calling for more volunteers, Lincoln, once committed to armed coercion, was moved without choice to the next stage of winning military victories. There was no single control of events as in the "regulated order" assumed by the Constitution makers. Lincoln himself said later that events had controlled him. As Lee knew, when guns were given the power of decision, then guns released their own voiceless forces which took direction of events.

As if recognizing that he was dealing with uncontrollable forces, Lee never referred to Lincoln. Since Lee was known to distrust the fanatical element of abolitionists in Lincoln's party (as, indeed, did most Northerners), he would have been aware of the danger of the growing power of a Radical group in Lincoln's government. Career abolitionists and professional South-haters and ruthless men of ambition, this combine in Washington was essentially disunionist. The Radicals were not working toward Lincoln's end of returning the seceded states to a republic as it existed before the secession. By July the U.S. Congress had felt it necessary to pass a resolution which — in effect repudiating the abolitionists who wanted to make slavery an issue — declared that the war was not waged for the "purpose of overthrowing or interfering with the . . . established institutions" of the seceded states. The purpose was to "maintain . . . the . . . States unimpaired; and as soon as these objects are accomplished the war ought to cease."

But how could men's resolutions contain passions that, already incited to the point of fighting to kill, would be played upon by the corruptions and violence unleashed in legalized mass action? After all, Lincoln had *said* the purpose of armed coercion was limited to the repossession of United States property, and promised there would be "no invasions of, against or amongst the people anywhere." Lee, recognizing this as an unrealistic promise before he came to Richmond, knew the logical extension of armed force was unlimited war, leading ultimately to extermination.

To prevent war being carried to its ultimate conclusion, the South must

submit or win independence. There would be nothing between, no negotiations, as some of the civil leaders believed. Independence would have to
be *won*, as it was in the Revolution, by military victories of a decisiveness
to break the enemy's will to support invading armies. In turn, to prevent
this it was inevitable that Lincoln must do what events indicated, regardless of recorded words. To achieve their independence the Southern leaders must also do what was indicated by events. This they were not doing.

Aware of Lincoln's preparations for forces to overwhelm the Southern
forces, Jefferson Davis simply waited, allowing the people's enthusiasm to
cool. As commander in chief, he had translated the Confederacy's political purpose of defense into a military policy of defense. It was a passive
defense that gave the initiative to the Federal forces and dispersed the dangerously inferior Confederate manpower on such excursions as Lee was
dispatched on.

As to his assignment, for once in his life Lee could not believe he could
accomplish anything on the job at hand. He recognized it as a hopeless
assignment. Writing his wife that he was traveling over a section he had
passed on his return from St. Louis twenty years before, he said, "If any
one had then told me that the next time I traveled that road would have
been on my present journey, I should have supposed him insane."

2

Lee was faced with the nebulous task of "coordinating" three prima
donnas, without any authority over any of them. With all his gifts and
application, nothing in his nature or experience qualified him for this type
of operation. In fact, his ingrained habits of consideration were a handicap — as he discovered on meeting the first of the three. Lee received a
very cool welcome when, on August 3, he rode into Loring's camp at the
advance base in the dirty mountain village of Huntersville.

Brigadier General W. W. Loring, a non-West Point career soldier, was
a self-assertive professional. Enlisting young from Florida in the Old
Army during the Seminole Wars, he had been brevetted lieutenant colonel in Mexico — where he lost an arm at Chapultepec — and commissioned colonel of a regiment of mounted riflemen while Lee was still
lieutenant colonel. A dark man with receding hair and piratical mustache,
at forty-two Loring was contumacious and opinionated, and openly
showed his resentment of Lee as a superior.

The other two personalities were political appointees which Davis had
made personally, negating Governor Letcher's efforts to keep untrained
prominent citizens out of command in Virginia. Henry A. Wise had been
the governor of Virginia during the John Brown insurrection, and his
closest contact to anything military was his relationship as brother-in-law

to the Federal general, George Gordon Meade. Davis authorized the fifty-four-year-old Wise to raise a "Legion" — infantry, cavalry and artillery — to act as an independent partisan force.

John B. Floyd, also a former governor from southwest Virginia, had been commissioned by Davis to raise a brigade of riflemen in competition with the regular recruiting in the state. Floyd, as Secretary of War during Buchanan's administration, had learned something about the equipment and organization required by troops, and to this extent was better qualified than Wise.

It happened that Floyd and Wise were political enemies and, as Floyd held seniority as brigadier general, he was most anxious to exercise this superiority over his rival. The Legion commander stayed as far as possible from Floyd's demesne in order to avoid his authority. Both avoided Loring.

Floyd wrote directly to Davis derogating the poorly disciplined and equipped force under Wise. As Wise had independently tried one abortive offensive, Floyd claimed that Wise's wretched campaign shook the mountain people's confidence in the Confederacy and showed his need of Floyd's guidance. Wise's campaign did show the need of somebody's guidance, though scarcely Floyd's. For protection Wise wrote appealingly to Lee.

At the end of one day in Loring's filthy, disorganized camp, Lee wrote Adjutant General Cooper: "They [Loring, Wise, Floyd] do not seem near a junction and I fear from their report, their command will not prove very effective after a junction is made."

Soon he learned that a regiment in Wise's Legion existed only on paper, and wrote the supposed colonel, "I regret to learn . . . that you have done nothing towards the organization of your regiment." The organizers of a company requested permission to disband because of the prevalence of measles and two deaths by brain fever. Lee wrote that a better reward for the men would be to reorganize the company. Men and women sent him letters petitioning the release of sons from the army. Maximilian Joseph Michelbacher, the senior minister of Hebrews of Virginia, wrote asking for a ten-day furlough for penitence and prayer for the Jewish volunteers with one or another of the three forces. Lee replied there was no way of telling when every man would be needed. Mrs. Martha Jane Randolph Codwise wrote to "Dear Cousin Robert," asking for information about her son, believed to be in Jackson's command. He was puny and should come home. Lee knew nothing about Jackson's command.

Every day revealed new details of unreadiness for action. In a mountainous region of little food produce, the slipshod supply services kept the troops on hand-to-mouth rations. Little grain was available and the horses had to rely almost entirely on grass. With the primitive medical service, illnesses held most of the regiments down to half of their paper rosters. Lee wrote Cooper: "I fear that little benefit can be accomplished and until sufficient supplies can be obtained, there can be little hope of effective operations."

The only possible remedy was for Lee to write Davis and ask for complete authority for himself. He simply could not bring himself to do this. Assigned his task as "coordinator," he tried to coordinate. Always preferring amicable exchanges, he tried tactful persuasion on the three willful men, each of whom was determined to get his own way in his private war with the other. Though Lee's approach gained limited results and he imposed some direction on the three commands, no combined effectiveness of action was possible without the authority to reorganize the whole operation under a single qualified command.

It is possible that Lee did not seek this authority partly because the purposes held for the campaign were unrealistic for the forces available with their weird trio of commanders. The population east of the mountains regarded the region as *Virginia* and, as reflected in the newspapers, the public expected the northwestern counties to be reclaimed. This accorded with the general purpose held by Davis. However, less sensitive to the loss of Virginia territory, the President was more immediately concerned with halting the Federal advances toward the Valley. On the ground, the three generals thought vaguely, each according to his own preferences, both of checking the enemy's advances and reclaiming the ground, but without a plan for either. The one move open to Lee was to simplify and clarify immediate objectives.

### 3

There were two main lines of enemy threat, and of possible counteroffensive. From the Federal-held position at Cheat Mountain, the Parkersburg-Staunton highway ran past Monterey directly into the middle Valley and to the Virginia Central Railroad. Fifty or more mountainous miles to the south the James River and Kanawha Turnpike ran through Lewisburg to Covington, a few miles from the terminus of the Virginia Central and within striking distance of the Virginia-Tennessee Railroad. The Virginia-Tennessee provided the only east-west railroad connection for the northern Confederacy, and on it the troops from western North Carolina and Tennessee had been hurried to build Loring's force in the Monterey area. The independent commands of Wise and Floyd were near Lewisburg where Wise, after his injudicious forward movement with his motley force, had fallen back for rebuilding at White Sulphur Springs.

By the time Lee arrived, McClellan had been succeeded by Brigadier

General William S. Rosecrans. A West Point graduate, "Old Rosy" had resigned from the army to enter civil engineering and, like McClellan, had offered his services to the Ohio volunteers. Genial Rosecrans had left a comparatively small force under Joseph J. Reynolds at Cheat Mountain while building for a major strike in the Kanawha area to the south. Once this major force reached Covington, the Confederates in the Monterey section would be outflanked and forced to withdraw.

As Lee clearly had to move before Rosecrans, he first gave his attention to Loring's force. This had the larger numbers, more than ten thousand, and the single command offered the only possibility of a quick offensive. But before Lee even reconnoitered the ground, the rains came. Beginning in early August rain fell every day. The valleys were filled with a damp, misty chill and the roads turned into quagmires. Loring's advance base at Huntersville was more than fifty miles from the railroad at Millboro, and the wagons bringing forward the provisions moved by inches axle-deep in the muck. Mules fell dead from the strain and sank, with only their ears protruding through the mud.

While the rain slowed all operations, Loring's unhardened, poorly organized and demoralized recruits allowed their camps to grow filthy. "Those on the sick list would form an army," Lee wrote his wife. "They bring it on themselves by not doing what they are told. They are worse than children, for the latter can be forced." Careful not to tread on the toes of the jealous professional, Lee suffered in silence as long as he could. A dirty camp, he said, "nauseated him," and he grew depressed by the rain. Suddenly, with only Walter Taylor and Colonel Washington, Lee moved out of the main camp and away from Loring.

They established an advanced base at Valley Mountain, where the vistas of mud inspired Lee to write his wife long descriptions of the dreariness. With the lack of equipment brought forward, the General shared a tent with Walter Taylor and John Washington. A great-nephew of George Washington, Colonel Washington was the last custodian of Mount Vernon. Lee grew very fond of him and was particularly touched by his religious devotions. They were all Episcopalians and at night each said his prayers before the others as unselfconsciously as kneeling in church.

Their mess was prepared by Meredith, a cook from the White House plantation. Perry, who had been a waiter in the dining room at Arlington, acted somewhat haphazardly as Lee's personal servant. It turned out that the General had to stir Perry out of the covers in the chilly mornings.

For the possibility of an offense on the detached Federal force at Cheat Mountain, Lee took to making personal reconnaissances of the terrain south and west of the mountain. As Lee began to envision an enveloping attack to surprise the enemy, he turned back the clock to the days when he was a forty-year-old engineering captain clambering through the rocks in Mexico. It was dangerous work and his plans advanced slowly, as his communications with Loring and Loring's subordinates were erratic.

In his rides he was growing accustomed to a new horse he had acquired, whom he named Traveler. A strongly built five-year-old, standing sixteen hands, Traveler was, Lee said, "a Confederate gray," with black points and small head. The horse and rider took to each other, and soon the big gray became Lee's favorite mount.

In the cramped conditions of the dismal mountain camp, Lee stopped shaving, and a full beard came out gray. The beard gave a patriarchal quality to the majestic composure and kindly manner that won for Lee the filial affections of the men in the ranks. At all times he moved easily among them and was always accessible. In their homesick misery, he embodied what the parochial Southern soldiers needed — a family figure. They gave him the deferential title of a familiar authority, "Uncle Robert" or "Mister Robert," slurred in their careless enunciations to "Marse Robert." He was not their commanding general in western Virginia, but he became then the men's leader, the one to whom they gave their implicit trust and devotion.

A bright interlude in his days was provided by his son Rooney, then a major commanding a cavalry squadron in the mountains. Lee wrote his wife that the big fellow was "as sanguine, cheerful and hearty as ever . . . He dined with me yesterday and preserves his fine appetite . . . I sent him some cornmeal this morning and he sent me some butter." The father was concerned that his son was out reconnoitering in the fine rain "without his overcoat, as I do not recollect seeing it on his saddle."

Lee was also concerned about his youngest son, Rob. Just reaching eighteen, he was determined to leave college and go into the army. General Lee had advised him against it. Then Lee wrote him that if, after considering all he had written him on the subject, Rob still wanted to go, the father would not withhold his consent. Lee wrote his wife, "I am unable to judge for him and he must decide for himself. . . . I pray God to bring him to a correct conclusion."

Then Lee wrote his wife on a strange subject. Mrs. Lee had left her refuge at Ravensworth and was traveling about for her health. Answering a letter of hers, on September 9, Lee wrote, "As to the reports which you say are afloat about our separation, I know nothing. Any one that can reason must see its necessity under present circumstances. They can only exist in the imagination of a few. So give them no heed. . . . Everybody is slandered, even the good. How should I escape?"

Lee made no further reference to these rumors which evidently were never published. He wrote much more about "the slanders" that were printed. Newspapers were beginning to snipe at the government for its lack of action and, as Lee had entered the army with such fame, some tart attention was given his failure to drive the Federals from western Virginia in the five weeks he had been there. Mrs. Lee wanted to publish a paragraph from one of his letters to her as a refutation. Lee wrote her that he preferred "to take no notice of the slanders you speak of" and reminded her that his private letters were not "for the public eye." Even to his wife, to whom he wrote continuously during this period of little action, he was careful about what he put in writing.

Lee was anxious for his wife to establish herself somewhere for the winter but he could think of no place, in neighborhoods familiar to her, that he could recommend as safe. "Perhaps you had better make up your mind to board somewhere, and let the girls do the same, and then you can move according to circumstance." As for expenses, he wrote, "Very little is necessary for me and you can have all the rest." At that time his Confederate army pay was worth approximately 100 cents on the dollar.

Mary Lee characteristically deferred making a choice. Instead, in the middle of September she went to Hot Springs. Five miles south of Warm Springs and between the separate Confederate forces, the fashionable spa was scarcely a safe retreat. However, by the time she was settled at the baths, her husband's attempted offensive in the Cheat Mountain area had come to an end.

Early in September, while Rosecrans was advancing cautiously in the Kanawha region, Floyd wrote Lee that the enemy threatened great harm to civilian property. Lee wrote, September 7, "I can not believe that the enemy will carry out their threat of burning and laying waste the countryside. It is intended to intimidate. The sentiment in America will not tolerate it."

Nevertheless, he hurried preparations for Loring's army to dispose of the Federal forces under Reynolds on Cheat Mountain. After Lee's personal reconnaissances had been completed, he designed an assault that would catch Reynolds by surprise. The attack was to open in the early morning of September 12.

Rain fell heavily during the night and provided the factor to set in motion a chain of failures among Loring's five brigadiers. While Lee waited, the key unit designated to lead the action never moved. In some of the units the inexperienced recruits had their powder ruined by the rain. Other officers throughout Loring's inchoate force found various reasons for doing nothing.

Lee grew excited at the failure of the first combat action he had ever prepared and galloped recklessly from command to command. His party rode almost into a body of Federal cavalry. The blue-uniformed horsemen fell back from an encounter with a skirmish line and, looking to their own safety, overlooked Lee. By ten o'clock, when Reynolds, alerted, was rushing up reinforcements, Lee realized Loring could accomplish nothing against a prepared enemy.

Lee reported officially only to the governor, pointing out that "this . . . is for your own eye." He expressed his personal feelings about the fiasco to his wife. "I can not tell you my regret and mortification at the untoward events that caused the failure of the plan. I had taken every precaution to ensure success and had counted on it."

In thinking he had designed a foolproof plan, Lee had much to learn about commanding troops in action — especially the troops of an informal citizen-army which, without the machinery of a regular establishment, was largely dominated by personalities. The deficiencies of Loring's supply services alone caused Lee to order the forces withdrawn the next day. Nor did Lee appraise the effects of the weather on the mountainous terrain. Green soldiers in the action, who looked back from the perspective of later experience, wrote that it would have been hard even for veterans to function well in that mud. For the miserable men with Loring, it was impossible under the slack command structure.

With Loring's withdrawal for food, Lee tacitly abandoned any plan of an offensive at Cheat Mountain. Lee kept his disappointment to himself, but he did not try to hide his grief over the death of John Washington. The colonel had begged Lee for permission to ride on a patrol with Rooney's cavalry. The small scouting party ran into an ambush of enemy pickets and three minié balls passed through Washington's body.

If Valley Mountain could be called "Lee's first battle" — in the sense that he directed an attack for troops he did not command — the deepest impression on him was Washington's death. He wrote Governor Letcher, "Our greatest loss is the death of my dear friend, Colonel Washington." Then he wrote a letter breaking the news to Washington's daughter.

4

No sooner had Lee eliminated the possibility of an offensive against Reynolds than he learned that the bottom had dropped out of the Floyd-Wise command in the Kanawha region. Against Lee's advice, not orders, Floyd had fought Rosecrans and been forced into a retreat. While Wise evaded Floyd's orders to join him, Rosecrans was advancing on two fronts. All choice was removed for Lee. He must go to resolve the clash between the two old politicians.

Lee directed Loring to shift to a defensive position and then follow him southward with the bulk of his troops. With only Walter Taylor, Lee rode through the wet valleys where the trees had turned russet and colored leaves layered the mud. He arrived on September 21 in the chaos of Wise's camp on Sewell Mountain.

There Wise had placed his miserably organized force in the path of the Federal advance west of Lewisburg. As aggressive as a wildcat, ex-Governor Wise was so totally ignorant of military matters that he did not know enough to recognize the danger to which he exposed his troops. East of him at the foot of the mountain, in a village called Meadow Bluff, Floyd was trying to enforce his orders on Wise to fall back on his position. After his one defeat, Floyd had retreated to Meadow Bluff shaken in mind at the encounter. However, Lee perceived that Wise's position on Sewell Mountain presented the stronger front.

Lee was saved from the dilemma by Davis. He recalled Wise from his command of independent partisans and placed his force under Floyd. With Floyd's chief enemy having been removed from Sewell Mountain, Lee then tactfully suggested that Floyd bring his brigade to the stronger position. By then Loring had marched his forces down to the new front, and Lee — with both Floyd and Loring more amenable to guidance — arranged the three separate commands into one defensive force.

The Federal advances came to a halt at the Confederate stand. Lee hoped to invite an attack, and fight a defensive battle. With Wise's bewildered relics and Floyd's southwestern Virginians more eager to fight one another than anybody else, and Loring's troops having already displayed their unreadiness at Valley Mountain, Lee did not feel that he could justify an offensive battle against Rosecrans. But Rosecrans refused to attack. During the night he removed his army and withdrew farther into the western mountains.

In early October, Lee then played with the idea of trying to mount an offensive into the lost counties. Everything worked against it. The rains came again, reproducing the problems of hauling supplies to the front. The men subsisted from day to day. Their morale was poor and, in an advance, they would be campaigning in country that Lee found to be more hostile than friendly. Spies lurked everywhere. With winter approaching, Lee did not feel the force with him to be capable of the decisive military action necessary to reclaim the disaffected counties.

While Lee had been in the mountains, an anti-secession convention, meeting at Wheeling, had passed acts severing the western counties from Virginia. In an intra-secession movement, an act was passed on August 29 providing for the formation of a new state, and this was to be followed by a plan for the "legal" partition of Virginia. Since the Constitution required a state to give its consent to the formation of a new state out of its territory, a "Restored Government" of Virginia had been formed at Wheeling for the purpose of giving consent to the partitioning.

Later Lincoln recognized this "Restored Government" as representing

Virginia and, as he said, in the "expediency" of a "war measure," admitted the new state to the Union as West Virginia (June 20, 1863). The authority for the admission, fourth section of the fourth article of the Constitution, held its curious contradictions. "The United States shall guarantee to every state in this Union a Republican form of government . . . and shall protect each of them against invasion."

Once the counties west of the Alleghenies began the drift toward becoming a Union state, there was really nothing Lee could have done to hold the region in Virginia. A complete army, given the time, material and officer personnel to become professionally trained and equipped, could only have opened a second front — and merely maintaining such a front would chiefly have given the Confederacy a backbreaking burden in supply. With the force on hand and the prevailing conditions, Lee had done all possible by stalling the enemy's advance into the Valley and to the railroads. This practical part of the vague, general assignment was, as a matter of fact, a very solid achievement. It removed the enemy's threat from the west.

The public did not see it that way. The newspapers, with an inexplicable purblindness about the political realities and the physical conditions in the mountains, denounced Lee for not advancing. As this was the only action with which he had been associated as far as the public knew, his stock took a big drop. He became regarded as no more than a name, with nothing behind it when it came to fighting the enemy.

Lee read the papers, and so did the officers around him. It was not in his nature to defend himself against attacks made in ignorance, nor, as a soldier, to explain military conditions to the public. He was, however, not indifferent. He did not need the support of praise, as his father had, any more than he needed fame. His work for advancement in the Old Army had been for the practical considerations of his family, and those considerations ceased to obtain in the financially poor, makeshift organization of the Confederate forces. Nonetheless, Walter Taylor could see that the newspaper abuse bothered him — perhaps hurting his pride or sense of justice. Taylor asked Lee why he suffered the attacks in silence when the facts were all wrong.

Lee told him, Taylor wrote, "that, while it was very hard to bear, it was perhaps quite natural that such hasty conclusions should be announced, and that it was better not to attempt a justification or defense, but to go on steadily in the discharge of duty to the best of our ability, leaving all else to the calmer judgment of the future and to a kind Providence."

At least the future vindicated him about the three prima donnas. Later in the war, Floyd was dismissed from the service after disgraceful behavior at Fort Donelson in Tennessee; Loring was relieved from command in Jackson's army after insubordinate conduct under that iron disciplinarian, and ended his Confederate career without distinction in the Western armies; Wise in time made the adjustment of acting as a brigadier in a chain of command, though until nearly the end he operated more on detached service than as part of regular commands.

5

Recalled to Richmond, Lee arrived on October 31, looking forward to a trip to Shirley. Mrs. Lee was there, and Lee had not been with his family since he left Arlington in April. His daughters were scattered, in school or refugeeing with friends. But Lee was not able to join his wife at Cousin Hill Carter's. Davis gave him another assignment in coordination, or, as Lee wrote his daughter Mildred, "another forlorn expedition." This time he would leave Virginia as the President's expediter and hurry to bolster the toppling South Atlantic coastal defenses.

With the lesson of the western mountains in mind, Lee asked Davis before he left for a definition of his authority. Davis assured him he held the powers of a full general. With this authority it was his ticklish task to persuade the state-minded governors of South Carolina and Georgia, Francis Pickens and Joseph E. Brown, to permit their state troops to be transferred into the Confederate forces where the assortment of volunteer and militia regiments could become part of the regular organization. The political state consciousness of the governors was so intense and provincial that, though both Brown and Pickens had sent troops to the Virginia theater, large bodies were maintained on state soil outside the Confederate organization.

The problems presented by this dispersion were by no means academic. The Federal fleet was threatening the small, ineffective sea island forts on a three-hundred-mile coastal stretch from south of Charleston to the mouth of the St. Johns River in Florida. Landing parties constantly committed depredations along the rivers, showing the vulnerability of the region to inland attacks that could, at the least, wreck the vital Charleston and Savannah Railroad. The day before Lee arrived in Charleston two of the sea island forts off the Georgia Coast fell. It was clear to him that only the lack of coordination between the Federal naval and army commanders kept amphibious troops from establishing land bases between Charleston and eastern Florida.

Lee established headquarters at Coosawhatchie, "a decrepit and deserted village," as he called it. As the coastal area was formed into a new department, of which he became commander, Lee formed a more imposing staff than any he had previously worked with. Captain T. A. Washington, as assistant adjutant general, Captain Joseph C. lves, an engineering officer, and Lieutenant Colonel William G. Gill, an ordnance officer, joined the faithful Walter Taylor, along with several South Carolinians who served temporarily as aides. Soon the staff was joined by Major Armistead Long, a brilliant artillerist from the Old Army, who was to become a permanent member. A thirty-six-year-old Virginian of distinguished, somewhat dandified appearance, devoted and highly intelligent Long worked sometimes as military secretary as well as informally as chief of artillery.

Mrs. Lee, who had moved from Shirley to her son's home across the Peninsula at the White House, now thought of joining her husband. Ignoring his advice of places to establish herself in safety, she had grown bored with her gypsy life as a refugee. Lee wrote to discourage her from joining him. He said he was seldom at the inaccessible town of Coosawhatchie. Referring to her dawdling habits, he said, "This place is too exposed to attack for the residence of a person as hard to move as you are. You would be captured while you were waiting 'a moment.'" Mrs. Lee compromised by remaining with her daughter-in-law and grandson at the White House.

As Lee wrote, from Coosawhatchie he traveled to all points of the Coast. When his trips were nearby he returned to headquarters in time to have supper by candlelight, after which he wrote messages and papers to eleven or twelve o'clock at night. Since he was a very early riser, the strongly built man functioned on little sleep. As concerned the safety of Mrs. Lee, it was true that Federal actions were spreading beyond tests of arms between armed forces. Though Lee expected the means to the end of Federal victory to get pretty rough, he was outraged at the deliberate crippling of public resources — as when the Federal fleet sought to block Charleston's harbor by sinking stone-laden vessels in the main channel.

On that he wrote the new Secretary of War, Judah P. Benjamin, "The achievement, so unworthy of any nation, is the abortive expression of the malice and revenge . . . It is also indicative of their despair of ever capturing a city they design to ruin, for they can never expect to possess what they labor so hard to reduce to a condition not to be enjoyed."

Privately Lee showed he was also displeased by the weak efforts put forth by many Southerners. He wrote his daughter-in-law Charlotte, "Our country requires now every man to put forth all his ability, regardless of self." To his daughter Annie he wrote that this was not being done.

"Our people have not been earnest enough, have thought too much of themselves and their ease, and instead of turning out to a man, have been content to nurse themselves and their dimes, and leave the protection of themselves and families to others." Then, referring to the criticisms that still rankled, he wrote, "To satisfy their consciences, they have been clamorous in criticising what others have done, and endeavored to prove that they ought to do nothing. This is not the way to accomplish our independence."

The war had also complicated his problem of manumitting Mr. Custis's slaves in the five years allotted in the will, and placing the freed people. He wrote Rooney, "If the war continues, I do not see how it can be accomplished, but they can be hired out and the fund raised applied to their establishment hereafter. If, however, you can not otherwise carry on your farm [without them], they might continue as they are until circumstances permit me to emancipate them. If emancipated under present conditions . . . I do not see what would become of them. I think it, therefore, better to continue them as they are for the present time."

Most of all his thoughts were of his family and the home they had lost. "I think of you all," he wrote to Annie, "in the busy hours of the day and the silent hours of the night, and the recollection of each and every one whiles away the long night, in which my anxious thoughts drive away sleep. But I always feel that you and Agnes [the middle sisters, close to one another] at those times are sound asleep, and that it is immaterial to either where the blockaders are or what their progress is in the river. I hope you are all well, and as happy as you can be in these perilous times to our country."

Then he wrote of the memories evoked by a letter from her. "I am much pleased at your description of Stratford and your visit. It is endeared to me by many recollections and it has always been a great desire of my life to be able to purchase it. Now that we have no other home, and the one we so loved has been so foully polluted, the desire is stronger with me than ever. The horse chestnut you mentioned in the garden was planted by my mother."

To his wife, he wrote of Arlington, "It is better to make up our minds to a general loss. They cannot take away the remembrance of the spot, and the memories of those that to us rendered it sacred. That will remain to us as long as life will last, and that we can preserve. In the absence of a home, I wish I could purchase Stratford. That is the only other place that I could go to, now accessible to us, that would inspire me with feelings of pleasure and local love."

Though his thoughts turned to the scenes he associated with happier times, Lee found he could make positive accomplishments in his job. Working with Pickens and Brown was far simpler than trying to produce harmony between Loring and the homegrown politicoes. Within a few months, he had brought into the field twenty-five thousand troops, with the fundamentals of organization and reasonably well equipped. This work had been no more than a less taxing duplication of his hurried preparations of Virginia's defenses. More testing to his talents, though no more exciting, were his arrangements for containment of the enemy's amphibious forces.

Freed from the self-limitations imposed by "coordinating," Lee worked in broad concepts. Giving orders instead of advice, he displayed for the first time in action the cast of his military thinking. When he went to the South Atlantic, the defensive structure there, as all over the Confederacy, was dispersed over a broad area with a scattering of forces attempting to cover all approaches. (In the Confederate West, the long line across northern Tennessee was giving Albert Sidney Johnston problems that paralyzed the talents of this highly regarded soldier.) Given his first initiative, Lee evolved a defense basically different from that of the prevailing policy.

Right off, he abandoned the small forts on the sea islands, which only provided the enemy with targets for local successes. Then he abandoned any attempt to protect the Charleston-Savannah Railroad along its entire length. Indicating his fundamental difference from dispersed, static defense, he concentrated his forces — while the units were being organized and equipped — *at strategic points*. The strongpoints were built inland, beyond the range of the ships' big guns. To protect those positions from gunboats ascending the inland waterways, he put the gloriously caparisoned recruits to building obstructions in the rivers.

At every strongpoint selected, Lee used his engineering skills to construct works that were advanced for their day as field positions. Wasting none of his Fort Monroe and New York harbor experience, for the big coastal guns mounted at Savannah's Fort Pulaski, he laid the foundations of a defensive structure that lasted throughout the war. In fact, so impregnable was the defensive system he constructed in three months that neither Charleston nor Savannah, surviving constant and heavy bombardment, was taken from the sea nor by flanking amphibious operations.

In making this unsung achievement, which stabilized the coastal defensive front, Lee not only demonstrated his gifts of diplomacy when operating with clearly defined authority. He showed a courteous imperviousness to the outrage of citizen-soldiers whose ideas of chivalric war he offended. The plantation princelings and the city dandies found digging with picks and shovels alien to the pageantries of war, and anyway it was not white man's work. Both men and officers, often of the same social background of privilege, could be difficult to discipline.

At that stage of the Southern states' armed defense, the elected line and field officers (through colonel) were neighborhood leaders more anxious to be liked than to apply discipline. Politically appointed brigadiers regarded their men as constituents rather than as soldiers, and some of those, like Wise, were themselves ignorant of the rudiments of command. Some professionals shrank from antagonizing the self-assertive volunteers, while others did antagonize them by playing the martinet. Lee's way, natural to him, was essentially the same as when he served as superintendent at West Point. There was a tolerance for the human being inside the uniform and a mildness in the discipline. He never had to assert authority because authority was inherent in his presence, a paternalistic authority which, with his impressive clan head appearance, gave reassurance to uprooted men.

The only strong resentment of Lee came from an Ohioan, Roswell Ripley. A thirty-nine-year-old West Pointer, Brigadier General Ripley, after marrying into a South Carolina family, had resigned from the Old Army to enter business in Charleston. In command of the district of South Carolina, Ripley was as contumacious as Loring had been. But Lee was no longer in a position where he relied on his preference for amiable exchanges. He acted on his habit of command, and Ripley received the same treatment as any soldier.

However, when Lee was hurriedly summoned back to Richmond on March 2, the public knew no more of his accomplishments on the Coast than in the mountains. The Confederate lull after First Manassas had been broken in 1862 by successful Federal offensives in Tennessee and off the North Carolina Coast, and the people, disillusioned and lacking heroes, looked for scapegoats. As Joe Johnston had written Davis, Lee had not struck a single blow for the Confederacy — at least, none where the glory lay. In his home state there were those who began to refer to Virginia's formerly number one soldier as "Granny."

### 6

The Richmond Lee returned to in the bleak first week of March, 1862, was a different city from the state capital to which he had come the spring before. Richmond had become a nation's grim capital. Gone were the enthusiastic local preparations begun under Governor Letcher and the confident talk of the battle that would end Lincoln's attempt to govern a free people by force. Gone too were the early commanders with whom Lee had worked on Virginia's defenses. Philip St. George Cocke, the first commander of the Potomac, had resigned from the army because of ill health and then committed suicide. His successor, Bonham, after being himself superseded by Beauregard, had resigned. Returning to the more familiar political arena, Bonham came to Richmond with the Confederate Congress. Daniel Ruggles had been shunted off to the Western armies.

In the city itself Brigadier General John H. Winder, a sixty-two-year-old professional soldier from Baltimore, had established himself as provost marshal, and his "Baltimore plug-uglies" — as the natives called his military police — made life miserable for the soldiers who came to town without leave to see the sights or to get a ride home for a visit. From jails extemporized in tobacco warehouses came the howls and moans of the Confederate prisoners. Winder was also in charge of the Federal prisoners, who had been foolishly placed in the overcrowded capital. Scattered throughout the city were hospitals of all sizes, in which local ladies worked as volunteer nurses.

During all the changes, Virginians soon came to think as Confederates, and the Confederacy had raised grave doubts of its ability to defend itself in what had become full-scale war. In West Tennessee the fall in February of two river forts, Fort Henry and Fort Donelson, uncovered Nashville and led to the first loss of a state capital. Along with this blow to morale was the tangible loss of Nashville's industries and supply depots. By the first of March the Confederates under Albert Sidney Johnston had retreated, closely followed, to Corinth on the border of Mississippi.

Closer to home, Roanoke Island, a key position in the North Carolina Sounds, fell to an amphibious force under Ambrose Burnside, and this reverse was felt particularly in Richmond. One of its crack militia units, the Richmond Light Infantry Blues, suffered severely at Roanoke Island and lost their captain, O. Jennings Wise, the son of ex-Governor Wise and a former Richmond newspaperman.

Brigadier General Wise himself was in command of the district, and he repeated his personality clashes with his superior, Huger, the pompous commander of Norfolk. The "permanent" Confederate Congress, then in session in Richmond, followed the familiar routines brought from Washington and appointed a committee to fix the blame for the disaster. The scapegoat was the brilliant Judah P. Benjamin, whom the President had unwisely placed in the War Secretary's post. This was a key spot, and Benjamin not only knew nothing about military affairs but Davis had appointed him in the face of popular opposition. Urbane Benjamin refused to defend himself by exposing Confederate deficiencies and cross-purposes in command, and the reproaches spread to his friend Jefferson Davis.

Congress and the people had had their confidence shaken in the President as commander in chief since the innocent days when he made his triumphal arrival into the city. Davis had also lost some early supporters — the first two Secretaries of State and the first Secretary of War — and made some enemies, but these were only contributory causes of the disenchantment. Basically, as it became clear that the Confederacy could have no life except by surviving a determined invasion, it became clear that the military defenses were too much for a one-man job, especially with Davis surrounding himself with civilians.

To remedy the situation, Congress passed a resolution to place a general in the War Department, without prejudice to his field rank. It was assumed Davis would supplant the disliked Benjamin with Lee, since the President seemed happy to use Lee as his executive, anyway. As Davis was familiar with Lee's behind-the-scenes achievement, he greatly admired him, and members of Congress were aware of this, as well as being themselves aware of Lee's work. Davis, however, did not want Lee officially in the war office.

Then Congress went further and passed a resolution to create "the office of commanding general of the armies of the Confederate states" to "be charged, under the direction of the President, with the general control of military operations, the movement and discipline of the troops, and the distribution of the supplies among the armies . . . and may, when he shall deem it advisable, take command in person of our army or armies in the field." This office — with Lee as its occupant — would be similar to the post of general in chief held by McClellan in the Federal armies.

There was never a chance that Davis would do anything except veto this measure. It came too close to invading his realm of authority as commander in chief, and he wanted to keep the War Department completely subordinate to him. The moves in Congress did force Davis to effect a compromise that satisfied everybody except Lee. Shifting Benjamin to the State Department, Davis installed in the War Department George W. Randolph. Recently commissioned brigadier, Randolph was the former commander of the Richmond Howitzer Battalion who had become Magruder's chief of artillery. To appease Congress and keep Lee where he wanted him, Davis ordered Lee "assigned to duty at the seat of government, and, under the direction of the President, is charged with the conduct of military operations in the armies of the Confederacy."

To civilians this sounded like an approximation of the commanding general post. Lee knew better. It returned him to an approximation of his duties when Davis first came to Richmond — only now the tedious details of office work would embrace the whole Confederacy and not merely Virginia. He wrote his wife, still at Rooney's White House, "I do not see either advantage or pleasure in my duties. But I will not complain, but do my best. I do not see at present either that it will enable me to see much more of you. In the present condition of affairs no one can foresee what may happen, nor in my judgment is it advisable for any one to make any arrangements with a view to permanency or pleasure."

What Lee was not saying was that military conditions in Virginia looked as if one concerted push by the enemy would bring down the whole system of scattered, dispersed defenses. For the third time in a Davis assignment Lee was called upon in an emergency, and in this he was powerless to act at all.

7

In beginning his dismal duties in an atmosphere of general apprehension, Lee endured the personal pain of seeing his last son leave college to go into the army. "Little Rob," as Lee often referred to him, came to Richmond, put up at the Spotswood, and the next morning his father went with him to get his overcoat and blanket. "God grant it may be for his good," Lee wrote his wife. "As He has permitted it, I must be resigned."

Lee was also saddened to attend the bedside of Bishop William Meade during his last hours. The former Alexandria rector called him Robert and recalled the days, in Lee's mother's lifetime, when the boy used to say the catechism to him. But Lee had little time for personal feelings. He could only rarely see his daughter Mary, then staying with friends in Richmond.

The President called on him at all hours for fruitless consultations, some of which properly belonged in the functions of a general staff and some in the War Department. Since Davis operated as his own staff and usurped many of the functions of the war office, Lee's duties as an executive were made more confusing by lack of defined purposes and, again, by lack of authority. It worked out that Lee was "charged with the conduct of military operations" that were not important enough for Davis to concentrate on personally but which he wished to retain "under the direction of the President." That came in the area of Davis's obsession with the shift of troops from one defensive point to the other.

In his need of omnipotence, Davis worked all hours to prepare against every known contingency. These defensive preparations gave him the illusion of being protected against the chances of war, but actually they nullified the possibility both of unified action toward a strategic end and of exploitation of the enemy's commitments. While the charts of his widely dispersed defensive garrisons gave Davis a sense of security against the threat of the unexpected that would be outside his control, the enemy was presented with a static system against which he could operate without fear of counterdevelopments. As these dispersals were antithetical to all of Lee's principles of warfare, his work was done without a sense of bringing independence any nearer.

Lee's most significant achievements, and most thankless, were in those areas unprovided for in Davis's departmental charts. All departments — commissary, quartermaster, medical, engineering, transportation, ordnance, and countless subdepartments — had been formed along the existing United States models. In this the Confederate bureau faithfully reproduced the inefficiency inherent in bureaucratic red tape. Where a rich, established nation could afford the luxury of waste (at least when opposed to a poor, improvised nation one-fourth its size), the poorer, smaller country, struggling for its very existence, needed to utilize the maximum of its physical potential. Since the unimaginative organizations failed to accomplish that, the bureaucratic system made it difficult to discover the source of shortages or complete lapses.

Some department heads labored manfully. Semi-autonomous operations, like Gorgas's ordnance department and the armament manufacturing at the Tredegar Iron Works, performed minor miracles in producing cannon, powder, ammunition and rifles. In all too many cases unmet emergency needs were ignored on the principle that they might go away. Case-hardened bureaucrats, like Northrop in the commissary department, devoted their talents to legalistic explanations and developed deftness in shifting the blame to others. Lee, in his habit of doing the best he could with whatever task was assigned him, performed countless of the unheroic, vital chores that otherwise would have not gotten done.

Lee seemed to find no pleasurable diversions from the fretful work that confined him in the noisy office. Though his horses were stabled in Richmond, he evidently did not take the relaxation of a daily ride. His routine consisted of the one-block walk from the Spotswood Hotel to Ninth and Main, which the blustery March weather turned into a wind tunnel, and then up the hill to Mechanics' Hall. At intervals he would be called from the room, overheated by the potbellied stove, for a quick cold journey along the foot of Capitol Square to the President's office in the old Customs House. For his main meal at midday he went back to the hotel, and presumably dined with members of his staff. At night, nothing indicates that he left his room. Judging from the unusually few letters he wrote his wife and children, he must have been nervously worn by the day-long suppression of agitation from picayune chores, Davis's interruptions and the uninspired attitude of those bureau officials who were time-servers even in a revolution.

Lee was among the men who assumed an individual responsibility for his sphere as if the total operation depended upon him. He worked through the existing system, such as it was, without being protected by the "organization." Nothing of a buffer existed between him, as autonomously responsible, and the fate of the nation. In this, he perpetuated the character of his earliest Virginia ancestors who, in a wilderness, had assumed total responsibility for their own fates. As he had written from South Carolina, Lee believed that only by individuals assuming this total responsibility could the whole, formed of these parts, successfully maintain itself against invasion.

He believed this even while daily encountering all too few of the completely responsible men. He worked with men as they were, and one of the most difficult for him was Joe Johnston. To his other tasks had been added the maintenance of liaison between Johnston and his mortal enemy, the President.

8

Johnston was one of those men who brought their habit of thinking intact from the Old Army. He did depend on the organization, and never himself thought in terms of the whole. Nor did he adjust his attitude to the special needs of a revolutionary movement. He was most cavalier in assuming that such gritty problems as subsistence and transportation, or rush engineering jobs on bridges and fortifications, would be attended to as in a nation with working machinery and unlimited resources. At the same time, Johnston promoted disruptions in the supporting services by holding communications with Richmond to a minimum and whenever possible avoiding the President in his role of acting chief of staff.

Before Lee assumed his duties, the deteriorating relationship between Davis and Johnston had reached a climax when the general withdrew from his fortifications on the Manassas line (March 8-9) and fell back to Fredericksburg. He and Davis had agreed on the evacuation, as all signs pointed to the imminence of a move by McClellan's Army of the Potomac. Their differences arose over details, especially where Davis interfered with troop organization and Johnston evaded the President's wishes by procrastination. Then, when Davis's directives over the withdrawal became profuse and contradictory, Johnston simply moved without advising the President and broke communications with Richmond.

On the Federal side, McClellan also went his own way. Defying first the clamorous civilians who had learned nothing from McDowell's premature offensive, then the Radicals in Lincoln's government who demanded action for the sake of headlines (as well as devious purposes of their own), and finally Lincoln, McClellan used seven months in perfecting probably the most meticulously organized and handsomely equipped army ever in existence. By then, no longer in favor and removed from the general-in-chief post, the formerly hailed "Young Napoleon" was forced to work through a new Secretary of War, Edwin Stanton, who at least by his actions appeared to be McClellan's avowed enemy.

Stanton, a Washington lawyer from the Midwest, was a bitter, treacherous man, driven by choleric energy and appetite for power. Though a Democrat and a slippery politician, he was among those men whose aggressions found release in the hostile aspects of abolitionism, and he acted with the Radicals in the bonds of common hatred of the South. And this group, committed to prolonging the war until slavery could be made an issue, was vehemently opposed to everything the conservative McClellan stood for.

Handsome young McClellan, with his gallant appearance and dramatic movements — always riding his black horse at a gallop — was a complex man whose methods were basically at variance with his public "image." He had persuaded Lincoln, against the President's and Stanton's preference, to give reluctant approval to a waterborne offensive against Richmond. In this, transporting his army to Fort Monroe, he would advance eighty miles over the flat Peninsula with both flanks protected by gunboats on the York and James rivers, and his naval supply supporting him to within striking distance of the Confederate capital. This invasion route, far more imaginative and promising than a straight land approach south from Washington, implemented a conviction of McClellan as well as expressing his fundamental character.

What he aimed at was a largely bloodless campaign. As had his predecessor, Scott, he believed in overwhelming the secessionists with a minimum of the destructiveness attendant upon invading armies occupying the land in bitter ground-fighting. In terms of restoring the Union this would achieve a settlement without the rise of hatreds and a lasting divisiveness. At the same time, by avoiding the hazards of a war of maneuver, he would insure victory by massing armament the Confederates could not match. This would enshrine McClellan as hero. But, on this road to fulfilling his early promise as "the savior of the nation," "Little Mac" played the double game of assuring his government of his intention to crush the Rebels in battles which he did not expect to fight. The original Napoleon had not been so bombastically purple in his heroic pronouncements.

Joe Johnston, never taken in by McClellan's verbal heroics, had not expected McClellan to attack his fixed works at Centreville. When Johnston slipped away from Manassas, he adroitly placed his army on the Rappahannock, where he could move to counter McClellan's advance from any direction. Davis, naturally antagonized by being kept in the dark about Johnston's withdrawal, made an issue over Johnston's abandonment of great quantities of food, guns and supplies.

Lee was outside all that. He was drawn into the main theater when the ships of McClellan's armada appeared off Fort Monroe in late March. Magruder wrote him on March 20 of signs of the enemy being reinforced from ships — "the whistling of steamers and the sound of drums." By March 24 Magruder and Huger wrote definitely of the ships arriving and the enemy's swelling numbers. No one knew that these troops came from McClellan's army (though that was a reasonable assumption), nor could anyone hazard their objective. The Federals might be aiming to reinforce Burnside for an inland thrust into North Carolina in the region south of Norfolk, or at Norfolk itself, or Richmond by way of the Peninsula. Norfolk seemed likely. This was the base of the *Virginia*, the ironclad rebuilt from the scuttled U.S. frigate *Merrimack*, with plates rolled at the Tredegar Iron Works. This was the first of the Confederacy's inventive contrivances used as substitutes for a navy. As the U.S. Navy's wooden ships were helpless against this monster, the *Virginia-Merrimack* blocked McClellan's use of the James River.

The problem for Lee was that he must assist in shuttling troops from one threatened point to another in accordance with plans that, not his own, were alien to his thinking. In Davis's system defensive units were spread across the state from Huger at Norfolk to three small, separated forces in the southwestern mountains, without any plan to coordinate their action nor any military authority responsible for the whole. Johnston, while acutely conscious of his area of authority, was concerned primarily with his own army. With this army, the basis of his strategy was to keep it out of harm's way. Lee's first job (something Davis did not want) was to draw troops from Joe Johnston's army in middle Virginia to Magruder on the Peninsula.

In the beginning of the ticklish business of removing troops from a general's command, Lee established an accord with his old friend. Johnston seemed pleased to be in communication with another soldier and appeared cooperative in spirit. When Lee asked if Johnston could "move" from twenty thousand to thirty thousand men to the Peninsula, Johnston answered that he could "bring" twenty-five thousand men. He would leave a force at the Rappahannock to mask the movement, while holding Jackson's small detached force in the Valley.

The next day a telegram was sent Johnston, asking for ten thousand troops at once, and the brief harmony was over. Obeying the order, Johnston protested to Lee (not to Davis) against this division of force. Ten thousand troops would be an insufficient addition to contain an enemy's movement on the Peninsula, while weakening his army against a thrust from the north. Though this normally would represent Lee's line of thought, Johnston's arguments took a specious turn. The enemy north of the Rappahannock looked quiescent if Johnston was to "bring" twenty-five thousand men for the Peninsula; but if ten thousand men were to be taken from him, the enemy on his front appeared menacing.

It was understandable that any general would resist a hacking away of his army. As he could not be expected to give his human resistance as an argument for the integrity of his army, Johnston's point was, "We can not win without concentration." Since, by his own statements, the potential danger on his front seemed as great as the then unknown size of the danger on the Peninsula, neither place could be logically selected as the point of concentration. While "concentration" made a good academic argument, under the circumstances it was impossible to escape the conclusion that Johnston had advanced it to prevent the dismantling of his own army.

Lee wrote soothingly of the importance the President attached to a strong line along the Rappahannock, to protect the Virginia Central Railroad connecting the capital with the fertile Shenandoah Valley, and attempted to reestablish the accord. Johnston ignored Lee's letter. That was March 28. During the following harried week in Richmond, with daily and hourly messages from Magruder bringing information of the enemy's growing strength at Fort Monroe, Johnston remained silent. He neither asked for information about the Peninsula nor sent any about his own front. Lee, presumably under Davis's instructions, continued to withdraw troops from uncommunicative Johnston, until by April 4 thirty thousand men were on their way to Yorktown.

On April 5, McClellan made, for him, a precipitate move. He tried to turn Magruder's works at Yorktown and take the fortified old river port in the rear. From "Prince John's" Old Army reputation as a bon vivant, McClellan apparently did not take him seriously, and the maps supplied by old General Wool at Fort Monroe did not indicate the extent of Magruder's ingenious fortifications. The Warwick River and its meandering tributaries crossed Magruder's narrow front, and by building dams at five fords (making them impassable) he flooded the naturally boggy country. General Keyes commanded the Federal corps at the head of the flanking movement made in a dismal rain. He brought his troops to a slithering halt in the swamps when guns opened from where depots were supposed to be. He advised McClellan of a strongly fortified front which could be forced only at a high cost in life. McClellan's ardor for a rapid movement quickly cooled.

Unknown to the Confederates, on this same day McClellan was advised by Washington that his largest corps, McDowell's, was to be held from him to protect Washington. It happened that, on March 23, Stonewall Jackson had been repulsed in an attack at Kernstown, outside of Winchester. Though he fielded no more than five thousand troops, his aggression either convinced Stanton or gave him an excuse to claim that the thirty-five thousand Federal troops under Banks were needed to protect Washington from the Valley route. At the same time Brigadier General James Wadsworth, a Republican political general in charge of the Washington defenses, protested to Stanton that McClellan was leaving him with only second-line units in the twenty thousand men designated for the Washington forts. Washington was a sensitive spot to the Republicans, with their insecure tenure, and many military decisions involving the capital were made for political considerations. But Stanton's act did seem to support McClellan's belief in his enmity. The War Secretary withdrew one-fourth of the army, which McClellan had painstakingly built for his invasion, to stand guard where even Wadsworth admitted no Confederates threatened. And in the forts 408 guns commanded all approaches. To make it complete, McDowell and Banks were placed in separate departments responsible to Stanton.

With this disruption to his army and plans, McClellan settled down to take Yorktown by siege. Maybe he would have anyway. He had brought along in his siege trains fifty seacoast guns which needed to be ferried to the front and mounted on stationary platforms. But McDowell provided him with an excuse, or a rationalization, for abandoning rapid movement.

Having failed to overrun Magruder, he could do nothing until Yorktown was evacuated. With crossfire batteries at Gloucester Point across the York River, the heavy guns in Yorktown held the United States gunboats at bay and blocked McClellan's use of the York as the ironclad *Virginia* blocked the James.

From McClellan's deliberateness after his April 5 sortie, the Confederates suspected that he planned to undertake siege operations. Though Magruder had no more than twelve thousand infantry and the Federals fielded upwards of one hundred thousand of all arms, McClellan had then made it plain that Richmond was his objective and he could gain nothing by attacking a fixed position at Yorktown. When this became certain, the bulk of Johnston's army was shifted to the Peninsula and Johnston was brought on personally to assume command of the new main front.

On April 13, Johnston was formally given command of all troops in Tidewater Virginia, including Norfolk, while retaining command of the scattered forces in middle Virginia. This was all he had asked for, in concentration and in scope of authority. He was not satisfied. After one day at Yorktown he returned to Richmond and requested an audience with the President. When Lee was asked to the meeting, he knew that his attempt at establishing harmony had failed. Instead of being a "coordinator" again, he was — of all things he dreaded — to be drawn in between factionalists.

## 9

Lee climbed the staircase to the second floor of the Government Building for the afternoon meeting called by the President. This was not to be one of the routine and futile discussions that wasted his time. Once again he had to choose sides in what amounted to hostilities, with an old friend on the opposing side. He and Johnston were no longer intimates, and their military relations were strained, but Lee still regarded him as a friend.

Lee found Davis looking thin and haggard, his features sharpened by recessed cheeks. New War Secretary Randolph was already there. Then dapper Johnston arrived, bringing with him two impressively large men, Major General Gustavus Smith and Major General James Longstreet.

Smith, a handsome Kentuckian, was a former "big name" at West Point whom Lee had met in the engineers in Mexico. Later resigned from the army, Smith became street commissioner of New York City, and such was his reputation that when he volunteered after First Manassas Davis commissioned him with seniority over all officers below Lee and Johnston in Virginia.

Longstreet, a burly laconic man, wore a bushy beard over rather coarse features, and steady blue eyes looked at the world in aggressive self-confidence. Born in South Carolina of people of Dutch antecedents from New Jersey, his strongest state attachment was Georgia, where his uncle, Judge A. B. Longstreet, was a widely known and esteemed scholar. A paymaster major in the Old Army, he had been given a Virginia brigade before Manassas and by his assured handling of troops had risen rapidly in Johnston's estimation. Longstreet and Smith were poker-playing companions at Johnston's sociable headquarters.

Davis told Johnston to state his proposal. With no beating about the bush, Johnston stated flatly that Yorktown was indefensible against McClellan's heavy artillery. Since, then, withdrawal was an eventual necessity, he wanted to retire at once. He did not want to fight on the lower Peninsula at all, nor with his available numbers. He proposed a withdrawal all the way to Richmond, where a concentration could be built by stripping coastal garrisons from North Carolina to Georgia. Again Lee heard the academically convincing argument of concentration.

Before Lee said anything, Randolph spoke up. He talked urgently against the evacuation of Yorktown on the grounds that Norfolk would be uncovered, forcing the *Virginia* to be scuttled. With this ironclad the only obstacle to the Federal Navy in the James River, gunboats could be at Richmond by the time Johnston was. Though this was a sound argument, and none could deny that gunboats could force the evacuation of the capital, Johnston's point was that the abandonment of Yorktown was inevitable.

Then Lee came in, very carefully. He pointed out indirectly that Johnston's proposed concentration at Richmond isolated his movement from the complex of military factors of which Yorktown was only a part. Burnside had recently occupied New Bern, on the North Carolina coast, and removal of troops from his front would invite an inland invasion aimed at the Weldon Railroad. Protection of this lifeline of Richmond with the Coastal South was basic in any strategy. Then, a wholesale removal of troops from South Carolina and Georgia would not only expose the Coastal front which Lee had just stabilized but politically precipitate something close to another secession movement.

As a "presidential adviser" and not a policy maker, Lee could say no more. But clearly his concepts were different from Johnston's. Always he wanted to engage the enemy as far from the capital as possible. Never by choice would he concentrate, as Johnston planned, for a purely defensive stand that could exert no effect on the enemy's arrangements. Even tactically Johnston's proposed concentration offered dubious advantage. If the Confederates abandoned other positions — announcing the intention of assembling at Richmond — the Federals had more men, shorter lines and better transportation for doing the same thing.

Lee's unexpressed concepts, deriving from his character as a soldier, were fundamentally antithetical to both Davis's scheme of defense and Johnston's plan within it. Where Davis personally needed to provide against all contingencies, Johnston, ingrained with the Old Army principle that the best record is achieved by the fewest mistakes, was absorbed with avoiding the enemy's intentions. But Lee, without their self-protectiveness, had never forgotten the lessons of Scott's military opportunism. Like Lincoln in the political sphere, he possessed the implicit self-confidence to go with unfolding events. He could of course recognize that the evacuation of Yorktown was eventually inevitable. Time, however, would give him the opportunity to seek favorable developments and to discover means of "upsetting the enemy's prearrangements."

Lee knew McClellan, Joe Johnston's intimate friend from the Old Army, who was in many ways similar. From his extensive preparations and methodical methods of approach, as well as his quick shift to siege operations against inferior numbers, McClellan showed his own need of certainties, of eliminating the possibility of human error. Knowing that McClellan would give them the time, Lee could forcefully support Randolph in disapproving of an immediate evacuation, without developing his own private ideas.

Nothing that Lee or Randolph said made any impression on Johnston. His mind was made up. The harangue went on all afternoon, with Davis mostly listening. The two camps separated for dinner, and then returned to drone over the same points until the exhaustion of boredom ended the unsatisfactory conference. Before the men parted, Davis gave the order to Johnston: Yorktown must be defended.

When Lee left the meeting, he could not know that Johnston had no intention of obeying the President's order. Johnston later wrote, "The belief that the events on the Peninsula would soon compel the Confederate government to the necessity of adopting my method of opposing the Federal army, reconciled me somewhat to obeying the President's order." By this he meant he would make his stand at Richmond and not, as the government expected, on the Peninsula. He would, of course, remain at Yorktown until McClellan's siege guns were moved up into position, and this was all that Lee immediately counted on. Time.

For, while Johnston was planning to cross his government — as McClellan was his — Lee developed a surprisingly Machiavellian course of his own. He opened a third operation between the conflicting controls of Davis and Johnston. Politically conservative Lee, nonsecessionist and reluctant Rebel, was the one who brought to the secessionists' struggle true revolutionary thinking. While Davis elaborated Constitutional theories of their rights and Johnston acted as if the United States was behind him and not McClellan, Lee took the big risks — personally and militarily. He maneuvered to circumvent Davis's departments and Johnston's areas of authority by preparing a counterstroke during the time McClellan used to move up into position the siege guns capable of throwing 176 tons of metal a day into Yorktown.

## CHAPTER VIII

# "Richmond Must Be Defended"

I N APRIL'S lovely weather, gloom gathered in the war offices building. The staff officers and clerks in Lee's office collected the rumors and gossip that circulated through the War Department on the floor below. From some unknown source a distorted version of the meeting with Johnston had been picked up and War Department circles were saying that Johnston had been *ordered* to evacuate Yorktown and retire to Richmond. As this was Johnston's private purpose, perhaps some leak from his headquarters had gotten mixed up with fragments of news gathered about the conference. This was frightening information to men with families in the city. It was also information that could be soon known in Washington.

Spies infested Richmond. A rounded-up group of spies, in order to save their own skins, testified against Timothy Webster, the most resourceful spy to operate in the city. Webster was publicly hanged at the Fair Grounds at the western end of Franklin Street, and the spectacle caused the first traffic jam on that stately street. Apparently all the prostitutes who had flocked to the wartime capital hired hacks for the occasion. But no one thought the death of Webster and dispersion of his operators ended spy activity in Richmond.

However, the gloom was not caused only by the fear of McClellan's army following Johnston to Richmond. There was a general sense of collapse. In the War Department the clerks talked of one newspaper's prediction that it would all be over by June 15. Early in April the Confederacy's Western Army failed to win a crucial battle at Shiloh, on the northern border of Mississippi, and Albert Sidney Johnston bled to death from a leg wound he ignored during the battle. Later in the month New Orleans fell. In Virginia the feeling was that there were too many Federal troops in the state, and nothing since Manassas indicated the Confederate commanders would do any better than those in the West.

Davis became the object on whom the feelings of apprehension were released. After being privately baptized in his home, the President had received confirmation in St. Paul's Church. A wag in the war office said, "I think Mr. Davis is turning for help to some Higher Power than England and France." But J. B. Jones, a fiction writer from Baltimore serving as clerk, heard more sinister motives whispered around the water cooler. Cromwell and Richard III had professed Christianity before their usurpations of power. Already Davis was reducing aristocratic Randolph, Jefferson's grandson, to the status of clerk.

Even to Lee, respecting Davis for doing his best, it was obvious that the President was doing too much himself in military operations and that War Secretary Randolph lacked authority. And whatever Lee suspected about Johnston's withdrawal, he did write his daughter-in-law Charlotte, trying to run the White House in Rooney's absence, to sell off the corn and wheat as quickly as possible. McClellan's army would pass that way. Yet it was the combination of Davis's distraction, Johnston's incommunicativeness and Randolph's subordination that made possible Lee's independent action between all lines of authority.

On April 20 the generalized apprehensions in the war offices building became suddenly narrowed to Richmond. McDowell's corps, which had been withheld from McClellan, started moving southward from Alexandria to Fredericksburg. Besides the immediate threat to the Virginia Central, McDowell's force could have for its ultimate objective only Richmond — and junction with McClellan. Between McDowell's thirty-three thousand and Richmond stood only Field's brigade, twenty-five hundred on paper, at Fredericksburg. McDowell's movement brought his force into the area of Johnston's authority, but Johnston did nothing. It was at this stage Lee began to act without consulting Johnston.

First, Lee presumably obtained Davis's permission to initiate some troop movements. In the absence of records, this is presumed because nothing was more jealously guarded by the President than the authority to move troops, even a regiment, from one place to another. (In addition to the authority, the details of troop disposition fascinated Davis, and the absorption seemed to bolster his sense of security.) Lee had then gained the President's confidence, and Davis never dreamed that the patient expediter planned to introduce cause-and-effect strategy into Virginia's defenses.

Neither Davis nor Lincoln had any comprehension of the strategic principle in which movement was initiated against one point to *effect* the enemy's operation at another point. This was the chief reason why Lincoln opposed McClellan's waterborne invasion: he was never convinced by McClellan that the threat of the Federal Army at Richmond would force the Confederates to concentrate there — and, hence, away from Washington. For the same reason Lincoln permitted Stanton to immobilize upwards of seventy thousand troops for the protection of Washington while McClellan's army was distant. It was Lee's purpose to keep the Federals immobilized in protection of Washington — and, hence, away from Richmond.

After one year (almost to the day) since he had offered his services to his state, the desk-general was going to put into practice, in a modest way, his theory of "disrupting the enemy's prearrangements." His immediate objective was to immobilize McDowell at Fredericksburg. The key figure in this operation was to be Major General Jackson, then in the Shenandoah Valley. Returned to obscurity since the day at Manassas that won him his public sobriquet of "Stonewall" (his men called him "Old Jack"), this Cromwellian warrior was chafing at a peripheral assignment that held him inactive in observing Banks's Federal force.

Simultaneously with developing the strategic move with Jackson, Lee began to collect some weight of numbers and armaments to place in McDowell's path from Fredericksburg. As far as Davis, Johnston and Randolph's gossipy War Department knew, that was all Lee was doing.

2

When Lee started his quiet moves, the Confederate troop dispersals across middle Virginia would have been irresistible targets to any aggressive Federal general. But Davis's scattered and uncoordinated units were spared by the fact that two lawyers, Lincoln and Stanton, had taken military operations over from the professionals, and the exposed commands were, for the moment, uselessly employed rather than endangered.

Westward from Field's brigade at Fredericksburg, Dick Ewell was stationed east of the Blue Ridge with a force of about eighty-five hundred — an infantry division, with artillery and some cavalry. In the Valley, Jackson had built up his force with new conscripts to about eight thousand of all arms. West of him in the Alleghenies, Edward Johnson had a brigade of something around three thousand, and in the southwest were other isolated oddments. Lee's purpose was to combine the forces of Jackson, Ewell and Johnson for a Valley counteroffensive while strengthening Field's brigade.

Fredericksburg was on the southern bank of the Rappahannock River, whose northern bank rose in cliffs to command the small city. Field withdrew his troops south of the river, passed through the hilly streets of charming city houses and took up a position on the ridge south of town. Charlie Field, a stockily built professional who had been a lieutenant in the 2nd Cavalry when Lee commanded, could be counted upon neither to panic nor to permit his small force to be gobbled up. To his lines the Richmond, Fredericksburg and Potomac Railroad brought the fresh units Lee detached from garrisons along the South Atlantic.

Since Lee avoided the "stripping" of these garrisons which Joe Johnston had advocated, with the authority of Davis's trust and his own diplomacy it was simple for him to make small withdrawals from each department. In this way he aroused no local protests nor dislocated the defensive systems he himself had devised. From the twenty-four thousand mostly state troops in North Carolina, Lee shifted north Joseph R. Anderson's four-thousand-man brigade. A West Pointer whom the government was soon to transfer to the management of his own cannon-producing Tredegar Iron Works, Anderson had pronounced administrative abilities and Lee placed him in charge of the growing force at Fredericksburg. Then, from the thirty-two thousand mostly state troops in South Carolina and Georgia, Lee brought up Maxcy Gregg's fine brigade of thirty-five thousand South Carolinians. From North Carolina, Lee also drew a couple of regiments, another odd regiment and two field batteries from around Richmond. Attracting no attention, he soon collected more than ten thousand troops, supported by guns, at Fredericksburg. While not a formidable force, the combined brigades attained a significance beyond a mere observation detail.

Lee's maneuvers with Jackson were trickier. He had no authority over the Valley commander. Before Johnston left his Rappahannock line for Yorktown, he specifically instructed Jackson and Ewell to communicate with him through the adjutant general's office. Instead, presumably on the President's orders, their infrequent and (until April 21) routine messages were forwarded from the adjutant general's office across the hall to Lee. As Johnston neither sent orders nor asked information from the detached commanders, Lee exploited this looseness of organization to edge into Johnston's area of authority.

Lee was not personally acquainted with the thirty-eight-year-old Jackson, nor had he corresponded with him since the early days when Jackson was at Harper's Ferry. However, he must have seen enough of Jackson's recent correspondence to know that the Valley commander was the one Confederate in Virginia who shared his own cause-and-effect view of crippling McClellan's plans. In early April, when Longstreet was temporarily in command of the Rappahannock line, Jackson had written several letters to Longstreet suggesting a collaborative movement against Banks's Federal force in the Valley. In these letters Jackson revealed his chafing to get at the enemy and, instead of merely observing, to seize the initiative for the purpose of disrupting the enemy's plans. "If Banks is defeated, it may greatly retard McClellan's movements."

To this strategist Lee wrote first on April 21, describing McDowell's concentration at Fredericksburg. Then, without explanations, he made the simple suggestion: "If you can use General Ewell's division [east of the Blue Ridge] in an attack on General Banks, and can drive him back, it will prove a great relief to the pressure on Fredericksburg." Though Lee gave him alternative choices, that was the line — as Lee evidently expected — Jackson pounced upon.

At that time McDowell, with Shields's division temporarily detached, approached Fredericksburg with thirty-three thousand men. In the Valley, Banks, with Shields's division, fielded twenty thousand directly in front of Jackson. Blenker's division, also detached from McDowell, was traveling north of Winchester with ten thousand. Scattered Federal forces in the Manassas area numbered about sixty-five hundred, and scattered forces in the Alleghenies — under Frémont, Schenk and Milroy — numbered another nine thousand. Lee and Jackson were going to attempt to immobilize these seventy-thousand-odd soldiers, not counting the garrison troops in the Washington forts, with fewer troops than in Banks's single command.

General Banks, the former Massachusetts governor, held the key unit in the Lee-Jackson plan. Prior to April 21, Banks and Jackson had the same orders — to observe the other. Beyond that, when Banks grew convinced there was no harm in Jackson's force, he was to send reinforcements to McDowell. As of April 20, since Jackson had retired southward after his Kernstown battle in late March, he remained quiescent in a camp east of Harrisonburg near a pass over the Blue Ridge. So little mischief was anticipated that Brigadier General James Shields, temporarily under Banks, wrote directly to the Secretary of War (in the Federals' own disarranged chains of command) asking permission to return to McDowell and join a movement in support of McClellan.

Jackson used Lee's April 21 letter as the authority to change the Federal attitude about his innocuousness. Stonewall Jackson was naturally hidebound in demanding observances of the regular channels of command. But, in his determination to break the inaction of waiting on the enemy's initiative, he also took advantage of the smeared command lines to open a correspondence directly with Lee. By April 29, Jackson, addressing Lee as "Commanding C.S. Army," offered three possible offensives. The one Lee liked proposed that Jackson join Edward Johnson west of Staunton to form a combined force to dispose of Milroy in the mountains, and then — with danger removed from the west — to bring the joint force back to the Valley. During Jackson's absence, Ewell would move into the Valley on Banks's front, where he would be ready to strike when Jackson returned with Johnson.

Lee observed the military amenities by avoiding giving specific instructions to an officer technically in Johnston's command. Writing Jackson that he must use his own discretion, the "military adviser" managed to indicate his preference for the offensive which combined the three separate forces.

Using this as his authority, Jackson secretly moved his troops away from Banks's front. Through the mud, with complete secrecy he started his little army to the Alleghenies on what became Jackson's "Valley Campaign."

### 3

The same day that Lee wrote Jackson, May 1, a clerk brought him a telegram Johnston had sent Davis. Lee read that Johnston was to evacuate Yorktown immediately. For a week Lee had received messages from Johnston which seemed to be preparing Richmond for his withdrawal from the Peninsula. McClellan's massing artillery made "certain" the result at Yorktown, he said. But then, only two days before, Johnston had suddenly abandoned all his suggestions for the defense of Richmond and, to Lee's surprise, proposed a general offensive that bore no relation to the realities. "Collect all the troops we have in the East and cross the Potomac with them, while Beauregard, with all we have in the West, invades Ohio . . . Please submit this suggestion to the President."

If nothing else, it would have been logistically impossible to move and concentrate the scattered units in the East anywhere near the Potomac before the Federals massed twice the number. In the West, Beauregard, who had succeeded Albert Sidney Johnston, was then trying to rebuild the battered army at Corinth, Mississippi. He was only allowed this breather because Henry Halleck, commanding Federal forces in the West, was preparing siege operations instead of attacking. Lee spared the President the shock of reading Johnston's fanciful flight. He wrote Johnston that the "feasibility" of a move to the Potomac had been considered for some while. As for "the proposed invasion of Ohio by General Beauregard," Lee simply said, "however desirable, it is feared at this time it is impractical."

Then, with no further reference to the general offensive, Johnston wired the President that he was evacuating Yorktown immediately. Caught by surprise, Davis himself telegraphed Johnston to ask if the safety of his army would permit them time to remove the public property from the Norfolk Navy Yard. When Johnston ignored this telegram, Davis followed his first wire with an incomprehensible message. "It is a necessity that you should send General Smith or General Longstreet to the Army of the North [the troops in Middle Virginia]. I dislike to tax you at this time, but it is unavoidable and admits of no delay."

The only objective Davis could have had in mind for the large divisions from Johnston's army was Fredericksburg, which McDowell then occupied. Since the President could scarcely be unaware of Lee's work in that area, his senseless message to Johnston appeared to be a manifestation of the strain to his overtaxed nerves. Johnston also ignored that message.

Davis forgot the move that "admits of no delay" and asked Lee to ask Johnston if he could not delay his withdrawal a few days. Lee sent his wire on May 2. Johnston ignored it.

Lee was helpless to do anything except keep his own control in the irrationality engulfing him. In the collapse of Davis's system, the President and Johnston themselves seemed to be suffering some kind of collapse of their own. It was fantastic that the commander in chief of a nation would permit a field general to break off communications and that the general of the nation's main army wanted to isolate his actions from the complex operations on which he was dependent and of which his army was the center.

A chain of emergencies was set in motion by the evacuation of Yorktown, beginning with the fate of Norfolk. Lee, imprisoned in the office, thought of his crippled wife at the White House, with their daughter-in-law and grandson. At any day McClellan's army would be there.

Johnston had abandoned Yorktown on the night of the 4th, but the news reached Lee, Randolph and Davis indirectly. Johnston was having nothing to do with any of them. They did not even know if Johnston had made any preparations for saving the ordnance, ammunition and stores accumulated in Norfolk. Davis hurried off Randolph and Stephen Mallory, Secretary of the Navy, to the doomed port city.

Shortly after the two dignitaries arrived in Norfolk, a staff officer from Johnston reported to General Huger with orders for the immediate evacuation of Norfolk and the Navy Yard. On the scene, where they discovered no imminence of danger, Randolph and Mallory would not have it. They wrote out an order giving Huger the authority to delay evacuation until the portable property could be removed.

The Confederates were allowed a week to complete the evacuation which Johnston had, without consulting Richmond, ordered immediately. By ignoring the general, as he had ignored the authorities, the forces at Norfolk saved the stores, started the melancholy task of scuttling the *Virginia-Merrimack*, and put Huger's soft-bodied garrison troops on a march westward through the flat, peanut-growing country which produces Virginia hams. Huger had no detailed orders from commanding officer Johnston for his troops. He was simply to "withdraw." As he had been earlier in communication with Lee, Huger wrote Lee for instructions. Lee assumed temporary responsibility for these orphaned troops from Johnston's area of command. For want of any other destination, he ordered Huger's division to Petersburg, twenty miles south of Richmond on the railroad.

Still no word came from Johnston of where he planned to make a stand or if he planned to. The only information Lee could get came from the garbled stories of stragglers from the army and civilian fugitives. Mc-

Clellan had overtaken Johnston's mud-slowed columns at Williamsburg, the former Colonial capital drowsing across the main highway up the Peninsula, and a rearguard action had turned into a fair-sized battle. Both sides sustained upward of two thousand casualties. Johnston's lightly wounded, accompanied by the ill and the exhausted, the shocked and the lost, dragged their way into Richmond's streets. Past Lee's open window crept the disheartening trickle, intermingled with carriages and wagons crowded with men, women and children fleeing before the enemy and clutching a few personal belongings.

Finally on May 7 a message came from Johnston. Lee's eagerness for information sank into bewilderment. Johnston told nothing of any plans. Lee learned that the army was at the crossroads town of Barhamsville, not far from the Pamunkey River, in the vicinity of the White House. Beyond that the burden of Johnston's message seemed to be an apprehension over Richmond, with McClellan establishing an advance base under protection of the gunboats. Since Johnston must have foreseen this inevitability when he argued for a defense at Richmond, and when he abandoned Yorktown for that ostensible purpose, it looked as if he might be preparing the war offices for an evacuation of Richmond too.

This message of foreboding reached Lee at the time he was occupied with a threat to Richmond more immediate than the future effect of gunboats on the Pamunkey River. As soon as the *Virginia-Merrimack* was scuttled, the James would be open to gunboats all the way to the Richmond docks. The only potential obstacle was a river fort eight miles below the city where a sheer cliff, Drewry's Bluff, rose on the south side in an elbow of the river. As it was one of those operations that fitted nowhere in the maze of departments, the work had been done mostly by farmers in the neighborhood, and the crude earthen gun positions were far from ready to take on the U. S. Navy.

Under the impetus of a group of worried Richmonders, led by the chief engineer of the city's defenses, War Secretary Randolph went beyond making an endorsement to be passed on into other offices, and placed the project in the personal charge of Custis Lee. On May 5, the day of Johnston's rearguard action at Williamsburg, General Lee's oldest son used his new authority to begin hauling heavy timbers to reinforce the earthworks where engineers were rushed. Naval personnel from Norfolk, including Lee's brother Smith, came to help mount the heavy guns into position. Ships were laden with stone and sunk in the river to narrow the channel. This would force ascending ships to turn broadside to the guns as they made the sharp turn in one of the loops (called "curls") in the James River. General Lee, the fort expert, rode daily down the river to inspect the work in progress.

When Lee came back to his office on May 8, a scorching letter from Joe

Johnston was on his desk. Complaining of the lack of recognition of his authority in the area, he had a list of indictments. Foremost was the charge that Lee had given orders to troops under his command. This referred to Huger's division, which Johnston's evacuation orders had left abandoned at Norfolk. "My authority does not extend beyond the troops around me," he raged. "I therefore request to be relieved of a merely geographical command."

Then, as if he had not asked to be relieved of command, Johnston went on to accuse the government of not furnishing *him* with information of the other departments under his command. He must be informed "without delay" of the position and number of his troops in the Fredericksburg area.

Unthreatened by the infantile tantrum, Lee saw it for what it was: Johnston was covering the guilt of his own uncooperativeness with an attack, and counting on Lee's long-suffering to take no action on the request to be relieved of command. Lee simply ignored that part of the letter and answered each point reasonably. But on the matter of Jackson and Ewell, Lee displayed a casuistry unsuspected by Johnston.

"I do not recollect your having requested information relating to the other departments of command to be forwarded you by other means than the usual course of the mails, and supposed the commanders were in direct correspondence with you." To this he added that, as he suspected Banks's objective might be to join McDowell, "I have telegraphed my apprehension to both Generals Jackson and Ewell to place them on their guard."

This was true as far as it went. It gave, however, no hint of the correspondence with Johnston's subordinates which was leading even then to the opening of a second front in the Valley. Later in the day after he wrote Johnston, Lee received a message from Jackson. He announced a victory over Brigadier General Robert Milroy at a place called McDowell in the mountains. While Johnston kept his plans for his army to himself as he badgered Lee about maintaining his areas of authority, the patient "Granny" in the President's pocket had quietly developed a separate line using the otherwise idle troops in Johnston's command.

### 4

With engineers rushing the work at Drewry's Bluff against the day the *Virginia* would have to be scuttled, Lee received a message from Johnston on May 8 which strongly suggested that he was repeating his Yorktown tactics in preparing the authorities for a continued withdrawal beyond Richmond. "We depend upon the *Virginia* for the defense of the James River," Johnston wrote. "The batteries on the south side [of the James River] are useless." As he evidently referred to Drewry's Bluff, officially

Fort Darling, he was no more than belatedly announcing the fears which Randolph had expressed in the April conference.

Three days later, May 11, the *Virginia* was scuttled. The next day, when Federal gunboats started up the James River, Johnston wrote asking Lee what plans had been made for supplying his army in the event Richmond was evacuated. With only Drewry's Bluff between the city and the gunboats, when the talk of Johnston's planless retreating spread from the war offices to downtown Richmond, panic began to arise in the population.

Jefferson Davis sent his family south to Raleigh. Cabinet members and workers in the war offices hurried to obtain passage on the suddenly crowded trains going south. British neutrals in the city and a horde of suddenly neutral businessmen besieged Winder's passport offices on Ninth and Broad Streets for clearance out of the doomed city. As the caravans moving in front of McClellan's advance continued to rumble into the city from the east, other lines of traffic streamed across the bridge to the south and on roads to the west. By May 14 the President, a man of great personal courage, had been so infected by the rising hysteria that he called an emergency Cabinet meeting.

A message came to Lee summoning him to a meeting at the White House. Leaving his office alone, he climbed the brick walks through Capitol Square, its trees and shrubs and grass then in the full flowering of May. Emerging from the square at the Bank Street gateway, he walked under the shade trees along Eleventh Street, crossing Broad, and entered the section called the Court End of Town.

Since John Marshall's day a number of lawyers (including Aaron Burr's defense attorney during his treason trial) had made their residences in the regular squares laid on the flat plateau above Shockoe Valley. Marshall's square red-brick country-style house looked old-fashioned among the town houses built between 1810 and the 1840's. Though Franklin Street was the later fashion, the Court End of Town — with the handsome houses then draped with the lavender of the briefly flowering wisteria — remained a fine neighborhood, and many of the Confederate officials rented homes there.

At the very end of Clay Street, at the edge of the drop to Shockoe Valley, stood the large-roomed gray-stuccoed mansion called "the White House." Lee passed a sentry box beside a hitching post and mounted the white stone steps to the brief portico. The colored major-domo of the Davis household ushered him into a hallway, which opened immediately into the grand parlor. Through this, Lee glimpsed the huge columns on the portico in the back and, beyond, the garden which Mrs. Davis liked to work in. Then the majordomo, who was elaborately officious, directed Lee to the stairs, high and steep and curving. Pausing briefly after the climb, he went into a medium-sized oblong room. There the glummest-faced men he had ever seen in his life were gathered around a table.

As soon as Lee seated himself, Davis turned to him. In his drawn face, the President's good eye looked as lifeless as his glass eye. He told Lee the meeting had been called to discuss the next line of defense after Richmond was abandoned.

Richmond abandoned! Lee stared at the President as if he had not heard him correctly. Then, glancing at the silent men — even debonair Benjamin as gloomy as the others — Lee lost his famed composure. The powerful emotions, so habitually controlled that non-intimates suspected him of coldness, rushed to the surface. "But," he said in a loud voice, shaken with passion, "but Richmond *must* be defended."

The power of his emotion filled the room, and that was what the men remembered. That, more than the words, shook them out of their despair. No man there had ever before heard Lee speak except in his mild bass nor seen a hint of the strong feelings beneath the courteous composure.

Davis was steadied and probably relieved. It would have been his natural preference to defend the capital to the end. Logically, without the arms-producing center, the end would come swiftly anyway. As the production center was also the transportation hub for troop movements and supplies throughout Virginia, so it was the citadel of defense for the three-hundred-mile front from the Atlantic to the Alleghenies. With Richmond evacuated this front would collapse, exposing the South Atlantic states to invasion from the north and severing railroad connections with the Confederate West except by way of Atlanta. McClellan had recognized this in making Richmond his objective. If he captured Richmond, even Johnston's army could not be long maintained in the field. Yet, so general was the defeatism spread by Johnston's planless retreat that only the passion of Lee's conviction gave the President and the Cabinet the determination to defend the capital.

That meeting in the second floor room was one of the crucial turning points in the history of the then divided republic.

The decision to defend Richmond gave no assurance that it could be defended against the United States gunboats of the James River fleet, then steaming from Hampton Roads into the river. Lee, back in his office, dismissed thoughts of Joe Johnston's feelings about authority. He wired Huger at Petersburg to hurry on a brigade to the fort on Drewry's Bluff. The next day the ships came.

On the bluff gunners fired their pieces over the newly turned earth mounds. Along the banks sharpshooters made life miserable for the navy personnel. Trapped broadside in the narrowed channel and unable to get the elevation for their guns, the gunboats began to retire downriver. In the jubilant relief at turning back the U. S. Navy, the people repeated in parlors and bars and hospitals the joking taunt of John Taylor Wood. From a sharpshooter's perch on shore, President Taylor's grandson had yelled at the fleet commander, "Commodore, that is not the way to Richmond."

## 5

General Lee did not join in the jubilation. He did not know what was happening to his wife at the White House and he could not imagine what Joe Johnston was up to. Without waiting for the outcome at Drewry's Bluff, Johnston had crossed his army over the Chickahominy River, the only natural physical barrier between Richmond and McClellan. Lee, along with everybody else in Richmond, had expected Johnston to make his stand at the Chickahominy.

Since no official heard anything from Johnston, Lee could only deduce that when Johnston had proposed to fight McClellan at Richmond he meant literally to make Richmond a fortress. But this seemed incredible. Johnston had protested that he could not defend Yorktown because of McClellan's superior artillery, and McClellan would bring the same artillery to Richmond.

On May 17, Lee learned that Johnston was indeed bringing his demoralized troops to the outskirts of the city. Lee learned this only indirectly. It happened that Postmaster General John Reagan had started to ride eastward to meet some of the Texas regiments. Soon Reagan galloped back to tell the President that Johnston's advance units were camping in the breastworks three miles from the city streets. These fortifications were the crudest kind of lines, hastily thrown up during the first months of the war.

The stunned President rode out himself and asked Johnston what were his plans for defending Richmond. Johnston turned him away like an important personage dismissing an unwanted newspaper reporter. Back in his office, Davis wrote a note demanding that Johnston state his military intentions. This he had submitted by his aide-de-camp, Colonel Custis Lee. The General's son returned with the information that Johnston refused to commit himself.

This was when Lee came in. By then frantic, Davis asked him to write Johnston. Lee wrote that "the President wishes you to confer with him about your future plans, and for that purpose desires you to see him at his office." Lee's letter was not acknowledged.

By then it should have been obvious that Johnston had no plans. The only reasonable explanation for Davis not relieving Johnston of command was that he had no one else except Lee, whom he was determined to retain as military adviser. As for Lee, Johnston's nearness to Richmond created new problems. Johnston began to assert active authority over his detached forces, and Jackson wrote Lee of a disturbing order from Johnston.

Johnston's order came just after Jackson's division (augmented by Edward Johnson's brigade) had returned to the Valley, united with Ewell, and the combined forces were ready to fall upon Banks. This political general, deceived by the apparent quiet on his front, had already sent Shields's division eastward to rejoin McDowell at Fredericksburg. At this stage Dick Ewell received a message from Johnston ordering him to follow any Federal troops eastward if they left the Valley.

Ewell, though thoroughly trained in subordination by his years in the Old Army, was reluctant to see Jackson's carefully prepared offensive ruined by the order of a distant commander. With stout courage, "Old Baldhead" told Jackson he would ignore the order — to follow Shields from the Valley — if Jackson, as his immediate superior, would give him the authority. Jackson immediately wrote the order, with the proviso that it would not obtain if Ewell received a contradictory order from Johnston at a later date. On May 17 Johnston wrote the superseding order: "We want troops here; none, therefore, must be kept away unless employing a greatly superior force of the enemy."

When Ewell showed Jackson the order on May 20, Banks had taken alarm and was in retreat northward down the Valley. Jackson, profoundly depressed, brooded over the gratuitous wreckage of his offensive and the prospect of returning to a supine observation of the enemy. Out of this brooding, he sent the telegram which Lee received on the 20th. "I am of opinion that an attempt should be made to defeat Banks, but under instructions just received from General Johnston I do not feel at liberty to take action. Please answer by telegraph at once."

What Lee did on receipt of this message was a carefully kept secret. Since later in the day Jackson put his troops in motion after Banks, it can only be assumed that Lee wired him the authority, and neither of them retained a copy of the message.

Johnston remained unaware that his orders had been overridden. On May 18, after reconsidering his earlier order, he sent two letters which gave authority for the offensive to continue. "The object you have to accomplish is the prevention of the junction of General Banks' troops with those of McDowell . . . The whole question is whether or not General Jackson and yourself are too late to attack Banks. If so, the march eastward should be made. If not (supposing your strength sufficient) then attack."

As these messages revealed, Johnston was a sloppy thinker. He neither followed a consistent line nor bothered to familiarize himself with the details of the distant front under his authority. Divided between his natural leaning toward a mathematical concentration at Richmond and the advantages of keeping McDowell immobilized at Fredericksburg, he sent contradictory, haphazard orders as he changed from day to day. If Lee and Jackson had not developed the campaign during April there would have been no choice of an offensive; and had Ewell followed his first orders, Johnston's change of mind would have come too late. The forces in Johnston's command were prepared to assume an offensive because of factors which, fortunately for harmony, remained unknown to Johnston. The offensive also held an objective beyond Johnston's orders. Jackson opened the campaign on Lee's suggestion "to drive him [Banks] back toward the Potomac, and create the impression, as far as practicable, that you design threatening that line."

Lee's unannounced maneuvers had resulted in the opening of a second front, designed according to his singly held purpose of keeping McDowell at Fredericksburg. But when Jackson put his small army in motion, at first this achievement did not loom large. In the last week of May, Johnston, having backed his army into the environs of Richmond, waited incommunicado while methodical McClellan pushed his advance to within six miles of the city. There he began preparations to repeat the siege operations which at Yorktown Johnston had said made the result "certain."

6

With Johnston assuming active charge of practically all troops in Virginia, Lee was reduced to the most mundane chores of the expediter. The President continued to call on him for consultations on distant points, but in Virginia his work revolved around details that wore at even his granite patience. In the backwater of his office, he learned that McClellan had established his advance base at Rooney's White House, the second Lee residence occupied by the enemy within a year. However, he was relieved to hear that Mrs. Lee had been ceremoniously conveyed through the Federal lines by an escort personally provided by McClellan, and went with her daughter-in-law and grandson to a temporary haven with kinspeople of Charlotte Lee in Hanover County.

While Johnston established camp with his full force (53,688) to the east and northeast of the city, McClellan divided his approximately one hundred thousand into two large prongs separated by the Chickahominy River. This swampy stream, after coursing southward about fifteen miles to the northeast of Richmond, at five miles to the northeast of the city swung on a relatively straight course eastward for about ten miles. There it curved in an arc to the south and crossed the Williamsburg Road at Bottom's Bridge, twelve miles from Richmond. On its eastward course the sluggish river, swollen by recent rains, spread to from one-half mile to one mile of swamp inhabited only by moccasins.

Two corps of McClellan's army were south of this stretch of the Chickahominy, pointed straight at the eastern part of the city across the flat, water-drained land of small farms and large belts of tangled timber. Three corps were spread to the north of the Chickahominy. There Porter's advance corps occupied the crossroads town of Mechanicsville six miles to the northeast of Richmond. Completely confident in front of Johnston's supineness, McClellan made no effort to disguise his intention of pushing out Porter's corps to make juncture with McDowell, who would come down from the north.

Lee could only watch, with whatever thoughts, when Johnston also announced his intention of trying to meet the Federal concentration at Richmond. The ten-thousand-man force Lee had established in front of McDowell at Fredericksburg was drawn closer to Richmond, halting at

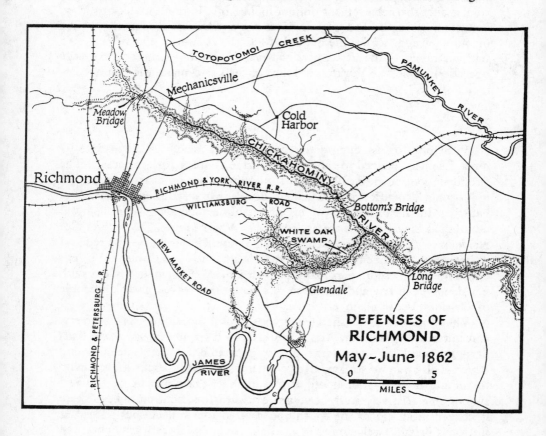

DEFENSES OF
RICHMOND
May~June 1862

Hanover Junction about twenty miles to the north. As the Virginia Central crossed the Richmond, Fredericksburg and Potomac there, on its way to the Valley, this indispensable railroad was left unprotected to the west. To the east of Hanover Junction, near Hanover Court House, Johnston placed a brigade of four thousand newly arrived in Virginia. Another unit Lee had managed to shift from North Carolina, the brigade was commanded by L. O'Bryan Branch, a Princeton graduate and prominent citizen.

Through no fault of his own, Branch had been carelessly detached by Johnston and placed where he could appear to threaten McClellan's line of communications with his White House base. McClellan gave Porter's corps some battle practice in overrunning these inexperienced troops. Somewhat cut up, Branch's regiments fell back on the other three brigades, drawing closer to Richmond. With the way open for the juncture of McDowell and McClellan, the only other forces in Virginia were Jackson's at the northern tip of the Valley.

However, it soon became evident that Jackson's force had achieved Lee's purpose. Following Lee's suggestion, Jackson had driven Banks across the Potomac, and exposed his own tiring men to the hazard of advancing as far as Harper's Ferry. There this small mobile force — something over fifteen thousand before casualties and straggling — showed itself to be worth an incalculable number fixed in garrisons. In a perfect illustration of the result of cause-and-effect strategy, Lincoln held McDowell at Fredericksburg against Jackson's threat in the Valley. He sent Shields's tough division back to the Valley to join Frémont from the west, while other units were rushed from the north in an effort to close in on Jackson from three sides.

In Richmond, Lee did not know at once of the full measure of success of the Valley campaign. For in late May, McDowell began what appeared to be the long-dreaded movement toward Richmond. Actually McDowell was only exercising his softening troops. Not knowing this, Joe Johnston decided to attack McClellan's corps north of the Chickahominy on May 29 before McDowell could arrive.

Not announcing his plans to Lee or Davis, he hurriedly made slovenly arrangements for an assault that could only have ended in disaster. He was saved from this by timely intelligence sent by the alert Jeb Stuart. McDowell was returning to Fredericksburg. Johnston, having worked himself to the point of attacking before McDowell arrived, then decided to attack the two Federal corps south of the Chickahominy two days later, May 31.

Lee, along with even the clerks in the war offices, was aware of all the shuttling of troops, but Johnston's only communication was to ask Lee to order forward Huger's division from Petersburg. By Friday, the 30th, with civilians in downtown Richmond talking openly of a coming attack, Lee grew restless in his inactivity. Waiting in the city at the imminence of battle was, staff officer Long reported, "by no means to his taste." He turned to Colonel Long and told him to ride to Johnston's headquarters with a message. General Lee did not wish to interfere but wished to offer his aid in the field in any way his services might be of value.

Darkly elegant Long, with his trim mustache, returned to the Ninth Street office with the report that Johnston expressed gratification at the message. Lee would of course be welcome, but what he could most do was to send reinforcements. There was nothing Lee could answer to that. To the fifty-four thousand (in round figures) Johnston had brought from Yorktown, Huger had added about five thousand troops, camped near the field. The force Lee had assembled at Fredericksburg aggregated, with Branch's brigade, roughly fourteen thousand. A few days before, these troops had been formed into a new division under A. P. Hill, promoted to major general at the same time. This new division had shifted to the Meadow Bridges, a crossing of the north-south line of the Chickahominy about two miles northwest of Mechanicsville. There was not another regiment available, though one more brigade, pried out of the South Carolina Department, was taking the cars to Richmond. In effect, Lee's services were declined.

That night a heavy rainstorm broke over the city, flooding the Chickahominy and threatening the bridges that connected the divided parts of McClellan's army. Seldom was a general presented with the opportunity Johnston had now to bring military destruction on a part of the enemy's army.

McClellan's two corps suddenly isolated to the east of Richmond totaled little more than thirty-five thousand. As discovered in reconnaissance by D. H. Hill's division, these troops were indifferently fortified across most of their front. None of McClellan's heavy guns had been moved forward. Eliminating A. P. Hill's new division and parts of Magruder's twelve thousand — held to guarding the crossings of the Chickahominy in the Mechanicsville area — Johnston could mass more than fifty thousand men on a narrow two-mile front.

On Saturday morning, the 31st, Lee was in his office early, waiting for messages from the field. He waited and waited. Not a message came, not even a rumor, and no sounds rose above the even rumble of the street noises. The President did not send for the military adviser, and in the War Department building routine work went on in the offices. When noon passed, General Lee could stand it no longer. He summoned one of his new staff officers, Aide-de-camp Charles Marshall, a former lawyer and kinsman of the Chief Justice. With bespectacled Marshall as his companion, Lee mounted a horse and rode toward Church Hill on the way to the front.

### 7

As Lee rode through the shaded residential streets, no sounds drifted in from the fields beyond. At Twenty-fifth Street the city houses came to an abrupt end, and Nine Mile Road, passing the edges of Oakwood Cemetery, ran without suburban transition between fields soaked from the rain of the night before. Off the road Lee and Marshall found Johnston's headquarters house empty. Continuing eastward along Nine Mile Road, they soon saw the scattered debris that indicated the forward movement of troops to battle. Lee rode on down Nine Mile Road in the direction of the Federal position.

At about five miles from the city Lee saw the first body of troops, three brigades of Smith's division taking their ease alongside the road. Beyond them a brigade from Magruder's command stretched idly across the road and in front of another road that forked off to the north, toward the New Bridge crossing of the Chickahominy. Where the New Bridge Road forked off stood the building called Old Tavern. Across Nine Mile Road from Old Tavern, Lee saw a group of horses and couriers outside an abandoned farmhouse. When Lee dismounted in the farmyard, he heard the sound of rifle fire drifting across the heavily timbered bog that separated Nine Mile Road from the Williamsburg Road.

Leaving Richmond, those two roads followed roughly parallel courses. The Williamsburg Road ran due east for seven miles to the crossroads called Seven Pines, and the Nine Mile Road curved from northeast to southeast to Fair Oaks, a stop on the York River Railroad. From Fair Oaks, Nine Mile Road ran to Seven Pines, one mile to the south. This stretch formed McClellan's main line. McClellan's advanced line extended about one-half a mile toward Richmond from Seven Pines and Fair Oaks.

The farmyard, where Lee paused listening to the faintly blown sound of the firing, was at the point of greatest distance between the two roads — two and three-quarters miles. The rattle of rifles seemed to come from the Seven Pines area. From the farmyard Nine Mile Road slanted sharply southeast through dense, wet timber for about two miles to McClellan's picket line advanced from Fair Oaks. From that area, in front of the idle troops posted across the road, came neither sound nor movement.

Lee and Marshall entered the farmhouse, Marshall going into a room on the west side of the house where the staff officers from Johnston's army were sitting around chatting. In the room on the east side of the house, Lee found a tense-faced Johnston sitting in stony silence with Major General Smith, his second in command, and Brigadier General Chase Whiting. Like Smith, Whiting had been a big name at West Point and had enjoyed a closeness with Johnston since he had served as Johnston's chief engineer at Manassas. As Whiting was then temporarily commanding Smith's division, the presence of the three generals inactive in a strained atmosphere indicated that something was going very wrong with Johnston's battle.

Johnston received Lee with none of his famed charm in evidence and offered no information.

Lee ventured the remark that he heard firing when he approached the house.

"It's only artillery," Johnston said, dismissing the subject.

Though it had sounded like rifle fire to Lee, he said no more. In the room it was true that nothing could be heard except the occasional rumble of guns, no more volume than was made when batteries practiced on one another. As was learned later, an acoustical freak prevented the sound of the rifle fire from being heard in the eastern side of the house. In the west room, Marshall and other staff officers heard the firing. Because of Johnston's secrecy none of them knew this was the signal he was waiting for to announce the opening of his battle at Seven Pines.

When Lee arrived, it was after two o'clock. Despite the absence of welcome, Lee found a chair and seated himself. He had determined to find out what was going on.

Shortly after four o'clock one of Smith's staff officers, Major Jasper Whiting, burst into the room. He was bringing a message from Longstreet at Seven Pines. Longstreet was driving the enemy, the message stated, but he urgently needed support on his left — from the Fair Oaks area — to sustain his drive. Johnston sprang up as if released from a trance.

He ordered Smith to his brigades guarding the swollen Chickahominy. He ordered Whiting to advance the other three brigades. Saying nothing to Lee, he left the house with Whiting. Lee could not force himself on the suddenly energized general. When he paused in the front doorway, he saw President Davis and an entourage riding down the road from Richmond. Johnston, evidently seeing the group at the same time, hurriedly mounted his horse and went with Whiting at a fast canter toward Fair Oaks.

Lee waited until President Davis rode up, and they tried vainly to find out from one another what kind of battle was going on. Davis had also heard the rifle firing from Seven Pines, and from the stationary sound it was obvious that the enemy was not being driven. In front of them on Nine Mile Road, Smith's three brigades under Whiting were slushing forward on the muddy road with a clatter of accouterment and shouts of officers.

One brigade was commanded by big John Hood, Lee's companion at Camp Cooper years before. Hood's men turned off into the dripping woods on their right, toward the flank of Longstreet somewhere across country around Seven Pines. Whiting's own brigade took the lead, under romantic-looking Evander McIver Law, a scholarly young South Carolinian. Then came the brigade of Johnston Pettigrew, the distinguished and much admired North Carolinian. Lee observed that no guns went forward with the infantry.

Lee and Davis turned their horses into the churned mud of the road and followed the rear of Pettigrew's gray-uniformed soldiers. When Lee and Davis started forward, musketry began rolling from straight ahead, around Fair Oaks. This was immediately joined by the deeper blasts of Federal cannon. After riding something over a mile between the heavily foliaged woods, Lee and Davis came out on a large cleared field on their left, enclosed on three sides by timber. Pettigrew's men, deployed across this boggy field, were moving north toward the Chickahominy and then east. Evidently Pettigrew was moving to support Law's brigade, fighting alone at Fair Oaks. Ominously, flashes of rifle fire streaked in the woods toward the river, on Pettigrew's left flank when his troops turned east to come up alongside Law.

Lee and Davis paused in this open field behind an action that was rapidly growing chaotic. Second-in-command Smith hurried forward the last two brigades of his division, and these still-faced men deployed across the bog of the smoky field into the fire pouring from the woods on Pettigrew's left.

Robert Hatton, leading the first brigade, was shot dead from his horse. Gigantic Wade Hampton, leading the second brigade, was dismounted with a foot wound, and stood on one foot yelling for the surgeon to come and extract the bullet. Pettigrew's men had gotten into line on Law's slim front, but without their leader. He had been left for dead in the wet brush. All three supporting brigades had lost their commanding generals.

Then Hood's bewildered regiments stumbled back out of the woods on the right. They had found nothing resembling a flank reaching north from Longstreet at Seven Pines. Piling up on the road among the wounded and stragglers, Hood's men milled around under the edges of the firing. Several of them toppled over into the churned mud. The confusion was total in the fading light of late afternoon.

While Lee sat his horse, staring into the bedlam, suddenly somebody running past yelled that General Johnston was being brought off the field severely wounded and maybe dead. Dusk was deepening then. Lee and Davis quickly rode through the random fall of metal to the western edge of the clearing. Two staff officers were bringing the slight figure of the commanding general out of the range of overshot artillery bursts. Lee and Davis dismounted and hurried toward him.

The flush was gone from Johnston's cheeks and, though conscious, he had obviously taken a heavy wound. Davis, his ready sympathies for suffering overcoming his accumulated resentments, knelt by Johnston's side and asked if he could do anything. Johnston shook his head. Lee stood silently watching, waiting until his once intimate friend could be lifted into an ambulance.

In the falling light, the ragged fire continued in a battle which, from what Lee could see, had no pattern. With Davis he went looking for Major General Gustavus Smith. The handsome Kentuckian, looking himself somewhat shaken, had not been taken into full confidence about Johnston's plan of battle. From what he had learned, there had been some "misunderstanding" between Longstreet and Johnston. Longstreet was supposed to have led an attack down Nine Mile Road with his division, supported by Smith's division under Whiting. D. H. Hill, supported by Huger, was to open the battle by an assault at Seven Pines. Longstreet had taken the wrong road, piling up three divisions at Seven Pines and not getting into action there until mid-afternoon. Smith's division had waited alone all day where Lee first found the troops, ready to go in.

By the time of their late attack at Fair Oaks, McClellan had gotten supports from north of the Chickahominy. Old "Bull" Sumner, Armistead Long's father-in-law, had defied the shaky bridges and late in the afternoon put two divisions in action near Fair Oaks. His quickly formed lines caught the assault forces in front and flank as they went in piecemeal. Without further details, it was clear that Johnston's opportunity against McClellan's two detached corps had come and gone. The problem now was to hold off possible counterattacks.

There was also the problem of a commanding general. Smith, ignorant of either Johnston's detailed plans or the total situation, looked on the verge of nervous collapse. Manifestly he would not do. Davis advised Smith to hold his present position until he learned the condition of affairs at Seven Pines, though it was obvious the enemy had not been driven there. It was then dark.

Lee and the President turned their horses toward the road to Richmond. They picked their way through the jam of ambulances and debris of what Porter Alexander, Johnston's chief of ordnance, called "a phenomenally mismanaged battle." The supporting services had been mismanaged too. Little provision had been made for the wounded, upward of five thousand when all had been found in the black bogs. When Lee and Davis reached the road, wagons and hacks and coal carts, any vehicles on wheels, were hurrying toward the shouts and the moans where lanterns flickered through the darkness. Beyond the last of the disorder the two men rode quietly. Away from the battle area a fresh night fragrance rose from the fields and woods.

Suddenly Davis turned in the saddle and told Lee he would be given command of the army. Davis was reluctant to part with Lee as a military adviser. In that capacity Lee had suited the President's purpose ideally: Davis could consult with Lee, get his advice (with no obligation to use it) and depend upon Lee for performing multitudinous chores in the details of operations — all without relinquishing any of his authority to Lee. Davis probably told Lee he would like to depend upon him for consultations, since Lee did continue as an unofficial adviser.

Having reached the decision, Davis told Lee to make his preparations at once. He would write out the order as soon as he got home.

Lee never referred to the conversation in writing, nor in letters to any of his family. One point in his reactions would be safe to assume. At last, his duty coincided with his inclinations. After thirteen months, he would attempt something he had never done in thirty-seven years as a soldier — lead troops in combat.

## CHAPTER IX

# "A New Impulse from . . . Headquarters"

L EE rode out Nine Mile Road again on a warm June 2, this time to begin his new life as commanding general in the field. About a mile
and a half beyond the abrupt ending of the old streets of Church
Hill, he came to a farm on the north side of the road and dismounted at a
modest, comfortable house. It was owned by Mrs. Mary C. Dabbs, a
widow, usually referred to as the Widow Dabbs. The house was called,
without a possessivè, the Dabbs House. There a headquarters flag was run
up, and Lee and the officers of his personal staff selected bedrooms. The
front room downstairs was the general office, and Lee's office was in the
back. He did not plan to spend much time in it.

Among the first letters to go out was one Lee himself wrote to daughter-
in-law Charlotte. Her baby, Lee's grandson, had died during an illness.
Shortly after this, he had the personal mission of going to fetch his wife.
She had been caught a second time within Federal lines and decided,
against all advice, that she might as well take her chances in Richmond.

McClellan had been severely criticized for providing Mrs. Lee with a
guard while she was at the White House, and he showed his contempt for
(what Francis Blair called) "parlor knights" by having the crippled lady
escorted to his own headquarters for her second passage out of his lines.
Lee sent Major W. Roy Mason for her with a carriage. From McClellan's
headquarters the former heiress of Arlington was driven past the last sentries in blue uniforms. At the Chickahominy the carriage rumbled over
the series of wooden bridges called the Meadow Bridges and, passing
among the gray-uniformed men of A. P. Hill's "Light Division," drew up
at a farmhouse.

There her husband, gray-bearded since she had last seen him about fourteen months before, hurried to the carriage. It was also the first time she
had seen him in the uniform of a Confederate general. Above dark-blue
trousers almost covered by high boots, he wore a regulation double-
breasted gray coat opened narrowly at the collar to reveal a black bow tie
against a glimpse of white linen. The coat collar was decorated with the

three stars in a wreath which was the insignia of all general officers, with no distinction between brigadiers and full generals.

Mrs. Lee's changes were of a different nature. The General looked at a greatly aged wife. The hardships of her life as a transient and the unending anxieties had taken a toll of the crippled woman, on whom the ravages of arthritis had advanced to a stage where she could scarcely walk. But she was safe.

Lee moved his wife into the Spotwood. Yet, though so close at the Dabbs House, Lee wrote his wife as if she were still at some distant place. The need for imposing discipline on the lax organization left by Johnston would not permit him to set the example of riding into town.

Lee had assumed command most unobtrusively. General headquarters had been a remote place to the soldiers in Johnston's day, and Lee's first published orders did nothing to indicate any change. Lee wrote the Special Orders in the third person, to be signed by Walter Taylor. Usually Lee's official communications were formal and rarely reflected anything of the man as his personality came through in personal letters. But in the address to be read to the troops he surpassed himself in flat stiffness.

"The unfortunate casualty that has deprived the army in front of Richmond of the valuable services of its able general is not more deeply deplored by any member of his command than by its present commander. He hopes his absence will be but temporary, and while he will endeavor to the best of his abilities to perform his duties, he feels he will be totally inadequate to the task unless he shall receive the cordial support of every officer and man."

That was not the full speech, but it suggests that Lee was aware that he was received by the army with something less than enthusiasm. His unseen accomplishments (such as introducing strategy with Jackson's Valley Campaign) were so generally unknown in the army that even Jeb Stuart wrote his wife of his disappointment in Lee. In any case, it was not Lee's way to try to arouse men to his service by words. Distrusting appeals to the emotions, to passion and prejudice, Lee handled words with the precision with which he would handle dangerous weapons. Unless joking, he observed this care in personal as well as official letters.

Lee assumed command in the same way he took on any task: within a master plan, he worked at the details, one day at a time. He worked for the cumulative effect. From the beginning, he worked with the advantage of holding an unique place in the commander in chief's personalized system.

Having won Davis's trust by tact in personal exchanges and selflessly successful application to the details of operations, Lee increased his influence by acting as the exact opposite of Johnston. He communicated with the President constantly and advised him in advance of any plan he contemplated. Then, by going through the form of conferring with Davis, Lee gave him the impression that everything was shared between them. Though such consideration was natural with Lee, he could not have been unmindful of the effects of Johnston's stubborn refusals to take the commander in chief into his confidence. The result for Lee was that he became at that stage the only field general on either side to enjoy the complete confidence and support of his government.

During this period his area of authority extended unofficially considerably beyond the army. Through his discreet activities as the President's consultant, Lee had developed the habit of working in terms of the total Virginia theater in relation to the Atlantic Coastal operations. Though he had also conferred on operations in the West, his detail work was concentrated in the East. He carried this area of broad, undefined authority into his field command, and protected it by maintaining the spirit of the relationship that had existed with Davis before he took command of the army. Winning this position was an achievement of Lee's character, and this achievement was of profound significance in determining the nature of the war.

When Lee came on, the Federal government — despite the Radical bloc that wanted a long drawn-out war — was still committed to a quick decision to achieve a settlement before the entangling issue of slavery became introduced. McClellan, though working on a timetable maddeningly slow to Lincoln, was in his deliberate fashion within about one month of completing preparations for siege operations that would make the military decision in Virginia and the Eastern seaboard decisively final. However, to the deterioration of his already poor relationship with Lincoln and Stanton, he continued to promise immediate action while continuing to call for McDowell. (In point of fact, by early June two of McDowell's large divisions had been sent him.)

Lee, reading McClellan's intentions by his actions, understood him perfectly. It was obvious that McClellan regarded the abortive attack at Seven Pines as an isolated, local flare-up and anticipated no change in the Confederate defenses waiting supinely on his schedule. In turn, Lee depended on McClellan's methodical approach by "regular stages." But, accepting the inevitable consequences of a position war against McClellan's unmatchable siege guns, Lee had no intention of waiting for McClellan to complete his preparations. He planned "to pry" McClellan out of his works and force him into the open, to fight the kind of battles McClellan had shown he wanted to avoid — a war of maneuver.

This plan expressed the principles of warfare Lee had held since he came to Richmond: to get off the defensive, seize the initiative and "disrupt the enemy's prearrangements." What he had worked out with Jackson on a small scale against McDowell he intended to employ against Mc-Clellan in a grand-scale counteroffensive.

Nor was the purpose of this counteroffensive — the first in the war in Virginia — so simple as merely lifting the siege of Richmond. His objective was "to drive our enemies back to their homes," and, as he wrote Davis, "change the character of the war." In his first, flatly worded address to the army he showed where he expected to fight by the name he gave the force gathered in front of Richmond — "the Army of *Northern* Virginia."

Lee needed to use no time in making decisions. His concepts had long been formed and, without waste motion, he began immediately to put them into practice. His problems were the details, the complex of physical details, large and small, between the plan and the execution.

2

Execution of plans, involving staff officers, was a matter of personalities. The staff officers were like the nerves carrying impulses through the body of the army. In selecting officers for his personal staff, Lee's primary consideration had to be the men's adaptiveness to the tone he established in the intimacies of shared living routines, including meals together. For the routines of his military household reflected the regularity with which he conducted his life.

While the men were adjusting themselves to life at headquarters, Lee personally set an example he did not intend the officers to follow. Around the house he wore a white linen jacket. He had caught a slight cold which he believed came from wearing the heavy uniform during the June heat. He had not previously in his life mentioned being affected by the heat, but the sun beating down on the damp flatland outside of Richmond at times produced a humid closeness that was almost suffocating. Hundreds of soldiers were ill with upper respiratory ailments, and under vigorous exertion older men sometimes fainted. Except for forty-seven-year-old Colonel Chilton, who did not exert himself vigorously, Lee's staff officers were much younger than he.

With the younger men he was, as always, cheerful, kindly and considerate, neither remote from them nor inviting intimacies. The staff officers' respect and affection deepened into reverence as they shared his hours under all conditions. Taylor, Long and Marshall wrote about him without recounting a single anecdote. The consistency of his behavior was awesome.

In selecting those talented for the specialized work of staff, Lee had to rely largely on instinct, as the shortage of experienced soldiers sent most men from the Old Army into field command. To businessman Taylor and lawyer Marshall, in Richmond he had added as aide-de-camp Charles Venable, a mathematics professor. Venable worked into the field of inspections, while Marshall gradually assumed some of the duties of military secretary. Taylor took charge of the clerks at the Dabbs House in assuming responsibility for the office routine. All three developed in the important communications area of delivering and receiving oral messages, which required coolness, tact and judgment.

Military secretary Armistead Long had trained in artillery under McClellan's chief of reserve artillery and Lee's Old Army friend, Henry Hunt. Lee had Long operate as liaison with his chief of artillery, Brigadier General William Pendleton. A new man brought in from the engineers, Captain T. M. R. Talcott, was the son of Lee's old friend. The young Talcott served as liaison with Major W. H. Stevens, the chief of engineers whom Lee had inherited from Johnston. The only Johnston legatee on Lee's personal staff was Captain A. P. Mason, who served temporarily as assistant adjutant general.

Where Lee brought in the likeliest Old Army man, for chief of staff, he encountered his single disappointment. Colonel Robert Hall Chilton, whom Lee had known in Texas, had resigned from the Old Army as paymaster major and served in Richmond in the adjutant general's office. An intelligent, conscientious man and absolutely devoted, Chilton had grown accustomed to paper work that involved no decisions. He brought no initiative to the job of assuming responsibility for knowledge of the operations of the army. Unknown to Lee in the hurried June weeks when he was preparing to mount his offensive, he had in effect no chief of staff.

With these members of Lee's personal staff, the general staff was completed by officers in charge of the supporting services — ordnance, commissary, quartermaster, medicine, engineering, the judge advocate general, and such. Through them it was Lee's rush job to tighten the loose organization he had inherited. Unlike McClellan's army, which had been built organically from the center into a single structure, the troops in front of Richmond were a hastily collected hodgepodge.

An army in name only, it was composed partly of Johnston's old Manassas army, with all the laxity of his indifferent administration; Magruder's Yorktown force, which had never been harmoniously incorporated with Johnston's army; Huger's recently arrived division, whose commander had been the victim of a collusion between Johnston and Longstreet in falsely charging him with the muddle at Seven Pines; and the newly formed large division of A. P. Hill, which had never acted with the other units in combat. In addition, brigades from North Carolina on the south side of the James River were still in Holmes's department and would operate *with* Lee's Army of Northern Virginia rather than being a part of it.

As Davis had refused to permit Johnston to form the divisions into the semi-autonomous units of corps, and as Johnston's sociable headquarters had been separated from the units, there was a sprawling lack of cohesiveness in the total force. The place-conscious soldiers identified themselves with their regiments, usually formed from a single locality and containing the cross section of a community — mechanic and doctor, carpenter and lawyer, dirt farmer and princely planter, the ignorant poor of the backwoods and the educated sons of baronial families, all learning to share equally the short rations, the wet camps, the dangers and the resisted discipline. Many could scarcely conceive of a community as large as a fourteen-thousand-man division, and few could expand their consciousness to identify themselves with *the* army.

The staffs of the brigades and divisions were often family or neighborhood affairs. The commanding officers, liking the familiar, appointed cousins and friends and even sons. Hardly any of these staff officers had had regular military experience, and not much in the surrounding slackness — where hard drinking was commonplace — offered the recent civilians any models for development. With little communication with general headquarters in Johnston's day, brigade command related only to its division and thus formed thirty-odd command levels, also without a strong sense of *the* army.

Without announcing it as his intention, Lee worked to bring the separate communities into unity with general headquarters as one means of tightening the whole organization. By personally supervising details, Lee's own frugalities and abhorrence of waste, his distaste for disorder, all were reflected in the countless small changes he introduced.

With his practiced economy of effort, he worked from sunup to past sundown each day looking after what Davis called "the proper adjustment of even the smallest parts . . . the minutest details" of the machine of a well-organized, well-disciplined army. From Davis down to Major Joseph Brent, a lawyer serving as Magruder's chief of ordnance, observers commented on the gradual formation of the parts into a cohesive whole. Brent mentioned "the new impulse from Lee's headquarters" by which "the network of a general organization was cast over the whole army."

Lee rode much about the lines, usually accompanied only by Armistead Long, visiting the generals and letting the men become familiar with the composed gray figure on his gray horse. As in South Carolina and Georgia, he endured the ire he aroused at putting the men to dig. He wrote the President, "Our people are opposed to work. Our troops, officers, community and press. All ridicule and resist it. It is the very means by which McClellan has and is advancing. Why should we leave to him the whole advantage of labor? Combined with valor, fortitude and boldness, of which we have our fair proportion, it should lead us to success. What carried the Roman soldiers into all countries but this happy combination . . . There is nothing so military as labor, and nothing so important to an army as to save the lives of is soldiers."

What the soldiers soon came to see was the safety provided by the works which they had so protested at digging. With the protective works, advanced pickets obviated the necessity of holding men idly under arms at all hours. The ennui was lifted, and their labors became part of the general movement and preparation. Then, as excess baggage was sent to the rear, and broken-down vehicles and animals sent back to depot for refitting, the atmosphere of sprawling dirty villages disappeared. Slovenly camps changed into lines where troops were ready for action. This brought an inevitable soaring in morale. The men could feel themselves part of a total organization directed by a single purpose.

Equally visible was the change in the artillery. There was not enough time to form an effective organization of the conglomeration of gun batteries loosely attached to divisions, but Lee did what was possible. The nominal chief of artillery was Brigadier General William Pendleton. A rector from the church in Lexington, in the faraway days of his youth Pendleton had crossed Lee at West Point. Pendleton, a limited man of limitless devotion to independence, was detail-minded, longwinded, and humorless. As he was actually in charge of an overlarge artillery reserve, he got around little to the batteries attached to divisions. Armistead Long, using Lee's authority, tightened slack by working from battery to battery. Ignoring hurt feelings, weak batteries were pulled out of line and combined in an effort to stabilize the size (four guns, eighty men) and the performance. Division chiefs of artillery were appointed to maintain the efficiency of the individual batteries and provide a small reserve for each division.

Also using Lee's "great powers," young Porter Alexander as chief of ordnance made "unheard of improvements" in the wagon trains that supported the guns. This increased the mobility of the artillery along with the morale of the gunners. As part of the new mobility, the old heavy smoothbores — which Johnston had favored against McClellan's massive armament — were replaced by handier field pieces. For Lee, not planning to meet McClellan on his own terms, was preparing against the day when his works would temporarily hold the Federals while he moved a striking force into the open. In that his basic strategy was involved in a race against time.

In the early weeks of June, McClellan had not brought forward any of his semi-mobile siege guns — the heavy pieces which moved on gun carriages, though slowly and cumbersomely. Nor had he yet used the York River Railroad to move forward one of his fifty seacoast guns — 100- and 200-pounder mortars, 13-inch howitzers, that had to be mounted on stationary platforms. To retard the advance of those monsters, Lee on the spot invented the first railroad gun ever to be fired in warfare. The York River Railroad ran from near McClellan's White House base into the Federal lines south of the Chickahominy, and from Fair Oaks station on to Richmond. To move between Richmond and Fair Oaks, Lee mounted a heavy gun on a flatcar, covering the front with a shield of railroad tracks and making a small mobile fort.

Within the limited time, Lee overlooked nothing that could be done. Yet, acting always within his character, he never gave any sense of hurry or tension. Not one soldier around Richmond, from private to major general, suspected that a big offensive was growing rapidly to maturity. There was nothing to leak to the enemy. The generals Lee had selected in his mind to lead the offensive knew nothing until they were called to his headquarters on the Monday afternoon of June 23.

3

Before this meeting with four generals, Lee had held a conference of his general officers when he had first assumed command. His purpose in calling the first conference — at a house called "The Chimneys," on Nine Mile Road near the front lines — had been to learn the attitudes of the men with whom he was to operate. To sound them out, he asked if the army should take a position nearer Richmond or attempt to resist further advance where it was. To Lee's concealed disapproval, a number of the officers expressed themselves strongly in favor of withdrawing nearer to Richmond. Though Lee made no reply to this defeatist attitude, he said privately to Marshall, "If we leave this line because they can shell us, we shall have to leave the next for the same reason, and I don't see how we can stop this side of Richmond."

President Davis, taking a ride for exercise away from the demands of his office, happened to notice the horses gathered outside The Chimneys, and dropped in on the conference. When Davis entered the room, he said, "the tone of the conversation was quite despondent." Opinionated Chase Whiting, the intimate of the former commanding general, was trying to demonstrate to Lee how withdrawal was inevitable. With paper and pencil, he was diagramming for Lee's benefit the enemy's irresistible approach by small advance points from which McClellan's engineers would construct "successive parallels." Whiting was growing eloquent as he put himself in McClellan's place against a cautious opponent, when Lee suddenly said, "Stop, stop! If you go on ciphering, we are whipped beforehand."

Davis, having seen enough of retreats that avoided the enemy's intentions, nodded in agreement at this expression of Lee's attitude. Lee, for his part, had discovered what he wanted to know about his general officers. Prolonged waiting for an attack by a superior force had exerted a demoralizing effect. He did not call any of them together again until the June 23 meeting, which he restricted to division commanders, and did not include all of those.

Between the two meetings, Lee had opened a new correspondence with Jackson out of which he developed the strategic details for his offensive. His first plan had been to reinforce Jackson heavily for a counterinvasion from the Valley. But only one more brigade could be drawn from the South Atlantic defenses, and Jackson's men were in hard case from their four-hundred-mile campaign. In early June he was retiring, heavily laden with captured supplies, to the middle Valley, followed by Frémont and Shields.

Lee then planned to reinforce Jackson sufficiently for him to drive back the enemy. After the Valley was cleared, he could slip down to Richmond for a joint movement against McClellan. To this end, Lee sent to the Valley the new brigade from Georgia, three thousand under Alexander Lawton. Then, under Whiting, he sent Hood's and Law's brigades from the former division of Gustavus Smith. Johnston's outwardly imposing second in command had collapsed when the army briefly devolved on him during the second day of the Seven Pines battle. After that anti-climactic action, when McClellan restored his original lines, Smith was temporarily invalided out of the army. His division was dissolved.

When Lee sent Lawton and Whiting to the Valley, since it was not possible to keep such information from Washington, he made the move as ostentatious as possible to play on the fears of Lincoln and Stanton for the capital. However, by the time these reinforcements reached the Valley, Jackson had defeated Frémont and Shields on successive days, June 8 and June 9, and the enemy had voluntarily retired northward. With Lee's purpose of clearing the middle Valley already achieved, he moved immediately to the final stage of his planning — to bring Jackson secretly from the Valley to the Richmond area north of the Chickahominy.

When the generals came to the Dabbs House on June 23, Jackson's whole force — minus some cavalry left for screening the front — was en route to Richmond. Jackson had left his vanguard fifty miles from the city and ridden through the night to attend the meeting.

With his recent Valley Campaign the greatest event in the East since First Manassas, Jackson was the most famous soldier on the continent when he entered Lee's private headquarters office in the back room on the ground floor. Tired, dusty, wearing a wrinkled plain uniform, his pale eyes peering nearsightedly over his rust-colored beard, the shy soldier looked anything except the "Stonewall" around whom the legends were growing. Lee offered him refreshments after his long ride, and he took a glass of buttermilk.

Of the others present, Jackson was well acquainted only with D. H. Hill, his brother-in-law. Harvey Hill was a slight, bearded man of austere appearance who held himself erect with difficulty against a chronic spinal ailment which sometimes forced him to stoop. A West Pointer, he had been an educator in his native North Carolina before the war. Hill was among those gifted scholars who found trouble in accepting the intelligence of others, and his caustic criticism made him enemies in the army. As he suffered from dyspeptic attacks, Hill attributed to his ill feelings the occasions when he spoke with a very harsh tongue. But he was a superior soldier, a fine leader of men, with quick and bold reactions. In the futilities at Seven Pines, Harvey Hill had shown himself to be, as they said, "an honest fighter." When relaxed, as in the meeting, he was agreeably informal and literate in his comments.

The other Hill, A. P., had known Jackson at West Point, though they had never been intimates. Powell Hill, without Lee's classic handsomeness, was a good looking man of thirty-seven. He wore a red-fox-colored beard below high cheek bones and he had strikingly intense eyes, deep set and hazel. Of middle build, he moved with grace and wore his short shell jacket with style. From Virginia's horse country, Hill was a highstrung and sensitive man for a professional soldier. Very much at ease in society, he was a favorite with Richmond hostesses. Of all general officers Powell Hill had the warmest manner and, though inwardly reserved, had a great capacity for arousing affection. With his new division only one month, Powell Hill alone was untried as a division leader in combat. But Armistead Long, on an inspection tour, praised the fine condition of Hill's Light Division and predicted a brilliant future for their ardent commander.

Jackson, both Hills and Longstreet were all family men. Jackson and Harvey Hill were devout Presbyterians, and Powell Hill was a somewhat careless Episcopalian. Longstreet, without any excessive professions of faith, had been deeply sobered during the winter when three of his children died in the scarlet fever epidemic in Richmond. Before that, the bluff, physical-type man had been a tippling stalwart at the poker sessions in Johnston's headquarters. Since then he had foresworn the garrison-style pleasures of army life and, at forty-one, with a revived ambition for glory in the field, he had devoted his enormous energies to his command.

Though he had bungled his big chance at Seven Pines, Longstreet managed — with an unsuspected capacity for rationalization and Johnston's help — to make blameless Huger the scapegoat for the deranged battle. As of the Dabbs House meeting, Huger was generally regarded as the failure who had deprived Johnston of a victory. Longstreet, having convinced himself Seven Pines had been, in fact, Huger's fault, was undisturbed in his self-confidence.

When Lee first assumed command, Longstreet ("Old Pete" to his men) had feared for the high place he enjoyed in Johnston's esteem, and had taken to dropping in at general headquarters to discuss the front with Lee. Lee's courteous attention and apparently unguarded discussions reassured the big fellow that his position in relation to the commanding general was unchanged. He overestimated the influence he exerted, but Lee did value the soldier's self-reliance and welcomed his initiative.

In his first battle, Lee planned to rely on the inititative of the men he had selected to go with. Never forgetting his lessons with General Scott, Lee intended to follow the pattern that had worked successfully in Mexico; he would plan the tactics in detail and leave the battle to the subordinates. They could exploit the developments. This demanded greater trustfulness in Lee than it had in Scott. He was not facing ineptly led Mexicans but an extraordinarily well-organized enemy, with superiority in numbers and armament. Perhaps Lee, with his own capacity for self-subordination, was too trustful. When a soldier revealed an incapacity for command, Lee was quick to get rid of him. But where leaders demonstrated ability, Lee assumed that they, like himself, would give always their best.

Two of his division commanders he obviously adjudged better suited to holding the lines in front of Richmond than for maneuver in the complicated plan of offense. Magruder was excitable and, as admirers of his pointed out, lost some of his "chivalric" aplomb when forced to cooperate with others. Huger, though unjustly under the cloud from Seven Pines, had not shown himself to be energetic in camp, and his troops were largely untried. In the greatest hazard any general had so far taken in the war, Lee assigned the twenty-odd thousand troops of these two Regular Army men to the lines in front of Richmond. He did this on the chance that McClellan would not attack when Lee withdrew the bulk of his force to the north side of the Chickahominy.

Nor was this the full measure of the risk which Lee was preparing to take. What he outlined to the four generals gathered on that Monday afternoon was a plan posited upon driving the enemy while effecting the most difficult maneuver in warfare — the meeting of two widely separated forces at the right time and place and in proper coordination on a designated battle area.

4

In Lee's offensive, the joint keys to prying McClellan out of his works east of Richmond were the York River Railroad and the Chickahominy

River. The York River Railroad, supplying McClellan's army from the naval supported base at the White House, was the lifeline by which he maintained his mobile city in a hostile country. In simplest terms, Lee planned to overwhelm the Federal troops north of the Chickahominy and, placing his own forces on the line of the York River Railroad, force McClellan to leave his works east of Richmond and cross the river to protect his line of supply.

To reconnoiter McClellan's dispositions on his line of supply from north of the Chickahominy to the White House, on June 12 Lee had sent Jeb Stuart from Hanover Court House with twelve hundred troopers on a reconnaissance in force. The flamboyant young cavalry chieftain became carried away by the spirit of adventure. Instead of returning west to Hanover Court House, keeping to the north of McClellan's lines, Stuart led his excited horsemen first east to the rear of McClellan's lines, there crossed the Chickahominy, and then returned to Richmond south of McClellan's lines — riding around McClellan's whole army. This bravura exploit, "Stuart's Ride Around McClellan," created the wildest enthusiasm in Richmond, making the young cavalrymen the darlings of the crowd. However, the results of Stuart's ride did not make known to Lee the disposition of McClellan's forces north of the Chickahominy.

On June 23, McClellan had four of his five corps shifted south of the river. From the Chickahominy southward across the Williamsburg Road, Franklin, Sumner, Keys and Heintzelman — approximately seventy-five thousand — faced the city six miles away, which Lee planned to guard with only the divisions of Magruder and Huger. North of the river in the Mechanicsville area there was the single corps of Fitz-John Porter, still waiting for McDowell. The first stage in Lee's offense was, in effect, to pinch off Porter's projecting pincer — one of the two arms extending to close on Richmond. Recently strengthened by McCall's division from McDowell's stationary corps, Porter, supported by some cavalry, fielded approximately thirty thousand of all arms — including especially some powerful gun batteries.

Regardless of the unknown Federal numbers, a known factor was the strong position Porter occupied behind the wet banks of Beaver Dam Creek. A rise behind the creek gave Porter's guns a field of fire across the tilting plains of approach. The road eastward from Mechanicsville — which Lee's assault forces would have to follow — crossed Beaver Dam at a virtually impregnable position. A dammed millrace there provided a water barrier, approached by boggy ground at the foot of a hill, with a sharply rising hill on Porter's side. To the south, on Porter's flank, the ground sloped away through heavy brush into the swampy edges of the Chickahominy. While Lee did not know how many Federal troops were on the north side, he recognized that only a small number would be required to defend Beaver Dam Creek at Ellerson's Mill. Basic in his plans was the avoidance of this deathtrap, and that was where Jackson came in.

Jackson was to march to the field from the north, by way of Ashland, by a route that would place him east of the headwaters of Beaver Dam Creek — on the same side of the defensive position as Porter. When Jackson's presence on the Federal flank and rear forced Porter to withdraw eastward, abandoning his outpost at Mechanicsville, the bridges across the Chickahominy would be uncovered. This would open the way for Lee's surprise main thrust by troops to be drawn from the lines in front of Richmond.

Longstreet and D. H. Hill would cross the river where the bridges had been destroyed over the nearly mile-wide stretch of the sluggish water and spreading swamps directly below Mechanicsville. Two miles to the west and slightly north, where the Chickahominy ran its north-south course, A. P. Hill would cross at the Meadow Bridges. These three large divisions, approximating thirty-five thousand men, would pursue Porter eastward over two roads, driving him along the Chickahominy toward the York River Railroad. Jackson would form on the Federal flank, bringing up to more than fifty thousand infantry — plus Stuart's cavalry — the force designed to drive the Federals on the north side.

At this stage, according to Lee's plan, McClellan would leave his works on the east side of the river, to cross over to support his detached wing and save his line of communications. Lee's self-assurance in exploiting developments was indicated by his absence of any plan beyond the maneuver that set the developments in motion. From his original detailed plan, he became a battlefield opportunist.

After Lee explained the details of his plan to the generals, he reached the question of time. For an unexplained reason, perhaps to show his trustfulness or to give the four dissimilar men an opportunity to conduct an informal discussion without his presence, Lee then left the room. The element of time really concerned only Jackson.

Longstreet and D. H. Hill, pulling their men out of line secretly at night, were scarcely eight hours of marching from the Mechanicsville bridges. Most of A. P. Hill's division camped on the ground from which the men would move out to cross the Meadow Bridges. One of his brigades, Branch's, would march northward to an unguarded crossing, at Half Sink, higher up on the river. There Branch would make contact with Jackson and act as liaison between Jackson and Powell Hill. When Jackson was known to be on the ground, A. P. Hill would begin the movement across the Chickahominy. When did Jackson think he could get there?

"On June 25," Jackson answered promptly, placing the time barely two days ahead.

There was an uncomfortable silence from the others. Counting that day, the 23rd, Jackson's vanguard would have to move about forty miles in two days to reach the battle area on the morning of June 25, and the rear of his strung-out forces would be miles behind. This might be normal marching time for his famed "foot cavalry" on the open Valley roads, but he was entering narrow, poorly mapped roads winding through densely brushed country, where enemy horsemen could retard him. For wagons and guns to get up with the rear of his long columns, he was cutting the time dangerously close.

As worn as Jackson looked, he was suffering an even deeper fatigue than he showed or than he realized. Under six weeks of stress Jackson, not robust at best, had drawn heavily on his reserve resources and was approaching a collapse from stress fatigue. Not yet having reached the state of clinical exhaustion, he was still unnaturally exhilarated and, in something like euphoria, rashly allotted his columns only the two days.

Longstreet suggested that perhaps another day had better be added. Jackson agreed. When Lee returned to the room, the generals told him they could be ready to open early June 26. With the fresh impression of Johnston's Seven Pines disaster resulting from the lack of written orders, Lee advised them that details in writing would be sent each one. In ending the meeting that prepared for his first battle in thirty-seven years as a soldier, Lee did not indicate by his manner that anything more than routine business had been disposed of. He shook hands with the generals and the men separated outside the house.

Jackson returned to his horse for another fifty-mile ride and a second night without sleep. He was in the final flare-up of his false energy before depletion set in. Nobody paid any attention to the drain he was placing on his system before his decisive part in the new army's first counteroffensive.

5

The day after the meeting Lee carefully composed the battle plans for General Orders No. 75. On the following day, the 25th, when the orders were to be delivered, McClellan threatened the whole plan by opening an offensive on the Williamsburg Road scarcely five miles from Richmond.

Near King's School, on the south side of the road, the two picket lines were separated by a half mile of entangled bog, the eastern edges of White Oak Swamp. McClellan attacked in force across this dreary stretch, driving Huger's pickets back on their main line of works. Huger's right flank had just been reinforced by Robert Ransom's brigade of green North Carolinians, transferred from Holmes's south of the James Department. When the sound of battle rolled across the flat country to Lee's headquarters, he called for his horse and put Traveler at a canter on a cross-country lane leading to the Williamsburg Road.

On the scene he observed that Huger's troops were standing steadily behind the freshly turned red clay soil of their new lines. Ransom's Tarheels on the flank, in their baptism of fire, were fighting as well as the comparative veterans. McClellan's push, in moderate strength, seemed to gather no momentum. On Magruder's adjoining front the only action was the noisy exchange of nervous pickets, though a Federal cannonade from across the Chickahominy rolled with unusually deep volume. Lee faced a dilemma. Either McClellan had heard of Jackson's advance down from the north and was opening a counteroffensive or McClellan by chance was making a local advance in his long-range plan to move forward by "regular approaches."

It happened that McClellan *had* heard of Jackson's advance, through the information provided by a well-informed deserter. But he was not opening a counteroffensive in reaction to Jackson's movement. The direction of Jackson's march had led him to assume that Jackson was threatening his supply line with the White House. McClellan did not anticipate a general offensive by a combination of Jackson and the Confederates in front of Richmond. Before he heard of Jackson's advance, McClellan had planned to begin his regular approaches on the 25th with the objective of moving in front of the swampy stretch of ground on the Williamsburg Road sector.

This was preliminary to a larger move, planned for the next day, to take the Old Tavern line on Nine Mile Road. To that end he had moved the first of his siege guns to positions across the Chickahominy from Magruder, and the 4½-inch rifled Rodmans were making the deep roar Lee heard on the north bank of the river. The Old Tavern line was important because it would open to the Federals the New Bridge crossing of the Chickahominy, closer to Fitz-John Porter by nearly three miles than the bridges McClellan was using north of Fair Oaks. On June 25, with Magruder on the high south bank and Federal artillery on the north, New Bridge was then closed to both sides. But it was fundamental in Lee's battle plan to drive Porter east of the broken bridge, so that his own divided army could be connected. In Lee's race against McClellan's schedule, it turned out that each planned a major move on June 26.

Lee's decision to proceed with his own offensive was based on sound judgment and ignorance. He correctly deduced that the action at King's Schoolhouse was local, unrelated to his own combined offensive with Jackson. He did not, could not, know that McClellan planned a larger offensive the next day against Magruder. Nor did he know that three-fourths of the Army of the Potomac was in front of Magruder's and Huger's twenty-two thousand. In relying upon his judgment of McClellan's intentions toward small, deliberate advances, Lee gave no heed to apprehensions. Not worrying about what the enemy *could* do, Lee concentrated only on what *he* was going to do to upset the enemy.

Given little attention, this decision of Lee was of a boldness that had not appeared before in Confederate strategy. Though the risk was greater than he realized, he could not have taken any risk without his habit of thinking affirmatively in the tangibles of what he could do without imagining disasters that might transpire.

When darkness ended the small action on the Williamsburg Road, Lee returned to his headquarters. After eating with his staff, he wrote his wife a note. Though he gave not the slightest hint that the next morning's sun would bring the most crucial day of his life, he did reflect the turn of his thoughts.

"I have been on our lines on the Williamsburg road since noon, dear Mary, and having finished my dinner find it near 10 P.M. with a great deal to do tonight. It is therefore impossible for me to see you. Indeed I should have to wake you up to do so. I therefore must deny myself the pleasure and hope we may meet many happy days yet. I know your prayers and well wishes are constantly with me, and my trust is that a Merciful Providence may hear and answer them. Give much love to Custis and all the girls."

## CHAPTER X

## "Our Success Has Not Been as . . . Complete as I Would Have Desired"

ON THE Thursday morning of his big day Lee, with members of his staff, left the Dabbs House for the scene of action. Though the sun was high on the bright, warm day, no sounds came across the Chickahominy from the direction of Jackson's approach. Before leaving, Lee punctiliously had written the President that he had received a message from Jackson saying he was running late. Instead of bivouacking beyond Ashland the night before, it was night when his van had reached the town twenty miles north of Richmond. However, Jackson's note stated that he was starting out at two-thirty that morning, with no more than twelve miles to his designated spot at the headwaters of Beaver Dam Creek.

When Lee rode away from the Dabbs House he heard the intermittent rattle of picket fire along Magruder's front and the occasional blast of guns. Lee had not been informed that Magruder's batteries had been banged around the day before by those Federal siege guns firing from across the Chickahominy, nor that Prince John was already growing alarmed over his inability to answer the enemy's newly placed artillery. Evidently feeling no apprehension for his Richmond defenses, Lee turned his horse onto a country lane leading from Nine Mile Road to the Mechanicsville Turnpike. On the turnpike, as he neared the high ground above the Chickahominy, Lee reached the rear columns of Longstreet's and Harvey Hill's divisions. The men, having moved from the lines around midnight, were lounging in the shade along the roadside.

In front of the waiting troops a slight rise projected to the edge of a bluff, from which the ground dropped sharply to the valley formed by the Chickahominy. Near the edge rose high mounds of earth, behind which gunners stood at the pieces of heavy artillery guarding the approaches to the city. Lee assumed from the lounging positions of the cannoneers and their idle conversation that no signs of Jackson's approach had been observed.

Lee dismounted behind the earthworks on the left of the road. Adjusting his field glasses to his eyes, he brought into focus the terrain around the village of Mechanicsville, at the top of the rise on the other side of the river. The dark clots of Federal soldiers scattered about the few houses at the crossroads village stood as still and neat as toy figures arranged on a board. Nothing moved on the road down which Branch's brigade would approach, bringing the news of Jackson's arrival. For the commanding general there was nothing to do except bear the ordeal of waiting for the one element on which his whole design of action depended.

As he waited, he began to be nagged by second thoughts about Mc-Clellan. Certain that by then McClellan was aware of Jackson's movement, he wondered if McClellan's advance on the Williamsburg Road the day before had been made to discover whether Lee had moved troops from his front. As of yesterday he had not moved any, but McClellan might well be contesting Jackson's advance. Confederate cavalry pickets had been driven off the road of Jackson's march and the telegraph wires near Ashland had been cut. Yet, as he had no alternative between abandoning his offensive and waiting for the actual developments, Lee passed the dragging hours holding on to his own composure.

Early in the afternoon, when the sun had grown hot, Major Brent came to him with a message from Magruder. The general wished to inform Lee that nothing untoward was happening on his front. Brent observed that Lee's tie was pulled around in his collar and, though his face held the familiar expression of confident calm, he looked a little disheveled. In his own strain, Lee recognized that excitable "Prince John" had grown uneasy, and he smiled at the naiveté of sending Brent with his innocuous message.

"I suppose you have come to find the cause of our delay," he said, "for General Magruder must be anxious. We have been waiting for General Jackson." Then Lee asked Brent to remain there until he had a message to send Magruder.

Shortly after Brent arrived, around three o'clock, the tranquillity over the distant countryside was broken by the crackle of rifle fire from the direction of the Meadow Bridges. Immediately, Lee saw the dark figures around Mechanicsville withdrawing from the village, retiring slowly across the farmed plain that sloped eastward a mile to Beaver Dam Creek. From the woods to the northwest, where they had been guarding the Meadow Bridges, more Federals fell back, firing. Then a six-gun Federal battery on the plain unlimbered and threw bursts beyond their own withdrawing soldiers.

Between the blasts Lee heard the distant sound of fife and drums coming nearer over the country roads that jogged at a succession of angles from the Meadow Bridges. Then a red battle flag fluttered out of the timber, where an elbow in the road turned toward Mechanicsville.

"Those are A. P. Hill's men," Lee said quietly, with no indication of his relief. Powell Hill's crossing of the Chickahominy meant that Jackson was coming on to the field.

To Brent, Lee said, "You may tell General Magruder that we'll reach the New Bridge tonight." Whatever happened in front of Richmond, the army would be connected.

Through the light smoke drifting across the farmland, Lee could see the five brigades of Hill's Light Division deploying one by one off the road. The forming battle lines stretched across the plain from Mechanicsville to a dip in the ground more than a mile northward. The blue figures and their guns had withdrawn eastward beyond the thickets bordering the slopes down to Beaver Dam Creek. From the far side of the creek Lee saw the sudden puffs of smoke as batteries opened on Hill's lines. Then, one of Hill's batteries trotted out on the field. The cannoneers quickly unlimbered and brought six guns into action. Almost immediately the guns, men and horses were engulfed in the smoke and sprayed earth from bursts from the enemy batteries.

Lee, seeing that Jackson's approach was not causing Fitz-John Porter to withdraw from his strong position, realized Powell Hill's men would be in a very exposed position if Jackson did not hurry. He decided to cross over to Mechanicsville.

Riding to the road leading down between the artillery positions, Lee found it clogged with almost motionless columns of D. H. Hill's sweating troops. By the time Lee forced his horse's way to the marshy river bank, he learned that no engineers had been brought forward to replace the wrecked bridges. This was the first lapse in the execution of his plans, that called for Hill and Longstreet to cross when the Federals withdrew from Mechanicsville. But only one brigade — commanded by Lee's Charleston detractor, Roswell Ripley — had laid planks and was just reaching the far side. A supporting battery was stuck where the swamp deepened. Lee halted and watched the gunners, splashing through the brackish water, trying to lay a crossing for their pieces. Lee waited until the bridge section was laid. Then he rode on across, pushing his horse up the half-mile slope to the crowded village.

At about five o'clock he encountered an excited Powell Hill. He told Lee that Jackson had not come yet. He, Hill explained, had advanced on his own initiative, anticipating Jackson, as he feared the whole day would be lost if he waited any longer. Lee absorbed the shock of this without speaking. Hill's breach of discipline had been made in the cause of initiative, of a sense of responsibility for the commanding general's plan, and Lee had no heart to criticize this eager personal involvement. The trouble with Hill's anticipating Jackson was that, with the bewildering silence from Jackson's area, Hill's troops were being drawn into a battle where Lee never planned to fight.

Immediately north of Mechanicsville two of Hill's brigades, in picture-book fashion, had advanced in gallant front toward the enemy. To avoid the artillery fire sweeping the plain, the men had plunged over the brow of the slope leading down to Beaver Dam Creek. There they clung to the hillside in the brush, exchanging fire with the Federal infantry. Farther north, where the banks of the creek were shallower and the thickets denser, Joseph Anderson had gotten parts of his brigade to the enemy's side. The men, pinned down by enemy fire, were holding on desperately and waiting for Jackson.

Right in front of Lee, where the east-west road to Cold Harbor led to Ellerson's Mill, dark-bearded Dorsey Pender was bringing out his North Carolina brigade from the bottoms. On his own initiative, he had tried an attack on Porter's left flank. One of his regiments was across the Cold Harbor Road, south of it, and aggressive young Pender wanted support to go back to take a Federal battery in flank. He talked first to his immediate superior, Powell Hill. Then he asked grim-faced Harvey Hill, who had just ridden into the village, about sending in Ripley's brigade on his right.

Evidently the discussion reached Lee, though not the part about taking the Federal battery. To Lee and to A. P. Hill the point was for Ripley to support Pender in turning Porter's flank by an advance along the heavily entangled woods beyond the Federal guns where the ground sloped down to the Chickahominy. But everybody was giving orders, as Lee did not assume active command of the field.

Then President Davis rode into the dusty village at the head of a large entourage composed of uniformed aides and civilians. Back at Fair Oaks, the President had so far forgotten proprieties that he had ordered forward one of Magruder's brigades late in the action in Johnston's battle. At Mechanicsville he again became carried away. He ordered D. H. Hill to send in Ripley's brigade, then formed in line of battle on the hill between the village and the river. Whether or not Lee was aware of Davis's giving an order to his army, he was outraged to see the President and members of the government making a tourist attraction of his battle. He rode up to the group and faced Davis with a sternness close to anger.

"Mr. President," he said in a tone of voice never before used between them, "who is all this army and what is it doing here."

"It is not my army, General," Davis answered with unaccustomed meekness.

"It is certainly not my army, Mr. President, and this is no place for it."

Abashed, Davis said, "Well, General, if I withdraw perhaps they will follow me."

This exchange, the first unpleasantness between the two men, was the only indication Lee gave of his thinly held control. The pieces were not coming together according to his plans, and in the confusion of the wrecked village, with shells bursting unnoticed around him, he faced the collapse of his first battle.

Around six o'clock Lee presumably learned that the van of Branch's brigade had appeared on the road from the northwest. This indicated that Jackson was approaching. Staff officer Marshall said that Lee considered it best to allow the attack of Pender and Ripley to proceed, to prevent Mc-Clellan from moving troops against Jackson which might block the juncture of the two forces. From this it appeared that Lee agreed to the make-shift arrangements in progress rather than assume command of the action. With his total plan then exposed to McClellan, there was little else he could do except let the unwanted action develop and hope that Jackson would come up.

No one seemed to supervise Ripley. This vain and quarrelsome former Regular Army officer had not arrived in Virginia until June 1. After Seven Pines his brigade of North Carolina and Georgia regiments was placed in D. H. Hill's division as partial replacement for heavy losses. Ripley led the green troops straight ahead in parade ground lines. With colors fluttering above them, the rigid men marched across the cultivated fields of Cosby's farm on the south of the road. Past the house and outbuildings, the lines moved to the slope down to the creek and millpond. Instead of drifting to the right, where the wooded hillside above the Chickahominy led beyond the Federal flank, Ripley sent his doomed men directly down the slope to the marshy ground around the creek. There packed Federal soldiers waited behind abatis on the opposite bank.

When the Federal rifles opened, the dreadful slaughter lasted until the inexperienced troops could find wet spots, where they burrowed into the earth behind bushes and small trees. When the sun was setting, around seven-thirty, one of their batteries unlimbered on Cosby's fields and sprayed the enemy, breaking the density of fire coming at them. After darkness came, around eight-thirty, the survivors began to climb out of the pit, leaving their dead. By nine o'clock the last firing faded off across the front and the fighting was over for the men.

For the commanding general the problems of the battle were just beginning. From all that was visible his whole offensive had been wrecked at the outset. Jackson was presumably halted somewhere off Porter's flank and rear, with the Federals then possessing more information about his whereabouts than did Lee. Jackson's advance, intended as a surprise for McClellan, had turned into a mystery for Lee. If McClellan suspected that

Longstreet and D. H. Hill had been withdrawn from the Richmond front, he could walk over Huger and Magruder and into the city. McClellan could — but would he?

With this question, Lee faced a different kind of a test than arranging battle plans and directing subordinates. This was a test of himself. Lee subscribed to the theory that an aggressive initiative under some conditions gave the aggressor control of the enemy's mind. The conditions were partly determined by the nature of the opposing commanding general. Put into practice against a Napoleon, the theory could produce disastrous results. Lee was staking not only a battle on his assessment of McClellan, but the nation's capital and indirectly the nation. Consulting no one, Lee determined to act on his appraisal of McClellan — that he would not attack the Richmond front.

From nine o'clock on Lee quietly watched the brigades of Longstreet and D. H. Hill sloshing across the Chickahominy, completing the division of his army *after* McClellan knew an attack was coming from north of the river. Lee of course was following his own inclinations in the decision to continue to press with the initiative. But there was something deeper. He recognized that independence had to be won by decisive military victories, and to win big he must take big risks. Since his trap had failed and the enemy was prepared, he could only win by fighting what he had designed to achieve by manuever. Though A. P. Hill's precipitate move had cost some casualties, it had cleared the north bank of the Chickahominy and the whole assault force would be in position the next morning. By then certainly Jackson would be on Porter's right and rear.

Lee ordered the new dispositions between nine and eleven that night in the noisy backwash of the battle in Mechanicsville. His wagons had not crossed the river and he ate no supper. He was joined by Longstreet, burly and unruffled, Harvey Hill, somber at the losses in his division, and Powell Hill, graceful in his tight shell jacket and quiet after the emotional drain he experienced in battle. They talked until eleven o'clock. Then Lee, keeping his disappointment and anxieties to himself, rode back across the river.

Temporary headquarters had been established, probably by Armistead Long, at a pleasant farmhouse on the plateau back from the gun positions on the edge of the bluff. The family had fled, and the weary soldiers had the house to themselves. Lee slept four hours.

2

Friday morning was another bright and sunny day, and not long after sunrise (around four-thirty) Lee was back in the debris around Mechanicsville. Nothing indicated that he recognized that his battle plan had been

too grandiose for inexperienced generals unaccustomed to operating together. However, with the new extemporized orders, he did assume a
loose command of the field at the opening action.

The men of A. P. Hill's brigades, having slept where the fighting ended,
started shooting across Beaver Dam Creek. It was soon evident to Lee that
only a holding force opposed them. McClellan had ordered Porter to
withdraw from the strong position in the early morning hours. As Jackson could not be depended upon to stay out of action on Porter's flank and
rear the second day, McClellan had ordered the withdrawal in preference
to bringing troops from in front of Richmond to oppose Jackson. There
was another naturally strong position to which Porter could retire.

When Porter's rear guard, supported by horse batteries, began to pull
out, Lee ordered forward Gregg's brigade over the crossing at Ellerson's
Mill, where the corpses lay from the evening before. Gregg's was the only
unused brigade in A. P. Hill's division. Its commander, Maxcy Gregg,
was a courtly, graying planter in his late forties, a scholarly gentleman and
fervid with zeal. His regiments were formed of privileged South Carolinians who were among the earliest volunteers after secession. Though inexperienced in combat, the men were as zealous as their leader, and advanced
without flinching over the desolate ground.

On the other side of Beaver Dam Creek, the Cold Harbor Road cut
abruptly to the north, and by eight o'clock Gregg's eager troops were
marching up the road behind the Federals' position of the day before. The
men passed abandoned equipment, burned wagons, and stragglers who appeared out of the brush to give themselves up.

Lee's salvage plan was working better than seemed possible the night
before. McClellan had neither shifted troops from south of the river to
Jackson's front nor exploited the opportunity to advance against the
weakly held Richmond front. Unknown to Lee, McClellan had abandoned his limited advance planned against Old Tavern for the day before
when he learned for a certainty that Jackson was marching south from
Ashland. Also, McClellan had been, as the saying went, "imposed upon"
by Magruder. Called "the Great Demonstrator," Magruder stirred his
troops to make such threatening gestures that McClellan's generals were
not sure but what they were about to be attacked.

With McClellan acting according to expectations, Lee expected the
Federals to make a stand in the Cold Harbor area. Cold Harbor Tavern
was at an intersection of roads that led to McClellan's White House base
and to the Grapevine Bridges that joined McClellan's forces north and
south of the Chickahominy.

After A. P. Hill's division had been started in columns of march directly along the line of retreat on the Cold Harbor Road, Lee put Longstreet's division on a parallel country road to the south. Harvey Hill's

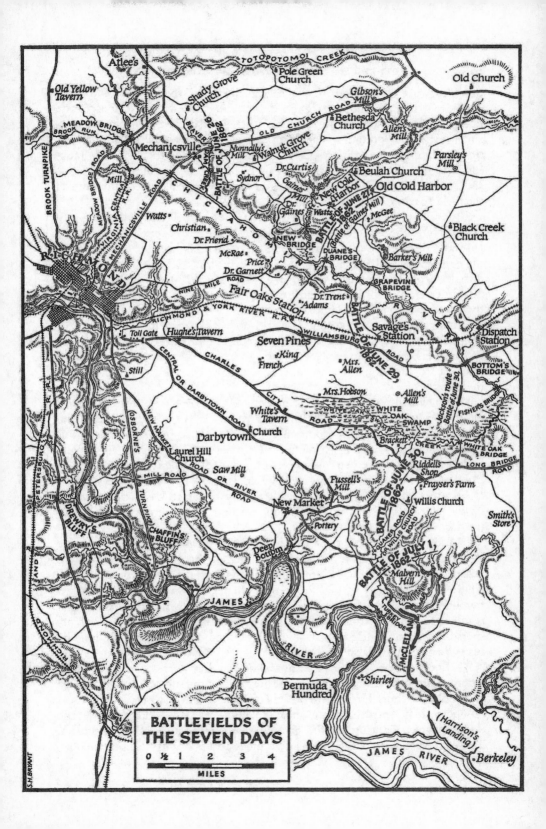

BATTLEFIELDS OF
THE SEVEN DAYS

0  ½  1    2    3    4
MILES

S.H.BRYANT

brigades were started on a road to the northeast that led to Old Cold Harbor. When all troops were in motion, Lee crossed the creek and rode behind A. P. Hill's columns of fours. When Jackson joined them, the pursuit by the four columns would approximate the original plan, with the significant difference that McClellan was prepared for them. As for Jackson, Lee had dispatched Captain Walter Taylor to Hundley's Corner — Jackson's designated point of arrival on the day before — to guide him to the Cold Harbor Road.

Around ten o'clock, word was brought Lee that Jackson with his van had arrived where the road from Hundley's Corner ran into Cold Harbor road at a right angle turn to the east. Lee pushed his horse ahead alongside the columns of Hill's men until he reached Walnut Grove Church, a short distance from the juncture of the two roads. A seedy-looking Jackson was talking to A. P. Hill in the shady yard of the country church. Lee joined them and Hill rode on off with his troops.

Lee sat down on the stump of a tree and Jackson, without warmth or animation in his face, stood in front of him as Lee began to talk in a low voice. Jackson made no explanation for going into bivouac two miles from where a battle was plainly heard. It would have been difficult for Jackson to explain.

When he had returned to his army four days before, after his second all-night ride, he had collapsed in the exhaustion of stress fatigue — a depletion of the adrenal cortex from which rest did not restore him. During his absence his army, not fully recovered from the Valley Campaign when their eastward movement began, marched badly. The Reverend R. L. Dabney, a Presbyterian clergyman whom Jackson had persuaded to serve as his chief of staff, was not fitted to bring order to the long columns. After Jackson's return, while he slept through the afternoon, a full day was lost in closing up the army.

Already behind when the van moved out from Ashland the day before — and not at two-thirty, as Jackson planned — the troops made excessive delays in clearing the road of obstructions left by enemy cavalrymen. There was no energy in Jackson to urge them. Not once did they hear his familiar "Push on, men, close up." By five o'clock, when Jackson at last reached Hundley's Corner with his van, his marching columns — interspersed with guns and wagons — were stretched out for miles behind. The rear was not up by dark.

By Lee's orders, the enemy should be moving across Jackson's front when he arrived, and Jackson should join in the pursuit via a road toward Old Cold Harbor. Except for a light screen of cavalry, the enemy was nowhere to be seen. From the heavy volume of fire Jackson heard, the Federals were fighting on the ground they were supposed to evacuate. The edge of the battle was about two miles across heavily timbered country from Jackson, and he had no notion of what was happening or what lay between him and the battle. In the apathy of his depletion, he did nothing. Before darkness came, he went to sleep to try and get a good night's rest. Not restored, in the morning he was surly and irritable as the troops resumed their march, and it was in that state that he listened to Lee's new plans for him.

Lee expected the Federals to make their stand atop the hill on the far side of Powhite Creek, a stream that ran from north to south through a sharp valley to empty into the Chickahominy. The roads followed by A. P. Hill and Longstreet led directly to Powhite Creek. Jackson — supported by D. H. Hill — would turn the creek north of the pond at Gaines' Mill to deploy on the Federal flank. Without the element of surprise, it was a repeat of the plan made for Beaver Dam Creek. Though no records were kept of this conversation, Lee's plans were made clear in a wire he sent Huger.

Jackson nodded his understanding and turned abruptly to his horse, an ugly sorrel. He mounted in a short-stirrup perch and the horse moved off in an awkwardly gaited trot. With the start of Jackson between the two Hills, all the pieces had at last come together in Lee's plan. Further to relieve his anxieties, Porter had then retired east of the New Bridge, opening a passage between Lee and Magruder. The two parts of his army were no longer dangerously separated.

Lee rode to the Hogan farmhouse, overlooking the river above the opened New Bridge, and sent the telegram to Huger. In informing Huger, Lee showed the rise of his optimism by suggesting Huger keep alert for Federal withdrawals from his front. Lee believed the bulk of McClellan's army was then on the north side of the river with him. This was Lee's first serious miscalculation: McClellan had sent only one division across to support Porter.

Shortly after noon Lee heard the expected crackle of rifle fire from the vicinity of Gaines' Mill, where the Cold Harbor Road crossed Powhite Creek. He took to the saddle again to go to the scene of action. Though he expected the battle to be fought by his subordinates, he wanted to be on hand for an action so casually improvised.

Strangely, as he approached Powhite Creek, the firing receded ahead of him. When he reached the hill leading down into the valley by Gaines' four-story brick mill, the only troops he saw were A. P. Hill's. They were hurrying up the opposite hillside in the heat. Powell Hill was not in sight. At a mile or more ahead of Lee, to the east, he heard the thunder of guns rolling above the rattle of the rifles. Lee rode down the hill, across the creek, and up the other side, where he had expected Porter to stand.

There he found only an advanced enemy camp that had been overrun and pillaged by Maxcy Gregg's lead brigade. The only Federals he saw on the plateau were a few prisoners going to the rear. Three-quarters of a mile across the open stretch ahead of him, the east-west running road bent at a left angle in an area called New Cold Harbor. A mile to the north the road reached the white frame tavern at Cold Harbor, locally called Old Cold Harbor to distinguish it from New Cold Harbor. The action seemed to be in the New Cold Harbor area.

Lee rode to the angle where the Cold Harbor Road turned north. There a private road continued to the east and from it another private road bore off to the south. Lee halted at a clearing beside the private road, across which several of Hill's brigades were deployed. The men were moving toward a woods grotesquely entangled with draping vines and briary underbrush. The woods dipped and climbed again, and from the unseen valley between, rifle fire rose in heavy volume. But the blasts of guns Lee heard came from an opposite plateau. Porter had found a position not shown on Lee's maps.

In the clearing just beyond the bend in the road, Lee joined Powell Hill. Hill was sitting at ease in his saddle, his deep-set eyes peering under the brim of a black felt hat. He told Lee that Gregg had located the enemy beyond a winding stream, part swamp, part creek, called Boatswain's Swamp. He was deploying his brigades for an attack. Lee's brief survey showed that the unmarked course of Boatswain's Swamp provided the enemy with the strongest position he had ever seen. It was a natural fort.

Paralleling the road from Old Cold Harbor for a mile to where Lee and Hill were mounted, and then south for another mile, Boatswain's Swamp changed from a slippery high-banked creek in the center and to the right into a broad soggy ditch approached by a morass from the center toward Old Cold Harbor. At the Old Cold Harbor end, the swamp swung around as if designed by nature to protect the flank of an army occupying the crest. D. H. Hill had arrived at Cold Harbor tavern to find the enemy in position across his front. He had immediately deployed a brigade across from Porter's swampy flank — occupied by Sykes's U. S. Regulars — and it had drawn back under the plunging fire of Sykes's guns.

At the southern flank of the line, the hill above the swamp ended in a sheer bluff overlooking the boggy ground that sloped to the Chickahominy. On the bluff, gun batteries swept the field. Longstreet was moving his division into woods facing that end of the line, below Powell Hill, and making no effort to turn the flank by way of the open fields commanded by guns. There was no chance here for a flanking maneuver as at Cerro Gordo or Contreras. The enemy must be attacked where he was, and Lee did not know the Federal strength.

With the reinforcement of Slocum's division, Porter numbered scarcely thirty-five thousand infantry and artillery. The numbers seemed greater because the rifle fire was concentrated in three tiers behind light works on the hillside above the swamp, with the Federal soldiers firing from stationary positions, and artillery was massed. Where Lee looked into the valley, obscured by the jungle of foliage, the Federal guns brought a terrible sense of wreckage with their metal bursts crashing among the entangled trees, tearing off branches and tossing up geysers of muddy vines. The violence confirmed Lee's impression that Porter's natural fort was manned by considerably more than thirty-five thousand. As he had wired Huger he believed the "bulk of McClellan's Army" was on his side of the river, he may have estimated as much as twice thirty-five thousand were available to Porter over his entire front.

This was another test for Lee. Circumstances were forcing him to assume command of the field, and he had never before directly ordered men into combat. It was a point where many able strategists lost their poise and others lost their decisiveness. Lee could not bring more than fifty thousand men, infantry and artillery, to the assault even when all troops had come up. As attacking troops were bound to suffer heavier losses than an enemy in Porter's powerful position, sweeping all approaches with his destructive guns, Lee was forced to the decision of staking everything on his belief in the valor of the men. Counting on their valor, he could count in advance on the thousands of the most valorous who would never leave that valley.

No observer — and they were plentiful in his clearing — noticed any hesitation in Lee or change of expression. It was passing three o'clock and Jackson had not yet appeared. Acting in anticipation of his arrival, Lee expected the Federal line would have to be extended when Jackson joined Harvey Hill on Porter's right flank. When the weight shifted away from A. P. Hill's front in the center, Longstreet would deliver the attack for the decision below Hill on Porter's left. Longstreet was sent orders to prepare for his advance. Then Lee quietly told Powell Hill to advance his men in assault as soon as Longstreet was in position.

3

Hill's men, smarting from their setback of the day before, plunged down through the thickets to the boggy bottom with high yells. For a short while Lee could follow the course of units by the sound up the opposite hill. There the units hung. Some fell back. Others made advances, and then they too fell back. As Lee and Powell Hill lost sight of the brigades when they vanished into the brush, so the brigadiers in turn lost sight of their separate regiments in the smoky thickets over the bog, and colonels could only see the men immediately around them. Soon the assault resolved into separated fragments fighting for their lives on countless small fronts. To Lee it became evident that not only were Hill's bitterly engaged troops making no progress; they were standing off counterattacks.

This was not the confusion of disarranged plans as the day before. He was looking into the face of battlefield defeat. He could see it in the slack faces of soldiers, recoiling out of the valley and stumbling in shock among the stretcher-bearers and the crawling wounded. He could hear it in the explosions falling among Hill's batteries, whose gunners seemed only to draw fire upon themselves. On the road near Lee, Willie Pegram had going the two guns he had salvaged from the wreckage to his battery the day before. This shy, bespectacled twenty-one-year-old Richmonder, who had left college to volunteer in a gun battery, looked like a misplaced scholar as his eyes strained through his glasses to see the effects of the fire. Nothing dimmed the roar swelling from the guns on the opposite plateau. Obviously Hill's men could not hold out against the tornado sweeping through the bottoms. If they broke, the army would be cut in half, and it would be all over.

Then, from the left, Lee saw the welcome sight of the columns of Ewell's division, veterans of Jackson's Valley Campaign. Dick Ewell, looking like a startled bird with his bulging eyes and wild mustachios, said he did not know where Jackson and the rest of the force were.

In advancing, Jackson had taken a fork in a road that led to the back of the large millpond of Gaines' Mill. There they heard firing in front of them, instead of along Powhite Creek. When the march was retraced to get on the enemy's flank, as in Lee's orders, Ewell's division had gotten in the lead. He became separated from Jackson's division and the two brigades forming Whiting's division.

Lee could not worry about where Jackson was again. Ewell's first two brigades were hurried into the action across the private road leading to the McGehee house. Lee watched the self-confident veterans brush contemptuously past Hill's shattered brigades, yelling taunts at their fellow Confederates. Lost from view when the men went slithering across the wet ravine, the two brigades shuddered to a halt at contact with the wall of fire. Before momentum could be regained in the slippery footing, Federal brigades on their left began to press forward in counterattack. Encountering the difficulties of the obscuring terrain that had beset Hill's brigades, the tough, proud troops found themselves struggling merely to maintain their positions in the foggy brush.

The third brigade, going in on their right, did not even do that. Dick Taylor's Louisiana brigade broke for the only time in its career. Taylor, grandson of President Taylor, was ill that day, and his colorful regiments went in with their pelican flag under senior colonel Isaac Seymour. Seymour was shot dead from his horse, order was lost in the bedlam in the thickets, and the men began clawing their way out of the valley.

Again Lee saw troops under Jackson's command appear separately and in uncertainty. These were the two brigades with Whiting, appearing out of the woods between Lee's clearing and Old Cold Harbor.

It seemed that on the road to the tavern, Whiting had received some garbled order delivered by Jackson's quartermaster, Major John A. Harman. Vain Whiting hated Jackson, whom he had known as a dull plodder at West Point where he was a ranking cadet. Uncooperatively, he halted the head of the column in the road until Chief of Staff Dabney had, on his own initiative, sent him forward cross-country toward the firing. Losing their way in the woods, his troops had emerged by chance where they were most needed.

Lee ordered John Hood and Evander McIver Law to bring up their columns and deploy on Hill's right. Before these troops were in position to go in, Lawton's big brigade came out of the woods farther toward Old Cold Harbor. These were the Georgia replacements attached to Jackson's own division, and it is not certain if Lee immediately saw the troops in their bright new uniforms. Lawton was directed off Ewell's mangled left by an unnamed staff officer, evidently attached to some unit in Ewell's division. On his own responsibility Lawton advanced the three thousand Georgians, and their Enfield rifles fired the first solid volume since Hill's initial attack.

At the same time, off Hill's right, Longstreet also acted on his own initiative. Earlier he had received orders to make a demonstration to relieve the weight on Hill. After advancing fully deployed, Longstreet decided a demonstration would be futile and decided to prepare for a full-scale attack on the formidable Federal left. While Longstreet was preparing his assault, at about five o'clock Jackson came trotting into the clearing on his ugly-gaited sorrel horse.

Lee turned to him and said in a flat voice, "Ah, General, I am very glad to see you." Then, to make the reproach plainer, he added, "I had hoped to be with you before this."

Jackson, his pale eyes staring myopically under his cap's visor, mumbled something. He made no explanation of having waited for two or more hours at the Cold Harbor tavern while the brigades under his command wandered their way through the strange woods, all coming out at different places. Two brigades from his own division were not on the field yet.

Then Lee said, "That fire is very heavy. Do you think your men can stand it?"

"They can stand anything," Jackson answered in a loud, grim voice. "They can stand that."

John Esten Cooke, a novelist then serving on Stuart's staff, recorded that Lee then gave Jackson orders in a voice too low for any of the nearby staff officers to overhear.

At that stage the battle was hanging in the balance. The enemy *had* to be driven or Lee's whole counteroffensive would collapse right there. In fact, with McClellan's communications unthreatened, Lee would be forced to hurry his survivors back to protect the Richmond front. Since there was no time or place for strategy, Lee told Jackson to place the brigades of his own division — as they came onto the field — in the gaps in the line curving from Longstreet on the right to D. H. Hill. Harvey Hill was still hovering off the enemy's right flank. When the line was complete, the whole force would move forward.

It was late in the day to mount an assault for a decision, but it was also too late to do anything else. Lee demonstrated here his willingness to risk a decisive defeat in committing himself to win. It also showed his personal aggression.

Some time after six o'clock the last of Jackson's brigades, having emerged from the woods west of the Cold Harbor Road, were forming in line. By then Hill's and Ewell's troops were finished. Remnants of the Light Division huddled along a rise above the last soggy dip to the swamp and maintained an irregular fire. But they had fought out the troops facing them, too — Morell's division, then McCall's in as replacements, then two brigades from Slocum's fresh division sent over by McClellan. As the sun began to sink, and Longstreet began to exert pressure on Porter's left flank, McCall's brigades were pulled out of the center and shifted to meet Longstreet pushing on their left.

Lee did not know that McCall's brigades left the center. He did reason that, with Longstreet massing on the right and D. H. Hill advancing on the left, the successfully held center would be the last place a fresh assault would be contemplated. The assignment went to the two brigades under Whiting, already in line behind Hill and extending his right southward from the road leading to the Watt house.

After giving Whiting the order, Lee turned to tawny-bearded Hood, and told his former lieutenant that none of the day's fighting had dislodged the enemy. As Hood remembered it, Lee said, "This must be done. Can you break his line?"

"I can try," Hood replied without hesitation.

Hood rode down to the two lines of his four regiments, the men fixing bayonets in the final pause before going in over the ground strewn with the corpses and untended wounded of Hill's men. The solders were under orders to advance as rapidly as possible without firing, getting quickly over the slick banks of the creek and on up the hill to close with the bayonet. The sun was setting when they suddenly moved forward with a determined rush. On their right Longstreet's long lines simultaneously swept forward under their red flags.

When the forward movement passed over the rise where Hill's survivors continued their fight, Hood showed the instincts of the born fighter and a fighter's instinctive reactions. Surveying the advancing lines he saw a gap broadening between Law, on his right, and Longstreet's left. Acting by reflex, he pulled the 4th Texas out of line and, followed by the 18th Georgia, put the men at a slanting run behind Law to come out into the gap. The 4th Texas had been Hood's original Confederate command, and the men plunged down the slope at a point where the Federals were closest to the creek. One-fourth of the regiment fell before the Texans reached the bottom. There the whole line, Hood and Law, scrambled across without a pause to fire.

The two brigades began scrambling up the opposite hill, their bayonets flashing in the dusky light and their high screams ringing over the din. The Federal troops in the first defensive tier began to waver. Porter's men were tired by then. Many of their rifles were fouled from the long firing and there was something irresistible about the line of bayonets coming at them through the smoky brush.

The first line started to fall back onto the second. As soon as the Federal soldiers exposed themselves by rising from behind their light works, Hood's and Law's men fired for the first time. Three thousand rifles crackled at close range. Under that rain of lead at their backs, the fought-out Federals broke. Scrambling their way up the hill, dropping rifles for speed, they rushed over their own second line and carried those defenders with them. The third line went before the first two reached it.

The second and third lines did not join the rush. Those men fell back firing. The casualties made no impression on the Confederates. Native-born Virginians were leading the 4th Texas. Colonel John Marshall, fifty-year-old Austin newspaper editor, was shot dead off his gray horse. The lieutenant colonel was Bradfute Warwick, a twenty-three-year-old Richmonder who had fought with Garibaldi while studying medicine in Italy. Warwick picked up a fallen battle flag and led the way to the crest of the hill. There he fell, wounded, dying a week later in his father's house. The 4th Texas had lost half its personnel when the survivors burst out on the plateau in front of the small house of the Watt family, where Porter had his headquarters in the center of his great position.

Hood had Georgia troops as well as Texans in his brigade, and Law's Alabamians breasted the hill at almost the same time. At about the same time Virginians in Longstreet's brigades came storming up on the hill. But Lee never forgot what came to be called "Hood's Texans." From then on the "Texans" became synonymous with shock troops in Lee's mind. It was an army victory, a soldiers' victory, and the key to it might well have been cool-headed John Hood, who meant what he said when he answered Lee, "I can try."

4

The engagement called Gaines' Mill was not over when John Hood made his breakthrough. But Lee knew then he had won his first battle. All of Longstreet's large division crowded up on the plateau where Porter's left had stood. At the other end of the line D. H. Hill pushed hard against Sykes's retiring Regulars. Officers tried to organize their scattered units for pursuit in the deepening dusk. There was too much confusion on both sides.

A few Federal cannons still blasted away while hundreds upon hundreds of Federal foot soldiers were being gathered up as prisoners. Entire regiments had been cut off by Hood's break. A woebegone cavalry charge was attempted by Jeb Stuart's father-in-law, Philip St. George Cooke, with a U. S. Cavalry regiment. That ended with a stampede in reverse, the horses overrunning Federal gun batteries and carrying off artillery horses in the rush. Sykes's Regulars held steady in their withdrawal, and two fresh brigades, sent over late by McClellan, served as a rallying point for the disordered retreat by the other divisions.

Lee's one certainty when night closed over the farms of the plateau was that the Federals had been driven from their strong position, leaving more than a dozen fine U. S. artillery pieces, thousands of rifles, and military stores beyond the dreams of the short-rationed Confederates. Also on the field were thousands of Confederate dead and wounded, approximating eight thousand when unofficial counts were in — the high cost in casualties to troops attacking a strongly defended position. It was a battle Lee had to win, and he did not count the costs. As he had answered Whiting's Johnstonian calculations of disadvantages, "If we cipher, we're whipped before we start."

Yet it was a melancholy field with the darkness disturbed by the cries and groans of the wounded, the flickering lanterns of medical parties, the rustling movement of men looking for friends and the hungry looking for forage. Wagons had not gotten up and most of the troops with empty stomachs lay down on the field where night found them. Lee's message to the President held no elation. Thanking Almighty God for the victory granted them, he wrote, "I grieve to state that our loss in officers and men is great."

Some time after dark, Lee returned to the Hogan house and ate his simple supper. Though not a Spartan by nature, he had grown up on country-style cooking, liked the plain foods of his region, and ate to appease his hunger rather than to enjoy a connoisseur's sampling of victuals. He was joined at the temporary headquarters by Longstreet, establishing himself as the right hand, and by Jackson, who thus far had done nothing to justify his reputation. In the easy conversation that followed victory and a full stomach, the men talked of preparing to advance at daylight. They would finish off the shaken McClellan on the next stand he made to protect his supply line. The logical stand would be where the York River Railroad crossed the Chickahominy at Dispatch Station, only six miles east of the battlefield.

The next morning, Saturday, June 28, Lee received some baffling information. When he returned to the jammed clearing at New Cold Harbor, Lee was informed that the enemy had vanished. Probing patrols by Longstreet and Jackson flushed only bodies of stragglers. These Federals had been left behind when Porter had retreated during the night across the Chickahominy to the main body of McClellan's army. Lee hurried off Stuart's cavalry, supported by Ewell's division, to Dispatch Station. While beginning wreckage on the railroad, the troops must discover the whereabouts of McClellan. Soon a courier galloped up to Lee with the message that the enemy had abandoned the north side of the river completely. The railroad bridge across the Chickahominy was burned. Stuart was pushing on to the White House base. With him would ride the colonel of the 9th Virginia, Rooney Lee, whose home it was.

While Lee was riding over the scene of Sykes's stand near the McGehee house, he encountered another son. Rob was a gunner in the Rockbridge Artillery, a battery composed mostly of college students and founded by Reverend William Pendleton at Lexington. Instead of numbering the guns, the rector had named them Matthew, Mark, Luke and John. The commanding general found his son asleep under a gun carriage. After another cannoneer prodded him awake, the begrimed boy and his father exchanged a few casual words, and the commanding general rode on. He had some private figuring to do.

McClellan had crossed Lee by refusing to leave his works to fight for his supply line. Yet, McClellan could not remain in the works in front of Richmond when he was depending upon the several hundred tons of supplies delivered daily to him by the railroad. In trying to read his opponent's mind, Lee had no way of knowing that McClellan was involved with confusing nonmilitary considerations. The formerly hailed "savior of the Union" was fighting fundamentally for his reputation.

From the beginning, McClellan's plan for crushing the dissidents with a single decision — the capture of Richmond by use of his superior armament — depended upon an orderly progression of his schedule. Since he had been in Virginia he had suffered the loss of his government's confidence and a succession of interferences. These had resulted in his own developed fixation about the coming of McDowell and a habit of giving meaningless promises to Lincoln and Stanton, whom he regarded as inferiors with temporary authority. Suddenly the initiative was seized from him, and the issue ceased to be governed by his schedule of operations. He needed to improvise, to invent a new combination. Between his own ambitions and his tenuous relations with his government, McClellan seemed unnerved by the unexpected turn. He shrunk from taking any risk at all.

He thought only of saving his army and particularly of saving the twenty or so siege guns he had by then brought forward to his lines. Once Porter's worn corps completed the crossing to the south during the night of the 27th-28th, and the bridges connecting McClellan with the north side were destroyed, he had saved his army — and his siege guns — at the cost of the campaign against Richmond. For, cut off from the base at the White House, he had no alternative to withdrawing from the lines to which he had advanced in front of the city. He did have an alternative in the way of withdrawal.

The logical and the safest way was a retreat down the Peninsula, back the way he had come to the base at Fort Monroe. This, however, would be an admission of defeat, and lead to the destruction of his ambitions by the hostile elements in the government. To avoid this failure, this palpable "retreat," McClellan decided to "transfer" his army across the Peninsula to the James River twenty miles below Richmond.

Back in the middle of June, Jeb Stuart's ride had alerted McClellan to the exposure of his base, and he had made preliminary plans with the navy to establish another base on the James River. On the night when Porter crossed the Chickahominy, McClellan sent orders to move everything possible by water from the White House to the James. Before leaving, the base troops were to destroy all stores that could not be immediately piled on ships, along with locomotive engines and freight cars. More than three thousand wagons were loaded to be moved across the Peninsula, and a herd of cattle.

At his Richmond lines, everything from the lavishly supplied camp that could not be loaded on the wagons was to be put to fire or abandoned. By the time the wagons and the army made it across the narrow roads, passing over the White Oak Swamp on the way, McClellan expected or hoped that the navy would have established a point on the James River where the army would retire under the protection of the gunboats and where the men and animals could be supplied.

McClellan later arranged a rationalization for his withdrawal to the James. He called it "a change of base" and pointed out the weaknesses of the White House as a supply depot. But the James as a base lacked at least one feature in relation to McClellan's plans — a railroad to move to the front the seacoast guns by which the evacuation of Richmond could be forced. Once on the James he would have tacitly abandoned his method of taking Richmond. Once he left the York River Railroad, his campaign by siege was over. For support of his rationalization, however, McClellan had never revealed to his government that he planned to take Richmond by siege operations.

Since these considerations of McClellan's were unsuspected by Lee and the generals with him that morning, their first reaction to finding the north side abandoned was a baffled disappointment. Lee's whole carefully devised plan had been for the purpose of prying McClellan out of his works for a battle in the open, and Longstreet said flatly the strategy was "unsuccessful." Some of the generals were convinced that McClellan would not retire when so close to his goal and believed he planned to overrun Magruder and Huger.

As on the night before, Lee faced the possibility that McClellan *could* drive into Richmond and again decided that he would not try. Once McClellan declined battle in the open, Lee seemed to expect him to retreat. Where or when was something else, and Lee could not begin a pursuit until McClellan evacuated his heavily fortified lines.

Lee sat his horse in the informal field headquarters in the clearing by the Cold Harbor Road, where the procession of ambulances moved haltingly toward Richmond. Coming from the city, groups of men from the supply services in Richmond passed Lee on their way to glean the field. From them it was obvious that in the capital the battle was regarded as a great victory that would lift the siege of Richmond. The President did not come out to Gaines' Mill, after his chastening experience at Mechanicsville, and during the day sent no word of his thoughts. But lifting the siege, as important as it was, had been incidental to Lee. He had set out to destroy McClellan's army as an effective unit. That remained his purpose.

Around noon Lee saw the first clouds rising east of McClellan's line. The retreat had begun. As he peered at the dust, its general direction away from the Seven Pines-Fair Oaks area could be either down the Peninsula or toward the James. In the uncertainty Lee sent off a staff officer with an order to Dick Ewell. He was to follow the Chickahominy from Dispatch Station to Bottom's Bridge, where the Williamsburg Road crossed the river, and see if the Federals were going down the Peninsula.

Simultaneously, on the south side of the river cavalry patrols tried probing eastward along the roads fanning southward from the Williamsburg Road. Federal picket lines had all approaches blocked. Between the Chickahominy and Fair Oaks an ill-timed assault made by political general Bob Toombs in Magruder's division was heavily repulsed at the main Federal lines. They seemed as strongly posted as ever. An attempt of Longstreet's guns to rake the Federals on the other side of the river aroused a smothering fire in answer. Lee knew he was losing a day by inability to gain positive information, but the army was, as he reported, "compelled to wait until his [McClellan's] purpose should be developed."

It was a dragging wait during the long, warm afternoon. By the end of the day Lee was satisfied that McClellan was moving toward the James. However, the only action he could take was to dispatch orders for early movement the following morning. Longstreet's engineers were to cross the river at daylight "to test the presence of the enemy." Magruder and Huger must be prepared to move out as soon as the Federals' intentions were discovered. These were only generalized directions toward the first step in organizing a pursuit. In moving across the Peninsula, McClellan would expose his army to attack, and if Lee could devise a trap he had another chance for the battle that would "destroy the enemy."

At dusk Lee rode back to temporary headquarters at the home of Dr. William Gaines, from whose grounds McClellan had fired his siege guns at Magruder across the Chickahominy. After supper, during the early hours of the night Lee began to evolve his second improvised plan in two days. Either he completed the plans early or he grew tired. When Brigadier General Jubal Early came to confer with him at eleven o'clock, he saw Lee sound asleep in bed, and he tiptoed out of the room.

## 5

On the hot, close Sunday morning of June 29 McClellan was gone from in front of Richmond. The miles of trenches stood deserted, and the squares where the city of men had bivouacked looked like a ghost camp. Tents were still standing, some with furniture, and rows of meat barrels, boxes of crackers, real coffee and tins of fish, trunks and camp chests bugged the eyes of the first Confederate soldiers to gaze on the splendor. Lee did not allow the men time to forage. They had to hurry to get on McClellan's rear guard.

Lee had crossed the river to Nine Mile Road. He met Magruder at the clearing by Fair Oaks near where he had watched Joe Johnston's chaotic fight not quite a month before. Colonel Chilton had already carried a message to Prince John ordering him to advance his division quickly on McClellan's line of retreat. Magruder was later to complain that Chilton had rushed him along so fast that he could not confer with his brigadiers.

Magruder was in a highly nervous state. He had suffered extreme tension from the three days of occupying those lightly held lines with nothing behind him, and for three nights had gotten little sleep. Worse for the famed gourmet (whose table was the delight of his staff), Magruder had lost his appetite and gotten some medicine from the doctor for what he called indigestion.

Lee did not notice the strain on the resplendently turned out Prince John. He was concentrated on explaining Magruder's part in his newly devised plan. The basic factor in Lee's tactics was the White Oak Swamp. This was a small, ugly version of the Chickahominy that spread its swamps across McClellan's route to the James River. Lee calculated that McClellan, with his wagons and livestock, would not get across White Oak Swamp before the following day. Lee's plan was to catch him in flank and rear at the crossroads at Glendale, a point of congestion on the Federal line of march, the next day.

Longstreet and A. P. Hill, recrossing the river at New Bridge, would move down the Darbytown Road to where it intersected the Long Bridge Road. There the two divisions would turn northeast on the Long Bridge Road, aiming for Glendale, where McClellan's columns would be branching off into the Willis Church Road. Hill and Longstreet would approach the front of McClellan's advance at an angle. Simultaneously Huger, having left his lines across the Williamsburg Road, would move down the Charles City Road, which intersected the Long Bridge Road at Glendale squarely on McClellan's flank. Magruder's job was immediate. He was to inflict as much damage as possible on the rear guard to slow the retreat and make certain that McClellan's columns were strung out in line of march the next day.

Lee explained to Magruder that Jackson, after rebuilding the Grapevine Bridges, would cross the Chickahominy to support him on his left. Magruder should advance cross-country between the Williamsburg Road and the York River Railroad, with Jackson — including D. H. Hill — coming up between his left and the river. These orders seemed clear enough, and Magruder nodded without questions.

Leaving him, Lee rode on along Nine Mile Road in its stretch behind McClellan's abandoned main lines between Fair Oaks and Seven Pines. Over at the Williamsburg Road Lee went to Huger's headquarters, to watch that sluggish general get his brigades moving onto the Charles City Road. When Huger rode off, Lee remained at his headquarters as a conveniently located center of operations. As the sun climbed, the forenoon grew hot. Lee seemed more relaxed than during the two preceding days. His army was safely reunited, the hazard to which he had exposed Richmond was past, McClellan was known to be in full retreat, and Magruder's troops were in motion in pursuit.

In this relaxation, Lee reverted to the preferred methods of command he had used the first day, at Mechanicsville. It was the traditional method for a commanding general to operate from a central headquarters (as did McClellan) where he would be in communication with all parts of the field. In following it, Lee also believed that placing responsibility on subordinate generals developed their initiative. This choice to operate from a general headquarters that day, with loosely and newly organized units of command, was the first serious mistake that exposed Lee's inexperience as a field general.

While his elaborate battle plan for Mechanicsville reflected inexperience, it failed because of human agencies — which Lee had optimistically believed could be controlled by mutually understood details of operation. But when he stationed himself on the Williamsburg Road, in comparative remoteness from Magruder's developing pursuit around Fair Oaks, Lee made a more basic mistake. He assumed that the parts of an army would function cooperatively without a central control of operations. This central control of operations depended upon staff work, and Lee had not then designed his staff to exercise this control.

In Lee's studies of Napoleon and experiences with General Scott, he had found no model of staff work to serve the changing needs which new technologies brought to warfare. (The advance work being done by the German general staff was not revealed until the Franco-Prussian War.) The most fundamental change brought to war was the rifled musket, the rifle. Where the less accurate smoothbore's range was fifty yards for effective shooting, the rifle had an effective range of two hundred yards when fired by the average soldier and of four hundred yards when fired by good marksmen. With a Whitworth rifle, a sharpshooter was effective at half a mile. In 1862, no general commanding on either side had yet appreciated the profound effect of this increased firepower, especially on assaulting troops. Nor had any other general, any more than Lee, devised at that stage a staff essentially different from Napoleon's or Scott's.

McClellan, a natural and superior organizer, had had nearly a year in which to perfect coordination between the parts of his army. But much of McClellan's attention had gone into the supporting services. He had supplied and equipped the Army of the Potomac as no other force ever on earth before. In fact, the soldiers were overburdened with supplies, with nonessentials and luxuries that did not tend to make troops hard, lean and mean. Without the wasteful abandonment of material, the army would scarcely have been mobile. One of the reasons why Lee was slow to accept McClellan's abandonment of the White House base was that his frugal mind could not conceive of the waste of a nation's resources on that scale.

McClellan happened to have in Brigadier General Randolph B. Marcy (as Napoleon had in Louis Berthier) an enterprising chief of staff, with energy and initiative. Marcy, McClellan's father-in-law, like Berthier, assumed many of the functions which, in a later period, became defined as the duties of an operations officer. When formalized, the duties of an operations officer were to maintain knowledge of the movements of every unit in his own army and, in cooperation with intelligence (the G2 section of modern staffs), knowledge of the disposition of the enemy's forces. Marcy only approximated these functions and, when pressed by other matters, did not maintain contact with the various units.

Lee had nothing approaching even the idea of an operations officer. If he expected Chilton, as chief of staff, to assume some of these functions, he never indicated it. That Chilton was a disappointment was evidenced by the alacrity with which Lee sped him back to the adjutant general's office when, later in the war, Chilton expressed a wish to leave the field. Lee's lack of comment on the subject would not in itself mean anything, since he continued to hold Chilton as a man in high regard and would have spared his feelings. However, aside from Lee's never mentioning operational functions which Chilton might have handled, in his first campaign he did nothing himself to remedy the lack or to show awareness that it existed. He simply seemed to accept this vacuum between headquarters and operations.

Of course, with all his experience in the army and his practical, correlative intelligence, he had been an army commander only twenty-eight days and was leading in combat for the first time in his life. Yet, from the day he began with Virginia's forces, Lee had demonstrated as few did an understanding of the nature of a citizen-army and adapted himself to the special needs of an extemporized force without the machinery of an established government. This understanding implied, of all things, an appreciation of the limitations of individuals, and Lee had displayed this in countless instances. With Magruder specifically, when the landing of McClellan's army threw him into a near panic at Yorktown, Lee had appraised the situation and, with never a reproach, by encouragement had steadied him into making a fine stand. But on assuming the personal responsibility of taking an army into combat, Lee turned to the familiar methods of traditional command in which he ignored the already demonstrated limitations of subordinates.

The "chivalric Magruder," as Davis called him, a generous, guileless and appealing man, had been best known in the Old Army as an artillerist and stager of pageants, and his most famous exploit was his season as social lion at Newport. During his three-day defense he had shown himself to be mercurial and excitable, and leading an attack would make even higher demands upon him. Jackson, with his gaudy reputation from the Valley Campaign, had failed to cooperate properly in the two battles that involved him. Though Lee knew no more than Jackson about the apathy of stress fatigue, Jackson looked dour and lethargic. Huger had been so slothful that Lee had reprimanded him for absence from headquarters during action on his front.

In that period Lee appeared to expect his generals to be aroused by combat to realize their fullest potentials, to transcend their normal limitations. Battle was the ultimate test for their cause. Along with this expectation, however, he gave such simple assignments — in comparison with the grandiose strategy at Mechanicsville — that nothing was required of the subordinates beyond rudimentary techniques of command. Between his expectations of the men and the simplicity of their assignments, Lee assumed that the units of his army *would* operate according to orders, and it never seemed to occur to him that staff officers could be sent to investigate what was actually happening.

6

An investigation into Magruder's pursuit would have discovered a complete breakdown in all staff work, the division commanders' as well as the commanding general's. At the beginning, Magruder's largely inexperienced troops came under a sizable volume of enemy fire shortly after the lead brigade deployed into the densely screened woods east of Fair Oaks. Unable to view the front and fearful of firing into Jackson's troops expected on the left, Magruder halted and waited for Jackson. When no word came from Jackson, Magruder (who employed his staff officers more than anyone) sent off a courier to ask when Jackson was coming. He would be delayed, Jackson's engineering officer reported, rebuilding the Grapevine Bridges.

Huger had not come up on his right. This was a misunderstanding of Magruder's, but he expected Huger there. He sent off Major Brent to Lee's headquarters. Brent, the lawyer who was learning about staff work as he went, apparently brought Lee the first message from the pursuit forces. He reported that Magruder expected an attack from a heavy Federal force in his front and asked that Huger come up on his right.

This surprised Lee, and he seemed, according to Brent, "a little incredulous." A Federal rear guard would scarcely attack. Lee apparently assumed that Magruder's well-known excitability was creating phantoms. He asked Brent if he personally had observed the enemy and formed an opinion of its numbers. The major said he had made no reconnaissance.

"But what do you think?" Lee asked. "Is the enemy in large force?"

From Magruder's headquarters Brent would not have seen the Federals at all through the heavy woods. In point of fact, they were posted in great force. Heintzelman's and Sumner's corps and Slocum's division, strongly supported by artillery, comprised half of McClellan's infantry.

Avoiding Lee's question, Brent replied formally, "General Magruder has instructed me to say that he finds the enemy in strong force in his front."

Lee smiled, Brent thought, in appreciation of his loyalty to Magruder. Clearly not believing the report, Lee sent neither Long nor Chilton, the trained soldiers on his staff, to check it. Instead, to be on the safe side, he told Brent he would order the last two of Huger's brigades to retrace their steps and move east along the Williamsburg Road to Magruder's right. If, however, no action opened by two o'clock, the brigades would be with-drawn.

Brent was not instructed to inform Lee that Jackson had not come up on the left. Lee, assuming he was there, did not ask. Brent rode off.

On the Williamsburg Road couriers brought Lee messages from other fronts, one very saddening. Jeb Stuart reported finding two squares miles of McClellan's supply base burning along the riverfront at the White House, and Rooney Lee's home reduced to ashes. McClellan had left strict orders to protect the house in which Martha Washington had lived when she married General Washington, and St. Peter's Church, in which both had worshipped. Horses were stabled in the church, and an arsonist from a New York regiment set fire to the house before leaving the base on a transport.

From Magruder's front, however, came nothing until late in the after-noon. Then it was the sound of rifle fire crackling above the thunderous roll of artillery pieces. Lee did not ride to the sound of the firing. His mind was manifestly on McClellan's retreat across White Oak Swamp and catching him there the next day. He continued to expect the strong ad-vance force he had ordered to drive what he presumed to be a rear guard. The firing beyond Fair Oaks did not swell appreciably, and from the scat-tered sounds he could estimate only that the enemy was not being driven. At the end of the day, he sent Walter Taylor to Magruder.

The purpose of Taylor's mission is vague and his part in the sequence of mishaps is unclear. It is not known when or through whom Lee learned what happened on the "pursuit."

Several hours before Taylor left Lee, around two o'clock, Huger de-cided he was not needed and withdrew from Magruder's right without informing Magruder. Shortly afterwards Heintzelman, also deciding he was not needed, withdrew his corps from the Federal left without inform-ing anybody. Each force, unknown to itself, had an open flank. Then, Magruder was informed that Jackson was not coming, as he had been ordered to "other important duty." Just as Magruder had decided to at-tack without Jackson, he discovered that Huger was gone. Hastily dis-patching a brigade to cover his right, he ordered the five other brigades forward. Completely out of self-control, he gave the order for "each commander to attack the enemy in whatever force or works he might be found."

Magruder's "command," as it was called, was a loose organization of three half-divisions (two brigades each), and only one was commanded by a trained soldier. With one brigade off to the Williamsburg Road, the other five pressed separately into the jungle at different speeds of advance. Only one brigade, Kershaw's, made it all the way to the Federal main line in the clearing at Savage's Station. This was a large farm at a stop on the York River Railroad, and in the open fields beyond the house McClellan had established a field hospital for twenty-five hundred wounded and sick. The brigade commanded by Joseph Kershaw, a lawyer from Camden, South Carolina, attacked with "great fury" — as the Federal generals reported — but the only result was to bring Lee's attention for the first time to the name of Joe Kershaw.

The other brigades did not come up in support or extend the line of attack; a couple of them never got into action at all. Though Kershaw's assault pierced Burns's brigade, the Federals had reinforcements at hand, and the isolated attack was contained as dusk gathered. On the Williamsburg Road, Sumner had by chance also discovered his flank was open and hurried troops over to clash with Paul Semmes's regiments in a brief, bitter fight in the dusky woods north of the road.

As the light was fading along with the action Magruder galloped his horse (he always rode at a gallop except for short distances) to the left of his line to talk with one of his politically appointed brigadiers, Howell Cobb, of Georgia. While there, Major Taylor came looking for him. In Magruder's official report, which Lee endorsed, he wrote that Taylor "informed me that General Jackson had orders to cooperate with me, and that there was some mistake about the orders directing him elsewhere." Because of a later communication from Lee to Magruder, it can be deduced that Magruder had told no one about Jackson's "other important duty" before he talked with Taylor. Taylor wanted to go then and see Jackson himself. Darkness had fallen, and under the intertwined branches of the trees it was as black as a cave. Without seeing Jackson, Walter Taylor made his way back to Lee and told him of the conversation.

Also, it can be deduced that by the time Taylor had gone off Lee already possessed some general information about the sputtering out of Magruder's disordered attack. He had written a message to Magruder expressing his "regret" at the little progress made in the pursuit. After Taylor returned, Lee added a postscript to the letter: "I learn from Major Taylor that you are under the impression that General Jackson has been ordered not to support you. On the contrary, he had been directed to do so and to push the pursuit vigorously."

In this message, Lee strangely seemed to blame Magruder for believing Jackson had not been ordered to his support. By then Lee knew that Jackson had not crossed the Chickahominy to cooperate on Magruder's left as ordered. As typical of Jackson since he had been on the Peninsula, he had not communicated with Lee all day. What the "other important duty" was never became known. Yet, there is no record that Lee ever queried Jackson about this or reproached him for not following orders.

Based on his actions, and those only, Lee seemed to judge Jackson on his potential and continued to expect him to live up to his Valley reputation. With poor Prince John, Lee seemed to judge him also on potential. In his case, Lee reached the right estimate on wrong evidence.

Jackson's failure to come up on Magruder's left made an immeasurable contribution to Magruder's gradual loss of self-control. His promising officers, like Kershaw, all mentioned the unsettling effect of waiting for Jackson's troops on their left. And, although it was Magruder's sense of uneasiness rather than reconnaissance that filled the woods in front of him with Yankees, they were there. Without Jackson, even a well-coordinated assault most likely would not have driven them.

None of this was known to Lee when he decided his former fellow cadet would not do. Lee had evidently seen enough of Magruder's susceptibility to alarms. Though Magruder happened to have good reason for his alarm at Fair Oaks, he had not know the reason any more than Lee did.

Magnificent-looking Prince John was in no sense a timid man. But when acting in concert with others — as pointed out by Armistead Long, one of his many admirers — he lost his poise. Magruder seemed to be made anxious by his responsibility in another's battles. His imagination took over, replacing skills with apprehensions, and he became a creature of irrational impulses. It is possible that Walter Taylor described to Lee Magruder's highstrung condition. In any event, he ceased to figure prominently in Lee's further plans. The pursuit was to be given to Jackson.

As an aftermath of the futile fighting (The Battle of Savage's Station), a terrible electric storm broke the sultriness in the middle of the night and the camps were drenched in the downpour.

## 7

The next morning the blue of the sky looked as though the storm had washed it clean, and before the sun began to climb the air was fresh and soft. This was the big day for Lee, the closing of the trap on McClellan at the Glendale crossroads, and he put behind the disappointment of yesterday's feeble pursuit. The sun was not long up before he was dressed, had finished breakfast, and was riding with his staff along the Williamsburg Road toward Magruder's headquarters. Near Seven Pines he saw Stonewall Jackson alone in the middle of the road, motionless on a small sorrel, with his staff of mostly young men farther down the road.

A young artillerist, Robert Stiles, not fully recovered from a light wound, was propped against a nearby pine. As he saw Jackson, the still figure looked much worn down, and from his dingy little cadet cap to his outsize boots he seemed "one neutral dust tint." According to Stiles, Lee, "absolute perfection" in "every detail of dress and equipment," dismounted when he neared Jackson, pulling off his right gauntlet. Jackson moved quickly then, "flung himself off his horse," and advanced to shake hands. His horse, called "Little Sorrel" by his men, trotted back toward the staff group, the flapping stirrup cups catching the glint of the early light.

In a brief conversation, Jackson seemed more animated than since he had reached the Tidewater. Following the Battle of Gaines' Mill, he'd had two uninterrupted nights' sleep and two quiet days. By no means restored from the clinical exhaustion, he had a little rise in energy and, momentarily free of the apathy, was eager to get at the enemy. Lee, ordering him to take over the pursuit, talked over the details of Jackson's closing on McClellan's rear, while the other columns attacked him front and flank at the Glendale crossroads. With everything clearly understood between them, Jackson signaled for his horse, and then vaulted awkwardly into the saddle.

Lee stood for a moment watching him ride away, evidently reassured by Jackson's determined manner. Resuming his ride, Lee began to see and hear the evidence of McClellan's hurried retreat. At Savage's Station, Mc-Clellan had left his twenty-five hundred wounded and sick, along with medical supplies which some idiot vandals had ruined. Hillocks of food supplies still smoldered, exploded ammunition dumps had left craters, and unharmed tools and equipment would fill a warehouse. At intervals mules bearing us on their flanks charged out of the wet woods and from clumps of brush Federal stragglers appeared to give themselves up. The road of the retreat was literally carpeted with discarded blankets and overcoats. Scattered dead of both sides lay unburied.

At Magruder's headquarters Prince John seemed more excited than ever. He had not gone to bed until three-thirty, when Jackson himself finally appeared, and then had slept one hour. He nodded vigorously when Lee told him to march his six brigades down the Darbytown Road, closing on Longstreet and A. P. Hill.

Lee rode back up the Williamsburg Road to the Darbytown Road turnoff. Soon he approached the strung-out colunms of the Longstreet-Hill force. The sun was turning the day uncomfortably warm, and the men had marched hard in the humid heat the day before, but the columns held a good pace and troops were cheerful. Lee rode alongside the marching ranks to the head of the column. The advance, with skirmish lines out, had swung left into the Long Bridge Road, which crossed the Peninsula from roughly north to south. The sun was almost directly overhead. Scrub woods enclosed the road on both sides, swallowing up the lonely figures of the skirmishers, pushing tensely through the brush.

Suddenly rifle fire rattled along the skirmish lines. The columns halted in the road and regiments from the lead brigade deployed into the entangled woods. They had hit the skirmish lines of McCall's division. General George A. McCall, ex-Regular Army, commanded the "Pennsylvania Reserves," sent from McDowell to support Porter, and A. P. Hill's men had fought them at Mechanicsville and Gaines' Mill. McCall's line was only one and one-quarter miles from the Glendale crossroads, where McClellan's columns were branching off into the Willis Church Road to the river. They had him.

Lee turned his horse off the road into a clearing as the shouts of cannoneers and the rattle of swab-buckets swinging on chains under the pieces announced the approach of a gun battery. Excitement began to rise. The improvised plan was working, the trap closing. Longstreet and A. P. Hill joined Lee in the clearing in a far different atmosphere from the gloom at Mechanicsville.

The plan was working even better than Lee realized. The four divisions McClellan had left at Glendale were not yet in position, and the Willis Church Road, forking off to the river, was jammed with wagons. McClellan's siege guns had just crossed White Oak Swamp, where the prized pieces were temporarily halted more than two miles away from the crossroads. Franklin's two divisions, posted there as rear guard, were resting after the passage over White Oak Swamp. The greater part of the two Federal corps which preceded the wagons had reached Malvern Hill and, below it, the advance brigades were at the River Road. McClellan himself had ridden on to the James River. Leaving his army, he was conferring with Naval Captain John Rodgers about a site for a new base to which he could retire. Though these details were unknown to Lee, his improvised plan gave him the opportunity to cut the Federal Army in half.

Lee's clearing was in countryside similar to the ground on the north side of the river. Mostly flat, the land was divided between small to middle-sized clearings of farmland and the timber with its matted screens of vines, briars and underbrush. At intervals boggy little streams coursed through murky ravines. By direct airline, Lee would have been between two and three miles across country from the Charles City Road at the point where Huger should be in position to open on the flank of the Federals at Glendale. At noon Lee received a message from Huger stating that the road had been obstructed, but it was then about cleared.

At this reassuring news, in preparation for Huger's joint attack, Dick Anderson's brigade of Longstreet's division was fully deployed and advanced. The wiry men drove McCall's skirmishers back on their main defensive line on the edge of the woods facing the cultivated fields of the Wilcox farm. Longstreet's other brigades and one of Hill's began to deploy off the road and form lines of battle.

During the wait for Huger to open, Lee received a message from Magruder. His six brigades had completed their march and were halted by

A. P. Hill's rear guard on the Darbytown Road. Lee dictated an order for Magruder to rest his men there, and be ready to support Hill and Longstreet.

At half-past two came the welcome sound of a blast from one of Huger's batteries. Everyone was so alert that orders were scarcely necessary. The cannoneers hurried their guns forward, the men trotting beside the gun carriages, and in a few moments the pieces were unlimbered and roaring. The soldiers in the skirmish line increased their firing.

Into the clearing rode President Davis, erect in his saddle and very military-looking with his Confederate gray waistcoat and dark gray coat and breeches. As he and Lee remembered their sharp passage at Mechanicsville, they greeted one another with especial cordiality. Davis was not followed by sightseeing politicians and Lee was not under so much strain. As the Federal guns began answering Longstreet and shells burst around the clearing, Lee did suggest the President move to a safer place.

Then Powell Hill, with his social ease, rode up and told both of them they were in his area of command and must obey his orders. They must withdraw from the clearing. As the commanding general and the President, with several members of their staffs, turned their horses about and started back, a shell burst over the precise spot where the group had been gathered.

After Lee had withdrawn to another clearing on a slight rise, the good-natured atmosphere began to pall. Three o'clock passed and no more sounds came from Huger's position on the Charles City Road. Federal guns were roaring over there — where Slocum's division was posted facing west — but from Huger nothing was heard. It was also past time for Jackson to have opened on the Federal rear, two miles to the north of Glendale.

There Franklin had destroyed the bridge after crossing. His two divisions, posted on high ground above White Oak Swamp, overlooked the small jungle through which the brackish stream coursed. Jackson, in position on the opposite side, with thirty guns going, was not heard above the Federal artillery where Lee waited. Neither Jackson nor Huger sent any messages. Again Lee did not send staff officers to discover what was holding them back.

At four o'clock, with apprehensive tension having replaced the earlier excitement, the commanding general received a message from an unexpected source. Tom Rosser, a black-haired, powerfully built Virginian of the West Point class of 1861, had only recently been commissioned colonel and given a regiment of raw volunteers. Unattached to Stuart's main body of cavalry (still on the north side of the Chickahominy), Rosser had been reconnoitering between Glendale and the River Road. Where the

Long Bridge Road intersected the River Road at New Market Heights, Lee had placed old deaf Holmes, who had crossed the James River with three brigades, artillery and a little cavalry. Unknown young Rosser had informed both Holmes and Longstreet that he had discovered Federal columns retiring hurriedly and in confusion to the James River. Longstreet was preoccupied with placing his own brigades and Holmes, stupidly placing his men on defense, paid no attention. Enterprising Rosser sent the information directly to Lee.

This must be investigated. Evidently not trusting any of the officers with him for important reconnaissance, the commanding general left field headquarters and rode down to the River Road to check Rosser's report. Looking upward from the River Road to the crests of Malvern Hill, what Lee saw was not troops but wagons, and moving rapidly. The jam at Glendale had broken in the four hours since noon. Moving by two roads — one a woods trails discovered by Keyes — McClellan's wagons were making it to the safety of the river.

When Lee thoughtfully turned back west on the River Road, he encountered Holmes, hurrying forward six guns and a regiment. He told Lee the rest of his command was being put in motion. Lee ordered Holmes to open fire on the enemy wagons to halt their movement. The parts of the Federal Army around Glendale were still separated and exposed to Lee's designed attack from three sides. But the attack had to come soon.

Lee galloped back to his post on Long Bridge Road. He found Longstreet, whom he had left in charge of the field, still waiting on Huger and Jackson. It was then around five o'clock, and Lee ordered Longstreet to deliver his assault. When Jackson and Huger heard him fully committed, one or both *must* come in.

Neither did. The two divisions of Longstreet and A. P. Hill, totaling under twenty thousand, attacked from first to last upwards of forty thousand Federal troops. McCall's division was broken and routed. Guns were overrun and captured. To the support of the four Federal divisions around the crossroads, a brigade was withdrawn from in front of Huger and two brigades from in front of Jackson. Lee watched the gray-uniformed men rush into the enemy's fire with spectacular fury, disregarding casualties. The momentum of the charge reached its crest, and then hung suspended. Ominously, Lee saw the thinned, disordered lines waver under the weight of counterattacks. Outwardly nothing changed in Lee as he watched Powell Hill send in the last brigade on the field.

When Lee had been absent on the River Road, Longstreet — exercising his temporary field command — had sent Magruder to support Holmes. Though Lee had recalled Magruder, there was no possibility of his tired men returning before dark. On the River Road, feckless old Holmes accomplished nothing. A few shells from the Federal guns on Malvern Hill discouraged his efforts to halt the escaping wagons.

When dusk began to cover the cleared fields and the woods, Lee saw by the flickers of rifle shots that his scattered units were going to hold to the point of their farthest advance. Only a little more than a mile short of Glendale, inexplicably those survivors of Gaines' Mill fought on alone with no support coming from the other two sides of Lee's perfectly designed trap.

The answer to the silence from the Charles City Road and the White Oak Swamp lay in the minds of men, outside any of Lee's tactics. Huger at best had grown sedentary from too many years in the even tenor of garrison life and, after being held up to the public as the villain of Seven Pines, fear of making mistakes reduced him to stupefied inanition.

On Huger's approach to Glendale, his lead brigade had been commanded by William Mahone, a small, slight Virginian who, in concern for his health, carried his own cow attached to his headquarters wagon. Billy Mahone had been a successful civil engineer before the war. Instead of clearing the obstructions the enemy left in the road, he decided to use his engineering skill and cut a new road through the woods. While his men hacked through the woods, the enemy extended the obstructions on the road. Huger came up and watched this battle of the axes, while his columns moved at the rate that a road could be cut. When at last around noon he emerged at the foot of a cleared hill, whose crest was occupied by Slocum's division, Huger opened with the one battery heard by Lee. When the enemy replied from the usual alignment of Federal rifled artillery pieces, Huger broke off fire and called it a day. Even when enemy troops were removed from his front to stem the Longstreet-Hill attack, he was not aware of it.

Two miles to the north of Huger at the crossing of White Oak Swamp, Jackson suffered a return of the apathy that overcame him when confronted by a problem not readily soluble. When he sent work parties to rebuild the bridge across the swampy stream, enemy sharpshooters on the wooded hillside across from the creek repeatedly drove them off. When Jackson tried to shell the enemy out of the woods, his own guns were outranged by Federal batteries posted on top the opposite hill. Dilemma.

His cavalry found a cowpath crossing to the north, and Wade Hampton, recovered from his Seven Pines wound and temporarily commanding one of Jackson's brigades, found another crossing with solid approaches that would support a footbridge for infantry. Jackson told Hampton to build the bridge. When Hampton reported the bridge was ready, Jackson, without a word, got up from where he was sitting and walked away. He sat down again. He wrote a letter to his wife, telling her he longed for the peace that would reunite them. He inquired after his colored Sunday school in Lexington. Decision became a physical impossibility, the effort overcoming him with drowsiness. After nightfall brought an end to his struggle against nature, he fell asleep during supper in the midst of chewing a mouthful of food. Rousing himself, he said, "Let us get a good night's sleep and see what we can do tomorrow."

No tomorrow would ever bring such possibilities for the destruction of the enemy's army as the trap Lee had set for that Monday, June 30. Such a possibility came once in the lifetime of an army. Lee recognized the magnitude of the opportunity that he had literally watched slip through his fingers, and the burden of that frustration was more than he could hide.

His disappointment was apparent to those near him, though, Longstreet said, "the composure with which it was borne indicated the grander elements of his character, and drew those who knew his plans and purposes closer to him." D. H. Hill, no admirer of Lee, observed that "he bore grandly his terrible disappointment." But the effort at composure, the lack of release in any kind of outburst, took its toll.

8

When July first broke hot and clear on the close countryside, General Lee showed the strain. He was not at his best. His thinking lacked the sharp clarity with which he had improvised the Glendale trap. Early in the morning he rode near the then deserted crossroads. His dark eyes brooded over the Willis Church Road down which McClellan's columns had escaped. Longstreet joined him there, his hearty humor unruffled by yesterday's disappointment. Then Harvey Hill, riding ahead of his troops in Jackson's column, rode up looking very subdued.

He had talked to a preacher friend of his who lived in the neighborhood, Hill told Lee. The Reverend W. L. Allen described the Malvern Hill plateau, where McClellan could make a rearguard stand, as a most forbidding position. After repeating the description of the difficult approaches to a half-circle plateau, where the powerful Federal guns could sweep, Harvey Hill said, "If McClellan is there in force, we had better let him alone."

Longstreet laughed. "Don't get scared," he said, "now that we've got him whipped."

Lee said nothing. He was impatient to start a pursuit. What to do about McClellan's defensive position could be decided when his troops found McClellan there. The worst of it was that the pursuit had to be made with the three forces that had already failed him — Huger, Magruder, and Jackson. The divisions of Longstreet and A. P. Hill, which had consistently done all that could be asked of men, were in no condition for further fighting that day.

Magruder's hard-marched men had relieved Hill's troops across the Long Bridge Road after midnight. Prince John himself compulsively placed the lines. With only two hours' sleep in seventy-two hours, and with the adverse effects of morphine in the medicine the doctor had given him, Magruder had grown so excitable that some uncharitable observers thought him drunk. Even his loyal staff officers had been shocked at irritability in the "chivalric" superior who was usually so thoughtful. Mounted at daylight, the poor gourmet was so undone that for breakfast he chewed at a chunk of bread while in the saddle. His orders were to follow Jackson down the Willis Church Road.

Jackson rode up at the head of his column, including Ewell's division, then returned from north of the Chickahominy. Lee rode across to the Willis Church Road to meet the dingy-looking general who had again failed him. Again Jackson offered no explanation. Lee could only hope the hero of the Valley Campaign would come to himself in the low country. He simply ordered Stonewall to follow the pursuit until contact. At least appearing alert after a long night's sleep, Jackson rode off with his van, Whiting's two brigades.

Last to get started would be Benjamin Huger. Before learning from Longstreet that morning that the enemy had vanished from his front on the Charles City Road, Huger had sent out two of his brigades to his right — southward. Armistead and Wright, encountering no enemy, had followed a woods trail to come out on the Long Bridge Road where the burial details were working near the scene of the action of the day before. Lee ordered those two brigades to the support of Jackson's right, and sent an order to Huger to bring on his other two brigades. Huger, undisturbed by the disappearance of Lewis Armistead and "Rans" Wright, started the other brigades in motion without coming personally to see Lee on the Willis Church Road.

Not only was Lee placing the pursuit in the trust of three failures, but jamming their combined troops on the Willis Church Road was poor logistics. Jeb Stuart was only then on his way back from north of the Chickahominy. The mounted detachments at hand had found the heavily brushed country to be difficult for cavalry operations. Lee, judging the little cavalry nearby to be useless, never seemed to think of sending out reconnaissance parties to look for other approaches to the base of Malvern Hill. He located neighborhood guides to attach to the advancing forces and seemed bent only on getting in motion the troops that had unaccountably been held out of the battle of the day before. When Jubal Early, an aggressive brigadier with Ewell, said he was worried that McClellan might escape them, Lee answered with untypical impatience.

"Yes, he will get away because I can not have my orders carried out."

From that remark, Lee seemed to hold no optimism about the pursuit. Accompanied by Longstreet, whom he had asked to ride with him, Lee moved on down the Willis Church Road for a look at McClellan's defensive position. He found Malvern Hill as forbidding as Hill's friend had described it.

The Willis Church Road took an oblique turn and climbed a quarter-of-a-mile hill between wheat fields to the crest. On the broad plateau the road ran between the driveways to modest plantation houses on either side — the Crew house and outbuildings in a grove on the right and the West house on the left. Beyond the Crew house to Lee's right the ground sloped abruptly away to a field of shocked wheat below. Immediately in front of the house's farmyard, this slope became a sheer bluff at the top of the hill which his assaulting troops must climb.

Beyond the West house on Lee's left rose a fringe of entangled woods along one of the inevitable boggy banked streams, Western Run. The small jungle of this stream, crossing the Willis Church Road half a mile from the foot of Malvern Hill, formed McClellan's right flank as the abrupt drop beyond the Crew house formed his left.

When Lee's first troops, moving forward on the road, became visible on the heights beyond, Federal batteries immediately opened. Once again came the sickeningly familiar crashing of metal fragments through the trees and foliage. In preparation for whatever might develop, Lee sent the division of "honest fighter" Harvey Hill off the right of the road to negotiate the troublesome creek crossing under artillery fire. He was too oblique to face the foot of the hill. Whiting's two brigades, the van of Jackson's force, were sent off the road to the left.

There the clearing of the Poindexter farm spread northward from the fringe of brushy woods along Western Run to another growth of timber. Lee observed that the Federal artillery fire came the heaviest on his left, where Hood's and Law's brigades were deploying their lines to move up toward Western Run. He deduced that McClellan regarded this as his more vulnerable flank.

As badly as he felt, Lee determined on a personal reconnaissance of the ground along Western Run. At the same time he gave Longstreet the responsibility for a reconnaissance of the ground in front of Malvern Hill, from a position about a mile and one half from and immediately facing the Crew house. A wooded hill rose there, whose crest seemed as high as the Malvern Hill plateau, and Longstreet was instructed to appraise, he said, "the feasibility of aggressive battle." He was also to lead Magruder's six brigades into position on D. H. Hill's right.

Longstreet rode confidently off on the assignment of a sort Lee had done as a captain in Mexico, while the commanding general surveyed the ground nearby. Lee did not seem to have any definite purpose in mind, though he had placed himself where he could observe what Jackson did with the troops under his command. Something after one o'clock Longstreet returned in a very sanguine humor, despite the report that Magruder had taken the wrong road.

The Willis Church Road was also called the Quaker Road, and the Quaker Road was what Magruder had been ordered to follow. There was also another Quaker Road, called nothing else, and three local guides had all assured Magruder that his road, dwindling off in the woods, was *the* Quaker Road in Henrico County. Magruder's aimless travels seemed unimportant to Longstreet because of the discovery he had made on the crest opposite the Malvern Hill plateau. In a clearing there sixty to eighty guns could be placed. If Jackson placed a like number in the Poindexter farm clearing, a crossfire could be brought on the Federal guns that would open the way for an infantry advance.

This prospect lifted Lee's spirits. But his mind was tired, his frustrations goaded him to get at McClellan before he got away, and he did not think with an objective appraisal of the elements on the field. Immediately Lee sent orders for Jackson's guns to be moved up and sent Longstreet back to his clearing to supervise the placing of the batteries. It did not occur to either depleted Lee or exuberant Longstreet to consider where the guns would come from to form the massed artillery on the crest. With Longstreet started off again, Lee told Chilton to write an order, and his nominal chief of staff wrote a garbled and unmilitary message to go to the division commanders.

"Batteries have been established to rake the enemy's lines. If it is broken, as is probable, Armistead, who can witness the effect of the fire, has been ordered to charge with a yell. Do the same." Chilton signed the order.

When the couriers rode off with that vague order, Lee lost control of the battlefield, and the action was directed by a sequence of unrelated happenings.

9

Lewis Armistead was selected as the observer by the chance that his brigade had advanced by a woods trail, instead of along the crowded Willis Church Road. By following a ravine that paralleled the base of Malvern Hill, he and Wright had come out on D. H. Hill's right in front of a fence that marked the edge of the Crew house wheat field. Armistead, a forty-five-year-old Regular Army man, had spent the earlier months of the war with Huger in garrison duty, and he and his Virginia regiments were very eager for field action. Armistead knew nothing about the one-thirty order, which had gone to division commander Huger, and on his own ordered up a couple of batteries around one o'clock. When Longstreet returned to his clearing between one-thirty and two, the batteries supporting Armistead were already being knocked about by return fire, and Armistead asked him for more guns.

Colonel Chilton had then ridden to Magruder's command to direct it to the field by a crossroads. Longstreet sought out Magruder, with the van of his troops, to ask him about artillery support. Magruder had thirty guns under division chief of artillery Colonel Stephen D. Lee. These were then in the rear of the column, and Magruder said that he would advance them as fast as he could. Longstreet's euphoria at his assignment quickly evaporated before the gritty details of making a reality of his suggestion. By two-thirty he could determine from Jackson's few guns in action, never more than two batteries at one time, that the massed artillery bombardment was as puny from Jackson's position as from Armistead's. He concluded that the idea was a failure. He rode away from the elevation and on back to his own command, never trying to find Pendleton's large reserve artillery.

Fussy Pendleton, obsessed with details, had been following the army with his many guns since Savage's Station, and was then looking for the commanding general to get some orders. The Reverend Brigadier Pendleton never found Lee, nor did Lee, any more than Longstreet, evidently think of Pendleton.

By three o'clock Lee also realized the bombardment was a failure. By then he probably began to resign himself to the day's passing without an attack on McClellan. Jackson had established field headquarters at Smith's place, north of the Poindexter farm, and Lee joined him there. No suggestions came from Jackson. His troops, waiting for orders, were huddling against the artillery fire roaring across Western Run.

Unknown to Lee, also at three o'clock Armistead ordered a local advance against Berdan's Sharpshooters, who had ventured too close under the protection of the shellfire from their own guns. Armistead's Virginians, released from their long inactivity as soldiers, ran forward after the retiring sharpshooters' line of skirmishers. Parts of Wright's brigade impulsively followed the chase. With gray-haired Armistead keeping up with them, the enthusiastic troops ran forward for a quarter of a mile before they halted beneath a slight rise at the foot of Malvern Hill. As the men would be too exposed to Federal artillery in returning to their position without Berdan's Sharpshooters screening them from Federal artillery, Armistead and Wright decided simply to stay where they were.

An hour later Magruder reached the field with the first of his wandering brigades, and was handed Chilton's note: "Armistead . . . has been ordered to charge . . . Do the same." Though written around one-thirty, the time was not on the message, and Magruder assumed the orders were current.

Magruder could see Armistead's point of advance, with parts of Wright's brigade. Others of Wright's regiments and Mahone's brigade were ready to go in. Most of the artillery fire did seem to be coming from the Federals, but a few guns were maintaining their fire, and Magruder's own batteries were toiling toward the clearing on the elevation. Accused of lacking vigor in his pursuit at Savage's Station, Magruder did not delay a minute. He dispatched staff officer Captain Dickinson with a message to Lee indicating that he was on the field and ready to exploit Armistead's advance.

Just before Captain Dickinson reached the commanding general, Lee's flagging hopes had been partly revived by a message from Whiting. He had seen movement around the old house back on Malvern Hill which indicated that parts of McClellan's forces were withdrawing. Though this was little to go on, it was what Lee wanted to hear. When Captain Dickinson then reported that Magruder was ready to follow up Armistead's *advance*, Lee responded with his hopes and did not consider the excitability of the author. Almost in reflex, he told Dickinson to tell Magruder to advance.

Careful Captain Dickinson asked that the order be put in writing. Lee dictated, "General Lee expects you to advance rapidly. He says it is reported the enemy is getting off. Press forward your whole line and follow up Armistead's success . . ." He included some details of troop disposition and hurried off Magruder's staff officer.

Lee lingered at his temporary headquarters near the gateposts in Smith's farmyard, to be accessible to any messengers, until around five o'clock. Then he heard the high yell of advancing Confederate troops drifting across the bottomlands. He started his horse down the Willis Church Road for the scene of action. At Western Run he turned to his right and found a crossing below where D. H. Hill's five brigades were preparing to move forward. Out of the brush bordering the swampy creek, he rode up the wooded hill toward the country road which Magruder had used in getting to the field.

Alarmingly he began to pass among strung-out columns of Magruder's brigades, feeling their way through the woods to the front. The faces of the men showed exhaustion from all their marching. A glance showed the ranks seriously thinned by stragglers unable to keep up.

Lee emerged at a clearing near the crest, turned to survey the field of Malvern Hill, and beheld an appalling sight. The remnants of three brigades — Armistead, Wright and Mahone — were clinging to the hillside under the brow of the hill near the Crew house. Wright and Mahone clung to the western face, trying to fire over the top, and Armistead, under the cliff to the front, was only seventy-five yards from the Federal guns. In the wheat fields some distance from the hill, two of Magruder's brigades were wavering in making an obviously late move in support. The Georgians of portly Howell Cobb and the Mississippians of white-haired Barksdale had advanced across the open fields in parade-ground formation, as the still and writhing figures in their wake testified, but men could advance no farther into the gale of metal sweeping at and over them.

On the other side of the Willis Church Road, D. H. Hill had started closer to the base than Cobb and Barksdale. Lee saw one of his brigades advanced to within two hundred yards of the crest. There the Alabamians had sought shelter under a slight rise. The other brigades had halted at various spots farther down the hillside. Stragglers from Hill's stout troops were pouring to the rear in droves. Obviously Harvey Hill had done all he could alone, and Lee saw no evidence of help coming from Jackson across Western Run.

Before he found Magruder, Lee turned to Lafayette McLaws, a bushy-bearded professional who commanded the two brigades Lee had passed drifting in the woods. With his sure instinct for ground, Lee directed McLaws to the front, though the two brigades — Kershaw's and Semmes's — were reduced by straggling to no more than fifteen hundred exhausted men. Then Prince John Magruder himself came to Lee and reported that Huger had refused to release Ransom's brigade in support because Magruder had neglected to send the order through Huger. Lee sent a personal order for Ransom to advance to support the three isolated brigades near the Crew house.

Behind Lee, Colonel Stephen D. Lee's artillery battalion was suffering frightful casualties in struggling toward the clearing, as the road was under the fire of Federal guns. Colonel Lee had a few half-manned howitzers firing for what good they could do. Young Willie Pegram, from A. P. Hill's division, was directing the fire of one gun still in action.

Magruder's last two brigades began to emerge from the woods behind D. H. Hill's men, then hugging the ground against the brutal antipersonnel fire of large-bore howitzers run forward from Colonel Hunt's artillery reserve. Kershaw and Semmes came out to Hill's right, and their fifteen hundred obviously could not live through the bursts crashing from the hill. The men said shells that "looked like lampposts" came hurtling from the heavy reserve guns posted farther back on the plateau.

When dusk began to settle over the hillsides strewn with gray-clad corpses and wounded, and indomitable Harvey Hill began to withdraw his men down the slope and out of range, Lee stared at a scene of irretrievable disaster. He watched anxiously for Federal counterattacks. As darkness began to gather over the countryside, the Federals showed they were satisfied to have repelled the assault. On their perch near the Crew house, where Armistead, Wright and Mahone prepared to settle for the night, it had looked close for a little while. The fire of the survivors of these three brigades had been accurate enough to drive off one Federal battery and force a call for reinforcements. Gradually the Confederate fire had grown weaker, to fade off at darkness.

Over where Harvey Hill had fallen back, Jubal Early led forward the first of Ewell's brigades. Those troops were just reaching the front after pushing through the melee of ambulances and stragglers jamming the Willis Church Road. Late in the day Jackson had ordered those reserves forward, but he had given no orders to Whiting, along Western Run, to support Hill directly. Except for the belated appearance of tobacco-chewing Early, Jackson might as well have not been on the field. Lee saw Early's men deploy in the darkness to form a line among the dead against surprise. Then he turned his eyes away.

In riding off the field, he passed the field headquarters Magruder had established. Captain John Lamb, who had devotedly attached himself to Magruder, was spreading blankets on the ground for the exhausted Prince John. Lee paused there and he could not help himself. He asked Magruder why he attacked.

Lamb recalled that Magruder answered stoutly, "In obedience to your orders, twice repeated."

It was true enough. It would be pointless for Lee to say he had sent the second order on the assumption that Magruder's brigades were on the field and in hand. If a commanding general made assumptions, he was responsible for the consequences. The deeper truth was that Lee had never been in possession of his full faculties, nor ever exerted directing command of the field. He must have known that. A competent performance by Magruder, with fifteen thousand men available, some help from Jackson, with something approaching fifteen thousand, might have made a difference. But the responsibility for the battle was his. He must accept the costly failure as his own.

He rode off to find his own bivouac.

10

To the men around Lee, the important point was that McClellan was gone from their front. The worn Federals were retreating through a foggy rain along River Road to the three-mile river front and wharves of Berkeley plantation. The Federals called it "Harrison's Landing" from the name of the family who, masters of the great plantation, had given the country a signer of the Declaration of Independence and a President. The minds of McClellan's soldiers were not on past heroes as their boots turned the wet wheat fields into paste, and ambulances carrying thousands of sick and wounded churned along the seventeenth-century driveway toward the transports and the protecting gunboats.

A desultory pursuit was started, joined in by Jeb Stuart, whose cavalry had returned to the army at the end of the day before. In the cold rain, over dirt roads turned into churned mud, the tired men of Longstreet and A. P. Hill made little progress. McClellan's rear guard turned on Stuart when his horsemen came too close.

This seventh day, of the Seven Days Battle Around Richmond, was taken by the commanding general largely as a day of rest, or comparative rest. That morning he established headquarters in the parlor of the Poindexter house, where a fire was built against the sudden chill. Longstreet came there, wet and out of humor. The day before had not gone well for him, and his troops, of whom he took meticulous care, looked in a shape he did not like. Jackson came, dour and uncommunicative, and sat in the gathering formed of Lee and staff officers. Then President Davis came from Richmond, full of military talk and suggestions, but not at all the autocrat he could sometimes be. The men in the parlor could see that the commanding general, for all his deference — perhaps partly because of it — was in charge of military operations in Virginia.

The next day Lee bestirred himself and his army, and the following day, the Fourth of July, he returned once again to one of his personal reconnaissances. He wanted to discover if there was any way to get at McClellan on the flat lands of Berkeley plantation. He summed up his findings in a letter to the President. "I fear he [McClellan] is too secure under cover of his boats to be driven from his position. I discover no intention of [his] either ascending or crossing the river at present. Reinforcements have joined him, and his sick, wounded and demoralized troops have been sent down the river."

On that casually worded note to Davis, Lee's counteroffensive campaign ended. To the people in Richmond, freed of the siege, and throughout the Confederacy, the retreat of McClellan's great army from the gates of the capital changed — as Lee had wanted — the character of the war. The siege of Richmond had symbolized the besieged state of the whole Confederacy. The lifting of that siege, in a bold driving counteroffensive, revivified a people who had been enduring invasion with flagging hope. A surge of aggressive spirit swept through the struggling young nation.

As Richmond had symbolized the besieged state, the "deliverer" of their citadel symbolized the fresh wave of hope and the surgent will to carry the war to the enemy. Lee emerged in those seven days as the authentic Confederate hero, a people's god, and the most famous soldier in the world.

Only Lee seemed disturbed by the mistakes made by himself and others, and to live over with regret the lost opportunities. His army had suffered losses of twenty thousand, less than one thousand of which were listed as "missing." Nearly one-fourth of his total command, approximately eighty-five thousand of all arms, the casualties were borne most heavily in the divisions of A. P. Hill and Longstreet. Jackson sustained only a few in his own division, and useless Holmes reported only fifty-odd casualties, mostly wounded by long-range gunfire. Likewise in the artillery, a few batteries took brutal casualties: Willie Pegram's Richmond battery lost three-fourths of its personnel, while the gunners with Pendleton's reserve went unharmed.

Looking back at the men who had failed him in crucial moments — Jackson repeatedly, Magruder, Huger and Holmes — Lee could regard his ambitious counteroffensive as a proving ground, a crucible, for the organization he had commanded less than four weeks when he took the soldiers into battle. It had also been a testing ground for Lee.

He had not used his artillery well. Malvern Hill was only the tragic climax of sending foot soldiers against Federal guns. In wasting the huge artillery reserve, Pendleton had been something less than inspired. Either Armistead Long, on the staff, or Porter Alexander, in ordnance, would have shown the initiative to bring the batteries up. Yet, the responsibility was Lee's. He had also allowed Jeb Stuart to remain too long on the north side of the Chickahominy. While it was doubtful how much cavalry could have accomplished in that country, Stuart was a tireless young man of great enterprise and daring.

Judged by later changes in his use of artillery and cavalry, Lee must have studied those areas in which his execution had not been up to his concepts. In the almost nonexistent staff work, on his staff and throughout the army, Lee appraised the failures of functioning in detail without recognizing the fundamental lack of the equivalent of an operations officer. For him to conceive of this specialized function would have been advanced thinking in staff operations, and Lee never had any advanced ideas on staff. What he did was to develop the efficiency of staff work within the existing system.

In doing this, Lee came close to acting as his own operations officer. He was never again by choice as remote from the field as at Mechanicsville nor were general headquarters ever again the vacuum they were at Savage's Station and Glendale. His own staff became more actively employed in maintaining communication and his subordinate generals developed the habit of communicating with headquarters through their own staff officers.

After the Seven Days, Lee could not truly reproach himself for the poor staff work of his subordinates. He had had no way of knowing how the division commanders would operate in relation to general headquarters in combat. After he found out, in a painful discovery, he tried by his usual methods of tactful suggestion to establish greater efficiency in the separate staffs. Admitting that "relatives and friends" made "agreeable" headquarters companions, he gave a strong hint that they might not be the best suited for the staff work that won battles.

He made one general criticism that was directed at nobody. When writing his report the following year, he listed as the costliest of all lapses the want of "correct and timely information." He attributed this lack "chiefly" to the low, heavily wooded country, in which McClellan's troops and troop movements were concealed. But Lee obviously felt that, with all the effects of the obscuring terrain and his own inadequacies, McClellan would have been crushed if the men who failed him had acted with ordinary competence.

"Under ordinary circumstances," he wrote in his report, "the Federal Army should have been destroyed." The wake of McClellan's retreat showed how near the thing had been for him. Droves of stragglers were gathered up, until prisoners totaled more than four thousand, including two generals. More than three thousand wounded and sick were left abandoned. More than fifty fine guns fell to Lee's army, thousands of rifles, and supplies that required days for the quartermaster and commissary departments to collect.

Viewing all this after the campaign, back at the Dabbs House on July 9 he wrote Mrs. Lee, "Our success has not been as great or complete as I would have desired, but God knows what is best for us." With this acceptance of a controlling Providence came the affirmation to look realistically at what had been accomplished. "Our enemy has met with a heavy loss from which he must take some time to recover and then recommence his operations."

The "recommence his operations" was the key to Lee's achievement, both as he accepted it and as it was. In executing his basic strategy, "to disrupt the enemy's plans," Lee had frustrated the purposes of the Federal government. He had also changed the nature of the armed conflict between the sections. After Lee's offensive, armed coercion ceased to be the fiction of "suppressing a combination." The possibilities of "a settlement" belonged in the past, and it was soon forgotten a settlement had ever been the purpose. Whatever Lincoln called the use of force, after the Seven Days it became a full-scale war of subjugation.

Now the struggle to subjugate a people must proceed to those logical extensions of war — the destruction of communities, the laying waste of the countryside, the upheaval of a society — which Lee had foreseen and which McClellan and Scott had sought to avoid. It had been the professional soldiers who drew back from systematic mass murder, knowing war carried to its logical conclusion established its own means and its own ends. Even under McClellan's policy of restricting the invasion to fighting between armed forces, nothing could prevent the disruption of civilian populations nor the irreparable losses of personal property that resulted from a combination of military necessity and irrepressible hoodlumism.

At Shirley, just in passing on its way to the next plantation, the Federal Army left a wasteland in its wake. Lee's Cousin Hill wrote in his factual farm diary, "They have ruined crops and everything, killed cattle, hogs and sheep . . . We tried to mend some fences not burnt and save some corn . . ."

At Berkeley, where the army tarried, the fields were ruined for the foreseeable future, woodland and shade trees from the primal forests vanished into campfires, outbuildings burned. Nothing stood except the shell of the manor house and its two nearest dependencies. The dining room table, at which Presidents had sat since Washington's day, was chopped up despite the protests of one of the soldiers. "Rebels have no rights," the vandals answered, and started on the piano, the chairs, the chests, the tables, until not a stick of furniture was left.

At Westover it was the same, all along the river row that had been a Carter domain when Lee's mother was growing up and where Lee as a child had been introduced to the regulated order perpetuated from one generation to the next. Even worse than the plague of war that struck his kinspeople were the losses in Lee's own family. With Rooney's home and furniture burned, the plantation was reduced to a debris which could yield nothing as long as the war lasted. The land was the same waste at Arlington, where the furniture was all gone and the house polluted beyond the possibility of use. After all the accumulations across three centuries, the great-granddaughter of Martha Washington and the grandson of Charles Carter were homeless, without a place of refuge to offer their daughters. And the use of force was just approaching the stage of unrestricted war.

The losses that were yet to come to his land removed from Lee any sense of satisfaction from his accomplishment in wrecking the Federal plans against his state. His son Rob said that Lee showed no elation at the victory hailed by everyone else. Rob had come down with an undiagnosed illness after the battles, and for recuperation went to stay with his mother at the Spotswood. When Lee was back at the Dabbs House, he visited his thinned-out son and crippled wife in the cramped quarters of the hotel. He did not want to talk of the fighting with his family. Exchanges were on such comfortably mundane matters as getting lighter clothes from his trunk.

On his visits to his wife he slipped in and out of the city unobtrusively, avoiding its crowds. When Lee did encounter acquaintances he had known in an earlier period, he showed no change at all in his emergence as the greatest soldier on the continent. Vice President Stephens wrote, "What I had seen General Lee to be at first — childlike in simplicity and unselfish in character — he remained, unspoiled by praise and by success."

This continued to be true of Lee. Nothing changed him. It was as if his completeness depended not at all on externals. Rob attributed his changelessness to his "practical, everyday religion." Walking among men as a king, born to rule, he walked before God with the humility that reduced triumphs and misfortunes alike to the test of himself in the eyes of Eternity. As he was the perfected product of an age in Virginia that was passing, so he reflected its religious attitude at its finest distillation: whatever happened in the external world, at his own center he felt as unthreatened as a child in the house of loving parents.

This personal security gave a selflessness to his compassion, so that he could and did suffer with this wholeness for others. While the city he had saved proclaimed his name, Lee in the hot back room at the Dabbs House looked ahead to the suffering to come.

# PART FOUR

# The Hope of a Nation

## CHAPTER XI

# "To Change the Theatre of War"

THE EVILS Lee feared in the new phase of war came suddenly and not merely in the faceless horror of war. They came in the personal policy of a general named John Pope, the only opponent Lee faced who aroused in him a sense of personal outrage. Lee respected McClellan and regarded most of the officers in his army — many of whom he still thought of as friends — as soldiers doing a job. This Pope was a different breed. Inflated with minor successes in the West, won against the Confederacy's poor command situation in the Mississippi River area, he came storming into Virginia as a darling of the Radicals. While Stanton was playing a treacherous game with McClellan, Major General Pope was given command of a new "Army of Virginia," composed of the forces of Banks, Frémont and McDowell, totaling about fifty thousand.

Inherent in all of Lee's objectives was a moral concept, of which his life had been the execution, and from the beginning Pope's behavior violated his structure of values. Operating in north-central Virginia where no Confederates opposed him, Pope became the first soldier to declare war on the civilian population through a series of harsh orders.

Soldiers were to live off the people, a measure Scott had refused to take against the avowed enemy in Mexico. All males within the Federal lines were to be arrested, and those who refused to take the oath of allegiance to the United States were to be driven out. Any person within the lines who wrote a letter to a Confederate soldier was to be adjudged a spy and become subject to the death penalty. Carried away by this order of ruthlessness, one of his brigadiers, Adolph von Steinwehr, immediately arrested five civilians in the little Valley town of Luray to be held as hostages. Whenever one of his soldiers was shot by a guerrilla, one of the hostages would be put to death.

Lee wrote a letter of protest to McClellan, stating that retaliatory measures would have to be taken. Though Pope partially drew in his horns, something ugly had come into the struggle, and something of the principles on which McClellan had fought began to fade. Men encouraged to impress foods from the civilians soon became pillagers and vandals.

There was none of the restraint once voiced by a colonel of McClellan's from New York State, who had said that soldiers must remember they and the Southerners were one people, and acts must be avoided that tended to widen the breech. With Pope came the violence of hatred.

In studying Pope's snorting and pawing, Lee revealed his distaste by avoiding the word "defeat" in writing about his plans against Pope. He used the words "suppress him." With McClellan's army recuperating by the river at Berkeley and receiving reinforcements, Pope in middle Virginia presented the same problem that had confronted Lee when he first came to Richmond as military adviser. The main Federal Army was on the Peninsula threatening Richmond, and a secondary army in middle Virginia could either cooperate against Richmond or operate against the railroads. By middle July, Pope showed the intention of operating against the railroads. By occupying Culpeper, he placed his army only thirty-five miles from Fredericksburg to the southeast and less than thirty miles from Gordonsville, a key stop on the Virginia Central, to the south and slightly west.

Since the Virginia Central had to be protected, Lee's preferred solution was a variation of his May-June strategy when he had immobilized McDowell and concentrated at Richmond against McClellan. Lee wanted to contain McClellan while he dispatched a force to dispose of Pope. The trouble with this plan was that he lacked the available manpower to send off a sufficient force without risking the capture of Richmond before the detached troops could get back. There was also a complicating element in the presence of Burnside's force on transports at Fort Monroe. Giving up operations off the Carolina coast because of the heat, Burnside was poised where he could move either up the James to McClellan or up the Rappahannock to Fredericksburg, where he could reinforce Pope. Burnside's movements became a key in the solution of Lee's problem.

Lee began a careful study of the known factors and available information, in a deductive process whose results came to be called "genius." It was a genius for the tireless evaluation of each detail. Acting as his own intelligence officer, he collected oddments of information from Federal deserters, from Confederate prisoners returned in the prisoner exchange opened with McClellan, from rumors gathered by his own forces and from the impressions of observant natives. He weighed these against the probabilities of the enemy's objectives and his own intentions. At no time thinking defensively, all the time he was trying to anticipate the enemy's plans in order to disrupt them before they evolved.

With his total confidence in his ability to exploit developments, Lee began a series of small moves. By all falling into place and growing into larger moves, they gave the impression of a master plan from the beginning. Actually, Lee worked from day to day, one move at a time, each controlled by unwavering concentration on one purpose.

First, to give some immediate protection to the railroad, on July 13 he sent to Gordonsville Jackson and his original Valley command. Here Lee was also resolving his reservation about Jackson's inexplicably flat performance during the Seven Days by returning him to the semi-independent command in which he had flourished. Working as a unit in coordination with others in a larger plan had been a problem to Jackson outside Richmond only as any unfamiliar operation would have presented a problem to Jackson in his clinical apathy. After the battles, he wrote a preacher friend that he had felt sicker than at any time since the Mexican War, but the ill feeling was not of a nature of which he could report himself sick. With nearly two weeks' rest, Jackson's natural energies began to be restored when he was stimulated by a return to the rolling Piedmont country where complicated problems did not come immediately at him.

When Jackson expressed the opinion that Gordonsville and not Fredericksburg was Pope's objective, Lee sent on Jackson's cavalry from Hanover Junction. Lee sent Jeb Stuart and part of his command to Hanover Junction, with orders to reconnoiter the Fredericksburg area. In his messages to the distant commanders, Lee seemed much surer in dealing with broad fields of maneuver than he had in directing his units in combat in the close confines of the swampy country outside the capital.

Then on July 27, with some of his lightly wounded beginning to return and two brigades of reinforcements on the way from South Carolina, Lee, in his eagerness to get at Pope, sent to Jackson the large division of A. P. Hill. This transfer of Powell Hill to Jackson's force resolved a command problem.

Hill had clashed with Longstreet, who, emerging as the big man under Lee, had been assigned a loose grouping of forces which included Hill's division. It happened that during the Seven Days a Richmond newspaperman, John Daniel, served as a volunteer aide on Hill's staff, and after the battles wrote an heroic account of the Light Division. Longstreet felt that his part in the campaign had been slighted, and he had his literate chief of staff, Moxley Sorrel, write an anonymous correction to the paper. Since Sorrel's anonymity was no secret in the army, the next time the amiable staff officer brought an order, Hill refused to receive him. Longstreet shifted the personal matter to military protocol and placed Hill under arrest. Courtly, sensitive Powell Hill adhered to the personal basis and challenged the superior officer to a duel. When Hill was transferred to Jackson's command, cordial relations were not reestablished between Hill and Longstreet.

During Lee's moves while his army rested and refitted, he was engaged in other troublesome details of reorganizing his army. Magruder, who had been slated to go to Texas before the Seven Days, left the Army of Northern Virginia after writing the War Department a long apologia on his performance. Inept Holmes was transferred to Arkansas, and sluggish Huger was made an inspector in the ordnance department. Neither was to be seen again in Virginia.

Magruder's loose command was reorganized and distributed between two professionals, Lafayette McLaws and stately D. R. ("Neighbor") Jones. Richard H. Anderson, a quiet, reserved professional from South Carolina, was promoted to major general and given Huger's former division. Holmes's five brigades, returning to the south side of the James, were not formed into a division. They came temporarily under the command of D. H. Hill, whom Lee had placed in charge of operations south of the James. The organization of the army remained fluid at that stage, as Lee was cautious in assigning men to division command. As shown in the Seven Days, he placed a large trust in his subordinates — too much, Longstreet thought — and individual failures in responsibility in generals he inherited did not shake his preference. He was to be careful in selecting men who could be trusted with initiative.

While Lee was juggling his units to find the right combinations, his troops were dispersed in digging on a new defensive system of works to the southeast of Richmond on both sides of the James River. Drewry's Bluff was strengthened and extended as a fort on the land side. Across the river on the north side, a series of earthen forts, under the supervision of Colonel Jeremy Gilmer, formed a line up to the Darbytown and Charles City Roads. Works were also started at Petersburg, twenty miles to the South.

The immediate purpose of this ambitious project was to retard any movement by McClellan, as the stronger the works for containment the more men Lee could detach for Pope. Lee started works as far south as Petersburg because McClellan's James River base opened the possibility of an advance on the south side of the river that could isolate Richmond from the Coastal states. While Lee could not know that Washington had vetoed McClellan's suggestion for a move south of the James, it was natural for him to assume that McClellan would think of it, for it was a movement which Lee particularly feared.

Also unknown to Lee was McClellan's fight with the Lincoln administration for his military life. With McClellan's enemies among the Radicals in the ascendant, Lincoln had given up on McClellan. He did not make a clean break. Major General H. W. Halleck, a military theoretician, had been brought in as general in chief to do the hatchet job. With no taste for the work, Halleck entered into a drawn-out argument with McClellan over McClellan's preference for reopening a campaign against Richmond from where he was, with his army swelled to forbidding proportions by Burnside. Finally on August 3, with Burnside sailing to Fredericksburg, Halleck sent the peremptory order that McClellan was to abandon the Peninsula and start embarking his army on transports.

Before the ax fell, McClellan had shown a lot of movement in his camps, and on August 5 startled Lee by marching his army back to its Malvern Hill position. Two days later McClellan returned to his camp and began to embark his sick and wounded as the first steps in dismantling his army. Lee would have been more mystified by this advance and withdrawal except that, while McClellan was at Malvern Hill, he learned that Burnside had landed in Fredericksburg. From then on, Lee grew certain that no offensive action was coming from McClellan.

A week later, when he received information that Burnside had started west to join Pope, Lee took his second big risk on the basis of his judgment of McClellan. He sent off Longstreet with a command of ten brigades while the large Federal Army was still in camp twenty miles from Richmond.

Earlier in August Jackson had fought Pope's vanguard at Cedar Mountain, and that firebreather had halted his hitherto unopposed advance on Gordonsville. Pope had made camp in a vulnerable position between the two sides of the triangle formed by the Rappahannock and its southern fork, the Rapidan, and Lee was hurrying troops to catch him between the rivers.

Almost immediately after Lee so dangerously reduced his army at Richmond, he received the reward for his boldness. D. H. Hill, from observations on the south side of the James River, sent him positive information that units of McClellan's army were leaving Berkeley. Though this reassured Lee about Richmond, he knew that McClellan could have no other destination than a juncture with Pope. If McClellan reached Pope before Pope could be defeated, the combined forces would be too much for Lee's manpower to take on. It was going to be a race.

2

At the open depot at the foot of Broad Street hill, Lee climbed aboard a Virginia Central coach on August 15. As the train rattled across Hanover County, Lee looked out of the open window in the direction of Hickory Hill. This was the plantation of Charlotte Wickham Lee's family where Lee's wife had recently gone from Richmond with her daughter-in-law. When Lee arrived at the little railroad junction town of Gordonsville, he wrote Mrs. Lee, "I passed by you Friday morning when you were asleep. I looked very hard but could see nobody. I should have liked so much to stop to have waked you all up. I was afraid at such an hour I should not have been welcome. But welcome or not I was obliged to go on and here I am in a tent, instead of my comfortable quarters at Dabbs' . . ."

Before leaving Richmond he had written a note to Custis, saying that he was sorry not to see him and Mary. He sent for keeping an extra summer underjacket which needed mending and a straw hat, which he evidently felt would not be dignified when he took the field.

At the new camp spreading out from the town in the low hills, Lee suffered a bitter disappointment in his plans for the "suppression" of Pope. His battle plans were arranged to trap Pope's army incautiously camped within the triangle formed by the Rapidan and the Rappahannock rivers, and at the same time to cut Pope's supply line on the Orange and Alexandria Railroad.

Before Lee could open his assault on the unsuspecting braggart, Longstreet needed to wait a day to supply his troops. Then the cavalry, on whom depended the wreckage of Pope's communications, was late in arriving. By then Jeb Stuart had been promoted to major general and his enlarged cavalry divided into two brigades, one under jovial, high-living nephew Fitzhugh Lee and the other under Wade Hampton. Stuart was enthusiatic about Fitz Lee and he had brought Lee's brigade to Hanover Junction, leaving Hampton at Richmond. Here began one of those sequences of small events that grew into a single large consequence.

When Stuart went personally to join Lee at Gordonsville, he did not stress urgency to Fitz Lee as he ordered him to follow on with his brigade. Fitz took an indirect course in order to gather some forage, and Stuart, assuming Lee would push on, was furious. To find his cavalry and hurry them forward, Stuart rode with only his staff on the road eastward from Orange to Fredericksburg, and at a little place called Verdiersville near the Wilderness the group went to sleep on the front porch of a farmhouse. They were south of the Rapidan, whose crossings were guarded by Longstreet's infantry.

One of the brigadiers in Longstreet's large, loose command was Bob Toombs, a fifty-two-year-old Georgian and among the most prominent citizens in the Confederacy. Before the war he had been a hugely successful lawyer and planter, and one of the outstanding Southerners in the U. S. Congress. In the Confederacy, tempestuous Toombs had started as Secretary of State but, finding that office too small for his ego, sought the true glory of the field. Toombs developed a loathing for discipline and West Pointers (he challenged D. H. Hill to a duel after Malvern Hill) and never forgot that his troops, or "followers," were also his constituents. Thus it was that Toombs decided the night was too unpleasant for his men to stand guard duty and removed the regiment guarding one of the Rapidan crossings. A Federal cavalry patrol rode unmenaced into Lee's lines.

Early in the morning these riders missed capturing Stuart only because of the speed with which he, a superb horseman, broke from the farm-house, taking the farmyard fence like a race rider at full gallop. In his flight Lee's cavalry chief left behind his plumed hat and his dispatch case. This dispatch, containing one of Lee's orders, was delivered to General Pope. By this concatenation of human failings, Lee's dispositions were discovered by the enemy.

After Lee postponed his attack to August 20, Pope had gotten the wind up. From Clark Mountain, south of the Rapidan, Lee stood and watched through his glasses the last of Pope's white-topped wagons disappearing in the distance, toward the Rappahannock. Turning to Longstreet, he covered his deflated feelings by saying, "General, we little thought the enemy would turn his back upon us thus early in the campaign."

Accepting human failures as he had accepted them at the Seven Days, Lee wrote only to the President, ". . . but the cavalry had not got up . . . and this delay proved fatal to our success."

With no repinings, he crossed his army over the Rapidan, and his columns shuffled over the dusty roads in the warm weather toward the Rappahannock, behind which Pope retired. Time became Lee's enemy in discovering a way to get at the suddenly reluctant Federal general, for McClellan would soon be coming. Each day lost Lee more of the advantage he had gained by his risk in moving his troops away from Richmond before McClellan actually started to leave Berkeley.

For two days, Lee probed the crossings of the Rappahannock, finding an alert Pope guarding all approaches to his new defensive position. Late on the 22nd Jackson tried a wide turning movement, beginning a crossing above Pope's right flank. At the end of the day a storm brought a downpour that isolated Jubal Early's brigade on the north bank of the river in one of the blackest nights the men had ever seen. On the 23rd the immediate problem became the rescue of Early's regiments from Pope's side of the flooded river.

While this was going on, Jeb Stuart returned from a night raid behind Pope's lines designed to cut his lines of communication at the railroad bridge at Catlett's Station. Though the bridge had been too wet to burn, the cavalry brought back something that delighted Lee more than news of a burned bridge. Stuart had on his staff a herculean Prussian baron, Heros von Borcke, who had run the blockade to offer his services to the Confederacy, and the major with the German accent delivered to Lee papers the cavalry had collected in Pope's hastily vacated headquarters at Catlett's Station.

Rooney came in to see his father, for the first time since the Seven Days. He told of having narrowly missed capturing Louis Marshall, the son of General Lee's sister Ann, at Pope's headquarters. It had been a bitter pill to Lee that his nephew had served on Pope's staff ("I'm sorry to find him in such bad company," he had written in a letter), and he wrote in high good humor of Rooney's exploit to Charlotte. "His cousin, Louis M., is said to have escaped at the first onset, leaving his toddy untouched."

Lee had reason for his good humor: the papers captured in Pope's headquarters revealed the Federal plans. Pope was to hold his line along the Rappahannock until McClellan joined him. Once certain of Pope's defensive intentions, Lee immediately planned to maneuver him out of his position. His plan against Pope took no time to develop. Simplicity itself, it would be totally unexpected because its audacity defied the basic rules of warfare.

With only fifty-five thousand men at Gordonsville, Lee planned to send off Jackson's command of twenty-three thousand on a wide march around Pope's right flank to get on his rear at his supply depot at Manassas Junction. Not only would Jackson be on Pope's line of supply, about which the Federal general talked so airily, but between him and Washington. Longstreet would continue to face Pope, masking Jackson's movement, until Pope of necessity withdrew from the Rappahannock. Then Longstreet would move out to unite with Jackson in the area of the war's opening battle, at Bull Run.

Lee was not necessarily looking for a battle there. In fact, his maneuver to force Pope's retreat was designed to avoid the casualties entailed in an attack across the Rappahannock against the superior Federal guns. With Lee's faith in his ability to control military events as they took shape, he would welcome a battle in northern Virginia if circumstances developed favorably for the commitment of his inferior numbers and armament.

Lee wrote the President on August 24 in terms of vague flexibility. "I think I can feed the whole army here . . . At first there will be difficulties, but they will be softened as we advance and relieve other parts of the country and employ what would be consumed and destroyed by the enemy. The theatre of war will thus be changed for a season at least, unless we are overpowered . . ."

Lee was not only continuing the exchange which formed a basis of their relationship, but diplomatically maneuvering to draw the troops in the Richmond area to his own army. Aware of the President's fixed policy of defending at all points, he knew that Davis was particularly sensitive to Richmond. Yet, Lee was also aware that in this period in their relationship, characterized by his own ascendancy, Davis's faith in his generalship outweighed many of the President's native predilections. Lee had acted on this.

After removing a few units from the Richmond lines, Lee tried a feeler on Davis to discover his state of mind about moving more troops away from Richmond. He asked the President could Richmond be held if he followed Pope?

This was a little sudden for Davis's orderly arrangements. "The [Federal] retreat presents a case not originally contemplated . . . To be self-reliant against a sudden attack" at Richmond, he wrote, "the divisions of D. H. Hill and Lafayette McLaws should be retained at Hanover Junction, and the five brigades originally under Holmes should be retained south of the James." Then Davis revealed his need for certainties by pointing out that "nothing certainly" was known of McClellan's army having retired farther east than New Kent Court House. For Lee it had been enough to be satisfied of McClellan's intent to withdraw.

However, to indicate his faith in Lee, Davis wrote that he had confirmed the orders Lee had left with Gustavus W. Smith. After his collapse at Seven Pines, Johnston's former second in command had returned to duty, and Lee, unwilling to trust Smith with troop command, had placed him generally in charge of the Richmond defenses.

Having broken the ice, Lee informed Davis that he intended pushing northward from the Rappahannock, and took a bolder course to get the troops from Richmond. In his dispatch to Davis he wrote, "The whole army I think should be united here as soon as possible. I . . . will direct General Smith to send on McLaws, D. H. Hill and other available troops. Should you not agree with me in the propriety of this step please countermand the order and let me know."

The next day, August 25, Lee went further, as far as he ever went with Davis. "I believe a portion of McClellan's army has joined Pope," he wired. "Expedite the advance of our troops."

Davis's answer was one of his finest responses. "Generals Hill and McLaws, at North Anna [River], ordered to join you. The brigades of Ransome and Walker start from here this morning." After giving an outline of the defensive structure around Richmond — with only one brigade at Drewry's Bluff and one across the river at Chaffin's Bluff — Davis wrote, "Confidence in you overcomes the view which would otherwise be taken of the exposed condition of Richmond, and the troops retained for the defense of the capital are surrendered to you on a renewed request."

Despite Davis's fine expression of confidence, five days had elapsed since Lee had opened the diplomatic correspondence. On August 26, when Davis wrote his reply, Lee was already in the midst of the boldest maneuver yet undertaken in the war. Without waiting for the reinforcements, his army was advancing toward the Washington area, where one hundred and fifty thousand Federal troops were gathering.

3

Late in the afternoon of August 26 Lee's tent was struck, his clothes and camp chest were piled into a headquarters wagon, and his saddled horse was brought him by a courier. A Navy Colt was carried in a saddle holster, from which Lee never removed it. On his sword belt he wore no sidearms. He swung his solid weight into the saddle, joined Longstreet and, followed by their staffs, rode westward away from the Rappahannock lines. Longstreet's troops were already on the road. To face Pope's army across the river, Lee left only Dick Anderson's new division — the first of the units he had pried away from the Richmond defenses and the only one to reach him.

This was well into the second day since Jackson had begun his swing around Pope's army, and Lee decided that Pope must by then be aware that Jackson was on his rear. Pope had been aware of Jackson's movement since the first day, August 25, but he assumed Jackson was returning to the Valley. Then, when reports reached him of enemy troops in his rear on the 26th, since Stuart's riders were fanned out in front of the infantry, Pope assumed it to be another cavalry action. With only Anderson's six thousand in his front, Pope believed "heavy forces of the enemy still confronted us . . ."

Lee had pretty well estimated Pope from his braggadocio. Along with his ferocity against civilians, Pope had boastfully derided McClellan for thinking in such terms as "lines of communications" and stated that *his* "headquarters were in the saddle." Around Lee the officers had made the obvious comments about where Pope's brains were.

Lee, with his army split three ways and out of communication with Jackson fifty miles away, showed so little anxiety — at least outwardly — that he spent a social evening on the 26th at the home of the Marshall family, near the village of Orleans. Mrs. Marshall did herself proud in serving a dinner for Lee, Longstreet, and some of their staff officers. The company of ladies and the sociability around a dinner table recaptured momentarily for Lee the spirit of happier times. Colonel Long said he threw off the sternness of his intense concentration against Pope and assumed the manner of "the genial cavalier." Even Longstreet emerged from his laconic reserve and made himself "entertaining."

The next morning, though the generals left at dawn, Mrs. Marshall started them on their way with a country-style breakfast. In the unaccustomed relaxation following heavy meals, Lee, with his staff and couriers, rode without concern to the front of Longstreet's marching columns and then on ahead of the troops. Suddenly a quartermaster came galloping toward them, yelling, "the Federal cavalry are upon you."

It was too late to consider the rashness of having sent off all of Stuart's cavalry with Jackson. It was too late for anything except the reflex action of the group of staff and couriers, about ten men, to form quickly across the road in front of the commanding general. They had no sooner filled the road with their horses than a column of John Buford's cavalry appeared over the rise immediately ahead of them. The Federal patrol paused. The officer in charge assumed the still group in the road to be the advance of some of Stuart's cavalry. After an agonizing measure of time, the Federals wheeled around and rode off. General Lee never made reference to his near escape from capture, another of those small events by which the course of the war could have been changed. But he no longer rode at the head of Longstreet's column.

Late in the day a courier brought Lee welcome news from Jackson. Marching fifty-four miles in two August days, his troops reached Pope's vast supply depot at Manassas Junction, on Pope's rear and between him and Washington. On that same day, the 27th, Pope began withdrawing from the Rappahannock line to go after Jackson. Two corps from McClellan's army, then on the way to the Rappahannock line, were directed to hurry to the Manassas area. Pope's belated moves were more or less assumed by Lee. He knew nothing positive about McClellan's units; he knew only that the Manassas area would be the destination of all available troops from McClellan's army. And if they got there before Longstreet did, Jackson's twenty-three thousand marchers could be gobbled up.

With Lee, Longstreet's troops were following Jackson's line of march west of the Bull Run Mountains. But John Buford, recently commissioned brigadier general in Pope's cavalry, was a very enterprising professional soldier and harassed the head of Longstreet's column to retard the movement to unite with Jackson. It was mid-afternoon of August 28 before Longstreet's van turned into Thoroughfare Gap for the passage of Bull Run Mountain to the east. Largely due to Buford, the passage was blocked by a Federal division, well supported by guns.

The check was part of the risk Lee had taken in dividing his army, and he had to get through — if only to save Jackson. The Gap was a narrow passage, in places no more than one hundred yards wide, with precipitous walls strewn with boulders and entangled with mountain ivy. Lee saw that from their side of the Gap Longstreet's men could get no batteries in position. The late hours of the afternoon faded into dusk with no dent made in the enemy's stand.

Lee ordered quick reconnaissance parties to search for other passages to the north and south. As darkness fell, he learned of a smaller passage three miles to the north, Hopewell Gap, and of a trail near Thoroughfare Gap. Lee ordered Longstreet to send three brigades under sturdy, plain-featured Wilcox on a night march through Hopewell Gap and to send John Hood over the trail. Hood was then commanding the two brigades that, formerly under Whiting, had been the heroes of the Gaines' Mill breakthrough.

During this danger, Lee showed his tremendous self-composure. He accepted the invitation to dinner at the nearby home of a Mr. Robinson and, giving not a hint of his anxiety, made himself as agreeable as the two nights before at Mrs. Marshall's. For all he knew, half the Federal Army might be arrayed against him the next morning, blocking his juncture with Jackson. But Lee also believed that a braggart such as Pope could not be a good soldier.

Pope himself ruined his great opportunity to keep the two parts of Lee's army separated. He did it with orders reflecting a state of total bewilderment. On the day of August 28, finding Jackson gone from Manassas Junction, Pope assumed him to be trying to get away after his raid. Forgetting the larger part of Lee's army, he rushed a concentration of his units to bag Jackson. McDowell on his own responsibility had placed Rickett's division at Thoroughfare Gap when Buford advised him of Longstreet's advance.

During the day of the 28th none of Pope's countermarching could find Jackson. He was resting his men in the woods at a place named Groveton, near the town of Gainesville on the Warrenton Turnpike. At the end of the day, Jackson, fearing he would not be found, opened fire on a Federal column passing his front. This was another of McDowell's divisions, commanded by General Rufus King, a very tough outfit formed of troops from the northern area of the Midwest. The two forces rushed together in a stand-up brawl which lasted until night, when both sides were probably glad to break it off.

Pope elected to believe that King had caught Jackson, and carefully laid his plans for the destruction of Stonewall the next morning. The plans were sound enough — except for overlooking the existence of the rest of Lee's army. During August 29 Pope, without feints or flanking movement, sent five Federal divisions in frontal attacks against Jackson's thin front. Jackson's three jaded divisions were back of a railroad cut southwest of Sudley's Ford at Bull Run, where McDowell had crossed in the Battle of First Manassas. Jackson's line buckled here, wavered there, A. P. Hill's men fought out of their ammunition and threw rocks, but the front held.

While Jackson was holding on, Lee was advancing with Longstreet's van. Ricketts, isolated and uneasy, had withdrawn his division from Thoroughfare Gap during the night. With Hood in the lead coming up, there was none of the fumbling of the Seven Days. Hood's two brigades came up on Jackson's right as if making an often-practiced drill maneuver under parade-ground conditions. Hood formed across the Warrenton Turnpike and at right angles to it. The following columns turned off the road to Hood's right and left, faced to the front, and came up in lines of battle to extend Jackson's position.

The last brigade up, unattached to any division, formed as Hood's reserve. This brigade was commanded by Nathan G. ("Shanks") Evans, the unsung hero of First Manassas who later, at Ball's Bluff, wrecked a Federal advance and cast the first blight on McClellan's reputation. But nobody wanted this wiry, cold-eyed army professional from South Carolina. The reason was what he called his "barrelita" — a Prussian orderly who carried on his back a keg of bourbon whiskey, from which Shanks was wont to refresh himself with the result that Shanks became "unruly," as Moxley Sorrel said.

After Evans's brigade got in line, immediately behind Hood, batteries clanged into position with the shouts of cannoneers. The guns began to roar, drawing an answering fire, and acrid battlesmoke drifted across the turnpike. A staff officer from Longstreet came galloping up to Hood with a message. Shortly thereafter an officer in the 4th Texas rode along the line saying, "Steady, boys, steady." One of the Texan survivors of the Seven Days said, when he heard those words, "I knew the ball was about to open."

4

General Lee established an informal field headquarters in a cleared field about a quarter of a mile back from the front, where he sat on the stump of a tree. Though the country was mostly open — corn fields, orchards and farm meadows — Lee's range of vision was obstructed by the rolls of the ground and a belt of woods facing the lines. He could observe, however, that when all of Longstreet's troops were in line nothing more than random artillery had greeted the deployment. Deciding the situation offered a promising opportunity for attack, Lee used a method of command that was to be fateful to his future: he *suggested* to Longstreet that an attack was desirable. "General Lee was inclined to engage as soon as practicable," Longstreet said later, "but did not so order."

This suggestion from Lee expressed his natural preference in dealing with high-ranking subordinates who had won his trust. Having emerged as the most dependable performer on the Seven Days testing ground, Longstreet had been closely associated with Lee since then at headquarters and on the march. After the Seven Days, Lee abandoned operating with large, semi-independent divisions. As corps were still not included in the Confederation organization, Lee gave Longstreet command of a group, a wing, of new smaller divisions. The organization was very loose, nothing resembling the semi-autonomous structure of a corps, and Longstreet as its commander was the only centralizing element.

Longstreet felt his self-importance, and Lee's suggested attack was not to his taste. It was really antithetical to his style of fighting. Methodical and slow-moving, Longstreet liked to have everything just so before he went into action, and ideally he preferred the enemy to come at him. He was too imbued with army training to oppose Lee's suggestion and offer his own ideas. But he could take advantage of the absence of a direct order and ask to be allowed first to make a reconnaissance of the enemy's ground. As reliable Longstreet was the man who was to mount the assault, Lee agreed.

Longstreet was actually using delaying tactics to get his own way against the mild-mannered commanding general. After an hour or so he returned on his bay horse and reported that an attack would expose his right to Federal troops known to be moving from Manassas. Lee was not satisfied with this. He was preparing to send out his engineering officers on a reconnaissance when Jeb Stuart rode up with his red beard glistening in the sun. He reported that a heavy Federal column, with guns, was approaching toward Longstreet's right. This changed things.

Wilcox, with three brigades, was pulled out from Hood's left and moved to the right of the lines with D. R. Jones's division. Moving out, these troops soon encountered their old friend from the Seven Days, Fitz-John Porter, supported by McDowell. Porter and McDowell were approaching Jackson's flank under Pope's orders, given in ignorance of Longstreet's position on the field. Both columns halted, guns were run up and opened, and neither side was disposed to commit. Longstreet returned to Lee's tree stump and reported that he believed Porter's and McDowell's corps were too far from their main army to open a serious assault, but he had observed dust columns that indicated the approach of other Federals from Manassas. A few minutes later the tireless Stuart galloped in with the same report.

Lee was not impressed with these reports. He assumed, correctly, that Federal troop movements were too distant to exert a material effect on the battle here. He believed Pope, concentrating on Jackson, was open for a counterattack. Yet, again he held back from giving the direct order. Again Longstreet, stubbornly clinging to his own preferences, used delaying tactics under the guise of apparently reasonable suggestions. He pointed out that the day was far spent and a reconnaissance in force would open the way for a daylight attack. In his desire for harmony and the promotion of initiative in the men who were to direct the fighting, Lee allowed himself to be overruled. Longstreet, with soaring ambitions none recognized under his bluff exterior, was satisfied he had established ascendancy over the mind of the commanding general.

The reconnaissance made at sunset came to a discouraging end. Before Hood moved out, his front was attacked by King's division driving off Jackson's flank. King's troops, roughly handled by Jackson the night before, had the misfortune to catch Hood when his self-confident veterans were looking for a fight. After an half-hour's exchange, King fell back in the dusk, followed by Hood and Evans and Wilcox, then returned from his march to the right. After dark Hood and Wilcox reported that the enemy's ground was strong, and both of these stout soldiers felt a morning attack would be unsuccessful.

Lee retired for the night to a nearby cabin with the conviction that an attack was impractical. Up early in the morning, he wrote the President, "My desire has been to avoid a general engagement, being the weaker force," and he planned to return to maneuver. That day he expected to receive attack from Pope, which he did not fear, and at night he would withdraw his army across Bull Run at Sudley Ford, again placing himself on Pope's rear. The sun was up on a bright, warm day when Lee returned to his command post to await developments from Pope.

They were slow in coming, though Pope had convinced himself that the enemy was retreating. It was one o'clock before the "pursuit" began, with an advance against Jackson's front by the corps of Porter and Heintzelman, supported by King's and Jesse Reno's divisions. This was a heavy attack. A. P. Hill's division, on Jackson's left, nearly broke under the weight. At three o'clock, when two fresh supporting lines of Federals appeared out of the woods, Jackson sent a message to Lee calling for a division from Longstreet to support him.

Lee immediately ordered Longstreet to send the division. When the order reached him, Longstreet perceived that the advancing Federal lines were crossing the field of fire of his guns. Reasoning that the artillery could relieve Jackson instantly, while a division would require an hour to move to Jackson's support, Longstreet himself rode to give orders to the batteries. The cannoneers had already seen the opportunity and were ready to "commence firing." One, two, then three batteries began to scourge the flank of Porter's advancing lines.

Just when the guns were making themselves felt, an eighteen-gun battalion opened from a low ridge that commanded the field for two thousand yards. This was the reserve battalion of Stephen D. Lee, the young colonel whom General Lee had placed in charge of Magruder's divisional artillery when he assumed command. General Lee watched this reversal of the Seven Days, when his had been the men attacking into bursting shellfire, and he believed that no troops could live under it. He had his signal officer flag a message to Jackson: "Do you still need reinforcements?" Jackson's signalman flagged back, "No, the enemy are giving away."

The Federal troop movement told Lee that Pope had packed the bulk of his army north of the turnpike, in Jackson's front, and a large portion of the attacking force was falling back with its flank presented to Longstreet's long-waiting lines. Regardless of his morning's plans, Lee recognized the opportunity for counterattack to be too good to pass by. Immediately he sent an order — this time, an order — for Longstreet to advance his whole line.

That time Longstreet was ready. The enemy had opened itself to a counterstroke in which every advantage lay with Longstreet, and he sent his brigades forward with no delay. When the long gray line advanced under the blue-crossed red flags, Lee saw a cohesion that made all the blunders of the Seven Days seem like a rehearsal for this largely spontaneous charge. When the screaming troops rushed into the open Federal flank, one of Hood's Texans said it was like the popular song, "Hell broke loose in Georgia."

Though Lee's face showed no change of expression, it was noticed that he mounted Traveler and the gray horse kept close behind the infantry's advance. At the scent of sudden victory, for the first time Lee showed that he was as excited as any soldier. Longstreet said the heavy fumes of gunpowder hanging over the ranks were to the men "as stimulating as sparkling wine." To a Northern observer the Mississippians, including a famed company from the University, rushed forward like "demons" rising out of the earth. All of them had waited, it seemed, a long time for a fair crack at the enemy, when they were not running into massed artillery planted on impregnable positions.

The retiring Federals fought in pockets of resistance. Uneven lines falling back from Jackson's front ripped at intervals into the troops on Longstreet's left. Jackson's worn-out men, turning from their two days' stand, were slow in advancing to Longstreet's left. Through the fading light, Lee observed that Jackson's regiments were not moving forward very spryly, and he dispatched an order for Jackson to hurry.

The sun became overcast with low clouds and early dusk began descending over the widely scattered action. When Jackson's men began coming up, the Federal retreat broke into a rout. Disorganized units crowded together in fleeing across the bridge over Young's Branch and the Stone Bridge over Bull Run where the turnpike crossed. Lee, recklessly exposed to fire, rode forward with the troops trying to cut the Federals off at the bridges.

On the Henry House Hill, where Jackson had won his sobriquet the year before, some Federal units formed around Sykes's Regulars and refused to budge. By then order was going from the Confederate lines and darkness was gathering. A light rain began to fall. Gradually the efforts at pursuit dwindled off.

At night the last Federals recrossed Bull Run, in a cruelly magnified rerun of the first battle of the war the previous July. Total casualties, roughly twenty-four thousand, ran nearly as high as the total number of troops actually engaged at First Manassas (or Bull Run). Lee's losses exceeded nine thousand and Pope's exceeded fourteen thousand, more than four thousand of whom were gathered up as prisoners. Thirty pieces of Federal artillery and more than twenty thousand rifles had been abandoned on the field, and supplies were scattered for miles.

When the firing was dying off, Lee halted about fifteen feet from a gun. Captain Mason, of his staff, brought forward an unsightly-looking gunner carrying a sponge-staff in his blackened hand. His face was equally blackened from powder that had soaked in with sweat, and his ragged clothes were stained with red clay. Lee had grown accustomed to private soldiers addressing him and, when Mason said, "General, here is someone who wants to speak to you," Lee said, "Well, my man, what can I do for you?"

"Why, General, don't you know me?" asked a surprised young voice.

Lee showed his relaxed humor by, Rob said, being "very much amused" at his son's appearance. He told Rob he was glad to see him safe and well. Then the inheritor of Romancoke plantation returned to his battery companions to clean the pieces and look after the horses, and his father rode through the drizzle to a field where a freshly built fire marked the site of headquarters for the night.

### 5

The next morning, August 31, the rain was coming down steadily, and Lee pulled on rubber overalls and threw a poncho across his shoulders. He rode over the wet fields — "nasty and soggy," Longstreet said — to Bull Run and crossed to the other side. Rifle fire crackled from an enemy skirmish line ahead, warning him that Pope's rear guard was alert and waiting.

Longstreet, from his personal observations of Lee, felt he "was quite satisfied with the results of the campaign, though he said very little." Still, military logic demanded that Lee try to finish off Pope in a pursuit. Longstreet's troops were called off from their grisly chore of burying the dead, to be put in motion forward, and a courier brought in Jackson for orders.

This was a different Jackson from the Seven Days. Totally vindicating Lee's judgment of his potential, this was the Stonewall Jackson of the Valley Campaign on a larger scale, the aggressive strategist with whom Lee had corresponded in April. Beginning with the Second Manassas campaign, Lee and Jackson developed an intuitive understanding in operations which had first been suggested in their spring correspondence. They developed also a deepening personal respect and warmth for one another that grew into a strong affection beneath the formalities of their exchanges. When Lee gave Jackson instructions for his part in the pursuit, Jackson replied with the single word "Good," which he invariably used when satisfied. Then, without a smile or another word, he rode off on his little sorrel.

Everything worked against the pursuit. During the afternoon the rain turned into a violent electric storm, the Confederate troops were tired and two more of McClellan's corps reached Centreville during the day. If Lee's attack on Pope had been delayed one more day, four-fifths of McClellan's infantry would have been on hand to support Pope's army. Having cut it that thin, Lee was understandably "satisfied" with the results of the campaign which ended with Pope's demoralized remnants carrying McClellan's veterans with them into Washington and under protection of the forts.

During the day, while Lee was standing with some officers in a woods, a sudden shout — a false alarm — caused Traveler to start forward. Lee grabbed for the bridle, tripped in his overalls and pitched forward. He caught himself on both hands, so that he did not strike the ground, and instantly was back on his feet. Colonel Sorrel, in the group, said that it was at once apparent that Lee's hands were "badly damaged," and a surgeon was called for. The doctor discovered a bone broken in one hand and, said Sorrel, "the other was nearly as bad with the twist and the strain." Both hands had to be put into splints and, to Lee's acute irritation, he ended his glorious campaign riding in an ambulance.

In wiring President Davis of the victory, Lee wrote that the nation owed its gratitude to God and "the valor of our troops." He had never held any doubts about the fighting qualities of the soldiers, but their employment in the Second Manassas Campaign also owed considerable to the lessons of the Seven Days. In abolishing the unwieldy divisional organization (with inadequate leaders on three of them), Lee approximated a corps organization by giving wings to Jackson and Longstreet, with each responsible for the divisions under him. With Jackson out of his doldrums, this naturally made for more efficient communication with general headquarters, and Lee and his subordinates all used their staff officers more effectively for maintaining contact. Stuart's cavalry helped in reconnaissance, as did the open country, and information about the enemy was brought promptly to general headquarters.

But, with all the improvements in operation, essentially Lee was able to clear Virginia of invading forces, combining more than twice the size of his own army, by his total commitment to one clearly conceived and steadfastly held purpose. Amid the divisions in the Federal government's war and the apprehensive dispersals of the Confederate government's defense, Lee brought the first single, controlling hand.

With this, in three months since he had taken over the heterogeneous outfits huddled in front of Richmond, Lee had returned the attempt at use of force back to where it had begun. There was, however, one significant difference from the eviction of invading troops after First Manassas. This time the farmland between the Potomac and the Rappahannock lay ravaged from the passage of the Federal armies, and Lee's army could not subsist for one day where Joe Johnston had spent the idle months — as the people said — "before the Yankees came." These man-made barrens would determine what Lee did with his victory.

## CHAPTER XII

## "Only Heroes Were Left"

VARIOUS AREAS of confusion grew up around Lee's move after Second Manassas, and Lee's purposes are not entirely clear. After the war when a cousin of his asked why he had crossed the Potomac and gone into Maryland, Lee replied that he had gone to feed his army. Looking back from a distance it was natural for Lee to reduce the factors in his decision to the one problem which came to haunt his mind above all others. Colonel Lucius Northrop's bureaucratic commissary department showed its inability to supply the army as soon as Lee moved away from Richmond, and from Second Manassas on Lee said that he gave more thought to subsisting his men and animals than to all other military problems together.

However, Lee did not have to go into Maryland in order to feed his army. He could have fallen back to the untouched part of Virginia south of the Rappahannock or shifted west to the Shenandoah Valley. Only if he wanted to affect the military decision, since his army could find no subsistence where it was, did he have to enter Maryland to feed the army. As Colonel Marshall pointed out, if Lee moved backwards, in terms of purely military considerations this would remove the threat of his army from Washington and permit the Federals to return to the interior of Virginia in greater force, as they had the year before. Beyond this, as Colonel Marshall and Lee's own words make clear, Lee was thinking in terms of the morale effect of a withdrawal on the people of the North. He was thinking of morale effect in the larger political concept that embraced bringing to an end Northern support of the war.

By arranging his known words, buttressed by Marshall's views, it is possible to deduce that Lee's ultimate purpose was to start a movement for peace. Marshall wrote that the Federal government depended upon "moral" causes, including the "popular belief that the war would end soon and successfully." Conversely, a victorious Confederate Army loose in the North, presenting a threat to its major cities, could make the attempt to defeat the new nation appear a hopelessly drawn-out, disruptive struggle toward an uncertain end. There was no question that the Northern will to support the war was flagging and large segments of the population were passing from indifference to opposition.

Lincoln had then prepared the Emancipation Proclamation in recognition of the need of a crusade to bring popular support to the war.

At the same time Lord John Russell was considering extending England's official recognition to the Confederacy in the community of nations, and it was assumed that France would follow England's lead.

This was a period of balance when it seemed possible to achieve independence.

As if aware of the forces that might then tip the balance, Lee acted with more urgency and with less deliberation than at any period since he had been a Confederate. Lee saw the last of Pope's departing wagons on September 2, and on September 3 he wrote Davis, "The present seems to be the most propitious time since the commencement of the war for the Confederate Army to enter Maryland." Nothing previously had been said by anybody about entering Maryland. But on August 25, the day Jackson started on his march around Pope, Lee had written his wife: "I think we shall at least change the theatre of the war from James River to north of the Rappahannock. That is part of the advantage I contemplated."

At that period the men in the army, as well as in the government, were convinced that many Marylanders would rally to the Southern cause if free of Federal force. It was felt possible that the slaveholding state would declare for the Confederacy. The Maryland volunteers with Lee made constant assurances that only the presence of the army was necessary to bring out Southern sympathizers. In the letter to Davis, Lee wrote: "If it is ever desired to give material aid to Maryland and afford her an opportunity of throwing off the oppression to which she is now subject, this would seem the most favorable." Then, not specifically referring to Maryland, he wrote, "I am aware that the movement [north of the Potomac] is attended with much risk, yet I do not consider success impossible." On the next day he wrote again and said, "Should the results of the expedition justify I propose to enter Pennsylvania."

Several days later General Lee talked to Brigadier General John G. Walker. Walker was a forty-year-old professional soldier from Missouri whose two-brigade command reached Lee after the Manassas Campaign. Walker recorded that Lee said Harrisburg, Pennsylvania, was "the objective point of the campaign." Lee planned to wreck the long bridge of the Pennsylvania Railroad over the Susquehanna a few miles west of Harrisburg. With the Baltimore and Ohio already in their possession, Lee said, "there will remain to the enemy but one route of communication with the West, and that very circuitous, by way of the Lakes. After that I shall turn my attention to Philadelphia, Baltimore or Washington, as may seem best for our interests."

This constituted Lee's known military purpose. It has been customary to treat as a separate matter Lee's September 8 letter to Davis suggesting peace proposals. However, there seems the probability that Lee planned to recommend the peace proposal to Davis once his army was safely across the Potomac. From Frederick, Maryland, fifty miles northwest of Washington, Lee wrote Davis:

"The present posture of affairs, in my opinion, places it in the power of the Government of the Confederate States to propose with propriety to that of the United States the recognition of our independence.

"For more than a year both sections of the country have been devastated by hostilities which have brought sorrow and suffering upon thousands of homes, without advancing the objects which our enemies proposed to themselves in beginning the contest.

"Such a proposition coming from us at this time, could in no way be regarded as suing for peace, but being made when it is in our power to inflict injury upon our adversary, would show conclusively to the world that our sole object is the establishment of our independence, and the attainment of an honorable peace. The rejection of this offer would prove to the country that the responsibility of the continuance of the war does not rest upon us, but that the party in power in the United States elect to prosecute it for purposes of their own. The proposal of peace would enable the people of the United States to determine at their coming elections whether they will support those who favor a prolongation of the war, or those who wish to bring it to a termination, which can but be productive of good to both parties without affecting the honor of either."

Davis did not acknowledge Lee's letter and subsequent events made it too late to act upon. But at the moment when Lee wrote Davis, it would seem to express for him the underlying and ultimate purpose of his campaign.

Though the invasion to Pennsylvania was certainly Lee's military objective (whatever results he hoped for), he felt that even if the expedition fell short of his most ambitious goals it would serve a good immediate purpose to cross the Potomac into Maryland. Here he was working with a short-range objective that he could settle for within the long-range objective. This was summarized in his official battle report written the following year.

Stating that northeastern Virginia was freed from the presence of Federal soldiers, he wrote, "The war was thus transferred from the interior to the frontier and the supplies of rich and productive districts made accessible to our army. To prolong a state of affairs in every way desirable and not to permit the season for active operations to pass without endeavoring to inflict further injury upon the enemy, the best course appeared to be the transfer of the army into Maryland."

The advantage of this, as he pointed out in a letter to Davis, would be to relieve Virginia's farmlands of invading troops so that the farmers — especially in the northern end of the Valley — could harvest their crops. Because of Lee's willingness to settle for this limited gain, and his later lack of reference to the potential gain from a protracted invasion, his larger intentions have been obscured.

When Lee was making his plans in September, in support of his larger intentions he suggested to Davis that Braxton Bragg mount a similar movement to the Ohio River. Bragg, who had superseded Beauregard in Mississippi, was a fine organizer. With a rebuilt army Bragg skillfully used railroads and ferryboats to make a great swing to Chattanooga, Tennessee, passing completely around the Federal forces. From there on August 28, in conjunction with Kirby Smith's small army in Tennessee, Bragg started northward for a marching campaign into Kentucky — actually more of a divided state than Maryland was.

With all the elements involved Lee acted so quickly that he seemed hurried to "strike while the iron was hot." He wrote frankly to Davis that the army was "not properly equipped for an invasion of the enemy's territory. It lacks much of the material of war, is feeble in transportation, the animals being much reduced, and the men are poorly provided with clothes, and in thousands of instances are destitute of shoes. Still we cannot afford to be idle, and though weaker than our opponents in men and military equipments, must endeavor to harass, if we cannot destroy them."

In his official report, again stating that the army was not equipped for invasion, he wrote, "it was yet believed to be strong enough to detain the enemy upon the northern frontier until the approach of winter should render his advance into Virginia difficult, if not impracticable."

In the haste of his determination to avoid a victory without fruits, Lee did not consider the physical toll of the Manassas Campaign on the men. He also seemed to regard the barefooted marching as a hardship the men would have to endure rather than to take into account the possibility that men would break down from the suffering on the hard Maryland roads. Also, many of the cavalry horses had become "unserviceable, from want of shoes or overwork." Lee left behind the cavalrymen, whose horses had broken down, to gather the enemy's abandoned supplies from the battlefields.

September 4, when Lee put the unrested army in motion to the northwest, marked the peak of his ascendancy in his relations with the President. Davis was as obsessive about the defense of Richmond as Lincoln was about Washington, and against all his apprehensions he had almost stripped the capital's garrisons to send troops to Lee. McLaws's relics of Magruder's command came up and D. H. Hill's division; and Wade Hampton's cavalry brigade joined Stuart. Not assuming victory, Lee urged Davis to continue the work on the fortifications on three sides of the city. In the event of defeat, Lee did not fear the advance of Federal troops on his line of withdrawal. He feared another waterborne invasion, though on this point he could have put his mind at rest. Having been talked into it once, Lincoln would never consider that again, nor any maneuver that removed a Federal force from between Lee and Washington.

Lee did not wait for Davis's approval of his suddenly broached plan. Resting his army only briefly in rich and comparatively unscathed Loudoun County, where the gaunt horses enjoyed good grazing, on September 5, Lee pointed his army to the Potomac ford near Leesburg. By the 7th Lee was dictating a routine message to Randolph from "Headquarters, two miles from Fredericktown, Maryland." That night, with his hands still in splints, Lee slept in his tent in Best's Grove.

2

In Frederick the streets of red-brick houses flush on the sidewalk were not dissimilar to the rows Lee had seen as a child in Alexandria. Frederick's streets, however, looked comparatively grim, and not only because in Alexandria the fronts had been brightened by white paneled doors and shining brass knobs. In Frederick the doors were closed tight in unwelcome, and most of the citizens who appeared on the streets looked at the Confederates either in detached curiosity or outright hostility. Merchants were reluctant to take Confederate money for their goods. The only visitors to the noisy encampment were romantic young ladies who, their sentimental sympathies with the South, wanted to meet the famous soldiers. Only these young ladies, and a few fascinated boys, were not repelled by the soldiers' ferocious and motley appearance.

In all truth, "Mr. Lee's company" — as a countrywoman in Virginia called the troops — looked more like a bandit horde than any kind of army ever imagined. The handsome uniforms which the men had worn away from home had just about come apart. The weatherstained, colorless trousers were raveled at the bottom and gone at the knees and seat; jackets, out at the elbow, were almost in tatters, and rips and tears were mended crudely or not at all. Hats were shapeless with floppy brims, and those men who were not barefooted or walking in homemade sandals of rags wore flap-soled rust-colored shoes.

Gone were all the shining accouterments of war. Blanket rolls were slung across the left shoulder, and across the other a cord supported the mostly empty knapsack that swung back of the left hip. Hanging to the knapsack was the all-purpose tin cup. On a cord looped over the neck hung the cantten. The men themselves, unshaven and shaggy-haired, were gaunt and brown, with fierce bright eyes and a swagger in their stride, and carried with casual pride their gleaming rifles. The rumbling drawl of their voices was incessant; they never stopped talking, and laughter burst from them in sudden violent streams.

The only uniforms that suggested the pageantry of war were worn by the officers. The two officers who were the center of interest, Lee and Jackson, made themselves scarce. Lee could not ride because of his bandaged hands, and Jackson in his shyness remained in his tent with closed flaps.

Jackson's shyness was no pose. His ambitions fulfilled by accomplishment, he shunned any attendant publicity. Newspaper correspondents were not permitted in his camp and he never read anything about himself in the papers. In privacy, he showed a good humor in Maryland, despite the chilly reception. Not even Lee was more dedicated to *winning* their independence by aggressive action, and he had wanted to take the war to the enemy since First Manassas.

Partly because Jackson shared Lee's desire for the offensive and partly because he excelled in semi-independent ventures, Lee began to regard Jackson's troops as a mobile, striking force. At Frederick, Lee asked Jackson to his tent to confer on the first operation of their advance.

When Lee crossed the Potomac, the Federal garrison at Winchester moved north down the Valley to Harper's Ferry and united with the troops there guarding supplies and installations. Lee had hoped his presence at Frederick would cause the Federals to abandon Harper's Ferry, as they lay across his line of communications with Virginia via the Valley. When the Federals remained, Lee decided he would not detach a force merely of a size to drive them off; he would build Jackson's strength to a size sufficient to envelop the garrison at the bottom of the cup of mountains. In that way he would not only lose fewer men, he would also capture all the garrison and the supplies. Typically, he sought advantage beyond the solution of the problem.

Jackson was so pleased at the prospect that he essayed a joke, saying he had been neglecting his "friends in the Valley."

Lee replied, "Some of your 'friends' will not, I fear, be delighted to see you."

Jackson's own command consisted of Jackson's own former division, Ewell's division and A. P. Hill's large Light Division. Both Jackson's and Ewell's divisions were under the temporary command of brigadiers. Charles Winder had been killed at Cedar Mountain and Dick Ewell had had a leg amputated as a result of a wound taken at Second Manassas. Ewell, the army's "character," was a combat officer at heart and, in the neighborhood where he had played as a child, he sneaked away from Jackson to direct fighting in the lines. Jackson's strength was built by the divisions of McLaws and Dick Anderson, normally with Longstreet, and the two brigades of John G. Walker.

Lee and Jackson were relaxedly discussing the details when Longstreet made a surly entrance into the tent. Longstreet was showing the first effects of feeling he had established influence over Lee. When Lee had mentioned to him the possibility of sending a force to Harper's Ferry, Longstreet had protested against dividing the army in the enemy's country. As Lee had not replied, Longstreet assumed he had won his point. Longstreet, beginning to fancy himself as a strategist, was insensitive to nuances in personal exchanges, and failed to distinguish the difference between Lee's encouraging a subordinate's initiative in combat and Lee's making the strategic decisions for which he alone was responsible. Failing to make this distinction, Longstreet was outraged at finding Lee and Jackson cozily preparing an action he had advised against.

Apparently unaware of Longstreet's displeasure, Lee dictated a carefully worded order for the campaign. Copies of Special Orders No. 191 were sent to various commanders. On the next day, September 10, the ragamuffin army made its raucous way out of Frederick into the rolling country to the west. At Middletown, Jackson, with his augmented force, branched off, and Longstreet's reduced columns pushed on to the pass in South Mountain. Behind him the decrepit wagons creaked for miles, rolling up clouds of dust. D. H. Hill's division followed as rear guard. Last came Stuart's cavalry, the horsemen looking "like circus riders" to Leighton Parks, a boy who watched in awe the passing of the laughing troopers.

But when Lee's army had gone, the three most important cigars in history were left behind. Because D. H. Hill had been informally in Jackson's command, Old Jack had punctiliously sent his brother-in-law a copy of Lee's Special Orders No. 191. By chance Jackson's copy reached Hill before the copy from Lee's headquarters. Some officer, probably of Hill's staff, wrapped three cigars in the extra copy, signed by Assistant Adjutant General Chilton. When Hill's men moved off their camp grounds, the cigars in the wrapper were left behind.

When the Federal Army reached Frederick, a sergeant picked up the trophy and absentmindedly read the writing on the wrapper. In a minute he ran with the paper to his captain. From the captain Special Orders No. 191 went to the colonel, from the colonel to the brigadier general and from him to McClellan's headquarters. As a final turn in "the fortunes of war," one of McClellan's staff officers recognized Chilton's handwriting. He authenticated the order that laid before McClellan the complete disposition of Lee's divided army.

McClellan had just been restored to command and, given his second chance, had been encouraged by the cheers of his troops to show his enemies that he was still the man of the hour. Making a quick reorganization of his forces — including the demoralized units from Pope's army — he had moved out quickly from Washington and reached Frederick two days after Lee's army left. With Lee's dispositions in his hands, McClellan moved immediately to the vulnerable spot in Lee's line of march — Turner's Gap in South Mountain. Once McClellan crossed South Mountain he could strike between the two parts of Lee's army.

At the same time he started Franklin's corps toward Crampton's Gap farther south. Crossing to west of the mountain there, Franklin would be on the rear of McLaws's division. In the envelopment of Harper's Ferry from three sides, McLaws was north of the Potomac River and separated from the rest of Jackson's troops. In this occasion when the element of luck entered, Lee's audacity had exposed him to a defeat that could wreck his army.

### 3

On the night of September 13 Lee was in camp at Hagerstown when a courier brought a message from D. H. Hill. Hill had crossed South Mountain to Boonsboro, where the wagon train was halted, he reported, when he had received an alarming message from Stuart. Infantry supporting the Federal cavalry was forcing him back to the pass through South Mountain. Stuart had added that, from the campfires he could see, it looked as if McClellan's whole army was pushing for Turner's Gap.

Lee absorbed this information and immediately reached a decision. Since no word had come from Jackson at Harper's Ferry, he determined to detain McClellan at Turner's Gap. Orders were hurried off to Harvey Hill to return to South Mountain and hold the pass. Lee told Longstreet to march his division back to support Hill.

Longstreet, in the assurance of what he considered his influence over Lee, protested the order. He suggested they move to Sharpsburg, where Jackson could rejoin them and concentrate the army. Lee brushed aside the objection without explanation. It was obvious that unless McClellan were checked he could reach Sharpsburg before Jackson left Harper's Ferry.

Stubbornly, Longstreet refused to admit that he had again failed in his influence on the commanding general, and the next morning wrote Lee a letter. In giving his reasons for not returning to South Mountain, Longstreet did not mention his pride in the condition of his troops. A superb administrator, he took great care of his men and resisted exposing the tired troops to a forced march in the warm weather.

Lee did not acknowledge the letter. His mind on the untypical speed and certainty of McClellan's movements, Lee, his hand still bandaged, mounted Traveler and started for South Mountain. When Lee, riding at the head of Longstreet's column, reached the western side of South Mountain, he learned at once that Harvey Hill was hard pressed and Longstreet's support desperately needed. Lee sent Longstreet up the hill with his worn men, their jackets stained with sweat, panting as they climbed.

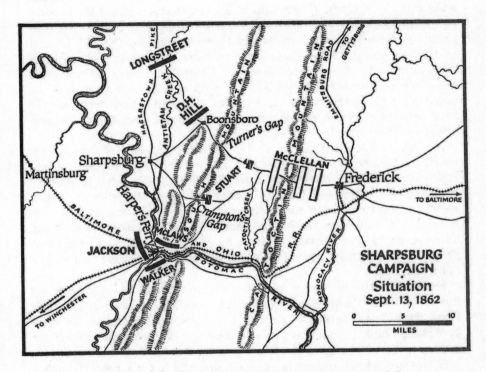

The gap, cutting down four hundred feet in the thousand-foot mountain, spread for five miles and was crossed by five roads, including the main National Road. Its jagged plateau was cut up with small ridges, woods, fences and stone walls, and crisscrossed with country roads and trails. Lee, using his staff as he had not at the Seven Days, dispatched Long and Venable on personal reconnaissance missions in the gap. Possibly because his hands were still painful and he handled the reins with difficulty, Lee remained at the foot of the western slope.

There Long and Venable and other officers told him that Harvey Hill had covered the five-mile front with a force reduced by straggling to five thousand. Hill had not deployed his troops too skillfully and, early in the morning, Garland's brigade alone had taken the shock of Cox's full division. When Samuel Garland tried to rally the shaken men, he went down mortally wounded, and his demoralized North Carolinians broke. By the time a fragment of these was re-formed, Ripley had wandered off with his brigade. Hill had been saved only by the slowness of Cox's supports forming, as it was three in the afternoon before the first of six more fresh divisions came into action against him.

When Longstreet's men clambered into the gap, Hill's left was engulfed. Under the fierce leadership of Robert Rodes, a thirty-three-year-old Virginian whose only military training had been at V.M.I., his Alabama brigade held on to their shattered lines against Meade's full division of Hooker's corps. The fought-out men were saved from being physically overrun by Longstreet's supports. Longstreet's later arrivals were spreading south of the National Road to prop up the whole front, and the pass could be held until night fell. But McClellan had a third fresh corps at hand, and there was no choice except for Hill's and Longstreet's thinned units to withdraw during the night.

At dark, as Lee heard the firing die off in the gap, he was hoping that the day gained would bring news that Jackson had taken Harper's Ferry and would be free to reunite the army. He was brought news of another sort. Franklin's corps had forced Crampton's Gap to the south, defended mostly by cavalry, and in the morning would be in the rear of McLaws, isolated on the northern bank of the Potomac. Lee looked squarely at the developments so inexplicably wrought by McClellan, and in the most undramatic possible way reached the decision that the campaign would have to be abandoned.

He would retire the troops with him west by way of Sharpsburg to the Potomac, where the river ran from north to south. Just west of Harper's Ferry the Potomac turned to a course from west to east, and McLaws, to save his command, could move west to the north-south course of the river and cross there. At eight o'clock Lee sent off a courier with a message to McLaws to abandon his part in the reduction of Harper's Ferry. Crossing the river to the west, he was to feel his way to Lee's part of the army. Lee said nothing of this to Hill or Longstreet.

Later that night, while the troops were clattering down through the gap bringing their wounded, Lee was given a message from Jackson. The nature of Jackson's message is known only by a dispatch Lee immediately sent Davis: "Believing from a report from General Jackson that Harper's Ferry would fall next morning, I determined to . . . retire to the vicinity of Sharpsburg, where the army could be more readily united."

On the indefinite hope raised by Jackson, Lee withdrew from the finality of retreat. He would halt his army at Sharpsburg on the chance that Jackson rejoined him before McClellan attacked. At 11:15 he sent another message to McLaws, asking him to change his route to make his way to

Sharpsburg, if possible. Lee did not fully commit himself to making a stand at Sharpsburg.

At midnight he conferred with his former college-mate, Brigadier General Pendleton, and instructed him to move most of his reserve artillery across the Potomac for the purpose of protecting a line of retreat. Pendleton's reserve had been drastically reduced since the Seven Days, as Lee built up the batteries attached to divisions. After withdrawing Stephen D. Lee's twenty-gun battalion, Pendleton carried only forty pieces. Colonel Lee, just short of thirty, was a West Point graduate from Charleston, South Carolina. After reorganizing Magruder's artillery, he had caught General Lee's eye at Second Manassas by his alertness, initiative and the deadly precision with which his guns were handled.

And so, after all the directions of governments and all the plans of generals, because an unidentified officer dropped three cigars in a wrapper, two armies were gathering at a town of no strategic interest to anybody on the banks of Antietam Creek.

4

Lee rode to Sharpsburg during the morning of September 15 with the exhausted, apprehensive troops of Hill and Longstreet. Both of the commands were drained by the uncounted hundreds of men whose bodies had given out or who could walk no farther on bleeding feet. For whatever reason men fell out on a march, they were all called "stragglers." The survivors who crossed the creek into Sharpsburg numbered less than twenty thousand infantry.

The town lay along a ridge on the Hagerstown Road about one mile west of Antietam Creek, with rolls in the country between Sharpsburg and the creek and west to the Potomac. Some of the surrounding fields were in pasture and in others the corn grew high. Rail fences crisscrossed the land. North of the town stood the East and West Woods, and beyond the woods Antietam Creek flowed two miles to the east of the road. Without any strong natural features, the ridged country outside the brick houses of the town offered generally favorable ground for troops on defense. Whether or not Lee had then determined on accepting a battle at Sharpsburg, he placed his infantry in positions to receive attack and posted his guns.

During the morning, Lee received the long-awaited message of Jackson's capture of Harper's Ferry. Aside from clearing his line with the Shenandoah Valley, it was a haul that seemed to justify the risk of having divided the army. Eleven thousand Federals were taken prisoner, who would be useful in returning Confederates through the prisoner-exchange;

73 rifled guns, of the type used so effectively against them, and 13,000 rifles became Confederate property; unassorted volumes of supplies would be added to their scanty stores.

McLaws, who had not received Lee's two night messages, had saved his command from Franklin's corps by facing a couple of brigades to the rear. They held off the Federals streaming down through Crampton's Gap until the Harper's Ferry garrison had capitulated. Then McLaws's troops made their way down Maryland Heights to cross to the south bank of the Potomac and join their fellows. To hearten his resting soldiers, Lee had the good news read to them. When the fragment of an army learned they would be joined by Jackson the next day, the men raised a spontaneous cheer of relief.

During the day, while McClellan's army approached, Lee reached his silent and never-explained decision to make a stand where he was. It can only be assumed that Lee felt unwilling to abandon his high dreams for the campaign and return to Virginia after scarcely more than one week on Maryland soil. With the critical reduction of his army, it would not seem that he could have reasonably expected to do more than repulse McClellan's army. McClellan would field more than eighty-five thousand of all arms; Lee would have scarcely forty thousand, infantry and artillery, when the troops from Harper's Ferry reached him.

Since Lee never sought battles in which he could do no more than repulse the enemy, his natural aggressiveness as a soldier came into play. It went against the grain to quit the field without battle. Yet, it could not have been instinct alone. The troops with him had heroically demonstrated their sharing of his will to win, supported by an ability to endure and a furious skill in fighting. On the other side McClellan had demonstrated an extreme distaste for committing troops to offensive combat. Lee, with his heart, must have hoped for a victory, or there would have been no reason not to withdraw across the Potomac and save his attenuated army from battle.

To support Lee in his decision, McClellan, after the hard action at South Mountain, returned to his deliberate methods. It was eight in the morning of the 15th before McClellan's first troops reached the western foot of South Mountain. Fitz Lee's cavalry brigade retarded the advance, and it was not until two o'clock that Lee saw the dark blots of the Federal vanguard approaching the other side of Antietam Creek. Late in the afternoon the Federal gunners opened in an unconvincing feeling-out, and that was all.

Lee evidently depended on McClellan not to do anything that day. Having slept only a few anxious hours the night before, Lee retired early in a tent pitched near the town.

The next morning the Federal guns began to fire more in earnest. From a rise east of Sharpsburg, Lee stared across the creek at the gathering masses. With his bandaged hands, he could not use field glasses well. Younger officers made surveys through the glasses, and as late as noon no evidence was seen of enemy advances. Though McClellan was taking his time to get all his troops into position, Lee's control seemed almost unnatural when he showed no relief at the arrival, around noon, of Stonewall Jackson and John G. Walker. Expecting Lee to look careworn with anxiety, Walker said, he found him instead "calm, dignified and even cheerful."

Lee put the sweating troops of Jackson and Walker into line as the men trudged onto the field in their motley uniforms. Longstreet's and D. H. Hill's defensive line was laid along the ridge between the town and the creek, with Longstreet extending southward from the Boonsboro Road and Hill northward. Hood's two brigades were placed at an angle north of Hill's lines, running from Hill's left to the Hagerstown Road. In Jackson's command, A. P. Hill had been left at Harper's Ferry to parole the prisoners and supervise the captured material. The two diminished divisions with Jackson joined Hood's left at the Hagerstown Road and faced to the north. Jackson's line extended toward the Potomac, with his flank protected by Stuart's cavalry and Pelham's horse guns. Walker's two brigades were placed off Longstreet's right, south of the Stone Bridge across the creek.

During the afternoon Hooker's corps crossed the Antietam to the north of Sharpsburg where the creek, two miles east of the town, was beyond the range of Lee's guns. While the Federal cannon across the creek deepened its volume, Hooker's corps made an advance on Hood's position in the East Wood. The attack was not pushed. McClellan seemed to be announcing where his thrust would come on the next day. There was nothing Lee could do with the knowledge. Every soldier in the vicinity had been placed in line.

When the sun went down, the divisions of McLaws and R. H. Anderson had not reached the field. Having first crossed to the south of the Potomac into Harper's Ferry, these troops were marching up the west bank on the north-south course of the river and could not be expected up before mid-morning of the next day. Before that McClellan, with every man and gun in position, was certain to open his attack.

Lee could only be thankful that McClellan had held off that day. At least the worn men with Longstreet and Harvey Hill enjoyed a full day of rest, and Jackson's and Walker's men had the afternoon to lie down after their marching. The last thing Lee did before going to his cot at ten o'clock was to pull Hood's two brigades out of line so that the men could get something to eat and a few hours' sleep before the next dawn brought another kind of test to the Army of Northern Virginia. Before Lee turned in, a bleak drizzle began to fall.

5

The Federal guns opened fire at three in the morning of the 17th. By daylight of a muggy morning the first division of Hooker's corps was advancing on the three of Jackson's brigades, under Lawton, that had relieved Hood in the East Wood. Stephen D. Lee's artillery battalion, posted off the road near the small Dunker Church, fired over the heads of Lawton's troops and slowed the opening advance. Then Hooker brought up thirty-six guns to cover his infantry. Worse, Federal batteries across the Potomac began to get the range of Lee's battalion. Jackson's men were suffering from artillery fire when the re-formed Federal assault rolled through the East Wood. Jackson's veteran brigades were splintered, and thousands of the blue-uniformed soldiers came storming through the woods.

From the crash of battle, before any reports came, Lee ordered Hood's men to break off their rest. Around six o'clock these tough troops went in on a counterattack with the confident pride gained at Gaines' Mill and Second Manassas. The shock of their rush rocked back the Federal advance. Then the Federals re-formed with fresh troops and came on again. Unsupported, Hood's two brigades suddenly gave ground. Three of D. H. Hill's brigades shifted front and tried to stem the tide. The fighting was close up and savage, rifles against rifles, between men toughened in combat and experienced in group killing. For both sides it was the hardest fighting of the war. Colonels and generals fell like privates.

Again the Federals came on. Swarming across the road, their lines approached the high ground of Dunker Church, where the guns of Stephen Lee that were still in action could not fire because of the Texans fighting desperately in front of them. Early's brigade with parts of Jackson's division made a stand in the West Wood near the disputed ground at the Dunker Church. Those were the last troops Lee had on his left. The three of Jackson's brigades, temporarily under Lawton, were through for the day when the shattered men staggered out of the East Wood. Lawton was wounded, the colonel on his own brigade was down, and the Georgia brigade was brought out by a major.

On the Federal side the units that were broken backward were also nearly all finished for that day. By mid-morning Hooker's corps was almost a wreck. Mansfield's fresh corps was then on the field and hammering at the critically damaged Confederate left. At nine o'clock Lee did the only thing possible. He removed Walker's two brigades from the right and ordered them hurried past the town to the corn field between the two woods.

On Lee's wide-open right this left only one gun battery at the Stone Bridge and two regiments, the Georgians of Bob Toombs. This was the gray-haired politico who had been put under arrest for removing his regiments from guard duty on the Rappahannock back in August. Lee gave Toombs the job of keeping Burnside's corps from crossing the bridge and engulfing the army's right. Though the numbers were desperately few, Bob Toombs was not a rash choice to command a last-ditch stand. The tempestuous willfulness that kept him from being a good soldier would give him a fierce joy in the act of defying an enemy army corps.

Lee simply had to forget about the Stone Bridge on his right when Walker's two brigades went running into the scattered action in the corn field. As with Hood before him, Walker's rush rolled back masses of advancing Federals. And, as against Hood before him, the great clots of dark-clothed troops re-formed and rolled back. Their thrust broke off Walker from Early in the West Wood. A sudden gap appeared in the Confederate line and fresh Federals poured in, a whole division of them. They were Sedgwick's division of a third corps, under old "Bull" Sumner, newly arrived on the field.

At this moment of crisis, around eleven o'clock, Lee was searching — with no outward sign of desperation — for any troops not engaged. Walking wearily toward the town came the first of McLaws's soldiers, completing their march from Harper's Ferry and a fording of the Potomac. Lee rushed them toward his broken left. There was no possibility that the men, trying to hurry on their springless legs in water-soaked shoes, could reach the gap before Sedgwick's division came through.

But ahead of McLaws the action had lost all form, with fragments of both armies scattered in no resemblance to battle lines. Into this patternless melee old soldier Sumner had put his head down and plunged. He advanced Sedgwick's closely packed battle lines into an open alley between precisely Walker, in the corn field, and Early re-forming in the West Wood. The gap became a gauntlet when Early's and Walker's soldiers turned sidewise and poured a merciless fire into the flanks of Sedgwick's tight lines. Before the trapped troops could adjust to the two blind side attacks, McLaws's puffing men approached their front. When McLaws's lines opened with point-blank fire, Sedgwick's division disappeared, losing 2200 men.

At this stage of the seesaw action, Lee left his headquarters in the center and rode toward the Dunker Church to make a personal survey. While he was there, with cut-up batteries limping past him on their way to refit, Lee showed the strain on his control. A skulker crossed in front of him carrying a squealing pig. Despite Lee's strictest orders against foraging, men had made way with pigs and chickens and corn in the field. This was the first one Lee had seen. All his tightly controlled tensions broke. The back of his neck turned red, a sure sign of the anger rising in him, as he coldly ordered the man arrested and sent to Jackson, who was to have him shot.

When the pig stealer got to Jackson, Stonewall thought he could use him better by putting him in the line where the firing was the hottest. The ragged soldier stood up well to his test and emerged unscathed. Armistead Long said, "He lost his pig but 'saved his bacon.'"

By the time Lee returned to his command post outside of Sharpsburg, the weight of a new attack was shifting to the center. These were the two other fresh divisions of Sumner's corps. They were advancing where D. H. Hill had only two brigades left, well posted in a sunken road. Again in the nick of time, R. H. Anderson's reduced division arrived on the field, following McLaws, and Lee hurried him forward in support of Hill.

All day Lee had for the first time in any battle exercised complete control of the field. Except for D. H. Hill with Jackson's two divisions, Longstreet was generally in charge of all the other units. Not taking the time to work through Longstreet, Lee personally moved the various units about interchangeably. Longstreet assumed responsibility for the brigades immediately in front of the town.

Longstreet, wearing a carpet slipper because of a bruised heel, had joined Lee on his rise east of the town. A hot sun had broken through the early clouds, and the two men were outlined against the sky. D. H. Hill rode back to join them. With the support of Dick Anderson, and the rapid fire of his guns, Hill seemed to have the new Federal advance against his center under control. All day Lee's cannoneers had concentrated on the advancing enemy infantry and simply suffered the punishment inflicted by the enemy's rifled guns firing from two rises across the Antietam. Though many guns had been knocked out of action, and the remaining pieces were served by skeletal crews, the surviving gunners were blasting away as if in perfect safety.

When Hill rode up, Longstreet was in the jocular humor that battle action usually brought to his spirits. Making a joke of it, he suggested that D. H. Hill dismount, or move away an interval, as he would draw artillery fire to them. A moment later a shot struck the forelegs of Hill's horse, and the animal crumpled forward. Hill instinctively threw his right leg over the saddle to dismount, but the position of the horse prevented his getting off.

Longstreet laughed. "Try it the other way," he said. Then, "Throw both legs over the pommel and see if you can't get off that way."

As Hill climbed over the neck of the dying animal, the members of the staffs relieved their tension by laughing at his awkward dismounting in the midst of shells bursting around them.

When Hill returned to his command, quite suddenly and unexpectedly the center of his line collapsed. It happened by one of those freaks that come when overwrought men are long exposed to danger and responsibility. When Sumner's divisions of French and Richardson were checked at the sunken road, segments worked around one flank to try to get an enfilade fire on Rodes's Alabamians. Rodes ordered his right regiment to "break back" and front the enemy on its flank. The rattled colonel of the regiment seized on the word "back," and ordered his regiment to the rear. The Federal troops, heartened by the sight of a withdrawal as well as having an open flank presented to them, swooped down the sunken road. The other regiments of Rodes's brigades were forced to follow the first to the rear. With the gate open, the whole Federal line rushed at the position.

The combative Rodes had momentarily removed his attention from his lines to attend to a wounded staff officer. When his senses could record the disaster, the hurrahing Yankees were pouring into the sunken road where only Confederate corpses remained. Dick Anderson's brigades were swept along with Rodes's men and almost ceased to exist as military units. Scarcely a Confederate gun continued to fire. The road was open between the two parts of Lee's army.

Again sixty-five-year-old Edwin Sumner commanded at the point of crisis. To support his two divisions who had made the breakthrough came Franklin's fresh corps, having marched up from Crampton's Gap. For the second time that day, Lee looked defeat squarely in the face. This time there were no more brigades that could make timely arrivals, no more units he could shift. Every man was engaged. His army stood on the brink of being cut in half and destroyed.

The issue was decided in the mind of one man, Sumner. Harvey Hill, never one to concede defeat, personally commandeered Robert Boyce's South Carolina battery and got the guns going with canister directly at the Federals then in the sunken road. He rounded up about two hundred men from various units, formed them quickly into a line, and sent the men at a suicide charge at two divisions. The assaulting line dissolved, but it was a charge. Then he hurried over a regiment from Walker's brigades, merely to present a line in front of the Federals. The 27th North Carolina was commanded by John R. Cooke, Jeb Stuart's brother-in-law, and his men fired their last cartridges as they built a little line of stones and fence rails.

While Harvey Hill was engaging in his makeshift heroics, Longstreet's staff came upon two unmanned guns of Miller's battery of the Washington Battalion from New Orleans. The five staff officers quickly dismounted, turned their bridles over to Longstreet, and themselves served the guns. The range was so short and the dark patches of the enemy so dense the temporary cannoneers could not miss. A handful of Miller's gunners, who had been off trying to find replacements for their dead horses, hurried back and took over their two pieces.

During this firing, Longstreet had noticed the lonely stand of Cooke's North Carolina regiment. Always liberal in encouragement with subordinates, Longstreet sent Major Sorrel to compliment Cooke and tell him that the fate of the center of the army depended upon him. Cooke was the son of Regular Army cavalryman Philip St. George Cooke, and, after studying at Harvard, had himself been commissioned directly into the U. S. Army. When Longstreet's staff officer reached him, the North Carolinians had run out of ammunition and were waving flags and cheering.

To Longstreet's message, Cooke said, "Major, thank General Longstreet for his good words, but say, by God Almighty, he needn't doubt me. We will stay here, by Jesus Christ, if we must all go to hell together. That thick line of enemy has been fighting all day, but my regiment is still ready to lick this whole damn outfit."

With the help of six guns raining canister into the enemy's masses, what Cooke's regiment licked was Sumner's mind. Beginning with his division under Sedgwick, he had seen too many units cut up on that bleeding field, and dimly through the smoke he could see clusters of Confederates moving on either side of the line where Cooke's North Carolinians waited with such apparent confidence. The clusters he saw were Anderson's disordered fragments, but he did not know that. Sumner ordered Franklin not to sacrifice his fresh corps and sent a message to McClellan of what he had done.

McClellan was on trial with the army. His enemies in Washington, who had bitterly protested his reappointment, were waiting for him to slip. As on the Peninsula, fear of the consequences of failure chilled his courage. He approved Sumner's withholding of the attack that would certainly have won him the battle, and perhaps much more. As McClellan saw it, Lee's whole army was committed to the center and its left. On Lee's right, Burnside's corps was finally getting across the creek at Stone Bridge, and Lee had almost nothing between Burnside and the town of Sharpsburg. McClellan decided the battle would be won there.

6

At his command post outside Sharpsburg, Lee did not know the final blow would be withheld from his wrecked center. The Federal soldiers were firing from their farthest point of advance, and the cannonfire from across the creek was still breaking over Confederate batteries and troops. Hoping to forestall any fresh troops coming against his center, Lee sent a quick message to Jackson to ask if he and Stuart could open a flank movement between the Federal right and the Potomac. Stuart's horse guns under young John Pelham had maintained a deadly fire all day, and the men were eager to shift off the defensive. Good-looking Pelham, of the West Point class of 1861, recklessly moved a gun out into the open to develop the Federal strength near the Potomac. He immediately drew the fire of Federal batteries posted all the way to the river. There could be no flanking maneuver from the Confederate left.

By the time Lee received this news, he was for the third time staring at defeat — this time from his right. Between two and three o'clock the battle shifted to its third phase when Burnside's corps pushed across the Stone Bridge. Toombs's two Georgia regiments had held up Burnside's crossing for hours in a triumph of defiance. Toombs retired his remnants back on a ridge and the gun battery kept firing. D. R. Jones swung his three brigades from their front on the creek's fords to face Burnside's divisions as the Federals formed to advance from the south. Burnside's soldiers were angry from having been held up at a bridge all day, and the heavy lines rolled through and over Jones's brigades.

Lee moved back to a rise west of the then crowded town, from where he watched the dark waves of enemy troops advance toward him. Directly in their front lay only the debris of Jones's brigades, with scattered fragments still firing. In a field of rank corn to the Federal left, Toombs's two regiments had worked their way toward the town and poured in a light fire on the flank. To Burnside's right, between Sharpsburg and the creek, Jenkins's brigade had faced south from the front of the town and formed in an orchard. Micah Jenkins was a scholarly young graduate of the Citadel, who had won his promotion by a great day in the futilities at Seven Pines, and his determined South Carolinians began damaging the right front of the Federal advance.

Near them were two guns from the "boys' battery" of Stephen D. Lee's battalion. In ages from fourteen to seventeen, the cannoneers of Parker's battery had served in the bedlam of the left until the boys were exhausted. In the crisis of Burnside's advance, enough survivors volunteered to get two pieces in action on the left of the road. Lee saw that these desperate measures were only delaying, slowing, the inevitable approach of Burnside's corps.

At about twenty to four, an artillery lieutenant with a spyglass in his hand moved past Lee with two guns he was moving into the Federal path. Lee, holding up his bandaged hands, asked the lieutenant, John Ramsay, to put his glasses on a dusty column approaching up the road from Harper's Ferry. At first Ramsay said the troops were flying the United States flag. Lee asked him to look again, farther to the right. Then the lieutenant exclaimed, "They're flying the Virginia and Confederate flags."

Lee said conversationally, "It is A. P. Hill from Harper's Ferry."

He had learned an hour before that Powell Hill, who had been ordered that morning to come up, was approaching the field. Of his arrival it was said, "And then A. P. Hill came up," and years later in Lee's dying delirium, he muttered distinctly, "Tell A. P. Hill he must come up."

Leaving one brigade at Harper's Ferry, Hill had started his five brigades at seven-thirty that morning. Driving troops that were worn to begin with through the muggy heat, Hill — with his jacket off, exposing a fireman's red shirt — reached the field with his van in seven hours. In another hour, the rest of the brigades were up and deploying. In the five brigades only 3500 men survived the march to go in on Burnside's flank. They were enough. Burnside's corps had sustained comparatively heavy losses in the pell-mell drive from the bridge to Sharpsburg, and they were neither in the shape nor the order to receive a flank attack delivered with the fury with which Powell Hill's men went in. Burnside's brigades receded back across the creek.

Suddenly, incredibly, it was all over. At no time since the opening gun had Lee held the slightest chance of doing more than repulse McClellan. Saving his army from destruction had been achieved by a succession of hairbreadth last-minute rescues. With a little unintentional help from Sumner and Burnside's long deliberation in front of two regiments, Lee had saved his army by his personal command of the battle. In an incalculable advance in technique since the Seven Days, his tactical execution had grown to match his strategy. Yet, it was more than techniques: it was the quality of leadership.

As the men identified themselves with the leader, they partook of his courage, his resolute decisiveness and will to win. At Sharpsburg the will to win became the will not be to defeated. Morally they felt the victors in repulsing more than two-to-one odds and a superiority of cannon that made of the battle "the artillerists' hell." Of the men who survived that campaign it was said, "only heroes were left." From Sharpsburg the legends began to grow of the valor of the Confederate soldier.

Strategically, however, the drawn battle was a loss. After waiting defiantly in front of McClellan the following day, while the appalling number of casualties were looked after, Lee had no choice except to retire into Virginia. Within two weeks, his campaign into the North was over. When Lee started the decimated army to the Potomac a few miles west of Sharpsburg, he left behind in Maryland the dream of exerting moral and political influences that could lead to the Confederacy's independence.

The soldiers summed it up crossing the river. On the way up, their bands played gaily "Maryland, My Maryland." On the way home, the men said bitterly, "Maryland, *their* Maryland."

## CHAPTER XIII

# "Subsistence Was Coming to Dictate Strategy"

WHEN LEE'S retirement back into Virginia removed the favorable conditions for offering his peace proposal, at the same time his retirement provided Lincoln with favorable conditions for issuing his Emancipation Proclamation. If Lincoln had issued the proclamation when Lee was invading Maryland and Bragg invading Kentucky, it would have seemed like a desperate resort and been seen for what it was — a measure to rally the weak and divided support of the war against former fellow citizens. The dramatic time for its release occurred when Bragg, refusing battle for Louisville, began to fall back toward Tennessee as Lee recrossed the Potomac. On September 22, three days after Lee was back in Virginia, Lincoln issued the proclamation.

The Emancipation Proclamation did not free any slaves. It *threatened* to free the slaves only in the sections of the South unoccupied by Federal troops *if* the secessionists did not lay down their arms by January 1, 1863. Since the slaveholders in Delaware, Maryland and Kentucky were not affected, nor the slaveholders in the South in areas already occupied by the Federals, the proclamation identified forcible emancipation only with *successful* rebellion. Lincoln made it clear that he regarded this "war measure" as an expediency when he said that if he could restore the Union without introducing the slave issue he would.

For the immediate purpose of arousing emotion by adding a moral crusade to coercion, the proclamation was the single most astute act in the whole resolution by arms. For the ultimate purpose of restoring a Union in harmonious concern for the common welfare, it was the single most divisive act since the republic was founded.

By stigmatizing all Southerners as fighting to preserve chattel slavery, it gave to the Unionists parts of the United States the illusion that their fight to "free the slaves" imbued the people with lasting and superior values in humanism. The very existence of the stigmatized South authenticated the North's righteousness, separated by a moral gulf from states which had been leaders in founding the original republic. For ultimately the Emancipation Proclamation, by dividing the regions on spurious moral lines, brought to an end the federated republic founded in 1789. That was the republic of which George Washington was the father. September 22, 1862, marked the beginning of a new Union, no longer a federated republic, of which Abraham Lincoln was the father.

This most certainly was not Lincoln's intention. In his secretiveness and pragmatism, Lincoln had in political-social action, as Lee had in military action, the illimitable self-confidence in his ability to take advantage of developments. Though he said that events controlled him and he did not control events — and this was true — Lincoln possessed the elasticity, along with the wonderfully evocative ambiguity of his words, to give an arrangement of logical progression to events. Like a cat, he could make any action appear to be what he wanted to do all along. But the Emancipation Proclamation released an amalgam of forces beyond his control.

There was an important aspect of the Emancipation Proclamation which came later to be obscured by the publicized moral aspect. The proclamation was employed as a punitive measure against the South. Early in the war, Union generals had begun running off slaves in the paths of their armies, and this practice was justified by Benjamin Butler, who called Negroes "contrabands" of war. During the Revolution the British had run off slaves as a matter of military policy, without trying to justify this means of weakening the enemy. The Federal practice was extended in July, 1862, when Congress passed the Confiscation Act, which provided that slaves were free if owned by persons supporting the rebellion. While removing slaves as working forces from the plantations would obviously hurt Confederate agricultural production, the promise of freedom could cause unrest among slaves in sections beyond Federal control.

When Lincoln went beyond the Confiscation Act, the New York *World* said, "He has proclaimed emancipation only where he has notoriously no power to execute it." But, in those areas outside of his control the proclamation aroused the fear of slave uprisings that diverted many men to the protection of large plantations and caused the abandonment of many small, isolated plantations. Actually, under this proclamation any slaveholder could retain his slaves by declaring loyalty to the Union. As the London *Spectator* stated, "The government liberates the enemies' slaves as it would the enemies' cattle, simply to weaken them in the . . . conflict. The principle is not that a human being cannot justly own another, but that he cannot own him unless he is loyal to the United States."

English Foreign Minister Lord John Russell said, "If it were a measure of Emancipation it should be extended to all the States of the Union . . . [It] is not granted to the claims of humanity but inflicted as a punishment . . . There seems to be no declaration of a principle adverse to slavery in this proclamation." In spite of the legendary figure of Lincoln as "The Great Emancipator," striking the chains from the slaves, there *was* no declaration of a principle adverse to slavery in the proclamation.

This is not to imply that Lincoln did not believe in emancipation. Like Lee, he believed in emancipation by state action, where the owners were to be compensated for the loss of property by the Federal government. He had unequivocally committed himself to disbelief in sudden emancipation as producing "a worse evil than slavery itself." Stating his conviction that a fundamental difference between the black and white races would make social and political equality impossible, Lincoln regarded the sociological problem of the freed Negro in the same light as did Southern emancipationists, such as Lee.

In going against his own convictions in this war measure, Lincoln offered the wispy hope that deportation would solve the problem. In this he was strongly supported by senators and congressmen from the bloc of states then called the Northwest — Ohio, Indiana, Illinois, Michigan, Wisconsin, Minnesota, and Iowa. These states, strongholds of white supremacy, feared that emancipation in the South would cause an influx of Negroes to the North.

Representative Samuel S. Cox of Ohio said, "If slavery is bad the condition of . . . Ohio with an unrestrained black population only double what we now have, partly subservient, partly slothful, partly criminal, and all disadvantageous and ruinous, will be far worse." In a June referendum on a new state constitution, Illinois voters approved an article that prohibited Negroes from settling in the state and denied suffrage to those there. Hostility to the Negro was shown by race riots and/or labor demonstrations of violence in Chicago, Detroit, Cincinnati, Cleveland, and Toledo. (Similar outbursts occurred in New York City, Brooklyn and Buffalo.)

Senator Lyman Trumbull of Illinois said in the Senate, "There is a very great aversion in the West — I know it to be so in my state — against having free Negroes come among us. Our people want nothing to do with the Negro . . ." He said the people of the Northwest were asking " 'What will you do with them [slaves] . . . we know it is wrong that the rebels should have the benefit of their services to fight us; but what do you propose to do with them?' "

Lincoln proposed, without evolving details, a colonization of Negroes. On August 14 in a conference with Negro leaders he told them, "There is an unwillingness on the part of our people, harsh as it may be, for you free colored people to remain with us . . . I cannot alter it if I would . . . It is better for us both, therefore, to be separated." Despite Lincoln's plan for colonization, and the assurances of pro-administration men that the abolition of slavery in the South would drain off the small Negro populations in the Northern states, the voters in the Northwest turned against the Republicans. In the October and November elections the states of the Northwest sent Democratic majorities to Congress.

Lincoln's deportation proposal was not among his more enlightened moves. In practical terms nothing came of it. No solution was provided for the problem that had occupied the minds of Southern emancipationists for half a century. Instead, beyond the people's worst fears, slaves were run off during the upheavals of war in an act which associated their freedom with hostility to Southern whites. This was made more pronounced by the use of Negro troops in the Federal armies. The actual conditions under which forcible abolition occurred deepened and complicated the sectional divisiveness by the effects on the Southern people.

The South's leaders and newspapers regarded the humanistic trappings as "misrepresentation" and "false pretense," covering the "sole purpose" of inciting servile insurrection. E. A. Pollard, of the Richmond *Examiner*, wrote, "A candid world" would interpret the proclamation as "an act of malice toward the master rather than one of mercy to the slave." This pretty well summarized the Southern reaction — though it also expressed sentiments of some in the North, where the proclamation was by no means received with unanimous approval.

The abolitionists rejoiced and advocated the arming of freed slaves. But, as they had been urging Negroes to kill white people since Nat Turner's insurrection in 1831, this represented nothing new from them. Chiefly, the Southern leaders were impressed by the extremes to which Lincoln's government would go to accomplish their physical subjugation. After that, Davis declared in a message to Congress, "a restitution of the Union has been rendered forever impossible."

Lee did not develop any of his personal reactions to the emancipation. It was written about and talked about at a time when Lee, back in Virginia, was occupied with the practical problems of emancipating Custis's slaves. Since the wreckage of the plantations made it impossible for the Negroes to engage in their accustomed agricultural work, Lee wrote Rooney that he did not see how he could execute the provisions of Custis's will while the war continued. "They can be hired out and the fund raised applied to their establishment hereafter . . . [but] if emancipated under present conditions, even if I could accomplish it, I do not see what would become of them." Later he wrote son Custis that he was trying to liberate all those "who wish it or can support themselves." Then he made his own personal preferences very clear. "Indeed," he added, "I should like to include the whole list at Arlington, White House, etc., if it can be done so as to finish all the business."

In a letter to his wife he revealed the highly personal aspects of releasing an individual in a dislocated society. Writing about Perry, the White

House dining-room attendant whom he had tried as his body servant, he said, "Perry is very willing and I believe does as well as he can. You know he is slow and inefficient and moves much like his father Lawrence, whom he resembles very much. He is also very fond of his blankets in the morning. The time I most require him out. He is not very strong either. I hope he will do well when he leaves me and gets in the service of some good person who will take care of him."

It might be said that the Emancipation Proclamation changed nothing for Lee.

2

General Lee never repined over the brevity of his invasion. Unchanged by success or misfortune, as Rob said, he fulfilled his duty in the design of Providence when he did the best he could. After all, he had achieved his short-range goal within the larger objective. Virginia was cleared of the enemy, and unmolested farmers harvested their fat crops in the northern Valley. In the rolling fields west of Winchester, Lee recuperated his men and rebuilt his army in the mellow autumn weather from September 19 to near the end of October.

His own headquarters were incongruously located in a rocky field that was difficult to ride over. Lee seldom used a house for headquarters for fear of enemy reprisals on the owner. Armistead Long, who selected headquarters sites, had picked the pleasant yard of a house. When Lee refused to occupy even the yard, Long in a pique selected the rough field.

Seven or eight pole tents were pitched with their backs to a stake fence. A stream of good water flowed close to Lee's tent. Wagons, stamped with US on their canvas, provided the sleeping quarters for the colored servants and the couriers, who lounged about headquarters near picketed horses. British visitors to the camp were surprised at the absence of handsomely accoutered aides and even sentries. Respect was the only barrier. This was commented upon by Lee's most distinguished visitor of the fall, Colonel Garnet Wolseley, later Field Marshal Viscount Wolseley. "While all honor him, those with whom he is the most intimate feel for him the affection of sons to a father."

Wolseley recorded the deep impression Lee made upon him. "I have met many of the great men of my time, but Lee alone impressed me with the feeling that I was in the presence of a man who was cast in a grander mould, and made of different and of finer metal than all other men." Mentioning that Lee's hair and beard were "nearly white," Wolseley recorded, "but his dark brown eyes shine with all the brightness of youth, and beam with a most pleasing expression. Indeed, his whole face is kindly and benevolent in the highest degree. In manner, though sufficiently conversible, he is slightly reserved; but he is a person that, wherever seen, whether in a castle or in a hovel, alone or in a crowd, must at once attract attention as being a splendid speciment of an English gentleman, with one of the most rarely handsome faces I ever saw."

Obviously Lee showed no outward trace of disappointment over the recent campaign. His soldiers seemed to be thoroughly enjoying themselves in the quiet aftermath. In the raucous camps, from which nightly singing arose, the men renewed their acquaintance with the taste of beef and fresh vegetables, along with receiving the bounty of an increased ration in their standard corn bread and bacon diet. For miles beyond the soldiers, horses peaceably foraged in the limestone grass of the meadows and fattened on grain. About the only activity was the repairing and mending the men worked at on the filthy rags that had lost all resemblance to uniforms.

Gray had become a symbolic color and was seen on officers as a thread through the motley. In the six weeks of rest in the beguiling autumn weather of late September through October, the soldiers received packages from home containing clothes left behind from their civilian days. Coats, pants, waistcoats were variously blended with surviving garments from the gallant uniforms which, during their ease, the men grew skillful and imaginative at patching. Since a sizable hole could not be inconspicuously covered, the men made large, square, forthright patches, some of bright contrasting colors, and one fellow sewed a red flannel heart at the seat of his breeches. Knitted socks came from home too, and mittens and mufflers, but not shoes.

Shoes remained the bugbear that burdened Lee in the care of his men. Some received a new government issue, but they were not as lucky as they thought when they walked in them a while. From the beeves Lee gathered, hides were were tanned, and prewar cobblers did a thriving business stitching new soles on mottled uppers. Numbers of men made a sort of sandal of the new leather, tied with thongs about their ankles. At the end of the interlude, all too many men were still barefooted.

With all the makeshifts and deficiences, the men, regaining their strength on the steady diet and physical ease, reached a peak of conditioning in which their stamina equalled their high spirits. Lee said the men were in the best shape physically since he had assumed command. The hard work and campaigning under Lee had purged the army of the weak and the malingerers, and the rehabilitated veterans of Lee's summer of 1862 were men proud of their toughness and capacity to endure. When the ten thousand stragglers returned from the Maryland campaign, along with the returned wounded from the Seven Days and Second Manassas, and some of the lightly wounded from Maryland, Lee had sixty-five thousand infantry — in physical condition the most powerful army he ever fielded.

Through the slowly grinding mills of the Confederate Congress, Lee was able at last to organize his army into two corps, with Jackson and Longstreet promoted to lieutenant generals. After the battle at Sharpsburg was over Lee, in his relief from the strain, had grabbed Longstreet's shoulders with his bandaged hands and exclaimed, "Ah, here's my old war horse." This tag caught on and was used to characterize Longstreet, but the flaws in his character — his jealousy of rivals and his desire to dominate Lee — remained unsuspected.

"The indomitable Jackson," as Lee referred to Stonewall in his report, had been particularly impressive in his heroic stand on the left at Sharpsburg, where he had fought without a major general in his command. Jackson's known flaw was his bad record with subordinates.

His most recent clash had been with Powell Hill. Released from arrest in order to fight his division in the Maryland campaign, Hill insisted on a court of inquiry and preferred countercharges against Jackson. Old Jack was not one ever to relent, and all of Lee's tact was required to avoid a court of inquiry. Lee trusted in time to heal the breach.

For Jackson's corps, it was only necessary to make a formal organization of the four divisions he had been commanding — A. P. Hill's, D. H. Hill's, Ewell's and Jackson's own former division. Jubal Early temporarily assumed command of Ewell's division, and fiery old Isaac Trimble, then out ill, was designated for Jackson's division.

Longstreet's divisional structure had been fluid since he had absorbed the former commands of Magruder and Huger, along with Walker's two brigades from Holmes's command, Whiting's two brigades under Hood, and Shanks Evans's unattached brigade. These were re-formed into four more or less equal divisions under McLaws, R. H. Anderson, John Hood and George Pickett, the latter two promoted to major general. Hood was everybody's choice for division command. Pickett, though deserving, had also been a personal favorite of Longstreet's since the long ago day in Mexico when Old Pete had watched the dandified young lieutenant with flowing curls scale the wall at Chapultepec. Walker's two brigades, remaining attached to Longstreet's corps, were placed under West Pointer Robert Ransom, with John R. Cooke promoted to brigadier for his stand at Sharpsburg. John G. Walker, whose brief stay with the army had won him high respect, was transferred to the West.

In the reorganization, many familiar faces were gone from the army. Along with the brigadiers who were killed, Georgia's outstanding political soldiers Toombs and Howell Cobb resigned from the army. Cobb left to make way for his rapidly developing younger brother and Toombs because his ego was cramped by the West Pointers whom he regarded as stiflers of all natural genius. Roswell Ripley, whose performance had fallen short of his gifts for criticism, was recalled to South Carolina, and pessimistic Chase Whiting, Joe Johnston's intimate, was sent to use his considerable engineering skill on the fort outside Wilmington. When Lee wanted to get rid of a soldier, he suggested to the War Department that his gifts could be more usefully employed elsewhere. Whiting was the last unwanted legacy of Johnston's army, and with his departure the Army of Northern Virginia totally reflected Lee, the identification between men and commanding general complete.

Lee regretted losing the fine artillerist Stephen D. Lee. Promoted to brigadier, he was transferred to the Western armies. However, his replacement, Porter Alexander, was soon to demonstrate that his extraordinary talents made him excel wherever he was placed. The young Georgia aristocrat had been urged more than any other junior officer to remain in the Old Army. A highly literate and sharp-edged perfectionist, Alexander had first displayed his superior intelligence and enterprise as Lee's chief of ordnance. Beginning with Stephen D. Lee's artillery battalion, he was to become the greatest cannoneer in the Confederate armies, if not in the war.

Lee never experienced trouble replacing artillery officers. That service drew educated men of privilege, with natural leadership and the trained intelligence that could be adapted to gunnery.

One morning, while the army was rebuilding its strength during October, Walter Taylor took Lee his personal mail. A little while later he was summoned to the General's tent at the hour during which they regularly reviewed the routine business of the day. To the young staff officer Lee seemed the same as usual. Back in his own tent, Taylor discovered that he had forgotten something. Reentering Lee's tent without any announcement, he was shocked to see the older man "overcome with grief." With tears wet on his cheeks he was staring at an open letter he held in his hand. His twenty-three-year-old daughter Annie had died after a brief illness in North Carolina. She had been refugeeing there with Agnes. As the two middle sisters they had always been close companions.

There was no time for mourning. From Harper's Ferry, McClellan had started southward on the east side of the Blue Ridge in the direction of Gordonsville. There he could threaten the Virginia Central. On October 28 the camp in the rocky field was dismantled and the rested army put in motion again.

3

While Lee was studying McClellan's intentions, the Federal Army suddenly veered off in the direction of Fredericksburg. Soon Lee learned he was facing a new opponent, Ambrose Burnside.

The Lincoln administration had reproached McClellan for not pushing a vigorous pursuit after Sharpsburg, and they had had enough of his maneuvering. He was removed from command for good. Lincoln and Stanton wanted direct action and they wanted it on the line they had preferred from the beginning — the straight overland route from Washington to Richmond through Fredericksburg. To get it they appointed a general without ideas of his own who would willingly do their bidding.

Tall, a little portly, with fine carriage and magnificent "sideburns," Burnside was a splendid-looking military figure and a genial, likeable man. He had been a classmate of A. P. Hill's in 1847, a year behind McClellan and Stonewall Jackson at West Point. Without ambition for the post of commanding general, Burnside dutifully and with considerable drive pointed his huge army (grown to 115,000) to the crossing of the Rappahannock at Fredericksburg. He was appointed on November 7, and on the 17th Sumner's corps occupied Falmouth, slightly upriver from Fredericksburg on the north bank of the Rappahannock.

Against the new threat, Lee was not as spirited as he had been in planning the summer offensives. Suspecting Fredericksburg was Burnside's objective, Lee, because the move seemed so obvious, could not convince himself that the Federals had abandoned strategy. Since Fredericksburg was near the Potomac wharves at Aquia Creek, Lee feared another waterborne attack, and one that might strike at the vulnerable area south of the James River. In early October, Lee had sent Stuart on a reconnaissance in force to discover if the enemy had any fancy intentions. Stuart had taken his cavalry across western Maryland in a raid that went to Chambersburg, Pennsylvania, and this spectacular exploit — in which again he encircled McClellan's army — was good for morale. Then on November 18 Stuart forced a passage across the Rappahannock on its northerly course west of Fredericksburg, and Lee learned for a certainty that Burnside was concentrating at Fredericksburg.

Fundamentally Lee did not want to fight there. He could not oppose the crossing at Fredericksburg, where the river was four hundred yards wide, because the high bluffs on the northern banks gave the Federal artillery a commanding position. On the south side of the river, back from the small city, a ridge called Marye's Heights gave Lee a formidable defensive position from which he did not believe his army could be driven. However, in repulsing Burnside, Lee would be in no position for the maneuvering that could exploit the repulse. As Jackson said, it would be a victory without fruits.

Lee preferred to fight on the North Anna River to the south, where he could oppose the river crossing and the terrain was favorable for maneuver. But for the second time subsistence became a deciding factor in his plans. South of the Rappahannock the country, free of large-scale invasion, was still producing foodstuff for the army and forage for the horses. Lee's reluctance to commit at the Rappahannock for such a non-strategic reason as subsistence was shown by the slow concentration of his army at Fredericksburg.

The first division of Longstreet's corps did not support the small observation at Fredericksburg until November 19, two days after Sumner's arrival at Falmouth. It was November 26 before Lee ordered Jackson's corps to come on. At the beginning of the Federal movement southward, Lee had left Jackson west of the Blue Ridge in hopes of an opening for a quick thrust, but Burnside's massing at Fredericksburg finally forced Lee to assemble his full army for the unwanted battle.

When Lee was preparing to leave a temporary camp at Culpeper, his son Rob walked in warmly bundled up in a Yankee overcoat. But he had no blanket, and no clothes, Lee wrote his wife, "but what he stood in." Lee was worried about him and gave his son a ride on one of his horses to Fredericksburg.

At Fredericksburg, Lee made some changes in his own wardrobe for the winter. He sent summer socks and drawers for Custis to put in his trunk in Richmond, to relieve the overcrowded valise he carried in his headquarters wagon. He asked Custis to have a vest made for him of blue, black or gray cashmere, or "cloth," with "rolling collar and army buttons." He also asked Custis for the loan of a Mexican bit to try on Traveler. The strong gray was a horse that liked to go and, Lee said, "my hands are weaker now."

In early December, while waiting for Burnside's assault to open, Lee suffered the second death in the family in two months. Rooney and Charlotte Lee's infant daughter died suddenly. Following the death of their first-born, Lee's grandson, it was particularly saddening. On December 10 Lee wrote Charlotte, "I felt that she would be such a comfort to you, such a pleasure to my dear Fitzhugh, and would fill so full the void still aching in your hearts."

Lee's family sorrows came when he was deeply distressed for the people near him, army and civilians. The weather was very cold, with much snow, and it was hard on Lee to see his men shivering in their thin clothes and the bloody tracks the bare feet left in the snow. Even worse was the "piteous sight" of the women, children and old men who made an exodus from their homes.

At Fredericksburg the first effects of the Emancipation Proclamation were seen in a new harshness in prosecuting the war. This was nothing like Pope's purposeless vindictiveness toward civilians. Coldly systematic, this fulfilled James McDowell's prophecy in Virginia's 1831-1832 slavery convention. Slavery would become a crusade with which, he had said, "in the name of liberty" the South would be held up "as the enemies of men whom it will be a duty to overcome and a justice to despoil."

Lee had not planned to defend Fredericksburg. The charming small city, built in the eighteenth century, was essentially residential, a center for Rappahannock River planters and in no sense a military objective. General Sumner, however, ordered the civilian population to evacuate the city or suffer the consequences of shelling.

When the city authorities told him of Sumner's ultimatum, Lee could only suggest that the collision of the armies might make it advisable for the citizens to seek safety. The night the civilians moved out with bundles of their hastily gathered belongings a sleet storm broke over them, and no man who witnessed their exodus from the city ever forgot the sight.

4

As the days of bitter weather continued and the city was not shelled, some of the people, who had been unable to find shelter, crept back into their homes like wanderers in a ghost town. Also occupying the deserted city were the troops of the 17th Mississippi and parts of the 18th Mississippi regiments, in Barksdale's brigade of McLaws's division. White-haired William Barksdale, a newspaper editor, was one of the few passionate secessionists who served well in Lee's army.

Around two o'clock in the morning of December 11, Barksdale detected faint muffled sounds out on the river. Burnside was stretching his pontoons toward the city. Barksdale's troops were quietly aroused, and the men crept silently through the icy dark streets to the houses that lined the river. There the men moved into the basements, opened windows and, piling their equipment in corners, poked their long rifles over the window ledges. Around four in the morning the sounds were near enough to be heard distinctly, though the thick fog drifting over the water prevented the men from seeing anything. At a signal from one of McLaws's guns, the line of perhaps seven hundred men — covering the mile and a quarter of the city's front — opened fire *at the sounds*. The engineering work parties immediately abandoned the pontoons and moved back to safety.

Burnside's guns opened on the houses on the riverfront, and the Mississippians huddled in corners until the barrage was over. They returned to their windows when the bridge builders came out on the river again. By noon the riflemen had driven off ten attempts to stretch the pontoons to Fredericksburg, still firing at sounds as the battle smoke hung in the fog. For this stand "Barksdale's Mississippians" went into the legends as sharpshooters. Though not officially sharpshooters, this tough outfit contained a high proportion of self-reliant outdoor types, all of whom had been familiar with firearms since childhood and some of whom were squirrel shooters.

By one o'clock the goaded Burnside opened the heaviest massed shellfire of the war, 181 guns, on the city. From the main street Fredericksburg sloped down to the river, so that the streets were tilted toward the guns. With the guns firing from the opposite bank higher than the city, the shellfire came down with the effect of being fired from above. Within three hours, many of the handsome mansions had been reduced to rubble and fires were burning through the broken walls of the buildings still standing. Incredibly, the survivors of the two Mississippi regiments returned to the windows in the dust-filled, half-wrecked cellars and took up their sharpshooting at the pontoon builders.

By then bridges had been completed below the city, and Federal troops advanced into the smoking streets behind Barksdale's men. Then the men withdrew from their cellars, falling back through the streets and firing into the advancing Federals. Barksdale had long since surpassed his simple assignment of delaying the bridge building until the army was alerted to the crossing, and he had defied one order of McLaws to withdraw. The thing became purely personal with the middle-aged secessionist, and when his regiments fell back on the main army at dusk of the 11th the men received a great spontaneous cheer from all the Confederates who had witnessed their miniature battle.

The next day Burnside's huge army crossed the river, and during that night, the 12th-13th, its guns could be heard crunching on the frozen ground. By then Lee had every unit of his army in place, covering the ridge south of Fredericksburg and to the west, and in heavy timber on a lower ridge to the east, Lee's right. On the morning of December 13 a fog shrouded the countryside when Lee established field headquarters in about the center of the long line on a hill — called since then "Lee's Hill."

Longstreet and staff officers stood with him, Jackson came and went, as Lee waited for the fog to lift and reveal the Federal movements. Around eight-thirty he could hear muffled sounds, but the mist was not sufficiently clear to see for any distance. Then at ten o'clock the clear winter sun revealed to him Federal forces advancing in handsome lines toward the swampy ground on his right, where Jackson's troops were deployed and waiting in the woods. Cannonfire opened on both sides, slowly building into a volume "at once terrific and sublime" — as seen by British war correspondent Francis Lawley.

Lee, totally free of strain, watched more calmly then the visitors. Meade's assault made a brief, shallow penetration in the swampy woods before the Federal troops were driven out with heavy losses, leaving prisoners behind. The assaulting lines re-formed and came on again in uninspired doggedness. Jackson's defense was put under none of the pressure such as at Sharpsburg, and the streams of lead pouring from his troops dissolved the attacking lines.

For Lee, too, the battle bore no resemblance to the tension of Sharpsburg, when he had spent the long day rushing exhausted units from one part of the field to another. Here he was only a spectator, at last enjoying the view of his army, unthreatened and unspent, throwing back masses of the enemy. Speaking aloud his thoughts, Lee revealed the elemental contradictions resolved in his nature.

Staff officer Cooke and Francis Lawley heard him say in a grave and measured voice, "It is well this is so terrible. We should grow too fond of it."

There spoke the powerful natural aggression, expressed through the techniques which he had mastered, and embracing and controlling the aggression was the moral value that judged war to be terrible. (Other versions quoted Lee as saying, "It is well that war is so terrible." But the "this" referred immediately to the awesome panorama unfolding below him, and *this* triumph would seem to have inspired the observation — with the clear implication that "this" battle meant war, as did the "it" in "we should grow too fond of it.")

Around noon the Federal attack shifted to the Confederate center, below Lee. Sumner's "Grand Division" of some twenty-seven thousand appeared from the streets of the city, crossed the bridges over a little canal and formed on a plateau at the bottom of the hill rising about a quarter of a mile to Marye's Heights. When the dark blue waves started uphill, the battle degenerated from war into "carnage." The open approach of the assaulting troops was swept by Parrott guns, rifled guns and howitzers, and the defending infantry fired from behind the stone wall of a sunken road on top of the ridge.

Lee had to do nothing. Poor Burnside, given the unsought command on the understanding that he must attack, sent wave after wave of fresh troops on the doomed attack up the hill. Of the nine thousand Federal soldiers who fell on the hill, not one even neared the stone wall. Some of the defending troops on the sunken road played cards between assaults. Before the day was over Burnside had lost upwards of thirteen thousand men. Lee's losses were something over five thousand, with an unusually high percentage of lightly wounded to killed and seriously wounded.

Yet, it was not the kind of victory that elated anybody. Jackson was particularly upset at not being able to open a counterassault on the battered enemy, but Lee could not attack toward the river because of the Federal artillery on the high northern bank. Lee could only hope that Burnside would renew his assaults. Lee's untouched left offered the enemy more favorable conditions for attack, and Lee waited two days. Burnside, however, had enough of sacrificing men even to please the government. During a wind and rain storm the night of the 15th-16th, he withdrew his army back across the Rappahannock.

Before his army retired, some of his troops sacked the city in the most wanton acts of vandalism yet committed in the war. In houses that had withstood the bombardment, silver was carted off and soldiers began throwing china at the walls in orgies of hoodlumism, while others ripped linen and hauled furniture out onto the street to form bonfires. Around the fires drunken men danced attired in women's clothes taken from the houses. Captain Oliver Wendell Holmes wrote in outrage at the carnival of destruction. The future Supreme Court judge said that such barbarism would never be forgiven by the civilization at which it was directed.

There was no doubt that the sack of Fredericksburg contributed its part in hardening the will of the Southern people to be free of the United States. At the same time the Confederate victory did Northern morale no good. Federal prisoners seemed disgusted at the war. Their letters home expressed a deep antagonism to Negroes. The freed slaves who came into their camps were often not well treated and sometimes shamefully.

But to Lee, discounting the shift in morale, the battle held no significance. Disappointed that Burnside had gotten off with no more damage than his frightful casualties, he seemed to put the campaign out of his mind and wrote more family letters than in months.

On the 16th, Lee wrote Mrs. Lee on the nagging problem of liberating the Custis slaves. Those who had jobs in the city or on the railroads could remain where they were and simply be furnished with the proper papers. Those hired out in the country could do the same or continue on the farms in their current status if they chose. "I should like if I could to attend to their wants and see them placed to the best advantage," he wrote. "But that is impossible."

On Christmas Day he wrote his wife and his youngest daughter, Mildred, at school in North Carolina. To Mrs. Lee he revealed his feelings about the human effects of the war. "But what a cruel thing is war. To separate families, and to separate and destroy families and friends, and to mar the purest joys and happiness God has granted us in this world. To fill our hearts with hatred instead of love for our neighbours and to devastate the fair face of this beautiful world. I pray that on this day when 'peace and good will' are preached to all mankind, that better thoughts will fill the hearts of our enemies and turn them to peace."

After his letters he went for dinner to Jackson's headquarters, very snug in the one-room building of the office on a plantation. Jackson had done well for his guests, and Lee relaxed in the gentle banter he practiced with the shy soldier who had become his intimate friend. Also with his staff, Lee continued to show only a cheerful face, and even played a modest joke on the young staff officers. Nondrinking Lee knew that some of his staff officers enjoyed an occasional glass and, when a demijohn was delivered to his tent, he invited his staff in. "Perhaps you gentlemen would like something to drink." He was very amused at their expressions when they lifted tin cups of cold buttermilk to their mouths.

The cluster of headquarters tents was pitched on the edge of an old pine field, near a grove of forest trees that supplied their campfires. For miles to the east and west below Fredericksburg the soldiers built camps that were to serve as winter quarters. Crude huts went up along with tents, and at nights group voices drifted across the winter countryside, singing "Lorena" and "Sallie, Get Your Hoecake Done." Across the river Burnside also went into winter quarters, and the year of 1862 ended with the armies fighting the cold rather than one another. In this quiet aftermath to the Battle of Fredericksburg, the biggest impression made was the serenade given the Rebels by a Yankee band, which ended the concert with "Home Sweet Home."

## 5

After the first of the year Lee acquired another new opponent, "Fighting Joe" Hooker. Unlike the modest Burnside, Hooker, a coarse man, had lusted after the commanding general's post and pulled strings to advance himself. Once in command, he sought to justify his appointment by the appearance of activity, and almost daily created some kind of alarm.

"He is playing the Chinese game," Lee wrote his daughter Agnes. "Trying what frightening will do. He runs out his guns, starts his wagons and troops up and down the river, and creates an excitement generally. Our men look on in wonder, give a cheer, and all subsides 'in status quo ante bellum.'"

There was actually little Hooker, or anyone else, could have done under the conditions of the ground. As Lee wrote his wife, "We are in a liquid state at present . . . We have mud up to our eyes . . ." What worried Lee was the effect of the intense cold on his short-rationed men. In January and February, he began to become seriously concerned over the inability of the Confederate commissary department to get a subsistence diet up to his troops. "I am willing to starve myself, but cannot bear my men and horses to be pinched," he wrote.

Then to Custis he wrote a glumly prophetic appraisal. "Our men and animals have suffered much from a scarcity of food and I fear they are destined to more. I am doubtful whether I shall be able to retain my position and may be at last obliged to yield to a greater force than that under command of General Hooker." Looking at the specter of hunger, he wrote, "We shall lose the moral advantages we had gained and our men may become discouraged."

In writing to members of his family, Lee could not include independent-minded Mary. His oldest daughter had decided she wished to go visiting behind the enemy lines in King George County. There she was out of communication with all the family. Lee wrote his wife, "I heard of Mary yesterday by one of our scouts. She was well." He made no further comment about her.

During that winter Lee began to write urgent warnings to Richmond of the consequences of continued failure to supply his men and horses. The warnings went unheeded, even when he reported that the men were reduced to a ration of one-quarter of a pound of salt meat. Lee also went unheeded when he put his finger on a danger spot in the distribution system. He wrote directly to Davis in reporting the "great delay in the running of frieight trains" on the R.F.&P., and urged the replacement of its superintendent, Samuel Ruth.

A native-born Pennsylvanian, Ruth was a traitor to the Confederacy. He was arrested in 1865 and after the war petitioned the United States government for financial compensation for his services. In the winter of 1863 Lee did not know that Ruth was a traitor, but he did know that the railroad was being operated to the disadvantage of his army. For Ruth's replacement, he suggested a Captain Sharp, in the quartermasters, and wrote Davis, "I beg Your Excellency will cause such directions to be given as the case admits of, and that I, at least, be informed what supplies I can rely upon."

The petition, unusually strong for Lee, did not move the President. The railroads represented one of Davis's problems that remained insoluble through his inability to allocate authority, and the harassed, nerve-wracked man evidently dismissed Lee's appeal as only another item in his railroad troubles. It turned out to be a costly dismissal, as emboldened Ruth worked with a ring of active Federal agents.

The acute food shortage in the winter camp pinched at headquarters, and sometimes Lee's staff officers complained of the poor diet which Lee insisted on sharing with his soldiers. The sparse rations were at least more temptingly served since Meredith, the Negro from the White House, had been replaced by Bernard Lynch, an Irishman, called "Bryan," who acted as mess steward. Among the presents showered on Lee (including a mattress) was a lot of chickens too few in number for Lee to attempt to share with the others. Bryan killed these to serve when distinguished guests were present, such as Colonel Fremantle of the British Army and Captain Scheibert of the Prussian engineers.

Before it became the turn of the last hen to be roasted, she had developed the habit of going daily into the commanding general's tent and laying an egg under his cot. His staff officers were certain the hen showed this preference because of Lee's love of animals and fowls. The commanding general enjoyed an egg with his breakfast, and the hen became a fixture at general headquarters.

While fighting off starvation, Lee used the relatively quiet months to resume the unending work on reorganizing his forces toward building a more efficient weapon. In the infantry there were more replacements to be made among general officers. At Fredericksburg, A. P. Hill lost another brigadier, the knightly Maxcy Gregg, whose South Carolinians had been the first out-of-state troops to parade in Richmond after Virginia's secession. Howell Cobb's younger brother, Thomas R. R. Cobb, was killed in his first battle as brigadier, and John R. Cooke was wounded out with a bullet in the center of his forehead. Personally attractive D. R. ("Neighbor") Jones, who Lee said was a favorite of his, died of a heart condition.

In the artillery Lee at last had the time to form the various batteries that had been attached to divisions into four-battery battalions, commanded by a lieutenant colonel. The battalions were formed in a group as corps artillery to be commanded by a chief of corps artillery. To compensate for Brigadier General Pendleton's limitations as chief of artillery, without hurting the feelings of the devoted Confederate, Lee wished to extend the authority of the chiefs of corps artillery and give them also the rank of brigadier. President Davis, growing more obsessive over organizational details, refused corps artillery chiefs the rank of brigadier. Lee, as he had learned to do in so many other legalistic details, simply gave the men the authority without the rank.

Lee also sent to Davis a plan for reorganizing the staff of the whole army. While he did not recognize the need for an operations officer as such, he largely compensated for the lack personally by the more effective use of his staff officers. By Stuart's enterprise and accuracy in reconnaissance, and by sifting all available sources of information, Lee also fulfilled the functions of an intelligence section. But the staffs of some of the division and brigade commands, without such a guiding control as Lee's, performed inadequately. This, Lee wrote, was largely due to ignorance, as many of these men had been drawn from civilian life, and some of the professional soldiers had never previously commanded more than a company. In suggesting a remedy for this Lee was very advanced, loosely anticipating the School of Staff and Command.

He advocated the formation of "a corps of officers to teach others their duty, see to the observances of orders, and to the regularity and precision of all movements." He recommended the reduction of the number of "aids" on all staffs, including his, and giving specially trained assistants to the chiefs of staff and inspector generals. This was Lee's most original insight into the needed changes in staff work demanded by the larger armies since the days of their training and Mexican War experience. "Some of our divisions exceed the army General Scott entered the city of Mexico with." Lee was very detailed in recommending the ranks and duties of officers in this proposed reorganization.

Davis ignored the suggestion, and Lee was forced to face the next campaign with recognized limitations which he was not permitted to correct.

Lee also recognized that he needed more men in order to win victories of a size to affect the decision. He wrote the Secretary of War: "In view of the vast increase of the forces of the enemy, of the savage and brutal policy he has proclaimed, which leaves us no alternative but success or degradation worse than death, if we would save the honor of our families from pollution, our social system from destruction, let every effort be made, every means be employed, to fill and maintain the ranks of our armies, until God, in His mercy, shall bless us with the establishment of our independence."

Nothing was done. He had developed, for him, an unusually strong resentment of the Confederate Congress, and expressed his feelings in letters to Custis. On February 28 he wrote him, "What has our Congress done to meet the exigency, I may say *extremity*, in which we are placed? As far as I know, concocted bills to excuse a certain class of men from service, and to transfer another class in service, out of active service, where they hope never to do service."

Lee's urgency could not be communicated to Davis and the Cabinet. Davis was becoming increasingly preoccupied by small actions. Late in December, Federal Major General John G. Foster struck inland from New Bern, North Carolina, and cut the Weldon Railroad. Even though Foster returned to New Bern, Davis grew apprehensive over the local action. Lee of course recognized the raid as a feint, designed to disperse forces, and in the middle of January went to Richmond to confer with Davis.

When Lee arrived in the city, a high cold wind was blowing. On the familiar streets around Ninth and Main, civilians and soldiers looked pinched by the cold. There was nothing left of the air of prosperity that had characterized Richmonders when Lee had first come to the city. Overcoats were frayed, shoes cracked, and men without gloves pushed chapped hands into their pockets. Along Main Street red flags fluttered in front of former stores that had been turned into auction houses. These new bazaars were jammed with a conglomerate assortment of personal belongings sold by Richmond families — silver candlesticks, tea services, ostrich plumes, satin evening wraps, Waterford punchbowls, feather mattresses, opera glasses, and silver chamber pots. The customers around these auction houses seemed mostly strangers, bold-faced women and sharp-eyed men in derby hats.

Among the strange men in the city were speculators and hoarders of scarce products. In January, 1863, the Confederate dollar was worth 33⅓ cents against a gold dollar, but many food products had soared to prices beyond any relation to the rate of exchange. Staples such as meat, potatoes and meal had increased in price about five times since Virginia had entered the war, but coffee and salt, scarce and hoarded, cost thirty times as much. Molasses, a favorite staple of the people, cost nearly ten times as much, at $8.00 a gallon, and was rapidly rising. Calico had risen from 12½ cents a yard to $2.25. Ladies' bonnets were not to be had at milliners', though some second-hand bonnets could be found in the auction houses.

In the war offices the workers were still talking about the ravages committed at Fredericksburg, and war clerk Jones said, "The Emancipation Proclamation, if not revoked, may convert the war into a most barbarous conflict."

Against this background of suffering, Lee must have been surprised by the attitude of Jefferson Davis. In the President's office Lee discussed the North Carolina situation. Davis seemed influenced by the fears of Governor Vance, and Lee partially quieted him by promising to send two brigades to North Carolina. But, aside from this local concern, Davis and other officials seemed oblivious to the physical plight of Lee's army and of the Confederate citizens. According to Longstreet, Davis was assured that the war would soon be over and their independence established.

Lee's reaction to this is known only through Longstreet's laconic comment. "General Lee did not share in this belief."

After only two days in the depressing wartime capital, Lee returned to his own army.

### 6

When the enemy's new campaign opened it did not immediately threaten Lee's front, but it involved his army. It began in mid-February when the Federal IX Corps landed at Newport News, near Fort Monroe on Hampton Roads, accompanied by deepening threats inland from the North Carolina coast. These moves came at a time when Lee recognized that the Army of the Potomac needed to open some maneuver to extricate itself from the unprofitable position across from Fredericksburg. On his immediate front, Lee expected Hooker to try to turn his position by crossing the Rappahannock farther to the west, as to the east the river widened and the ground was swampy. Against this move he had dug strong works back of the fords for miles beyond the city. The objective of the Federals at Fort Monroe was less certain.

While by then Lee had realized that another waterborne invasion would not be attempted, because Lincoln's and Stanton's fears for Washington held the invading army between Lee and the capital, the Confederate leaders were sensitive to subsidiary threats to the area south of the James River. Thus, when the IX Corps appeared at Newport News, across the river from Norfolk, the Confederates assumed it held one of three objectives — Charleston (where Beauregard was in command), the reinforcement of the inland movements in North Carolina (threatening the Weldon Railroad) or, in conjunction with garrison troops at Norfolk and Suffolk, an advance on the south side of the James River.

To meet these scattered threats, Lee had to employ his own army. To make his problem more involved, the command situation in the area between the James River and Wilmington had grown chaotic. Under Lee's authority Gustavus Smith vaguely exercised command of the department from the James River to Wilmington. Chase Whiting was at Wilmington, Marylander Arnold Elzey at Richmond, New Jersey native Samuel French had a small force in southeastern Virginia, and D. H. Hill had been sent to organize the forces in his native North Carolina. Instead of interrelating these subdepartments, Smith was nursing his bitterness over his lack of advancement in the field and exercised control nowhere. To quiet Davis's apprehensions after the Weldon Railroad was hit in December, Lee had sent off the fine two-brigade division under Robert Ransom. When professional soldier Ransom reached North Carolina, also his home state, he promptly wrote a letter to his friend Colonel Chilton, describing Smith's inefficiency.

As Ransom intended, Chilton showed the letter to Lee. Lee could not have been surprised, as he wrote more letters to Johnston's former second in command than to anyone else. Lee always showed when he distrusted a subordinate on detached duty by constantly writing him advice and encouragement. Giving up on Smith, he forwarded Ransom's letter to Davis. The President called Smith to Richmond where, after being assigned to innocuous duties, the former "big name" resigned. To fill temporarily the vacuum left by Smith, when Lee learned of the Federal IX Corps at Newport News, he detached Longstreet with two divisions, Hood and Pickett.

Longstreet was given a dual assignment. His immediate objective was to protect the south side against an advance by the Federals at Newport

News, while remaining close to the railroads at Richmond in the event he needed to be recalled hurriedly to Lee. Secondarily he was to supervise, under Lee's authority, the more or less interrelated points of defense between the James River and Wilmington.

This detachment of Longstreet produced an effect which Lee did not comprehend. Expecting every trusted subordinate to do his best, Lee experienced his most significant lapse in understanding. Longstreet had then grown jealous of Jackson and, with his delusions of fitness for grand strategy, he cherished a secret desire for independent command. The Department of North Carolina offered him this.

Including his own two divisions, the garrisons, cavalry and scattered troops under his authority totaled 41,500, a force of small army proportions. To give employment to these troops, Longstreet distantly directed some operations against New Bern and Washington, North Carolina, which came to nothing. Then he turned his attention to collecting food supplies in southeastern Virginia (south of the Norfolk-Suffolk area) and into eastern North Carolina.

From that region General French had been drawing supplies, particularly bacon, for his small force. As Northrop's commissary department could not seem to gather the farm products and ship them to central points of distribution, Longstreet was to perform this commissary work on a scale to bolster the low meat rations in Lee's army. To do this, he wrote Lee, he would be required first to fight the Federals around Suffolk, as well as the IX Corps across the James River at Newport News. This was what Longstreet really wanted — to wage an independent campaign in which he could win a victory on his own and not as somebody's "war horse."

During all of March his letters to Lee showed that his campaign had become the most important factor in the East to him. He asked for more troops from the main army to support his offensive, and advised Lee on how he could defend against Hooker with fewer troops by retiring southward to the North Anna River. Though it was not Lee's intention to retire anywhere on defense, but to get at Hooker as soon as the weather cleared and the roads hardened, he wrote patiently to Longstreet. A withdrawal to the North Anna, he wrote, "throws open a broad margin of our frontier and renders our railroad communications more hazardous and more difficult to secure." He did want the supplies, though it was impossible to reduce his own force further for a commissary expedition.

Then, at the end of March, Lee wrote Longstreet that all reports indicated that Burnside's IX Corps had left Newport News on transports, headed for the West. With the removal of this threat from the south side and North Carolina, the original reason for Longstreet's detachment ceased to exist. By then Longstreet was committed in his own mind to a campaign, based on the excuse of collecting supplies, and Lee became un-authoritative in his relations with Longstreet.

Though Lee had shown that he shrunk from overriding a subordinate's initiative, his laxness in command with Longstreet may have been partly caused by an illness which put him to bed at the end of March. From a throat infection, Lee developed severe pains in his chest, back and arms. Though not so diagnosed, the symptoms probably indicated pericarditis. Along with this, he may also have suffered from hypertension, as the ruddy glow of his face was becoming florid. In his uncomfortable and weakened condition, he seemed uncertain about Longstreet's employment and extended him the latitude of placing him on his own discretion.

On April 2, he wrote Longstreet that, as Burnside's IX Corps was gone and the force against him reduced, he should be strong enough to move against the Federals. However, as the enemy remained behind an en-trenched position, Lee feared that Longstreet could "accomplish but little, except to draw provisions from the invaded districts. If you can accom-plish this it will be of positive benefit. I leave the whole matter to your good judgment."

Longstreet showed no judgment at all for a commander of a detached force who should hold his troops ready to rejoin the main army for partic-ipation in the next major campaign. On April 11 he committed his two divisions and other troops to a siege of the fortified small city of Suffolk. Lee had advised him that such an operation would probably accomplish nothing, and Longstreet's dull, futile siege only proved Lee right. The result was that Longstreet's independent operation kept him away from the army when Lee had to meet Hooker.

Before Longstreet committed his mobile force to this siege, a new fac-tor contributed to Lee's uncertainty over Longstreet's divisions. While recovering from his illness, he was drawn into more complications about the employment of his army by the new Secretary of War, James Sed-don. Randolph had rebelled at being reduced to Davis's "clerk," as he was called, and when the President overrode Randolph's one assertion of au-thority, the Secretary resigned. With Lee's successes in Virginia and con-ditions at least outwardly better in the West, Congress forgot about its demand for a military man in the War Department, and Davis was free to appoint an intimate from civilian life.

Seddon was a scholarly lawyer who, because of his poor health and his wife's wealth, lived in handsome style on a plantation west of Richmond and acted as a dilettante in politics. Though his chronic catarrhal condi-tion gave him an emaciated appearance, which he accentuated by affecting a foolish-looking skull cap, Seddon was a man of charm and quiet force. Assuming office with the President's support, Seddon intelligently left many organizational details to experienced subordinates and the Adjutant

General's office. He concentrated on the major factors in what had then become three major fronts — Virginia, Tennessee (the middle Confederacy) and the Mississippi River.

By April, Seddon had grown convinced that the West was the sector that needed attention, particularly Bragg in Tennessee, where it was presumed Burnside's IX Corps would strengthen Rosecrans. At this period around Richmond the belief in Lee's invincibility had developed an unspoken assumption that Lee could work his miracles and at the same time support other fronts with units deached from his army. As Longstreet's two divisions were already detached, Seddon suggested that one of these be sent to Bragg.

Lee was courteously cold to this proposition. He pointed out that Longstreet felt he lacked the troops for his operation as it was, "and has applied for more of his corps to be sent to him." If troops were taken from Longstreet, his operations would be arrested and "deprive us of the benefits anticipated from increasing the supplies of the army." This was only the negative point. Affirmatively, Lee needed all his troops to assume the offensive again, always with his purpose of disrupting the enemy's dispositions.

Though Seddon was sound in concentrating on the West, he had fallen into Davis's mental habit of shifting troops to prop up fronts where the enemy would be met according to his arrangements. What the West needed was not more troops, but another Lee to use the good soldiers available. Since this was not possible, Seddon expressed a general tendency in wishing to employ units from the winning combination. Lee's counterproposal was simple and typical.

Charleston was being threatened in the East, while in the West Pemberton on the Mississippi, as well as Bragg in Tennessee, faced an enemy offensive. Joe Johnston, recovered from his wounds, had gone West as department commander. On April 9 Lee wrote Seddon, "The readiest method of relieving the pressure upon General Johnston and General Beauregard at Charleston would be for this army to cross into Maryland." This could not be done, he advised, until the roads hardened and the army obtained "a certain amount of provisions and transportation." Beginning with Longstreet's detachment, subsistence was coming to dictate strategy.

This plan, which Seddon and Davis tacitly accepted, was posited upon Hooker's not attacking before Lee was ready to move. Hooker, not having to wait for bacon or the collection of animals scattered for forage, failed to accommodate. On April 29 Fighting Joe opened his long-prepared offensive with what he called "the finest army on the planet." In size, organization, and the materials of war, it was. He fielded 138,378 men of all arms, of whom 12,000 cavalry gave him the largest mounted force yet in the war.

To meet this offensive Lee had, with Longstreet away, not appreciably more than 62,000 of all arms — odds of more than two to one. Yet, even on the 29th, when Hooker's assault opened, Lee could not bring himself to send Longstreet the direct order to return his divisions to the army at once. He wired the war offices in Richmond that "all available forces had better be sent forward as rapidly as possible." In a second wire, he included Longstreet specifically. In forwarding Lee's wires to Longstreet, Adjutant General Cooper wrote on the second, "The Secretary, in view of the above, directs the return of your command, or at least such portions of it as can be spared without serious risk . . . These movements are required to be made with the utmost dispatch."

Three days later, on May 2, Longstreet wrote Cooper, "I cannot move unless the entire force is moved, and it would take several days to reach Fredericksburg. I will endeavor to move as soon as possible."

Because of the latitude extended Longstreet, Lee was to meet Hooker with only three-fourths of his infantry and without his "old war horse." He was also to meet a boldly imaginative offensive, a practically perfect battle plan to secure the flight or destruction of Lee's numerically inferior force.

## CHAPTER XIV

## "Let Us Cross Over the River"

O N A WARM Sunday, April 28, Lee went with Jackson to the Yerby home, where Mrs. Jackson was staying with their seven-month-old daughter. Jackson remained to spend the night, and Lee returned to his tent at the woods. Just after daybreak he was awakened by Captain James Power Smith, one of Jackson's staff officers. Colonel Venable had told Smith it would be all right for him to enter Lee's tent.

Lee rose up, swinging his feet outside the covers, and sat on the side of the cot. Smith told the General that Federal troops were crossing the river below Fredericksburg under cover of a heavy fog. Lee showed no surprise. Smith said that he spoke "playfully."

"I thought I heard firing," Lee said, "and was beginning to think it was about time some of you young fellows were coming to tell me what it was all about. Tell your good general that he knows what to do. I will meet him at the front very soon."

Early on the foggy morning Lee rode to the hill from where he could dimly see two Federal corps massing near the river. These troops, under Sedgwick, did not advance, but began to dig lines under the protection of their batteries on the northern banks.

Sometime later in the morning a courier rode up with a report from Jeb Stuart. Federal infantry had crossed the Rappahannock at Kelly's Ford about twenty-five miles to the northwest. The force was advancing southeast toward two fords across the Rapidan, Germanna and Ely's. Twelve miles west of Fredericksburg the Rappahannock forked, and these two fords crossed the southern branch, the Rapidan, a short distance west of the fork. After six o'clock Lee learned that the heavy force — the corps of Meade, Howard and Slocum — had crossed the Rapidan fords and were advancing toward him on his side of the Rappahannock. Between this force on his flank and Sedgwick on his front, Lee was in a position where it looked as if he must fight two battles with something more than fifty thousand infantry, or save his army by retreating between the two forces.

Only two days before, Lee had written the President, in requesting the return of troops belonging to his army, and said, "from the condition of our horses and the amount of our supplies I am unable even to act on the defensive as vigorously as circumstances may require." Yet, immediately he perceived the box he was in, his reaction was to strike the enemy. For, if Hooker had Lee caught between two parts of his army, seen another way, Hooker's army was separated with Lee dividing it.

A factor Hooker seemed to have overlooked was the nature of the country, called "the Wilderness," into which he was putting his army. This was a somber stretch of woods, fifteen miles square, where only a few farms cut clearings in the desolation. Entangled vines and high-growing matted underbrush formed dense screens over footing made boggy by small streams that slithered between shadowed banks. The Wilderness became the key for exploiting unpredictable elements. Lee could always wait patiently for developments.

That night, by the light of a brilliant moon, three of Jackson's divisions moved out of their position east of Fredericksburg, and R. H. Anderson's division fell back from its position along the Rappahannock fords. In the misty dawn of April 30 Anderson's columns advanced west on both sides of the road through the open farm country east of the Wilderness. Around noon Anderson's skirmishers made contact with Federal cavalry in a large clearing on the edge of the Wilderness.

Called Chancellorsville, the clearing consisted of the grounds around the substantial brick house and outbuildings of the Chancellor family. At that time it was occupied by a widow, Mrs. Sanford Chancellor, a young son, six daughters, and a number of refugees from Fredericksburg. Hooker took over the house as his headquarters and herded the sixteen women and children into a back room, where they were kept under guard.

On encountering the Federal cavalry, Anderson fell back to a defensive position and sent the information to Lee. Lee, still on the heights overlooking Fredericksburg, wrote Anderson at two-thirty. "I hope you have been able to select a good line and fortify it strongly . . ." As Lee had never before used fieldworks in open maneuver, he made it plainer that he wanted Anderson to throw up entrenched lines. "Set all your spades to work as vigorously as possible." Lee had earlier sent forward two engineering officers to draw lines for entrenchments.

When Lee sent this message, he and Jackson and other officers were studying the movements of Sedgwick's forty thousand infantry on the plain below Fredericksburg. The racket raised by the Federal troops convinced Lee that Sedgwick was only demonstrating. From the steady bits of information flowing in from Stuart, Lee concluded that, as Sedgwick was a feint, the movement around Chancellorsville constituted Hooker's main attack. Jackson and the other officers did not share Lee's conviction but, unshaken, Lee determined to stake the fate of the army on his judgment.

He was working with one significant advantage. Back in April Hooker had sent off the bulk of his cavalry, under George Stoneman, in a destructive raid on railroads and civilian property. At that time, as one of Stuart's brigades was in the Valley and another gone south for forage, Lee had with him only the brigades of Rooney Lee and Fitz Lee. Though it was hard to leave farm families unprotected against these raids, Lee detached only two regiments under his son to prevent the destroyers from settling down too comfortably to their work. By this choice Lee retained most of Stuart's five thousand troopers for screening and reconnaissance, while Hooker, with only Pleasanton's brigade, was forced to move blindly.

Once Lee decided to attack Hooker, he placed a force of about ten thousand along the ridge, where Burnside had been repulsed, to contain Sedgwick. With forty guns and Barksdale's brigade of marksmen (from McLaws's division), the bulk of the force was Early's division of Jackson's corps. Jubal Early, the handsome darkness of his youth lost with a rough gray beard and a rheumatism that stooped his figure, was a profane, irascible and bitter man. Trained at West Point and an anti-secessionist lawyer from western Virginia, Early had been so outraged by the actions of invading forces in his state that he directed all of his virulence at the enemy. As he was also a fighter of steely skill, Lee knew that only heavy attacks — not demonstrations — would budge "Old Jube" from his naturally strong position.

In the eventuality that Sedgwick expanded his demonstration into an attack, Lee planned for Early's holding force to retreat southward and cover the wagon train. Jackson's three divisions and McLaws's were ordered to move west to join Anderson.

On the morning of May 1, when the ground was still covered by a fog rising from the river, Lee lingered on the heights overlooking the wrecked city to be sure that Sedgwick was only demonstrating. Around noon, when no threats had developed, Lee left the little force under Early and rode west. Halfway to Chancellorsville the road divided into the Turnpike and the Orange Plank Road, the latter swinging in a loop below the Turnpike until the two roads rejoined around Chancellor's clearing. A few miles east of Chancellorsville, Lee met Jackson on the Plank Road, and soon discovered a strange situation.

Jackson had joined Anderson and McLaws at eleven that morning and, when the combined line left the rifle pits to press against the Federal advance, curiously, Hooker began to fall back. Lee surveyed the suspicious action of four corps giving ground before five divisions.

On the day before, the three Federal corps making the advance from the Rapidan had been joined by three divisions from other corps, and Hooker's flawless troop movements had amassed approximately eighty-five thousand men of all arms in the Wilderness. On the night before, Hooker had said, "The enemy must either ingloriously fly or come out from behind his defenses and give us battle on our own ground, where certain destruction awaits him."

Inexplicably, Hooker began to fall back. Unable to gain any information with his small cavalry force, he might have been unsettled by lack of visibility in the creepy jungle, where his great army bunched on narrow roads like tunnels through the green maze. Then there was the story that Fighting Joe, a chronic heavy drinker, had foresworn the bottle for his big test and in so doing had put the cork on his courage. A chronic drinker would certainly suffer some trauma in going suddenly on the wagon, and there was the aura of Lee's invincibility (he had wrecked three reputations) over these mottled lines advancing so fearlessly with their bright and deadly rifles. For a fact, when Hooker, to the consternation of his officers, changed his advance into a withdrawal, a loss of nerve seemed the only explanation.

Lee, having come to attack, warily studied the conditions to see where he might strike. Late in the afternoon he rode toward the right, toward the Rappahannock, and discovered large Federal forces drawn back in strength with their flank resting on the river. At sunset the Federals, having withdrawn into the fringes of the Wilderness around Chancellorsville, made a stand. Hooker's troops quickly cut down trees and formed a deep abatis of entangled branches in front of a line they fortified with logs. Outnumbered here nearly two to one, it would be suicidal to attack a fortified position surrounded, as Lee said, "by a dense forest filled with an entangled underbrush."

The Federal right, stretching off into the murky dusk of the Wilderness, remained the only possibility for an assault. In exploring the possibilities of a turning movement on Hooker's right, Lee gambled security on his faith in Jackson as a collaborator.

2

Before dark Lee met Jackson in a small clearing in a pine wood off the Plank Road. There a country road ran southeast to Catherine Furnace, which the Wellford family had reopened to contribute ore to the Confederacy, and the family was then in residence in a substantial house on the property. Through the dusky woods in front of the two generals came the flickers of the sporadic fire of skirmishers, and a sharpshooter banged away from a perch in tree branches. Couriers moved the horses farther back in the woods, and the generals seated themselves on a log. Both wore long double-breasted gray coats and high boots. Lee's gray felt hat with the brim slightly curved at the sides sat squarely on his head, and Jackson's battered cadet cap perched over his eyebrows.

Jackson could not believe that Hooker's actions indicated a serious assault, and he said his opinion was that the whole force would be back across the river by morning. Lee answered that he hoped Jackson was right. However, in the event he wasn't, it would be a good idea to attack the Federal right. Lee called for Major Talcott, his staff engineer, and Captain J. K. Boswell, Jackson's chief engineer, and the two young men were directed to reconnoiter the front. Since the groping at the Seven Days, Lee regularly employed staff officers on the type of reconnaissance he had done with Scott.

It was full night when the two engineers went off. While they were gone, Jeb Stuart rode up, dismounted, and joined Lee and Jackson. The stocky cavalryman was one of the few who took liberties with Jackson, making jokes that brought pleased smiles to the plain, brown-bearded face. Stuart reported that Fitz Lee had discovered the Federal flank to be "in the air." The line halted in the jungle where there was no physical position, such as the river on the Federal left, on which to anchor. Light works bent back to face south, but the west was open and little to no cavalry was in evidence. This seemed to be the opening Lee was looking for.

Shortly afterwards Talcott and Boswell returned to confirm Lee's impression of the strength of the Federal front, which was further strengthened by guns massed in several clearings. This report decided Lee on a turning movement of the Federal right flank. "Now," he muttered, spreading maps out on the ground in front of him, "how can I get at those people?"

Jackson recognized Lee's words as the rhetorical question he was apt to speak aloud when puzzling over a problem. He said, "Show me what to do, and we'll try to do it."

After a while Lee had it. Jackson could move south beyond the Federal flank, then march west until he could turn back north on the Brock Road to reach the Plank Road in the rear of the fortified lines stretching on both sides of Chancellorsville. Stuart's cavalry would cover the movement.

This was the kind of maneuver that pleased Jackson. Asking no questions, he arose from the log, "his face lit with a smile," an observer remembered. "My troops will move at 4 o'clock."

An early riser, Jackson needed his sleep and he wandered off into the shadows to make a bed on the ground. Reverend B. L. Lacy, a chaplain in Jackson's corps, then joined Lee. Lacy had once had a church near

Chancellorsville, and General Stuart had sent him to give Lee detailed information about the crossroads and the distance. It would cover about twelve miles and troops would be concealed most of the way. Then Lee went back to a small, open space in the pine woods where, under the boughs, he spread his saddle blanket, arranged his saddle as a pillow, and covered himself with his overcoat.

When Lee awakened before sunrise, Jackson was already up, seated on a cracker box beside a fire built by a courier. Jackson had been chilled by the early morning air, and he was sipping coffee from a tin cup brought him by Armistead Long. Lee found a cracker box for himself, and soon the two generals were joined by the Reverend Lacy and Captain Jed Hotchkiss, Jackson's topographical engineer. Young Hotchkiss was a New England schoolmaster who had been teaching in Virginia when the war came, and his mapmaking, utilizing an uncanny eye for ground, had been a vital part of all Jackson's campaigns — except the Seven Days, when Hotchkiss had been absent. With Hotchkiss and Lacy, Jackson worked out the final details of his march, tracing the course with his finger.

Then Lee asked, "What do you propose to make this movement with?"

"With my whole corps," Jackson replied promptly.

Lee showed his surprise. Jackson's plan would use two-thirds of the available force. "What will you leave me?"

"The divisions of Anderson and McLaws."

Lee's audacity in redividing his already divided army was being more than matched by Jackson. Neither Anderson's nor McLaws's divisions was complete: Barksdale's brigade was posted on Early's left and, from Anderson's division, Wilcox's brigade was guarding Banks' Ford between Fredericksburg and Chancellorsville. For the minimum of eight hours required for Jackson's van to complete the march to Hooker's rear, Lee would be facing the bulk of the Federal Army with not more than fourteen thousand infantry.

Also, neither McLaws nor Anderson was a general Lee would trust to command the action of the troops left behind. Lafayette McLaws had shown steady competence and no more. Dick Anderson, quiet and likeable, had personality problems related to the bottle. Once committed to action he showed the qualities of what Lee called "a capital officer" — he had quick reflexes, was cool in decision, prompt in acting and tenacious in fighting. But normally the Regular Army soldier from South Carolina was low keyed, slow to move and inclined toward irresolution. And holding off the Federal Army would require more than a stout defense, for fourteen thousand men on a three-and-a-fourth-mile front would give a density of less than three men per yard. The only safe defense would be

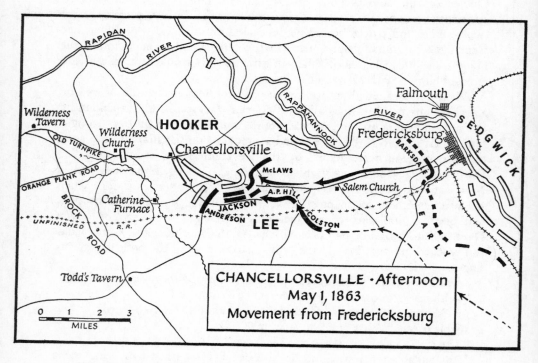

CHANCELLORSVILLE · Afternoon
May 1, 1863
Movement from Fredericksburg

a spirited demonstration, to give the impression that Lee meant to follow up the advance of the day before. Lee would have to do the job himself. Not to be outdone by Jackson's boldness, he decided it could be done.

"Well," he said to Jackson, "go on."

### 3

Jackson walked to the campfires where, just before daylight, his men were eating their scanty breakfasts. Rapidly he issued orders through his tightly knit staff, of which the chief of staff was the widely esteemed Sandie Pendleton, a young graduate of Washington College in Lexington and the son of General Pendleton. The troops were quietly pulled out of line and formed in columns of fours on the road. Guns were placed between the columns, including the reserve battalion then commanded by Porter Alexander. Finally the wagons came up. The sun was shining brightly on that May second morning when the tattered men started down the woods-lined road to Catherine Furnace, their sleeves brushing against the dogwood blossoms.

Jackson took his place near the head of the column, riding his small

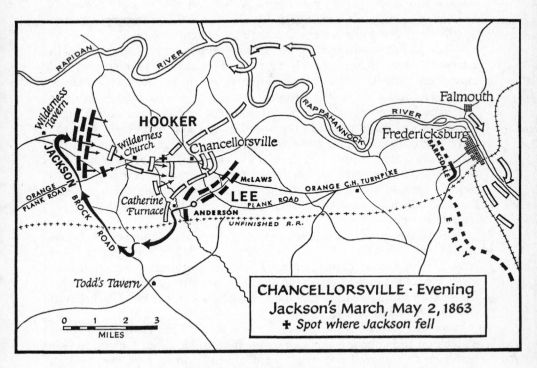

CHANCELLORSVILLE · Evening
Jackson's March, May 2, 1863
✛ *Spot where Jackson fell*

sorrel horse, Fancy, which his men called "Little Sorrel." Moving down the road, he passed General Lee, watching from the roadside. Jackson, his face flushed a little, reined in for a few final whispered words with the commanding general. Then he rode ahead. Past the clearing at Catherine Furnace, Jackson's advance columns — moving behind Fitz Lee's cavalry brigade — pushed into a crude trail opened for the ore carts. The going grew hard through there, and Jackson rode along the columns with his familiar chant, "Close up, men, push on, push on."

By eleven o'clock Federals on the cleared rise of Hazel Grove had observed the passage of Jackson's column, and batteries opened fire. Jackson's wagons were shifted to another road and the columns kept moving. Then Dan Sickles sent two divisions from his III Corps to Catherine Furnace to develop the situation. Only one regiment, the 23rd Georgia, remained at the furnace clearing as rear guard. Falling back into the cut of an unfinished railroad, this regiment was gobbled up. Before Sickles could realize that he was in position to cut Lee's army in half, his two divisions were hit on both sides.

Jackson had hurried back two of A. P. Hill's brigades, supported by Brown's artillery battalion, and Dick Anderson threw in Carnot Posey's brigade and supported it by Wright's. When Lee shifted Billy Mahone's brigade to occupy the ground left by Wright, the line was stretched so thin that a soldier could not even reach to the man next to him.

While all this was happening behind him around noon, Jackson, as if in a fatalistic state of believing his march was impervious to incidents, had moved on with the head of the column to the Brock Road. This sliced northwest through the impenetrable maze. As Jackson said, if Hooker had kept his cavalry, the turning movement would have ended right there. But the road stretched open ahead. It was past noon then, with the sun beating down from a cloudless sky, and men began to faint and fall out of line from the pace. "Push on, men, close up," the soldiers heard in their dulled senses above the shuffle of feet over the dusty road. At two o'clock Jackson and the van of the column reached the Orange Plank Road, three miles west of Chancellorsville and directly in the rear of Hooker's army.

Around that time Hooker, anxious to recover his confidence, had convinced himself that Jackson's movement heralded the beginning of a retreat. This would hardly coincide with the aggressive action of the seven brigades Lee was directing on his front, but, as the threats on his front at Chancellorsville were not developed in force, Hooker believed what he wanted to believe.

Jovial Fitz Lee, all business that day, had reached the Plank Road ahead of Jackson and done some quick reconnoitering. He asked Jackson to ride with him to a cleared rise where he could look down onto the enemy's camp. Where the Brock Road intersected the Plank Road, the Plank Road again diverged from the old Turnpike, which was about two and three-fourths miles farther north. From the clearing where Fitz Lee led Jackson, he could see that the Turnpike would mask his approach on the unsuspecting Federal camp spread out before him. Jackson's face grew radiant as he surveyed the carelessness of Howard's XI Corps — Germans, called "bounty troops" by the Confederates. The men were laughing and smoking and, what added a glint to Stonewall's eyes, beeves were being driven up and butchered.

Returning to the Brock Road, he ordered his first division up to move across to the Turnpike and deploy. This was the former division of D. H. Hill, temporarily commanded by Robert Rodes — furious Rodes, tall and bony-faced, chewing nervously on the edges of his tawny mustache. Next came Jackson's old division, temporarily commanded by Raleigh Colston, a Frenchman and the adopted son of a Virginia doctor. Educated at V.M.I., thirty-seven-year-old Colston had yet to distinguish himself beyond adequacy.

At three o'clock Jackson sent Lee a brief message. His leading division was up, and "the next two appear to be well closed." A. P. Hill's last two brigades had left Catherine Furnace only an hour before after breaking off their action against Sickles. At four o'clock Rodes's van reached the Turnpike and began to deploy. At six o'clock both Rodes and Colston had formed in line of battle across the Turnpike. Jackson, watch in hand, studied the scene.

Then Jackson said, "Are you ready, General Rodes?"

"Yes, sir."

"You can go forward, sir."

The hush of the spring evening was rent by the eerie, high-pitched screams of some eighteen thousand men bursting out of the thickets on the peaceful camp of Howard's Germans. Two divisions broke almost before they were hit. Clots of blue-uniformed soldiers fired irregular volleys before they were engulfed in the backward rush of their fellows. Falling back, running back, abandoning haversacks and stands of arms, the two divisions degenerated into a mob fleeing from the advancing lines. Buschbeck's third division took a position behind riflepits and, aided by batteries, made a stand against the assaulters. Rodes's and Colston's intermingled lines were losing order in their rush through the matted vines and clinging underbrush, with prisoners filtering through their ranks. After about three-quarters of an hour, Buschbeck gave way, and the rout of the XI Corps, Hooker's right, was complete.

It was then approaching eight o'clock and dusk was deepening. As Rodes's and Colston's men reached the clearing east of Dowdall's Tavern, the lines of the tired men grew hopelessly disordered. Across their front thirty guns had opened from Hazel Grove, and a couple of brigades had been rushed forward to dig desperation lines along a creek bed. Sickles was hurrying across from Catherine Furnace. No troops were sent back from Chancellorsville. When Jackson's battle was heard, Lee had turned his day-long demonstration into actual attacks. Though the assaults were light, they pinned down the Federal troops.

Jackson, flushed with excitement, was trying to hurry the deployment of A. P. Hill's six brigades to replace Rodes and Colston in line of advance. Jackson had determined to advance Hill's Light Division on a slicing attack toward the river in the gathering darkness, to cut Hooker's army off from its line of retreat across the United States Ford.

Jackson rode with Hill across to the Plank Road, where Hill's right brigade was beginning to advance. Seeing all of Hill's troops ready to move forward, Jackson told Hill where he wanted him to attack. It was then night, and Hill told Jackson he knew nothing of the topography. Jackson sent Captain Boswell ahead to explore the line of advance and report back. Then he and Hill, with their staffs, rode forward down the road.

In the distance a Confederate battery had opened in the darkness, and a gale of return artillery fire swept the Plank Road. Jackson's party turned around and, to get out of range of the shell bursts, the horses were hurried. To the 18th North Carolina, of Jim Lane's brigade, the rush of horses sounded like a cavalry patrol. A wild charge of enemy cavalry had been made earlier. The fine riflemen of the 18th North Carolina poured a volley into the woods and across the road.

Horses and riders fell. A slug entered Jackson's right hand and two lodged in his upper left arm, one just below the shoulder. When he dropped the reins, Little Sorrel bolted into the woods. An overhanging bough struck Jackson in the face. His cap was swept off and he rocked back in the saddle, clutching at the reins with his injured hand. Captain R. E. Wilbourn, of his staff, grabbed Little Sorrel's bridle. When the horse ceased its plunging, Jackson slid off into Wilbourn's arms.

A group gathered quickly. He was laid on the ground near the road under a pine tree. Powell Hill, all differences forgotten, cradled the wounded man's head, ripped open his left sleeve, and tried to staunch the flow of blood. A main artery had been severed. A staff officer was hurried back for Dr. Hunter McGuire. Three men formed a litter and started carrying the still form through the woods. A shell burst over the party and one of the litter bearers fell. The wounded man was dropped, his bleeding hand striking the ground, and he groaned once. That was the only sound.

At Dowdall's Tavern, he was lifted into an ambulance. Dr. McGuire gave him whiskey and morphia as the ambulance, preceded by several soldiers carrying pine torches, lurched across the fields from which Howard's corps had recently fled. Jackson's plan for the night attack, to cut Hooker off from the ford, was forestalled by other disasters. Powell Hill, returning to advance his troops, was struck by shell fragments and wounded. Captain Boswell was killed making his reconnaissance for the line of advance. Colston and Rodes, temporary division commanders, knew nothing of Jackson's plans and began to grow anxious for their own safety.

In the tent of a field hospital set up beyond the range of artillery fire, Jackson was covered with blankets, and given more whiskey. Against the pain and the weakness, in his rigid, clammy face the thin lips were compressed so tightly that the impression of his teeth could be seen. But he uttered no sound, except occasionally to inquire after other wounded. He kept his mind clear by a tremendous effort of will. At two o'clock, Dr. McGuire told him that chloroform was to be administered and asked him if, should it be found necessary to amputate his arm, it would be all right to do it at once.

"Yes, certainly, Dr. McGuire," he said, "do for me whatever you think best."

He was put to sleep and his left arm was amputated two inches below the shoulder.

4

Captain Wilbourn left the field hospital before it was known that Jackson's arm would be amputated and reached Lee's camp at two-thirty on the Sunday morning of May 3. Aroused by the voices, Lee climbed out of his blanket on the ground and listened to Wilbourn's report of the battle. Wilbourn saved to the end the mention of Jackson's wound, which he tried to present casually as only a fleshwound. Nonetheless Lee moaned when he heard of his friend being wounded, and tears sprang into his eyes.

"Ah, Captain," he said, "any victory is dearly bought which deprives us of the services of General Jackson, even for a short time."

Then Wilbourn tried to tell him some of the details of the wounding, but Lee could not listen. "Don't talk about it," he said. "Thank God, it's no worse."

He forced his mind to turn to the carrying on of the work left unfinished by Jackson. Wilbourn told him of Jackson's plan for cutting Hooker off from the United States Ford. It was too late for that. The vital thing was to join the two wings of his army, separated by about two miles. With the wounding of A. P. Hill, there was not a major general in Jackson's corps to whom the command could be given. At three in the morning Lee dictated a note to Jeb Stuart, giving him temporary command of Jackson's corps, with orders to drive forward to unite the army.

In his first command of infantry, and a corps at that, thirty-year-old Jeb Stuart demonstrated the extensiveness of his gift for warfare. He had Hill's division, the men fed, attacking down the Plank Road before daylight. His reserve lines were forming to go in. Hooker had a good position, as the Confederates knew, with defensive lines easily made strong in the jungle of the Wilderness. Counting Howard's corps as temporarily lost, after other casualties he still had at least sixty thousand infantry, while Lee had fielded only forty-two thousand infantry before casualties. But there was a feeling too among the Confederates that Hooker's army was beaten.

It was true that Hooker's poise was gone. Early in the morning Hooker's unnerved command presented Stuart with the one advantage he needed: he withdrew his guns and troops from the cleared eminence of Hazel Grove. In a short time Alexander, rushing batteries there to supplement his own battalion, had forty guns going at one time to play over the Federal lines. That probably made the difference — as the Federal troops to the west gave ground after repulsing three of Stuart's attacks — that and the defensive turn taken in Hooker's mind. He had directed his engineers to draw a new defensive line north of the Turnpike. This formidable line formed two sides of a triangle, with one flank secured on the Rappahannock and the other on a bend of the Rapidan.

In contrast with the safety on Hooker's mind, Jeb Stuart — a golden figure with the plume in his hat and the yellow sash — was riding up and down his lines singing at the top of his bugling voice, "Old Joe Hooker, won't you come out of the Wilderness." Almost carelessly he threw his last reserves into the attack, and the men responded with the confidence of driving against an opponent with no fight in him. By ten o'clock the right brigades of Hill's division made juncture with Anderson, pushing westward under Lee's direction. The army was joined.

Hooker's people fell back from Chancellorsville, and Lee's united lines swept into the clearing, where the Chancellors' brick house and outbuildings were blazing. Lee rode forward to meet Stuart at Chancellorsville. When he rode into the clearing, the troops saw him. The sight of their leader acted as a signal, Colonel Marshall said, "for one of those uncontrollable outbursts of enthusiasm which none can appreciate who have not witnessed them. The fierce soldiers, with their faces blackened with the smoke of battle, the wounded, crawling with feeble limbs from . . . the devouring flames, all seemed possessed with a common impulse. One long, unbroken cheer . . . rose high above the roar of battle . . . As I looked on him in the complete fruition of the success which his genius, courage and confidence in his army had won, I thought that it must have been from some such scene that men in the ancient days ascended to the dignity of the gods."

Even with the air of calm composure which Lee maintained, he must have felt the pride of achievement. As a soldier, he knew that by breaking every rule of warfare he had carved one of the world's military masterpieces. Yet, it was a lonely triumph with his great collaborator off wounded and, after the moment of acclaim had passed, the completeness of the victory was destroyed by two messages delivered to him in the clearing around the burning buildings.

The first was a note from Jackson, saying that he had survived an amputation of his left arm. Lee's profound emotional reaction was enough in itself to overshadow the sense of triumph. Immediately he turned to Marshall and dictated a note whose sentiments showed Lee to be speaking out of the self-denial of his deep affection.

"General, I have just received your note, informing me that you were wounded. I cannot express my regret at the occurrence. Could I have directed events, I would have chosen for the good of the country to be disabled in your stead.

"I congratulate you upon the victory, which is due to your skill and energy."

The second message to Lee revealed that he would not be able to cap his victory by driving Hooker into the river. Sedgwick had driven Jubal Early from the heights overlooking Fredericksburg. Even then the Federals were marching west with nothing between them and Lee's rear except Wilcox's brigade, left on guard at Banks' Ford.

The night before, Hooker had ordered Sedgwick to make the attack as a means of relieving him. All during the morning Old Jube had fought off the assaults with a savage defense. Then, under a flag of truce, Federal parties had climbed the heights to gather their wounded, and they saw the small force opposing them. With this knowledge, Sedgwick threw his full weight behind an assault, and Early's thin lines could not contain it. He retreated southward, as ordered, and Sedgwick began a hurried march west. Cadmus Wilcox pulled his brigade back from the river into Sedgwick's line of march and fought a hard, skillful delaying action. He could do no more.

Lee had no choice except to break off his attack on Hooker and rush McLaws back to the support of Wilcox. At the same time Lee was forced to continue the appearance of an assault to prevent counterattacks from Hooker. By the end of the day Sedgwick had been checked at Salem Church, but he was still on Lee's rear.

For the next day, since he was too weakened to attempt more against Hooker, Lee decided to finish off Sedgwick. Anderson was sent back to get on Sedgwick's flank, and Jubal Early, returning behind Sedgwick, was coming up on his rear. Caught on three sides, with the river on the fourth, Sedgwick recrossed the Rappahannock at a ford. Hooker's offensive was over.

By May 5, Lee at last gathered his forces all together and planned the final push to drive Hooker to the river. Fighting Joe did not wait for it. During a heavy rainstorm he retired his army across the Rappahannock. On the morning of May 6 nothing remained in Lee's front except the debris of a withdrawing army.

By then Jackson had been transferred to comfortable quarters in the Chandlers' house at Guiney's Station, on the R.F.&P., and his wife and young daughter had come to be with him. During the week pneumonia set in, and by the end of the week he was sinking fast. Around noon on Sunday, Sandie Pendleton visited him, and Jackson asked, "Who is preaching at headquarters today?"

Major Pendleton told him it was the Reverend Lacy, and that everybody was praying for him.

"They are very kind to me," he said, and soon after that his mind began to wander. Then he lapsed into a coma.

Suddenly he cried out distinctly, "Order A. P. Hill to prepare for action. Pass the infantry to the front. Tell Major Hawks . . ." his words faded off and once more he fell into unconsciousness.

Late in the afternoon he spoke in a low, quiet voice: "Let us cross over the river and rest under the shade of the trees."

## 5

Lee, who had refused to the very end to accept the possibility of Jackson's death, openly wept. The loss of "the great and good Jackson," as Lee and Stuart called him, was recognized as irreplaceable. He would be lost as a man for whom Lee had developed the warmest affection and deepest respect, and as a soldier with whom went the combination that had made possible the army's most brilliant maneuvers. Lee realized that without Jackson another Chancellorsville could not even be attempted.

In the shock of his loss over his friend and collaborator, Lee was called to Richmond as adviser in a crisis on another front — a crisis that again involved the reduction of his own army. In the West, where Joe Johnston was commander of the department that included two major armies, Bragg's in Tennessee and Pemberton's at Vicksburg, Johnston refused to assume responsibility for either army. Though he was experiencing his usual difficulties with the hated Davis, Johnston received strong support from Seddon in the War Department. Seddon tried to get him to act in spite of the unhealthy system of departmentalization.

Johnston compromised by advising Pemberton to abandon his various garrisons and concentrate against Grant. Grant, having failed to make progress directly against Vicksburg, had crossed to the west bank of the Mississippi, then recrossed to the south, and was marching northward along the river. As Johnston's suggested concentrations conflicted with the controlling policy of the President, bedeviled Pemberton tried to do both and did neither. By the middle of May, Grant had Pemberton backed up into Vicksburg, while Johnston, with remnants of Pemberton's forces outside the city, hovered off the periphery of the action.

To save Vicksburg, Seddon proposed to send out one or both of the two divisions — Pickett's and Hood's — that had just returned with Longstreet to Lee's army. In this suggestion Seddon revealed the extent to which Richmond had come to regard Lee as a magician. At Chancellorsville, in addition to losing his top subordinate, Lee lost thirteen thousand men, 21 per cent of his army, and without Longstreet he would field barely forty thousand infantry. With this small force, it would be impossible to sustain the maneuver which had kept the enemy in the northern part of the state. Lee could only go on the defensive, fall back toward Richmond, and expose his army to the threat of starvation. He simply could not make the Richmond authorities see that his army was destitute and, unless he could operate in a country where subsistence could be gathered, the army would dissolve from hunger.

Since he could not convince the officials that he required men and food for those men to perform his miracles, Lee appealed to Davis, Seddon and the other Cabinet members on the grounds of strategy. As tactfully as possible, he pointed out that sending a detachment from his army to the West would not, due "to the uncertainty of its employment," insure a success at Vicksburg. However, the reduction in his army would almost certainly force him back in the Richmond lines where the army had been bottled up a year ago. Then the government would be confronted with two sieges instead of the one at Vicksburg. Davis, then ill, shuddered at the thought of giving up the ground in Virginia from the Rappahannock to Richmond.

Then Lee offered his counterproposal. As he had said back in March, when Seddon wanted to send his divisions to Bragg, Lee repeated that the best way to relieve the situation in the West was to mount an invasion of the North. To that end he would require the return of all his detached units. Also he suggested that Beauregard move up into Virginia with a skeletal army which could pose as a threat to Washington while Lee crossed the Potomac.

Though Lee offered this, at the Richmond conference, as a specific counterplan to sending off his divisions to the dubious command situation in the West, an invasion had been his purpose all spring. Had his army been physically able, he would have moved north before Hooker opened his offensive. By then, campaigning in the North was an absolute necessity for maintaining his army in the field.

This urgency never reached Davis and his Cabinet, but all except one of them did comprehend that Lee was essentially presenting the most effective use that could be made of the one successful army in the Confederacy. Whatever they thought of the invasion plan, the individuals followed the maxim of sticking with a winning horse. Except for Postmaster General Reagan, the Cabinet voted not to break up a winning combination in an effort to prop up a loser.

In Richmond Lee had found his wife — staying at their friends the Caskies' — suffering severely and virtually helpless. Under the successive stresses on his emotions, while battling to keep his army intact, Lee was not sharp in appraising the nuances where personal relationships entered military policy. The ill President had agreed to Lee's invasion proposals in general, but the details, where they conflicted with his structure of dispersed garrisons, were something else.

Lee did not enjoy the ascendancy in his relationship with Davis which he had known the summer before. During the months when Lee had been away from Richmond, Davis had come increasingly to occupy himself with the charts of troop disposition and reverted to his natural tendencies to disperse troops in defensive garrisons. Once these arrangements were made, in Davis's neurotic need for certainties they remained fixed as if imbedded in cement.

Missing the subtle quality of the change, Lee did not suspect that Davis had no slightest intention of disrupting his charts to return Lee's veterans to him. This unsuspected interference from Davis came when Lee was faced with the painful task of reorganizing his forces to adjust to the loss of Jackson.

No replacement would be capable of commanding a four-division corps. Since the two-corps structure had originally evolved in adaptiveness to the personnel, Lee now reshuffled his units to form three corps. Longstreet would remain commander of the First Corps, minus Anderson's division. Jackson's former Second Corps, minus A. P. Hill's division, would go to Dick Ewell, then recovered from his Second Manassas wound. Ewell was not the ideal choice. However, he was the ranking major general in the Second Corps, he had shared Jackson's Valley triumphs, and his selection was inevitable. There was a question of how much psychic damage Ewell, a wiry physical type, had suffered from his leg amputation, and the question of how much initiative he would show when removed from Jackson's iron discipline.

In his corps, "Old Baldhead" would be well served on one division by Jubal Early and on another by Robert Rodes, promoted to major general for his Chancellorsville performance. Jackson's former division, with its ill luck in commanders, went to a newcomer to the army, Edward ("Allegheny") Johnson. A rough-hewn character of Regular Army background, Johnson had commanded with Jackson in the early part of the Valley Campaign, and was considered to be knowledgeable, a strong leader and dependable.

It was mainly in the new Third Corps that the reorganization suffered from Davis's troop dispositions. To be commanded by A. P. Hill, promoted to lieutenant general, this corps was formed of Anderson's division, a four-brigade division from Hill's former six-brigade division, and a new division formed of two brigades from Hill's old Light Division and — as Lee intended — the two brigades under Robert Ransom and John R. Cooke which Lee had sent to North Carolina for the winter operations. Refusing to return these veterans of the army, Davis substituted brigades of his own choice.

One of these brigades was composed of partly battle-innocent Mississippians commanded by the President's nephew, Joseph R. Davis, an amiable lawyer who had never been in combat. The other brigade was composed of North Carolinians, commanded by the distinguished Johnston Pettigrew. Pettigrew had won vast admiration in Virginia before he was wounded at Seven Pines, but he was a stranger to Lee's army.

Lee wrote through Seddon, saying, "I . . . dislike to part with officers and men who have been tried in battle and seasoned to the hardships of the campaign in exchange for wholly untried troops." Davis, as a theoretician, was insensitive to the intangibles that made a whole greater than the sum of its parts. To him the same number of men equaled the same number of men under Lee's leadership. These two brigades of strangers added to the makeshift quality of the new corps with two new major generals untried at division command. Dorsey Pender, the dark-bearded, twenty-nine-year-old North Carolina professional soldier who was close to Hill, was promoted to command the four brigades from the old Light Division. The new division went to Henry Heth (pronounced Heath), Hill's fellow Virginian and West Point classmate.

Along with the reshuffling of units and general officers in the two corps led by men new at corps command, Longstreet's dependable First Corps was hurt by a reduction in the strength Lee had counted on. Two of Pickett's five brigades were withheld on guard duty by Davis, and one of these, commanded by brilliant and inspired young Micah Jenkins, was an unusually large outfit, for which Lee continually petitioned Davis.

Lee's confidence in the invasion was gnawed at by these presidential interferences that weakened his army. He saw in Davis's reversion to a practice of dispersed defense a divergence between the official policy and his own strategies that had maintained a war of maneuver. With a note of discouragement, he wrote Seddon, "If the Department thinks it better to remain on the defensive, and guard as far as possible all the avenues of approach and await the time of the enemy, I am willing to adopt this course. You have therefore only to inform me."

On the other hand, Lee wrote, when the hot season decreased the enemy's activities on the Atlantic Coast, the garrisons could be lightly held and a large enough force put in the field "to make some impression on the enemy." That was in reference to his suggestion for a subsidiary army under Beauregard, as well as for the full complement of veterans for his own army. "Unless that can be done," he wrote in understated prophecy, "I see little hope of accomplishing anything of importance."

Lee was not informed that he was desired to remain on the defensive. In effect, Lee could do what he wanted with what force he had, but no changes were going to be made to support his offensive. He perceived that the invasion, far less powerful than he had planned, was to be a lone operation isolated from the undeclared policy of defensiveness. With his veterans held guarding railroad junctions, in actuality his offensive was divorced from the preoccupations of Davis and Seddon.

When Lee put his army in motion in June, in a final effort to reclaim at least the two brigades detached from Pickett's division, he wrote Davis in desperation. "I am quite weak . . . and it is now too late to accomplish all that was desired."

He could no longer reach Davis. The President was then growing compulsive in his concentration on his organizational charts, with pins indicating troops at all points that might be threatened. Seddon, an honest, intelligent man, was a civilian dealing in abstractions and knew nothing about the realities of Lee's army. Davis's compulsions and Seddon's limitations blinded them both to the psychologically bad timing, with all else, of interfering with Lee's army when he was adjusting to Jackson's death.

The absence of Jackson lay like a shadow over the whole planned invasion. Lee held none of the high hopes as in the invasion of the summer before. The movement away from the Rappahannock — that began slowly, piecemeal, on June 3 — was made in the spirit of necessity. It was a grim necessity, a desperate necessity, his first major move without the unreserved support of his government, and without Stonewall Jackson.

To his wife he wrote, when his lonely movement was beginning, "Kiss my daughters for me, and you must all remember me in your prayers, and implore the Lord of Hosts for the removal of the terrible scourge with which He has thought best to afflict our bleeding country."

## CHAPTER XV

## "It Was All My Fault"

ON SUNDAY, June 28, General Lee found himself in the embarrassing circumstance of being in the enemy's country without his cavalry. Lee's tent was pitched in Shetter's Woods, a local picnic grounds outside the thriving small city of Chambersburg, Pennsylvania, where the major portion of his army had been camped for two days. For those days, while his men rested and the supplies garnered from the fat countryside were distributed, Lee had tried to hide his mounting apprehension over the disappearance of Jeb Stuart. On that Sunday afternoon he restlessly left his tent, and came out into the grove to stare off at the South Mountain range to the east. His staff officers detected the signs of anxiety under his tightly held control.

As failure in executing an assignment would never be associated with the tireless, prescient Stuart, Lee could not suppress the fear that some ill had befallen his former cadet. Before they left Virginia, while the army was making a leisurely shift from the Rappahannock to the Shenandoah Valley, Stuart's cavalry had been surprised at Brandy Station and entangled in the toughest fight of its history. Stuart had gathered there the largest mounted force he had ever commanded, more than nine thousand troopers, and the cavalry had been pressed to its ultimate limits before driving back the troopers newly commanded by Brigadier General Alfred Pleasanton.

In the heavy casualties, Lee's son Rooney went down with a wound, and Farley, the scout and Shakespearean scholar, was killed. Earlier, in the spring, the appealing young Pelham, commander of the almost legendary horse artillery, had been killed, bringing grief to Stuart. Lee had faced the cold fact that the Yankee troopers, riding better mounts than the personally owned and fading horses of the Southerners, were catching up with the performance of Stuart's native-born riders. Under Pleasanton they had gained in confidence and aggressiveness. When the army had shifted to west of the Blue Ridge, Stuart's men were continually pressed in guarding the passes. As always, the cavalry had screened the infantry, but men and horses were worn to the bone by the constant riding and fighting.

When the army started northward west of the Blue Ridge on June 23, Lee left Stuart with the discretion either to follow the army for his assignment of guarding the mountain passes to the east or to move northward east of the mountains and establish contact with the infantry north of the Potomac. It was a garbled as well as a discretionary order as it pertained to Stuart's way of going, but his assignment was made unmistakably plain: he was to protect the right of the advance column, Ewell's Second Corps.

Ewell had for advance cavalry Albert Jenkins's raiders from western Virginia, borrowed for the occasion. Undependable for orthodox work, these wild riders had served Ewell well enough as he marched north with little serious opposition, taking the Federal garrison at Winchester on the way. Passing on through Chambersburg ahead of the main column, Ewell headed north for Carlisle, with Jubal Early's division branching off for York. That was all right for Ewell with the main army behind him. By the time Lee reached Chambersburg he had to know what was happening on the other side of the mountains. Where was Hooker — and where was *Stuart?*

The one notion that never occurred to Lee was that Stuart would abuse his discretion, go glory hunting and get himself cut off from his own army. Incredibly, that was exactly what was happening. More than Lee realized, Stuart's unimpressive victory at Brandy Station had wounded the ego of a very young man as vain as he was gifted. A figure as colorful as Jeb Stuart naturally attracted enemies and ill wishers, and the newspapers had not let him off easily for his narrow squeak with Pleasanton. Stuart was thinking about his reputation when he undertook the assignment of covering the army's right. He planned to combine duty with the glory of riding around Hooker's army.

After the infantry was on its way down the valley, Stuart rode east of Hooker's army, intending to circle it. The trouble was that Hooker moved northward paralleling Lee's line of march, and his army remained interposed between Stuart and Lee. On Sunday the 28th, with Lee anxious in Chambersburg, Stuart was off on a side adventure in Maryland to capture 125 new US wagons drawn by handsome mules. This prize slowed down his men and horses, all deeply tired when the ride north began.

Going across Maryland toward Pennsylvania, the exhausted men dozed on their horses, some not even coming awake when they fell off. Inexhaustible himself, Stuart kept them moving, trying to turn the head of Hooker's column and fighting off cavalry sent to block his line of march. On the Sunday that Lee stared at the silent hills, hoping for a sight of his horsemen, Stuart was riding his cavalry out of the campaign. Forced by then to struggle for the survival of his command, he would end up trying to discover the whereabouts of his own army.

In Shetter's Woods, a Mrs. McLellan, who visited Lee's tent, was impressed by the "strength and sadness" in his face. She came to appeal to him for food for a number of families who faced hunger as a result of the Confederates' impressment of cattle, hogs, flour and molasses. Mrs. McLellan explained that the men of the community were afraid to ask because of the depredations of their own soldiers in the Southern states. After Lee suggested that she send a miller to inform his commissary officers of the amount of flour needed for the emergency, Mrs. McLellan impulsively asked for his autograph.

"Do you want the autograph of a Rebel?" he asked.

"General Lee, I am a true Union woman and yet I ask for bread and your autograph."

Writing "R. E. Lee" on a slip of paper, he remarked on the cruelties of war and said, "My only desire is that they will let me go home and eat my own bread in peace."

Lee proclaimed his lack of aggressive intent in the General Orders No. 73 written to his soldiers at Chambersburg. "The commanding general considers that no greater disgrace could befall the army, and through it our whole people, than the perpetration of the barbarous outrages upon the unarmed and the defenseless, and the wanton destruction of private property that have marked the course of the enemy in our own country . . .

"It must be remembered that we make war only upon armed men, and that we cannot take vengeance for the wrongs our people have suffered without . . . offending against Him to whom vengeance belongeth, without whose favor and support our efforts must all prove in vain."

Moving into the enemy's country did not revive his hopes of anything positive coming of the invasion. On his way to Chambersburg, he had made one last forlorn appeal of support for his move. In a letter to Davis, he urged that troops from the North and South Carolina garrisons go to build a force to act on the offensive in conjunction with Bragg, and that "even an effigy" of any army under Beauregard be brought to middle Virginia. Those moves, he wrote, "would do more to protect both states from marauding expeditions than anything else."

Then he wrote another letter in which he went further than he ever had with Davis. Lee came right out with a criticism of the government policy. Already having undermined his campaign, it had totally reverted to the defensiveness which everywhere controlled military operations before he assumed command. "It seems to me that we cannot afford to keep our troops awaiting possible movements of the enemy, but that our true policy is, as far as we can, so to employ our own forces as to give occupation to his at points of our selection."

Lee realized that, though he was occupying enemy troops at his point of selection in Pennsylvania, it was not enough. What he could not then accept was that, beyond the employment of his own reduced army, he had lost all influence over Davis in military operations. Davis still sought his opinion, but they were talking about different things.

With this discouraging background for the invasion which, after the reduction of its scope, he had undertaken half reluctantly, at Shetter's Woods came the premonition of ill in the mysterious absence of the one subordinate who had given the commanding general reason to depend upon him absolutely. Nightfall did not bring an end to this day of foreboding for Lee.

At ten o'clock he was seated in his tent, fully dressed, when a tap came on his tent pole. It was Major Fairfax, a staff officer of Longstreet's, with an alarming story brought by a spy. Lee had little faith in paid spies. But this civilian was vouched for by Seddon, and Lee was desperate for information. Harrison, a strongly built brown-bearded man, showed the signs of travel and spoke in a tired voice. Two Federal corps, he told Lee, were close to the mountains on the opposite side and in possession of the knowledge that Lee's army was at Chambersburg. Also, Hooker had been superseded in command by Meade.

On both counts this news was ominous. Lee would take his fantastic risks against the Popes and the Hookers, but George Gordon Meade was another breed. A high-principled gentleman from Pennsylvania and a friend of Lee's from the Old Army, Meade was the type of general, Lee said, who would make no blunder. "And if I make one," Lee added, "he will make haste to take advantage of it."

Late that night Lee went to his cot puzzling over how to avoid blunders against an alert enemy when he had no cavalry to tell him where the enemy was.

2

Lee's immediate resolution was to advance A. P. Hill's new corps in what amounted to a reconnaissance in force. On Monday, June 29, Hill's shaggy, tawny men started east for a pass in the mountains that led down to a little roadside town called Cashtown. Many of Hill's men were attired all or in part in the new butternut-colored government issue uniform and the men moved out in the careless well-being of full stomachs.

Lee remained with Longstreet's corps at Chambersburg, still hoping for news of Stuart. Equally mysterious was the absence of the two brigades, Beverly Robertson's and William E. ("Grumble") Jones's, which had been left at the Blue Ridge passes in Virginia. They were to follow after the infantry was clear of danger from surprises. These two brigades had not operated regularly with Stuart, and he had left them behind because he distrusted Robertson and bad blood existed between him and Jones. In another confusion of orders, this cavalry remained for days staring at the empty passes in the Blue Ridge long after Lee had crossed the Potomac. Lee sent orders back for them to hurry forward. Finally, John Imboden's cavalry, another western Virginia outfit borrowed for the invasion, was operating off Lee's left. Their attention to the forage and the victuals on their journey kept these irregulars far away.

It was one of the few times when his staff recognized his efforts at self-control, as he paced restlessly outside the tent. Yet when he was approached by John Hood, Lee immediately assumed a manner of cheerful composure designed to protect a subordinate from knowledge of his own anxieties.

"The enemy is a long time in finding us," he said. "If he does not succeed soon, we'll go in search for him."

The next day in a drizzle the camp was broken and Lee moved out with Longstreet's two complete divisions, Hood and McLaws. Pickett's division, reduced by the President to three brigades, waited at Chambersburg as rear guard until some cavalry showed up from somewhere. Orders had already been sent to Ewell at Carlisle to abandon his march on Harrisburg, and for him and Early to move south for a convergence of the army east of the mountains. With the army moving, as one of his officers said, "like a blindfolded giant," Lee thought it well to bring his infantry units together.

At the end of the dismal day, Lee camped west of the mountains. That night a courier came from A. P. Hill. The new corps commander reported that Pettigrew's brigade, going to the town of Gettysburg for supplies, had collided with a Union force that seemed to be principally cavalry. Pettigrew, the scholarly North Carolinian newly with Heth's division, had discreetly returned to Cashtown at the eastern foot of the mountain. There was nothing in the report to alarm Lee. Gettysburg was a busy county seat of something over three thousand inhabitants, and its only importance was as the hub of five roads that intersected in the town square. According to the report of Harrison the spy and other indications, Meade's army was at some distance from Gettysburg, and would have no reason to converge there.

This was true enough. However, Lee overlooked the use that the Federal cavalry commander would make of his collision with Confederate infantry. Buford had sped the information to Meade, and early on the morning of July 1 the van of the Army of the Potomac was hurrying to the town between two ridges in a rolling farm country.

Also the next morning Pettigrew, with Heth's full division, started back to Gettysburg to acquire the shoes said to be there. Sustained by the fat rations the men had been issued in Cumberland Valley, the army marched with the lowest incidence of straggling in its history. But many men were barefooted, the Northern roads were hard, and indulgent Pow-

ell Hill would not permit his soldiers to be deprived of shoes because of
some enemy cavalry. As a precaution he advanced Pender's four brigades
from the old Light Division in support of Heth.

In moving out from Cashtown, Harry Heth took routine precautions
against contact by deploying his brigades on both sides of the road, with
lines of skirmishers in advance. They moved out between five and six
on a sultry morning, crossing wheat fields and stubble in the rise and fall
of the country chopped up by countless fences and stone walls. The men
were impressed by the small size of the carefully worked farms, with
their big stout barns overshadowing the houses, and by the puny groves
and widely scattered woods. The three lines of skirmishers had advanced
five miles under a sun growing hot when they were met by the sudden
crackle of carbines and the whine of minié balls.

This was only the cavalry the men had been alerted against. With the
pace slowed, the lines continued to press forward. Around ten o'clock
Heth's first two brigades were no more than one mile from Gettysburg.
At this point their front was crossed by a wooded ravine, at the bottom
of which coursed a brook called Willoughby Run.

Here their advance lines were swept by the exploding shells of six guns
of Regular U. S. Artillery. While the men looked for cover, Willie Pegram ran up his twenty-gun battalion on the fence-lined road and opened
up. As the answering fire grew no heavier, Heth concluded that the
enemy cavalry had merely received some artillery support. Eager in his
first action as division commander, without reconnaissance he carelessly
ordered his two advance brigades forward down the wooded slope to
Willoughby Run.

Lee's army worked on the principle that each unit was the equal of
any other, and Heth's brigades had been put in motion according to
where the men had camped the night before. By this chance, the brigade
on the right of the road was the smallest in the corps, 1048 officers and
men whose heavy Chancellorsville losses had not been made up. These
Alabama and Tennessee troops were commanded by James Archer, a
forty-six-year-old Marylander boasting a fine record with Hill. On that
first of July morning Archer, a slight man with a long black beard, was
suffering from some weakening ailment.

On the left of the road went the brigade commanded by the President's
combat-innocent nephew, Joe Davis. Only two of the Mississippi regiments were experienced. The 11th, formed around a nucleus of University of Mississippi students, had distinguished themselves in Virginia
in the first year. But as an outfit, Davis's brigade, strangers to the
army, would be considered unseasoned.

On the right Archer's troops, after climbing a fence to cross the creek
at the bottom of the ravine, entered a thick woods. There the men were

caught in a galling fire on their front and flank. They soon recognized the enemy, from the black hats, as the Iron Brigade, of Doubleday's division of Reynolds's I Corps. Outnumbered two to one at the point of contact and not knowing what forces supported the Iron Brigade, Archer's men, like any sensible veterans, got out of those woods as fast as they could. Archer, trying to rally them at the fence by the creek, was physically overpowered by a ferocious Irishman. He became the first general officer captured during Lee's command.

On the left of the road in the open, Davis's Mississippians were not caught by surprise, and their accurate rifle fire drove the first line of Federals in their front. Only a gun battery continued to fire as the men advanced to follow up their success. The cut of an unfinished railroad paralleled the turnpike there, and Davis put his men down into that to advance in safety beyond the battery. While the bunched men were moving in the cut, fresh troops Abner Doubleday had rushed to the road came up precisely where they found the Mississippians trapped in the narrow tunnel below them. The only thing Davis's men could do was run the gauntlet, leaving hundreds of dead and wounded.

With his two lead brigades in disordered retreat, Harry Heth kept his poise. He formed his next two brigades on defense, re-formed Archer's men under Colonel B. D. Fry, and brought up the gun battalion of David McIntosh, Pegram's brother-in-law. Then, too late, he did what he should have done before he blundered into Union infantry: he waited for A. P. Hill and orders. Against the strongest orders of Lee to avoid a general engagement, because Jeb Stuart wanted to ride around the Federal Army and Hill's men needed shoes, the two armies collided at Gettysburg.

3

Lee was riding across the mountain, with Longstreet, when he heard the rolling thunder of the guns and the rattle of musketry. Soon he recognized the sound to be too heavy for an engagement against cavalry. Leaving Longstreet, he spurred his gray horse forward. By the time he and his staff had ridden into the village of Cashtown, the heavy and continuous sound clearly indicated a general engagement.

Moving between the wagons and reserve artillery of Hill's corps, Lee showed impatience as well as apprehension. For the first time he spoke openly about the absence of the cavalry. Colonel Long said he "intimated that Stuart's disappearance had materially hampered the movements and disorganized the plans of the campaign."

Then he found A. P. Hill and asked him what was going on. Under the tension of commanding alone on the front in the enemy's country, highstrung Hill had become afflicted with what was apparently an in-

testinal disorder. He was very pale and the look of sickness in his face
reflected his weakened condition. Powell Hill said he did not know what
was happening, though Heth had strict orders not to bring on a general
engagement. Lee started on to the road, and Hill, calling for a courier to
bring his horse, forced himself to mount and follow Lee to the scene of
action.

Lee soon passed among Pender's deploying troops. Around two o'clock
he pulled off the road where he could survey the scene of Heth's debacle. Order had been restored then, and the Federals were not advancing from Willoughby Run. From the town in the distance, however, a
whole corps of dark-clothed troops was moving out. Before Lee had to
make a decision, his attention was caught by a column approaching from
the north. The gray-butternut motley could only be his own troops,
quickly identified as Rodes's division. Marching toward Gettysburg
under Lee's order of the 29th, Rodes was fortuitously coming upon the
field precisely where and when he was most needed.

Unknown to Lee, Rodes's superior, Dick Ewell, was in a disturbed
state of mind. The newly appointed lieutenant general had been angry
with disappointment when Lee had recalled him from Carlisle, just as he
was completing preparations to capture Pennsylvania's capital at Harrisburg. Marching southward, he had grown agitated when he had received
orders the night before to proceed to Gettysburg *or* Cashtown. From his
experience in Jackson's corps, Old Baldhead wanted to be told precisely
what to do. That morning he had marched by a road that as far as Middletown could lead to either place; then a message sent from punctilious
A. P. Hill informed him that the Third Corps was moving on Gettysburg. Traveling himself in a carriage, because of the discomfort of riding
with his wooden leg, Ewell then directed Rodes to Gettysburg.

When Rodes heard the sound of firing ahead, on his own he had deployed his advancing brigades from the road to a paralleling and partly
covered ridge. Lee saw these veterans of Harvey Hill's old division at the
same time he saw the Federal corps moving out from Gettysburg in lines
of assault. Harry Heth came up and asked if he could attack. Lee was not
ready. Through his field glasses he was watching Rodes's division take
the assault of a full corps — Howard's Germans, of the Chancellorsville
disaster, anxious to remove the blight from their record.

Just when it looked as if Rodes was in serious trouble, Lee observed
another column under red battle flags coming up at an angle on Rodes's
left. This was Early's division, returning from York. With a fortuitous-
ness no one could have planned, Early's line of march brought him up
on Howard's flank and Old Jube struck instantly. Then Lee told Heth to
go forward.

Heth had three brigades ready by now, with Pender's division deployed in support. When Hill's two divisions advanced, Rodes shifted to attack, and the Federals began fighting at right angles to one another on two sides. In front of Hill's troops, the going was bitter, with chunks ripped out of their lines by the fire of enemy batteries. But northwest of Gettysburg Howard's "bounty troops" gave way. One of their generals fled into town, where he hid in a shed for the next three days. With their flank gone, the Federals in front of Hill fell back into Gettysburg.

Hill's men pursued as far as the top of a ridge west of town. There the disordered regiments halted to rest the exhausted men, bring up segments of troops strung out behind and attend to the wounded scattered across the countryside.

Troops from Ewell's two divisions drove all the way into the town from the northern side, gathering up five thousand prisoners in the chaos in the streets of the snug little city. About the only firing came from snipers in houses south of the street that ran through the square. Most of the remnants of the two Federal corps were making their way to the safety of a hill south of town, climbing to the crest on which spread the stone-walled Evergreen Cemetery.

Lee had followed behind Hill's irregular lines. Halting in the road at the bottom of Seminary Ridge, he stared at the clumps of Federals forming on the hill to the south of Gettysburg. In a short while he asked A. P. Hill if his men could advance from their ridge across the shallow valley of farmed land and seize the opposite hill. Very solicitous of his troops, "Little Powell" thought his men too spent. Also their ammunition was about gone, and no wagons were up. However, his guns could support an advance made by any fresh troops.

Lee then sent Walter Taylor with a message to Ewell to seize the hill rising south of Gettysburg. As he would have with Jackson, he added a fateful discretionary clause — "if practicable," without bringing on a general engagement. After dispatching the message, Lee waited with growing bewilderment for the sound of Ewell's guns. The afternoon dragged on and nothing happened. Hancock's corps of Meade's army was hurrying to Cemetery Hill. Colonel Long, making a quick reconnaissance, told Lee this hill extended into a powerful position formed by a precipitous ridge, Cemetery Ridge, facing west. Around six o'clock, with the silence continuing, Lee began a circuitous ride to Ewell's headquarters north of Gettysburg.

On the way he passed soldiers gathering fence rails for campfires, with no thoughts of assaulting anything more than a henhouse. Light was beginning to fail when Lee reached the Blocher house, whose back porch overlooked an arbor. Ewell with two of his generals was back there. He and Lee greeted each other with restrained courtesy. Lee, ten years older, had never known Ewell intimately. Lee had come to question the

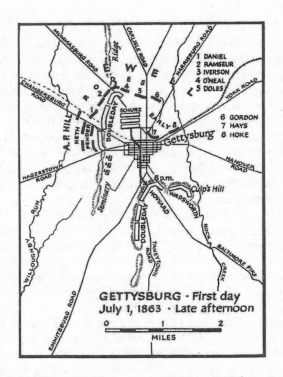

**GETTYSBURG · First day**
**July 1, 1863 · Late afternoon**

1 DANIEL
2 RAMSEUR
3 IVERSON
4 O'NEAL
5 DOLES

6 GORDON
7 HAYS
8 HOKE

0          1          2
MILES

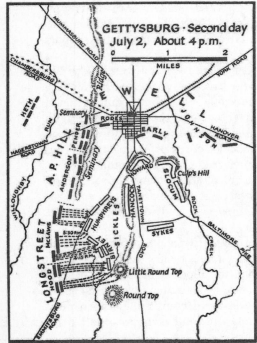

**GETTYSBURG · Second day**
**July 2, About 4 p.m.**

0          1          2
MILES

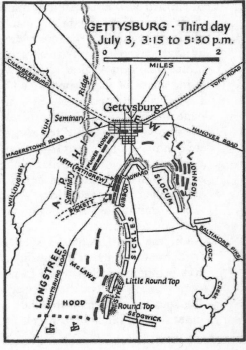

**GETTYSBURG · Third day**
**July 3, 3:15 to 5:30 p.m.**

0          1          2
MILES

new corps commander's lack of action, but one look at Ewell's stricken face and he needed ask no questions. The good combat soldier, Jackson's quaintly lovable subordinate, had become paralyzed by irresolution in the lonely sphere of high command. Cemetery Hill had not been taken because Ewell had lost the will to act.

It was too late to discuss the failure to take the strong position that would have completed the success of the day's action. The problem now was to get the hill, and its extension into forbidding Cemetery Ridge, before the enemy was solidified there. Without his usual amenities, Lee opened the conversation by asking about the condition of the troops. To his surprise Rodes answered, and this combative Virginian had turned defense minded. He had taken heavy casualties in fighting off the XI Corps, and his division was in poor condition.

Then Lee asked Ewell directly, "Can't you, with your corps, attack on daylight tomorrow?"

Ewell, his bulging eyes glazed, sat rigidly in his paralysis. It was Jubal Early who answered. This fierce fighter also had turned defensive. His survey of Cemetery Hill and its eastern extension, Culp's Hill, had convinced him it was too late to make an attack there. Curiously, Ewell showed a deference to his dark-eyed saturnine subordinate. It looked as if he needed to depend on someone. Encouraged, Early grew so bold as to suggest to Lee that, from his survey, he believed the other end of Cemetery Ridge was vulnerable. Ewell stirred at this suggestion of somebody else making an attack, and heartily agreed with Early.

This defeatist attitude in the Second Corps, his old striking force, disturbed Lee. Speaking his thoughts, he said, "Then perhaps I had better draw you around to my right, as the line will be very long and thin if you remain here. The enemy may come down and break through it."

Again Early answered, quickly assuring Lee that on defense they would be immovable. The rough terrain would favor whichever side was on defense. Again Ewell agreed with his subordinate. Voicing his groping throughts, Lee said tentatively that he would try an attack from his right, and suggested that Ewell's corps could at least demonstrate in support. Then, unable to accept such supineness from Jackson's old corps, he said Ewell might turn his demonstration into an attack if it seemed practical.

With the proviso of "if practical," Rodes and Early joined Ewell in saying that they certainly *might* do that.

That was the best Lee could get out of them. Disheartened, he remounted Traveler and in the deepening dusk rode back between campfires to the Chambersburg Turnpike. Across the road from a house on Seminary Ridge headquarters had been established, and staff officers were laying their blankets in the orchard. Lee wearily dismounted. He faced a long night ahead in which he must find ways of occupying the enemy's strong position with an army without the Jackson combination.

After supper other generals joined him — Pendleton for a time, and Longstreet, having ridden ahead of his troops whose van was camped five miles back. Discarding plan after plan, Lee worriedly tried to reach a resolution in which the suddenly undependable Second Corps would not be wasted. Finally he made up his mind to shift Ewell's corps around from the north of Gettysburg, removing the hinge at Cemetery Hill, and placing the troops under his own eye in position to support an attack from Seminary Ridge. An order was written out and sent to Ewell.

Late in the evening Lee was surprised to see Ewell awkwardly dismounting outside headquarters. The devoted Confederate had not been satisfied with the impression he had left with the commanding general, and he recognized Lee's change of plan as indicating a lack of faith in him. After Lee had left him, Ewell had heard from Edward ("Allegheny") Johnson, commanding his third division. Arriving after the day's action, Johnson's division had been moved to the east of Gettysburg in front of Culp's Hill. He advised Ewell that Culp's Hill was not occupied. Ashamed of his earlier indecision, Ewell rode over to general headquarters to tell Lee that he would attack in the morning.

Lee changed at once. The tired lines of anxiety lifted from his face, his brown eyes brightened and he spoke with decisiveness. With Ewell attacking from their left, Longstreet would attack from their right with the two fresh divisions of his corps. The main attack would be Longstreet's; Ewell, an adjunct, would not commit until Longstreet was engaged on Cemetery Ridge. A. P. Hill, with two of his divisions cut up, could demonstrate from the center. His third division, Anderson's, had arrived at Seminary Ridge after dark, and those unengaged brigades could exploit any opening developed by Longstreet. Stuart, he had learned, had reached Carlisle. Lee ordered the cavalry to move forward, and, though the troopers would be in no condition to accomplish much, at least Stuart would be on hand.

"Gentlemen," Lee said in the confident voice with which they were familiar, "we will attack the enemy as early in the morning as possible."

4

After a before-dawn breakfast, Lee was at a cleared stretch on wooded Seminary Ridge when the sun came up on July 2. Behind his grassy knoll and to the right were Spangler's Woods. To his front the ridge sloped down to the fence-lined Emmitsburg Road, running at an angle along the floor of the shallow valley between Lee and Cemetery Ridge.

To his left on the opposite ridge he saw the trees in Evergreen Cemetery, and about a mile and a half to the south, his right, the rocky columns called Little Round Top and Big Round Top. Immediately in front of the Round Tops the country was very rough, with huge boulders rising out of the marsh on either side of Plum Run. Northward, nearer Lee's position, there was a wheat field, and then a large peach orchard fronting on the Emmitsburg Road. Behind these fields the ground rose in a readily negotiable slope to the crest of Cemetery Ridge. Studying the ground, Lee planned an attack from the Emmitsburg Road on his right, the flank posted in front of the Round Tops. The assault lines were to sweep obliquely northward to the open stretches of the hillside, aiming for the crest in what would be the Federal left.

As he peered through his glasses, Lee caught glimpses of the movement of Meade's army hurrying to occupy the ridge. As yet there seemed no density of concentration. In mentally preparing to commit his troops, Lee showed no change in the habitual mask of composure — "a kinglike quality," one of Ewell's staff officers described it. He did show the strain of maintaining it by restlessly moving about. The successive failures of his subordinates were taking a toll in tension, and he was encountering a new problem in command where least expected — Longstreet.

After his period in independent command, Longstreet had returned in a state of afflatus to an army from which the rival Jackson was gone. Though he had outwardly appeared to be his usual bluff self, his postwar writing revealed his unhealthy inner condition as of the morning of July 2.

His recollections showed that Longstreet's conviction of his ascendancy over Lee gave him the attitude of operating as an equal with Lee, as if they were co-commanders of the army. He adverted repeatedly to his disapproval of certain things and to the approval that he had given others. His fundamental criticism would have established the military principle that the commanding general must submit his orders for subordinates' approval and adapt them according to the subordinates' preference. As Longstreet would never have defended such a principle in its general applications, obviously he held himself in a special category, not subject to rules obtaining for the other corps commanders.

The background of Longstreet's July 2 disturbance was revealed entirely by him. Longstreet said that before the army moved north he had told Lee that he preferred to fight defensively, and Lee had promised him that the invasion would be offensive only in strategy while defensive in tactics. As Lee was alive when this statement was made, he disclaimed any knowledge of the conversation and said he would never have thought of giving such a promise. With his opportunistic flexibility, it seems most unlikely that he would have. The probability is that Longstreet, who was very free with suggestions, did make a proposal about defensive tactics, and Lee, as usual, listened politely. This was enough for Longstreet to believe he had influenced Lee to accept his way.

Then, on the afternoon of the day before, Longstreet had joined Lee while Lee was waiting for Ewell to attack. According to Longstreet he made a long speech, with fully rounded sentences, advising Lee not to attack the Federals on Cemetery Hill. He should shift southward, around Meade's left, take a strong physical position between Meade and Washington, and there await attack from the Federals. Neither Lee nor his staff made any reference to this conversation. Probably Lee was too preoccupied with the battle he was directing to do more than brush aside a proposal from a corps commander who had just arrived and whose troops were not yet on the field.

As this exchange was reported after Lee was dead, various of Lee's generals pointed out the rather wild impracticality of Longstreet's idea. To begin with, the army was not gathered — Pickett was a day's march away — and Lee had no cavalry. On the grim factor of subsistence, the men would be unable to forage while in motion, and their impressed supplies were already giving out. The most damaging item against the move was that Meade hoped Lee would do it: he had taken precautions to meet Lee's army away from Gettysburg. Lee would be moving over narrow roads in close country, with miles of wagon train, on the arc with Meade on the shorter distance of the base. Meade could hit Lee's strung-out army at points of his own selection long before Lee concentrated at a strong defensive position. Finally, even if Lee did succeed in taking a defensive position, nothing compelled Meade to attack. But Lee, for want of supplies, would have to keep moving.

As these details were not explained to Longstreet, early in the morning of July 2 he joined Lee at his informal command post near Spangler's Woods and made his proposition again. Again Lee, his mind crowded with the responsibilities of getting the whole action started, dismissed the proposal without discussion. From this point on, Longstreet's behavior revealed the resentful, intransigent humor of a rejected collaborator. As at Second Manassas, he began a delaying action in order to get his way.

Before joining Lee, Longstreet had not gotten his van — five miles from Seminary Ridge — off to an early start, nor did he advance the men with any urgency. While Meade was rushing to man the two-mile line from Cemetery Hill to the Round Tops, Longstreet took no move to hurry his troops forward. His loyal chief of staff, Moxley Sorrel, said, "As Longstreet was not to be made willing, and Lee refused to change or could not change, the former failed to conceal some anger. There was apparent apathy in his movements."

Lee could not have failed to notice Longstreet's ill humor. McLaws, ahead of his troops, had joined Lee and volunteered to lead a skirmish party with Captain Johnston of the engineers on a reconnaissance. Longstreet forbade him to leave his division so sharply that McLaws found him "irritated and annoyed." Evidently Lee was too busy to take any heed of Longstreet's surliness.

At about eight-thirty, when the rear troops of Longstreet's two divisions were coming up behind Seminary Ridge, Lee said quietly to Longstreet, "I think you had better move on."

Assuming Longstreet would move his two divisions to the assault area and open his attack, Lee then rode around to the north of Gettysburg to confer with Ewell on coordinating with Longstreet. Lee saw that Ewell's brief flare of decisiveness had faded. The rocky masses of Culp's Hill were then occupied, and poor Old Baldhead had lost the spirit of attack of the night before. However, as Ewell did appear self-controlled and his troops were in good position, Lee reverted to his plan for a demonstration that "might" develop into an actual attack when Longstreet went in. At around ten o'clock Lee started back to Seminary Ridge.

By then Longstreet's guns should have opened. Instead, a silence lay over the whole field. Riding west of the town, Lee grew more impatient than his staff officer Long had ever seen him. From the Gettysburg-Cashtown Road, he pushed Traveler up Seminary Ridge to the crest. The army lay spread at rest exactly as he had left it. Everyone near him saw his shock. Nobody seemed to know where Longstreet was. Lindsay Walker, A. P. Hill's huge chief of artillery, pushed himself up from a shady slope, and said he thought Longstreet was in the valley west of Seminary Ridge. Looking bewildered, according to Colonel Walker, Lee rode off through the woods. Around eleven o'clock Lee found Longstreet and his staff idly lounging. In the two and one-half hours since Lee had left him, the stubborn man had managed to do absolutely nothing.

While Lee had been gone, Longstreet had offered Hood an explanation for his tacit disobedience. "The general is a little nervous this morning; he wishes me to attack; I do not wish to do so without Pickett. I never like to go into battle with one boot off." Pickett was just being relieved of his duty at Chambersburg by the appearance of Imboden's dubious cavalry. He could not reach Gettysburg until the end of the day.

When Lee found Longstreet, he immediately ordered him to move out. Even then, Longstreet tried one more delay. He would like to wait until Law's rearguard brigade got up. Lee's frayed control was evident to those familiar with him. Francis Lawley, passionately pro-Confederate correspondent of *The Times* of London, was an intimate at general headquarters; he sometimes dined with Lee and, when sick on the march to Gettysburg, was conveyed in an army ambulance. Lawley said, "Lee struck me as more anxious and ruffled than I had ever seen him before, though it required close observation to detect it."

As Law's brigade was due in half an hour Lee, having waited that long, agreed to wait for its arrival. But Lee remained with Longstreet while waiting. Around noon the van of Law's Alabamians, grimy with sweat and dust, began turning off the road into the shadowy valley. Twenty-seven-year-old Evander McIver (pronounced McKeever) Law, lean-faced and romantic looking, was a scholarly graduate of The Citadel. He had been operating an academy in Alabama when the war came, and his brigade of Alabama volunteers had accompanied Hood's on the breakthrough at Gaines' Mill. When he rode toward Lee and Longstreet at the head of the column, his regiments were completing a forced march of twenty-four miles between three in the morning and noon — the best marching of any unit on either side in the campaign.

It was nearly an hour before the last of the ranks came up. By the time the steaming men had rested briefly and filled their canteens, it was one o'clock before Longstreet stolidly put the first of his two divisions in motion south, to the right of the Confederate line. Lee rode the first mile with Longstreet to see the troops on their way. Then he turned his gray horse about and pushed up the wooded hillside to the open knoll in the center of the field. There, in front of and midway between A. P. Hill's three divisions, he took up another wait. Lee assumed that when Longstreet, frequently slow to get started, finally got his troops in action, he would do what was indicated. This was the culmination of Lee's misreading of Longstreet that had begun during his independent command in the late winter.

5

Lee, waiting on the grassy slope to hear the action open to the south, had made the same mistake as many others in his appraisal of Longstreet: he judged him entirely by his exterior. The burly man with the steady blue eyes and expression of stolid self-reliance was one of the most unruffled of all generals in battle. His presence was reassuring to soldiers and subordinates alike, and since the Seven Days he had been fixed in Lee's mind as a dependable quantity on a battlefield. His own self-command was suggested by the strong control he exerted over his major generals and brigadiers, along with the superb discipline and high morale of his troops. His men, capable of great endurance, went unfaltering where ordered and, when Longstreet wanted to fight, the war did not produce a better combat leader.

The flaw within lay in his middle-life surge of ambition. He deluded himself that his desire for independent command was equated by the necessary capacity for high strategy. In this delusion, Longstreet possessed extraordinary powers of convincing himself of anything he wanted to believe. At the deranged Battle of Seven Pines, where he commanded the field, he had convinced himself that Huger was at fault — though he was forced to distort and rearrange events, suppress facts, and tell outright lies. When he wasted two crack divisions at the siege of Suffolk, he saw nothing of the dismal futilities but only the glory of independent command. The year after Gettysburg, when he failed on a more heroic scale at the disastrous siege of Knoxville, he again convinced himself that others were to blame, and arrested generals right and left. By these powers of self-deception, he had been unable to accept the reality of his failure to impose his strategy on Lee.

Until one o'clock, he had repeated the Second Manassas tactics of procrastination. At Second Manassas no harm had resulted, due to Jackson's men having stood up under two days of brutal, massive assaults until the enemy was exposed for the counterthrust of Longstreet's rested, compact brigades. Second Manassas was Longstreet's ideal of a battle, that and Fredericksburg, where in a strong position he had received attack. There was no Jackson at Gettysburg to set up the enemy for Longstreet — though A. P. Hill and Ewell had cut up two Federal corps pretty badly the day before — and Meade was under no military nor political necessity to attack. When Lee ordered Longstreet to attack as directed, not only was he forced to fight the kind of battle he did not like: his illusion of dictating the strategy was shattered when Lee overrode his procrastinating methods, and Longstreet's ego suffered a violent shock.

In this shock Longstreet lost control of himself. He became like a sulky child who, forced to do something against his will, followed the letter of the order in willful stupidity. He showed this by insisting, over his subordinates' protests, on executing the exact details of Lee's orders even though all the generals with him *found the conditions to be different from what they were when Lee issued the order.*

Lee had given the order at eight-thirty in the morning. Longstreet managed to consume three hours in moving by circuitous routes three miles, and it was four o'clock when his first brigades reached the Emmitsburg Road across from the Round Tops and the peach orchard. Lee, in the absence of Stuart, had used an engineering officer to reconnoiter the Little Round Top area, and Captain Samuel Johnston — partly by bad luck and partly by the limitations of a one-man reconnaissance in the chopped-up country — had brought wrong information. He reported that the end of Cemetery Ridge around Little Round Top was unoccupied. Lee planned his attack obliquely from the Emmitsburg Road to Cemetery

Ridge on the assumption that his own line overlapped the Federal flank. The assaulting lines were supposed to catch the Federal flank at an angle.

Instead, as soon as John Hood and Lafayette McLaws looked at the Federal position, each recognized that Cemetery Ridge was occupied in strength all the way to Little Round Top, and the enemy's defensive line overlapped their own right. For Longstreet to attack obliquely, according to the letter of Lee's order, would be to expose the flank and rear of the assaulting columns to the enemy. Worse: directly in front of Hood's deploying brigades on the flank, Birney's division was posted at the western base of Little Round Top in the rugged country around Plum Run. Across the road from McLaws's brigades, other parts of Sickles's corps crowded the peach orchard. "Thus," McLaws said, "was presented a state of affairs certainly not contemplated when the original battle order was given." He believed if General Lee knew the conditions he would call off the attack.

Longstreet did not apprise Lee of the changed conditions. Instead, he held McLaws and Hood to the letter of Lee's eight-hour-old order and commanded them to attack obliquely in echelon. McLaws delayed execution in the face of Longstreet's peremptory commands which ignored the existence of Sickles on McLaws's front. Hood showed more initiative. He sent out scouts, who found the country open south of the Round Tops. A flanking movement to the right could take Little Round Top in reverse, and the occupancy of this spiky height would control the whole ridge held by Meade. As Lee's original orders manifestly did not obtain in the present conditions, Hood suggested the flanking movement to Longstreet.

Longstreet refused to consider any alternative to an obstinate, senseless execution of the order precisely as Lee had given it in the morning. Twice again, in defiance of all military protocol, Hood urged Longstreet not to send his troops on the hopeless assignment. Twice Longstreet answered stubbornly, "General Lee's orders are to attack up the Emmitsburg Road."

None of this was known to Lee, waiting as he had all day to hear Longstreet's guns open. With a general of Longstreet's reputation for dependability, Lee would not think of sending a staff officer to investigate his conduct of the battle. Late in the afternoon, he finally heard the crackle and the rolling thunder. Then, much later, through his glasses he saw the edges of the assault columns start climbing up Cemetery Ridge. Unsuspected by Lee, this movement was no part of his battle plan.

## 6

It had happened that when Hood stoically led his men out of the woods into what he knew to be a doomed movement, he was struck by a shell fragment. When the big man was carried from the field, command devolved on Evander McIver Law. Law's brigade was on the extreme right, and, before the assault, Law had also proposed the flanking movement to Hood. When the command came to young Law, he simply disobeyed Longstreet's order. Instead of following the suicidal order to move obliquely across the enemy's front, he sent his brigade straight ahead.

The other brigades in Hood's division had started obliquely. Under searing fire, their lines were forced to drift to the right to form on Law. There was shuffling and confusion in making the drift. Huge boulders rose in the men's path, and gaps were torn where clusters of men fell. When the disordered lines, carrying Birney's division before them, reached the rocky mass of Devil's Den, Law did what he had wanted to from the first. He took the survivors of his own brigade around the southern base of Little Round Top and started the men clambering up the slippery face.

When Hood's attack had opened, Little Round Top had been unoccupied except for some signal men and Meade's engineering officer, General Gouverneur Warren. With no time to check with Meade, Warren on his own initiative diverted reinforcements in a rush to the edge to which Law's panting men were climbing. It was only a brigade, Vincent's, but it was enough to give a temporary check to Law's remnants spread out on the cliff.

Law's Alabama troops, after the forced night march, had wandered three hours more with Longstreet back of Seminary Ridge before assaulting over the forbidding countryside. The scramble up the stony cliff had used their last reserves of energy. When Vincent's brigade was supported by more fresh troops, Law's scattered men were too exhausted to fight any more. They halted yards and minutes away from the objective selected spontaneously and disobediently by the twenty-seven-year-old brigadier.

After Hood's attack had developed, Longstreet ordered McLaws to go in on frontal assault. While tacitly abandoning the oblique attack to which he had mulishly adhered, Longstreet rode about shouting orders that did nothing to establish control of the action. Kershaw's and Semmes's brigades, attacking alone, pushed to the wheat field north of Hood's front, driving Humphreys's division as Hood had driven Birney. Sickles's corps was close to a wreck.

Then Barksdale's Mississippians crashed through the peach orchard, going to the foot of Cemetery Ridge. Brigades from Hancock's corps and Sykes's corps were hurrying to contain the thrusts. Barksdale, his long white hair like a plume, fell mortally wounded, as did seignorial Paul Semmes. With their generals down and no central control directing the separate movements, the isolated fragments went forward under the instincts of veteran soldiers to reach the crest.

In the more open country to the north of Barksdale's drive, three brigades from Anderson began going in. They also advanced separately. Low-keyed Dick Anderson, under no one's immediate direction that day, remained at ease under a shade tree and assumed no active responsibility for his front. Though then in Hill's division, he had been ordered by Lee to cooperate with Longstreet. Longstreet had ordered him to put his division in action by brigades as soon as McLaws's assaulting lines connected with his right flank. The "by brigades" instruction referred to the original order of attacking in echelon. After Longstreet had abandoned the oblique attack, as a consequence of Law's committing his brigade straight ahead, he had not advised Anderson.

These brigades of Anderson's were the troops that came dimly, through the smoke, into Lee's view. Assuming the late attack was directed by Longstreet, Lee did nothing to stir Anderson's two idle brigades into support of Wilcox and Wright. Rans Wright, moving out last, had benefitted by the earlier attacks that had entangled three Federal corps, and Lee could see his Georgians push up the ridge just south of the Codori barn. They went all the way to the crest of Cemetery Ridge, in the center of Meade's position, and it looked close to victory there. It was. Then Lee saw Meade's sharply handled supports come up to force Wright's isolated regiments back down the ridge.

From his command post in the center of the strung-out front — reaching from the Round Tops north to Gettysburg and bending back east to Culp's Hill — Lee had exercised no direction at all. Having informally attached Anderson to Longstreet, his former corps commander, Lee understandably expected Longstreet to direct Anderson. It was also understandable for him to leave the demonstration in the center to A. P. Hill. But Powell Hill was still sick, and both of the two divisions with him were without their commanders. Hill's friend Dorsey Pender went down with a wound from which he died. Heth was briefly out from having caught a shell fragment on his head; he had gotten a new hat in Cashtown, too big for him, and the paper stuffing inside the band saved him from a more serious or perhaps mortal injury. Virtually leaderless, Hill's men, recovering from the hard fight of the day before, engaged in desultory firing at intervals that never approached anything like a convincing demonstration. Though it was understandable for Lee to exercise no personal command over Anderson and Hill, he was not the Lee of Sharpsburg and Chancellorsville.

Probably he was feeling ill by the end of the day, for during the night he had suffered a severe attack of diarrhea. None of his staff, sharing the same food and water, was afflicted. This was the first recorded instance of strain, outwardly controlled, affecting Lee physically. Obviously the strain, caused by lapses in command, had also affected the mental powers of Lee that usually imparted decisiveness of action to the units of the army.

At dusk, as Longstreet's fragmentary attack was dying off, Early's division of Ewell's corps mounted a furious attack east of the town that carried all the way to the plateau of Cemetery Hill. Through the gathering darkness Lee could see the flashes of rifles where Early's brigades advanced to within sprinting distance of Meade's headquarters. Once again timely Federal reinforcements pushed the isolated assaulters back down the hill while, this time, the five fine brigades in Rodes's division remained practically idle in an arc around Gettysburg. This was the Robert Rodes whose aggressive leadership had first attracted attention amid all the blunders of Seven Pines. Spots throughout the army reflected the limp command.

Lee had come, with reason, to expect the units of his army to work in coordination in execution of his orders. First, on the way north on the invasion in which he was losing heart, he was placed under stress by the apprehension over Stuart's absence. Next, when a meeting engagement swelled into an unwanted battle, he had been robbed of capitalizing on the collision by Ewell's paralysis of will. Then Longstreet, the one experienced corps commander, exposed him to the prolonged nervous tension of waiting. Though Lee never knew the details of Longstreet's disordered behavior, he knew the assault had failed, though very narrowly, while potential reserves remained unemployed.

All these command lapses in the enemy's country, in taking their toll of Lee, prevented him from recognizing the extent to which the succession of individual failures affected him personally. Lee did not seem to be aware that he was not at his best. In this unawareness, he also failed to recognize the extent to which the Army of Northern Virginia had become a one-man army. As was said by Major Justus Scheibert, the sympathetic observer from the Prussian Army, Lee did not then realize that operations which had been possible with Stonewall Jackson were no longer possible without him.

That night, when the last firing sputtered off after nine o'clock, Lee made his way in discomfort to the tent near the road at the foot of Seminary Ridge. No generals came to his headquarters. Longstreet did not even send a message. Lee planned alone, while his staff officers wrote out his orders by candlelight.

His mind working in its habitual concreteness, Lee looked only at the knowns. He believed Meade had not been driven because of "a want of proper concert of action." But Meade's army had been shaken at both ends and spread, and the center could be pierced — if the army performed in proper concert of action. Believing this was possible, Lee sent out the orders for an assault early the next morning. Ewell was to attack Culp's Hill from the north, keeping the Federal defenses spread, while Longstreet attacked the center. Hill would remain to support Longstreet. With Ewell handling a diversionary attack, Lee put his trust for the main thrust in his old dependable, Longstreet.

## 7

In the slanting light of early morning, Lee, weakened by the diarrhea attack that had continued through much of the night, was at his command post before the camp stirred. Except for cannoneers placing their guns in position, silence hung over the gray, grisly field. Lee planned to advance the batteries of Longstreet's and Hill's corps to build the heaviest artillery barrage on a single point in the war.

In manpower, the odds were not as heavy as those Lee had been facing. Out of Meade's one hundred thousand of all arms in round figures, he fielded about eighty thousand infantry before casualties. Also before casualties, Lee fielded about sixty thousand infantry out of a total force brought to about seventy-five thousand by the twelve thousand mounted troops — counting the irregulars of Jenkins and Imboden. In the first two days Federal casualties had been heavier than Confederate, due to the five thousand prisoners taken on the first day. So Lee was not trying for one of his strategic miracles. He devised an unimaginative, orthodox assault, based upon his faith in the prowess of his troops and the artillery preparation.

When the sun came up, men began stirring from their bivouacs. Thousands in the stretches along the wheat field, Devil's Den and Little Round Top had slept where night had brought a halt to their fighting. As soon as their units were re-formed, these troops would be ready to resume battle where they were. Hill's men were ready on Seminary Ridge. Ewell's troops were in position for their supporting attack to be delivered at Culp's Hill. There was, however, no news from Lee's one fresh division, Pickett's. These troops had halted only three miles from the field yesterday afternoon, and during the night Lee had sent Longstreet orders to bring up the three all-Virginia brigades of 4500. Nothing had been heard from either Pickett or Longstreet.

Lee mounted his gray horse and rode down the western slope of Seminary Ridge to an open field, where Longstreet had made his headquarters in a small schoolhouse. Outside the school, little bigger than a shed, Lee found Longstreet and his staff officers taking their ease. As soon as Lee dismounted, Longstreet began to harangue him. He had made arrangements to renew the attack by his right, "with a view," as he stated in his official battle report, "to pass around the hill [Little Round Top] occupied by the enemy . . . and gain it by a flank and reverse attack."

In Longstreet's postwar writings, he changed the meaning of what he had written in the report Lee saw. He wrote that he adverted to his first day's proposal of moving "around to the right of Meade's army," to another location entirely, and there "maneuver him into attacking us." Under the circumstances of July 3, such a movement would have been unthinkable. Ewell was engaged with the enemy five miles away and wagons were spread in fields as far back as Cashtown. The Federal Army would have to be reduced to the role of a spectator to permit this slow, cumbersome movement to develop and proceed across its front. Furthermore, Longstreet would be guilty of the rankest insubordination to advance such a proposal after Lee had issued his orders for an early morning attack and the other two corps, with Longstreet's own artillery, were in position to open the assault.

But what Longstreet actually had done, according to all official reports, in itself amounted to insubordination. He had failed to execute Lee's orders for an early attack. Without advising the commanding general, he was preparing a separate movement unrelated to Lee's plans for the whole army.

In all the controversial accounts of Gettysburg, it seems evident that Lee flatly dismissed Longstreet's proposal of taking Little Round Top in reverse. Longstreet said Lee had grown "impatient with talk," and Lee, in his battle report, simply wrote, "General Longstreet's dispositions were not completed as early as expected."

Yet, after Lee told Longstreet the attack was to be made at the Federal left center as ordered, the balky subordinate then suggested changes in the details of that assault. Hood's and McLaws's divisions, much cut up and scattered, would be exposed to enfilade fire when they advanced. (This was the objection raised by Longstreet's subordinates the day before and which he had overruled.) Let Pickett's fresh division, he suggested, go in with A. P. Hill's rested divisions and strike at the exact center. To this alteration Lee resignedly agreed.

Lee is very difficult to explain in that early morning encounter between the two men. Powerfully built Longstreet, ten years younger than Lee and glowing with robust health, stood with his heavy features set in stubbornness. Lee, in the illness induced by anxiety, looked much older close up than when he rode past his men. The white was thickening in his gray beard and in the hair worn fluffed over his ears, and lines of care showed in the classic façade of composure. In agreeing with Longstreet's last-minute change of his battle, up to a point Lee was acting as he habitually did in permitting a trusted subordinate some latitude in tactics which he was to execute. Beyond that, Lee was preoccupied with many details concerning the whole of his faulty organization. As soon as he saw that Longstreet had not prepared to attack, while Longstreet was making his counterproposals to thwart Lee's will, Lee was thinking that he must get a message to Ewell to delay his assault on the Federal right at Culp's Hill.

It was not a question of Longstreet's "disapproval," as he wrote in his postwar apologia. Lee did not ask for his approval; he gave him an order. Nor did Longstreet deliver the impassioned monologue in opposition to Lee's assault which he attributed to himself thirty years later. This contradicted his battle report, along with those of his subordinates, and such mutinous behavior would have been commented upon by the staff officers, who scarcely mentioned the brief exchange. Longstreet's inventions were, as in his case against Huger, designed to give an after-the-fact rationale to his own obstructionist behavior. It is significant that Lee never showed any awareness of having been opposed by Longstreet. As far as Lee knew and recorded, Longstreet wanted to change the nature of the tactics for the attack *at Gettysburg* and, for that reason, had not completed his dispositions as ordered.

When all the elements that never happened are removed, when it is realized that Lee was unaware of Longstreet's mental state (about which Longstreet himself seemed somewhat confused in retrospect) and that Longstreet was known to have procrastinated before, the drama of Longstreet's later arrangement becomes reduced to a tired, ill, overburdened army commander dealing with a balky subordinate who, once he got moving, was the only dependable corps commander on the field. It does not explain why Lee, instead of assuming direct control of the assault himself, entrusted complete responsibility to a general with Longstreet's attitude and known limitations.

Longstreet had deliberately delayed the day before, and on that morning his delay amounted to tacit disobedience. Longstreet's responsibility included organizing the assault force, though Longstreet, essentially a defensive fighter, was known to be slow to commit to attack. In organizing the assault force, Longstreet was given responsibility for effecting cooperation with A. P. Hill, some of whose troops Longstreet was to direct in the combined assault, when only the coldest surface civility existed between these antithetical types whom earlier Lee had been forced to separate to avoid a duel. Only the day before, Dick Anderson, newly attached to Hill and missing Longstreet's strong control, had dangled between the two corps commanders. Nothing suggested that Longstreet, certainly not in his uncooperative attitude, was fitted to assemble and direct a frontal attack for which he was solely responsible.

The only possible explanation for Lee's not assuming personal direction was the effect of the physical weakness. The following month he wrote that he was becoming "more and more incapable of physical exertion," and could no longer give the necessary personal supervision to the field. This was true. With his heart condition that had begun with the spring attack, the prolonged physical and mental stress and the growing burden of responsibility brought a steady decline. Outwardly his magnificent carriage was unaffected, his massive torso was still erect and his head high on his strong neck, but he felt the weakening he tried to conceal. It can only be assumed that the effect of the illness on July 3, combined with the worry over the breakdown in coordination between the parts of his army, deprived him of the full possession of the combination of those faculties that had produced his successes.

In the Maryland invasion, fate had intervened with the three cigars. In this Pennsylvania invasion, the human element intervened with the personality flaws of three men — Stuart's vanity, Ewell's indecision, Longstreet's frustrated ambition — and the effects of the combination on the fifty-six-year-old commander. For Lee, on the assumption that Longstreet would, as had Jackson at Chancellorsville, organize and deliver an effective assault on his own, rode back through the woods to his command post, and began to wait as he had the day before.

8

Beginning at seven in the morning, the hours dragged by. Below Lee's knoll, where the guns were advanced near the Emmitsburg Road for the proposed barrage, the cannoneers' jackets turned dark with sweat as the men waited nervously in the open under the rising sun. Lee showed his own impatience by a sarcastic reprimand of a handsomely mounted staff officer riding in front of the guns. Sharpshooters banged away at one another and occasionally some battery blasted. From beyond Gettysburg, to the east, came the sounds of a furious action.

Lee's orders for Ewell to delay his attack, which Lee had sent when he discovered Longstreet was not ready, were too late. After two days of incomplete performances, Dick Ewell had faithfully executed Lee's night order to attack early "in conjunction with Longstreet." Allegheny

Johnson's division attacked Culp's Hill before daylight, and the attack continued during the morning hours while Lee waited for Longstreet to form.

At nine o'clock the last of Pickett's division, which had received no orders to hurry, reached the shaded western slope of Seminary Ridge. Lee evidently did not notice that the men, of this designated spearhead of the assault, broke ranks and stretched out on the grass. He was listening to Ewell's lonely fight fade off. Allegheny Johnson, commanding Jackson's old division, had occupied Slocum's corps until ten o'clock, and then the veterans could do no more. At that hour Lee's hopes for "concert of action" were in the past. Ewell's action in the joint assault had come and gone before Longstreet started arranging the assault force.

The arrangements permitted by Lee were loose to begin with. Six brigades from the divisions of Pender and Heth formed one assaulting column. As Hill assumed his troops were to be employed by Longstreet, he took no active part himself. Knowing that his numbers were much reduced, he did suggest to Lee that his whole corps be used. However, he did not mention to Lee, even if he knew the details, that the six brigades would number no more than ten thousand. The adjoining assaulting column was formed of Pickett's 4500 men. Pickett's right was supposed to be supported by two brigades from Anderson's division. But neither Hill, Anderson nor Longstreet assumed responsibility for Wilcox and Perry. Pickett and his men seemed to regard Hill's brigades as supports to their attack.

Just before noon, when the tension of the waiting grew unbearable, Lee mounted Traveler and rode along the western slope of Seminary Ridge down to a swale and a patch of woods. The woods were like an oven, and Pickett's men showed visible signs of suffering from the wait in the heat. When the men saw Lee, they were under orders not to cheer and the troops silently lifted their tattered hats. Two of the brigades were commanded by Old Army men, Lewis Armistead and Robert Garnett. Garnett was ill, wrapped in a blue coat. Stern-faced James Kemper was a Virginia politician who had inherited the brigade superbly trained by A. P. Hill, with which he became a forceful leader.

Around one o'clock when Lee returned to his command post, Longstreet sent a note to Porter Alexander. The twenty-seven-year-old colonel was that day temporarily in charge of First Corps artillery. Alexander's seventy-five guns had been in position near the Emmitsburg Road since daylight, while he waited for the order to commence firing. As eager as he was to open, he was profoundly disturbed by Longstreet's note.

"If the artillery fire does not have the effect to drive off the enemy or greatly demoralize him, so as to make our effort pretty certain, I should prefer that you not advise Pickett to make the charge. I shall rely a great deal upon your judgment and shall expect you to let General Pickett know when the moment offers."

This cloudy note, as Alexander wrote, "suggested at once that there was some alternative to the attack, and placed on me the responsibility of deciding the question . . ." Alexander coolly sent off a courier with a message to Longstreet saying that if there was an alternative to this attack it should be considered carefully, as all their ammunition would be used "to test this one." The courier found Longstreet asleep, propped against the snake fence on the side of Spangler's Woods. Longstreet sent the reply: "The intention is to advance the infantry if the artillery has the desired effect of driving the enemy's [artillery] off, or having other effect such as to warrant us in making the attack . . ."

Though this assured Alexander that the cannonade was to open, he felt deeply the responsibility of deciding whether or when Pickett should attack. With no more delay, he opened fire from his seventy-five guns. Hill's batteries joined in and several long-range British rifled guns from Ewell fired at an angle. The Federal batteries immediately answered. One of Pickett's men said, "Such a tornado of projectiles it has seldom been the fortune or misfortune of any one to see." The sky became "lurid with flame and murky with smoke," and sulphurous clouds eclipsed the light and shadowed the earth "as with a funeral pall."

Despite the awesome spectacle, the confusion and injuries caused in the rear of the Federal lines, the Confederate guns were overshooting. No significant damage was done Meade's batteries nor the infantry lined behind walls along Cemetery Ridge. After Alexander had kept his guns going until ammunition was running low, he sent Pickett a note, "If you are coming at all you must come at once, or I can not give you proper support . . ."

The good-looking, dandified George Pickett mounted in excitement and rode to show the note to Longstreet. Pickett was eager to go in. He had never enjoyed one of those big moments in the war and he had a personal reason for wanting it now: the thirty-eight-year-old widower was engaged to a young girl. When Longstreet said nothing after reading the note, Pickett said, "General, shall I advance?" Longstreet, still without speaking, nodded his head. Pickett gracefully remounted, spun his black horse and galloped back to his lines. The three Virginia brigades were put in motion.

While Pickett's troops were preparing to leave their covers, Longstreet left his staff and rode to Alexander. The young artillerist told him that the nine howitzers he planned to move out with the infantry were missing. Also his ammunition for supporting the attack was nearly gone. The Reverend General Pendleton, nowhere in sight, was responsible. After

Pendleton's feckless performance at Chancellorsville, Lee had abolished the artillery reserve and, evidently to save the devout gentleman's feelings, left him as nominal chief of artillery. As an arrangement, it was worse than having no chief at all. Pendleton fussed at details, such as moving the nine howitzers without telling Alexander, but neglected to see that the light ordnance wagons that followed the guns had been replenished after the previous day's fight from the heavy ordnance wagons with the wagon train.

When Alexander told Longstreet the situation, Longstreet shouted, "Go and stop Pickett right where he is, and replenish your ammunition."

Alexander evaded the order. He said he had too little reserve ammunition to accomplish anything and, during the break to bring that up, "the enemy would recover from the effects of the fire we are now giving him."

Longstreet then said that he had never believed in the charge and would stop Pickett then except that General Lee expected it. He never thought to inform Lee that the infantry would not be supported by batteries as Lee had planned in his battle order. Of all the lapses in command, the only one Lee criticized was the failure to notify him of the lack of artillery ammunition to support the charge. Had he known of that, he would have called it off.

Knowing nothing of the details involved in mounting the attack, Lee saw Pickett's three brigades file out of a ravine in Spangler's Woods about four hundred yards in front of him. The guns had ceased firing to allow the infantry to pass. As the Federal batteries faded off, the troops came out in the open in a hush over the field. As soon as the lines started advancing the Federal guns reopened, firing anti-personnel ammunition, and geysers spouted in and around the troops. Gaps appeared in the ranks before the lines advanced ten paces.

At the same time, Hill's six brigades emerged from the shadowed woods along the crest of Seminary Ridge. Their battle lines advanced down the open stretch of ground toward the fences on both sides of the Emmitsburg Road. Nearing the road, with a wake of dead and wounded behind them, the two forces drifted closer together without making contact. As the men climbed over the fences and started up the hill, Pickett's brigades passed the Cordori barn in aiming for the projection of a stone fence on the crest. Hill's men, with their left flank fallen away, were pushing for the road along the plateau of Cemetery Ridge. Pickett's right flank was mangled by enfilade fire. Neither Wilcox nor Perry was ordered forward to cover his flank.

Near the projecting stone fence, Pickett's men came under rifle fire and had themselves the first chance to fire at the enemy. By the time the survivors reached the stone fence, the enemy had been driven away and not a man nor a horse stood to the guns in the projecting angle. But scarcely one-third of the men were left, and all order in the units was lost. Garnett was down dead, Kemper seriously wounded, and Pickett was frantically sending off staff officers to call on Longstreet for support. Bunched together, more like a crowd, handfuls of the survivors climbed the stone fence behind Lewis Armistead. Armistead's black hat was waving on his sword above his uncovered gray head and he rushed to the first of the abandoned guns. As he placed his hand on the hot barrel, his body arched in pain and he fell mortally wounded.

The remnants plunged straight ahead through the smoke toward Meade's reserve line. These Federals were planted solidly along the road. Other Federal forces loomed out of the smoke on the right. Some of Pickett's remnants fell still fighting, others surrendered within the Federal lines, and others started the long way back. North of the stone fence salient, the wave of Hill's men also began to recede. At a distance of about three-quarters of a mile Lee watched the debris of the assault wash back down the hill and across the road.

His expression unchanging, Lee mounted Traveler and rode down from his command post to meet the survivors and send them back to the protection of Seminary Ridge. Pickett rode up, just short of hysteria, and cried out that his division was wrecked.

"Come, General Pickett," Lee said quietly, "this has been my fight and upon my shoulders rests the blame. The men and officers of your command have written the name of Virginia today as high as it has ever been written before."

For Lee the battle was not over with the repulse of the assault. There were counterattacks to guard against and the care of the shattered men who made it back to their own hill. One-third of Pickett's 4500 made it out, some of those slightly wounded or injured, and Hill's six brigades suffered almost as heavily. Everywhere the commanding general rode among the troops, re-forming their units and getting them to places of safety.

"Don't be discouraged," he kept saying. "It was all my fault this time . . . All good men must hold together now."

His army was not wrecked. Only three brigades of thirty-seven on the field were hurt beyond immediate repair, and the gunners stood steadily to their pieces with no indication that the cannoneers had less than twenty rounds per gun. Local sorties were made against Lee's right, but nothing serious developed in the way of a counterattack. For the whole three days Meade's army had been hurt at least as much as Lee's, both suffering around twenty thousand casualties.

As a soldier in a North Carolina regiment said, "Both sides got the worst of it at Gettysburg." Meade, however, did not have to win. He needed only not to lose, not to have his army driven from its strong position. For

Lee to suffer the final repulse, after having victory dangling just beyond his grasp for two days, was to lose the whole campaign.

Even while he was comforting the men and rearranging the units, his mind already turned to the long retreat that was the only course left him. The guns possessed the ammunition for only one small action, food was running low, and every third foot soldier in the army was either wounded or lost.

### 9

That night no would-be collaborators came to share the sorrow that, once inside his tent, Lee's staff saw bared on his tired face. During the early hours of the night he wrote out specific orders for Longstreet and Ewell to follow on the retreat. Then he rode to A. P. Hill's headquarters to work in detail the line of march which his troops would lead. Sometimes during those desolate hours Lee recognized, perhaps without conscious thought, the collapse of the methods he had used when Stonewall Jackson commanded a corps. For the end of the campaign he assumed command of every aspect of the retreat, giving the most exact instructions, with no provision for anyone's discretion.

When Lee returned to his headquarters tent late at night, his exhausted staff officers were asleep. The only person stirring was General Imboden who, with an aide, was waiting to receive instructions for escorting the ambulance train. When Lee wearily dismounted, before he spoke to the cavalry leader he threw his arm across the saddle and rested on it. As Imboden saw him, "The moon shone full upon his massive features and revealed an expression of sadness that I had never before seen upon his face." To break the embarrassing silence, Imboden ventured to say, "General, this has been a hard day for you."

Lee raised his head and, making no effort to hide his grief, he said, "Yes, it has been a sad, sad day for us." Suddenly he straightened and spoke in a voice choked with emotion. "I never saw troops behave more magnificently than Pickett's division of Virginians did in that grand charge upon the enemy. And if they had been supported as they were to have been — but, for some reason not yet explained to me, were not — we would have held the position and the day would have been ours."

After staring off into the night, as if reliving the scene, he said in an anguished voice, "Too bad. *Too bad.* O, too bad!"

Slowly the emotion passed, and the habitual control asserted itself. Courteously he invited Imboden into his tent to examine the maps. "We must now return to Virginia," he said.

# PART FIVE

# The Hero in the Long Retreat

## CHAPTER XVI

# "I Cannot See How We Can Operate With Our Present Supplies"

THE NORTH, then and since, made much more over the Battle of Gettysburg than did the South. It was the only battle fought on Union soil and, as Maryland was considered a border state, climaxed the only Northern invasion by a major army. At that time Lee's army, never defeated, was the most famous armed force in the world. When his hairy, hard-bitten troops crossed into Pennsylvania, with the advance force under Ewell threatening the state capital at Harrisburg, excited alarm spread throughout the East. Militia units were called out and messages streamed back and forth between governors and Washington. Because the Federal forces made a defensive fight on their own land against Lee's legendary army, sentiment attached a greater significance to the battle than it actually had.

On July 4, the day after Lee's repulse, Vicksburg was surrendered to Grant. As well as freeing Grant's army for other operations, this brought the whole Mississippi River under Federal control and sliced off the Confederate West. Under these circumstances, Lee's lone army could not have accomplished anything decisive. Lee himself had not expected to make any accomplishments on the scale that he had hoped for in the Maryland invasion the year before. Lee saw the invasion almost entirely as a desperation measure necessary to evict the Federal forces from Virginia and to subsist his army.

There was the added element of Lee's having said that the best way to relieve the Confederate West would be by a Northern invasion. Lee had proposed his invasion long before the Vicksburg crisis and, having no faith in the muddled Confederate command situation in the West, had fundamentally been keeping his own army intact in order to sustain maneuver. At that, *if* the absence of his cavalry had not forced him to fight sooner than he intended and *if* the starved-out Confederate forces at Vicksburg could have prolonged siege indefinitely, then Federal troops might have been diverted from the West. But this consideration was incidental to Lee, and also, he was forced to make his invasion with less strength than he had planned.

While Lee was of course disappointed not to win at Gettysburg, from all his letters and known comments he seemed to feel that the primary objective of the campaign had been achieved. His strongest expressed feeling about the battle itself was his "grief" over the casualties. In that battle the tragedy of the third day's assault had unrolled before his eyes. To his daughter-in-law, Charlotte, he wrote, "The loss of our gallant officers and men throughout the army causes me to weep tears of blood and to wish that I could never hear the sound of a gun again. My only consolation is that they are the happier and we that are left are to be pitied."

As Gettysburg became a point of discussion, Lee made more comments on it than he did on any other battle. With one exception, nothing that Lee said immediately following the battle was changed in his later reflections. The exception occurred in the last year of his life, five years after the war. Then to two trusted intimates — his cousins Cassius Lee and Professor James J. White, former infantry captain — Lee said he would have won the Battle of Gettysburg if Stonewall Jackson had been with him.

It is possible that Lee did not come to this realization until the details of the battle were remote. It is also possible that he was unwilling to state this in writing and that then, with his own end approaching, he spoke unguardedly in private conversation. Most likely it was a combination of both. This exception, however, was in the realm of an "if."

As the battle was fought, Lee steadfastly maintained three points: the absence of the cavalry forced him to fight under unfavorable conditions where he did not want to; the units of the army did not achieve coordination; the responsibility was his. However much he had been failed by subordinates, he never veered away from the admission that he was responsible for the conduct of his subordinates and that he had expected too much of his soldiers.

At the same time it should be stressed that in the retreat from Gettysburg, the battle did not hold to Lee its historic significance. Nor did it to the men in the army. It was on the retreat that Lee's army came the closest to disaster, and Lee and his men faced the threat with no suggestion of defeatism.

2

The first to leave Gettysburg were the wounded. During the night of the 3rd and the morning of th 4th thousands were hastily treated and placed on the floorboards of springless wagons. Hundreds more, too seriously wounded to be moved or having suffered amputations, were left in private homes and in the (now Gettysburg) college. Thousands more with light wounds, "the walking wounded," gathered at the wagons forming in a meadow off the road to Cashtown. Shortly after noon, just before the wagon train of wounded was ready to start, a torrential downpour broke.

The blinding sheets of water continued to fall during the afternoon, flooding the meadow. Pouring through the canvas sides of the ambulances, the water drenched the wounded men lying on the floorboards. Horses and mules, blinded by the water and frightened by the wind, became hard to manage. Around four o'clock the head of the wagon train was gotten in motion behind a screen of Imboden's cavalry, and started for the pass over the mountains.

During that day Lee had remained on Seminary Ridge, watching for any move from Meade. The troops maintained their position, while preparing to move out that night. After dark A. P. Hill's soaked soldiers moved down from Seminary Ridge and formed their columns in the muddy Fairfield Road. Hill's troops were to push to the Potomac crossings at Williamsport and Falling Waters, going by a different route from the wagon train.

It was daylight of the 5th before the road was cleared of Hill's columns, guns and wagons. Longstreet's corps then moved out in the muggy light under rain that had changed into a steady drizzle. General Lee rode out with Longstreet's columns. The road was not clear for Ewell's corps, which formed the rear guard, until late in the afternoon. Except for some harassment of the wagons by Kilpatrick's cavalry, the enemy did not interfere with the beginning of the retreat.

Late in the afternoon of July 6 Lee, with Longstreet's advance columns, reached Hagerstown near the Williamsport crossing. It was then that the threat began for Lee's army. Federal raiding parties had destroyed the pontoon bridges over the crossings, and the swollen river was too high to ford. Stretched along the banks at Williamsport were the miles of wagons of the wounded. Imboden had escorted the train of agonized men to safety with only minor mishaps, although at the river the wagoneers had had to fight off Federal cavalry until rescued by advance regiments of Stuart's troopers. But numbers of the untended wounded had died along the way, including generals Dorsey Pender and Paul Semmes. Other dead were being lifted out of the wagons after the halt, and among the moans rose cries of men begging to be killed to be relieved of their misery.

General Lee ordered engineers to begin reconstructing a pontoon bridge and started the wounded across the river in commandeered ferry boats. All of Lee's orders were very specific, many in writing. The ferry boats ran day and night, while warehouses were torn down for the timber to be used on the new bridges. However, the work proceeded slowly, and it was learned that Meade's army was approaching. Food was running low. The guns had ammunition for only one small action.

At this crisis Lee did not immediately show any alarm, nor did the soldiers. The band of the 26th North Carolina from Hill's corps serenaded Lee in his tent, and Walter Taylor came out and thanked the musicians. On July 7 Lee was brought letters from his wife and Agnes that turned his thoughts to personal affairs.

After Rooney had taken the heavy leg wound at Brandy Station, he was put in bed at Hickory Hill, the Hanover County home of his wife's family. A Federal raiding party came by and, before the eyes of his wife and mother, dragged the wounded man from bed and sent him on his way to prison at Fort Monroe. Lee immediately wrote his wife and Charlotte.

On July 12, while Meade's army was drawn up for attack across his front, he wrote his wife at greater length after receiving another letter from her. "I am very glad to hear that Fitzhugh suffered but little by his removal. I trust he will soon be well. We must expect to endure every injury that our enemies can inflict upon us and be resigned to it. Their conduct is not dictated by kindness or love, and therefore we should not expect them to behave otherwise than they do. But I do not think we should follow their example. The consequences of war are horrid enough at best, surrounded by all the amelioration of civilization and Christianity. Why should we aggravate them? I am very sorry for the injuries done the family at Hickory Hill and particularly that our dear old Uncle William in his 80th year should be subjected to such treatment. But we cannot help it and must endure it."

On July 8 he had written to the President that the condition of the army "is good and its confidence unimpaired." Then on July 10 he wrote the President that "the Potomac continues to be past fording . . ." The bridges had not been rebuilt, all the wounded had not yet been ferried across, nor had the five thousand Federal prisoners who were also being sent across the river by ferry. That night he wired the President, "the enemy is gradually making appearance against us."

Actually on the 10th Meade had driven in the Confederate outposts. The next morning, the 11th — the day before he wrote his long letter home — Lee looked more "visibly anxious," Alexander said, than he ever saw him at any other approaching action. Alexander also noted that "Lee in person" saw to "the placing of Longstreet's corps."

However, there was no indication of any personal strain at all between Longstreet and Lee. Imboden recorded that he had been in Lee's tent when Longstreet, wet and muddy, came in and Lee greeted him most cordially, calling him "my old war horse." Imboden said that this "cordial greeting" between them was "a sufficient answer . . . to the statements of alleged ill feeling between the two men growing out of affairs at Gettysburg." Imboden wrote this twenty years later, when Longstreet's attack on Lee, made after Lee's death, had aroused the bitterest feelings between

Longstreet and his former brother officers. This controversy gave the impression that discord had existed at Gettysburg. The point was that Lee never held any ill feelings toward Longstreet nor did Longstreet show any toward Lee during the war.

On the day after the battle, when his preferences for strategy belonged in the past, Longstreet came out of his sulks. As far as observers noticed, he returned to his usual "good humor." Lieutenant Colonel A. J. L. Fremantle, an observer from the Coldstream Guards, recounted that he met Longstreet "in a high state of amusement" over a message brought under flag of truce. The message stated that "General Longstreet was wounded, and a prisoner, but would be taken care of." During the afternoon of July 4 Longstreet talked a long time to Fremantle about the battle. Fremantle wrote, "He said the mistake they had made was in not concentrating the army more, and in failing to make the attack yesterday with 30,000 men instead of 15,000." (Lee had planned for the attack to be made with more than twenty thousand infantry, to be accompanied by guns.)

Neither to Fremantle nor to any of the intimate guests of the high command did Longstreet refer to his proposal to move the army away from Gettysburg into a defensive position between the enemy and Washington. In the Gettysburg campaign, these European visitors amounted to a small club of Confederate sympathizers. The center of the group was composed of Colonel Fremantle; Fitzgerald Ross, an English captain in the Austrian Hussars; Francis Lawley, whose stories in *The Times* of London were virtually Confederate propaganda, and Major Justus Scheibert of the Prussian Engineers. Scheibert had shared the tent of his fellow Prussian, Major Heros von Borcke, the gigantic baron who served as Stuart's volunteer aide-de-camp. After von Borcke went out wounded in the cavalry action preceding the Gettysburg campaign, Major Scheibert made himself useful on Stuart's staff and presented to the cavalry leader six Yankees he had personally captured.

These "foreign Confederates" shared more unguarded conversations with Lee and Longstreet than the generals in the army. Fremantle and Lawley were at Longstreet's headquarters during his meetings with Lee, and Captain Ross reported Lee as talking freely about the battle during the muddy ride of the retreat. None of the four, all of whom wrote of the campaign, mentioned Longstreet's proposal nor any conflict between him and Lee. Nor did anyone refer to the impassioned objection Longstreet later claimed he made on the morning of July 3 to that day's assault, including his alleged reiteration of his preferred withdrawal away from the field.

Longstreet referred to his first day's proposal to shift to Meade's right — which he evidently did make to a preoccupied commanding general during the late afternoon of July 1 — in a letter to his uncle written three weeks after the battle. Judge A. B. Longstreet was a scholarly and revered lawyer in Georgia, and in a spontaneous release to him, on July 24, Longstreet revealed what probably were his true feelings about Lee at this time. He also suppressed any mention of his aberrant behavior on the second and the third days and presented himself as an ideal subordinate.

"I consider it a part of my duty to express my views to the commanding general. If he approves and adopts them, it is well; if he does not, it is my duty to adopt his views, and to execute his orders as faithfully as if they were my own . . . As we failed, I must take my share of the responsibility. In fact, I would prefer that all the blame should rest upon me. As General Lee is our commander, he should have the support and influence we can give him. If the blame, if there is any, can be shifted from him to me . . . I desire . . . that all the responsibility that can be put upon me shall go there and remain there. The truth will be known in time, and I leave that to show how much of the responsibility of Gettysburg rests on my shoulders."

When Longstreet wrote this, no one had placed any responsibility for Gettysburg on him. While later Longstreet lost this generous impulse in a postwar effort to aggrandize his reputation, there is no reason to suspect that the sentiments expressed in his emotional letter did not reflect his feelings to Lee once he passed beyond his balkiness in the battle.

Certainly during the threat at Williamsport, Longstreet acted as if his two days at Gettysburg were a forgotten interlude in his support of Lee. With an inexhaustible energy that awed Fremantle, the big fellow performed in every way that would tend to assure Lee he was the old dependable.

On the 12th it looked to Lee as if Meade, with his army all in position, was ready to attack. Having arranged his troops in lines of defense, Lee waited prayerfully. In the letter he wrote his wife that day he said, "Had the river not unexpectedly risen, all would have been well with us . . . The waters have subsided to about four feet, and if they continue, by tomorrow, I hope, our communication will be open. I trust that a merciful God, our only hope and refuge, will not desert us in this hour of need."

During the 12th Meade contented himself with reconnaissance. For the 13th Meade proposed to his corps commanders that the whole army make a demonstration in force, to be converted into an attack if an opening was discovered. Meade allowed himself to be overruled by the majority of his corps commanders and let the 13th pass. During that day Major John A. Harman, Jackson's former quartermaster, completed a rickety bridge across the river at Falling Waters. Also during the day, Meade reconsidered and decided to attack on the 14th — one day too late.

At dusk of July 13, when Lee's army was ready to begin its withdrawal,

The first known portrait of Lee, believed to have been painted by William E. West in 1838, when Lee was thirty-one. The original painting is at Washington and Lee.

From a portrait of Mrs. Lee painted by William E. West during the same period
her husband's portrait was painted in 1838. Mrs. Lee was then twenty-nine.

Photograph from a daguerreotype (not in existence) believed made before Lee
went to the Mexico War in 1846, when he was thirty-nine.

Photograph taken in studio of Minnis and Cowell, Richmond, probably in January, 1863. Taken prior to his serious illness in the spring of 1863, this picture of Lee, at about the time of his fifty-sixth birthday, shows him in the full vigor of his wartime leadership.

The familiar photograph taken by Brady shortly after Appomattox, in the rear of the house at 707 East Franklin Street, Richmond, catches Lee before the fire of battle had died, and shows the look of "resolution" so often mentioned by his soldiers.

This photograph taken in the Boude and Miley studio in Lexington in 1870, perhaps in January, is among the last pictures taken in the last year of his life.

Photograph of Mrs. Lee in her wheelchair in the Lexington years.

Shirley, the home of Lee's mother and a second home to him. Photograph by David Ryan, courtesy of Mr. Hill Carter.

THE ARLINGTON HOUSE — 1860

From an engraving, dated 1860, of Arlington, birthplace of Mrs. Lee and later the home of the R. E. Lee family.

Lee's office in the basement of the chapel at Washington and Lee.

Lee's funeral, with Washington College in the background, the chapel he built in the foreground. The burial vaults for the Lee family are now part of a museum of Lee memorabilia in the basement.

another rainstorm broke and rain fell nearly all night. Where the roads were not hard surfaced, men and guns struggled through the churned mud that, Alexander said, "became canals of slush." Bonfires were lit along the banks of the river to light the entrance to the shaky bridge.

At daylight of the 14th only Ewell's corps and the wagon trains had crossed the bridge. The weather cleared then and Lee crossed over at the head of Longstreet's column. Longstreet's men got over safely and then Hill's columns began to cross. At near noon only Heth's division remained on the northern bank when Federal cavalry attacked, supported by guns.

Two of Heth's brigades drove off the cavalry with a sharp volley of rifles. Among the few casualties, Brigadier General Johnston Pettigrew fell mortally wounded. This distinguished North Carolinian had been captured at Seven Pines, where, wounded, he had been left for dead, and had only recently returned to Virginia after being released in the prisoner exchange. Pettigrew was the sixth Confederate general to be killed in the Gettysburg campaign.

After driving off the cavalry, Heth's rear guard moved to the bridge. Before his last columns reached it, a heavier Federal force advanced on their rear. Heth's weary veterans continued across the shaky bridge, leaving behind only their stragglers.

John Esten Cooke was standing close to Lee near the southern bank of the river when Heth's last brigades trudged across the bridge. Cooke said that Lee then showed the fatigue of the strain and loss of rest. When Lee looked at these last troops on the bridge, "as it swayed to and fro, lashed by the current, he uttered a sigh of relief, and a great weight seemed taken from his shoulders." Stuart brought him a cup of coffee and Lee, Cooke wrote, "drank it with avidity, and declared . . . that nothing had ever refreshed him so much."

The next day he wrote his wife a short letter in which his jerky sentences reflected his exhaustion. "The night we recrossed [the Potomac] it rained terribly . . . Yet we got all over safe . . . We are all well. I hope we will yet be able to damage our adversaries when they meet us, and that all will go right with us. That it should be so, we must implore the forgiveness of God for our sins, and the continuance of His blessings. There is nothing but His almighty power that can sustain us. I hear that Mary has found you. I hope she is well. Give love to all."

3

Lee was no sooner back in Virginia than his personal fortunes took a sharp turn for the worse. His army had just halted for a rest in the Valley when he learned that Rooney's life was threatened by the Federal prison authorities at Fort Monroe. In July the Confederate administration, goaded by the atrocities committed by some of the invaders, had selected by draw two Federal officers in Libby Prison to be hanged in retaliation for the execution as spies of two Confederate soldiers in Kentucky. On July 16 Fort Monroe wrote Robert Ould, in charge of prisoner exchange, that General W. H. F. Lee would be hanged when the Federal officers were. Lee faced the inevitable without uttering a protest.

When the retaliatory measures were dropped, Lee never tried to express his relief. He continued to be deeply disturbed by Rooney's exclusion from the prisoner exchange, as Charlotte's health had begun to decline dangerously while her husband was in prison. Lee started writing long letters to his wife about the family when he established temporary headquarters at Culpeper, in the "horse country" northwest of Fredericksburg.

While Lee's army had been resting in the northern Valley, Meade crossed the Potomac east of the Blue Ridge, and Lee marched his troops through the passes to keep his army between Meade and Richmond. On July 24 the three corps began to assemble in and near Culpeper. Two days after Lee arrived he wrote his wife at Hot Springs.

Mrs. Lee had been prostrated when Rooney was dragged off in front of her, and also her arthritis had grown extremely acute. She had become confined to a wheelchair, except for short movements on crutches. Mary had returned from her solitary wanderings and went with her mother, as did Agnes. Since the death of her sister Annie, Agnes had been staying with her mother. Henry Taylor Wickham, a kinsman of Charlotte Lee, said that Annie's death "was a shock to Agnes from which she never recovered . . . She became quiet and pensive."

Wickham was a young man in the house of Hickory Hill when Agnes was staying there with her mother, and he is the authority for a romance — often vaguely rumored — between Agnes and her cousin, Orton Williams. According to Wickham, Agnes was in love with the young soldier but rejected him because of his heavy drinking. Evidently to show his worthiness, Williams volunteered for an espionage mission at the time Lee was preparing his invasion. Passing through the Federal lines with forged papers, he was caught. To whatever extent his mission had been motivated by Agnes Lee, Orton Williams was hanged on June 8, 1863.

Lee made no reference to Agnes's love affair, but only to her health. "I hope my poor little Agnes will be able to throw off her neuralgia and that you will all return [from the Springs] full of health."

Lee was concerned that no one would be with Charlotte, who had gone to the Bath Alum Springs. "She is suffering in health as well as from her separation from Fitzhugh. [Though Lee had given his son the name of Rooney as a child, after he grew up, Lee referred to him as Fitzhugh.] She writes as if in distress and sadness. You must try and cheer her. It now cannot be avoided and we have only to submit. I hope his exchange may be soon effected. But nothing can be done to hasten it. The more anxiety shown on our part, the more it will be proscrastinated by our enemies, whose pleasure seems to be to injure, harass, and annoy us as much as their extensive means enable them."

On August 4 Lee shifted his army south of the Rapidan River to Orange Court House, south and a little west of Culpeper, and about forty miles almost due west from Fredericksburg. This was the first time Lee's army had been south of the Rapidan River since he had prepared his campaign against Pope the year before.

The rolling country of Orange County was farmland, and at that time was rather lean in food produce. Many of its younger men were in the army and farms had been hit in a couple of raids, but the people were hospitable in spirit and shared all they had. There were some fine houses in the county, including Montpelier, the home of former President James Madison, which had been decoratively expanded by the architect who built the Capitol in Washington.

General Lee's headquarters were on the extensive grounds of another "spacious" house, as Sorrel saw it, belonging to Mr. and Mrs. Erasmus Taylor. Over Lee's protests, Mrs. Taylor sent buttermilk, loaf bread, ice, and vegetables every day to Lee's headquarters. The Taylor house was constantly crowded with young girls, and dances and picnics were continuous. Lee seems not to have participated in any of the entertainments. His troubles follow him to Orange.

At that time the United States was confiscating property for tax arrears in sections occupied by Federal forces. By demanding that property owners pay in person, the tax collectors made it almost impossible for Southerners in the armies to make the tax payments. Lee wrote Custis, who acted as his executor for civilian affairs, about the difficulties of finding the proper persons to pay his taxes to.

"I have nothing now not in the hands of the enemy except $5,000 in Confederate State bonds, which are not taxable, I believe, and $5,000 or $8,000 in N.C. bonds, I forget which . . . I own three horses, a watch, my apparel and camp equipage. You know the condition of the estates of your grandfather. They are either in the hands of the enemy or beyond my reach. The Negroes have been liberated, everything swept off of them, houses, fences, etc., all gone. The land alone remains a waste." (Arlington was confiscated in January, 1864.)

Also by the time Lee was settled at Orange Court House he began to be disturbed by the appearance of criticisms of his "failure" in Pennsylvania. He seemed less disturbed for himself than for the reflections on the army. After reading a detailed criticism in the Charleston *Mercury*, he wrote the President:

"I much regret its general censure upon the operations of the army, and it is calculated to do us no good either at home or abroad. But I am prepared for similar criticism and so far as I am concerned the remarks fall harmless . . . To take notice of such attacks would I think do more harm than good, and would be just what is desired . . . No blame can be attached to the army for its failure to accomplish what was projected by me, nor should it be censured for the unreasonable expectations of the public. I am alone to blame, in perhaps expecting too much of its prowess and valour.

"It however in my opinion achieved under the guidance of the Most High a general success, though it did not win a victory. I thought at the time that the latter was practicable. I still think if all things could have worked together it would have been accomplished. But with the knowledge I then had, and in the circumstances I was then placed, I do not know what better course I could have pursued. With my present knowledge, and could I have foreseen that the attack on the last day would have failed to drive the enemy from his position, I should certainly have tried some other course. What the ultimate result would have been is not so clear to me."

The criticism began to spread from the newspapers to talk in Richmond. As Lee wrote, the people had expected too much. Worn by their privations and wearied of the state of siege, the people of Richmond had seized upon the rumors that drifted back after the first day at Gettysburg and induced themselves to believe that Lee was about to end the war. Thomas De Leon, an observant dandy in the wartime capital, wrote of the wild expectations: "We had captured Meade and forty thousand prisoners. Washington was at our mercy; and Lee would dictate terms of peace from Philadelphia!"

When the true news came, exaggerated by Northern sources, De Leon said, "Down to zero dropped the spirits of the people; down to a depth . . . only the deeper from the height of their previous exaltation."

Simultaneously came the news of the surrender of Vicksburg — frankly called by President Davis "our disaster in the west." As the depression spread throughout the Confederacy, "the groan of inquiry and blame" arose, said De Leon. The question centered on Lee, whose army was supposed to be invincible. "Why had the campaign failed?" A new kind of rumor started. Presumably some of this talk reached Lee, for on August 8 he offered to resign from the army. He wrote Davis:

"I know how prone we are to censure and how ready to blame others for the nonfulfillment of our expectations . . . The general remedy for the want of success in a military commander is his removal . . . I have seen and heard of expression of discontent in the public journals at the result of the expedition. I do not know how far this feeling extends in the army. My brother officers have been too kind to report it, and so far the troops have been too generous to exhibit it. It is fair, however, to suppose it does exist, and success is so necessary to us that nothing should be risked to secure it . . . I cannot even accomplish what I myself desire. How can I fulfill the expectations of others?

"In addition, I sensibly feel the growing failure of my bodily strength. I have not yet recovered from the attack I experienced last spring. I am becoming more and more incapable of exertion, and am thus prevented from making the personal examinations and giving the personal supervision to the operations in the field which I feel to be necessary . . . I hope Your Excellency will attribute my request to the true reason, the desire to serve my country, and do all in my power to insure the success of her righteous cause."

Longstreet later wrote that "General Lee suffered during the campaign from his old trouble, sciatica," and simplified Lee's letter as an application "to the authorities for a change of commanders." President Davis saw Lee's request to be relieved in another light and wrote the kind of fine expression he was capable of. In a long letter, personal and warm in tone, he wrote, "I am truly sorry to know that you still feel the effects of the illness you suffered last spring, and can readily understand the embarrassments you experience in using the eyes of others, having been so much accustomed to make your own reconnaissances . . .

"But suppose, my dear friend, that I were to admit, with all their implications, the points which you present, where am I to find that new commander who is to possess the greater ability which you believe to be required? I do not doubt the readiness with which you would give way to one who could accomplish all that you have wished, and you will do me the justice to believe that if Providence should kindly offer such a person for our use, I would not hesitate to avail of his services.

"My sight is not sufficiently penetrating to discover such hidden merit, if it exists, and I have but used to you the language of sober earnestness when I have impressed upon you the propriety of avoiding all unnecessary exposure to danger, because I felt our country could not bear to lose you. To ask me to substitute you by some one in my judgment more fit to command, or who could possess more of the confidence of the army, or of the reflecting men of the country, is to demand an impossibility.

"It only remains for me to hope that you will take all possible care of yourself, that your health and strength may be entirely restored, and that the Lord will preserve you for the important duties devolved upon you in the struggle of our suffering country for the independence which we have engaged in war to maintain."

Lee said no more about resigning, and the public never knew about his letter. If, as is probable, Lee really did want to resign, this could indicate that he felt he had passed the stage where he could bring into play *that best* which he knew to be required. Also, despite the warmth of his exchange with Davis, there was possibly a sense of frustration, even a futility, in his view of a future in which his methods would no longer be used. Controlled by the policy of dispersed defense which, as he said, "tried to meet the enemy everywhere at points of his selection," he would be fighting by a program in which he had no faith.

To Mildred, at school in Raleigh, he wrote words which he must have used for his own comfort. "The struggle which you describe you experience between doing what you ought and what you desire is common to all. You have only always to do what is right. It will become easier by practice, and you will always enjoy in the midst of your trials the pleasure of an approving conscience. That will be worth everything else."

### 4

In this low period for Lee, he was faced for the first time with a serious shortage of manpower for his army. He had not been able since the Seven Days to field as many men as he wanted and needed, but at Orange Court House his army shrunk to a different dimension. Almost the only replacements for the heavy losses at Chancellorsville and Gettysburg were returned wounded and prisoners returned through the prisoner exchange. Some conscripts, who had previously evaded conscription, reluctantly went into the ranks, but many of these soon deserted. Lee wrote constantly to the War Department urging a round-up of the exempts who managed to avoid the conscription acts. Though noncombatant bureaux were certainly well manned, they continued to be ineffective in collecting both exempts and deserters. In the North Carolina mountains, deserters established communities.

The coming and going of the unwilling conscripts, as well as the (sometimes profitable) safety of the exempts, tended to undermine some of Lee's most stouthearted veterans. The men most affected were those sickened or wasted by malnutrition and those drawn to their homes by piteous appeals from their family. Wives and mothers, starving and frightened on farms isolated in the midst of desolate fields, wrote letters begging the soldiers to come home to help them. Lee vainly used his fading strength in composing letters in which he suggested remedies and warned the authorities of the consequences of failure to provide soldiers with a subsistence diet, shoes and warm clothes for the coming winter. Nothing depressed Lee more than his inability to bring any changes in Northrop's bureaucratic Commissary Department. Lee used Imboden's cavalry west of the Blue Ridge entirely for rounding up beeves.

Though the morale was high among the soldiers as a whole, Lee was beginning to experience difficulties in providing the men with the quality of officers who had led them during the past year. The drain of the shallow pool of general officer material forced Lee to replace seasoned brigadiers with men of bare adequacy. His regiments began to suffer from the lack of uniformity in the ability of colonels, who fell like flies in leading their troops in battle. Yet, Lee alone seemed to realize that the Army of Northern Virginia was past its peak.

Then in late August, Lee was called to Richmond for another conference on the use of troops from his army in other sectors. When Lee passed through the streets on his way from the Virginia Central depot, the gloom of midsummer had lifted from the people. The warm weather was pleasant rather than hot, and the faces on the streets had lost the pinched look of winter. Though few except strangers looked prosperous, the men and women appeared reasonably cheerful considering their evident poverty: at least, they did not give the general impression of seeming downcast.

In the President's office it was different. With all the optimism of early spring gone, Davis grimly presented Lee with the conditions in what he called "this trying hour."

For Lee it was, in a way, like his old days as military adviser. Davis, gaunt and pale, mentioned threats from one end of the Confederacy to the other. Lee, who a war clerk said "looked well" after his month's rest, conscientiously discussed all the points on which his advice would not be followed. Charleston was under siege, useless as a port, and Beauregard was in what had become a chronic state of alarm. From Wilmington, the last open port to connect the nation with the rest of the world, Whiting wrote, "I see danger not far off." But obviously the key point for the continuing life of the Confederacy was Chattanooga.

On the border of east Tennessee and north Georgia, Chattanooga was literally the "gateway" to Atlanta and the interior of the eastern Confederacy. By the stupidity of the Federal high command in dispersing Grant's victorious army after Vicksburg, the Confederates west of the Alleghenies had to contend only with the one army of Rosecrans approaching Chattanooga. With Western Department commander Joe Johnston removing himself from this critical point, the defensive force was commanded by Braxton Bragg, then the most hated and least respected general in the Confederacy. As in the spring, the only solution that occurred to the President was to shift troops from Lee's army to support Bragg.

Longstreet was anxious to take his corps to the West to open an offensive there, leaving Lee to shift to the defensive. In fact, while Lee was still in Richmond, Longstreet wrote him suggesting that, taking only the brigades then detached from the army, he put himself "in General Bragg's place." Bragg could take over Longstreet's corps. Lee did not recommend Longstreet for army command.

With little confidence in the results of an offensive by Bragg's army, Lee agreed to send Longstreet with Hood's and McLaws's divisions and most of the First Corps artillery. In writing he said, "Should General Longstreet reach General Bragg in time to aid him in winning a victory, and return to this army, it will be well, but should he be detained there without being able to do any good, it will result in evil."

For Charleston and Wilmington, despite Lee's assurances, two brigades were sent to Charleston. This was a game of musical chairs which returned to Longstreet's corps units then detached in exchange for units from Longstreet's divisions. With Jenkins's large brigade, which had been withheld from Gettysburg, sent to Longstreet, Pickett's division was reduced to Montgomery Corse's unused brigade and the three leaderless, decimated brigades of the charge. Lee earnestly urged that Pickett's division be kept intact for recruitment, as "it will be more efficient, united." Davis dispersed these four brigades in North Carolina.

Lee returned to Orange Court House on September 7 to see his First Corps off the next day. Within two weeks Lee received the news that confirmed his fears over a Western invasion with Bragg's army. Rosecrans had grown lax with overconfidence, and Bragg caught the divided Federal Army south of Chattanooga. With a powerful assist from Longstreet, Bragg's army defeated Rosecrans at Chickamauga on September 19-20. But the neurotic Bragg made no pursuit and permitted Rosecrans to retire safely back into Chattanooga. Bragg's discontented general officers sent Davis a resolution declaring their lack of confidence in the inept commander. Longstreet lost all his aspirations for personal glory in the West and wrote War Secretary Seddon for Lee. "We need some such great mind as General Lee's."

Typically of Davis when one of his favorites was attacked, he supported Bragg and dispersed the complaining generals, including Harvey Hill and Longstreet. Before Longstreet left Virginia, Knoxville had been occupied by the Federals, severing Virginia's railroad connections with Tennessee. Instead of returning Longstreet to Lee, Davis dispatched him to what became a long, futile siege of Knoxville. This left Lee for the fall campaign with an army of about forty-five thousand of all arms — barely more than half the size at the Seven Days.

In September, Lee fell ill again, with symptoms of angina pectoris. The attack was not as severe as the one in the spring and was diagnosed as rheumatic pains. Except for a passing reference to his continuing "rheumatic pains" in a letter to Agnes, Lee wrote nothing of his illness to his family. Mrs. Lee had gone from the Springs with Mary and Agnes to a safe place in the country near Lynchburg, where "paying guests" were accommodated. In October Lee wrote Mary there that, in answer to her letter, it would be "impracticable" for him to obtain supplies from the commissary as she suggested. As far as is known, Mary was the only member of Lee's immediate family who ever asked for any special favors.

Lee was recovering in a camp near Orange when he learned that two corps from Meade had been sent off to Rosecrans. With such army as he had, his instinct was to get off the defensive and take advantage of this weakening of the enemy. Though the scope of his accomplishment would necessarily be limited, he hoped at least to maneuver the Federals out of Culpeper, a strategic point from which Meade could strike in several directions. Fundamentally, he would again "disrupt the enemy's arrangements" and not wait on the enemy's time and place of selection.

5

Lee's circuitous movement around Meade's flank toward Washington, to draw Meade after him, was like an artist using his professional techniques when his powers were at a low ebb. Meade, his own army considerably reduced, played cautiously against the open maneuvers of an army whose hard striking powers he respected. By October 14, the Federal Army had retired gradually to the old stomping grounds at Centreville without giving Lee a single opening. There, his rear guard was exposed in withdrawing from Bristoe Station, and Lee ordered A. P. Hill to attack.

Betrayed by his impetuosity, Hill went in too fast. Heth's division suffered sharp casualties, and before a second assault could be formed, the enemy escaped from the field. Lee, giving a melancholy look at the dead, suppressed any reproaches at the subordinate whose guilt had been over-eagerness. Powell Hill personally endeared himself to the commanding general by a forthright admission of his mistake. "I attacked too impulsively," he said, and offered no excuses.

At that, for the third time Lee had the invading force on the defensive backed up at Washington. Had he possessed the men and the animals, and had they been physically fit, he would have crossed the Potomac again. But he no longer held that desperate choice. With subsistence failing to come up from Richmond, it brought gloom even to look at the war-made barrens where families for generations had lived in dignity and grace. For the first time Lee voluntarily took a backward step. He withdrew his army to the Rappahannock country, handy to the dubious supply lines by way of the Virginia Central. He also showed the grim stage the defense had entered by destroying the Orange and Alexandria Railroad as he retired.

Back in camp, he revealed to his wife that the wretched condition of the army reduced his moves to defensiveness. "General Meade I believe is repairing the railroad [Orange and Alexandria] and I presume will come on again. If I could only get some shoes and clothes for the army, I would save him the trouble." Though Lee continued to be troubled by what he called "rhuematic pains," he was relieved that his wife had returned to Richmond with her physical suffering less acute after her stay in the country. She sent him some flannel drawers and felt encouraged to attempt to make him a jacket.

Ceaselessly seeking ideas that might help the flow of supplies and relieve the burdens on the creaking railroads — often repaired from the enemy's raiding parties — Lee sent Seddon the sound suggestion of removing Federal prisoners from Richmond into the interior. The city's population had doubled during the war. With everyone suffering privations from the lack of distribution of foods, Lee pointed out that the prisons "increase largely the amount of supplies to be transported to the city." Lee wrote at a time when the Federal authorities were growing reluctant to continue the prisoner exchange, since the Confederacy was favored in the return of prisoners by their ratio to men under arms. Ten thousand returned soldiers meant incomparably more to an army of fifty thousand than to a nation with hundreds of thousands in the field. His suggestion was, of course, ignored.

Meade's army, with its great engineering corps, was not materially slowed by the necessity of rebuilding a railroad. By early November the Army of the Potomac was back at the Rappahannock. Lee withdrew behind the upper Rapidan in the region of Orange Court House and awaited developments. On November 26, Meade threw his army across the Rapidan at the Ely and Germanna fords, into the area of the Battle of Chancellorsville. Jeb Stuart, back in form, reported the movements promptly. Believing Meade was trying to pass his front on the way to Richmond, Lee moved out his two corps to attack the Federals in flank.

Meade, expecting Lee's army to be strung out along the upper Rapidan fords, turned west toward Lee. As it suited Lee even better for his smaller force to be attacked, on November 28 his men formed lines and dug in along Mine Run, a little creek that flowed south from the Rapidan. Since the field works his troops had thrown up at Chancellorsville, the soldiers had become adept at building earthen lines like low trenches — mobile forts.

On the next day Meade's army deployed for assault, and the powerful guns opened. Then Meade, perhaps remembering Lee's attack on his fixed position at Gettysburg, and aware of the tremendous firepower brought by Lee's soldiers, could not bring himself to commit his men against the Confederate works in that tangled, obscured countryside.

The weather turned bitterly cold while the armies faced one another for three days. Seeing the enemy was not going to attack, Lee's native aggressiveness sought ways of getting advantageously at Meade. Keeping Stuart's cavalry restlessly probing through the woods, he was rewarded by the information that Meade's flank was in the air and a turning movement possible. While Lee was carefully planning the details of a flanking movement, Meade also discovered that his flank was vulnerable. On December 2, the day Lee was to deliver his attack, Meade had vanished.

Lee immediately hurried his troops forward in pursuit. Soon he realized that Meade had safely recrossed the Rapidan and he could not conceal his disappointment. John Esten Cooke recorded that Lee, "with an air of deep melancholy," sent a message to Stuart that he was recalling his infantry to spare them useless exertion. Meade said it was so cold that sentinels froze to death at their posts. Lee's returning foot soldiers were warmed by spectacular blazes that flared up in the woods, started by the Federals' abandoned campfires. In spots "necklaces" of flames ran up the vines on tall trees, burning like torches against the winter sky.

Lee's staff saw that he continued to be agitated for a couple of days. Colonel Venable remembered his saying, "I am too old to command this army. We should never have permitted those people to get away."

The non-battle of Mine Run brought to its anticlimactic end the whole unprofitable fall campaign. Meade returned to Culpeper, which became practically a Federal advance base in Virginia, and Lee returned to his headquarters in a tent near Orange. It was often remarked that his soldiers noticed that he never took sumptuous headquarters in a house and their awareness of his sharing their privations was another element that endeared him to the men. With all fighting behind, the men started building crude huts for the winter, as the government could provide no tents for its soldiers.

However, for Lee 1863 had not done its worst.

6

Before Longstreet went west in early September, Davis had suggested that Lee take command of Bragg's army. Lee, not refusing, clearly showed his disinclination. On November 23-25 Bragg's demoralized army was driven from the field in the battles of Lookout Mountain and Missionary Ridge, and, as the men themselves had jeered at him in leaving the field, Bragg resigned his command on November 30. Lee, acting in his unofficial capacity as military adviser, wrote Davis urging the appointment of Beauregard. The command of the Charleston defenses did not need a full general, and Beauregard was free to assume command of the army. Davis replied with a telegram asking Lee if he could go to Dalton, in north Georgia, where the leaderless army had retreated.

This suggestion from Davis was stronger and, after Lee had diplomatically evaded the question, Davis asked him to come to Richmond. On December 9, when Lee once again took a jolting ride over the often-repaired Virginia Central, he expected to be ordered to Georgia.

After twelve days of conferences, Davis decided not to go against Lee's manifest wishes and his practical objections to his separation from the Army of Northern Virginia. Foremost among the objections was the fact that no general then with the army was capable of assuming command.

Lee did not mention Powell Hill. The formerly great division commander was temperamentally unsuited to higher command and was straining beyond his capacities at corps command. Of Ewell, Lee only said he was too feeble. Actually, the army's former "character" was suffering from some emotional disturbance, which Lee later described as disorder to his "nervous system."

While Ewell had been adjusting to his wooden leg, his childhood sweetheart and lifelong friend, "the Widow Brown" (as Ewell always referred to her), married him, her son said, out of pity. In camp along the Rapidan, the Widow Brown set up an establishment in an abandoned house which Ewell's disgusted staff officers called "petticoat headquarters." Jackson's old lieutenant, who needed a strong hand to guide him, had found it in his new wife, and it was saddening to see the dominance of the Widow Brown unsettling the simple-natured, good-hearted soldier.

What should have been obvious without Lee's objections was that he and the army were one and indivisible. The Army of Northern Virginia in the records, to the soldiers it was "Lee's army" and to themselves the men were "Lee's men." The consideration of his going to a strange army in an unfamiliar terrain, while a new commander took over the force he had personally forged in the crucible of shared campaigns, indicated the desperation in the thinking of the administration within its fixed policies and rigid departmentalization.

There was another personal reason of Lee's, which may or may not have influenced the President. Lee stressed that he did not feel physically capable of going to a new command where he might not receive "cordial cooperation." From the mentions of "infirmities" in his letters, the once powerful man, proud of his endurance, was obviously oppressed by his failing energies and the crippling pain that had persisted during the fall.

Davis, in respecting Lee's reluctance to leave his own army, refused to follow the advice of appointing Beauregard. He was too deep in the President's black book. Instead, Davis selected Joe Johnston, even though his ancient enemy had remained completely supine during the fall of Vicksburg. After various other matters had been discussed, Lee was free to return to his army on December 21.

It was hard for him to leave Richmond that close to Christmas. For the first time since leaving Arlington, Mrs. Lee and her daughters had a home of their own. It was a modest enough small wooden house they rented in midtown Richmond, but Lee experienced the pleasure and comfort of staying with his wife and children under their own roof. Charlotte, whose illness was growing worse, was staying in a house not too far away. But the man to whom duty was the foundation of his moral structure was compelled to deny himslf the luxury of special privilege. On Christmas Day he was back in the bleak camp with his men, writing his wife of his sadness at learning that Charlotte seemed to be nearing the end.

Referring to the closeness between Charlotte and Rooney, he said, "They seemed so united that I loved them as one person."

The next day Custis wired his father that she was dead. Rooney was then in prison on Johnson's Island, near Chicago, and it anguished Lee to think of the news reaching his son "in the bars of his prison." Lee wrote that he would not try to get away for the funeral, but would "bear my sorrow in silence alone. May God have mercy upon us all and have you in His holy keeping."

The unquestioning totality of his religious faith sustained Lee in the midst of the miseries that came to his family and that came, during the bitter winter, to the Confederate people. The sufferings of the civilians in the regions in which Meade had operated so moved Lee that he mentioned the ravages in his battle report. "Houses were torn down or rendered uninhabitable, furniture and farm implements broken or destroyed, and many families, most of them in humble circumstances, stripped of all they possessed and left without shelter and without food. I have never witnessed on any previous occasion such entire disregard of the usages of civilized warfare and the dictates of humanity."

Two years before in western Virginia, when the enemy had threatened to lay waste the country, Lee had written, "The sentiment in America will not tolerate it." Now, he was witnessing the beginning of the logical extension of resolution by war.

That was the winter when Sherman put his men on, what he called, the "pleasant excursion" of systematically destroying the town of Meridian, Mississippi. "I have no hesitation in pronouncing the work as well done. Meridian . . . no longer exists." That was the winter when a brigade of Negro soldiers under Brigadier General Edward Augustus Wild was sent into the region of northeastern North Carolina ostensibly "to clear the country of slaves and procure recruits for his brigade." Actually this was the first armed operation directed at the civilian population.

In Wild's report on introducing "a more rigorous style of warfare," he recorded that his colored troops "burned their houses and barns, ate up their livestock, and took hostages from the family . . . three women and one old man. Hanged one guerrilla . . ." The "guerrilla" was Private David Bright, of the 62nd Georgia Cavalry, passing through the region at the time. Twenty other prisoners were rounded up, who "had the benefit of a drumhead courtmartial." Showing callous indifference to the future relations of the white and black races, General Benjamin F. ("Beast") Butler, commanding the Norfolk district, threatened the people with further "visitations from the colored troops" if they did not expel from their region the bands of semi-regulars who operated near their homes as "Partisan Rangers."

In late February a joint cavalry raid — led by Colonel Ulric Dahlgren and General Judson Kilpatrick — struck at Richmond with the purpose of freeing the Union prisoners. Kilpatrick's column was hit by a small force of Wade Hampton's cavalry and veered off. Dahlgren's column reached the western outskirts of the city where, in the dusk, it ran into the light fire of a boys' battalion of Local Defense Troops. Hearing nothing from Kilpatrick, Dahlgren turned north, his troopers slowed down by silver and other loot from houses along the march. Companies of militia caught the raiders, killing Dahlgren and dispersing his force. Papers were purportedly found on Dahlgren's body which revealed his intention of killing Davis and his Cabinet and burning the city.

Lee wrote Meade asking if he countenanced such methods of warfare. Meade repudiated the purposes in the papers allegedly found on Dahlgren. In fact, he had not been in favor of the raid: that was one of Lincoln's ideas.

Nothing done by the enemy in the new phase of war aroused retaliatory impulses in Lee. Though deeply outraged, he was never tempted to violate his code of behavior. He was fighting, as he recognized, for the survival of his civilization. Even more fundamental to him was the survival of the personal concepts of honor, and honorableness, that had led him to identify with the Confederacy's cause.

Unquestionably the spiritual force which sustained Lee's convictions was a factor in sustaining the morale of his army during the long winter that stretched to April, 1864. To his men Lee personified their cause, and the patriarchal presence of "Uncle Robert" — a perfected ideal of their society — provided a source of inner strength. Only morale held together the shivering men who never got enough to eat and who almost daily at morning roll call were undermined by the absence of one or another former comrade who had gone over to the enemy for food.

During the winter Lee tried the expedient of granting furloughs to sixteen of every hundred men at a time, so there would be fewer to feed and some might find nourishment at home. This, as he wrote Seddon in January, only alleviated the plight to some extent. "Unless there is a change, I fear the army cannot be kept together." No change was made. Nobody listened to him.

Belatedly in February, Congress did pass a third conscription act, extending the age range from seventeen to fifty, and at least writing into the law a narrower restriction of exempted classes. The effects of this last-ditch measure were vitiated by the ways in which it was applied. Those under eighteen and over forty-five were, by another new act, placed in newly created reserve units restricted to defense of their states. Though listed on Confederate rosters, they were essentially state troops. The units were formed regionally, in groups of counties, and usually remained in their localities. Many of these reserves could have served usefully in supporting services, releasing able-bodied men for the armies.

The conscripts from thirty-six to forty-five were unwisely sent directly into veteran regiments as replacements for losses. The majority of these men, physically and/or mentally unfit for the abrupt transition into the lines, would have contributed more in fixed garrisons, from which veteran units could be returned to the army. Lee could not make Davis understand that veteran units were urgently needed for more reasons than their numbers. Thus, the unwilling conscripts were hustled from home life into the rough camps of hard-bitten veterans who, long inured to war, had developed a bawdy, earthy humor at the privations and dangers that shocked the newcomers. Most of these tarried only briefly. Against the insignificant permanent increase the new act brought to the army, the next month Lincoln simply called for seven hundred thousand men.

When April came, the fresh green of the trees and the wildflowers appearing along the roadsides did not bring for Lee the renascence of spring. The open weather brought another campaign against his capital, this one mightier than any before.

## CHAPTER XVII

## "Every Advance . . . Has Been Repulsed"

IN 1864 Lee's new opponent was a younger man, forty-two-year-old Ulysses S. Grant. Lee had never known "Sam" Grant. At West Point he had been a class behind Longstreet, with whom he formed a lasting friendship. Though his career at the Academy had been quite undistinguished, Grant had won the admiration of many Southerners with his fine horsemanship. Several years after the Mexican War, he dropped out of the Regular Army and had been living in purposeless torpor when the war came. Completely disinterested in the political aspects, Grant entered the service with volunteers and advanced rapidly on a habit of military successes in the West.

Lee knew almost nothing about this new man as a soldier. In the West Grant's chief characteristics as a general, pugnacity and stubbornness, had invariably been favored by divided and/or incompetent Confederate commands. When he was brought by Lincoln to Virginia, he was appointed general-in-chief of all the armies and given an authority far beyond that which any other general on either side had ever enjoyed. When Grant came to assume personal charge of the Army of the Potomac, all Federal purposes had been reduced to winning an outright war of conquest before the November elections. Lincoln abandoned his divided political-military purposes and gave the job of subjugation to Grant as a professional. With no questions asked, he became the instrument of the evolved policy of unlimited war.

Lincoln had to win before the fall elections because a continuing armed stalemate would, Lincoln conceded, give a Democrat a good chance of being elected on a peace program. Despite the crusade element injected by the Emancipation Proclamation, a war weariness spread across all classes in the North. Soldiers' disillusioned letters revealed that, far from a crusade, the invasion offered opportunities for self-aggrandizement, for plunder and speculation, and for the gross tyrannies of men suddenly placed in despotic power. Propertied families in the East, the South's natural allies, began to think it better to let the Southern states have their freedom than to destroy their civilization. Antagonism to Negroes was shown in numerous episodes in the North.

Politically the Democrats had no stake in the war and the will to conquest was sustained in the Republican Party. For the general population to return the Republicans to office, the war would have to be well on its way to being finished by fall. Toward this end, the Lincoln administration prepared a broad-fronted offensive of many minor strikes growing around two major advances to open simultaneously in Virginia and Georgia.

Grant's direction of a wide offensive in Virginia did not establish him against Lee in a classic duel. While Grant's unlimited powers permitted him to shift troops about as he willed, Lee's authority had been constantly narrowed until it was restricted to his own army. Even there he did not enjoy complete control of his troops. Most of all he held no control over the interrelating movements between Virginia and the North Carolina coast, including the railroads which supplied Richmond and transported troops. This single area of operation was divided into different departments, under different commanders, all subject to the President. In this way Grant's true antagonist was Jefferson Davis. This was a switch from the 1862-1863 period when Lee played on the fears and obsessions of Abraham Lincoln.

2

Davis's steady encroachments into Lee's area of authority after Sharpsburg made a serious extension during the Gettysburg campaign, when the area south of the James River was removed from Lee's command. While Lee had been worried about assembling his army for the invasion, D. H. Hill was in charge of this Department of North Carolina under Lee's general supervision. Hill proved to be so uncooperative that Lee irritably wrote Davis that the command lines should be straightened with Hill or he would rather not have responsibility for the department. In one of Davis's most fateful decisions in favor of bureaucracy, he took Lee at his word and erected a separate department beginning at the James River — or, across the river from Richmond. Even Drewry's Bluff, the river fort protecting the city, was placed in a department outside the authority of the field general defending the capital.

As it affected Lee the departmentalization of the military operations was more complicated, and more absurd, than that. In late April Lee deduced from the numbers of Federal soldiers transferred from the Atlantic Coast that Grant was forming a secondary army at Fort Monroe, to strike at the vulnerable southside of the James. This secondary army under Butler could either sever Richmond's railroad connections with the South or act as a pincer in conjunction with Grant against Richmond, or both. Trying to convince Davis of the danger, Lee urged him to concentrate troops from the Coastal garrisons, under Beauregard, south of the James. Instead, Davis formed yet another new department of which Beauregard became titular commander.

Within this grand department, George Pickett became commander of a sub-department under Beauregard. Neither Beauregard nor Pickett had any troops. Two of Pickett's scattered brigades were on the river fort east of Richmond but, as these troops were north of the James, outside his department. Two others were in North Carolina where Robert Hoke, semi-independent, was conducting a siege against the Federals in the inland coastal city of New Bern. Pickett himself, newly wed to a young bride, was — with his staff and one guard regiment — enjoying life in the pleasing small city of Petersburg. Beauregard moved from Charleston and established headquarters at Weldon, North Carolina, where he occupied himself defining the areas of his authority.

Dispersal and departmentalization were equally harmful in the West. Lee presumed to write the President advice which, if followed, would simplify the tasks of Joe Johnston. Though Johnston was jealous of Lee, and wrote spitefully of him in letters to friends, Lee retained some of the affection from the friendship of their early years and respected him as a soldier. In any event, he wanted any Confederate general to be successful in defending Atlanta against Sherman, who had already displayed a certain glee in systematized destruction. But the troops for Johnston's command were slow to assemble, the army was woefully deficient in basic needs, especially transportation, and, in defending Atlanta, his authority stopped short at the adjoining Department of Alabama. There another commander had his own fish to fry.

Within this constricting pattern, things took a fantastic turn. During the spring Davis was seized with an impulse to take the offensive in the West, and defense-minded Johnston was ordered to open an offensive campaign against Sherman. At a stage of the war when all troops were beginning to dig field works, the defense held a pronounced advantage. Though Civil War generals had been slow to progress beyond the lessons instilled from the Napoleonic era, by 1864 all adapted tactics to the new rifle and, behind works, experienced riflemen were almost certain to defeat an attacking enemy of equal size. Since Johnston's illy equipped army was little more than half the size of Sherman's confident veterans, an offensive would constitute mass suicide.

In the chronic misunderstanding between Davis and Johnston, the general did not give the President this fundamental reason for not mounting an offensive. He listed the lacks, all of which were valid, that had to be met before he could attack. Among the deficiencies was manpower, and

Johnston asked for troops from Coastal garrisons. By then the strains of office were driving Davis into a private world of his charts. He advised Johnston he could have reinforcements from the garrisons *after* he mounted the offensive.

Lee gave Johnston's cause such support as he could without offending the President. However, he was pressed to the limits of his persuasiveness to hold his own army together and try to reassemble its scattered units. In Davis's sudden offensive bug, he had considered detaching Longstreet permanently from Lee's army to permit his undertaking an offensive of his own. As it was, Pickett's division was still detached and two other brigades were in North Carolina.

The tightening control of Davis's bureaucratic methods not only threatened Lee and Johnston with insufficient troops to meet the enemy's major thrusts, it largely nullified the advantages to the Confederacy of having its defense reduced to two major fronts. As Richmond provided a buffer to the South Atlantic states from the north, the railroad center of Atlanta was a citadel to the west. Within the boundary of the line from Richmond to Atlanta, and on to Mobile on the Gulf, were the war plants that provided the armies with cannon and small arms, cartridges and powder, and attempted to provide clothing and shoes. Most of the railroads that gave the defenders the advantage of interior lines were operating. This potential advantage was meaningless in Davis's rigid structure. He responded like an exposed nerve to every peripheral thrust, and remained deaf to Lee's assurances that a concentration to defeat the enemy's major moves would cause the enemy to contract his broader operations.

### 3

While's Lee's anxieties about the total front and reassembling his own army made a drain on his energies, the rapidly aging man of fifty-seven managed to apply himself without distraction to the problems of the new enemy in his front. Grant would field a total of 140,000 men of all arms —a professional army built through bitter campaigns on the sound structure of McClellan's organization. Three infantry corps numbered 75,000 plus Burnside's corps of 20,000. Under Sheridan, a new aggressive cavalry leader brought in by Grant, the seasoned mounted army would number 12,500 troopers. In the Army of the Potomac (technically still Meade's) thousands served in the supporting branches, and in special details were soldiers whose numbers equaled a Confederate corps.

Against this force, Lee had along the Rapidan about 35,000 infantry, in Ewell's and A. P. Hill's corps, and nearby were 10,000 newly returned from Tennessee under Longstreet. Longstreet's futile campaign in the winter mountains had been severe on his men and they were in hard case on their return to Virginia. When Lee went to review them, the soldiers worked all hours trying to make a presentable appearance in their tatters. Then, when they saw the familiar figure on his gray horse, the men burst out crying. Tears shone in Lee's eyes as he silently greeted his veterans.

Along with this something over 45,000 infantry, there were nearly 5000 artillerymen and Stuart fielded 8400 cavalrymen — some newly recruited sixteen-year-olds and some middle-aged farmers whose places had been overrun. Not counting the small numbers in the supporting services or the colored cooks, Lee would field less than 60,000 against approximately 120,000 combat troops. When he managed the return of Pickett's division and the other two brigades, his numbers would run to about 67,000. However, when Grant was ready to deliver his "On to Richmond" offensive, these detached troops would not be with Lee for the opening of the campaign. To get Davis even to promise to send on his veteran units, he had to threaten to abandon the Rappahannock line and withdraw toward Richmond.

Even with what Lee had, only 35,000 infantry until Longstreet reached the army, it was not in his nature to plan defensively. Against Grant, it would be more important than ever before to disrupt the enemy's prearrangements, as Grant was trying to induce dispersals by a three-pronged offensive. In addition to the secondary force under Butler, which Lee feared would be directed at the southside of the James, a third force under Franz Sigel was poised to strike up the Shenandoah Valley. If Lee could drive Grant back on the major front, he had no worries about the other thrusts. Since his numbers were too low and the men's physical condition too feeble for him to consider an offensive of his own, he was forced to wait on Grant's move. But, when Grant moved, Lee planned to hit him and not wait to be attacked.

To meet this new man, Lee would change his habits of command. After Gettysburg, he could not again follow his inclination of planning a battle and trusting the tactical execution to the initiative of subordinates. Hagridden Ewell was irresolute and Powell Hill too impetuous. Hill seemed to have gone back physically too: his cheeks were sunken under the high-growing beard and his intense eyes, unless he was animated, showed a melancholy cast. During the spring his wife had another daughter and, at the new mansion in Orange Court House where the Hills spent the winter, Lee acted as godfather at her christening.

Longstreet had returned somewhat chastened from his ill-fated independent command. His personal record with subordinates was horrible. He hounded out of the army Dr. Jerome Robertson, who had succeeded to command of Hood's old Texas Brigade. He preferred so many charges against Lafayette McLaws that McLaws demanded a court of inquiry, which exonerated him of everything except a minor count. Significantly

Longstreet's most serious charge against McLaws was the very attitude on which he himself built his own case at Gettysburg — lack of faith in the superior's orders. He also carried on a feud with Evander McIver Law, in which his attempts to keep Law under arrest were manifestly so personal that the War Department refused further to entertain his charges and commanded him to restore Law to his brigade.

Longstreet got in the bad graces of the War Department with all his troublemaking. His vaporous schemes for an offensive, with which he could retain his independent command, were dismissed. Discovering he had no friends in Richmond, Longstreet seemed relieved to return to his "war horse" role.

He brought back his two divisions with new commanders. For the good of harmony Lee felt that McLaws should serve elsewhere. His division was temporarily assigned to Joe Kershaw, only the second nonprofessional soldier to be given division command. Rodes, the first, had been trained at V.M.I.; Kershaw, a resolute-looking man of forty-two, clean-shaven except for a blond, droopy mustache, had been a lawyer and a member of the South Carolina legislature. Having learned the lessons of command in two years as a consistently able brigadier, he brought a high enthusiasm to his assignment. But he was untried.

Hood, who had commanded the other division, had been wounded at Chickamauga, and he returned to duty with a wooden leg as a lieutenant general and administration favorite in Joe Johnston's army. Hood was succeeded, over Longstreet's bitter protests, by Charles Field. Formerly a lieutenant in Lee's 2nd Cavalry, Field had been long absent from Hill's old Light Division with a leg amputation. Despite the wooden leg, the powerfully built Kentuckian made a formidable appearance and suffered none of the disturbances that afflicted Dick Ewell. As a soldier, when he was wounded out of the Light Division, Charlie Field had been the hardest of any brigadier to replace. However, in taking over Hood's division Field had the handicap, along with his superior officer's opposition, of unfamiliarity with the troops to which the war office had assigned him.

Hill's corps also had a new division commander in plain, sturdy Cadmus Wilcox, who succeeded Pender. In Wilcox's four brigades from the old Light Division, not one was led by its original commander and not one of the new brigadiers was a professional soldier.

With this command personnel, Lee had to tailor his plans to fit the material. First, to gain the advantage his inferior numbers needed against Grant, Lee had to deduce in advance where Grant would strike. Trying to put himself in the mind of Grant, whom he knew to be a nonmaneuvering direct hitter, he eliminated the course to the east, by way of Fredericksburg. That way the Rappahannock would have to be crossed twice and a long lateral movement made before Grant could turn south at Fredericksburg. Then Lee eliminated the movement west, beyond Orange. Though the open country was favorable for maneuver and the Virginia Central could be threatened, Grant would swerve too far from the navy's supply services on the tidal rivers. That left only the forbidding country of the Wilderness, through which Grant could move in a direct line toward Richmond.

By May 3 Lee was convinced by reports that the mighty Federal army was preparing to move. With several of his generals he rode up the steep slope of Clark Mountain, a high mound rising near Orange Court House. From there, two years before, he had watched the wagons of Pope's army disappear northward. Now, gazing through his field glasses, he saw the movements in the tented city which unmistakably indicated preparations for advance against him. Evidently he had not discussed his theory that Grant would strike directly south through the Wilderness.

The other generals, dismounted, gathered around Lee on the grassy knoll. Powell Hill was, as a staff officer remembered him, "simple and cordial," wearing his plain shell jacket and creased black hat. Dick Ewell was "pale and haggard," but smiling gently. Since his marriage to the Widow Brown, he seldom gave his bravura performances of rages, and the color of personality was subdued. When away from his wife, Ewell came under the dominance of Jubal Early. Old Jube, one gray-bearded jaw swollen by the cud of tobacco he was chewing, surveyed the enemy camp with his dark, saturnine gaze. Burly Longstreet, physically unchanged by the hard winter's campaign, for once offered no advice.

Lee himself outwardly appeared to have retained his controlled vigor. Allowing for the whitening of hair and beard, the new lines of care in his florid face, he looked no different to his companions than when he had stood on Clark Mountain two years before. Brigadier General John B. Gordon wrote that the more you gaze upon him, the more his "grandeur grew upon you" filling "your spirit with a full satisfaction." With all his majestic composure, "he was genial as the sunlight of this beautiful day."

Suddenly Lee pointed a finger of his gauntleted hand. Grant would advance by way of the Ely and Germanna fords, he said. Hooker had entered the fifteen square miles of the Wilderness that way and turned east toward Lee; Meade had crossed the Rapidan there and turned west toward Lee. Lee expected Grant to advance straight ahead with the purpose of overrunning Lee's army wherever it was encountered. The Federal commander would use the methods that had worked in the West, believing that Lee had been winning only because he had not fought Grant. The staff officers with Meade, noting the condescension of the men with Grant, predicted that "Grant would find Lee and the Army of Northern Virginia a different proposition from Bragg." Lee intended to prove them right.

He planned to march his three corps westward along parallel roads to catch Grant's columns while strung out in the constricting roads of the Wilderness. Yet, while Lee was convinced that Grant would give him this opportunity, he could not commit his troops until Grant's army was actually in motion. Until Grant moved, Ewell and Hill would remain spread to the west of the area of Grant's expected crossing, with Hill about twenty-five miles away at the base at Orange Court House. Longstreet was southwest of Hill at Gordonsville. Lee took none of these generals into his confidence, as he swung up on Traveler and rode back down Clark Mountain.

Riding to his camp, Lee assumed alone the inherent risk in planning to catch Grant in flank. If Grant moved a striking force rapidly through the Wilderness, he would cross Lee's front and place the Federal army between Lee and Richmond. Lee took the risk on the appraisal he had made of Grant. He believed that Grant, with confidence in overwhelming a Confederate army wherever met, would move his forces in a compact unit, the infantry not advancing until the sixty-five miles of wagon trains and the herds of cattle were across the Rapidan. Grant's heavily laden army was equipped to operate in a ravaged country and not to maneuver. On this judgment Lee determined on the gamble in order to seize the initiative and not wait for the attack of the conqueror from the West.

That night in his tent at Orange Lee prepared to break up his simple headquarters. A package to be sent to Richmond was made up of his winter boots, an embroidered collar and cuffs sent by some lady admirers, and flannel shirts his wife had made for him. Mrs. Lee, in her invalidism, had become a great knitter, and Lee had written her two nights before that he had distributed 392 pairs of her socks to the Stonewall Brigade, Jackson's original command. He had also asked her to have Custis send up his summer boots, "the long pair," and his blue pants of summer cloth "without stripes."

On that last night before going out to meet the new enemy leader, Lee wrote no letters to anyone. He had earlier written Custis his feeling about this campaign of decision: "If victorious, we have everything to live for. If defeated, there will be nothing left for us to live for."

In all his warnings to the President and the war offices, Lee had never written the simple words "if defeated" — meaning the Confederacy. By the self-revealing letter to his son, Lee showed that he recognized 1864 as bringing the all or nothing campaign, and he was not sanguine.

4

There was always a strain of sadness in leaving an old camp. Men were forced to abandon the odd objects they had sentimentally acquired for their mud and log huts, and officers sent their personal belongings to the rear, as wagons were allotted only to general officers. Locks of hair and daguerreotypes were pressed in the backs of hunting-case watches or in small round lockets, sold to soldiers on both sides for articles of remembrance. Canteens were filled, blankets rolled, and into haversacks went rations of freshly cooked cornbread.

In the last-minute rush, many of the men received only half-cooked dough or raw meal. They were all cheerful enough, as they invariably were when marching toward the enemy, though the tone of the army was subtly changed from the preceding spring. In their resigned acceptance of the insufficiencies for waging war, the men reflected a resolute determination in place of their former casual assumption of ultimate victory.

Lee watched the ragged soldiers, whose brightness in the face of their hardships moved him to such sorrow. With his capacity for repose, he waited for them on his horse in the stillness of a statue. Around noon, May 4, the cheerfully talking men in Heth's and Wilcox's divisions formed their columns of fours on the plank-bedded road. Then Lee started his horse forward and the troops began their march away from Orange Court House to the cheers and waving of the ladies, children and old men who had been their winter neighbors.

Ewell's corps was already in motion on the parallel stone turnpike to the north. On another parallel road to the south, the Catharpin Road, Longstreet's two divisions would move out from Gordonsville. Longstreet, however, was a day's march farther from Grant's line of march than Hill and Ewell, and Lee would make contact from only two of the approaches. Also, as Dick Anderson's division would be left as rear guard until the wagons were well on their way, Lee had as immediately available for the contact barely thirty thousand infantry.

The approaches of the three roads toward and through the Wilderness were protected by Stuart's cavalry, the men on their worn mounts pressed by the aggressive tactics of Sheridan. The new Union cavalry chief, a former infantryman, worked with the purpose of defeating Stuart's horsemen in combat rather than in performing the orthodox functions of cavalry. Toward this end, Sheridan enjoyed a three-to-two superiority in numbers, incalculable superiority in the condition and reserves of horses, and the heavy firepower of a new seven-shot repeating carbine. As a result of Sheridan's pressing tactics, Stuart — while screening his own infantry and holding open the roads for their advance — was able to gain only general information of the Federal masses pouring across the two Rapidan fords and moving southward through the Wilderness.

The three corps of the Army of the Potomac — Hancock, Warren and

Sedgwick — had crossed the fords by the afternoon of the 4th. The soldiers carried three days of "full rations" in their haversacks, with three days of bread and "small rations" in their knapsacks. Behind the infantry came the "fighting" wagons, followed by the light spring wagons that carried the officers' personal luggage, all across the five pontoon bridges before the day was over. The heavy wagons would be twenty-four more hours in crossing, along with the herd of cattle which provided three days of "beef on the hoof" to each man. The puzzler for Lee, the crux of his gamble, was whether Grant's combat troops would move on through the Wilderness or wait for the heavy wagons.

After nightfall Stuart's reports indicated that Grant's infantry had halted in the tangled shadows of the Wilderness. Whether or not Grant would be there in the morning was the question troubling Lee when he went into bivouac just west of the Wilderness. Hill's van halted at a scattered cluster of farmhouses grandly named New Verdiersville and called by the soldiers "My Dearsville." In a clearing in the woods, a candle was lit in Lee's tent.

Before he could think of what Grant might be doing, messages of desperate alarm arrived from President Davis. Wires had been sent from Richmond to the telegraph office at Guiney's Station on the R.F.&P., and couriers had galloped across the dark countryside with the news. "Beast" Butler, the terror of civilians, was disembarking more than thirty thousand troops on the south side of the James River below Richmond. Between Butler and Richmond lay only the small garrison at the river fort of Drewry's Bluff; between Butler and Richmond's lifeline railroad to the south, at Petersburg, was the one regiment with George Pickett. Davis had not moved a single soldier from the Coastal garrisons to the area where Lee had urgently warned the Federals would strike.

With the enemy already at Richmond's back door, the President advised Lee of the dispositions he was then making to rush troops, piecemeal, to the threatened point. In these dispositions, Lee glumly perceived that Pickett's division and the other troops belonging to his army would be temporarily withheld at Richmond. This was necessary because Davis, completely removed from Lee's influence, was incapable of disarranging his charts in anticipation of the enemy's moves.

Nor could he distinguish between major and peripheral objectives. A full division formed in North Carolina under Robert Hoke, one of Lee's brigadiers, was being employed in a siege of New Bern while upwards of two hundred thousand Federal troops advanced in a multi-fronted offensive in Virginia. For Davis's telegrams also contained the news that enemy forces had, on the same day, opened offensives in the Shenandoah Valley and at the salt works in the southwestern corner of the state.

Lee forgot diplomacy. He came straight to the point in a letter to Davis, in which he gave the strongest of his countless admonitions on the principles of concentration.

"I fully appreciate the advantages of capturing New Bern, but they will not compensate us for a disaster in Va. or Georgia. Success in resisting the chief armies of the enemy will enable us more easily to recover the country now occupied by him, if indeed he does not voluntarily relinquish it. We are inferior in numbers, and as I have before stated to your Excellency, the absence of troops belonging to this Army weakens it by more than the mere number of men.

"Unless the force that it will be necessary to leave in North Carolina is able to reduce New Bern, I would recommend that the attempt be postponed, and the troops in N.C. belonging to this army be at once returned to it, and that Gen. Beauregard with all the force available for the purpose, be brought without delay to Richmond."

Having written Davis, Lee needed to call upon all of his cultivated self-mastery in order to clear his mind of the threatened disasters around him. Not only was he defending a city which might fall behind him while he engaged Grant. At this late hour, ten miles from collision with Grant's army, he was asked to assume direction of the action in the Valley. He knew nothing of those distant operations beyond the fact that the only Confederate force available was a scratch command of John Breckinridge, the bourbon-loving former Vice President of the United States. Though the militarily untrained Kentuckian brought to his command mostly a forceful presence, Lee wired Breckinridge to "take the general direction of affairs . . . for the present . . ."

With that, around midnight he prepared to go to bed, having successfully resisted the distractions of events beyond his control. In earlier preparing Davis, "he had done those things that he ought to have done," and in the darkness of the woods at Verdiersville he freed his mind for those tasks which God assigned to his talents.

When he arose before dawn the next morning Lee revealed the extent to which he cleared his thoughts of the possibility of Richmond falling behind him. At four o'clock Stuart sent the news that the Federals were still camped in the Wilderness, and by the relief Lee showed in front of his staff it was obvious his mind was occupied solely by Grant. While the night before he had hidden his apprehensions in silence, at breakfast he talked cheerfully and with relative freedom of his plans for suprising the enemy on his front.

Grant started his leisurely course southward through the Wilderness at five in the morning of May 5, expecting to find Lee — who had refused to defend the river crossing — on defense somewhere in his front. Warren's corps was moving along the north-south Brock Road (Jackson's passageway at Chancellorsville), with Hancock on a parallel road to the east. Sedgwick was waiting for marching room near the river. It was the course Lee would have himself designed for the enemy to follow.

In early light of a radiant May day Lee, ordering Hill's two divisions in motion, personally inspected the folding of the saddle blanket on Traveler and the tightness of the girth. Swinging into the saddle, Lee started the horse out at his fine pace of a fast walk.

Riding into the sun he rode beside Powell Hill, whose eyes were shaded by the floppy brim of his black hat. When the columns entered the rankly green entanglements of the Wilderness, with its somber memories of Stonewall Jackson, Stuart appeared at intervals out of the maze off their right. Jeb was turned out in his colorful finery, with an ostrich feather pinned in one curled-up side of his weather-stained hat. The grimmer days that had come upon his troopers had not affected his happy disposition ("Like the chief of a hunting party," one of his staff said). He reported that Sheridan's belligerent tactics were not piercing his screen off the flank of the marching columns.

Then from the left, from the interval between Powell Hill and Ewell, Major Campbell Brown of Ewell's staff appeared. Some of Lee's early morning buoyancy faded. Brown was the son of Ewell's dominating wife, and it was rumored that "The Widow Brown" had been finagling for him to get the chief of staff's job away from capable and popular young Sandie Pendleton. The sight of Campbell Brown seemed to remind Lee of the unhappy changes in the commander of the old Second Corps. Ewell's original orders — which, he said, were to his liking — simply called for him to march down the road until he struck the enemy. Lee amended that. He told Major Brown he "preferred not to bring on a general engagement before General Longstreet came up."

Such an order would never have been given Jackson. To Ewell it indicated that Lee trusted the soldiers to maintain themselves in a collision engagement, but he did not trust Old Baldhead's discretion. As it happened, the enemy seized the initiative and Dick Ewell, the ex-Border dragoon who reveled in simple combat, was drawn into the type of straight-on local action that suited his tastes and his talents. On the Plank Road, Lee heard the battle open around noon on the old stone Turnpike, hidden from him by two and three-quarters miles of the desolate jungle.

5

Ewell had observed the movement of Federal troops on the Brock Road and, on nearing this north-south passageway, started deploying the brigades of Rodes's lead division off both sides of the Turnpike. The men of J. M. Jones's brigade began to hack and claw their way to the right through the densest part of the thickets, unbroken even by a cowpath. The soldiers could see scarcely twenty yards in any direction. Before the lines were completely formed, Jones's regiments — containing a number of last-ditch conscripts — were caught in the wave of a full Federal division that came bursting out of the brush.

The Army of the Potomac was still theoretically commanded by Meade, under Grant's general orders, and this gnarly gentleman had initiated the movements in reaction to the presence of Ewell's troops on the Turnpike. When the gray columns had first been observed, Warren's V Corps had marched down the Brock Road to the Orange Plank Road, where the van turned west in the direction (unknown to the Federals) of A. P. Hill's approach. Meade ordered the three divisions of Warren's corps to contract along the Brock Road, to meet Ewell's advance. Believing Ewell represented no more than a delaying action to the Federal march, Meade told Grant of his intention to develop the Confederate strength. Grant immediately revealed his attitude of pugnacious self-confidence toward the fabled Lee. "If any opportunity presents itself for pitching into a part of Lee's army," he said, "do so without giving time for disposition."

Following those orders, Meade opened the assault with Griffin's division alone. Griffin advanced before the other two divisions of Warren's corps were in position on his left, or before the lead division of Sedgwick's division came up on his right — between the Turnpike and the river. Charles Griffin was a very tough customer and his seasoned troops rolled over Jones's brigade almost before the Confederates knew what hit them. Gentle Jones, a classmate of Grant's at West Point who had just won trust in his conquest of a bottle problem, was killed trying to rally his men.

As had happened to Jackson's assaulters at Chancellorsville, the momentum of Griffin's troops through the maze of matted vines made order difficult to sustain. As had not happened to Jackson's troops, supports were on hand to rain lead through the green thickets at the advancing troops. Rodes's other brigades had formed behind Jones. Furious Rodes was everywhere, his black horse flecked with foam.

Ewell came riding to the front on his flea-bitten horse, Rifle, and began piping commands in his high-pitched voice.

Following Rodes, the well closed-up columns of Jubal Early's division came hurrying forward. Ewell sent in Gordon's brigade to support Rodes's right flank stretching off through the woods. "The day depends on you, sir," he called shrilly.

At about the same time on the north side of the Turnpike, where the van of Sedgwick's corps had not made its way along the overgrown country lanes, "Allegheny" Johnson advanced the third of Ewell's divisions. A brigade of these hairy, ragged veterans of Jackson's old division came screaming out of the vines on Griffin's right flank. Griffin's repulsed attackers began to fall back. Their retirement began a concatenation of misadventures attributable almost entirely to the Wilderness.

As Griffin's men started backward, Wadsworth's division was groping its way forward to support Griffin's left. Instead of making contact with Griffin, Wadsworth's lead brigades encountered the brigades of Gordon and Junius Daniel. Blasted by close-up rifle fire spurting out of the green brush and turned about in the obscuring terrain before lines could be formed, the uncoordinated brigades of Wadsworth's division retired back onto the Brock Road.

As Wadsworth was retiring, Crawford's third division fumbled forward seeking Wadsworth's left. Crawford's lead brigade, lost in the mesh of vines, was enveloped by Gordon's brigade and horribly cut up before the units could disentangle themselves. The other brigades of Crawford's division could only fall back to the Brock Road. Because of the effects of the Wilderness, on which Lee had counted, seven Confederate brigades had thrown back a corps of 25,000 troops, while another Federal corps, in supporting distance, was unable to reach the field.

During the afternoon Warren's corps re-formed and Sedgwick's corps reached the field, between the Turnpike and the river. By then Ewell had his three divisions in position and well dug in. With the Federals' heavy guns nullified by the lack of open spaces for artillery batteries, the Wilderness gave every advantage to defending infantry, whose stationary lines were not exposed to the hazards of maintaining order while moving through the jungle.

As a combat soldier, Ewell had done all that anyone could ask. However, as a general, he had extended his capacities to their limits in maintaining his front in the local action. He divorced himself from the rest of the battle, though his right flank was widely separated from Hill on the Plank Road. When A. P. Hill came under heavy attack later in the afternoon, Old Baldhead showed no interest in the battle on the other part of the front. Looking after his own position, tidying up his entrenched lines, he asked no questions nor sent for any orders from Lee.

6

When Lee learned, through the volume of the firing, that Ewell was caught up in an action he could not even see, let alone control, at the same time he learned that the Turnpike was separated from the Plank Road by nearly three miles where they intersected the Brock crossroad. Whether from faulty maps or from a detail that Lee had overlooked, or both, he seemed surprised at the width of the gap between his two corps. As, with Hill's van, he approached the Brock Road, Lee grew uneasy about what the enemy might be up to in the obscured gap. Actually, Wadsworth's and Crawford's divisions were stumbling through the maze off Ewell's right when at two o'clock Lee reached the clearing of the Widow Tapp's farm, slightly more than a mile from the Brock Road.

Unknown to him, Getty's division of Sedgwick's corps was then hurrying to the vital intersection with the Plank Road. Hancock, whose van had reached six miles to the southwest at Todd's Tavern, was straining the men of his corps in a reverse movement over the narrow roads toward the intersection. Lee had caught the Federal Army in a more vulnerable position than he had expected or realized. A determined push by Heth's lead division would probably have carried the Brock Road before Getty was formed. Blocking the passageway, Heth would have divided the Army of the Potomac.

With no visibility through the murky green screens, none of Lee's generals imagined that their old, familiar opponent would be so carelessly and clumsily exposed by Grant. Also, in approaching the Brock Road, Heth's division had fought off enemy cavalry which for two miles waged a rearguard action as if infantry support were immediately behind. From the information available to him in the yard of the Widow Tapp's subsistence farm, Lee took the orthodox course of deploying Heth's brigades off both sides of the road to develop the enemy's front.

Lee had on both roads only five divisions, and he had to consider that at point of contact conscientious Harry Heth was one of those soundly trained, intelligent men of promise who never gave an outstanding performance. Also his four brigades suffered seriously from shifts in command personnel. After Pettigrew had been killed on the retreat from Gettysburg, his North Carolinians had not taken to his replacement, W. W. Kirkland. Both Archer's and Davis's brigades were temporarily commanded by colonels. Joe Davis, apparently thinking his uncle's confidence in him was misplaced, was on a leave that would become permanent. Archer, waiting to be exchanged as a prisoner, would die shortly after his release. Charlie Field's former and frequently orphaned brigade had found a good man in a Virginia professional, "Mud" Walker, but he had not been long in command.

With these factors controlling his decision, Lee did not display the qualities of "divination" sometimes attributed to him, when he failed to recognize that the intersection was virtually open. As a matter of fact, though Lee reacted quickly to changing conditions either in campaign strategy or battle tactics, his apparent divinations were based upon deductions from selective gathering and careful analyses of all available information. Standing in the yard of the Tapp farm, Lee was not satisfied with his deductions. He was divided between his desire to reach the Brock Road and his apprehension over involving Heth in a second engagement with that gap existing between Hill and Ewell's battle. Only Wilcox's approaching division would be available for any emergency. In another way, it was a struggle between impulse and the rudimentary principles he had so often defied. Here there was no Jackson among his subordinates with whom he could risk breaking the rules.

With his capacity for waiting for developments, while the van of Wilcox's columns neared the Tapp farm, Lee went with Powell Hill and Stuart, and some of their staff officers, to a shaded knoll rising to the north of the humble farmhouse. There in the relaxing warmth of the afternoon sun, the three generals seated themselves under a tree. The staff officers gathered nearby.

Lee's personal staff had by then been reduced to three — Venable, Marshall and young Walter Taylor, who had grown into a highly able assistant adjutant general. Talcott had earlier returned to the engineers and that spring Armistead Long returned to the artillery, assuming command of the Second Corps artillery. Misfit Chilton had returned to the adjutant general's office, accompanied by a diplomatic letter in which Lee expressed the hope that his talents would prove valuable in his new post. By then Lee had perfected the coordinating action with the larger general staff that directed the supporting services, and many of those officers worked around general headquarters during campaigns. At Lee's rest under the shade tree, Walter Taylor seems to have been the only officer present from his staff.

Suddenly Lee jumped up, calling something to Taylor. Out of a field of pines on the far side of the scraggly clearing, a line of blue-clad soldiers was emerging. Beside Lee, Jeb Stuart arose slowly to his feet, as Hill's chief of staff said, "looking the danger straight in the face." Powell Hill did not move as his intense hazel eyes thoughtfully surveyed the enemy soldiers.

With all the maneuvers of great armies, the complex plans of generals and the high policy of civilian leaders, the fate of the war hung for a countless beat of time in the hands of a group of unidentified soldiers under a field officer. The Federal officer shouted a quick order. As suddenly as they had appeared, the enemy soldiers, lost in the trackless brush, vanished back into the Wilderness. Around four o'clock on the afternoon of May 5 the chance to shorten the war passed.

The effect of this narrow scrape with capture was immediate on Lee. He ordered the lead brigade of Wilcox's division to turn off the Plank Road by the Tapp farm and probe through the jungle toward Ewell's right. The enemy's position in the gap between the two roads must be developed. From the sounds in Ewell's direction, his corps was at least holding its own. Having made up his mind to use Wilcox for connecting the separated forces, Lee was still swayed by his impulse to get to the Brock

Road. He wrote a note to Heth asking him if he believed he could carry the Brock Road intersection without bringing on a "general engagement."

Heth sent the honest answer that the enemy seemed gathered in force and he could not determine the extent to which an attack would develop the action. He could not see the enemy: he could judge his strength only from the weight of metal rattling through the vines. He was ready to attack, Heth said, if Lee gave the order — that is, assumed the responsibility. That was Heth, a dutiful subordinate.

The enemy saved Lee from making a decision. While Getty's division had been engaging Heth in skirmishing, Hancock's full corps had completed its forced march to the intersection and deployed. Hancock, the tall, combative professional with many Southern friendships from the Old Army, held the Rebels' fighting qualities in great respect. Before he opened his assault, he built a log breastwork in the event he should be forced back. Grant, anxious to open the assault, ordered Hancock to hurry in before he completed his usual careful dispositions.

As with the earlier rushed attack on Ewell, the assaulting units did not advance simultaneously and bring the full force of their numbers, around 30,000, against Heth. If they had, Heth's four brigades would have been overwhelmed. As it was, Heth's men were able to hold their ground against the weight of the first waves only because of the Wilderness as an equalizer.

7

As soon as General Lee heard the volume of fire rolling toward Heth's troops, he hurried off a courier to Wilcox with the order to bring his four brigades back to the Plank Road. Whatever might develop in the gap between the two roads, the clear and present danger to Heth was a certainty.

By the time Wilcox, excitedly galloping about on a white horse, brought his first brigade to Heth's left flank near the north of the road, he found Kirkland's North Carolinians engulfed by the enemy. Going to the rescue, Thomas's Georgians were immediately swallowed up in what a Federal officer called "bushwhacking on a grand scale." Men fought at right angles to one another and back to back. With the officers' vision restricted to twenty yards, "every man was his own general," a South Carolina private said. The objective became survival.

A. P. Hill had his greatest day as a corps commander. With Lee assuming command at the executive level, "Little Powell" was free to give that personal direction of combat in which he had excelled as a division commander. Like Ewell, he was fighting at the level for which his capacities fitted him. Handling two divisions only slightly larger than his old Light

Division, he transmitted to his men the emotional force that surged in him during combat. He exposed himself as recklessly as a field officer as he rode back and forth along the lines, personally placing two of Wilcox's brigades to support Heth's shaken units along the road.

Heth's three brigades on the south of the road were fighting prone from behind log works back of swampy ground. Above them a stand of saplings was sheared clean at breast-high level from the sheets of fire poured by the attackers. Untouched on the ground, with the stationary men getting off an average of two shots a minute, Heth's three brigades in ten minutes rained more than one hundred thousand slugs of lead into the packed masses floundering through the bog in their front. When Wilcox's two brigades gave a temporary check to Hancock along the road, normally contained Heth grew so excited that he ordered a local counterattack without informing Hill.

It had become a soldiers' fight and Lee could follow the battle only by the "crackling" of rifles which, a soldier said, "sounded like fire in a cane-brake." Such was the confusion in the blind fighting that as Heth sent his three brigades charging to the right of the road, Sam MacGowan (Maxcy Gregg's successor on the famous South Carolina brigade) was falling back from a counterattack along the road on Heth's left. Some of Heth's men made it all the way to the Brock Road, only to encounter fire from behind the log breastwork Hancock had prudently built before going in. When Heth's disordered lines started to fall back, the sun was going down, and the chaotic battle seemed near its end.

Then, as the right brigade was stumbling back to its original position, Jim Lane was appalled to see through the smoke two fresh Federal brigades advancing against his open flank. As he broke back a regiment to check this envelopment — from Hancock's last reserves — the whole Federal line surged forward again through the woods then dusky with smoke and the failing light.

The course of this firing told its own story to Lee, sitting his horse in the Tapp farmyard. He had not another regiment to throw into the path of the fresh tide of assault. Against a breakthrough, he grimly ordered most of the twenty guns in Poague's battalion placed in the clearing.

Twenty-seven-year-old William Poague was one of those naturals who, without military training, rose in the artillery, and he was only then coming into his own. Poague came from farm people near Lexington and, after graduating from Washington College, had just started law practice when war came. He enlisted in the Reverend Pendleton's Rockbridge (County) Battery and succeeded to its command in time for Jackson's Valley Campaign. In the reorganization after Jackson's death, he was given a battalion in Hill's corps and had just recently been promoted lieutenant colonel.

Lee selected his battery on the chance of its proximity rather than because of Poague's reputation. He was a slight man, with a thin and rather melancholy face elongated by drooping mustache and a scraggly, pointed chin beard. (Many young Confederate officers grew beards to make them look older.) As Poague stood solemnly beside his posted guns, Lee probably looked more to the failing light than to the gun battalion to save the day.

Colonel Venable expressed it for them all. Lee had sent him to observe Heth's stand in the shadowy woods north of the road. Jeb Stuart rode up on his own to take a look. As they watched Heth's fragmented units, with all lines lost, struggling to hold their ground against the waves rolling forward, Venable said to Stuart, "If night would only come."

It was almost dark when a courier rode up to Powell Hill with the alarming information that an enemy force was groping its way across the gap, between him and Ewell. Hill knew that Lee had no available troops to send to protect the already mangled left. Instead of sending the information to Lee, he acted on the impulsiveness that sometimes got him into trouble. Hill hurried forward the 125-man provost guard, the 5th Alabama, turning over the prisoners they were guarding to any noncombatants at hand. He sent the Alabamians into the darkening thickets with orders to shriek like banshees and fire as fast as they could load. The force that could hear but not see them was Wadsworth's division, which had lost its way around noon off Ewell's right. White-haired old Wadsworth, the politically appointed general, brought his bewildered troops to a halt to await attack.

That ended the long day for Lee. He left the Tapp farm for his headquarters tent pitched off the road a short distance back. Evidently he left without seeing Powell Hill. Hill's proud hour had come at the cost of nervous and emotional exhaustion. When he dismounted in the farmyard, a fire had been built beside one of Poague's guns, and Hill sat on the ground leaning back against a wheel of the gun carriage. With his eyes hollowed and cheeks sunken above his red-fox beard, Little Powell looked ill despite his happy smile.

The repulse of heavy odds on both roads brought a different reaction to Lee. It aroused his aggressiveness. In his headquarters tent, showing no ill effects from the day of tension, Lee cast his thoughts immediately to plans for the next day. When Longstreet's two divisions and Anderson came up, he expected to carry the fight to the enemy and disrupt Grant's advance by taking the Brock Road passageway. Lee's exhilarated projection of his thoughts to the next day was based, at least in part, on his appraisal of his new opponent.

8

In his underestimation of the Army of Northern Virginia, Grant had moved his army on a logistical program that ignored Lee's existence. He seemed to assume that, as in the West, the Confederates would permit themselves to be acted upon by his initiative, superior numbers and armament. When he found his flanks threatened, Grant reacted with a pugnacity that led to one of the clumsiest battles ever fought in Virginia. Absorbing appalling casualties, he threw his men in wastefully as if their weight was certain to overrun any Confederates in their path. In terms of generalship, the new man gave Lee nothing to fear.

But, as Grant had underestimated him, Lee underestimated the powers of recovery in the Army of the Potomac when commanded by a general as belligerently tenacious as Grant. As Grant had had no experience against an army as bold and skillful as Lee's, Lee had no experience against an opponent who took no count of his losses. Not expecting Grant to be able to resume an offensive by daylight the next morning, Lee based his plans for the next day on the arrival of Longstreet before daylight. This miscalculation of Lee's became involved in a curious command lapse that cut across the whole army like a crack in a structure.

That night after the shock of battle began to wear off, colonels and generals in Hill's two divisions crept about cautiously to discuss with one another the dangerous condition of their broken and irregular lines. The exhausted soldiers had fallen asleep where they finished fighting, without building fires. Regiments and brigades were all intermingled in small groups, some no larger than a squad. In places the lines of the enemy were so close that officers of both sides who moved a few steps in the wrong direction were captured. The interlocking treetops, with the vines and creepers, shut out the night light and in the underbrush along the ground it was as black as a cave. Some time after nine o'clock officers made their way back to division commanders Heth and Wilcox to report that "a skirmish line would drive both divisions."

Heth and Wilcox separately made their way to Powell Hill, propped up against the gun carriage wheel. They told him of the need to arouse the men and form them into orderly lines against any daylight attacks. Hill told them that General Lee's orders were to let the men rest where they were, as they would be relieved after midnight by Longstreet. Neither Wilcox nor Heth was satisfied, and Wilcox went directly to Lee's headquarters.

Before Wilcox said anything, Lee told him that Longstreet's, as well as Anderson's division, would be up to relieve the tired troops during the night. With this assurance, Wilcox, as he reported, "made no suggestion about the line."

Heth returned twice to Hill, and the second time Hill grew impatient. "Damn it, Heth, I don't want to hear any more about it. The men shall not be disturbed."

Evidently the visits of Heth and Wilcox aroused some anxiety in Hill, for around midnight he went back to Lee's tent. According to Colonel William Palmer, Hill's chief of staff, "General Lee repeated his orders — that is, Longstreet would relieve his men." Reassured that his troops were to be withdrawn, Hill, like Wilcox, did not mention the bad conditions of his lines to Lee. Expecting Longstreet to be manning the front before the enemy opened any action, Hill, very indulgent of his men, went to sleep relieved that their rest need not be disturbed.

In this lapse in communication, Lee did not change his orders because of a faulty assumption. When Hill had come to his tent, Lee knew that Longstreet would not arrive much before daylight. He did not mention this to Hill because of the assumption — having been told nothing to the contrary — that Hill's lines were formed in sufficient order to receive attack. Later in the year when Heth, in a private conversation, tried to shift the blame for his unpreparedness to Hill, Lee said, "A division commander should always have his division ready to receive attack."

In the midnight meeting in the candlelit tent, Hill and Lee missed the fundamental point in their communication because of the different effects on the two men of the release from the strain of the battle. When Hill assumed that Longstreet would take over his lines during the night, he spoke for himself as well as his troops when he said, "Let the tired men rest." Lee, while it was natural for him to assume order on his front, was thinking with his aroused aggression when he made no provision for Longstreet's arrival possibly later than daybreak. Each man made a completely reasonable assumption according to his temper at the moment.

Powell Hill left Lee's tent without knowing that Longstreet was still in bivouac on the Catharpin Road, five miles south through the Wilderness from Parker's Store, about two miles in their rear. Lee had expected Longstreet to reach the point of his bivouac at noon of the 5th, when he would rest his troops until around six, and resume the march toward the Brock Road. Around six o'clock, Lee had sent Colonel Venable with verbal orders for Longstreet to change his line of march from the Catharpin Road and cross over to the Plank Road. On Venable's return, he told Lee that Longstreet had not reached his bivouac until five in the afternoon and his troops were resting for a start at one in the morning. Lee then sent verbal orders for Longstreet to come at once.

These orders went sent by Major Henry B. McClellan, Stuart's young adjutant general. McClellan, from Philadelphia, was a cousin of the Federal general and had brothers in the Federal Army camped in the blackness of the Wilderness. He had been a schoolteacher in Virginia before the war and, as unassertive as he was zealous, was little known outside the cavalry. It happened that Major McClellan, accompanied by a guide to lead Longstreet's divisions across country, delivered his orders to Charlie Field, the new division commander whom Longstreet had not wanted in his corps. Probably not acquainted with young McClellan in the first place, the professional soldier — a former instructor at West Point — became every inch Old Army. He refused to accept verbal orders that conflicted with existing orders from his immediate superior. Around ten o'clock a fuming McClellan told his story to Lee and asked to be sent back with written orders. Lee said that by the time McClellan reached Field, Longstreet's troops should be in motion anyway.

In telling nothing of this to Hill and Wilcox, Lee evidently was trying to spare them worry, so that the generals as well as the men could rest undisturbed. Showing no outward apprehension himself, Lee went to his cot after midnight for another night of four hours' sleep.

## 9

Daylight came on May 6 with everyone tensely waiting for Longstreet. According to Lee's last arrangement with him, Lee had no reason to expect Longstreet appreciably before daybreak, but he certainly expected him when the morning began to grow light around five o'clock. At five o'clock Longstreet's columns were not visible on the Plank Road to the west.

A minor controversy flurried over Longstreet's "lateness" at the Wilderness, but Longstreet did not grow defensive about it. In his narrative, he omitted mention of having advised Lee that he hoped to be at his bivouac point by noon of the 5th, and stated simply that he came up at five, with his rear columns closing up "at dark" — well past seven. He also made no mention of McClellan's visit, stating that the guide reported from Lee at eleven. McClellan left the guide there not later than nine. After stating that he planned to move out at midnight (as a result of Colonel Venable's earlier order), Longstreet wrote, "At one o'clock the march was resumed."

Lee was not known to have made any comment on Longstreet's time of arrival, but Colonel William Preston Johnston wrote in a private memorandum, unpublished, that Lee told him Longstreet was "slow coming up." In the Gettysburg controversy, Jubal Early had written that Lee, in discussing the next day's plans at the end of the first day, had said Longstreet was "so slow." Contumacious Old Jube hated Longstreet, and his uncorroborated statement was viewed with some skepticism. But Colonel Johnston was another matter. The son of high-minded General Albert Sidney Johnston, he served on the personal staff of Jefferson Davis, was a friend of Custis Lee and uninvolved in any controversy. Close to General Lee after the war, Colonel Johnston left among his private papers an item headed "General R. E. Lee: Memoranda of Conversation May 7, 1868." Johnston wrote:

"He said Longstreet was slow coming up . . . that if he had been in time he would have struck the enemy on the flank while they were engaged in front. He said Longstreet was often slow."

Taken at face value, Johnston's recorded conversation would indicate that Lee accepted Longstreet's limitations as he was known to accept those of others, and kept his reservations to himself. Also, as he expected others to do the best they could, he expected Longstreet to give his very considerable best once he brought his highly disciplined troops into action. But Lee was oversanguine to have counted upon Longstreet's relieving Hill's men before the enemy came at them again. At five o'clock the vans of both of Longstreet's divisions were just completing their march through the Wilderness and emerging on the Plank Road at Parker's Store, out of sight of Lee at the Tapp farm two or three miles away. At precisely that hour, as Heth's and Wilcox's men were stirring from their sleep of exhaustion, their unprepared lines were struck by the full weight of the more than a corps gathered under Hancock.

Not hurried out on that assault before his dispositions were complete, and with Wadsworth's division driving in from the north of the road, the superior combat soldier overlapped both of Hill's flanks and struck across the road with irresistible force. General Lee had no more than returned to his informal command post behind Poague's guns on the Tapp farm than the shock to Hill's troops was made evident by the appearance of individual soldiers falling back out of the woods across the one hundred yards of clearing.

Slowly, though it must have seemed like sped-up time to Lee, the numbers of his withdrawing veterans increased, coming out of the fight in poor order or none at all. From the sounds in the brush, it was evident that some groups were resisting desperately and others were falling back with only light firing. Obviously no lines as such exsited. Lee knew the irregular front, beginning about a thousand yards away, was dissolving. Sitting motionless on his gray horse, Lee showed his recognition of approaching disaster by sending Walter Taylor to the rear to start the wagon train in motion away from the field. He showed his inner agitation by speaking "rather roughly" to Sam MacGowan. "My God," he shouted, "is this the splendid brigade of yours running like a flock of geese?"

MacGowan had taken his wounds in leading the South Carolinians in the

A. P. Hill tradition, and he answered stoutly enough, "General, these men are not whipped. They only want a place to form and they will fight as well as they ever did."

The trouble was there was no place to form. The only steady "front" was the Tapp farm clearing, occupied by Poague's sixteen guns. It was at this crisis that the mild-eyed young artillerist brought himself unforgettably to Lee's attention.

With growing groups of Hill's infantrymen falling back on either side of his guns, Poague's cannoneers showed their discipline by calmly loading their pieces with antipersonnel ammunition and shifting the huge carriage wheels to point the guns at the road. When the last of Hill's remnants left the woods, the first rush of hurrahing Federals along the road came almost on their heels. Firing over the heads of their own retreating infantrymen, Poague's gunners sent shell bursts into the dark-clothed masses packed on the road.

Lee, wreathed by the smoke rising from the guns, saw the pursuit on the road checked with terrible casualties. But Hancock's heavy, triumphant forces quickly diverged to either side. Soon to the right of the clearing, on the other side of the road, the enemy advanced through the entangled woods to a point across from the guns and even beyond. Only fragments of Hill's men were still firing. On Lee's side of the road about the last of Hill's troops were leaving the woods in front of the clearing. There Lee could see the enemy troops gathering in the screen of vines facing the clearing to rush the guns.

At this moment of wreckage facing one wing of his army, the first of Longstreet's troops deployed from the right of the road into the thickets. These were two brigades of McLaws's old division, eagerly led by Joe Kershaw in his new temporary command. The troops, long separated from the army, were also eager. Coolly opening their ranks to permit Hill's fugitives to pass to the rear, the men closed their lines and advanced a solid front to crash into Hancock's fluid forces.

While Kershaw was piling up the enemy south of the road, only a single thin brigade came trotting up the road to the clearing where Poague's sooty gunners were firing at point-blank range. Lee saw the first of the tawny soldiers when the lead regiment began deploying behind the guns. Pushing his horse to the guide of the line, he shouted, "What troops are you, my boys?"

"The Texans."

Lee excitedly took off his wide-brimmed hat and waved them on. Some impulse, of which Lee was unaware, was communicated to Traveler, and the horse moved forward with the advancing line. Except that Lee's whitening head was uncovered, the only outward change in his usual composure was a look of grim determination. He seemed not to realize that he was moving into the range of fire. To the appalled soldiers it looked as if he intended personally to lead the counterattack.

"Go back, General Lee," the men began to call, "go back." A sergeant grabbed Traveler's bridle, halting the horse. John Gregg, the long-faced, black-bearded new commander of the Texas Brigade, though unacquainted with the commanding general, rode to his side and urged him to go to the rear. Lee seemed not to hear them. In the anxiety which his massive features did not reflect, he had lost himself in willing forward his favorite shock troops.

At that point Colonel Venable, as he recounted, recalled that Lee had been looking for Longstreet. Venable galloped up to him and said, "General, you've been looking for General Longstreet. There he is over yonder."

Lee's brown eyes followed Venable's pointing finger to the powerful figure of Longstreet. He replaced his hat and slowly turned his horse about. He was again in command of himself.

Assured that Lee was safe, the less than one thousand Texans attacked as if life held no meaning. Their line fragmented on contact with the Federals at the far edge of the clearing. Then "Rock" Bennings's Georgians rushed in to support them and Law's Alabamians obliqued across the smoky clearing to go charging into the woods on the Texans' flank. The irregular lines of the advancing Federals rocked to a halt.

Across the road Kershaw got a third brigade out on his flank, extending the line. Then the psychological balance of battle began to shift. Though the six brigades of Field's and Kershaw's divisions had been halted by the violent collision, the initiative passed to them. The speed and unevenness of the Federal advance — around islands of resistance groups — had scattered their alignment when they met the solid fire of fresh troops whose order had not yet been affected by movement through the Wilderness. In the element of morale, the attacking troops were repulsed when flushed with apparent victory. The men had seen the white-topped Confederate wagons moving away in flight. Against the cohesive pressure of the six brigades, which barely covered the narrow front, Hancock's irregularly formed men began to fall back.

With the turn of the tide, the Federals came in for their share of command lapses. Hancock called for Gibbon's reserve division to come up on his left flank. Gibbon was waiting for Longstreet on the Catharpin Road. But Sheridan, trying to ride Stuart's horsemen into the ground (and taking a heavy toll of their personally owned mounts), had not discovered that Longstreet had crossed over to the Plank Road. So Gibbon stayed where he was, leaving Hancock's left flank open.

On his right flank, Hancock was trying to hurry forward Burnside's fresh corps to exploit the gap between the two roads. Burnside, a general of no high skills who never enjoyed the luck to cover his deficiencies, spent the morning wandering among the saplings and vine-draped trees trying to find a path that led in the right direction.

When no Federals approached in the gap off his left, Lee's discovery of Hancock's open flank on his right was enough to shake off the effects of the close escape from destruction. He turned immediately to plans for a counteroffensive.

First Lee eliminated the possibility of any help from Ewell's corps. The night before, in his own rising aggression, Lee had so far forgotten Ewell's limitations as to give him the choice of a decision. If the enemy had shifted sufficiently to the Plank Road front to make an attack from the Turnpike practical, Lee ordered, Ewell should strive to cut the Federals off from the river. If the enemy remained in strength on his front, Ewell should shift to his right to support Lee's proposed attack along the Plank Road. Ewell did neither. He simply rejected the initiative of making any decision. Going on as if he had never received the order, Ewell stoutly resisted the enemy's local attacks — designed to get him to do precisely that.

Lee turned to Hill's two divisions to close the gap by shifting to their left toward Ewell. Quickly re-formed, the men were, as MacGowan had promised, eager to have a go at the enemy with their lines in proper order. With the nagging worry of the gap between the roads at last off his mind, Lee began to organize a movement to turn Hancock's exposed flank.

The hastily improvised turning movement became something of a group affair. Lee's new and temporary chief of engineers, Martin Smith, established the precise location where Hancock's flank was in the air. One of Kershaw's brigadiers discovered an unfinished railroad that offered a concealed approach. Longstreet, with Lee's approval, selected four brigades from four separate divisions to form the equivalent of a division. These were all fresh troops except the Mississippi brigade, in Heth's division, that had been mishandled at Gettysburg by the President's nephew. Colonel Stone, acting in command, requested and received permission to take part in the attack. Finally, for leading the movement, Longstreet indulged Moxley Sorrel, his twenty-five-year-old chief of staff who chafed for combat.

Sometime after ten in the morning, Lee watched an elated Sorrel, one of the most attractive-looking men in the army, push his horse into the brush beside the color-bearer of the 12th Virginia.

10

When the troops in the flanking movement crept toward the railroad cut, Lee rode to the north of the Tapp farm. He wanted to know when

Hill established contact with Ewell's right. From random firing, he knew that Federal soldiers were then crowding into the maze in the gap between the two roads. Unaware of the whine of stray minié balls, Lee heard the high screams rising from the right of the Plank Road and by the course of the firing he recognized the pattern of a successful flank attack. Despite his anxiety over closing the gap, Lee had to ride back to the Plank Road to determine the extent of the success.

He gazed upon a total reversal of the early morning near disaster. The flanking movement had rolled up the enemy, driving all of Hancock's troops out of the woods south of the Plank Road. The road itself was crowded with disorganized Confederates. In the brush north of the road the Federal troops were falling back. It seemed an ideal situation for the formation of a full-scale stroke to seize the Brock Road. Ahead of Lee, Longstreet and some of his generals were riding up the road.

This time Longstreet was not waiting on the commanding general for orders to mount a decisive stroke. He was already telling Joe Kershaw of his quickly devised plan for a push to the Brock Road, to be accompanied by a second flanking movement sweeping beyond the Brock Road to drive north along Hancock's log breastworks. Micah Jenkins, the brilliant young South Carolinian who had grown despondent at their cause during the months in the Tennessee mountains, grew excited with fresh faith when his brigade was selected as the pivotal unit in the flanking movement. "We will put the enemy back across the Rapidan before night," he said.

As Jenkins spoke, from the woods on the right a few rifles crackled tentatively. Longstreet instinctively turned his horse in the direction of the firing and the mounted men nearest him followed. At this rapid movement, the volley from the woods grew heavier. Three men pitched from their horses. Courier Baum and Captain Dobie, Kershaw's assistant adjutant general, were killed instantly. Young Jenkins, with the words of hope fresh on his lips, went down mortally wounded. Longstreet was struck by a bullet high in the chest, lifting him in the saddle, but he held on.

While Kershaw galloped up the road shouting, "Friends! Friends! We are friends," Longstreet was laid at the foot of a leafy tree by the roadside. He was almost choked with blood. With his hat off, a nearby artillery officer said his forehead looked "white and domelike" above his weather-stained cheeks and bushy brown beard. As an ambulance approached along the cluttered road, Longstreet — calm against the pain and shock — told Colonel Sorrel to turn the attack over to Field. He was to hurry to General Lee and urge him to continue the great flanking movement. When he was lifted into the ambulance, his lids were closing and only a faint line of blue showed against the lashes.

Lee was riding toward the roadside group when Sorrel found him. On receiving Longstreet's message Lee, Sorrel recorded, "expressed concern" over Longstreet's condition and "his loss to the army." He was not stirred to the emotional reaction he had shown at Jackson's wounding in the same locality almost exactly one year before. Lee's respect for Longstreet as a soldier and comfortable intimacy with him as a man did not include the warmth of affection he had felt for Jackson. Absorbing the blow of the loss to the army, Lee turned immediately to the job left unfinished.

To Lee and Charlie Field, whom Lee left in command of the action, it was at once apparent that Longstreet had been too sanguine in assuming his troops were in the order to deliver an offensive stroke. To the south of the road the brigades were scattered in the woods and perpendicular to Field's lines advancing north of the road. The troops who had fired into Longstreet's party were those south of and parallel to the road. To Sorrel, Lee and Field seemed an awfully long time — from noon to four o'clock — straightening out the assault alignment. But Sorrel, like Longstreet, overlooked the nagging details in his excited vision of the great stroke that would finish off the enemy.

Then, as the Wilderness brought confusion to advancing lines, so the matted foliage gave protection to retreating troops. Even in disorder, the Federals were not driven from the field. North of the road the fighting never ceased entirely. As Field's brigades could gain little momentum in pushing their advance, Federal soldiers who had quit the field could be re-formed. By the time Field's brigades were aligned south of the road, Hancock had formed his fugitives behind the log breastworks.

Lee turned over the assault to Field and the attack was solidly delivered. It carried to the Brock Road, all the way to where the log breastworks were burning. By then segments from Burnside's corps had been shifted to the breastworks in support. The survivors of Longstreet's two divisions, with two of Hill's brigades, simply lacked the weight to carry the position. The second day of Grant's confident aggression ended with his army hanging on for its life in protection of its vital passageway and Lee "seriously disappointed." Venable believed Lee had conceived it possible to drive Grant back across the Rapidan.

It was clearly not enough for Lee merely to inflict a repulse upon the free-swinging Grant. As soon as he recognized that the Federal reinforcements would contain the flanking movement, Lee left the Plank Road with the desperate hope that some decisive action might yet be delivered by Ewell on the Old Turnpike. Riding behind Hill's lines, which finally closed the gap and connected with Ewell's right, he reached Second Corps headquarters while the light was fading.

When he dismounted, Lee looked at generals grouped in a dismal repetition of Gettysburg. Again Ewell, pallid and apologetic, showed the paralysis of will on being confronted with a decision. Again Jubal Early had established ascendancy. This time Old Jube had influenced Ewell against undertaking an attack around the Federals' right flank, which Brigadier General Gordon had found to be drawn in and exposed.

John B. Gordon, the thirty-two-year-old Georgia lawyer with the ramrod carriage, had attracted Lee's attention earlier. Along with the skills he had quickly acquired in troop leadership, he showed the constant application of mind and energies to the work at hand that Lee looked for in subordinates. As late as it was Lee, making no comment on Ewell's explanations, grimly ordered Gordon's flank attack to be made.

In the gathering dusk Gordon led a light force around the Federals' open flank and came storming out of the woods. The surprise attack rolled up a brigade and created considerable confusion, during which two brigadier generals were captured along with a number of startled soldiers. With night coming on, Gordon lacked the strength to accomplish more. At the end of this last of the might-have-beens, Lee did not accept Ewell's inaction with his usual equanimity, though he stifled any words.

Colonel Venable said that the views of Lee's "gentle temper," formed by observing him in ordinary circumstances, were "not altogether correct. No man could see the flush come over the grand forehead and the temple veins swell on occasions of great trial of patience and doubt that Lee had the high, strong temper of a Washington, and habitually under the same strong control." These repressions of anger took a toll unrealized by Lee. For his own condition, he would have been better off to release some of these feelings. But, except for occasional flare-ups with members of his staff, Lee did not reproach patriot-soldiers for doing the best they could — whatever he thought of that "best."

Judging from the short time before he removed Ewell from command, Ewell's best in the Wilderness was one of the trials to Lee's patience. Gordon remembered his "grim looks" and that his cold silence during Ewell's explanations "revealed his thoughts almost as plainly as words could have done." In Colonel Johnston's private memorandum, he wrote of Lee: "He said at the Wilderness, Ewell showed vacillation that prevented him from getting all out of his troops he might."

In the dark woods, Lee started Traveler toward the Plank Road. He showed no satisfaction at having directed one of the great tactical battles of the war, won by the poise sustained during two days of threatened disaster against twice his numbers, and by the cold nerve to promote a counterattack while a gap remained between the two wings of his army.

On the other side of the Brock Road, Grant went into his tent and threw himself face down on his cot. Charles Francis Adams said, "I never saw a man so agitated in my life."

Lee correctly estimated that, against the smallest force he ever fielded,

Grant's losses ran very high — seventeen thousand casualties, more than Burnside at Fredericksburg and as many as Hooker at Chancellorsville. Lee's army suffered less than half of that, and many of the casualties were lightly wounded who would soon return to duty. Yet, with more Federal mistakes committed than in any battle at the river, Lee could not exploit them. His numbers were simply too few and his subordinates too undependable. Now his one dependable corps commander would be absent for an indeterminate period. Lee had won a tactical victory that gained him no more fruits than Fredericksburg. He had not gained the initiative.

It was full night and Lee was tired when, on reaching the Plank Road, he gazed upon a scene of horror. The blackness of the Wilderness was sliced by the flares of brush fires sizzling along the ground, from which rose the moans and cries of the wounded. With animosities suspended, men of both sides groped through the jungle to give succor to the victims. Underneath the rise of voices came the rhythmic thud of picks and shovels. The survivors, without orders from headquarters, were digging lines of defense against the next day.

To Lee, staring at the firelit woods, there was no question of strategy for the next day, or even of what to do. The men were doing the only thing possible in preparing to protect themselves. With the failure to gain the initiative and too weak to attack, Lee could only wait for Grant's next move.

Turning away, Lee pushed his horse through the press of ambulances and stretcher-bearers and walking wounded on the dark road to his tent. He climbed down from the saddle in which he had spent the most of sixteen hours. In his tent, he dictated a brief, factual account of the battle in a telegram for War Secretary Seddon, listing the casualties among general officers.

Brigadiers J. M. Jones and promising young Micah Jenkins were dead and Leroy Stafford mortally wounded. Among brigadiers wounded was John Pegram, the West Point–trained brother of Willie Pegram, the young artillerist in Hill's corps. John Pegram had only just gotten himself transferred from the Western army to Lee's army, in order to be near his family in Richmond. Replacements must be found for those experienced soldiers and, of course, for Longstreet.

Before going to his cot, Lee would have to reshuffle his officer personnel in preparations for the next day and Grant's next move. He could *hope* that Grant would be foolish enough to attack him where he was . . . if Grant did, Lee *might* find an opening that offered possibilities for a counterattack . . . For the master of strategic maneuver, it had come to that.

## CHAPTER XVIII

## "We Must Strike Them a Blow"

BEGINNING on the warm Saturday of May 7, Lee could only be caught in passing glimpses as the action he directed unfolded. He was too continuously involved to write personal or official letters and the soldiers were so engulfed in the desperate, exhausting movement and fighting that few clear impressions remained to be recorded. Most of the battle reports of the 1864 campaign were later destroyed and, due to the high mortality among general officers, scant records were preserved. Yet, for two days the fragmentary evidence of Lee's direction revealed the parts of his army performing ideally in coordinated movements as of a single body responding to impulses from the brain.

At sunrise Lee was first seen for the day by Colonel Sorrel, summoned to Lee's headquarters back of the Tapp farm. Sorrel had been with the corps, Lee told him, since it began as a brigade, and the older man wanted to talk to him about a successor for Longstreet. As Field and Kershaw were new to division command, Lee did not mention them and he seemed not to have considered the absent Pickett. His preferences leaned toward Early, Edward Johnson and Richard H. Anderson, in that order. Sorrel answered frankly that Jubal Early's harshness had rubbed First Corps people the wrong way, and Allegheny Johnson was unknown to them. Dick Anderson — "chivalrous," Sorrel called the reserved South Carolinian — was remembered warmly from his period with the First Corps. By elimination Longstreet's command would devolve on Anderson, who had been less than inspired while with Hill.

Then, during Saturday afternoon Lee was seen sitting with Powell Hill on the porch of an abandoned house, facing a weedy field, where Hill had established headquarters midway between the Plank Road and the Old Turnpike. Lee, manifestly concerned about Ewell, was pausing on the return from his second trip to Ewell's headquarters. In the woods across from the field the facing lines were quiet. Grant had not renewed his attack. Suddenly Colonel Palmer came bounding through the front door. Up in the attic the young chief of staff had torn loose shingles to make a peephole for a fine marine glass he happened to have, and he

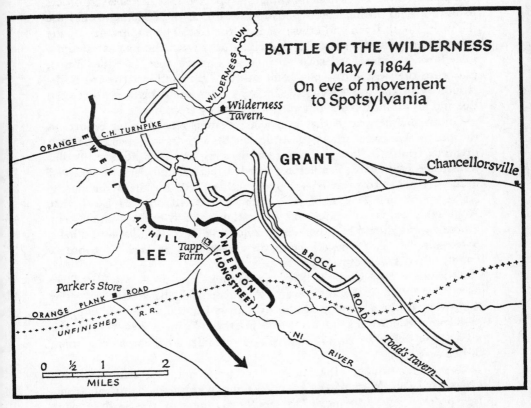

had seen guns and wagons moving southward from the clearing around Wilderness Tavern which he took to be Grant's headquarters. This supplied the evidence Lee needed to confirm his opinion that Grant would move southward across his front in the direction of Spotsylvania Court House.

Along with the quiet on the front — occasionally broken by a local feeling-out advance from the enemy — two earlier pieces of information gave Lee the clues. On his first trip to the Old Turnpike, Ewell advised him that the enemy was withdrawing from the Germanna Ford Road — the position of the Federal right. At noon Jeb Stuart sent a message of the enemy's cavalry pressing around Todd's Tavern, midway between the battle front and Spotsylvania, twelve miles to the southeast. Before Lee's second trip to Ewell, Walter Taylor sent a message to Stuart saying, "the general thinks . . . appearances would indicate an intention of the enemy to move toward Spotsylvania Court House." Stuart was instructed to find out about roads available for infantry and artillery.

Nominal Chief of Artillery Pendleton reported that he received orders to hack a road through the woods southward, as the Federals would use the main Brock Road and other roads to the east. The importance of the court house village was as a crossroads. Roads from the northwest there joined roads from Fredericksburg (near Grant's base at Belle Plain), ran on to the west and — most ominously — ran southeast toward Richmond. With the grave danger of Grant interposing his army between Lee and his capital, no one reported any urgency from Lee.

Colonel Palmer stated that immediately upon receiving his report on the porch, Lee sent orders to Anderson to withdraw Longstreet's two divisions from the lines at dark, rest the men, and then follow Pendleton's trace southward. Pendleton recorded that around dark he received orders from Lee to provide Anderson with a guide for the night march. At seven o'clock Walter Taylor wrote a dictated note to Ewell that Anderson's corps would be put in motion toward Spotsylvania Court House and he should be prepared to follow the next day. Taylor added a postscript that Lee's new headquarters would be at Parker's Store, a couple of miles west of the Tapp farm.

Alexander's First Corps artillery, finding no firing space in the Wilderness, was halted at Parker's Store. Alexander said he started his guns southward in the afternoon for Shady Grove Church, on a road roughly paralleling Pendleton's trace for the infantry. From Shady Grove, the conversion point, a road ran east to Spotsylvania. There was no glimpse of Lee that night.

The next morning, of a Sunday that grew hot, Lee sent a written order to Ewell. Most of the enemy having withdrawn from the front, Lee ordered Ewell to move "as rapidly as you can" to Shady Grove Church and provided him with specific directions for line of march. Lee sent another written message to Ewell saying that A. P. Hill had reported himself sick, and Lee would "be obliged" to borrow Jubal Early for temporary command of Hill's corps. Lee also reshuffled the brigades in Ewell's three divisions, in a Machiavellian device for evading the administration's rules of seniority, "so that General Gordon may take command" of Early's division. Lee wrote, "I shall proceed to Shady Grove Church." Ewell was to follow him.

Lee rode the twelve miles and arrived near the court house sometime before half-past two without anyone reporting having seen him during the whole day. At two-thirty from Spotsylvania he sent a brief telegram to War Secretary Seddon announcing that General Anderson "repulsed the enemy with heavy slaughter and took possession of the court house."

The information about the stand made by Anderson's two divisions and Stuart's cavalry was perhaps delivered to him by Colonel Venable. On the day before Lee had revealed his reservations about Dick Anderson by sending, Venable reported, "an aide-de-camp with Anderson under orders to keep him [Lee] constantly advised." Of May 8, Venable's recording of "Lee's arrival with Ewell's corps in the afternoon . . ." indicated that he had not ridden with Lee through and out of the Wilderness, as Lee actually arrived several hours ahead of Ewell. Venable's account of the great fight of the soldiers with Anderson sounded as if he were present.

None of Lee's previous audacity impressed Venable as deeply as the casual reliance he placed upon the troops themselves — under a new, untried commander — "to hold superior numbers in check until he could come to their support." Nor did any action directed by one of Lee's subordinates arouse more admiration in Venable than Jeb Stuart's stand in holding back the Federals until the brigades under Anderson got into line. But, in combination with Stuart's great hour and Lee's vindicated trust in his veterans to "maintain themselves against odds" — along with, of course, Lee's anticipation of Grant's move — finally the Federals were checked by the chance that Longstreet was not in command of the two infantry divisions.

When Anderson had withdrawn the infantry from the lines after dark on May 7, the woods designated for their resting ground had caught fire from the smoldering underbrush. Longstreet would have moved the men back farther to get their rest. Anderson, who may have been aware of his listless performanecs with A. P. Hill, was stirred from his usual deliberateness by his new responsibility. Having gotten a look at the miserable, stump-strewn trace Pendleton had cut for his men to travel through at night, Anderson started them southward without rest.

In the dark of the moon the men required six hours to cover eight miles. Then, on a cross-country road, the van reached a clearing beside a brook three miles from Spotsylvania Court House at first light around five o'clock. With the Sunday quiet unbroken, Anderson rested the men while they cooked their breakfasts of a chunk of fat bacon, a piece of hard tack and a cup of substitute coffee made of peanuts.

At six o'clock a message from Stuart started the refreshed column hurrying toward the open land on Spindler's farm less than two miles northwest of the crossroads town. For some while before daylight two brigades of Fitz Lee's cavalry had piled up the Federal night march by obstructing the Brock Road with logs and firing from the blackness of the woods. Around daylight Merritt's division of Sheridan's cavalry, supposedly screening the columns of Warren's V Corps, drew aside and called on the infantry to clear the road.

Warren, whose command had been badly cut up in the hurried first day's assault on Ewell, was very deliberate in deploying Robinson's lead division, and it was nearing seven o'clock when Fitz Lee's cavalry was driven out of the woods northwest of Spotsylvania. Supported by Breathed's battery, the dismounted troopers formed behind a light line of fence rails on Spindler's farm, and continued firing while Robinson deployed for attack. When Robinson's men, exhausted from the long night march behind the horses, moved toward the fence rails from one side, the first of Kershaw's troops came running up on the other side.

The Federal soldiers expected only cavalry and they fell back before the bayonetted rifles wielded by men fresher at that stage than they were. In an hour Robinson's division was wrecked beyond repair. Warren got his other divisions in and Anderson put Field's brigades in, and all the while Stuart kept his troopers extending the line until relieved by the foot soldiers.

It was Jeb Stuart the army remembered for that morning. Calmly sitting his middle-sized horse, in such a storm of lead that he invented excuses to send off his staff officers, he ignored the rushing about of Sheridan's units bent on driving Confederate cavalry. Sheridan's heavier forces were driving some of Stuart's light brigades off to the east and almost behind him around the village, but Stuart kept enough troopers with him while he personally placed in line the infantry coming up until Grant's path to Richmond was blocked.

The battle was by no means over when Lee reached the field. A small force had simply planted itself across Grant's line of advance. Other corps of Grant's army were developing a broader-fronted action when Lee assumed control. Yet, no glimpses came of Lee personally. It was the invisible control he exerted, as he had at Chancellorsville and had not at Gettysburg.

Ewell, returned to a simple combat assignment, made a flat statement of his work: "After a very distressing march through intense heat and thick dust and smoke from burning woods, my troops reached Spotsylvania Court House about 5 o'clock, just in time for Rodes to repel an attack, an attempt to turn Anderson's right." The diarist of the First Corps laconically noted ". . . and the enemy makes another attack on our position with their VI Corps, which is also repulsed, Rodes' Division being thrown on Kershaw's right and relieving the attack."

All of Ewell's corps was on the field when the fighting ended at dark. Hill's corps, having waited as rear guard, was being led forward by Jubal Early, with Little Powell following in an ambulance.

The next glimpse of Lee was on the following morning. With Anderson under Lee's eyes, Venable evidently had returned to headquarters. He reported that the General was up at three in the morning, having breakfast by candlelight, and left immediately for the front.

Lee rode to the front to prepare defensive lines on the assumption, made on Grant's observed tactics, that Grant would try to batter his way through the roadblock. That three o'clock rising, giving Lee between four and five hours' sleep, was to become a habit at Spotsylvania. Lee would be forced to resume personal field command, as the perfect functioning of the army's coordinated parts could not be sustained under the continuous hammering.

Jeb Stuart himself was drawn off with part of his cavalry when Sheridan, in his determination to defeat Stuart's cavalry, took twelve thousand troopers on a raid to Richmond. On the May 8 collision Stuart's coolly cheerful skill in handling the field, while Anderson hurried forward the veteran infantry, had made possible Dick Anderson's single great day as a Confederate. He was never to enjoy another. Then, within days of Ewell's competent work on Sunday, he began to fall apart, his physical decline accompanied by mental lapses. With the army becoming reduced to Lee and the soldiers, he had to do more and more himself.

2

Lee's return to direct, personal command of the troops did not come at once. For the first days of building the roadblock across Grant's advance, Lee largely left the front to his subordinates and devoted himself to supervising the most elaborate system of field fortifications then seen in world warfare. With maneuver impossible with the casualty drain on his small numbers, and expecting none from Grant, Lee drew on his long-ago engineering experience to design what amounted to mobile forts as an equalizer to Grant's numbers.

The hard manual labor of digging was extremely taxing to the underfed men but, though some fainted from exhaustion, none protested. They understood what "Uncle Robert" was doing; a tired soldier was more useful than a dead soldier. At intervals the men would be interrupted in their digging by a call from the picket line, "Yonder they come, boys!" Then they exchanged pick for rifle and fought off a local attack. The ragamuffins buried their dead, looked after their wounded and took up the picks and shovels again.

The position, selected by the chance of where Fitz Lee's troopers formed a line across the road, was naturally strong. Just south of the Wilderness, the country was heavily wooded around patches of farms, and Lee's left rested on the Po River as a flank. The Po was one of four small streams that wandered across the country converging to the east to form the Mattaponi River. While neither deep nor wide, its banks were abrupt and it presented a definite obstacle to troop movement. Beginning on Monday, May 9, Grant brought the weight of newly arriving corps to his left, away from the Po, while maintaining a continuous, solid front from the Po to Lee's right.

Lee's growing lines formed two sides of a triangle across a base about three miles wide. As most of these lines extended through or near woods, Lee's men also "slashed" the woods in their front — felling the larger trees with the branches toward the enemy. This removed the trees as protection for advancing troops while the interlaced, vine-draped branches impeded movement. Along the base of the triangle was the cluster of houses of Spotsylvania, where an imposing new court house had replaced the building in which Lee's father had been in jail. Lee's headquarters tents were pitched near the village.

One reason for the fragmentary personal flashes of Lee from May 7 to May 12 was that he wrote nothing at all to reveal anything about himself — no details of his days, his speculations and his evolving plans — and one of the reasons for this was his break in communications with Davis.

His communication with Richmond consisted entirely of terse telegrams to Seddon. Though it has nowhere been stated, Lee seemed very cold to the President after he learned on the way to meet Grant (the night of May 4) that not only were the troops belonging to his army (one and one-half divisions) being withheld, but nothing had been done to prepare to meet Butler's thrust south of Richmond. While Lee had been battling Grant from May 5 through May 9, an unorganized collection of troops was making a desperate stand which had thus far saved Richmond and/or Petersburg only because of the ineptness of "Beast" Butler, the sorriest of the surviving political generals with the Federal armies. Lee, in severing communications with the President, seemed to cut himself off from this back-door threat at Richmond.

He had done all he could in warnings and advice, all ignored, and any thoughts he gave to what might be happening at Richmond would only distract him from the twenty-hour-a-day task of thwarting Grant. If he did not contain the major thrust at the center of the multiple offensive, Richmond would be doomed anyway and the enemy's secondary advances would be of no consequence.

Yet, while Lee's hands had been full with the immediate enemy at other times, this was the only period of the war when Lee seemed concentrated entirely on the action in his own front. When he did resume communication with Davis on May 12, it was in flatly worded telegrams on the subject of returning the troops that belonged to his army.

This is not to suggest that Lee was acting in pique. He was never known to have done that, and in May he was confronting the greatest crisis until then in his life and in the life of his country. It is to suggest that, when he put Butler's threat out of his mind because of the futility of diverting his attention to an action then beyond his control, at the same time he put Davis out of his mind after writing him that strong letter on the night of May 4 — and in putting Davis out of mind he suppressed an impatient protest verging on anger.

Lee's obedience to constituted authority was instinct with him, both from his upbringing in an ordered, hierarchical society and his army training. This would not preclude a flare of resentment at the supreme authority who, by imposing his will, exposed Richmond to capture and withheld veterans from Lee's army for a crucial campaign.

Lee's achieved ideal of rising above hostilities did not mean he approved of everybody or never disapproved of an act of those he did love. It meant that he neither harbored grievances nor was motivated by animosities. Lee's absence of approval was usually shown by silence or by his way of reference.

For instance, while he never mentioned Lincoln at all, since it was necessary to refer to the forces opposing him, in his dispatches they were always "the enemy" and in conversation usually "those people." Yet, he prayed every night for those people, the enemy. One of his generals who aroused Lee's active disapproval was referred to as "that man." When his friend Pendleton failed so miserably at Chancellorsville that he was reduced to nominal command of nonexistent reserve artillery, Lee simply omitted his name from his battle report. Jeb Stuart had been deep in his affections since he was a cadet during Lee's superintendency at West Point, and of his defections in the Gettysburg campaign Lee wrote in his report, "In the absence of the cavalry . . ." without mentioning the name of the chief of cavalry.

Judging by his silence toward Davis, and the chilly, businesslike tone when he resumed correspondence, it would appear that Lee felt an angry disapproval of the President's bureaucratic immobilization of troops for the 1864 campaign in Virginia. In time the anger and disapproval would evaporate. Lee respected Davis as a person and, as President, he was a patriot doing the best he could. But in those May days at Spotsylvania when the upturned red-clay soil was forming lengthening mounds of works, Davis would not seem to have occupied a warm place in Lee's heart.

With Stonewall Jackson gone and Longstreet temporarily gone, with Stuart away and Powell Hill absent from illness, cut off from the commander in chief, Lee seemed more alone than at any time in the war.

3

Before daylight of May 12, an emergency brought Lee suddenly back to the immediate, personal direction of the army. The invisible direction of his preference ceased and again the patriarchal figure on the gray horse moved into the center of the action. The briefly perfect functioning of the parts collapsed at the center, around Dick Ewell.

Edward Johnson's division of Ewell's corps occupied the tip of a projecting salient, called the "Mule Shoe" by the soldiers, which Lee had been uneasy about. In the hurry of throwing up works, Lee had been forced to build along the lines formed more or less at random by the troops. Two stretches of lines met at a blunt point about one mile in advance of the adjoining lines on right and left. Lee's plan was to erect a new fortification across the open base of the projection, half a mile wide, but this line had not been begun as of the night of the 11th-12th.

Before going to bed on the night of the 11th, Lee had received information from the cavalry which indicated that Grant might be planning a shift to Lee's right. The information was sent by his son Rooney, who had been exchanged from the Federal prison in March, 1864, and returned to command in April as a newly promoted major general. As this report lacked the certainty of a reconnaissance made personally by Stuart, Lee ordered the corps chiefs of artillery to have their guns ready to roll early in the morning in the event sudden movement became necessary. A wet fog gathered in the woods during the night and, as no passage had been cut through the Mule Shoe salient to the base, Armistead Long thought it prudent to withdraw most of the twenty guns from the toe back to the road.

After the guns were withdrawn, Allegheny Johnson, as well as the soldiers not asleep, heard heavy troop movement in the wet woods in front of the salient. Johnson sent a staff officer to Ewell with the information. At first Ewell did nothing. Then, after considerable delay and another message from Johnson, Ewell sent an order for the artillery battalion to return to the Mule Shoe. He did not advise Lee of any of this. Just before daylight, the sleepy-eyed gunners were hauling their pieces through the black, clammy woods toward the toe when Hancock's whole corps surged over the breastworks. Johnson's four brigades were overrun so suddenly that the gunners, just reaching the lines, were rolled over by dark masses before they could even unlimber the guns.

It was the type of total breakthrough for which everyone involved with the defense tried to blame someone else. Beyond all the details of failures, fundamentally the soldiers were exhausted. Resting poorly in the dripping woods, the men were not alerted to receive the attack they assumed would come after daylight. These troops were the proud veterans of Jackson's old division, including the famed Stonewall Brigade, and the men scarcely fought at all. Around two thousand were captured, including division commander Johnson, futilely waving the hickory club he used in place of a sword.

The men who were not instantly killed or gathered up, stumbled their way through the foggy darkness toward the rear. Among those who escaped was Major Hunter, Johnson's assistant adjutant general. Covered with a black "rain overcoat" bearing no insignia, he rode out on a loose artillery horse, and it was Major Hunter who first saw Lee.

Startled by the firing after finishing his candlelit breakfast, he had galloped up to the open base of the Mule Shoe just before daylight. Hunter could tell the commanding general little more than that Yankee hordes were plunging unchecked through the blurred woods which Lee faced. Lee saw a single Confederate brigade forming to advance a breakline. These were R. D. Johnston's North Carolinians, just returned to the army and in the division for which Lee had used his stratagems to place John B. Gordon in temporary command. A Virginia and a Georgia brigade from the same division were at hand, forming Lee's only reserve.

As in the Wilderness, Lee's anxiety to close the breach aroused the impulse to lead the troops in person, only he seemed more consciously purposeful than in the dazed way he rode forward in the Wilderness. In the misty half-light outside the woods at Spotsylvania, he was clearly assuming personal command. A Virginia sergeant grabbed Traveler's bridle and Gordon dashed up to argue with his commanding officer. "These are Virginians and Georgians," Gordon shouted, and told Lee that if he would go back the troops would drive the enemy.

Lee moved aside for the men to advance, but he did not go to the rear. He remained where he was, though the agitation quickly passed. When shells began to explode around him, he began directing units with his familiar calm, as he watched Gordon's three brigades attack with the abandon of the Texans at the Wilderness. Soon their lines merged into the dark, loose masses advancing through the woods, and Lee could only wait to see if the tide would be checked.

Gordon enjoyed the luck of striking the enemy when all order had gone from his advance. Hancock had attacked in three waves and the second and third had excitedly crowded into the heels of the lines in front. Pushing through the darkness of the woods, with the muddy ground sliced by gullies, the three intermingled lines became like a mob when those in advance were raked by concentrated rifle fire from Gordon's brigades. The men in the front began pushing backward on those pressing forward and the mob began to mill around.

Almost simultaneously brigadiers on the right and left of the projecting salient reacted to the threat by moving quickly on their own initiative. From the base of the Mule Shoe, on Lee's right the divisions of Wilcox and Heth manned lines that slanted southeastward to the court house. On his left, Rodes's division held the lower part of the western side of the salient and joined with Anderson's two divisions. To protect Gordon's flanks against the overflow of the Federal masses, Jim Lane, the professor from Tidewater Virginia, broke back part of his North Carolina brigade on Gordon's right. On the left Dodson Ramseur went further.

Ramseur, a twenty-seven-year-old North Carolinian and West Point graduate, was one who wore a ferocious beard to hide the youthfulness of his face. The attempt was unsuccessful, as his gentle, trusting eyes suggested nothing of the warrior. In the mist of that early morning light, boyish-looking Ramseur marked himself for future promotion when he threw in his brigade against the solid masses that threatened to overrun his lines from the rear. Junius Daniel, another professional from North Carolina, advanced his brigade to Ramseur's support. Though Daniel fell mortally wounded, his men held back the tide.

By full daylight Lee saw that Gordon, incredibly, was nudging the Federals backward on the eastern side of the salient. But at the same time Rodes, on his nervous black horse, galloped up to General Lee with more bad news. A fresh Federal corps, Sedgwick's, was massing on his front outside and southwest of the salient. Warren's corps, attacking straight on, was already pinning down Anderson on Rodes's left. Ramseur and Daniel, of Rodes's division, were entangled in the salient and weakening. As invariably when faced with an immediate danger, Lee did not hesitate to strip a point of potential danger. He sent Colonel Venable off with a rush to advance all except one brigade of the division guarding his flank west of the Po River. This was Dick Anderson's former division, newly commanded by Billy Mahone. After a disappointing showing as a brigadier, hypochondriacal Mahone had finally come into his own on Longstreet's flanking movement in the Wilderness.

Again Lee revealed the excited anxiety beneath the outward composure by riding back to urge forward Mahone's first brigade, Nat Harris's Mississippians. He was riding at the head of the column beside Harris when artillery fire suddenly broke across their path. For one of the few times when under fire, Traveler reared. While his forefeet pawed the air, a solid shot passed under his belly, grazing Lee's bootheels.

"Go back, General Lee," the frightened soldiers yelled. "For God's sake, go back!"

With all appearance of self-control, he said, "If you will promise to drive those people from our works I will go back."

The soldiers shouted their promise and rushed forward into the woods. The Mississippians came up just as Ramseur's regiments were about done for. Their momentum started a backward Federal movement along the western face of the salient, on Gordon's left. Lee, perceiving that Wilcox's lines on the right of the salient were not under heavy attack, pulled Sam MacGowan's brigade out of line. The South Carolinians pushed into the smoky woods, stumbling over dead and wounded in the morass, to come up between Gordon and the brigades from Mahone. By mid-morning the mixture of brigades from two corps, with Rodes the only division commander on the ground, drove Hancock's corps back outside the works on both sides of the Mule Shoe and at the apex.

There began the grisliest fight ever fought in Virginia. The Confederates were trying to drive the Federals away from the works and the Federals were clinging to the outside. The men were fighting in muck deep enough for corpses to float in. The opposing soldiers fought so close that they tossed bayonetted rifles over the parapets as harpoons. Half-drugged with exhaustion and with all military purpose lost—for Hancock's men were back where they were before the breakthrough —the men of both sides went through the motions of combat all during the ghastly, endless afternoon. The survivors renamed the Mule Shoe the "Bloody Angle."

To break the stalemate, Grant sent in Burnside's corps on the right flank near the court house, where only Heth's division held the lines. The gun battalions of Poague and Willie Pegram poured such a galling fire into the packed lines that Burnside's assault dissolved with heavy losses. Along Anderson's lines to the left of the salient, all day Alexander's superbly served First Corps guns had broken up the successive efforts of Warren's corps to mount an assault.

By the end of the day, Grant had lost another seventeen thousand men, while Lee's losses—largely through the wreckage of Johnson's division— approached ten thousand, with a heavy toll in brigadiers. Grant lost corps commander John Sedgwick, shot by a Georgia sharpshooter at eight hundred yards with an imported British Whitworth rifle. A West Pointer with many Confederate friends, Sedgwick was sincerely mourned in Lee's army.

By nightfall Lee was building a new line along the base of the Mule Shoe, where he had wanted it all along. At full darkness the shattered survivors from the "Bloody Angle" made their way back to the new line, and after all the carnage the unmanned fortifications of the Mule Shoe formed only a ghostly parapet in the woods where the dead lay.

4

When Lee returned to his headquarters that night, after the decisive repulse of Grant's attempt to overrun him, he was delivered a message that extinguished any glow of victory. Jeb Stuart had died of a stomach wound in Richmond. Though Lee had been prepared for the worst by an earlier message that his former cadet was wounded, he could not control his grief. He turned quickly aside and went alone into his tent. Later, when a staff officer entered, Lee said in a broken voice, "I can scarcely think of him without weeping."

Because of the shaken condition of the army after the May 12 fight, Lee did not announce Stuart's death for several days, when the details were in. When Sheridan had taken twelve thousand troopers on a raid to Richmond, Stuart, even in racing his worn mounts to the protection of the capital, would not denude the infantry of cavalry. He took only three brigades. His roughly four thousand riders clashed with Sheridan on the flat farmland north of Richmond near a stage tavern called Yellow Tavern. The Federal weight was too much. Stuart, trying to rally his men, rode with his red-lined cape fluttering into the midst of the fighting and was shot in the stomach by a dismounted cavalryman.

As a military factor in the campaign, Sheridan's victory at Yellow Tavern accomplished nothing. He was driven away from the city's inner fortifications by guns manned by reserves and the rifles of the local defense troops — boys, old men, and government clerks, some of whom were veterans invalided out of the army by wounds that incapacitated them for active campaigning. But the by-product of Stuart's death was a crippling blow to the future campaigning of the army. Like Jackson, the chief of cavalry was literally irreplaceable, and in the tone of the army the last that was young and golden left with thirty-one-year-old Jeb Stuart.

In General Orders No. 44, in which Stuart's death was announced, Lee showed his awareness of his army as an historical force. "His achievements form a conspicuous part of the history of this Army, with which his name and services will be forever associated."

While Lee was suffering the double blow of his personal sorrow and the army's loss, Grant's belligerence was cooled down by his frightful losses and a fresh appraisal of Lee. As Meade predicted, Grant had found Lee and the Army of Northern Virginia a different proposition from Bragg and the betrayed soldiers in the West. Grant waited nine days after the "Bloody Angle" for thirty thousand fresh reinforcements to come up. Though various sorties were made and Grant shifted the weight of his army eastward, Lee kept his depleted men digging lines that blocked every approach. Grant grew querulous about Lee protecting his dwindling army behind these new-style fortifications: he thought it unsporting of Lee not to expose his inferior numbers to be overrun like the Confederates in the West.

Lee liked fighting behind works no more than Grant liked attacking them. Wanting of all things to return to maneuver, he reopened his correspondence with Davis for the purpose of making a juncture between his army and troops from the twenty thousand infantry which had been hastily gathered *after* Butler opened his attack between Richmond and Petersburg. Rushed piecemeal from Coastal garrisons, with detachments from Lee's army and the Richmond defenses, supported by a quantity of hurriedly assembled gun batteries, the hodgepodge force had been commanded during the emergency by what might be called a "galaxy" of Confederate generals.

Pickett happened to be on the scene; Robert Ransom, former division commander, had been in charge of Richmond's defenses and he defied Davis's departments by crossing the James River with a couple of brigades; D. H. Hill, without a command, came up from his North Carolina home as a volunteer; Whiting, commanding the forts at Wilmington, had been sent by his friend Beauregard; Braxton Bragg, then Davis's "military adviser," ruled in the war offices. After this collection of troops and generals had contained Butler, Beauregard — who had written a friend he had no intention of burning his fingers pulling Davis's chestnuts out of the fire — then made his elegant appearance at Petersburg.

Beauregard, organizing the ragtag force into divisions, at once instituted a counterattack on Butler. Though the poorly coordinated attack was not successful, Butler retired his army onto an isthmus formed by the juncture of the James and Appomattox rivers, where the land opening was only three miles wide. Beauregard needed only build lines across this opening, fortified by guns, and Butler was — as Grant said — "bottled up." When Grant perceived that Butler's secondary threat was over and his army immobilized, he sent orders for one of Butler's corps to join the thirty thousand reinforcements already coming to his army. Lee, anticipating this order of Grant's, then proposed joint action between his army and the force gathered under Beauregard.

Lee wrote Davis in detail of Grant's withdrawals of troops from Petersburg and other points to be concentrated in the Army of the Potomac. After stressing the necessity of countering this concentration with troops from the Richmond-Petersburg line, Lee made it as plain as he could in a May 18 telegram: "If the [Confederate] troops are obliged to be retained at Richmond I may be forced back."

Beauregard, working in his department independently of Lee, also saw that Lee could only conduct a defensive retirement unless a juncture was made between their two forces. Beauregard's proposals were customarily grandiose, but he adopted Lee's fundamental point of the need for concentration to mount a counteroffensive. Without that, Beauregard soundly predicted that Lee could only fall back, step by step, and the picture presented was one "of ultimate starvation."

Grant, Lee, and Beauregard, then, all recognized that the test was reduced to the two major armies whose courses would be determined by the numbers each could mass. Davis could not be persuaded to view it that way.

By then, Davis's inner anxieties had driven him to maintain an orderly structure of departments that fulfilled an increasing neurotic need to have control of everything himself. He had not been shaken in maintaining his departmentalized structure after it exposed Richmond to capture, which was averted only by a series of last-ditch improvisations made in spite of his departments. Nor did he absorb the reality that these desperate measures had been made necessary only because he refused to disarrange the system he controlled in anticipation of the enemy's moves. In supporting his own sense of security, Davis was also unable to disarrange his new structure in anticipation of the consequences of Lee's being forced to fall back toward Richmond. Since the President could not bring himself to act in anticipation of a situation not already existing, Lee and Beauregard were prevented from uniting in common purpose against Grant.

Davis's rigidity in continuing an existing situation went so deep that he gave strategic preference neither to Lee nor Beauregard: Lee was to contain Grant and Beauregard contain Butler (whose uselessness was recognized by his own superior). Though Lee had kept the enemy distant from Richmond since he had evicted McClellan two years before, it would upset Davis's organization to give him single command of the defense of the capital. Beauregard remained as independent of Lee as if he commanded on the Mississippi — and soon the two generals began to work at cross-purposes.

To maintain the two fronts, unrelated in Davis's mind, he did recognize Lee's need of replacements merely for the containment of Grant. To this end, he removed from Beauregard's department troops belonging to Lee's army — Pickett's division and the brigade formerly commanded by Hoke. Davis then considered shifting to Lee some of the units which Beauregard himself had said were not needed to keep Butler penned up. At this Beauregard took a different attitude entirely. When he had proposed his joint offensive, Beauregard suggested leading a wing of fifteen thousand *with* Lee. Once Beauregard understood that troops were to be sent from him *to* Lee, suddenly he found Butler such a menace that Richmond would be endangered if one soldier was removed. Lee's potential collaborator became his rival.

Because Lee was not immediately aware of Beauregard's change and because joint action between the forces was so obviously the single necessity, he was slow to realize that the two armies were to be kept separated in inviolable compartments and that his petitions to Davis had no effect whatsoever.

In hoping for at least some joint action, he was visibly cheered at the return of his veterans. Though, in dismissal of his advice, Pickett's four brigades had been separated while being re-recruited with conscripts, Lee did not realize the poor morale in the units which had only days before been reunited under their division commander. So eager was Lee to return to maneuver that he made no comparison when Grant's thirty thousand replacements were matched on his side by the accretion of the 2250 infantrymen in Breckinridge's two brigades. These troops, with help of teen-age V.M.I. cadets and some cavalry, had turned back Sigel's threat in the Valley and were coming on to Lee.

Lee must have begun to think a little wishfully, a little with desperation, when this total accretion of about 8500 troops — coming after losses of seventeen thousand — could stimulate him to hope for an opportunity to get off the defensive. But clearly his spirits rose when the army left the bleak lines around Spotsylvania Court House. Grant was at last in motion again and to Lee movement held the prospect of maneuver — even though he began the movement by falling back to within twenty-three miles of Richmond.

5

With his staff and a young cavalryman from the neighborhood to act as guide, Lee rode away from the court house town at eight o'clock at night of May 21. Ewell and Anderson had been started southward during the day, and only A. P. Hill's corps was left as rear guard when Lee's small party rode off. Through the night he rode toward the North Anna River, which he had selected as Grant's destination. The main highway to Richmond crossed the river there, and the R.F.&P. Railroad Bridge, and Lee planned to be waiting at the North Anna when Grant's van arrived.

Grant had started Hancock's corps moving away from Spotsylvania on the night of May 20-21, with other troops following the day of the 21st. He was moving on an arc that ran to the southeast and back to the southwest. Grant's line of march was again a matter of deduction on Lee's part. In moving southward Grant was leaving the area of the supply base of Belle Plain on the Potomac, and Lee presumed (correctly) that he would move in an easterly direction that made him accessible to the supply base of Port Royal on the Rappahannock. In moving southward from that area, to avoid crossing two rivers Grant would be forced to cross the Mattaponi back to the west. From there the logical completion of Grant's swing would bring him to the Richmond-Washington highway at the North Anna River, only two miles from the junction of the Virginia Central with the R.F.&P. at Hanover Junction.

In acting on his assumption, Lee was protected against surprise by two

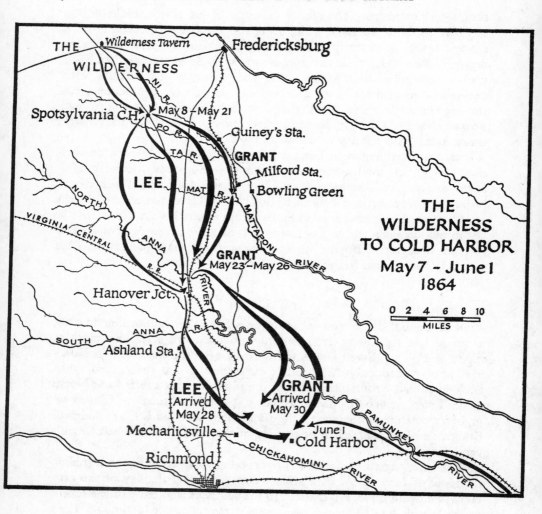

THE
WILDERNESS
TO COLD HARBOR
May 7 - June 1
1864

of the three cavalry brigades Stuart had left with the army — a brigade in Wade Hampton's division and one in Rooney Lee's division. Pierce Young's small brigade had, with its broken-down horses, gone to Richmond for refitting.

On the other side, Sheridan had not yet returned from his May 12 raid. Grant had no cavalry that could interfere with Lee's march to occupy the selected position, and Lee's foot soldiers were marching on the shorter distance of the chord of Grant's arc. Though Ewell's van left Spotsylvania twenty-four hours after Hancock, around noon of the

21st, there was none of the element of a race as on the way to Spotsylvania.

In Lee's exhilaration, he pushed himself physically on his night ride, and was also a little careless. Riding on the Telegraph Road, Lee's party was at times separated only by one mile from Federal flankers across country to the east. At three o'clock in the morning, having ridden seventeen miles in seven hours, Lee rested two hours. After taking a nap, he ate a scanty breakfast. Then he rode on six miles to the North Anna, where he saw the van of Ewell's corps wearily trudging down the hill to the river. The men had covered twenty-three miles since noon of the day before, marching most of the night.

Pausing to give orders for the disposition of the troops, Lee crossed the river and rode on to Hanover Junction. His headquarters tent was pitched in the angle formed by the crossing of two railroads. By nine-thirty, he was sending telegraphic messages to Richmond, and further heartened to find Breckinridge's two small brigades at Hanover Junction. Then, due to the wreck of Allegheny Johnson's division, Lee turned to reshuffle brigades to retain the structure of three divisions in Ewell's corps. By then A. P. Hill had returned to duty, releasing Jubal Early for his own division. For Gordon, who had temporarily commanded Early's division, Lee formed a new division consisting of Gordon's own brigade and two brigades salvaged from Johnson's division. Forming divisions of three brigades was a desperate makeshift, but at least Lee's new favorite would get a division of his own.

While Lee was making the quick reorganizations in the Second Corps, Hill's corps began crossing the river around noon, and the commanding general allowed all the troops a complete rest for the day. Though he was directly in Grant's path in his move toward Richmond, Lee did not put his engineers to drawing lines for defensive works. Thinking with his hopes, Lee expected Grant to avoid any more straight-on assaults of a fixed position. He thought Grant would try to turn him to the east or west. He revealed his own plans in a message to Davis the next morning, May 23.

"Whatever route he [Grant] pursues, I am in a position to move against him, and shall endeavor to engage him while in motion." Not yet knowing that Beauregard was working against him, Lee wrote, "I shall be near enough Richmond, I think, to combine the operations of this army with that under General Beauregard." Mentioning that no more troops were necessary to retain Butler in his entrenchments, Lee added that, as Grant's army was in the field, "it seems to me our best policy to unite upon it and endeavor to crush it."

On the same day Beauregard wired Davis that reports indicated reinforcements were coming to Butler. "If this be true, he may take the offensive soon. Then I shall require assistance." When Beauregard sent that message, Smith's XVIII Corps was under orders to leave Butler and reinforce Grant's army. Lee's call for an offensive operation was not acknowledged by the President.

Sometime during the day after sending off the latest of his futile appeals, Lee began to feel the effects of the physical and mental strain. He did not look at his best when, before noon, he rode to the high south bank of the North Anna to study the movements of the Federal forces gathering on the opposite side. On the porch of a red-brick house on the crest of the hill, he drank a glass of milk while watching the puffs of smoke shoot from enemy guns as Grant began to feel out the Confederate position. The milk in the glass did not shake when a stray cannon ball struck the porch column he was standing beside.

Sometime after noon he received a report that Federals were massing across from Ox Ford, two miles upriver from the highway bridge. Then he heard the roll of artillery to the west of that, and decided to make his own reconnaissance. By then Lee manifestly felt unwell, though he did not say so. But, instead of calling for Traveler, he asked for the use of a carriage.

He was driven along a country road that ran beside the tracks of the Virginia Central, parallel with the river. West of Ox Ford and south of the river, he passed the camps of Hill's troops spread in the mostly open farm country. Well beyond the terrain of the Wilderness, Hanover County consisted of substantial farms and fine houses between belts of timber — heavily foliaged but lacking the density of the Wilderness. Lee's carriage left the road and cut across a field to where a battery of horse artillery was firing. He climbed from the carriage and, between the roaring blasts of the guns, talked briefly with the battery captain. He ranged his field glasses across the countryside toward the river. Satisfied that the Federal movement was only a feint, he returned to his carriage.

That was the last report of anyone seeing him on the field. Lee presumably went back to his headquarters at Hanover Junction and gave in to his illness. That night he suffered an attack called "intestinal inflammation." From the time he left the gun battery, nothing definitely related him to the action that followed his departure.

The reports on the action itself were confused and reticent. With the officers and men of both armies bordering on exhaustion from the prolonged fighting, the units that clashed late on the afternoon of the 23rd fought below their potential and no general on the field showed a leadership of which he was proud.

Three miles to the northwest of Ox Ford, a belt of timber concealed a bad crossing of the North Anna at a ford by a gristmill, Jericho Mills.

Around noon the infantrymen of Warren's corps began to wade across, while engineers built a bridge for the guns and wagons. At three o'clock Powell Hill was informed of enemy troops gathering on his flank and he hurried off Wilcox's division, followed by Heth. Wilcox's attack was poorly coordinated but Warren's four divisions were not well established for receiving attack, and did no more than drive off Wilcox's four separated brigades. By the time Heth deployed, dusk was falling and he relieved Wilcox's scattered units.

General Lee apparently received the details the following morning when his control was undermined by acute ill feeling. Always irritated when he felt sick, Lee let loose his suppressed resentments and frustrations by lashing out at Hill. "Why did you not do as Jackson would have done — thrown your whole force upon those people and driven them back?"

Recuperating from his own illness, Powell Hill said nothing. After all, in sending forward one division to develop the unseen enemy in the woods, he had done precisely what Lee did in sending forward Heth toward the Brock Road in the Wilderness. Hill, with his reverential love of the commanding general, may have realized that Lee was striking out at more than him.

Lee soon regained his composure, though his temper remained edgy. He forced his mind to the problem of a Federal corps digging in on his left flank. The night before Hancock had rushed the bridgehead Lee left on the north bank of the river at the highway bridge, and this as good as announced the Federal intention of forcing a crossing on his right as well as his left. These enemy crossings would separate the two wings of his army by five miles, with a threat to its center by the good crossing at Ox Ford.

Sick as he was, Lee reacted instantly to the problem with his most single brilliant flash of tactical improvisation. As if in a dazzling vision, Lee conceived of a movement that transformed his danger into a trap for the enemy. The Ox Ford crossing between the two flanks became the pivot. There, where the southern bank was higher, Alexander's artillery could achieve dominance and, lightly supported, insure holding that crossing. From Ox Ford as the apex of a triangle, Lee bent his flanks back southeast and southwest at a 45-degree angle, resting on the marshes of Little River. Hill on the left, and Ewell and Anderson on the right, threw up works, forming the effect of a fort. This was accomplished within a few hours.

When Hancock pushed across the river as anticipated, instead of finding Lee fighting on two fronts, Grant found his own army divided on Lee's side of the river. Since Wright's corps had crossed at Jericho Mills to support Warren, and Burnside was committed to futile efforts to force a crossing at Ox Ford, Hancock's corps was isolated from the rest of the army outside the works of Ewell and part of Anderson's. Here was the opportunity Lee had sought to crush a part of Grant's army. Humphreys, Meade's chief of staff, conceded that Lee had the chance to overwhelm Hancock for "two or three hours."

But, in these two or three hours, Lee was too ill to ride to the lines and assume command. While he trusted Anderson and Ewell on the defense behind their works, he could not trust either to form an assault to be delivered against Hancock. Hill had his hands full watching Warren and Wright (who had succeeded Sedgwick). Lee, fretting, could only hope that Hancock would attack. Even doughty Hancock had enough of assaulting works. Once he saw the lay of the land, Hancock turned defensive and hurried his own men in throwing up works. When Hancock dug in, as were Warren and Wright outside Hill's works, Lee saw his brilliant trap end in a stalemate.

Not listed as one of the great engagements, not even on the battle flags of some regiments, the bloodless battle of the North Anna was as decisive a repulse to Grant as Gettysburg was to Lee. The difference was that Grant, who did not even attempt to assail the roadblock, was not forced to retire for supplies and refitting. The naval bases, shifting as he shifted, supplied his army and withdrew his wounded.

This defensive victory was no comfort to Lee when his worsening feelings forced him to return to his tent. "We must strike them a blow," he murmured over and over. "We must not let them pass us again. . . . We must strike them a blow."

### 6

Lee's intestinal inflammation did not pass as had the attack of diarrhea at Gettysburg. The illness settled in him, and Lee recognized that he was beginning to wear out. "I am not fit to command this army," he said, when the next move of Grant's compelled him to prod his mind, clouded with sickness, to a new concentration on the enemy's intentions.

His own counteroffensive had become only an inner goad. From the North Anna, he had written Davis, "If General Beauregard is in position to unite with me in any operation against General Grant, I should like to know it . . ." Not understanding Davis's fixations, Lee could not accept the finality of the obtuseness that prevented the juncture of the two forces.

However, though gnawed by his urge to get off the defensive, once again he must try — this time from the tent in which he lay ill — to anticipate his opponent for the negative end of thwarting him. "If I only had my poor Stuart," he said once, "I would know what those people are up to."

Grant had given up on the direct approach to Richmond and on overrunning Lee. Leaving the Richmond-Washington highway, he sent his troops on a rapid march east along the North Anna, which soon became the Pamunkey, to a crossing at Hanovertown northeast of Richmond. The country was brushy along the river and Lee's attenuated cavalry — suffering from a breakdown of horses — could not penetrate the screen of Sheridan's troopers, rested and returned to the army. For the first time Lee felt uncertain about Grant's intentions.

Riding in a carriage south on the Telegraph Road during May 27, Lee made his headquarters at Atlee. This stop on the Virginia Central was only nine miles from Richmond. To the east, where Grant's army seemed to be, the Federals could use a network of country roads to the capital. Such an approach, however, would result only in another defensive stand of Lee's behind the modern field fortifications of which Grant complained. Grant's most damaging stroke would be a swing back to the west to operate against the Virginia Central. Even though Lee was apprehensive over the railroad, he seemed to hope that Grant would make the move in which he could be caught in motion.

The day after his arrival at Atlee, Lee's sickness forced him to retire to a room in the house of the Clarke family. From there he dictated a message to Davis, saying he would "endeavor to give battle" where it was convenient to Beauregard. Now Old Bory knew, as Lee did not, that Davis had no plans for him except as a potential troop feeder to Lee. Thus, when Lee's message was passed on to him, Beauregard persuaded Davis that his own force was menaced by Butler. The President answered Lee: "It is doubtful if he [Beauregard] could be better employed at this time" — than by watching Butler's bottled-up force.

This was about when Lee finally realized that his army and Beauregard's were to be kept in separate operations. At the same time, he was reluctantly forced to commit part of his cavalry to combat, in order to establish the whereabouts of Grant. Since Stuart's death Lee had appointed no chief of cavalry, and added to his burdens by having the division commanders report directly to him.

For the reconnaissance in force Lee selected Fitz Lee's two-brigade division and to the one brigade then active in Wade Hampton's division added the half of a new brigade that had just arrived from South Carolina. These eleven hundred finely conditioned troopers had finally been released from their agreeable desuetude in one of the President's departments and, stung by the taunts of the ragged veterans, were an angrily determined lot of young men. They were also armed with rifles, at which they were very expert, instead of the shorter-ranged carbines.

The combined force met Gregg's cavalry division on the flat lands around a little country church. Enon Church was near the crossroads of Haw's Shop, in Grant's line of march away from the Pamunkey. Fighting dismounted to spare the troopers the risk of horses collapsing under them, with the battle-innocent South Carolinians vying with the veterans in courage, the force brought a firepower to battle Gregg to a standstill. For the first time facing even numbers, Sheridan — estimating the regiment and one-half of green South Carolinians as four thousand "mounted infantry" — called the Enon Church battle "an unequal contest." He was compelled to bring over Torbett's division to force the Hampton–Fitz Lee cavalry from the field, and there was no pursuit. This was a far cry from the days of glory under the plumed Jeb Stuart but the grim horsemen, in their orderly withdrawal, brought along Federal infantry prisoners from the V and VI Corps. By this sacrifice of his fading cavalry, Lee learned that Grant was pushing from the Pamunkey toward Richmond.

Still unable to accept completely this obvious move from Grant, in his apprehension about the Virginia Central, Lee left A. P. Hill's corps within five miles of the railroad and the Telegraph Road. To operate in Grant's front, Lee sent the tough veterans of the Second Corps, but not under Dick Ewell. The night before Old Baldhead, also reaching Atlee in an ambulance, reported himself sick and asked to be relieved temporarily. Having no intimacy of relationship with Ewell, Lee did not find it too hard to extend Ewell's leave into a permanent removal from command. To save face for the devoted soldier, Lee arranged to have him appointed commander of the Richmond defenses — something of a post for displaced generals.

Jubal Early, a brigadier in Jackson's heyday, assumed command of the old Second Corps, and Dodson Ramseur succeeded to command of Early's reduced division. While Lee sent orders from his sickroom at the Clarke house, Early spread his troops along the southern banks of the Totopotomoi Creek. This multi-fingered stream, moving sluggishly through swampy, thickly brushed banks, was Grant's introduction to the terrain of the Seven Days Battle. After all the hard marching to which Grant put his troops and despite his well-concealed movement, Lee was still in his path. Though Grant's front was blocked by only one corps, and that fielding less than two-thirds of its original numbers, the brush-lined water barrier reduced the Federal forward movement to probing by skirmishing.

While Early's men were skirmishing across the Totopotomoi during the afternoon of May 29, President Davis paid Lee a visit. The two men talked of the possibility of troops from Beauregard. Lee, having then accepted the rejection of his proposals for a joint movement, was simply asking for more troops. But Beauregard had convinced Davis that only four thousand of Butler's men — not Smith's whole corps — had gone from his front and to send any of his troops to Lee "would jeopardize the safety" of his position and "greatly endanger Richmond itself." That night Beauregard came himself to Lee's headquarters. The loquacious Creole talked so eloquently that Lee did not argue with him. Maybe he felt too sick. Anyway, he was not convinced.

On the next day Lee discovered that Grant's whole army had shifted eastward along the Totopotomoi and he lost his last apprehensions that Grant might swing back to the west to operate against the Virginia Central. Once he eliminated this possibility, Lee envisioned Grant's plan of advance to the last detail.

On the morning of the 30th he wrote to Dick Anderson that Grant would sidle from position to position along the Totopotomoi, turning the headwaters of another stream at Bethesda Church. This was on the Old Church Road to Richmond by way of Mechanicsville. From Bethesda Church Grant would fortify his line and move by his left flank, eastward, to the Chickahominy. "This is just a repetition of their former movements. It can only be arrested by striking at once at that part of their force which has crossed the Totopotomoi in General Early's front."

While Lee had caught on to his new opponent very quickly — outlining Grant's plans as if he had read the battle orders — his own goad to catch the Federals in motion had become an unrealistic obsession. It was as if the sick man was driven by a premonition that if he did not strike now the offensive would be gone forever. In a now or never desperation, he eagerly agreed when Early proposed an attack on the Federal flank reaching toward the Old Church Road at Bethesda Church. With Anderson replacing Early's troops along the Totopotomoi, Early could march by a rough road he had cut, paralleling the stream, to Old Church Road. Screened by cavalry there, Early's three divisions could deploy perpendicular to Grant's line north of the Totopotomoi, and roll up the flank.

Lee, as well as Early, refused to accept the reality that the potential for offensive action was drained from the army. Since leaving the North Anna, even the men's marginal subsistence diet had broken down. Units went for two days without food of any kind. Then the men received three hard biscuits and a slice of the fat pork they called "side meat," and which was used at home for cooking greens. A gunner in the Richmond Howitzers wrote that their hunger was an "unimaginable, all-pervading pain inflicted when the strength to endure pain is utterly gone. It is a great despairing cry of a wasting body . . ."

Along with the physical weakness of the starving men, the Second Corps had a makeshift quality in its command. Diminished brigades had been shuffled and new men replacing fallen brigadiers were unaccustomed to working together. Ramseur was a total stranger to his division. The 58th Virginia Regiment was down to sixty-eight men under a captain, and he was worried about his wife at home in the path of Grant's army. The soldiers were still deadly in the slow action fighting, such as defense and skirmishing, which drew on their individual experience in protecting themselves and employed their superior marksmanship. But coordination was difficult between units in the more taxing demands of group movements in assault, and the men were called upon for greater physical exertion.

At Bethesda Church combative Rodes sent in his division in something like an old-fashioned charge of Lee's veterans and began rolling up the Federal flank. The Federals reacted quickly, bringing up reserves to form a line and dig in. Early supported the initial assault with only one brigade. This merely sacrificed men and their new commander, young Colonel Willis, in a futile charge against the Federal works. In his first command of a corps, Jubal Early showed the need of experience in coordinating separate bodies in a single action. He made no use of the skill and contagious courage of division commanders Gordon and Ramseur. In the failure of his assault, he tried to blame Anderson for not cooperating. It was unhappily true that Anderson, after his one inspired hour at Spotsylvania, had returned to his lackluster competence and remained supine on Early's left.

Lee reproached neither of them as he had A. P. Hill at Jericho Mills. More typically, he accepted the limitations of the individuals it was his lot to depend upon. Also, when the dismal reports came in at the end of the day, the 30th, news arrived that drove everything else from his mind. His own spy system had discovered that Smith's XVIII Corps, from Butler's army, was arriving at the White House landing. The line of march of these sixteen thousand fresh troops would bring them up on the left of Grant's wide front, and Lee could not further thin his own line to move even a regiment out to meet Smith. With counteroffensives temporarily forgotten, Lee for the first time faced a threat to Richmond which he knew his army could not contain.

7

Ignoring protocol, Lee sent a telegram directly to Beauregard, who only the night before had insisted that Smith's corps was still on his front. Lee, having no authority in Beauregard's department, simply asked for Hoke's division as immediate reinforcements. Beauregard answered, "War Department must determine when and what troops to order from here." This broke Lee's tenuously held patience.

At seven-thirty he wired the President: "General Beauregard says the Department must determine what troops to send for him. He gives it all necessary information. The result of this delay will be disaster. Butler's troops will be with Grant tomorrow. Hoke's division, at least, should be with me by light tomorrow."

Lee had not sent a peremptory message since the period of his 1862 ascendancy, and he had never used such an unequivocal word as "disaster." Davis always acted when the enemy was at the door, as this gave him a certainty. Without disturbing his departments, he sent a message to Military Adviser Braxton Bragg, then at his home, to order Hoke forward.

At ten-fifteen, fifteen minutes before Bragg's order reached him, Beauregard sent Bragg a message saying that he felt "authorized by the President's letter of the 28th" to send Lee reinforcements. Anticipating the War Department's order, Old Bory made his record look better by appearing to act on his own. The four hours' delay, however, made it impossible for Hoke's troops to reach Lee by daylight of the 31st. It was dusk before the first of the brigades, softened by garrison duty, marched out the Cold Harbor Road to the position beyond Lee's flank.

During the day of May 31 Lee felt sufficiently better to leave the sickroom. He rode in a carriage to a new headquarters at Shady Grove Church, to be nearer the eastward shift of the armies. That night he learned that Sheridan had forced Fitz Lee away from the crossroads at Old Cold Harbor, where Lee believed Grant intended to make juncture with Baldy Smith's corps. Sheridan's presence there in force confirmed Lee's assumption. As the Federal soldiers threw up mounds of works in their sidling eastward, like a gigantic molehill stretching for miles, Lee grew convinced that Grant planned no assaults against the facing Confederate lines during his concentration for a turning movement at the crossroads tavern.

However, Smith's corps had not yet reached Cold Harbor, while Hoke's division had. Lee snatched at this small advantage and immediately issued orders for a daylight attack. They would overrun Sheridan at Cold Harbor and fan to the west to strike the head of the Federal infantry advancing in column.

Lee returned to the audacity characteristic of his grandest maneuvers to arrange a formidable force. He pulled Anderson's corps out of the line that was shifting eastward with Grant's shifts, and started the men by bypaths across country toward Cold Harbor. Since only Kershaw's lead division would join Hoke at the Cold Harbor Road by daylight, the opening attack would be delivered by Kershaw and Hoke, on either side of the road to Cold Harbor. When daylight came on June 1, Lee did not feel well enough to go to the field, but everything seemed ready just as he had planned it.

On the field Dick Anderson ordered Kershaw to open with a reconnaissance in force into the thickly vined woods on his front. Since Kershaw had been commanding the division, he had shown partiality for using his own old brigade, for which no new brigadier had been appointed. It happened that the senior colonel, Lawrence Massilon Keitt, had only recently brought his large regiment to Virginia from two years of comfortable idleness in a South Carolina garrison. Keitt's troops were as gallantly turned out as 1861 volunteers, and just as innocent of warfare. Thirty-nine-year-old Keitt, a United States congressman at twenty-nine, was one of his state's most distinguished citizens and it devolved on him to act in the tradition.

As one of the veterans saw him, "Keitt led his men like a knight of old . . . mounted upon his superb gray charger . . . preparing to cut his way through like a storm center . . . But every old soldier . . . saw at a glance his inexperience and want of self control." This "martyr to the inexorable laws of army rank" was knocked dead from his horse in the first volley from repeating carbines that showered out of the woods. When guns from Regular United States batteries started spraying the open field, his shocked men fled for their lives. In their abject flight, they carried along the veteran regiments from the brigade. The second brigade, its flank exposed, could only retire out of range of the fire from the woods.

The sequence of decisions that placed Keitt in charge of a reconnaissance in force finished off Lee's boldly conceived plan before its execution got started. For the third time in nine days, with the third corps commander, it became inescapably evident that Lee's army could perform no maneuvers without Lee in personal field command. Anderson's management of his affair was even sorrier than Early's two days before. For the non-self-seeking Anderson it could only be said that he blamed no one else, and there was some extentuation in the total inaction from Hoke on Kershaw's right.

Twenty-seven-year-old Robert Hoke had been a promising brigadier in Jackson's old corps when he was wounded out at Chancellorsville. When he recovered at home in North Carolina, he took part in a locally successful action that — amid the succession of gloomy minor disasters along the Coast — made Hoke a home-state hero. Upped to major general he returned to Virginia and was given a seven-thousand-man division in the operations against Butler. In the loose organization there it went unnoticed that he cooperated poorly with others. At the abortive Cold Harbor attack, though he was operating under unfamiliar conditions as a stranger to Lee's army, Hoke seemed content to rest on his reputation.

Three times illness had kept Lee from field command during opportunities presented by Grant's belligerent clumsiness. Though he would accept the illness as God's will, he could not escape the gnawing erosion of frustration. Then, too weak to ride, he missed the solitary journeys on Traveler which he later said gave him renewal to keep going.

Nor was Anderson's disappointing direction of an assault the worst. That afternoon the Federals attacked. By the time the divisions of Pickett and Field had come up on Kershaw's left, completing Anderson's corps, Wright's corps was in line to the west of Cold Harbor and Smith's new corps had arrived at the crossroads. In the attack of this combined force, Field and Pickett held, but Smith drove a wedge along a ravine where Kershaw and Hoke joined west of the Cold Harbor Road. Anderson sent Lee a message that night saying he needed reinforcements in order to hold his lines.

The message reached Lee in his new headquarters near Cold Harbor, which he had reached that afternoon. The group of headquarters tents was pitched in an open field on the hillside overlooking Gaines' gristmill in the shallow valley of Powhite Creek. The pleasant, cool-looking site was marred by the wreckage of the four-story brick mill, burned by Sheridan on his Richmond raid — an unsightly reminder of the changes since Lee, in his full vigor, rode past the mill on the way to delivering his first major assault.

On the next morning Lee, wearing an unmilitary sack linen coat in the humid heat, once again mounted Traveler, and rode out to look at the lines. He was frankly preparing that June 2 to receive attack. The brief penetration between Kershaw and Hoke had not been exploited and the break was repaired by strong fortifications built at a concave angle. To extend Hoke's right, Lee planned to post Breckinridge's two brigades on the Turkey Hill rise where Harvey Hill had fought at Gaines' Mill. But no one seemed to know the whereabouts of the troops from the Valley. Lee went looking for Breckinridge himself. At ten o'clock he found the Kentuckian and his men eating breakfast in Mechanicsville. He sent the brigades to their position.

During the hot, humid morning reports came to him of local forays from the Federals along the left of the six mile line. However, he held to his conviction that the main attack would be delivered in the Cold Harbor area, and shifted two of Hill's divisions, Mahone and Wilcox, to strengthen the right of his line. It was a thin line, with the flanks protected by the cavalry on their gaunt horses. But, though the soldiers had strained their last reserves of energy to throw up entrenchments, Lee relied on the men to maintain themselves behind connected works. There they would not be called upon for physical exertion nor would they be exposed to the inadequacies of command.

In the afternoon a cooling rain began to fall, breaking the sultriness of the day. Having done all he could, Lee returned to his hillside head-quarters, dismounted, and waited in his tent for the action to open.

The attack did not come that afternoon. At four-thirty the next morning, June 3, Lee heard the rolling thunder of battle, the volume so heavy that windowpanes rattled in Richmond. Before any messages reached Lee, the issue was decided. Though even the soldiers did not know it, Grant's attack was broken in fifteen minutes. The first Federal wave disintegrated before a volume of fire, rifles and guns, and succeeding waves only piled up the dead and wounded on the flat ground in front of the trenches. Within an hour seven thousand Federals lay on the ground, to make the highest casualties in that period of time during the war.

Grant, who had convinced himself that his hammering had shaken Lee's army to the point of demoralization, sent orders for his corps to renew the assault on their immediate fronts without reference to the movement of the other units. Through the morning, until ten o'clock, the Confederate soldiers could hear the shouts of officers, then a flurry of movement and a distant volley fired from the ground. The Federal troops were tacitly refusing to commit suicide by advancing upright into rifle range of those trenches. Finally these simulacra of assaults faded off, and Lee's baffled soldiers slowly realized that the climactic battle of Grant's month-long offensive had come and gone.

Grant's hammering tactics, that battered and bled Lee's army, had been a two-edged sword. In losing approximately fifty thousand men, about the amount of infantry Lee started with, Grant had bled the army he inherited of its veterans. Discouragement grew from, as the soldiers called it, "the butchering in the slaughter-pens" on the drive to the Chickahominy. Morning reports ceased to be called for because "the country would not stand for it, if they knew."

This was Lee's achievement. Perhaps, under the circumstances of his collapsing army and the restrictions of his own government, the 1864 campaign was his greatest achievement as a soldier. Lee knew it was not enough. In saving Richmond, he had lost maneuver. He was back to where he began when he took over the army from Johnston — a static defense which doomed them by arithmetic.

Lee's spirit as a man, not his mind as a soldier, rejected acceptance of conducting a doomed defense. In his hot tent above the millpond, he worried at plans and stratagems by which he might get at Grant's army and defeat it in the open. With hope transcending his realism, he ignored the evidence that the power for offense was gone from his army. He refused to accept the impossibility of the one action that could stave off defeat from the society to whose independence he had committed his life.

8

After Cold Harbor, Grant gave up on any more maneuvers that ended with Lee in his front. For nine days the armies faced one another across the hot, muddy stinking trenches. But the respite from action was nothing of a rest. Sharpshooters practiced their skills continuously and the intermittent bursts of artillery fire kept everyone from settling down. Sickness spread daily in the unhealthy confines of the foul trenches and survivors of the hardest battles succumbed to disease in their low resistance. The men dug at graves in those stifling June days. However, further drains on the men's stamina were checked by the freedom from physical exertion and the arrival of bacon run in by the blockade from Nassau. The bacon was so fat the soldiers called it "Nausea bacon." Onions were issued as an antidote to scurvy.

Very little was needed to restore the cheerful temper of the men. One of them joked to General Lee as he rode by that they would get so fat from food and idleness they would not be able to fight. Morale soared over their defeat of Grant and the conviction grew that he could never beat them. Lee looked further than the soldiers or the government. Riding restlessly back and forth as his health returned, he futilely sought some way to get at the Federal soldiers behind their own labyrinthine lines instead of waiting on what new moves Grant might undertake.

While Lee perforce could do no more than wait for the enemy's move, one that might give him an opening for a counterstroke, he had the time to write his wife frequently. Judging from his expressions of gratitude for various packages of food and clothing she sent him, Lee did not ride the few miles into Richmond to see her.

Since early in the year, Mrs. Lee had enjoyed the nearest thing to a permanent home since she left Arlington. Mr. John Stewart, a wealthy Scotchman who lived on an estate outside the city at Brook Hill, rented the Lees a handsome, spacious house on fashionable East Franklin Street near Capitol Square. Though its rear balconies overlooked a walled garden, facing the river only a few blocks to the south, it was not a restful residence. The echoes of battlefield thunder rolled in Mrs. Lee's bedroom and the streets were noisy day and night with the rattle of supply wagons going out to the fields, creaking ambulances coming in and the steady rumble of the wagons of dead on the way to the cemeteries.

Lee at this time must have considered the advisability of abandoning Richmond, to free his army from being chained to the defense of the capital. However, along with the harmful effect on the country's morale, it would have been an extremely difficult operation to remove the arms-producing facilities, hospitals, warehouses and government offices. In any event, Davis would never have consented. Then, the enemy's next move forced Lee to abandon his own nebulous projects in reaction against Grant's use of the initiative.

Before Grant moved his army, he opened operations on secondary fronts that threatened the supply lines to Richmond and the army. On June 6, Lee learned that a Federal force under David Hunter had occupied Staunton, the western terminus of the Virginia Central. The next day he learned that Sheridan had headed west toward Hunter. Two days later, June 9, Beauregard sent an urgent alarm that Petersburg was under attack by cavalry and infantry.

Lee took the three diversionary threats one by one. Against Hunter, he returned Breckinridge's two brigades to the Valley to support the poorly disciplined cavalry operating in the western part of the states. Against Sheridan's accomplished railroad wreckers, he sent to the Virginia Central the bulk of his cavalry — the divisions of Fitz Lee and Wade Hampton, the latter with the full new brigade from South Carolina (minus its sizable casualties) and Pierce Young's rebuilt small brigade. The attack at Petersburg he dismissed as a raid.

Then on June 11 the news from the West grew ominous. With the wayward cavalry of the Valley dissolving before the Federals, Hunter had moved south to occupy Lexington, the charming center of rural Rockbridge County, and the site of V.M.I. and Washington College. A small-bore Sherman, Hunter had put his men to the burning of the college buildings of V.M.I. and the home of former Governor Letcher, along with pillaging from civilians' homes. His next stop was obviously Lynchburg, an important railroad junction on the eastern slope of the Blue Ridge. From there Hunter could start east, meet Sheridan, complete the destruction of the Virginia Central, and come on to join Grant. Against this very grave danger, Lee had no choice except to detach troops from his own army.

Though this reduced his chances against Grant, Lee characteristically did not hesitate to make the full commitment necessary to crush the immediate danger. On June 12, the veterans of Early's corps, with their artillery, were pulled out of line and marched to the depot for a roundabout train trip to Lynchburg. Though Lee did not learn it until the next day, Wade Hampton had inflicted a decisive repulse on Sheridan at a stop on the Virginia Central, Trevilian Station. Sheridan did not admit that the tattered Confederate cavalry had repulsed him, but he abandoned his efforts to wreck the railroad, turned back from his assignment of making juncture with Hunter and brought his cavalry back to Grant's army.

Without Sheridan's support, Hunter retired before Early, and the threats from the Valley and to the railroad were removed. However, in sending Early to Lynchburg, Lee had thought beyond mere defense. He had ordered Early, after he disposed of Hunter, to move north down the Valley to create a counterdiversion by such threat against Washington as he could make with his small force. Hunter, by disposing of himself by flight into the mountains, made the assignment easier for a corps then reduced to eight thousand infantry.

The low estate to which Lee's army had been reduced could most clearly be realized by the fact that Early's eight thousand represented nearly one-fourth of the infantry. Not counting Hoke, who was to be detached from Lee, or the two brigades and stationary artillerists garrisoned on the north side of the river at Chaffin's Bluff, the corps remaining with Lee numbered barely twenty-eight thousand infantry. With these, and the two slim cavalry brigades under Rooney, Lee had to counter the next move of Grant's. This came on the night of June 12-13.

9

On the morning of the 13th Lee's pickets discovered miles of empty trenches and not a Federal soldier in sight. Not surprised by this, Lee crossed his diminished infantry over the Chickahominy to the flatlands where weeds and vines grew from the miles of works left from McClellan's siege two summers before. Lee had written Davis that he expected Grant to shift to the James River. In leaving Cold Harbor, Grant would march through the concealing brush along the north bank of the broadening Chickahominy about twenty miles east of Richmond, where he would cross to the south bank and move straight to the James. From there he could either advance on Richmond from a naval-supported base or move south of the James (as McClellan had wanted to) for an attack on Petersburg. In Richmond the general opinion was that he would advance against Petersburg.

Lee moved his troops on a leisurely march along the fan of roads his large 1862 army had used in the Seven Days Battle. Where McClellan had escaped Lee's trap at Glendale, Lee halted at a crossroads called Riddell's Shop. Twelve miles from Richmond, Lee could cover all approaches to the city or move to the pontoon bridge at Chaffin's Bluff for a shift to Petersburg. Around the time Lee reached Riddell's Shop he learned that Grant's army, as anticipated, was crossing the Chickahominy farther to the east on pontoons where the Long Bridge had been burned. This information came from a small cavalry brigade under Colonel Gary, also released from South Carolina and attached to the Department of Richmond.

Later in the day, near dusk, Rooney Lee reported that his two slender brigades had encountered Federal cavalry in their front. As the enemy was not employing Sheridan's usual belligerence, it was assumed the Federal horsemen were merely screening the approaches to Grant's main army to the east. Except for the plantations along the river, the country was so densely foliaged that it was impossible to detect any troop movements at a distance.

The next morning, June 14, Lee sent Hill's foot soldiers to support the troopers in pushing east across Malvern Hill and on to the River Road. Beyond Shirley, where Lee's cousin Hill Carter was struggling to get his crops raised, Federal infantry were encountered around Berkeley plantation and prisoners were collected from Warren's V Corps. From the defensive attitude of the Federal infantry, Lee wrote Davis at noon, "I think the enemy must be preparing to move south of the James River."

Later in the afternoon he wrote Davis that portions of Grant's army were believed to be at Westover plantation and farther east at the landing of Dr. Wilcox's plantation. "I see no indications of his attacking me on this side of the river . . . As his facilities for crossing the river and taking possession of Petersburg are great, and as I think it will more probably be his plan, I have sent General Hoke with his command to a point above Drewry's Bluff in easy distance of the pontoon bridge." By the end of the day Lee planned to move his army the next morning back to Chaffin's Bluff, from where by way of the pontoon bridge to Drewry's Bluff he could move quickly to Petersburg.

Before Lee went to sleep that night two messages from Beauregard relayed the information from signalmen that the Federal pontoons earlier observed being shipped up the Chickahominy had not been seen returning. This could indicate that the pontoon bridges had been used only in Grant's crossing of the Chickahominy at Long Bridge and that he was not yet crossing the James. Beauregard's messages, verifying Lee's own information that Smith's corps had sailed from the White House Landing, also mentioned that Smith had returned to Butler. With this suggestion of the possibility that only Smith had moved to the south side of the James, Lee changed his mind about moving to Chaffin's Bluff. The next day, June 15, he allowed his soldiers another day of rest in the quiet at Riddell's Shop, while waiting for more definite information on Grant's movements.

During that morning Colonel Samuel B. Paul, of Beauregard's staff, came to Lee's tent to request the return of the troops belonging to Beauregard's Department. Paul had brought along pages of figures to prove the need of the troops. Previous to Paul's visit, jealous-minded Beauregard had been addressing all his communications to Military Adviser Braxton Bragg. As many of Old Bory's messages had been false alarms — as late as June 10 he had wired, "Without immediate reinforcements we shall lose that city (Petersburg)" — and as Bragg shared Davis's dislike of the glory hunter, he had grown careless with Beauregard's stream of correspondence. It was only as a result of failing to gain an ally in Bragg that Beauregard finally sent his direct appeal to Lee for the return of his troops.

Since Smith had returned to Butler, Lee immediately acted on Beauregard's request. He sent orders to Hoke, already detached at Drewry's Bluff, that he was released to Beauregard's command. In the extensive Petersburg fortifications begun under Lee in 1862, Hoke would join the 2200-man brigade of ex-Governor Wise. Between Richmond and Petersburg, a makeshift division under Bushrod Johnson supported the guns containing Butler on the Bermuda Hundred line. Matt Ransom's large brigade of Johnson's division was then in the Richmond fortifications and Lee also returned Ransom south of the James. These troops completed Beauregard's command. Then Lee asked Bragg to call out the Local Defense Troops to support the stationary artillerists in the fortifications. (When the tocsin sounded their call to arms in the bell tower in Capitol Square, the clang reverberated through the rooms of Mrs. Lee's house.)

After Lee dispatched these orders, he waited around his headquarters at Riddell's Shop with a lack of urgency he had never before shown over determining the enemy's intentions. He had reached a place in his campaign against Grant where Davis's departmental system superseded him in command. As south of the James River was Beauregard's department, Lee was totally dependent upon Beauregard — or upon the War Department conveying Beauregard's intelligence — for information that located any part of Grant's army on Beauregard's side of the river. No word came from Beauregard. The only message from Richmond was a letter from Davis asking Lee's advice on the replacement of Bishop Polk, a lieutenant general in Joe Johnston's army who had been killed on Johnston's retiring movement toward Atlanta.

On Lee's own front the enemy cavalry continued active. Since Lee's responsibility was to remain in position to protect Richmond until he learned that Grant had crossed the James, he could not abandon the eastern approaches to the city on his assumption of what Grant would do. The James River dividing line between his and Beauregard's departments had finally become a wall isolating Lee from one part of the total operation.

On the other side of the wall, Beauregard was most anxious to keep his department to himself. After Lee effected the return of his troops, Beauregard immediately reverted to communicating with Bragg. Around noon he wired Bragg that Smith's corps had crossed to the south of the Appomattox River and was approaching Petersburg. Beauregard had then at Petersburg only Wise's brigade supporting the stationary guns in the fortifications. Advising Bragg that he would have to choose between defending Petersburg and the Bermuda Hundred line — the fortifications that bottled up Butler — Beauregard asked for an immediate answer. Bragg evaded the responsibility of deciding between the two points. He wired Beauregard that Hoke was on his way to Petersburg. Beauregard wired back a tart answer saying that he wished to know the War Department's preference between Petersburg and Bermuda Hundred, "as I fear my present force may prove unequal to hold both."

Before this emergency Bragg, as he had on the battlefield, became immobilized. He sent no answer at all, nor did he communicate with either Lee or Davis. As the President had appointed Bragg the coordinator between departments, a vacuum appeared at the coordination center between Beauregard and Lee.

Lee, in his woodsy headquarters, was unaware of the collapse in the operation of Davis's department system. He received no inkling of Beauregard's hairbreadth escape from his long threatened disasters late in the day of the 15th. Smith's corps had suffered from its rough handling at Cold Harbor, and his late afternoon attack failed to carry the Petersburg works defended by 2200 infantry because of his own caution and the lack of spirit in his troops. At dusk Hancock's corps, from Grant's army, arrived on the field. Only a breakdown in the Federal command prevented him from walking into Petersburg.

Beauregard's flurry of telegrams to the war offices reduced Bragg to complete inanition. Beauregard wired at nine o'clock, "I shall order Johnson [division at Bermuda Hundred] to this point [Petersburg]. General Lee must look to the defenses of Drewry's Bluff and Bermuda Hundred, if practical."

The abandonment of the Bermuda Hundred line meant that Butler's troops would occupy the railroad and highway connection between Richmond and Petersburg, cutting the two cities off from one another and isolating Beauregard at Petersburg. Bragg filed the message. Beauregard's own determination to avoid any collaboration that might bring Lee into his department resulted in Lee's going to his cot on the night of June 15 in total unawareness of the developments south of the James River.

At two o'clock in the morning of June 16, Lee was awakened by the delivery of a telegram sent him by Beauregard at 11:15 P.M. Giving no details of any kind, the message stated that Beauregard had abandoned the Bermuda Hundred line in order to concentrate at Petersburg. "Can not these lines be occupied by your troops? The safety of our communications requires it."

Sitting up on his cot in the still darkness of the wooded countryside,

Lee must have wondered why Beauregard informed *him* of the need to keep open communications after Bushrod Johnson's division was already withdrawn. Why had he not been informed by the War Department, through which all exchanges were conveyed? After all the controls exerted by the President over his army, Lee was suddenly faced with the absence of any central control at all. During the few hours of his sleep, the system had vanished.

At two o'clock in the morning, there was no time to clear with the President, then asleep in the White House. Lee could only act on his own discretion. He must hurry troops across the departmental boundary of the river to look to the emergency created by the absence of one single authority for the total operations.

10

Around nine-thirty on the Thursday morning, June 16, Lee reached the high earthen walls of Drewry's Bluff. The information filtering in to him there exposed a chaotic situation. Seven miles to the south Beauregard's abandoned lines at Bermuda Hundred were occupied by Butler's soldiers. From there Federal troops had fanned out across the flat countryside to the highway and the railroad. Lee learned that Pickett's division, the first troops to cross the river, encountered the enemy firmly blocking the way between Richmond and Petersburg. Lee called Field's division forward to support Pickett in driving Butler back inside the Bermuda Hundred lines. Of this desperate action in his department Beauregard seemed to know nothing at all.

Lee had sent Beauregard a telegram asking for information and received a wire — evidently the second sent by Beauregard — which crossed his. "The enemy is pressing us in heavy force. Can you not send forward the re-enforcements asked for this morning and send to our assistance the division now occupying the trenches lately evacuated by Johnson's division, replacing it by another division?"

This message airily assumed that the trenches abandoned by Bushrod Johnson's division had not been occupied by Butler and showed ignorance of the fight Lee was then making to reopen communications between the cities. Though Lee could assume that some of Grant's army was then in front of Petersburg, Beauregard did not say which, if any, of Grant's units were there. With the divisions of Hoke and Bushrod Johnson joining Wise's brigade at Petersburg, Beauregard then fielded fourteen thousand infantry — half the size of Lee's. Lee wired Beauregard that his 9:45 dispatch was the first that he had received and said, "I do not know the position of Grant's Army and can not strip the north bank of the James. Have you not force sufficient?"

Just before one o'clock Beauregard replied, "We may have sufficient force to hold Petersburg."

Later in the afternoon Beauregard wired that signalmen had counted forty-seven transports on the river by June 15. In reply Lee dismissed the transports as probably having returned Butler's troops and reverted to the main point. "Has Grant been seen crossing the James River?"

Glory-minded Beauregard later grew sensitive about the appearance on his record of his uncooperativeness, with the garbled, uninformative messages he sent Lee about the action on his front. After the war he concocted a clever, conscienceless narrative to show that he had showered Lee with "urgent calls" which Lee was too stupid to heed. In arranging his dishonest narrative, Beauregard omitted messages of his own, took Lee's out of context, and connected his selections with broad generalities that were outright lies.

Hence, about Lee's question — "Has Grant been seen crossing the James River?" — Beauregard later wrote, "This shows that Lee was still uncertain about his adversary's movements, and, notwithstanding the information I had already furnished him, could not realize that the Federals had crossed the James and that three of their corps were actually assaulting the Petersburg line."

However, Beauregard's answer to Lee's question, which he omitted from his narrative, was: "No information yet received of Grant's crossing James River. Hancock's and Smith's Corps are however on our front." Except for a telegram which Beauregard knew Lee had not received, this message — sent at seven in the morning — was Beauregard's first specific reference to any troops from Grant's army on his front. In point of fact, Burnside's corps was also at Petersburg on June 16, but Beauregard's answer to Lee shows that he did not know this at the time.

The most vital item omitted by Beauregard from his postwar fiction was the fighting of one-third of Lee's diminished army in his own department. "The Army of Northern Virginia was yet far distant," he wrote in dismissal of the battle which Pickett and Field carried on until eleven o'clock on the night of the 16th, forcing Butler back to the Bermuda Hundred lines which Beauregard had abandoned.

Unlike the "Gettysburg controversy" that grew around Longstreet's charges, Beauregard's persuasively written myth went unchallenged and is still generally accepted. He wrote long after Lee was dead and the complete telegraphic exchange, from which he made his edited selections, did not become available until the *Official Records* began to be published in 1901. As an indication of the little headway records can make against a myth, the impression remains that Lee's "whole army" (conjuring up a picture of its full powers as at Fredericksburg) sat idly in front of Richmond while Lee, dismissing Beauregard's "stream of information," stood muttering, "Where can Grant be?"

The fact was that restoring communications between Richmond and Petersburg was Lee's major concern when he crossed the James early in the morning of the 16th, in instant response to Beauregard's first message to *him*. Small though the scale was, the battle against Butler loomed very large to Grant as well as to Lee. Grant, on learning Butler was loose, diverted three divisions to the Bermuda Hundred front to solidify the line across the Richmond-Petersburg highway and railroad. Before these Federals arrived, early in the morning of June 17 Lee ordered an assault by Pickett to drive Butler out of the abandoned Confederate lines.

Since rejoining the army during the North Anna operations, Pickett's rebuilt division had not looked dependable and straggling had been heavy on the march out from Riddell's Shop at three in the morning. But in fighting Butler's illy led garrison troops, Pickett recaptured for that one brief hour the glory of Gettysburg. He drove the Federals back to their enclosure in a charge that looked as handsome as any ever delivered by the army. Had Pickett struck with less decisiveness it would have been too late. The speed with which Lee restored the Bermuda Hundred lines won a race of incalculable significance.

On June 17, however, Lee was still uninformed of the developments at Petersburg. During Pickett's assault, he wired Beauregard that at Drewry's Bluff he was cut off from all information. "Can you ascertain anything of Grant's movements?" Beauregard replied, "Enemy has two corps in my front. Nothing yet positive known of Grant's movements." Then, mentioning no urgent danger, Beauregard asked, "Could I not be sufficiently reinforced to take the offensive [and] thus rid of the enemy here?"

This was a baffling message to Lee. As Beauregard had mentioned the presence of Smith and Hancock on his front the night before, Lee could only assume these were the two corps Beauregard referred to. The lack of other Federal troops was implied by the request for reinforcements to drive off the enemy in his front. This left three of Grant's corps unaccounted for, and Federal cavalry had still appeared on Lee's front the day before.

Since Grant's army numbered around one hundred thousand, there was nothing to prevent his detaching Hancock's corps in support of Smith in an attack on Petersburg while advancing on Richmond with the three unaccounted-for corps. With Kershaw's division already at the river crossing in readiness to move to Petersburg, Lee had in front of Richmond only the fifteen-thousand-man corps of A. P. Hill. In reply to the request for reinforcements to assume the offensive Lee wired Beauregard, "Until I can get more information of Grant's movements, I do not think it prudent to draw more troops to this side of the river."

Lee had been trying to conserve the men and horses in the two thinned cavalry brigades, but he sent Rooney orders to make a forced reconnaissance. The troopers had already found the enemy cavalry absent from their front and during June 17 pushed ahead to Wilcox's Landing. There Rooney learned that the last Federal troops, the cavalry, had crossed the pontoon bridge the night before. Rooney started a courier back to his father with this positive information.

Before the courier covered the fifteen miles to Chaffin's Bluff and crossed to Drewry's Bluff, at four-thirty General Lee had received a telegram from Beauregard. Civilian sources reported thirty thousand Yankees marching from the river toward Petersburg. On this indefinite information, Lee shifted Kershaw's division to the south of the river and, as he had originally planned, started the withdrawal of Hill's corps to the pontoon bridges at Chaffin's Bluff.

By nightfall, after Lee had received the message from his son, a telegram of alarm came from Beauregard. Totally different in tone from the earlier messages that requested reinforcements for an offensive, Beauregard advised Lee that prisoners had been taken from the II and IX Corps, and prisoners informed him that the V and VI Corps were "coming up."

The first communication to identify more than Hancock's corps at Petersburg, this telegram was inaccurate in detail and revealed the primitive intelligence system operated by Beauregard. Warren's V Corps had been on Beauregard's front during the day of the 17th, while most of the VI had been diverted to Bermuda Hundred in the battle for the abandoned lines. The one element that had never occurred to Lee, while trying to get detailed information, was that four corps of Grant's army could be marching for three days toward Beauregard's lines without his being aware of their presence in his department or of the identity of those he was actually fighting.

Later that night, at ten o'clock, came the second of Beauregard's actually "urgent" reports. In this he said without reinforcements Petersburg would have to be evacuated. Lee, then knowing for certain that no troops remained north of the James to menace Richmond, acted with urgency. Kershaw's division, already on the south side, was hurried forward to report to Beauregard the next morning. A. P. Hill, pausing at Chaffin's Bluff, was ordered to make a night crossing of the river and make a forced march along the Petersburg turnpike the next morning. Lee prepared to abandon his isolated quarters at Drewry's Bluff and follow Kershaw to Petersburg.

For then, after all the needless strain caused by the divided command

and the breakdown of Davis's bureaucratic system, after it was too late to combine the armies for any operation except on defense, Davis was forced to rearrange his charts and give Lee complete authority for the Richmond-Petersburg sector.

This of all things was what Beauregard had striven by all means to avoid. In no exchange of telegrams had he ever hinted that he desired the cooperation of Lee himself. All he asked were troops from Lee's army to be shifted to his command to be used in situations he never defined until the night of June 17. For Beauregard knew that once Lee came into his department he would be reduced to second in command, as he had been at First Manassas and at Shiloh. Petersburg had been his first chance to win the glory all for himself, but it was simply not possible for him to get the Army of Northern Virginia without its commander.

II

Though Beauregard in his relationship with Lee was egocentric and un-stable, and in the excitement of the mounting emergency sent contradic-tory and uninformative messages, at the point of contact at the Petersburg fortifications he fought with courage and a resourceful skill in disposing his forces. Petersburg was situated on the south bank of the Appomattox and, with the river as a flank, works in depth extended for ten miles and almost enclosed the city. The Federals' attacks were delivered only along about three miles that faced to the east. Concentrating his fourteen thou-sand infantry in these sections, Beauregard defended with a depth of a little less than three men a yard, and an assortment of guns, firing from high-walled embankments, that blasted away with grape and canister until the cannoneers staggered with exhaustion.

Beauregard's collection of troops had served together in Virginia only one month, during which many of the units had been separated on differ-ent fronts, and no maneuver that demanded concert of action would have been possible. What was demanded was heroic determination not to yield, and this single spirit pervaded the troops battling from their dirt walls. Breeches made were quickly plugged by a shift in the lines and the men were not shaken when one of the redoubts was overrun and an old sta-tionary gun captured.

On the other side, the attacks were disjointed and feebly pushed. When a breech was made by sheer weight of numbers, there was no quick reac-tion to exploit it. The month-long campaign against Lee had crushed the offensive spirit of the Army of the Potomac, along with splintering the core of its veterans. Even so, the successive waves for three days of troops that must have numbered from first to last seventy-five thousand infantry

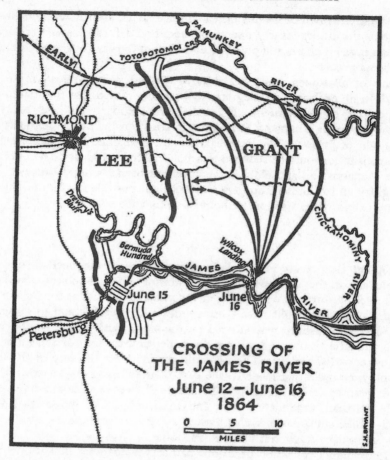

CROSSING OF
THE JAMES RIVER
June 12 – June 16,
1864

0    5    10
MILES

wore down the defenders. With casualties reducing the numbers in the thinly stretched lines, the fought-out troops would not have the resistance to stand off fresh assaults on the fourth day.

Beauregard recognized this at the end of the 17th, when he sent Lee his call of desperation. During the night he made fresh dispositions, withdrawing his men from the battered fortifications half a mile closer to the city. The engineers traced a new line and the exhausted infantrymen dug all night. The crude works gave protection only from bullets fired by an enemy infantry advancing straight ahead.

Early in the morning of June 18, the Federal lines of attack came on again and Grant's jaded soldiers were momentarily cheered when they entered the abandoned works they had assaulted for three days. Then, on discovering the unshakable defenders waiting for them in new lines half a mile farther on, the Federal soldiers could not regain their initial momentum in any unison. By the time their assault lines had re-formed and another of the poorly organized advances begun, the veterans of Kershaw's brigades were deploying at the new line.

The half-dazed soldiers of Bushrod Johnson's division did not need to see the red battle flags to recognize their own in the tawny, hairy faces shaded by floppy hats. Johnson's men tried to raise a cheer of greeting but most of them wept in relief. As these soldiers staggered away from the mounds of turned earth, Kershaw's relatively fresh men hurried to take their places, sliding their rifles across the loose earth of the trench. Right behind them the batteries of Porter Alexander's artillery rolled into line with a clanging of chains, and these mobile guns deepened the field of fire maintained by the stationary guns in the redoubts.

Just as at Spotsylvania, the issue was decided when the rapid crackling fire of Kershaw's marksmen poured into the press of men advancing across open country. At nine-thirty their right was extended by Field's division, scarcely three thousand survivors of the once great assault force of John Hood. Hood's old Texas Brigade was down to 435 men. These veterans still brought a heavy fire power and the Federal troops had lost taste for attacking works which spouted sprays of lead. As General Meade said, "the moral condition of the army" could not support another offensive.

Grant tried sporadic attacks throughout the day, but the attempt to take Petersburg was over. The forced march had brought the Federal troops to the Petersburg works in no shape to push home assaults, and the command in the Army of the Potomac was strained beyond the point of efficient coordination. When Lee rode out onto the fields behind the new lines, Grant's grand offensive against Richmond and Lee's army was finished.

When Lee rode up, Beauregard greeted him cordially and escorted him to a position where he could survey the new line. Beauregard was proud of the lines he had extemporized along the chord of the arc of the original fortifications. Lee found the lines well drawn, following the natural roll of the ground, and complimented Beauregard. However, beyond those lines Lee somberly looked across the flat countryside to facing lines which the Federal soldiers were also throwing up. In those Federal works Lee saw the final end of maneuver for both armies.

Since Lee had first moved out against Grant on May 4, his single, controlling purpose had been to maintain the maneuver that would avoid a siege. That, as Beauregard had said, presented a picture of "ultimate starvation." Before Grant left Cold Harbor, Lee had told Jubal Early, "We must destroy this army of Grant's before he gets to the James River. If he gets there, it will become a siege, and then it will be a mere question of time."

When he talked of destroying Grant's army with the force he had, Lee had been thinking with the heart of a man who could not conceive of his civilization being conquered. When he predicted the consequences of not striking the enemy a blow, Lee — as his government could not — looked squarely at the realities of the static defense of withstanding a siege. In that the contest was not between him and Grant, but between the Confederacy and the United States. By the fourth year of the war, the United States possessed the one weapon against which Lee was powerless — starvation.

This was the specter confronting Lee when he looked at the new lines at Petersburg that marked the end of Grant's campaign, and of all campaigns for himself.

## CHAPTER XIX

## "The Result May Be Calamitous"

IN JUNE Francis Lawley returned to Richmond after a trip home to England. *The Times* of London correspondent and Frank Vizitelly, the illustrator, had made the blockade run from Bermuda to Wilmington on the *Lillian*, and arrived in the Confederate capital during Grant's shift across the James. When Grant's campaign against Lee and Richmond collapsed at Petersburg, Lawley wrote *The Times* on June 27:

"If a man were landed in Richmond from a balloon after six months' absence, if he were taken along Grace or Franklin streets in this city on a summer evening, and told that two enormous armies are lying a few miles off and disputing its possession, he would deem his informant a lunatic. In every porch he would see a group of gaily attired ladies (I do not believe that 20 vigorous years of blockade would pale the lustre of ladies' toilet in an American town); he would hear many a light laugh, many a song issuing from open casements; he might pass an hour in conversation without being reminded that war is furiously raging, otherwise than by the suggestive boom of the faintly heard cannon . . ."

That was the way Lawley wanted to see it, and for Grace and Franklin streets the picture was not overly colored for a general impression that omitted details. What the ladies ran in through the blockade were fashion patterns from Paris. Their new dresses were ingenious reworkings of parts from older garments and, at least once, from a damask curtain. There were no dresses of new materials when even gingham had reached ten dollars a yard. The songs heard were likely to be sad, such as "When This Cruel War Is Over," which had caught Jeb Stuart's fancy just before he was killed. No songs at all came from the houses of mourning nor from the Franklin Street house in which Mrs. Lee lay ill, suffering a cruelly acute advance of arthritis.

Inside some of the houses rooms were almost bare, the furniture and decorations having been sold for necessities. Many of the houses were crowded with sick — civilians suffering from want of medicines, the old from malnutrition, and soldiers overflowing the hospitals. Mrs. Judith McGuire, occupying a house in the neighborhood Lawley passed, wrote on

June 24, "I have been much occupied nursing the sick, not only in the hospital but among our own friends."

Also, Grace and Franklin streets were a small part of the swollen city. In most sections Lawley could not have found even a pleasant façade, though in the "sporting section" on East Franklin the few blocks around the Exchange and Ballard hotels were riotous with a night life never before seen in Richmond. Many conscientiously overworked individuals, such as Mrs. Phoebe Yates Pember, matron of the huge military hospital on Chimborazo Hill, disapproved of the very idea of "gaiety" in such times. Though usually the sociable young ladies were diverting soldiers on leave or recuperating from wounds, Mrs. Pember daily confronted too much suffering and experienced too much fatigue in the struggle against deficiencies of medicine and food to have any heart for entertainment. She wrote a friend, "If Spartan austerity is to win our independence, we are a lost nation."

On June 22, referring to her hospital, Mrs. Pember wrote in a letter, "My Hotel is very, very full, most of the convalescing boarders [wounded soldiers] sleeping upon the floor. The fighting is so near that in some cases the wounded are brought in from four to five hours after the engagement . . . for the past three weeks there has been no day or night that the booming of cannon has not been the last sound at night and the first in the morning . . ."

At Chimborazo Hospital, young Dr. James McCaw's staff experimented with substitutes for medicines, with boiled rags for sponges in washing wounds (making great advances in antisepsis) and with horsehair for silk to be used in sutures. Since bricks and builders were scarce, advanced uses were made of light and air and space by building one hundred fifty one-story flimsy frame structures. Since personnel was scarce (all nurses were volunteers), experiments were made in occupational therapy, such as putting the convalescents on short tours of sentry duty and on light work on the soup boiler (a converted beer vat from a distillery). The result of the experiments was the lowest mortality rates of any hospital in the world until the sulpha drugs of World War II.

The Chimborazo grounds had the advantage of the location of an open bluff overlooking the river and, beyond the built-up part of the city, was the coolest spot in Richmond. That summer was intensely hot and Lawley, reporting that the "effect" of the heat was visible in the "pallor . . . in every countenance," described the citizens in general in the daytime as "pale shadows which flit along the shady sides of Richmond's streets."

On June 27, "the bright and hot" day of Lawley's letter, a head of cabbage sold for $10.00 in the public market, and formerly scented gardens in the rear of the mansions were being worked as vegetable patches. Between the ivy-covered brick walls urban farmers produced tomatoes and "snaps" (string beans) and some variety of green peas called cowpeas, which apparently sat heavily on the stomach.

On the next day War Clerk J. B. Jones wrote in his diary that, although he and his son had joint salaries amounting to $8000, "we have the greatest difficulty to subsist. I hope we shall speedily have better times, and I think, unless some terrible misfortune happens to our arms, the invader will soon be hurled from our soil."

This wishful thinking, untypical of Jones, reflected a largely unspoken desire for peace swelling among the people. The population, as if partly numbed by its day-to-day struggle for existence, had lost the capacity to make realistic appraisals — or even to think — of the larger, embracing struggle of the forces at war. Mrs. McGuire wrote in her journal, "We have had very little time to think of public affairs . . . While the cannon is booming in our ears . . . it is wonderful to me that we retain our senses."

At the same time, the more literate seemed aware that the Northern population was growing almost as weary of the war as were the invaded. The Northern attitude was expressed by William Swinton, historian of the Army of the Potomac. When Lee halted Grant's offensive, "with its mournful loss of life," where McClellan had reached by easy stages two years before, "there was at this time great danger of the collapse of the war." Had the war been restricted to Virginia, Swinton wrote "it would have been difficult to raise new forces to recruit the Army of the Potomac which, shaken in its structure, its valor quenched in blood, and thousands of its ablest soldiers killed and wounded, was the Army of the Potomac no more." Lincoln himself expressed concern during the summer over the chances of the Democrats, with McClellan as the nominee, to defeat the Republicans in the November elections.

Yet, there was relatively little comment from Confederate leaders on the hope that the United States fall elections could bring them peace with "independence." Davis seemed oblivious of the possible advantage to be gained in the political sphere by merely maintaining the stalemate into the fall.

Grant, in settling down to something of a joint siege of Richmond and Petersburg, had plainly turned to a long-range program of applying "attrition." As soon as Grant built trenches at Petersburg, Lee wrote Davis: "I think it is his purpose to compel the evacuation of our present position by cutting off supplies, and that he will not renew his attempt to drive us away by force."

Lawley wrote The Times of London of the stalemate: "the Federals willing to wound, and yet afraid to strike; the Confederates satisfied to repel attack, yet indisposed to assume the offensive." In the propagandistic turn Lawley gave his reporting, "indisposed" was chosen instead of the more factual "unable," but it was an otherwise accurate picture of the Richmond-Petersburg front.

However, as Swinton pointed out, the war was not restricted to Virginia. The other end of the line, at Atlanta, also needed to maintain a stalemate. In handling the Atlanta front, Davis reflected the general population's loss of capacity to think realistically, even within the framework of his departmentalization. Under the strains from without, pressing on his inner anxieties, he began to be driven by personal elements. Joe Johnston became the object on whom he could vent his needs to control the direction of events — or, give himself the illusion that the control was in his hands.

When continuing a stalemate into the November elections in the United States was the one, single hope of winning peace with independence, the tortured man became obsessive about forcing Johnston to get off the defensive and open a counteroffensive. Since an offensive by Johnston's army was then manifestly impossible, and as Davis's departmental restrictions prevented Johnston from using such strategic countermeasures as might have hurt Sherman, Davis's increasing prods at Johnston reduced the Atlanta front to the resumption of the duel between the two personal enemies.

2

Although Lee, his advice ignored, had not been able to give Johnston's cause any effectual support, the former failure in Virginia had done some growing as a soldier in the West. Discarding the habits acquired during his prewar experiences with the boundless resources of the U. S. Quartermaster Department, Johnston had learned to work with the limitations of the makeshift nation and, against Sherman, performed with the poised skill his admirers had expected of him.

Outnumbered two to one — with the usual Confederate inferiority in armament and deficiencies in the supporting services — he conducted a one-hundred-mile delaying action from Dalton to Atlanta, sparing his army serious injury during continuous fighting and movement. He repulsed Sherman with heavy casualties in the one full-scale battle, Kenesaw Mountain, fought ten days after Grant was halted at Petersburg. Since Sherman was operating in mountainous country, in which he depended upon one railroad for supplies, the deeper he advanced the more his lengthening line of communications became exposed to the disruptions of cavalry raids. By the end of June, Sherman had just about set himself up for Forrest. Though his numbers were declining, Nathan Bedford Forrest still commanded one of the most formidable forces of raiders the war produced.

In making his skillful retirement before Sherman, however, Johnston had not changed as a person. His personal letters revealed a mean, petty jealousy of Lee and in his exchanges with Davis he reverted to the evasiveness of his 1862 retirement to Richmond. It was natural for the President to suspect that Johnston had no more plans than before, and it was true that around the war offices assistants made jokes about assembling a fleet at Savannah to continue Johnston's retreat to Bermuda. Also, it was probable that Johnston himself had no more of a plan than in 1862. But he did have an enemy exposed, as McClellan had not been, to the crippling disruptions of raiders.

Sherman revealed his own anxiety over Forrest by organizing large mounted forces to strike from western Tennessee into Mississippi with orders to "punish . . . the people." Civilians must be shown that Forrest "will bring ruin and misery on any country where he may pass or tarry."

When Sherman introduced "ruin and misery" to the civilian population as a factor in cause-and-effect strategy, he was primarily acting as a professional soldier doing a job. No more politically minded than Grant, and showing a strong aversion for Negroes, Sherman was concerned with the successful subjugation of a people and not with the end of restoring the Union for which force was the means. Personally, he did develop a somewhat grisly gratification in his power to spread destruction, but this was an incidental effect in making humans the agents of extending war to its logical conclusions. Lee, also as a soldier, strongly supported Johnston in countering Sherman on strictly military principles. Civilians would have to suffer in order to employ Forrest against the railroad supplying Sherman. Lee advised Davis to concentrate the cavalry "on Sherman's communications."

Davis was not a soldier, though he liked to think of himself as one. During this crisis, he said to his wife, "Oh, if only Lee could take one wing and I take the other." What he presumedly wanted to do with the other wing was to lead soldiers in a glorious charge in the tradition of volunteers in the Mexican War. Beyond this heroic vision, it was characteristic of Davis to see the local rather than the general, to give preferment to the protection of places over cause-and-effect strategy, and he insisted upon doing that at Atlanta. He withheld Forrest from the major campaign in order to protect the interior against raids and, thus, achieved Sherman's intention for him. As Grant said, they were often helped by Davis's "genius."

Having nullified Johnston's only strategic factor, the President continued to demand an offensive and belabored the General about his plans. Johnston continued his evasiveness. On the Fourth of July, he withdrew his intact army into the outer fortifications of Atlanta, where he would have the support of the same sort of heavy guns as at Petersburg and presumed support from the thousands of able-bodied exempts whom Governor Brown placed in the militia. Up to this point Johnston had done all that could reasonably have been expected, and was in position to stalemate Sherman at Atlanta as Grant was at Petersburg.

But he still refused to deal openly with Davis, to take him into his confidence and try to discuss dispassionately the broad realities of the situation. Since Johnston would reveal no plans, Davis's obsession with an offensive became the bone of contention between the two wills. Johnston was either going to promise to do it or be replaced. To bring the test to a climax, Davis sent the malign Braxton Bragg to Atlanta to discover Johnston's intentions. As when Custis Lee had visited Johnston outside of Richmond in 1862, he refused to commit himself.

Then Davis asked Lee for his advice in replacing Johnston with John Hood. After Hood lost his leg at Chickamauga, the magnificent-looking tawny-haired soldier improved his time while recuperating in Richmond by winning the favor of the President. Returned to the Army of Tennessee as a lieutenant general under Johnston, Hood became — after Bishop Polk's death — the closest general in that army to Davis. As ambitious as he was combative, Hood, then thirty-three, let it be known that he was not averse to going over to the offensive. Knowing Hood for many years, Lee suggested the more experienced Hardee instead of Hood. William Hardee, a sound professional soldier, had long been associated with the Army of Tennessee.

On July 12, Davis wired Lee that he had replaced Johnston with Hood. Lee's reply was one of his baldest messages to the President. "Telegram of today received. I regret the fact stated. It is a bad time to release the commander of an army situated as that of Tennessee. We may lose Atlanta and the army too. Hood is a bold fighter. I am doubtful as to other qualities necessary."

This undiplomatic telegram, with its prediction of the loss of "Atlanta and the army too," accomplished nothing more than an expression of Lee's sense of foreboding about his collateral front.

3

That summer General Lee began drawing on his physical reserves to keep going at the stressful pace. Grant's turn from maneuver to a program of attrition wore away at Lee as it did at his army and the region's resources. Along with his supporting moral force, Lee was sustained by those habits of order, as deeply ingrained as instinct. He wasted no nervous energy in deciding what to do next, in compulsive hurry, or in worry about what he should do or had not done. All energy was directed in an even flow to acts of accomplishment on what could be done right then. In his letters to his family, he never referred to the past nor to the future. From sunup until the candles were blown out, he lived implicitly by the prayer, "Give us *this* day."

By these habits, within his faith in Providence, when Lee completed his assigned duties, he could rest totally. He could also find renewal in very simple things. With his personal staff he was pleasantly situated in the yard of a house on the north bank of the Appomattox, not far from the Richmond-Petersburg highway. From his reference to the owner as "a Mrs. Shippen," Lee had evidently not known before the lady whom he found to be "very kind." She sent the staff rolls and vegetables and milk, and twice, while they were having their dinner at sunset, she sent them "a tureen of delightful calf's head soup."

Lee wrote his wife of a special interest in Mrs. Shippen. After suffering long and severely from crippling rheumatism, she had, after a siege of pneumonia, improved considerably and was able to walk again. Lee wrote his wife of Mrs. Shippen in an effort to offer some encouragement toward regarding her own affliction as not hopeless. Lee felt deeply his own helplessness during her current attack. The three girls were then with their mother, and Lee wrote Mildred, "You must give her a great deal of love and say I wish I could see her and cure her. I fear both are beyond my power. It is impossible for me to leave here at this time."

It bothered him, too, that he could not even provide for his wife such simple needs as lemons. They were not to be had in the markets. A Mrs. Kirkland, of Petersburg, gave him two from her own trees, which Lee sent on with a dried-up lemon he found in his valise. Since lemons were unobtainable, he also sent advice, probably unheeded, for her to try to cultivate a taste for buttermilk. He urged her to get out of the city's heat as soon as she was well enough to travel.

Lee himself was showing an increasingly sensitive reaction to hot weather. His physical decline was not evident to those around him, though references to his appearance occasionally mentioned "a careworn" expression. However, he felt the heat more than his companions. Having endured one-hundred-degree Texas heat in a tent, Lee had first appeared to be bothered by hot weather in 1862 when he sought lighter uniforms. In riding the lines in the flat country outside Petersburg, he wrote, "It is perfectly stifling and then the dust is so dense that the atmosphere is distressing."

The effect of the hot, humid weather on him made Lee acutely sensitive to the suffering of the soldiers digging "in the extreme heat," constantly deepening and strengthening the trenches. Lee's distress for his men — extending also to the civilians in the area — seemed to involve him emotionally more than before. Always before, the suffering of the men and the hardships borne by the population could be regarded as sacrifices necessary to gaining some military end. Now he had nothing he could hope to offer as a reward.

Grant, in some purpose not very clear, moved up long-range guns with which at intervals he shelled the residential section of Petersburg. While some families were forced to leave their wrecked houses, and several churches were forced to close, aside from increasing human misery no result was achieved relating to a military decision. Mr. Platt, rector of the largest Episcopal Church, held services on Sunday, July 10, at Lee's head-quarters, The service was under the trees and Lee wrote, "We had a re-spectable audience. Some ladies, many officers and soldiers."

On that Sunday, Lee, in a letter to his wife, showed as he occasionally did that he still maintained a flash of his old turn of humor. "I saw some gentlemen from Fredericksburg today who said that every one is de-lighted that Grant is down here and that things in the upper country are flourishing and people reviving. Grant seems so pleased with his present position that I fear he will never move again."

Lee's light reference to Grant indicated no lightness in regard to Grant's operations. The dull, monotonous but continuous local strikes be-came the grimmest warfare Lee had ever experienced. Lee had no great respect for Grant as a general. During July he wrote Custis, "His talent and strategy consists in accumulating overwhelming numbers." Yet it was the deadliest form of wearing down, wearing out an enemy of inferior numbers and inferior resources. It would take a long time, far longer than the "all summer" Grant had declared he would continue his hammering. But, unless the political situation ended the stalemate by ending the war, the end was unquestionably, as Lee had said, "a mere question of time."

Grant employed a pendulum action, striking first at one end of the line beyond the works and then the other. Several miles south of Petersburg, he sent infantry in wrecking expeditions on the Weldon Railroad, hacking away at the Richmond-Petersburg lifeline with the South. Then north of the James, thirty miles from the attack on the railroad, a striking force thrust toward Richmond from the east. The Richmond fortifications were manned only by artillerists on the stationary guns, with Gary's small South Carolina cavalry brigade scattered in patrols to sound warnings. At each warning, Lee's emaciated foot soldiers hurried back across to the pontoon bridge to support the guns. With occasional thrusts directly at the Petersburg lines, which were kept under constant artillery and sharp-shooter fire, and occasional action north of the Appomattox along Butler's Bermuda Hundred front (then called the Howlett Line), the pendulum movements swung monotonously back and forth week after week, begin-ning in late June.

To parry these thrusts, while maintaining a stable front, Lee was work-ing with stretched-out units that bore little resemblance to the Army of

Northern Virginia. In July Jackson's old Second Corps was operating along the Potomac, where Jubal Early was trying a diversionary threat on Washington. The remnants of Longstreet's old First Corps were divided, with Anderson's control little more than administrative. Pickett's not too dependable division occupied the Howlett Line which the troops had re-taken in the June fight against Butler. Kershaw and Gregg, the latter down to barely three thousand including the sick, alternated between rushing to halt an advance at Richmond and holding a segment of the Petersburg trenches.

The network of trenches deepening to the east of Petersburg (the first in world warfare) was held by two patchwork divisions from Beaure-gard's old command, Hoke's and Bushrod Johnson's, along with various batteries and brigades released from the Coastal garrisons. Even "Shanks" Evans, accompanied by the orderly carrying the bourbon keg on his back, was welcomed back.

Lee's only intact corps was A. P. Hill's. Digging as they held the end of the lengthening line southeast of Petersburg, Hill's gaunt ragamuffins comprised the mobile force that was hurried at monotonous intervals to drive Federal infantry away from wrecking sections of the Weldon Rail-road. Lee saw Powell Hill frequently during the summer days. He was deeply fond of the warm and courtly younger man, whose passion for their cause seemed to grow as his strength wasted away and his body grew slight. Hill was at his best as a corps commander during this period when the greatest demand put upon him was to sustain the morale of his men while using every conceivable method of rotation to prevent their physi-cal collapse. Yet, with his emotional nature, Little Powell was not a type with whom Lee could consult.

Off Hill's flank was Lee's son, Rooney, with his two thinned-out bri-gades, containing several hundred troopers without horses. Supporting Rooney was a cavalry brigade commanded by young James Dearing. Re-signing from the West Point class of 1862, Dearing advanced to command an artillery battalion with Pickett until, after being briefly assigned to the horse artillery, he commanded cavalry operations around Petersburg be-fore Lee came. Lee saw little of his son, though enough to find that Rooney had regained his hearty spirits. But he heard very favorably of him and Dearing in late June when James Wilson, who had been two classes ahead of Dearing at West Point, led a force of five thousand cav-alry on the railroads to the southwest of Petersburg.

Rooney's command harried the rear of Wilson's force during its rail-road wrecking and pillaging of farms until Wilson turned with his own division to hold off Rooney, while Kautz's brigade (formerly with Butler) rode ahead to burn the railroad bridge at Staunton River. A band of mili-tia-farmers gathered on the opposite side of the river and, firing between the crotches of tree branches, opened on Kautz with shotguns and old smoothbore muskets. Kautz drew off and Wilson, following, started back.

He was heading for a Federal infantry force on the Weldon Railroad, not knowing that A. P. Hill had driven it off. Instead, some of Hill's infantry remained in the area and Wade Hampton had just returned with the major portion of the cavalry from the Trevilian Station fight with Sheridan. Rooney Lee's regiments, still following Wilson and Kautz on those horses that had not broken down, pressed the raiders into the infantry-cavalry force across their line of march. Wilson escaped by leaving one thousand prisoners, twelve guns, all his wagons and most of the loot, including silver stolen from homes and a communion service from a church. Rooney's dismounted troopers got some horses.

As disastrous as was the end of Wilson's raid, the damage done to the railroads — along with the sections wrecked on the Weldon — meant for Lee the detachment of work forces to repair the damage. Since he could not persuade the administration to form permanent work forces of men not qualified for army service, this in turn meant the detachment of more soldiers from the lines. It was when he rode along the trenches, looking at the toiling skeletons of men, that observers found his expression "careworn." On those rides along the lines, there were more ghosts than soldiers "present for duty" and, with more strangers than familiars among the officers, he must have sometimes seen the ghosts of "the good and great Jackson" and the golden Stuart with laughter lighting his face.

4

At the end of July Lee was forced personally, for the first time since Spotsylvania, to gallop to the front to a point of breakthrough. While Grant had been whittling away at Lee's army, his own troops fought far below the quality of performance of the Army of the Potomac before Cold Harbor. As Swinton had said, after the decimated veteran corps reached Petersburg they were "the Army of the Potomac no more," and the replacements — conscripts and paid substitutes — were neither eager nor trained soldiers.

The provost marshal general of the army, Brigadier General M. R. Patrick, wrote in his diary on July 18, "This army is nearly demoralized and the cavalry is no better than a band of robbers . . ." A few weeks earlier Patrick recorded a court-martial "for the trial of two men who had committed a crime upon the body of a Mrs. Stiles living near Prince George's Court House . . ." This was an area occupied by the Federal Army east of Petersburg. A few days prior to that Patrick recorded giving "the necessary orders for hanging Johnson, the negro, for Rape . . ."

Of the army's fighting qualities in that period, General Meade's statement that the offensive spirit had been drained was substantiated by the readiness with which Federal infantrymen gave themselves up as prisoners. Between June 22 and August 24, eight thousand Federals surrendered.

The emergency that arose on July 30 was not caused by any resurgence of offensive spirit, but by the blowing up of a segment of lines southeast of Petersburg. Lee's lines on that part of the front were thinly held at the time, as troops had been withdrawn to repel an infantry advance north of the James River. The soldiers in the lines, partly composed of garrison troops brought up from South Carolina, had heard the underground digging for several nights before July 30, but it seemed not to occur to either officers or men that the enemy would resort to blowing them up. Around daylight eight thousand pounds of powder exploded under the earth, tearing open a great hole they called the Crater. Burnside's corps, employing the first Negro troops used in combat in Virginia, came pouring through the gap.

When Lee rode into the level field about a quarter of a mile behind the dust clouds rising over the bedlam around the Crater, he saw soldiers forming thin lines on both sides of the gap and fighting furiously. The Confederates had been enraged rather than demoralized at seeing the bodies of their fellows tossed into the air, and the Negroes in the assaulting forces intensified their determination to fight to the last breath. Lee rode to the nearby Gee house, from where he sent orders to Hill to hurry forward Mahone's division.

When Lee watched Mahone's troops rush to strengthen the lightly manned lines, the fighting grew desperate around the edges of the Crater, where men stumbled and lunged in panting hand-to-hand struggles. Slowly it became apparent to Lee that the Crater itself was becoming a deathtrap for the attacking soldiers. Men crowded into the pit of shifting loose earth, littered with the dismembered parts of soldiers who had occupied the line above the blast, and had difficulty in getting out. Groups of Confederates ran up several of the newly introduced trench mortars to the edge of the hole to throw shells into the milling masses. The attackers caught in the pit began scrambling backward for safety.

Coordination collapsed in the accompanying assaults on the lines on both sides of the Crater, as too much had been expected of the effects of the explosion. Slowly the Federals were driven back along the whole segment of lines. When the smoke and dust drifted away, with the customary random firing replacing the shouts and high screams, Lee ordered the construction of new lines.

In the days following, while new fortifications were being built, the case-hardened survivors of the gruesome attack began to make jokes about it — telling how one sailing upward exchanged greetings with a friend on the way down. Yet the strain of life on the underfed men in the muddy trenches was beginning to gnaw at the soldiers' morale. Hundreds on the rolls were absent with illness and hundreds would be seen no more. Not a night passed without some soldiers stealing away in the dark. Some went home and some went over to the enemy for food.

In early August, anxious to relieve his best troops from the undermining ordeal of trench life, Lee experienced a little quickening of his spirit when he saw an opening through which he might return to maneuver on a limited scale. In mid-July, Jubal Early had demonstrated against the city of Washington with his ten thousand infantry and indifferent cavalry and then, too weak to do more, retired across the Potomac. There he lurked as a potential menace to the capital. As Lincoln wanted some experienced troops to support the Federal forces in the Valley, Lee hoped that Grant, in preference to reducing his numbers, would attack him in his works as a means of forcing the recall of Early. However, with the Crater disaster fresh in his mind, Grant took the course of detaching Wright's VI Corps and roughly 6500 of Sheridan's cavalry, then rested and refitted after the abortive raid that ended at Trevilian Station. Since Grant reduced his numbers at Petersburg, Lee felt emboldened to withdraw some of his tatterdemalions from the lines to operate once again in the open.

To this end, he sent Dick Anderson to Culpeper with a force composed of Kershaw's division and cavalry under Wade Hampton. Lee had then appointed Hampton chief of cavalry, in the conviction that the qualities of the militarily untrained South Carolinian were more needed than the professional training of his younger, more exuberant nephew, Fitz Lee. Hampton, forty-six years old and probably the richest planter in the South, was, like Lee, a man always in complete control of himself. Indifferent to military glory, he brought a serious-minded purpose and natural leadership to the defense of his society.

Lee could scarcely have expected to affect seriously the war in Virginia by returning to his old maneuver of placing forces on both sides of the Blue Ridge. Like an artist released from hack work, he grew interested in the play of strategy. Writing frequently and in detail to Anderson, Lee summarized his assignment with a general instruction. "Any enterprise that can be undertaken to injure the enemy, distract or separate his forces, embarrass his communications on the Potomac or on land is desirable."

Yet, even before all the cavalry joined Anderson, Lee was forced to recall Wade Hampton and his own division. On Sunday, August 14, Lee wrote his wife that he was "kept from church today by the enemy's crossing to the north side of the James River . . ." In that letter, written at night, Lee dropped in an unguarded line which revealed more of his inner feelings than a volume of his collected warnings and petitions to the government. Referring to recent depredations to churches — their "materials used, often for the vilest purposes" — he wrote, "We must suffer patiently to the end, when all things will be made right." The "end" obviously meant the end of life and marked a steady increase in Lee's references to the eternal peace when all struggle should at last be over. The war had changed his journey on earth into a struggle which he would "suffer patiently" until released.

The next day Lee received reports that the attack north of the James was developing heavy strength in a push from the White Oak Swamp toward Richmond, and could not be contained by the remnants of Field's division. As the lines in front of Petersburg could not be further weakened, Lee was forced to call on Pickett for a brigade and hurry a brigade from A. P. Hill to the Richmond-Petersburg Railroad. Rooney Lee's troopers were brought up from south of Petersburg and pushed their bony horses along the dusty turnpike to the Richmond lines. Then Lee decided he had better go himself.

A refreshing rain on the 14th had broken a long, dry spell, but clouds overcast the sky and the morning of the 16th was warm and humid when Lee established headquarters at Chaffin's Bluff. This was a fortified position above the landing where the pontoon crossed the James. From there, around ten-thirty, Lee wired the President that the Local Defense Troops had better be called out to man the fortifications. The Federals were pushing westward along the Darbytown and Charles City roads, where in 1862 Lee had moved his huge divisions eastward in developing the trap at Glendale.

The Federal attack was a small action in the annals of the war, but it was full-scale battle to the men engaged (a name on their regimental battle flags) and if the Federals broke through Richmond would be endangered. Wade Hampton, having been hastily recalled, brought his cavalry on the field in time to add the weight to halt the enemy's drive. As dusk settled over the marshy, brushy countryside, the Federals retired back across White Oak Swamp.

That night Lee established camp headquarters at Chaffin's Bluff. With the troops gathered, of necessity, in front of Richmond, Lee wanted to direct forced reconnaissance to discover the enemy's dispositions north of the James. Two days later, while his troops were skirmishing, Lee received a telegram from Beauregard — commanding at Petersburg during Lee's absence — asking for reinforcements to support Dearing's cavalry. Dearing reported a force of the enemy advancing against the Weldon Railroad. Back went Rooney Lee's riders to the turnpike for Petersburg. The night of the 19th it rained hard and rain was falling during the 20th when Lee got the news from Petersburg — inaccurate, but bad enough.

Beauregard had underestimated the Federal force on the Weldon Railroad, three divisions of Warren's corps, and only Heth's division had supported the cavalry in attacking the enemy on the railroad tracks. Though

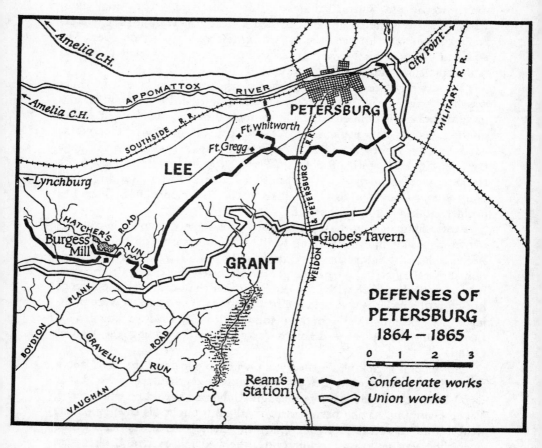

the Federal troops did not fight with much spirit, giving up 2700 prisoners, Warren had the men entrenched along the tracks and the light assault force could not dislodge them. At this news, Lee abandoned his brief camp at Chaffin's Bluff. On August 21 he rode back to Petersburg, through its shady streets and to the wet countryside beyond the last new lines.

At the placename of Globe's Tavern, about three and a half miles south of the outskirts of the city, Lee stared silently at the first disruption in his lines of supply — the first successful step of the enemy in isolating Richmond from the South. Though Globe's Tavern was another engagement not listed among the war's great battles, it was a turning point.

In meeting the constant pendulum swing, this time the shuttling of troops to Richmond caught the flank weakened and, perhaps more importantly, Lee away from the action. Looking at the break in the railroad, Lee felt it was futile to assemble sufficient strength to drive the enemy off.

To restore the break would cost "a greater sacrifice of life than we can afford to make," he wrote the President. Besides, with Grant's superiority in numbers "we could not prevent him from returning to it or to some other point, as our strength is inadequate to guard the whole road."

Appearing to accept the break in the Weldon Railroad as inevitable, Lee immediately made arrangement for his wagons to haul supplies from Stony Creek — on the railroad — twenty miles to his lines. He wrote Seddon in detail of the absolute necessity of getting corn from the South. His own supply was exhausted as of that day, and it would be a month or six weeks before the Virginia farmers harvested their fall crop.

Along with the presents that came to Lee from admirers, he personally received at his headquarters contributions sent to the army and in that period a Mrs. Fowlkes from southside Virginia sent some cloth for the soldiers woven on her place. In writing to thank her, Lee wrote what he accepted as the simple truth of their condition. "I am glad to find the patriotic women of the South are turning their attention to the manufactures of all kinds. To them the soldiers must look for clothing and subsistence."

Back at his regular headquarters in Mrs. Shippen's grove, Lee took ten days to compose an extremely long letter to Davis. Point by point, he traced the inevitable consequence of the government's failure to bring more men to the front. Though many of his points were only new or more emphatic versions of earlier suggestions, he described in graphic detail the exhausting effect on the men of interspersing digging with frantic rushes to one end of the line or the other, and he came out with a strong advocation of using Negroes to replace white men as teamsters, mechanics, cooks and laborers. "It seems to me that we must choose between employing negroes ourselves, and having them employed against us."

Lee touched a sensitive political spot, considering the governors' application of state sovereignty, by urging a rigid inspection of the rolls of exempts in all states. "Our ranks are constantly diminishing by battle and disease, and few recruits are received. The consequences are inevitable, and I feel confident that the time has come when no man capable of bearing arms should be excused, unless it be for some controlling reason of public necessity."

He also advocated bringing the reserve force, the militiamen unfit for campaigning, into forts and trenches. "Their mere presence in the works below Richmond would prevent the enemy from making feints in that quarter to draw troops from here . . . We could make our regular troops here available in the field." It would be difficult to guess whether Lee expected any results from his petition or was only doing his duty as he saw it.

5

On the day Lee wrote his carefully reasoned letter, September 2, Sherman's troops marched into the burning city of Atlanta. Hood, giving the President the offensive he wanted, had attacked until his decimated army was completely removed from Sherman's pathway into Atlanta. In seven weeks since Joe Johnston's removal, Lee's collateral front in Georgia was broken.

The elated reaction in the United States instantly removed the possibility of the Democrats winning on a peace program in November. Lincoln and the Republicans were assured of remaining in office until the job of subjugating the South was finished. The discouragement from Grant's early summer losses was forgotten and a new conscription act brought out such numbers that whole new armies could be created. With the passing of the possibility of a political change bringing peace, no rational hope remained for the Confederacy to gain its independence.

Lee had not been unmindful of the moral effect in the North of Grant's being stalemated at Petersburg but, as with other Confederates in Virginia, civil and military, he missed the wider significance of the fall of Atlanta. In one of his relatively rare written references to the war to his wife, Lee wrote her, "The fall of Atlanta is a blow to us, which is not very grievous and which I hope we will recover from."

If Lee's meaning was limited to military operations, he assumed that Confederate forces would be re-formed and regrouped as so often before in the West. Then, with the thousands of able-bodied men in the Georgia militia, a force would present an obstacle to Sherman's movement eastward into the interior from Atlanta. However, along with the reaction in the North, the fall of Atlanta exerted a profound effect in the Confederacy, both on the people (including especially the Georgia militia) and on Davis's military direction.

While Davis could not admit that his decisions caused the results at Atlanta, in the goad to prove the rightness of his course he became severed from rationality in relation to the war in the West. With Sherman in Atlanta and all of Georgia to levy on for supplies, Davis *then* permitted Hood's army to march away northward tearing up the tracks on the railroad from which Forrest had been withheld when Sherman was dependent upon it. By this demented move Sherman's path was cleared for a march across the state to the port city of Savannah. Actually, the fall of Atlanta in a brief siege presaged the dissolution of the last front in the West.

The decline in the people's morale would have been difficult to gauge. A growth of the despairing acceptance of the inevitable was most prevalent in the rural areas. Individuals on lonely farms and isolated plantations, often stripped of all means of subsistence and living in fear either of enemy raiding parties or slave uprisings, lacked the sustaining spirit of a group that came to dwellers in towns and cities. The more literate citizens and the influential newspapers appeared unshaken in their determination never to yield. Somewhere between this hard core and the defeatists ("Croakers," as they were called), probably the majority was not yet, not quite, ready to give up. At the same time the people were not willing to make further sacrifices. Certainly those who had never made any were not going to begin.

No change was observed in the morale in Lee's army. The heat had passed, the fall weather was pleasant and the men had adjusted themselves to life in the foul trenches. However, no changes were made to strengthen the army nor relieve the physical drain on the soldiers. The dribble of Negroes who formed work forces were put mostly on lengthening and strengthening the lines to the east of Richmond. In addition to those works, a system of large earthen forts ran from north of the city to the west, facing the open country rolling on high ground above the James River and the Kanawha Canal.

In Petersburg, among the families Lee visited, the spirit of resistance seemed actually to have been hardened by the shelling of homes and churches. With all the privations and makeshifts, the well-to-do families managed to continue the character of their gracious antebellum life. When Lee was not camped in the fortifications east of Richmond, he visited often in the homes of these passionate, charming Rebels. While recapturing a season of the social life he so deeply enjoyed, he encountered an attitude of morale that was no longer general in the Confederacy.

It was not that the spirit in Petersburg promoted any illusions in Lee. The issue remained for him "a question of time." But time was running out perhaps more rapidly than he realized. The conditions in the country that presumably supported his army were deteriorating at a rate in which his army was coming to support what remained of the country. In the true sense of humility — of walking humbly in the sight of God — Lee could not accept the reality that he, a solitary mortal acutely aware of his limitations, had become the primary factor in prolonging a war with the United States.

Yet the war had reached the stage where the lengthening lines from Richmond to southwest of Petersburg maintained the only stable front in what once was a border of one thousand miles. Lee — not the secessionist government nor its President, but Lee, a soldier who had offered his services to the defense of his state — represented the heart of the resistance of a society that must be crushed before the revolutionary forces could roll on unimpeded toward the formation of a new, unenvisioned America.

6

While Lee showed no awareness of the deeper implications of the fall of Atlanta, in his own Virginia theater the reverses were tangible collapses in military operations. His effort to play again at strategy with forces in middle Virginia came to a sudden, disheartening end.

In the Valley, Early had maneuvered skillfully for more than a month against a force of Sheridan's three times the size of his own. Sheridan commanded more than thirty thousand infantry and sixty-five hundred cavalry, all handsomely equipped and fatly supplied, along with Crook's mounted raiders operating in the area. On September 19 the two armies came to grips outside Winchester, and the weight was too much for Early's less than ten thousand physically weakened foot soldiers, with their poorly mounted, illy disciplined cavalry. Early directed his battle ably enough and his toughened veterans never fought harder, inflicting five thousand casualties on the assaulting forces. But the Federal cavalry with their repeating carbines got around a flank, forcing a break, and Early's troops fell back from the field at dusk in shaken order. Robert Rodes, at the fullness of his powers, was killed in the battle.

Early retreated south along the Valley Pike to Fisher's Hill, to make a stand where the Massanutten Mountain in the middle of the Valley narrowed the front to the west. Early was less skillful at Fisher's Hill, where Sheridan attacked on the 22nd, and weakened his line by trying to cover the whole front. Again the infantry fought stoutly, inflicting heavy casualties. But again the Federal cavalry drove into the left flank, and the whole line retired from the field in disorder. Early retreated south up the Valley and moved east to the foot of the Blue Ridge.

The end of Lee's wan effort at maneuver came when Kershaw and Fitz Lee's cavalry division were moved from Culpeper to the west of the Blue Ridge to strengthen Early. Sheridan did not pursue. With Early removed as a threat to the Potomac line, Sheridan put his men to a systematic destruction of the Shenandoah Valley as a source of food supply to the army and the civilians. Animals were slaughtered or taken, barns and fields burned, and no article of food — a peck of cornmeal, a chunk of fatback, a potato or a chicken — was left north of Staunton, in the middle of the Valley.

Lee stoically accepted this "reverse," as he called it, along with the end of his brief flurry at maneuver. It did not shake his determination to maintain his second front in the Valley, both to limit Sheridan's swath of desolation and to keep the Federal veterans detached from Grant. As he could not send another man, he appealed to Governor Smith (a former brigadier in Early's old division) to call out local troops in the Valley area. Yet, even as Lee strengthened Early with Kershaw, he was forced to detach Breckinridge's two slim brigades. They were hurried away to support a collection of raiding cavalry in defense of the salt works in the southwestern corner of the state.

This desperation policy of borrowing from Peter to pay Paul was manifestly coming to the day of reckoning, and on September 26 — having failed to stir Davis and the discontented, despairing Seddon — Lee tried an appeal to Braxton Bragg. Sending figures to show that Grant had received ten thousand more replacements than the men sent off with Sheridan, Lee put in urgent language the need at least for Negroes to replace teamsters, laborers and hospital attendants. "Unless they [the Negroes] are sent me rapidly, it may be too late."

This was not a scare warning. It was already too late. Three days later on September 29, Lee wired Bragg: "General Ewell [commanding the Richmond defenses] reports the enemy have possession of Fort Harrison. Order out the locals and all the other troops to his assistance."

Fort Harrison was a key position in the miles of fortifications which Lee had started under construction in 1862. The high earthen walls of Fort Harrison, enclosing three sides of a large square, formed a bend in the lines that ran continuously from Chaffin's Bluff to the New Market, or River, Road. These lines were not occupied by troops, but served as positions to which defenders could be rushed. Fort Harrison, similar to other and smaller strong points in the lines, was merely a well-protected position for heavy stationary guns, and only about fifty infantrymen were stationed there. Before sunrise on the morning of the 29th two corps (the X and XVII, then operating with the Army of the Potomac) rushed out of the woods below the slope leading to Fort Harrison. Overruning the half-awake pickets, the Federal soldiers scaled the parapets before the gunners could get off any shots.

From Fort Harrison northward the lines divided, forming an outer works and an intermediary works — actually the last lines before the unconnected forts scattered around the outskirts of the city. When the Federals, pouring through the fort, fanned out from the open end facing toward Richmond, they were already inside the outer works and immediately upon the unmanned lines of the so-called intermediary works. Between the assault force and Richmond stood only the few guns in position behind the parapets of a fortified point called Fort Gilmer.

Toward Fort Gilmer went running two veteran units still called brigades — the few hundred survivors of Hood's Texans under black-bearded John Gregg and the three hundred survivors of the Tennessee brigade Bushrod Johnson had brought to Richmond in May. A single battery galloped to the roadway leading to the open end of Fort Harrison and threw bursts into the troops spilling out.

Lee, not informed of the strength of the Federal breakthrough, wired Ewell to recover Fort Harrison. To support Ewell, Lee pulled Hoke's division out of the Petersburg lines, along with oddments from other units nearer the James, and called on Porter Alexander to take personal charge of six batteries. Orders were rushed to Rooney Lee to proceed to Richmond. Then, with his small staff, Lee mounted Traveler and once more started back to the north side of the James.

The sun was setting when Lee rode across the fields of Mrs. Gunn's farm to the back of Fort Gilmer. There he learned that Ewell, far from attempting to recover Fort Harrison, had experienced the fight of his life in holding Fort Gilmer. Reverting to the simple combat in which he was at home, riding everywhere on his flea-bitten gray horse, "Old Baldhead" had performed as in his days with Jackson.

The ditch in front of Fort Gilmer was ten feet deep and twelve feet wide and bodies of Yankees were piled up in there like cordwood. As at the Crater, Negro troops attacked in the first line and many were among the dead. The two small veteran brigades, first supported by the old men, boys and cripples of the Local Defense Troops, and late by other brigades of Field's division, had prevented any of the assault force from crossing the parapet and getting to the guns in the fort. These guns, later supported by Alexander's field batteries, never stopped firing. Before the steady, deepening rain of canister the assaulting force finally fell back across the field cluttered with cut-down trees.

Lee was not satisfied that the enemy had been contained in his breakthrough. He immediately planned an attack to be delivered early the next morning to recover Fort Harrison. He planned as carefully as in his greatest campaign.

Then, on the mild autumn morning of September 30 he watched the first breakdown of coordination in his troops in a limited action. Field attacked too soon and was repulsed. Hoke, waiting for the scheduled time of the assault, attacked when Field was falling back and was also repulsed. Lee did not watch this collapse in the rudiments of warfare with his usual composure. One soldier, seeing him wave the troops on with his hat, recorded, "I had always thought General Lee was a very cold and unemotional man, but he showed lots of feeling and excitement on that occasion."

He formed the lines for a second assault and, as at the Wilderness and Spotsylvania, tried to will the men forward until the position was carried. He could not accept their inability to coordinate when this attack went as disjointedly as the first. After the men again fell back, for a third time Lee waved the men forward. That attack was the weakest of all. The veteran soldiers recognized the hopelessness of exposing themselves further.

When Lee saw the men hurriedly withdraw beyond the range of the enemy's fire and huddle there, he then accepted the futility of further efforts.

Though new lines could be rebuilt to compensate for the loss of Fort Harrison, nothing could compensate to Lee for the loss in his troops of rudimentary efficiency. Officers showed the effects of the prolonged strain of containing a physically more powerful opponent that grew stronger as they grew weaker. The emaciated men showed the effects of operating in broken units, from which too many familiar companions had gone and the scared faces of conscripts tended to shake the veteran's confidence in the performance of his unit. All this Lee faced when he went that night to temporary headquarters at Chaffin's Bluff.

Nor was this the worst. Lee soon learned that the enemy had narrowly been turned back from an attack on the Southside Railroad, on which he had been forced to depend after the break in the Weldon Railroad. Running west from Petersburg to Lynchburg, at Burkeville the Southside crossed the railroad that ran from Richmond to Danville, on the North Carolina border. Since late summer, A. P. Hill's troops had labored at digging lines to the southwest in protection against Grant's new thrusts to the west — toward the Southside Railroad and an eventual enclosure of Petersburg.

The Federal advance on September 29 and 30 had been contained partly because Rooney Lee disregarded his father's orders to move to the Richmond front. On his own, he turned his troopers about to hurry to the support of Hampton's old division, then reduced and commanded by Galbraith Butler. On the 30th, the men in Heth's division laid aside their picks and shovels and marched to the cavalry's support in driving off the enemy.

When, in the aftermath of Fort Harrison, Lee received this news at Chaffin's Bluff, he first revealed his resignation to the inevitability of the end in Virginia. The reflection of his usually guarded inner thoughts was made indirectly in two letters.

First he wrote Wade Hampton that if Grant could not be prevented from extending to the west, he would reach the Appomattox and cut off Petersburg from southside Virginia. Then the army would be invested in the city. The only factor by which this could be prevented was an increase in manpower.

Lee's second letter, on the subject of bringing out exempts and Negroes, went to War Secretary Seddon. In this, saying that the failure to increase manpower "may be calamitous," Lee made his first reference to his inability to defend Richmond. "The discouragement of our people and the great material loss that would follow the fall of Richmond, to say nothing of the great encouragement our enemies would derive from it, outweigh, in my judgment, any sacrifice and hardship that would result from bringing out all our arms bearing men."

Since by then Lee could not reasonably have hoped for any significant action resulting from his many appeals for men to Davis, Seddon and Bragg, he showed that he had prepared himself — if not the government — for the end of the Richmond-Petersburg front by the very casualness with which he referred to "the fall of Richmond." Making only a passing reference, and this not as a warning, Lee almost put the fall of Richmond in the past tense by pointing to the results of the loss of the capital.

Shortly after writing these letters, he wrote his wife, then in the country. Lee had been to church in Richmond, and "heard Mr. Patterson preach a very good sermon on the subject of forgiving our enemies. It is a hard lesson to learn now, but still it is true and requires corresponding effort."

He could foresee the day, not too far off, when he would be forced to live with the enemy again. Against that day, he could only call on his faith in Providence for the strength to do each day the duty of that day as he conceived the tasks which God's will assigned him — one day at a time, until the end came.

"May a Merciful God watch over us all," he wrote his wife.

## CHAPTER XX

## "I Shall Endeavour to Do My Duty . . . and Fight to the End"

O N ENTERING the last stage, the gathering twilight of their hopes, Lee seemed possessed of a peacefulness as he had not during the spring and summer campaign when the issue still hung in doubt. This peacefulness contained nothing of resignation. He spared himself no more than in his most decisive battles in using all his skills and energy to contain the enemy on his front and all his powers of persuasion to induce effective action from the government in the support of his army. Judging only by his ceaseless efforts and air of calm resolution, his soldiers could — as most of his veterans did — believe Lee yet expected to win.

The more observant John Esten Cooke, who believed Lee to be beyond hope, wrote, "His countenance seldom, if ever, exhibited the least traces of anxiety, but was firm, hopeful, and encouraged those around him in the belief that he was still confident of success . . . It must have been the sense of having done his whole duty, and expended upon the cause every energy of his being, which enabled him to meet the approaching catastrophe with a calmness which seemed to those around him almost sublime."

In Lee's calmness was the quality of acceptance, as if he were cast in a drama of inevitable climax in which his role required him to fight as if the end were unknown. In this acceptance he ceased to be plagued by illnesses. After the summer's heat passed, he went into autumn's mild weather in good health. He reverted to his simple jokes in camp and to his familiar turn of humor when he revealed to Senator Hill that he was not insensitive to newspaper criticism.

"We made a great mistake in the beginning of our struggle," Lee said in apparent seriousness to Hill, "and I fear, in spite of all we can do, it will prove to be a fatal mistake. We appointed all our worst generals to command our armies, and all our best generals to edit the newspapers." Then he explained that he had made campaign plans that seemed perfect, but the actual battles developed defects, and, he said, "I occasionally wondered why I did not see some of the defects in advance. When it was all over I found by reading a newspaper that these best editor-generals saw all the defects plainly from the start. Unfortunately, they did not communicate their knowledge to me until it was too late."

He returned to the solicitousness for all his children which he had not been able to express during the spring and summer crises, and accepted philosophically the chance that placed his wife in the country while he was accessible to Richmond. During October, after the fall of Fort Harrison, Lee grew anxious about attacks north of the James and frequently remained at Chaffin's Bluff. By then Mrs. Lee was comfortably settled with friends at "Bremo," a stately and handsome plantation house also on a bluff overlooking the James River — about forty miles to the west of Richmond, in Fluvanna County. As it was painful for her to travel, and General Lee might return to Petersburg at any minute, she stayed where she was during the pleasant fall weather.

When no crises demanded his attention, Lee went into Richmond more often during October than since he had been in command of the army. On Sundays he rode in to worship at St. Paul's Church and sometimes on weekday evenings he relaxed at social gatherings as he did in Petersburg. He was seen at those "starvation parties," where refreshments were concocted of food substitutes and the ladies displayed the "new" dresses made at home in the latest Paris fashion models run in through the blockade. Though "always the dignified, patrician soldier in his bearing," as an observer found Lee, he was "thoroughly urbane" at the parties.

At first the young people feared he might share the disapproval of Mrs. Pember, the stern hospital matron. Constance Cary, who was to marry Jefferson Davis's private secretary, Burton Harrison, formed a committee to ask General Lee if he sanctioned their dances. "Why, of course, my dear child, my boys need to be heartened up when they get their furloughs. Go on, look your prettiest, and be just as nice to them as ever you can be."

In this acceptance, Lee did not voice his disappointment — by recorded word or in letters — when Jubal Early's front in the Valley suddenly collapsed in a single battle. After Early's September defeats, Lee had not been satisfied with his Valley operations. In this judgment, Lee seriously underestimated Sheridan's numbers and overestimated Early's. In exchanges, Lee continued to give "Old Jube" support and encouragement. But, anxious to employ the troops, he did stress the point that if Early could not make effective use of the veterans with him, some should be returned to Lee. Stung into action, Early planned a surprise attack on Sheridan.

On October 19, at Cedar Creek, his soldiers delivered an assault in the great tradition of the old Second Corps and rolled up the Federal lines. At the moment of regrouping for the final thrust that could carry the field, Early's resolution faltered. To the despairing consternation of his subordinates, he withheld the order. During this hiatus in command, his advance carried to Sheridan's bulging wagon train and officers lost control of the troops. Forgetting the enemy, the famished men began burrowing into the wagons. The Federals, given the time to reorganize, counterattacked when disorder had come to a large part of Early's infantry. The result was rout. Three thousand men were captured, mostly among the suddenly stuffed foragers in the wagons, and the gunners were forced to abandon twenty-three pieces. Young Dodson Ramseur, left wounded on the field, bled to death in a nearby house.

At this humiliation on the scene of past glories, the public and the army turned against the harsh-tongued man who had never bothered to make friends. Lee, even though in ignorance of the odds Early had contended against, remained staunch in his support of the soldier he knew to be a devoted Confederate. With all the bitterness in his personality, Jubal Early showed a selflessness in his devotion. He accepted the blame rather than divulge the disparate numbers in the Valley, which would expose the pitiful condition to which the Confederate forces had been reduced. Never reproaching Lee for having underestimated the enemy, he retained an undying and passionate loyalty, and was an effective defender against Longstreet in the postwar Gettysburg controversy.

At the time of Early's defeat, Lee was somewhat heartened by the return of Longstreet, whose self-vindications were long in the future. He returned to duty with his right arm partly paralyzed. In saying that he found Lee "worn by past labors," Longstreet referred to him as "our great commander." Beauregard, the other future writer of a self-justifying epic, had parted warmly from Lee in late September for a new assignment. Under Lee's urging, Davis had appointed Beauregard in charge of a department designed to control the operations of the erratic Hood. Old Bory, ever mindful of his hero's reputation, saw the handwriting on the wall and refused to involve himself in a doomed campaign. He exercised no active authority.

Lee placed Longstreet in command of the north side of the James, where he had then established permanent lines. These were occupied by Field, who was to be joined by Kershaw when he returnd from the Valley. As this would restore Longstreet to most of his First Corps, a new command was created for Dick Anderson. Declining steadily in efficiency and spirit, he may have been the first of Lee's high-ranking officers to lose heart. As an alternative to dismissing Anderson from the army, Lee formed the divisions of Hoke and Bushrod Johnson into a Fourth Corps that existed mainly in the tables of organization as a command proper for a lieutenant general.

On Longstreet's front east of Richmond, the Torpedo Bureau (which kept the James River filled with floating mines) supplied the troops with land mines to be planted in the area of the forts between Chaffin's Bluff and the River Road. General Rains, a torpedo expert, had first used land mines during McClellan's Peninsula Campaign. At that time, the Confederates were inclined to agree with McClellan's protest at this "barbarous warfare." Since then the deliberate desolation brought to civilians and communities, the atrocities of the hooligan element in the Federal armies, and Grant's use of underground explosives at the Crater, removed the scruples. Land mines were strewn at the rate of about one hundred a day, and Longstreet was able to hold the infantry in the works covering the Darbytown and Charles City roads.

Lee remained at Chaffin's Bluff after Longstreet was established, though there seemed to have been no consultations between them. Longstreet later wrote that he believed Lee was apprehensive about Grant's shifting his main army back north of the James for a full-scale attack at Richmond, but nothing Lee wrote, officially or privately, indicated this. He repeated his quickly formed conviction that Grant was trying to force him out of his position by cutting off supplies — as Grant was. During October Lee had no military intimate, as Jackson had been and, in a different way, Longstreet before he went West. Judging by an earlier letter, Lee remained at Chaffin's Bluff to make a personal appraisal of the enemy's dispositions.

## 2

Early on the hazy morning of October 27 a not unexpected report came that a heavy enemy force was advancing from the White Oak Swamp along the Darbytown and Charles City roads. Lee, showing his unimpaired confidence in Longstreet, turned the field over to him. Lee remained no more than an alert observer as the assault unfolded in strength — two corps, totaling twenty thousand infantry.

While Terry's corps advanced up the two roads between the gold and scarlet fall woods, Weitzel's XVIII swung over to the Williamsburg Road in the area of the Seven Pines battle. The attacks were slow to develop and Longstreet was never better in straight-on combat action. The new Federal corps lacked the sharp cohesiveness of the veteran Federal units Longstreet had faced in the Wilderness, and late in the afternoon, as rain began to fall, the joint assaults gradually collapsed.

Even while the firing was dying off, Lee was studying reports of a heavier attack developing south and west of Petersburg at the Southside Railroad. Again Grant had combined the pendulum swings, and this time the movement against the railroad was in earnest — thirty-five thousand troops, combining Warren's corps and part of Hancock's, with Gregg's cavalry division. This time, also, the thrusts came on the same day and Lee could not hurry back to Petersburg. He could only stay up to wait for the reports of A. P. Hill, in command of the sector.

By October 27, Lee's heavily fortified lines ran to the east of Petersburg south from the Appomattox River about three miles and then, south of the city, about three and one-half miles west to Battery 45 on the Boydton Plank Road. From here southwest for about six miles ran the lines that had so depleted Hill's men to dig to Hatcher's Run. These last lines were not intricate works. They were straight trenches six feet tall, with a six-foot ditch in front, lined with the sharp-pointed sticks called abatis. For several hundred yards in front all trees had been felled, both to provide firewood and to clear the approaches, and the soggy fields were littered with tree stumps. This desolate stretch ended at Hatcher's Run where the creek spread into the pond of Burgess' Mill. Lee learned that the Federal attack came west of Burgess' millpond, beyond the last lines, toward the Boydton Plank Road.

At eleven o'clock on the black night of the 27th, with the rain shaking his tent, Lee received Hill's telegraphed report. Hill and Wade Hampton had combined perfectly. Hampton's horsemen had delayed the Federal advance parallel to Hatcher's Run while Hill formed parts of Heth's and Mahone's divisions west of the millpond. By the time the assault force crossed Hatcher's Run, A. P. Hill's brigades, fully deployed, attacked. No failure marred the coordination among Hill's troops. Unlike the patch-work force that had tried to take Fort Harrison, Hill's men had operated together continuously and sustained their corps unity. As was almost ha-bitual during that period, coordination failed among the Federals. When Wade Hampton led a charge down the Boydton Plank Road, the Federals withdrew in poor order, leaving their wounded on the field. Also among the casualties were Hampton's two sons who served on his staff. One fell wounded and the other, going to his brother's aid, was killed.

Lee got no satisfaction from these repulses of the enemy. He felt no more than temporary reprieve from the calamity he began to refer to openly to the President. He no longer wrote the long letters of suggested remedies. Of the two battles on the 27th, he wrote only "at Burgess' Mill we had three brigades to oppose six divisions"; at Richmond, "two divi-sions to oppose two corps. The inequality is too great."

Lee knew it was going to become greater since Grant had broken off the practice of exchanging prisoners. Men lost in capture would be gone the same as those killed. To make it worse, the captured Federals would become a permanent drain on the Confederacy's inadequate supplies. This would further thin the army's subsistence rations by distributing food among a growing population of prisoners — especially the thousands insanely held in Richmond. Lee said simply, "Unless we can obtain a reasonable approximation to his [Grant's] force I fear a great calamity will befall us."

To do those things that could be done, Lee made an inspection tour of the lines in returning his headquarters to Petersburg. Apparently feeling that with Longstreet commanding, north of the James was as safe as he could make it, Lee, as he wrote, could "always find something to correct on the lines."

On the bright and frosty morning of November 1, he rode again across the pontoon over the James and looked at all the positions held between the river and Petersburg. The next day, which turned dark and dismal, he inspected the fortifications around Petersburg. After these two days of inspection, he wrote in a note to Davis, "the great necessity I observed . . . was the want of men." He did not ask for any more.

The next day, in a cold rain, he rode down to the end of the lines and pitched a camp several miles from Rooney's outfit. That night Rob, then transferred to his brother's staff, came and spent the night with his father. Rob was turned out in a new uniform and had acquired "a handsome horse." Rooney rode over the next day, the weather cleared and his two sons rode with him along the lines. Rob wrote, "We greatly enjoyed seeing him and being with him . . . and he seemed to delight in our ride with him along the lines."

Returned to his tent in Mrs. Shippen's grove, on a bright Sunday, November 6, Lee wrote of seeing the boys in a long letter to Mildred. She was at Bremo with her mother, and Lee had waited for a time of leisure to answer a letter of hers. In telling his favorite child that he had thought of her while waiting for an opportunity to write, he said, "Indeed, I may say, you are never out of my thoughts . . ." Then, as if suddenly aware of missing the exchanges in which he had given her personal guidance, he wrote Mildred as though no war existed.

"I hope you think of me often, and if you could know how earnestly I desire your true happiness, how ardently I pray you may be directed to every good and saved from every evil, you would as sincerely strive for its accomplishment. Now in your youth you must be careful to discipline your thoughts, words, and actions. Habituate yourself to useful employment, regular improvement, and to the benefit of all those around you . . . I was much pleased to hear that while at 'Bremo' you passed much of your time in reading and music. All accomplishments will enable you to give pleasure, and thus exert a wholesome influence. Never neglect the means of making yourself useful in the world . . . Give a great deal of love to your dear mother, and kiss your sisters for me. Tell them they must keep well, not talk much, and go to bed early."

When Lee reestablished headquarters at Petersburg, as the weather began to turn cool Mrs. Lee returned to Richmond. From there, she prevailed upon the General to abandon his tent for the coming winter. Lee had explained that "it is from no desire for exposure or hazard that I live in a tent," but the activities of an army's headquarters would "turn the dwellings of my kind hosts into a barracks." In late November Lee wrote his wife that a Mr. Turnbull "had sent his family off for fear of General Grant and his missiles," and his house became available. It was about one and one-half miles west of Petersburg, in a pleasant yard facing a road.

With the then permanent lines north of Richmond left to Longstreet, Lee became, at the Turnbull house, accessibly located behind the constantly extending lines around Petersburg. But the house was "dreadfully cold," he wrote his wife. "My door will not shut, so that I have a goodly company of cats and puppies around my hearth." The members of his personal staff found the house pleasant and Walter Taylor luxuriated in what had been the parlor. Colonel Taylor added to the staff a former classmate of his at V.M.I., Major Giles Cooke, who had served on Beauregard's staff.

Outwardly Lee's health still appeared good. In mid-November he wrote his wife that he did not yet require his flannel underwear, as the cotton she had sent him was "abundantly warm." He did mention that he had not seen Rooney earlier in the week when he went down to the cavalry camp, because it was a trip of thirty miles and "I can not go out of my way. My horse is dreadfully rough and I am very stiff and heavy."

Into the very end of November, the weather did not turn cold, and on the unmarred countryside around the Turnbull house Lee found "the bright sun and balmy atmosphere pervades every where." Very responsive to the weather, Lee sustained throughout the fall the cheerful humor in exchanges with intimates. In his letters to his wife, the absence of stress from battles was reflected in his jocular tone and fanciful turns of images in writing about the romantic affairs of young people they knew. He showed that he still liked "pretty ladies." He wrote, "Miss Jennie Pegram is at present agitating the thoughts of . . . soldiers in this city. I see her bright face occasionally as she flashes it on her beaux, but in pity she turns it away from me, for it is almost dazzling."

In his then frequent letters to his wife, he made almost no mention of the war. Of his army he wrote, after his wife had sent a batch of woolen socks she had knitted, "If two or three hundred would send an equal number, we should have a sufficiency."

The mild weather broke on December 9, during the last Federal action of the year on the Weldon Railroad. Most of the troops in Heth's corps were roused from their camps during the night of December 8, to push a march to the south to support Hampton's cavalry. The next day turned intensely cold and the men marched on frozen ground under low snow clouds. Many could not keep up. Before dark sleet began to fall. When the freezing men halted, they had difficulty in keeping fires going and those without captured Yankee tent flies and good blankets shivered through the night. The next day the sleet turned to rain. By the time the column reached the wreckage of the tracks and the smoldering ruins of houses, the weather had sent the Federal troops marching back to their lines.

After this, action was limited largely to sharpshooter sniping and the pounding of artillery shells. When Grant's potential for stretching his lines westward was increased by the return of Wright's VI Corps from the Valley, Lee could only counter by bringing to Petersburg the three skeletal divisions that remained of the Second Corps. Even with the return of wounded and men from details, and a sprinkling of conscripts, Jackson's old corps numbered only 8600 effectives.

Lee's young favorite, John B. Gordon, became acting corps commander, the first nonprofessional to hold the post. His three divisions were commanded by their senior brigadiers — Gordon's own by Clement A. Evans, a Georgia lawyer and state senator, Rodes's old division by Bryan Grimes, a North Carolina planter, and Early's (which had gone to the late Ramseur) by John Pegram, the only professional soldier. A handsome man of pleasing personality, Willie Pegram's brother was engaged to be married to Hetty Cary, a classic beauty and one of Richmond's most famous belles.

With the Second Corps strengthening the works in front of Petersburg, Hill's men were freed for the lines reaching west to Hatcher's Run. Jubal Early, discredited and miserable, was left in the Valley with a scratch force of infantry, called a division, under Brigadier General Gabriel Wharton, who had operated in the western part of the state. The total force contained a few batteries and two slim cavalry brigades under Tom Rosser.

Lee's increase in numbers, to counterbalance the Federal VI Corps's return, did not last long. The dissolution of the Confederacy's Western front began its inevitable effect on his own. In mid-November Hood, having nowhere else to go after finishing Sherman's supply line, embarked to the northwest on the mad expedition of retaking heavily fortified Nashville from the Federals. On the same day Sherman, living off the country, began his virtually unopposed march of burning and looting across Georgia to Savannah. On December 19 Hood was defeated by Virginian George Thomas at Nashville and the fragments of what had once been the Army of Tennessee began a disintegrating retreat over icy roads — fulfilling Lee's prediction that it would cease to exist as an effective force. Two days later Sherman entered Savannah. His next stop would be Charleston, in beginning a march *north* through the Coastal Confederacy.

Even while Sherman was approaching Savannah, a great armada set sail for Wilmington, the last open port. The only remaining force that could be called upon was Lee's army. On December 20, Hoke's division was put on the creaking railroads for Wilmington, where Braxton Bragg — with no more military operations of which to be the adviser — went to assume command.

Of this rapid deterioration of the defenses of the collapsing Confederacy Lee made no mention when he wrote his wife during the Christmas season. She had entertained friends for Christmas dinner in the Richmond house, and Lee told her, "I am unable to have any enjoyment of that kind now."

"Now" meant the time of bitter cold and snow, when he saw again the bloody prints of men's feet, when the strongest soldiers fainted from weakness after only a little digging in the frozen earth, when pinched faces turned to him in appeal whenever he rode down the lines and men called out, "General, I'm hungry." Their suffering chilled the cheerfulness he had presented to the world during the mellow autumn months and grief tore at him like personal sorrow. In Petersburg, too, time was past for even makeshift social gatherings, and for years afterward Lee's mind was haunted by visions of the haggard faces of the civilians, the men and women shivering in their frayed clothes.

On Christmas Day Lee went alone to church. There he met Colonel Talcott, former staff engineer and son of Lee's friend of Fort Monroe days. Colonel Talcott also seemed alone for the day and Lee brought him back to headquarters for a Christmas dinner. His staff had all gone off, "to more pleasant feasts," Lee wrote his wife. "We, however, had a nice turkey and potatoes."

Bryan, the Irish mess steward, was "greatly alarmed" over the disappearance of a saddle of mutton, which he feared had gone to the "soldiers' dinner." This meal was provided for the men by families all over the countryside contributing what they could from their own scant fare. "If the soldiers get it, I shall be content. We can do very well without it. In fact, I should rather they should have it, than I."

### 3

After the first of the year Lee, in the moral obligation that required him to act as though defeat could be held off, took a stand on the controversial issue of arming the slaves. The idea of forming regiments from Negroes, who would be emancipated, had first been introduced in January, 1864, by Pat Cleburne, an Irish major general with the Army of Tennessee until his death in Hood's Nashville campaign. Davis ordered the resolution suppressed, as he did not believe the Confederacy had then reached such an extremity. After the fall of Atlanta, when hope fell for the election of

McClellan's peace party, the idea of arming freed slaves began to be advocated in some newspapers and discussed in Congress. By then Davis, who placed the independence of the new nation above all considerations, favored the measure.

The opposition did not come, as might have been expected, from the big planters. A large majority of those had already lost their slaves, run off by the enemy, and the rest accepted the loss of theirs when the war was lost. In Richmond — where sugar was selling for $10 a pound and coffee for $12, calico for $25 a yard and flour $1250 a barrel — slaves, who sold for between $1000 and $1500 before the war, were bringing only from $4500 to $6000. The opposition came from a violent and vocal group of anti-administration obstructionists, including the Vice President, Alexander Stephens. This wispy constitutionalist headed a group of deluded men who still regarded the secessionist government as a political movement. Blind to the social revolution in progress, they believed that peace could be restored by negotiation with their fellow politicians across the Potomac.

On December 7 Governor Smith advocated the arming of freed slaves in his address to Virginia's General Assembly, and in early January Andrew Hunter wrote Lee asking for his support of the bill in the Confederate Congress. Lee, still regarding sudden emancipation to be an evil, had reached the stage, as Lincoln had earlier, where the immediate emergency outweighed his preference for long-range adjustments between the races. Making the point of expediency very clear in his January 11 letter to Hunter, Lee gave his support to the measure on the grounds of its necessity for the preservation of their independence.

Referring to the large numbers of Negro soldiers who had been hired as substitutes by Northern white conscripts, he wrote, "Many have already been obtained in Virginia, and should the fortunes of war expose more of her territory, the enemy will gain a large accession to his strength. His progress will thus add to his numbers, and at the same time destroy slavery in a manner most pernicious to the welfare of our people. Their Negroes will be used to hold them [our people] in subjection, leaving the remaining force of the enemy free to extend his conquest. Whatever may be the effect of our employing Negro troops, it cannot be as mischievous as this.

"If it end in subverting slavery it will be accomplished by ourselves, and we can devise the means of alleviating the evil consequences to both races. I think, therefore, we must decide whether slavery shall be extinguished by our enemies and the slaves used against us, or use them ourselves at the risk of the effects which may be produced upon our social institutions. My own opinion is that we should employ them without delay. I believe that with proper regulation they can be made efficient soldiers . . ." Along with giving freedom to slaves who became soldiers, he recommended that the measure be accompanied by "a well-digested plan of gradual and general emancipation."

With the introduction of Lee's letter, the debates in the Confederate Congress grew hotter and longer and more complicated, as the problem did present endless ramifications in the details. At the time also the members of Congress were concerned with another problem they felt to be more important — leadership of their armed defense. On January 15 Wilmington was captured, closing the Confederacy's last port. This isolated the people and their armies from the food and material of war that had slipped through the Federal blockade.

Sherman's march to Savannah had shown the Confederate defenses to have been an eggshell. The interior had been stripped of the power of resistance in order to support the frontiers. To help check Sherman's northern march, soon to start from Savannah, Lee had been forced to send to South Carolina Galbraith Butler's cavalry division accompanied by Wade Hampton. It was hoped that Hampton could rally South Carolinians to make a stronger stand than had the Georgia militia. Congress's one answer for the expiring nation was the appointment of Lee as commander in chief.

This solution was not confined to Congress. Jones, the sharp-eyed clerk in the War Department, probably expressed the sentiment of much of the population which genuinely respected Davis as a man and as a President. Saying that Davis's abilities eminently qualified him for chief executive of a nation whose independence was established, Jones said, "But he is probably not equal to the role he is now called upon to play. He had not the broad intellect required for the gigantic measures needed in such a crisis, nor the health and physique for the labors devolving on him." And Longstreet had written Lee in December, "On the subject of organization, I would also suggest that you take the matter in hand and arrange our entire system . . . and give our minds the right direction."

In early February Congress passed the measure appointing Lee commander in chief. Davis, though his proud and loyal wife bitterly opposed it, signed approval of the order appointing Lee on February 6. Lee recognized the appointment for what it was — a meaningless gesture of desperation primarily designed to remove Davis from supreme command — and showed no intention of assuming the authority of the office. To the end signing himself "Commander of the Army of Northern Virginia," Lee chiefly extended the range of his authority to the total operations involving his own army. He continued to defer to Davis on matters of large decisions and immediately wrote to assure him that nothing fundamental was changed between them.

"I know I am indebted entirely to your indulgence and kind consideration for this honorable position. I must beg you to continue these same feelings for me in the future and allow me to refer to you at all times for counsel and advice." Saying that he would be pleased to relieve the President of a portion of the work in maintaining "harmonious action" between the armies, he renounced any intention of assuming direction of distant operations, such as in Texas and the defense of Mobile. "I must . . . rely upon the several commanders for the conduct of the military operations with which they are charged, and hold them responsible . . ."

From his own situation, of struggling to hold together an army for the defense of twenty-eight miles of lines and railroads extending beyond, it would not have been feasible for him even to try to acquaint himself with the details of other organizations. In the realm of military policy, it was far too late to introduce any correlative strategy. The one practical action Lee could take was to appoint Joe Johnston (against the President's wishes) to the hodgepodge command forming to slow Sherman's northward march. He and Johnston would cooperate directly in joint plans involving their two armies without bureaucratic departmentalization separating them, though their cooperation then concerned only the closing operations of a hopeless defense.

One other act Lee might have taken was to remove inept Northrop from the commissary department. However, as a result of Lee's many outraged protests over food supply, Davis himself finally removed Northrop. At that late stage, also on February 6, Davis appointed an able, energetic man in Brigadier General I. M. St. John, *then* to bring efficiency to the army's food supply.

Actually, the most practical move Lee could make was to arrange terms to end the suffering of his dwindling band of followers. When he assumed the nominal supreme command, his thoughts were turning to means of reaching a peace settlement short of total surrender.

### 4

A few days before Lee's appointment, on February 3, three Confederate representatives met with Lincoln and Secretary of State Seward in the saloon of a steamer in Hampton Roads in a so-called "peace conference." This meeting came about through the visit to Richmond of Francis Blair, presumably speaking for the Lincoln administration in proposing terms for the discussion of a truce. If there was one point on which Davis suffered no delusions it was in the certainty that unconditional surrender would be Lincoln's only basis for peace. Recognizing the Blair proposition as an unofficial feeler of Confederate sentiment, Davis, with shrewd tactics, used the feeler for his own purposes.

To meet Lincoln he appointed two leaders of that deluded segment which believed in the possibility of a negotiated peace — Vice President Stephens and Judge Campbell, an assistant in the war office and former justice of the U. S. Supreme Court. Their group sought to give the impression that the war was prolonged only because Davis refused to open negotiations for the resumption of the old Union. In order to gain an accurate, unbiased account of the conference, Davis sent as the third man an intelligent and respected realist, R. M. T. Hunter. This former United States senator from Virginia was then a power in the Confederate Senate.

As Davis had anticipated, Lincoln gave uncompromising demands for unconditional surrender, with slavery abolished, as the only terms of peace. Stephens, shattered, went home to Georgia and Judge Campbell retired muted into the gloom of the war office. Then Davis revealed his own basic delusion. He believed that the Confederate people needed only to know of Lincoln's demand for an abject surrender to be freshly inspired to put heart back into the cause.

Ignoring the conditions in the shrinking area that remained of the country, he delivered to a Richmond audience an impassioned speech exhorting the people to rise up and continue forever their fight for liberty. Stephens, in a sort of pot calling the kettle black, said of the speech, "I looked upon it as little short of dementation."

While the speech accomplished nothing in arousing people whose bodies (as Lee wrote of his soldiers) could endure no more even if their courage could, it did show Lee and other leaders inclined to peace that the President was determined to carry on the struggle until total subjugation had been reached. Sometime in mid-February Lee met Hunter in Richmond to discuss what could be done, with Davis's attitude as it was.

At the time of their meeting, the end was approaching mercilessly through Sherman's northward thrust against only token opposition across South Carolina. Lincoln (as was soon to be articulated in his Second Inaugural Address) had come to justify the desolation brought by torch and sword on the moral ground of punishment for the evil of slavery, with Sherman as the personal representative of the God of Vengeance. His men were turned loose in a continuing riot of arson and pillage (boxes of silver and personal jewelry were shipped North) with no restraint placed upon the spirit of hoodlumism that spread through the army. From humblest to grandest, families were left in stricken destitution, areas were devastated for generations to come, and the march of terror reached its climax on February 17 in the burning of the state capital of Columbia. After the burning of Columbia, Charleston was evacuated. Only North Carolina remained between the millstones of Sherman and Grant grinding inexorably to a meeting.

In regarding the horrors that grew with the approaching end of total war, Lee personally had nothing more to lose. Hunter did. A fifty-five-year-old lawyer from the as yet undevastated Rappahannock River country, he had by hard work, clear-sighted ambition and careful husbandry become a plantation master and owner of slaves. Seeing his life's efforts on the verge of being wiped out, Senator Hunter had been moved by the offers of Lincoln and Seward (in the February 3 "peace conference") to compensate planters for the loss of their slaves.

Less personally, Hunter believed that if the Confederacy offered to surrender while its armies were still in the field, more favorable terms might be worked out in the details of a peace settlement. This probably represented Lee's position. However, Hunter said to Lee, when he proposed this to Davis the President turned on him as a "croaker." Believing his own influence lost and feeling bitter toward Davis, Hunter urged Lee, as commander in chief, to open negotiations for peace on the hope of bargaining on Lincoln's terms.

Lee told Hunter that he feared it "would be almost equivalent to surrender" if he personally advanced peace proposals. Then, Hunter asked, would Lee go to the President and tell him it was all over? Talking late into the night, Lee could not persuade himself that it was the proper thing for a soldier to recommend political action. Lee was being forced into a dilemma as to the nature of his duty — to the constituted authority who legally represented the falling country or to the men who looked to him for leadership.

As was said by Colonel Marshall, one of the staff officers closest to Lee: "Such was the love and veneration of the men for him that they came to look upon the cause as General Lee's cause, and they fought for it because they loved him. To them he represented cause, country, and all."

Yet, Lee's religious sense of the mortal's humble place in the Divine Design made it difficult for him to accept himself as the sole cause for which an army of men suffered and died. Every influence in the formation of his mind and character convinced him that only the President possessed the right to make the political decision that would end the men's purposelessly endured misery. But, Hunter recorded, Lee talked of the soldiers' destitution "with a melancholy air and tone which I shall never forget."

The men were supposed to be rationed a pound of cornmeal a day and one-third of a pound of bacon, but they were usually short-weighted on the cornmeal and the bacon was more likely to arrive every third day, sometimes once a week. On rare occasions the men received an issue of leathery, "blue" beef. On this diet, every third day a man's turn came to dig up earth frequently frozen to the depth of a foot. A soldier in Mac-Gowan's South Carolina brigade reported that the exhaustion of the men — "even those who looked strong and healthy, would pant and grow faint under the labor of half an hour" — was most apparent "when our meat ration failed."

Freezing in the loneliness of the icy pits on the picket lines where the winter winds swept across a bare ridge, the men were poignantly aware of the contrast across the lines. "All this time the enemy drank coffee, ate fat, fresh beef and good bread, and drank quantities of whiskey, as their roarings at night testified."

Officers to lead the men were themselves failing, and some of the best were lost in the small actions. Lee had just performed the melancholy task of writing a letter of condolence to beautiful Hetty Cary Pegram. Within a month after she stood with John Pegram at the altar of St. Paul's, she was back in the church at his funeral. Pegram had been the only professional soldier among the division commanders in Gordon's corps. In Hill's corps sturdy Wilcox, unwaveringly committed to independence, wanted a transfer to Texas, where the death of his brother left a widow and two young children without nearby kinsmen. Powell Hill himself was sick, more often at home than at his headquarters, and Dick Anderson was sunk in apathy. Longstreet was frankly seeking ways for a military peace.

Shortly after Lee revealed to Hunter his anguish over his troops, Longstreet told Lee of an exchange of his with the Federals which he thought worth developing. Though Longstreet's proposal offered only the faintest hope, Lee grasped at it as a possible solution for his dilemma.

On Longstreet's east of Richmond front, the Federal forces were commanded by General E. O. C. Ord, a professional soldier. Giving the written pretext of discussing means of halting the friendly barter that went on between the opposing troops, Ord arranged an interview with Longstreet. In the interview Ord, saying that his side thought the war had gone on long enough, suggested that Lee and Grant meet and "have a talk." Grant was prepared, Ord said, to receive a letter from Lee asking for a meeting and in a military convention "old friends of the military service could get together and seek out ways to stop the flow of blood." In other words, professionals would make the decisions.

When Longstreet spoke enthusiastically about this to Lee, he immediately arranged a meeting with Davis to discuss the subject of his writing Grant. Lee and Longstreet together went to the Confederate White House at night, where they found General Breckinridge.

The former United States Vice President had just succeeded Seddon, who, in early February, had resigned in despair from the War Department. As soon as Breckinridge grew acquainted with the condition of the armies and their supporting services, he approached Senator Hunter and urged him to try to persuade the President to seek peace. Thus, he was known to be in agreement with Lee and Longstreet.

When the three generals joined Davis in the little downstairs study, gathering before the fire in the white marble fireplace, each wanted to seek peace on the best terms possible. But, in the evidently rambling conversation, not one of them would tell the President they had reached the end of the power of resistance. The only definite result of the conference was that Davis agreed to Lee's writing Grant. He probably thought nothing would come of it anyway.

Lee himself did not believe that a meeting with Grant would achieve any settlement agreeable to Davis's demand for independence. He wrote Davis that he hoped "some good would result, but I must confess that I am not sanguine. My belief is that he will consent to no terms unless coupled with the condition of our return to the Union. Whether this will be acceptable to our people yet awhile I can not say." In what Lee left unsaid, he clearly indicated that acceptance of the return to the Union was inevitable.

On March 2, he wrote a carefully prepared letter to Grant. "Lieutenant General Longstreet has informed me that in a recent conversation between himself and Major General Ord as to the possibility of arriving at a satisfactory adjustment of the present unhappy difficulties by means of a military convention, General Ord stated that if I desired to have an interview with you on the subject you would not decline, provided I had authority to act. Sincerely desiring to leave nothing untried which may put an end to the calamities of war, I propose to meet you at such convenient time and place as you may designate, with the hope that upon an interchange of views it may be found practicable to submit the subjects of controversy between the belligerents to a convention of the kind mentioned. In such event I am authorized to do whatever the result of the proposed interview may render necessary or advisable. Should you accede to this proposition I would suggest that, if agreeable to you, we meet at the place selected by Generals Ord and Longstreet for their interview at 11 A.M. on Monday next."

Before Lee received Grant's reply, a sudden catastrophe brought to a climax his dilemma where his duty lay. Early's small band was destroyed by Sheridan at Waynesboro, a town on the pass across the Blue Ridge from Charlottesville to Staunton. When Sheridan's mounted force of ten thousand struck, Early's infantry "division" had shrunk to one thousand effectives, and, except for one hundred troopers who acted as skirmishers, his two lean cavalry brigades were forty miles away. The resistance of the one thousand disheartened infantrymen was so brief, before they surrendered, that Jubal Early barely escaped the field. Accompanied by Armistead Long, the chief of Second Corps artillery who had remained in the Valley, Early made it across the mountain north of the Gap. From there the small party began a fugitive's journey to Richmond. Later the two cavalry brigades that had escaped the action — Tom Rosser's division, numbering about twelve hundred — also started a roundabout way to Richmond.

To Lee this meant not only a humiliating end to the Valley front, but the return of Sheridan's mounted hordes to operate beyond his lines to the west. It was from there, protecting the Southside Railroad, that he had sent Wade Hampton with Butler's division to the forlorn assignment of checking Sherman in South Carolina — the only dispatch of troops from his army to another front at which he later expressed regret. With the menace of Sheridan due to approach his exposed right, Lee looked into the face of surrender. Until that hour the end of the struggle loomed, like one's own death, as a future, indefinite eventuality. Yet, by reflex he rejected the finality of his army's laying down its arms.

While he believed the Confederate *government* should seek a peace settlement which accepted their failure to win independence, it was another thing for him *personally* to commit to the act of surrender the loyal veterans who had suffered and endured because of their faith in his leadership. His identification with those men, involved with his own reaction against submission to force in the field, entered a new element in his divided sense of duty. Lee recognized this.

His usually harmonious nature was agitated by an inner division. On one of the rare occasions in his lifetime he needed advice on committing to a decision. He needed to be reassured that, if he permitted his army to continue the fight, he was doing what should be done and not what he wanted to.

5

The man he brought to the Turnbull house at two o'clock in the morning was John B. Gordon. Lee's respect for the thirty-three-year-old Georgian as a soldier had grown steadily, and he had come to know him personally since Gordon returned to the army as acting commander of the Second Corps. A young man to Lee, he had optimism balanced by the active, thoughtful intelligence he applied unceasingly to their military problems — in detail and in broad scope.

Gordon entered Lee's room to find a long table littered with reports from every part of the army. Motioning Gordon to a seat at one end of the table and seating himself at the other, Lee simply told Gordon to read the reports. These reports showed the actual detailed conditions of every unit as opposed to the paper strength on the roster.

"The revelation was startling," Gordon wrote. To the endless list of sick and missing, many officers had gone beyond the formal statistical report. They described in plain terms the emaciation of men listed as "fit for duty," and gave cases of proven veterans who showed indifference to orders or the consequences of disobedience, and evidence of temporary insanity. "All the distressing facts combined were sufficient, it seemed to me, to destroy all cohesive power and lead to the inevitable disintegration of any other army that was ever marshalled."

When Gordon had finished reading, Lee then gave him his estimate of general figures. He had no more than thirty-five thousand men fit for duty against a hundred and fifty thousand of Grant's, and to oppose Sheridan coming east from the Valley, Lee said he could field "scarcely a vedette." (Federal reports listed Grant's strength — excluding sick soldiers, detailed soldiers and the thousands in supporting services — as 124,700 effectives, including Sheridan.)

An army under General John Schofield coming east to join Sherman would bring up to eighty thousand the numbers against Joe Johnston's outside strength of fifteen thousand, including a skeletal corps from the Army of Tennessee. While two more division-sized corps from the Army of Tennessee (from which Hood had resigned) were making their way to Johnston, Sherman was already approaching North Carolina. After giving those facts Lee, Gordon said, "asked me to state frankly what I thought under these conditions it was best to do — or what duty to the army and our people required of us."

With Lee looking at him intently as he waited for the answer, Gordon said he saw three courses. He would name them in the order in which he thought they should be tried.

"First, make terms with the enemy, the best we can get.

"Second, if that is not practicable, the best thing to do is to retreat — abandon Richmond and Petersburg, unite by rapid marches with General Johnston and strike Sherman before Grant can join him. Or —

"Lastly, we must fight without delay."

Lee asked, "Is that your opinion?"

Gordon said that it was, and then asked if he might inquire as to Lee's.

"Certainly, General, you have the right to ask my opinion. I agree with you fully."

Since Lee agreed that the first choice was to make the best terms possible with the enemy, Gordon asked him if he had given his views to Davis and the Confederate Congress. Lee repeated what he had told Senator Hunter about the impropriety of a soldier recommending political action. Then Gordon grew emboldened to urge Lee to advocate peace negotiations. As Lee had already written Davis, on the same day he wrote Grant, announcing that he was coming to Richmond to discuss the proposed meeting with Grant, Lee compromised by promising Gordon he would go to see the President.

It was nearly sunrise when Gordon left. With only a few hours' sleep, Lee took an early morning train to Richmond. Judging from the nature of his Saturday meeting with Davis, before Lee saw the President he had received Grant's reply dated that day, March 2. In this, Grant declined to meet him. "I have no authority to accede to your proposition for a conference on the subject proposed. Such authority is vested in the President of the United States alone." With that matter evidently closed when Lee visited Davis, it is difficult to know what proposals Lee did make. In Davis's account of the "long and free conference," he made no mention of Lee's referring to peace negotiations. From this it would appear that Lee could not bring himself to go beyond the attempted meeting with Grant — which had come to nothing — and recommend to Davis that the government seek peace terms with the Lincoln administration.

All known from Lee's side is what Gordon recorded that Lee told him of the interview. Gordon wrote that Lee spoke with respect of the strength of Davis's convictions, "of his remarkable faith in the possibility of still winning our independence, and of his unconquerable will power." Then Lee added, "You know that the President is very pertinacious in opinion and purpose." This might indicate that Lee had tried to present his proposals and given up. Lee also said, "The Congress did not seem to appreciate the situation," though he had not talked with anyone in Congress. Actually it had been the President who "did not seem to appreciate the situation." Judging by both Lee's and Davis's accounts of their interview, Lee had been unable to intrude the dismal facts into the fantasy world of faith of a man he respected. In part he respected Davis because of the enduring quality of his faith, however blind.

While recognizing the hopelessness of Davis's dream of independence, since Davis's authority committed them to struggle until conquered, the nature of Lee's duty became resolved. It was — as he wrote his wife and told Gordon — "to fight to the last." With this resolution, Lee restricted his talk with the President to the practical moves open to the army.

Of the Saturday morning conference, in the little study, Davis wrote entirely about the military decisions they made. Lee told him of the plan to abandon the Richmond-Petersburg line and to seek to make juncture between his army and Johnston's. Davis accepted the need of abandoning Richmond without flinching. Not viewing this move as the beginning of the end, he asked Lee with some spirit why he did not commence his movement at once. Lee patiently explained that the animals were too weak to haul the wagons and the guns until the winter roads dried and hardened.

So remote was Davis from these realities of physical decline — though he had received more than one hundred letters from Lee pointing to the consequence of failure to provide subsistence — that he wrote of the exchange that Lee's delay in moving out of the Richmond-Petersburg lines was caused by his aversion "to retiring from the enemy . . . [as] his thoughts were no doubt directed to every possible expedient which might enable him to avoid retreat." Davis and Lee were talking from different levels of experience when they parted in agreement on the moves to be made.

It was raining when Lee walked through the bleak, winter streets to the house on East Franklin, and spent the first night with his family in a long time. The next morning, when the rain turned cold, he attended the communion service at St. Paul's and then returned to Petersburg. He began at once on plans for leaving Virginia and making juncture with Joe Johnston.

On that day Lee began to plan without the cold realism which had characterized all his military thinking since he cast his lot with his state. He ceased to calculate in terms of the possible. The move evolving between him and Johnston was desperation strategy based upon improbabilities.

There was nothing else he could do. To remain in the Richmond-Petersburg lines would be merely to wait for the certain end. The only strategy that constituted *fighting* to the last was the move to unite the two armies. In developing the details of this strategy, Lee worked as painstakingly toward its execution as if the physical conditions made it a possibility. Indeed, if his own undeluded analysis of his army's condition were not known, it could be assumed from his careful planning that he expected his strategy to succeed.

To prepare for the final contest as if he had a chance was more than his sense of duty to do the best he could each day. Since his duty as a soldier was to fight to the finish, in his own unconquerable spirit was the instinct to fight to win until he could fight no longer. He would never be self-defeated first.

6

When Lee and Johnston corresponded over their moves during March, Sherman advanced northward in North Carolina until the remaining strip of Confederate soil between the Federal armies was reduced to one hundred twenty miles. The Coastal flank was in Federal possession and raiding parties were coming in from the west. On March 23, Sherman combined with Schofield at Goldsboro, which was one hundred twenty miles west of the Confederate supply depot at Greensboro. South of Danville, Greensboro was connected to Richmond by a railroad that joined the Richmond and Danville.

Johnston's "army" of 13,500 had not been increased by the survivors of the Army of Tennessee, as men deserted the patchwork force as fast as the newcomers arrived. Even in the artillery, where the men's attachment to the guns usually prevented desertion, cannoneers left for home taking with them their personally owned horses. Johnston wrote Lee that his force could do no more than "annoy" Sherman. Yet, Lee allowed himself to consider Johnston's proposals although they differed in detail from his original intention of abandoning his lines to join Johnston.

Longstreet, following his conferences with Lee over peace proposals, again fancied himself as an adviser. When his personal friend Grant rejected a soldiers' meeting, Longstreet advocated turning to "heroic methods" for continuing the war and seemed to have wanted Lee to assume dictatorial powers. Longstreet showed himself about as far away from reality as Davis. By such measures as immediately putting the eight thousand to ten thousand noncombatants in Richmond into the trenches, he would collect one hundred thousand men, "with a good supply of rations." The rations would be provided by seizing all the gold to pay the farmers, as he had been "credibly informed that there was plenty of produce in the country which the farmers would cheerfully deliver in Richmond or Petersburg if liberal prices in *gold* could be paid them."

Lee's only objection, as Longstreet recalled, was that gold could not be found. At that time it took sixty-one Confederate dollars to buy one in gold, and there was practically no gold in the whole of the Confederacy, including its Treasury.

But Lee, in the uncertainties of his desperation thinking, agreed with Johnston and Longstreet on a compromise plan. In this plan he would hold his lines with part of his force, and send off selected troops to Johnston with which he could attack Sherman. Since Lee was acutely aware of the physical realities of the numbers of men and their condition, and the paucity of supplies (with or without gold), his attempt to execute this visionary plan could only illustrate the effect of prolonged stress on his judgment, as Davis and Longstreet were affected in their way. Once Lee shifted to plans that were no longer based on the known probabilities, he was working in a climate alien to his normal methods.

Within this atmosphere of desperation, Lee wrote Davis that, in order to hold his lines with reduced numbers, he must first force Grant to shorten ("curtail") his lines extending to the west. To do this he must deliver a successful assault that broke Grant's lines east of Petersburg. Attempting even a limited offense with the forces available was like a gambler's throw of his last coin on a long shot. If Lee lost, he would be no worse off. No further purpose would be served by husbanding his forces, as he had been by protecting the men from the casualties of attack.

For this all-or-nothing gamble Lee turned to his new confidant, Gordon, whose troops faced the weakest section of the enemy's lines. Lee asked him to explore the possibilities of a breakthrough. Gordon reported he believed the Federal lines could be broken at poorly constructed Fort Stedman, three-quarters of a mile from the Appomattox River.

At Fort Stedman the opposing lines were only one hundred fifty yards apart, the closest on the front. Of equal importance, behind Fort Stedman Gordon located three open-ended forts which could be taken from the rear. By occupying these positions, Gordon explained, an assault force could fan out to the right and left to enfilade the Federal front lines, cutting off the Federals between Fort Stedman and the river. Grant would then have no choice except to withdraw troops from the southwest to reoccupy the section of lines that divided his front. As diagrammed, the assault looked flawless, and Lee instructed Gordon to work out the details.

Since Jackson's death, Lee had so adjusted himself to the decline in quality in the high command that he failed to consider the limitations of enterprising young Gordon. Lee had been largely attracted to Gordon by his attitude and application, and he was a natural leader of men. One of his soldiers, in describing his martial appearance on a battlefield said, "He was so purty, it would put heart in a whipped chicken just to look at him." But, while his courageous determination and applied intelligence had mastered the skills of handling troops up to the size of division strength in action, he had never planned or executed a maneuver in sole command of a force as large and as self-complete in its operation as a corps. And Lee had given him the strength to approximate an army corps as of the spring of 1864. To the Second Corps's eight thousand, Lee added four brigades from A. P. Hill's corps and two from Bushrod Johnson's division.

Such was Lee's faith in Gordon in those dark days that he reverted to his preferred method of command and entrusted him with the whole operation with no more supervision that he would have given Jackson or Longstreet. As Gordon developed the details, his careful, ingenious plans seemed to justify Lee's faith.

During the night the obstructions would be removed from in front of the Confederate lines at Colquitt's Salient. Before daylight a force would creep out to silence the enemy pickets and clear the way for fifty strong men with axes to remove the abatis from in front of the Federal lines. Then three hundred picked men, wearing white strips across their chests, would rush into the Federal lines and, pretending to be Yankees, yell they had been ordered to the three forts in the rear. With these open-ended forts occupied, the main assault force would charge across the short distance between the lines, seize Fort Stedman and fan out to either side. Lee ordered the attack for March 25.

Before daylight Lee walked his horse up to the rear of the fortifications at Colquitt's Salient. In the night light he observed that Gordon had perfected every detail of his plan. The trenches were packed with waiting soldiers and every group was in position to carry out its assignment on schedule. At four o'clock a single rifle was fired as a signal.

Lee watched the silent men steal through the darkness in a flawless execution of the separate movements. In a matter of minutes thousands of shadowy figures were pouring through the gap in the Federal lines. Then their rifles began to crackle on both sides of Fort Stedman for a distance of about a quarter of a mile. Around daylight Lee received a message from a jubilant Gordon. Fort Stedman was occupied and the three hundred men were on their way to the three open-ended forts.

As the sun rose, guns began to blast from batteries in enclosed redoubts behind the Federal lines. Soon their volume of fire ominously deepened. Then another message arrived from Gordon. The picked men could not find the open-ended forts they were supposed to occupy. By seven o'clock Lee needed no messages to tell him that the fanning-out movement was halted.

A heavy rattle of rifle fire joined in with the roar of the guns to indicate that Federal infantry reserves had come up. Gordon's attacks on Fort Haskell and Battery 9 were repulsed in bitter fighting. Before eight o'clock the sounds made it apparent to Lee that the Confederates were pinned in and around Fort Stedman. The men were suffering heavily from shells streaming from the protected redoubts. At eight o'clock Lee sent Gordon an order to call off the attack and withdraw the troops.

For all the elaborate details Gordon had perfected, it was too late to remedy the fundamentals which, in his inexperience, he had neglected. Most of all, he did not use artillery. Having risen himself with foot soldiers, Gordon relied entirely upon the infantry. Once inside the Federal lines, it was a repeat of the 1862 story of men against cannons. Even in reliance on the infantry, Gordon was guilty of faulty reconnaissance. The open-ended mounds he mistook for forts were abandoned relics from the old Confederate works from which Beauregard had withdrawn to a new line. Thus, this key element in his plan evaporated.

In taking the hazard of the attack, Lee and Gordon had counted on the effects of the surprise, much as had Grant at the Crater. But the Federal gunners in their enclosed redoubts kept their poise, bringing confusion as well as casualties to the assault force, and the Federal infantry reacted quickly. After the war, Samuel Ruth, the traitorous superintendent of the R.F.&P. Railroad (whom Lee had vainly sought to get removed in the fall of 1862), listed his warning of the Fort Stedman attack as among the contributions for which he claimed financial recompense. No Federal reports mentioned having been warned and Brevet Brigadier General Abbott, an engineering officer at the string of fortifications under attack, reported, "It was a complete surprise, and was successful."

General Meade, in effect executive officer of the army, was off at City Point, Grant's naval supply base. After noon, when the Fort Stedman assault was over, Federal officers in the lines to the southwest decided on their own to take advantage of the shift of Hill's four brigades away from their front. Their quickly arranged attack overran the picket lines before

Hill's troops halted the push at the main works. But the Federals occupied these picket lines, which placed them threateningly close to Hill's main position on Hatcher's Run. In this attack eight hundred of Hill's men were taken prisoner.

Along with this consequence of the attack on Fort Stedman, Gordon's losses ran disproportionately high in men lost as prisoners. Nearly two thousand of his soldiers surrendered rather than make the return journey to their lines across the open ground swept by artillery. March 25 lost Lee between four thousand and five thousand men. At that cost, he also lost the last-throw gamble undertaken in the cloudy-minded compromise he made with Joe Johnston and Longstreet. Lee could only return to his original plan of abandoning the Richmond-Petersburg lines and try to move his whole army to Johnston.

When Lee rode away from the scene of disaster, on the way back to the Turnbull House he met Rooney and Rob. He did not try to hide his inner feelings from his sons. In the wishful planning of the Fort Stedman attack, he had ordered up Rooney's division with the possibility of exploiting the breakthrough by riding to cut Grant's communications. The lead columns of the horsemen were just approaching Petersburg and the two brothers pulled up at the sight of their father. Young Rob never forgot, he said, "the sadness of his face, its careworn expression."

## 7

Three days after Fort Stedman, Lee learned that his daughter Agnes intended to visit Petersburg — just when he also learned that Grant was massing troops to the west. With Lee preparing to abandon his position, Grant would race to turn the Confederate right beyond the last mile of works before Lee moved out, or to cut the Southside Railroad, or both. Lee reflected none of his anxiety in writing his wife that he could not "recommend pleasure trips now," nor did he take a position of parental authority with his daughter. In the letter to Mrs. Lee, he enclosed a note for Agnes, in which he left the decision to her. "I fear you have put off your visit too late . . . It would be very dreadful if you should be caught in a battle when the road would have to be used for military purposes and you cut off." Quiet, unassertive Agnes decided to come; she had lived with war too long for danger to change her plans.

In thanking his wife for a new bag of socks, Lee showed that he could still divert his mind at night by reading. He sent her a copy of the autobiography of his former supporter, General Scott, with the comment, "The General of course stands out very prominently and does not hide his light under a bushel, but he appears the bold, sagacious truthful man that he is."

He also told his wife that Rooney and Rob had dined with him the night before, and as always he drew comfort from his children.

He did not, however, get to see Agnes when she came to Petersburg. He wrote her on March 31 that, if she had come to his house at four o'clock that morning, "I could have seen you with my weary sleepy eyes," but he had to ride westward where Grant's forces had gathered for the thrust to the right of his lines. Nothing in his casual note indicated the urgency in his hurry to avert the immediate calamity of his open right being turned before he could move his army out.

The new chief of commissary, General St. John, had collected supplies at Danville, Lynchburg and Greensboro. For days the bony horses, scattered for forage, had been gathered, and the leaky, wobbly wagons put in the best possible condition for travel. However, the drying out of the winter roads had been halted by a downpour the night of the 29th, with the rain continuing through the 30th, and it was still drizzling on the morning of the 31st when Lee rode away from the Turnbull house. Also, at Richmond almost nothing had been done to prepare for the evacuation. And Grant's push had been readied by the return of Sheridan's cavalry, poised to strike that morning.

Sheridan, after taking a leisurely trip of destruction from the Valley, had posted his mounted force at Dinwiddie Court House. This was only a little more than seven miles south of the Southside Railroad, and the road to the tracks ran about three miles west of Lee's last, light lines. At least two corps of Federal infantry were known to be moving west to join Sheridan.

From where the relatively strong Confederate works ended at Burgess' Mill, Hatcher's Run coursed south and a little east, and Grant's infantry had crossed the run about five miles south of Burgess' Mill. West of Burgess' Mill, Hatcher's Run coursed almost due east and west, and the new Confederate lines to the west were built south of the stream — or with the stream behind them. Those works stretched for three miles along White Oak Road, loosely parallel to Hatcher's Run, and bent back on Hatcher's Run about three miles from the crossroad called Five Forks. At Five Forks, two roads from the south — one from Dinwiddie Court House — intersected the White Oak Road, and a single road ran on north to the Southside Railroad. Five Forks was the point Lee — on first learning of Sheridan at Dinwiddie Court House — had deduced the Federal advance would strike.

Since building new lines was now impossible Lee had for three days been gathering a mobile force at Five Forks. When all his cavalry was assembled — the three so-called divisions of the Lee cousins and Tom Rosser — the troopers would number about 5400, placed informally (without official written Orders from Headquarters) under Lee's nephew Fitz. Sheridan would field at least ten thousand cavalry. For infantry Lee hurried out along the White Oak Road three brigades from Pickett and two from Bushrod Johnson. This infantry force at Five Forks would number about 6400. Its artillery support would be guns commanded by Willie Pegram, from Hill's corps, then grieving over the recent death of his brother. The Federal infantry would number more than fifty thousand, of which — on the morning of the 31st — Warren's corps was moving westward across the Confederate front along White Oak Road.

With this small mobile force at Five Forks, only twenty-seven thousand infantry were left to occupy more than twenty-seven miles of works. Gordon's corps placed one man every two yards, no more than a skirmish line, for the six miles from the Appomattox River to the works that ran to the west from south of the city. Heth's division, in the last three miles of Hill's lines to Burgess' Mill, had the heaviest density on the whole front with one man per yard. In the lighter lines west of Burgess' Mill along the White Oak Road, three brigades under Bushrod Johnson were stretched to less than a man per yard. It was to these lines — along a low rise in the flat, wet ground, mostly covered with heavily brushed pinewoods — Lee rode early in the morning of March 31.

Characteristically he was not waiting to defend against Sheridan's fast movement around the open flank of his lines. Fitz Lee and Pickett were under orders to attack Sheridan as soon as he approached Five Forks. When Lee dismounted behind Johnson's skimpily held works, he wanted to observe the Federal infantry that was marching westward across the Confederate front. This enemy force might move into the three-mile opening between the end of the works and Pickett at Five Forks. Only a scattering of cavalry patrolled those three miles and served as a connection between the two forces. While Lee studied the dripping countryside, blue-clad infantry appeared across from the end of the works, advancing confidently toward the White Oak Road.

This was the lead brigade of Ayres's division of Warren's V Corps, moving a little carelessly with the information that only cavalry pickets patrolled the road beyond the works. Lee acted quickly to roll up their front by striking where the left flank was open. He hurriedly pulled Mac-Gowan's brigade out of Hill's lines on the other side of Burgess' Mill, and the South Carolinians joined the three brigades with Johnson forming in the woods north of the road. With Eppa Hunton, of Pickett's division, as one of the three brigades under Johnson, the extemporized force was formed of troops from three corps. Johnson's division was then all that remained of the Fourth Corps, formed for Dick Anderson, and Lee personally made the troop dispositions without the formality of going through the dispirited titular commander.

This local action at eleven o'clock in the morning, without a name, was the last charge Lee would see made by the troops of the Army of Northern Virginia. Certainly he must have felt justified in his decision that the men were not ready to quit by the manner in which the battle lines stormed from the woods into the open field. The enemy, rocked in the front, was ripped in the left flank by MacGowan's proud veterans, and the Federal brigade was thrown back on its division. Ayres's division in turn was forced back more than a mile, while Crawford's division, moving up in support, retired in confusion. Ayres withdrew across a little branch called Gravelly Run. There he joined Griffin's division, already formed in line along the banks of the creek.

Lee's four brigades were carrying the fight against a Federal corps when Miles's division, of Humphreys's (formerly Hancock's) II Corps, came up on the left of the slim attacking lines. When Wise's brigade was struck in flank and driven, with more Federal forces seen approaching the field, Lee ordered a withdrawal. In the afternoon Warren's re-formed corps, with divisions from two other corps, recovered the ground. At the end of the day the assembled mass moved against the works along White Oak Road. The four brigades, back in their lines and under Lee's eyes, stood steady to receive attack and the assault was not pushed vigorously.

While Lee's action occupied the Federal infantry, the cavalry under Fitz Lee, supported by Pickett, had driven Sheridan all the way back to Dinwiddie Court House. When night came Pickett, flanked by the troopers, camped only half a mile in front of the court house. From there he dispatched to Lee a message of the day's success.

Back at the Turnbull house, Lee realized that he had only postponed the inevitable turning of his lines. The force of fifty-three thousand Federal infantry, none the worse for its losses of two thousand, could move westward farther south of his lines (as it did during the night) and strike north from the Dinwiddie Court House area to Five Forks. Sheridan could be freed to strike farther west against the Southside Railroad or even the Richmond and Danville. Writing Davis of these grim facts the next morning, April 1, Lee dispassionately stated that the long-dreaded eventuality was at hand. The conditions, he wrote, "in my opinion oblige us to prepare for the necessity of evacuating our position on the James River [Richmond] at once . . ."

8

The break came with a suddenness for which Lee was unprepared. It also came with a completeness of which he was not informed. For the Saturday of April 1, Lee selected to return to the stretch of works thinly held by Bushrod Johnson, and left Five Forks to Pickett and Fitz Lee. The unexpected negligence of these two professional soldiers showed the soundness of Lee's earlier selection of sober-minded Wade Hampton over his nephew, for Fitz Lee and Pickett sacrificed vigilance to their appetites.

In late March the delectable shad, a delicacy to Virginians, ran in the rivers, and around noon of April 1 Tom Rosser had some of the fish baked. As another example of the effect on men's minds of prolonged stress in a losing cause, Fitz Lee and George Pickett left their troops to give themselves the pleasure of a shad-bake with Rosser.

During the early morning hours of the 1st, the Pickett-Lee force — on discovering the presence of Warren's V Corps nearby — had begun a withdrawal from Dinwiddie Court House. Sometime before noon, before Pickett and Fitz Lee took off, the troops reached Five Forks, a dismal spot in stretches of flat farmland and brushy pine woods. Pickett formed a line of about one and three-quarters miles with the five infantry brigades under his command. On the right Corse's brigade was posted along the northern edge of the cleared land of Gilliam's farm, with Rooney Lee's cavalry division (2400 full strength) on the flank along the western line of the Gilliam field. Corse's was one of the two of Pickett's brigades that had been left behind in the Gettysburg campaign, and its proportion of veterans was higher and proportion of conscripts lower than in the three of Pickett's brigades being drained by desertion. Even so, an immeasurable gap existed between the roster strength of "present effectives" and the men actually in the ranks.

On the left of the other four brigades, only one regiment from Fitz Lee's cavalry division was posted to connect with Roberts's small cavalry force, called a brigade, patrolling the three miles between Five Forks and the end of the lines. The remaining regiments of Fitz Lee's division (total strength 1800) were placed behind the infantry and strung along Ford Road, the road from Five Forks to the Southside Railroad. The wagons were parked on the far side of Hatcher's Run, with the 1200 dismounted troopers of Tom Rosser's two brigades and their sore-backed horses.

Against this force, parts of Sheridan's ten thousand cavalry engaged Rooney Lee and Corse on the right, while the seventeen thousand infantry of Warren's V Corps advanced from the southeast at an angle toward the left flank of the four infantry brigades which totaled less than five thousand. One of Sheridan's cavalry divisions flanked Warren on his left. On Warren's right Mackenzie's fresh cavalry brigade, brought over from north of the James, moved directly against Roberts's several hundred troopers scattered in patrolling the White Oak Road.

The Federal force, thirty thousand with the artillery, could scarcely have been contained under the best conditions — with the Confederates strongly entrenched and the defense directed by an alert, determined command. But the men were indifferently dug in, and Pickett and Fitz Lee had not told anyone when they quietly took their leave to join Tom Rosser at his fish-cooking fire on the far side of Hatcher's Run.

With Fitz Lee acting as chief of cavalry, his division was commanded by Colonel Tom Munford. Despite recommendations, Munford had not advanced since he came down from the Valley with Jackson's cavalry in the Seven Days, though his commission as brigadier was then waiting to be signed in the adjutant general's office. When Warren's three heavy divisions were seen deploying for attack — with Mackenzie's cavalry brigade already having occupied a point on the White Oak Road between the force at Five Forks and Johnson's lines — Munford hurried off a courier to his superior officer. When Fitz could not be found, Munford sent off a courier to Pickett. That courier also returned with his message undelivered. The senior officer on the field was Rooney Lee, but as neither he nor Munford knew that Fitz had left the front, there was in effect no officer in charge when the Federal assault struck around four o'clock.

With the scattered Confederate cavalry force off the infantry's left shoved aside, the force of Warren's corps, plus Devin's division of dismounted cavalry, rolled up the line of Pickett's four brigades from east to west. Within minutes the troops disintegrated as units. Hundreds fled into the woods and hundreds more simply dropped their rifles and surrendered to the masses swarming around them. Fragments in poor order tried to form with regiments of Munford's cavalry along the Ford Road perpendicular to the lines and facing east. But guns were overrun after Willie Pegram, personally serving a battery, was taken mortally wounded from the field by his friend and assistant adjutant general Gordon McCabe.

Sheridan's purpose was to drive the whole force west and isolate it from the rest of Lee's army. However, Corse and Rooney Lee held firm at the clearing of Gilliam's farm to the west. In fact, one of Rooney's brigades counterattacked and broke up a charge led by the flamboyant George Armstrong Custer. This was the state of the field when Pickett, riding through a gale of enemy fire along the Ford Road, reached Five Forks. Seeing that the Ford Road could not be held open, he formed his fugitives in the woods on Corse and Rooney Lee. Through the falling light, Corse and Rooney Lee made their way back across Hatcher's Run. There the disordered units joined Rosser's unengaged brigades and Fitz Lee's troopers who, under Munford, fought their way out.

Fitz Lee was completely honest about his dereliction, admitting that he had not expected the enemy infantry to attack that afternoon. Pickett presented a dubious justification in claiming that he preferred to defend at Hatcher's Run, but a message from Lee ordered him to hold Five Forks "at all hazards." Pickett, though a natural soldier, had experienced a decline in spirit during the winter and, with his young wife nearby, often reported himself "absent: sick."

From the rout Federal claims of prisoners ran from 4500 to Sheridan's boastful estimate of between 5000 and 6000. Confederate reports were by then few and scattered, but any figure above 4000 captured would have been mathematically impossible. Of the 6000 infantry engaged, uncounted hundreds were killed or wounded, with casualties heavy in Corse's brigade. Of the men who escaped through the woods, at least 1850 of the fugitives were recorded as re-forming with Pickett and Johnson by the next day. For the point of effectiveness, however, these men fled the field as individuals and, whatever the number of prisoners, the infantry force formed under Pickett ceased to exist as a unit. The cavalry, taking its own casualties, could not have approached 5000 in its numbers when the horsemen gathered during the night north of Hatcher's Run.

That night Lee was not informed of the extent of the debacle. Around five-thirty, T. S. Garnett, a young cavalryman, galloped up to Lee in the woods behind Johnson's works and told him only that the battle "had gone against General Pickett." Garnett had attended school near Arlington and Lee had been his boyhood hero since Lee was lieutenant colonel of the Second U. S. Cavalry and worshipped in the same church. As frequently when pondering over a new problem, Lee spoke aloud. "Well, Captain," he said to young Garnett, "what shall we do?"

Not knowing that Pickett's force was wrecked, Lee decided he could hold on one more day to prepare for the evacuation of his lines. To hold open the Southside Railroad he ordered, through Anderson, the withdrawal of the three brigades with Johnson from the works west of Burgess' Mill. These troops were to move through the night to join (what Lee supposed to be) Pickett's division on the Southside Railroad at Sutherland Station. As no more than an observation force in the three miles of abandoned works, Lee shifted a regiment and some sharpshooters from Heth's division. Then he rode back through the dusky woods to the Turnbull house.

In the headquarters room he dictated a message to Longstreet to come to Petersburg with Field's division, then increased with returned wounded and some conscripts to about 4500. As in any crisis, Lee never hesitated in weakening the sector less immediately threatened. North of the James remained only the remnants of Kershaw's division, less than two thousand, with the artillerists on the stationary guns, to oppose the two corps of the Federal force called the Army of the James. The Local Defense Troops were to be called out to the Richmond lines that night.

Lee indicated no reason for his postponement of the inevitable evacuation of the lines. Though the army would have been rushed to complete the withdrawal before daylight, and though he assumed Pickett's force to be off his right, perhaps, in the falling mental energies of hopelessness, he made the same sort of assumption his nephew Fitz had: he assumed that Grant would not directly attack his lines. Also he was tired to the marrow of his being.

9

It was no secret to Grant's army that Lee's works had been thinned to the strength of little more than a skirmish line. Also, for delivering an assault, the Federals had gained an incalculable advantage when — in the aftermath of the abortive Fort Stedman attack — Wright's VI Corps occupied the entrenched picket lines in front of A. P. Hill's works southwest of Petersburg.

After midnight of April 1-2, Federal guns began to roar at intervals along nearly the whole of the front, concentrating mostly at the works around the city. During this ominous, sporadic bombardment, the Federal infantry formed for a dawn attack. Wright's VI Corps massed close to the northern section of Hill's lines that stretched along the Boydton Plank Road to Burgess' Mill. In the darkness of those lines southwest of the city, the men of Heth's and Wilcox's divisions — paces apart — waited apprehensively, unable to sleep.

At 4:40 in the morning, in the first, dim, foggy light, the Federals attacked across the front from the Appomattox River to the northern section of Hill's line. To the east and immediately south of Petersburg, the troops in Gordon's corps, forced out of their front lines, made an orderly withdrawal to inner fortifications. There, strongly supported by artillery, the soldiers held with unshaken determination. But where Wright's corps attacked from close up to Hill's single line of works, the massed assault struck a segment manned by only two thin brigades of Wilcox's division. Before Lane or Thomas could even think of calling for reinforcements, their men were literally swept out of the trenches. These well-led veterans of Hill's corps did not break. The survivors of the two brigades fell back northward in passable order through the swampy woods.

Parts of the attacking force followed Lane and Thomas, whose men, facing the enemy, kept up an exchange of rifle fire. Other parts of the VI Corps moved southwestward along the Boydton Plank Road toward the bend in Hatcher's Run. Around seven in the morning a fresh Federal force — brought over from north of the James — struck from the front near where Hill's lines reached Hatcher's Run. Two of Heth's brigades in that segment fought only briefly. With disordered units of the VI Corps moving toward their rear along Boydton Plank Road, these troops mostly surrendered.

Before the swarming droves of Federals could extend their push farther westward, the four brigades in the area of Burgess' Mill — two of Heth's and two of Wilcox's — withdrew from their lines. In loose, somber columns of march, the men started across the fields and through the woods northwest for the Southside Railroad. Humphreys's II Corps followed these four mixed brigades, of perhaps as many as three thousand foot soldiers, and after three miles threw shells into the rear of the column and the wagons. Near Sutherland Station on the railroad, Heth halted to deploy the troops between a large house and a country church along the crest of an open ridge. Posting a few guns, as the wagons scurried past, he prepared to receive attack. From their easy triumphs in the breakthrough, the Federals were overconfident and two quickly delivered assaults were repulsed.

When parts of the II Corps settled down to this isolated fight, it was mid-morning. Then the Federal forces of three corps, scattered over miles of wooded country, began to re-form and return to the east — toward the inner fortifications that ran along the western outskirts of Petersburg to the Appomattox River. During this random action west of the inner fortifications — still firmly held by Gordon — Lee learned, slowly and painfully, of the developments beginning with the dawn breakthrough only by what he saw from the Turnbull house. Not one message had come to headquarters.

Apparently, like the soldiers, Lee had not been able to sleep through the night bombardment. When A. P. Hill came into his room before four in the morning, Lee was lying awake on his bed partly dressed, as if he had not removed all his clothes the night before. Lee looked exhausted. Powell Hill himself was on sick leave, staying with his wife and daughters in a house nearer Petersburg. Also awakened and alarmed by the firing, Hill had put on his uniform and gone first to corps headquarters for any information. Coming into the lamplight in Lee's room, his drawn, sunken-cheeked face revealed the ravages of the winter's wasting illness. His hazel eyes burned with the intensity of the emotion that caused him to say only four days before — while recuperating with kinspeople in Richmond — that he had no wish to survive the fall of the capital.

Shortly after Hill's arrival Longstreet came in, as vigorous and imperturbable as ever. He announced that the first troops of Field's division were on their way on the shaky cars rattling over the Richmond and Petersburg Railroad. While Lee, still lying on the bed, was instructing Longstreet to march his troops to Hatcher's Run, Colonel Venable rushed into the room.

Venable exclaimed that on the Cox Road, which ran in front of the gate of the Turnbull house, wagons and teamsters were "dashing rather wildly" toward Petersburg. A wounded officer on crutches had told him,

Venable went on, he had been driven from his quarters in one of the huts occupied by the sick and wounded of Nat Harris's Mississippi brigade a mile and a half back of the front line. This was Lee's first intimation that his front had been broken to the southwest.

Lee drew a wrapper around him and walked with Hill and Longstreet to the front door. In the early morning dimness the generals saw a line of skirmishers marching quietly toward them. Their uniforms could not be distinguished in the poor light. Lee at once told Venable to ride out and reconnoiter. Without waiting for orders, Powell Hill was already mounting his dapple-gray horse, in good condition from the months of rest. With Hill went his favorite courier, Sergeant Tucker, mounted on a poor beast he had just freshly groomed.

Soon after Hill and Venable rode off, Lee distinguished the blue uniforms of the advancing skirmish lines. As he recognized the enemy, their line halted. Apparently, made cautious by the rapid movement of mounted officers, the enemy troops waited in a swale for their main force to come up. Lee went into the house to finish dressing and, as he rarely did, buckled on his dress sword. Back out on the lawn, he mounted Traveler and surveyed the countryside.

Scattered firing crackled to his right, the west, and heavy continuous fire rolled on his left, around Petersburg. There was as yet no advance from the area where he had first seen the enemy skirmish line, though columns of smoke arose from houses set fire by shells. Beyond the Turnbull lawn seven guns from Poague's battalion — brought over during the night from the Bermuda Hundred line — rattled into position. These gunners were the only force of any kind between general headquarters and the enemy's army.

Lee's eyes were drawn to an approaching group of A. P. Hill's staff officers, and what held his gaze was Sergeant Tucker riding Hill's dapple-gray. The courier halted in front of Lee. His general, Tucker said, had been shot dead from his horse. Lee's eyes filled with tears and for a moment he struggled with the shock of grief. Then he said, "He is at rest now, and we who are left are the ones to suffer."

After another moment, he gave Colonel Palmer, Hill's chief of staff, the melancholy duty of telling Mrs. Hill. "Colonel, break the news to her as gently as possible."

Lee first learned from Tucker's account that the whole Hatcher's Run line was gone. Tucker had ridden with Hill two miles southwest of the Turnbull house, crossing the Boydton Plank Road to the west. As they continued westward parallel with the lines, everywhere they looked — fields and woods and abandoned winter huts — they saw clots of the enemy. When Tucker asked the general where they were going, Hill told him he had to find Heth. Then he said, "Sergeant, should anything happen

to me, you must go back to General Lee and report it." Shortly afterwards, riding down an open slope, they came upon two Yankee stragglers
at the edge of a belt of timber. Powell Hill, drawing his Navy Colt, called
on them to surrender. From behind trees, they fired.

Tucker had seen no Confederates. The disorder of the scattered Federal
forces told Lee that the enemy had completely overrun the lines and that
whatever was left of his Hatcher's Run force was cut off to the west. He
immediately sent a courier for Harry Heth, to come to headquarters and
assume command of the Third Corps. The message reached Heth when
the four brigades that had escaped to the west with him were preparing
to stand off the II Corps's attack.

Heth left the command, but could not make his way through the enemy
groups scattered across the countryside. While Heth was trying to reach
Lee, the four brigades were driven from their defensive position near
Sutherland Station. Largely as fugitives, the men made their way westward through the woods to the Appomattox River. Lee gave Longstreet
command of the Third Corps — what of it was left and when its units
could be assembled.

It was at this mid-morning point, when Lee knew the worst, that the
disordered Federal forces to the south and southwest began to re-form
and advance toward Petersburg. Lee's headquarters, three-quarters of a
mile outside the inner fortifications, lay in the line of advance. From the
Cox Road Lee watched the forming masses — the VI Corps and two fresh
divisions from Gibbon's corps from north of the James — as their supporting guns began to blast and rifle fire crackled from their skirmish
lines. Poague's guns opened in answer and Longstreet hurried out a skirmish line of two hundred men from the first arrivals of "Rock" Bennings's brigade.

At this time, around ten o'clock, Lee turned with complete calmness to
Walter Taylor and, as casually as if issuing some routine order, dictated a
telegram to the Secretary of War. "I see no prospect of doing more than
holding our position here till night. I am not certain that I can do that. If I
can I shall withdraw north of the Appomattox, and, if possible, it will be
better to withdraw the whole line tonight from the James River [Rich-
mond]. The brigades on Hatcher's Run are cut off from us . . ." Then,
after details for concentration near the Richmond and Danville Railroad,
with no change in his voice, he spoke the words that admitted the end of
his three years' struggle to protect the Confederate capital. "I advise that
all preparation be made for leaving Richmond tonight."

On 10:40 of the beautiful spring Sunday, this message was received at
the war offices across from Capitol Square. A messenger climbed the steep
block of Ninth Street hill to St. Paul's Church, and the penciled telegram

was handed to President Davis in his pew. He immediately left the church service and wired Lee: "To move tonight will involve the loss of many valuables, both for the want of time to pack and of transportation." During the February and early March talks between Lee and Davis in the White House study, the President had never once accepted the reality of Lee uncovering Richmond. No preparations had been made for evacuating the capital.

10

Before Walter Taylor and the telegraph operator left the Turnbull house after sending Lee's message, a shell whining over Lee's head tore into the house. Nearby, Poague's gunners were being smothered by enemy artillery fire. The Federal infantry was massed for assault, their rifle barrels gleaming in the April sun, and Lee's headquarters stood directly in their line of advance. When Taylor and the telegraph operator left the house, with the headquarters papers and personal luggage gathered in preparation for leaving, Lee murmured, "Colonel, this is a bad business."

Outside the inner fortifications the only breakpoints were two of those high walled squares called forts — Fort Whitworth and Fort Gregg — one mile and one mile and a quarter south of the Turnbull house. There were only two guns in Fort Gregg and three in Fort Whitworth, and Lee had divided the few hundred Mississippians in Nat Harris's brigade between the two positions. Into Fort Gregg also went some dismounted artillery drivers and a handful of Lane's North Carolinians who had fallen back following the first breakthrough — 214 men in all in the fort. Advancing toward them came the thousands in one division and parts of another from the XXIV Corps, from north of the James.

Federal columns from the VI Corps had reached the Cox Road, and were moving fast toward Lee's group. Poague's gunners had limbered up their pieces, the men clinging to the plunging horses, and were starting at a gallop for the inner fortifications. Lee stared at the advancing enemy with a look of suppresssed defiance, and said to a staff officer, "Well, Colonel, it has happened as I told them it would at Richmond. The line has been stretched until it has broken."

Then he turned his gray horse about and the group moved at a walk away from the Turnbull house. The house soon blazed behind them. Before Lee reached the earthworks in the suburbs of Petersburg, a furious shelling burst around his party, tearing up the ground and killing the horse of one of his staff. Ordnance officer Cooke was riding with Lee's party then, and he recorded Lee's instinctive reaction of anger. "He turned his head over his right shoulder, his cheeks became flushed, and a sudden flash of the eye showed with what reluctance he retired before the fire directed upon him." Lee seemed to realize that the shelling was aimed at him personally — as it was. Federal officers had recognized him.

When Lee rode over the earthworks of the inner lines he was lustily cheered by the remnants of commands — including Longstreet's arrivals from Field's division — posted behind the works that stretched one and a half miles from Battery No. 45 to the Appomattox. Inside the lines Lee missed the heroic defense of the two guns in Fort Gregg. It was not until one o'clock before Foster's division, at a cost of 714 casualties, overran the parapets of Fort Gregg in a hand-to-hand fight. Inside the garrison, the Federals found 55 dead Confederates, 129 wounded, and only 30 uninjured men. Though this was the last great stand made by veterans of Lee's army, the men who had endured that far — including the survivors in Fort Whitworth, who were withdrawn when Gregg fell — were as full of fight as any troops Lee ever led. As long as Lee was with them, the men still did not expect to yield to the enemy.

After the fight at Fort Gregg, to the surprise of the Confederate soldiers no attacks were pushed directly at the inner fortifications during the afternoon. In this breathing spell, Lee established temporary headquarters at the Dupuy house in the suburbs. There, with a composure that impressed every person who had business with him, he planned the details of his withdrawal, just as carefully as on the retirement from Sharpsburg and Gettysburg.

Guns were to be moved out of the works after dark, crossing to the north bank of the Appomattox, to be followed by the infantry. The troops from the Bermuda Hundred line and the forces in front of Richmond (including the stationary artillerists, a battalion of sailors, and oddments of service troops) were sent directions for lines of march for the convergence at Amelia Court House. This was on the way to Danville and Joe Johnston. Longstreet came in with Colonel Palmer, and Hill's former chief of staff helped Walter Taylor write out the orders from the rough notes taken in dictation.

Only once did Lee's outward calm break. In the early afternoon he was delivered Davis's telegram asking for more time for the evacuation of Richmond. Tearing the paper to pieces, Lee said, "I am sure I gave him sufficient notice." Within a moment he collected himself and dictated a coldly worded reply. "Your telegram received. I think it will be necessary to move tonight. I shall camp the troops here north of the Appomattox. The enemy is so strong that they will cross above us and close us in between the James and Appomattox Rivers, if we remain."

As an afterthought, Lee sent another wire. Saying that he had issued "all the necessary orders" for the evacuation, he told Davis he was sending an officer "to explain to you the routes by which the troops will be moved to

Amelia Court House, and furnish you with a guide . . ." Evidently Lee considered the possibility that Davis would want to leave Richmond with the army.

A little later, at three o'clock, he was delivered a letter from the President. Written the day before, the letter concerned methods of recruiting Negro troops. On March 16 Congress had passed the bill to enlist Negroes, though in an emasculated version of Lee's broad plans for emancipation, and Davis was ready to act. Reading Davis's letter, Lee's feelings of kindness were aroused for this man with his untouched dream of independence. He replied courteously in Davis's terms, just as if they had a future. He mentioned that he was willing to detach officers to recruit Negro troops and had sent their names to the War Department. Then, to make amends for his abrupt telegrams, he wrote in detail of the conditions that forced him to move that night.

At the end of the day, he sent his last message from the Richmond-Petersburg front to the war offices. It was necessary, he said, to abandon "our position tonight, or run the risk of being cut off in the morning." Though he could not know that Grant had planned a three-o'clock-in-the-morning attack, he could reasonably assume that Grant would not let him withdraw if it could be prevented. He did not write his wife or daughters.

After dark, when the guns began to move from the lines, Lee left the suburban house and rode out of Petersburg over the bridge across the Appomattox. On the north bank of the river, he dismounted at the mouth of Hickory Road, running west. There he stood for hours, holding the bridle in his gauntleted hand, occasionally giving orders as the troops filed past him in the darkness.

Only fifteen thousand survivors of the Army of Northern Virginia left Petersburg with Lee. To the north along other roads moved the remnants of Mahone's division, from the Bermuda Hundred lines, and the heterogeneous band from Richmond under Dick Ewell. To the west, numbers and whereabouts unknown to Lee, the separated survivors of Bushrod Johnson's division, Pickett's division, and Hill's two divisions floundered through the night in disordered groups making their way west along the brushy, muddy banks of the river.

When the last of the files was passing Lee, the earth shook and the sky was lit by glares of the exploding magazines around Petersburg. Seeing that the rear of his marching column was well closed up, Lee mounted Traveler and rode at a slow walk through the darkness.

## CHAPTER XXI

## "General Order No. 9"

LEE'S RETREAT, starting with the unrealistic purpose of moving south to juncture with Johnston, became in actuality a flight. It was the stumbling, crawling flight of a collapsing organism: the minds of officers collapsed with the bodies of the men. A collapse in the organization between the army and the supply services right at the outset lost Lee his one day's lead and brought starvation to the walking skeletons who, like Lee, were trying to do their duty and fight to the end.

On leaving Petersburg the troops with Lee, like the General, seemed relieved to be out of the trenches and the units marched well during most of the night of April 2-3 and the day of the 3rd. This main portion of the army consisted of Field's division under Longstreet in the van, the five thousand in Gordon's corps as the rear guard, with remnants from wrecked commands and artillerists from abandoned guns tagging along. For about twenty miles this column marched north of the Appomattox to Bevill's Bridge, where the river, coursing at an eastward slant from north to south, crossed their front. The overflow of the Appomattox from the recent rains had inundated the approaches to the bridge, and the columns were forced to turn north for five miles to Goode's Bridge. By early morning of the 4th Longstreet, with artillery and wagons, was across Goode's Bridge — back to the southside of the Appomattox — and moving for Amelia a little less than ten miles away.

Gordon waited for the arrival of Mahone's division, marching by a different road from Bermuda Hundred. Then Gordon crossed and Mahone waited at the bridge, guarding its eastern approaches, for the arrival of Ewell's force from Richmond. Ewell's crossing had been designated at a point farther north and west. The pontoons Lee ordered for Ewell never appeared, and his hodgepodge command, with its wagon train, was rerouted to the already overcrowded Goode's Bridge. By nightfall of the 4th Ewell had not yet reached the bridge. However, the fragments from the divisions that had moved west separately — Pickett's, Johnson's, Heth's and Wilcox's — reached Amelia or nearby during the day of April 4.

Until that stage, the only contact with the enemy had been Field's light skirmishing with cavalry as he moved to Amelia during the morning, and a cavalry attack at dark of the day before on some of Fitz Lee's troopers.

During the day of April 4, while the arriving units converged outside the little court house town, where one thousand disreputable-looking wagons were camped, John Esten Cooke found the troops with Longstreet and Gordon to be "still in good spirits . . . of excellent morale . . . and nowhere could be seen a particle of gloom . . ."

Allowing for some sentiment in the novelist, staff-officer Cooke was probably accurate enough in general about the moral condition of the soldiers in those two commands which had sustained their group unity. The same obtained for Mahone, waiting at Goode's Bridge, as his intact division had been outside all the action at the breaking of the lines. But Cooke's appraisal did not apply to all the survivors of the four divisions that — after the shattering experiences at Five Forks, the breakthrough and Sutherland's Station — had groped their way westward in fragments.

No brigade was prouder, or with more reason to be proud, than MacGowan's veterans, formed around the nucleus of the prewar volunteers of the First South Carolina and carrying the tradition of A. P. Hill's original Light Division. Somewhere between five hundred and one thousand of those soliders moved to Amelia, accompanied by their unshaken commander, Sam MacGowan. Of that march, J. F. J. Caldwell, an officer of the First South Carolina, wrote that what was left of their part of the army "was so crushed by the defeats of the last few days that it straggled along without strength, and almost without thought. So we moved in disorder, keeping no regular column, no regular pace. When a soldier became weary, he fell out, ate his scanty rations — if, indeed, he had any to eat — rested, rose and resumed the march when his inclination dictated. There were not many words spoken. An indescribable sadness weighed upon us. The men were very gentle toward each other — very liberal in bestowing the little of food that remained to them . . .

"About midnight [of the 3rd-4th] . . . the depression of spirits and exhaustion of the bodies of our men increased. They fell about and slept heavily, or else wandered like persons in a dream. I remember, it all seemed to me like a troubled vision. I was consumed by fever, and when I attempted to walk, I staggered like a drunken man."

Around noon of the 4th, when the men reached the main part of the army, Caldwell reported that, "we revived rapidly from our forlorn and desolate feeling." MacGowan's men drew moral strength from falling in on the regular units, suggesting the familiar organization of the army, and from the comforting presence of Lee. But those brigades that straggled up without the group spirit of MacGowan's, and those whose leaders were lost or demoralized, were cheered little by uniting with the army. What all the men needed most, even the stout-hearted, was food — and the rations that were to have been issued at Amelia represented the first collapse in operations.

In his last message from Petersburg to Breckinridge, Lee gave what he and his staff considered clear instructions for the delivery of rations to Amelia. "Please give all orders you find necessary in and about Richmond. The troops all will be directed to Amelia Court House." This message was received in the War Department at seven o'clock at night, and it is not clear if any action was taken on it. Before that St. John, the new commissary general, had learned from Lee's earlier telegrams that the lines were to be abandoned. On his own he wired Colonel Robert G. Cole, Lee's chief of commissary, for directions for the 350,000 bread and meat rations stored at Richmond. At some unknown hour Cole wired, "Send up the Danville Railroad if Richmond not safe."

The "if Richmond not safe" was a strange contingency, since Lee had wired at ten in the morning that the Richmond front must be evacuated. Whatever the fate of Richmond, the troops would need the rations at Amelia. Walter Taylor wrote later, "I am sure that General Lee gave verbal orders to the Chief Commissary . . ." It is possible that Lee neglected to do this, since usually competent Cole initiated no action himself. It is also possible that Cole, operating away from headquarters, was not informed early in the day of the orders sent for the abandonment of the Richmond lines. Evidently by the time Cole sent St. John his reply, the war offices had been reduced to chaos by the frantic preparations for the evacuation of Richmond. St. John reported that Cole's reply "was received . . . too late for action, as all railroad transportation had then been taken up" by government services.

The first train out of Richmond for Danville was commandeered late in the Sunday afternoon for the bullion remaining in the Confederate Treasury, guarded by the cadets of the Confederate Naval Academy. At dusk the President went to the next train with his Cabinet, members of government services and hastily collected records. This train pulled out of the depot at dark, leaving hundreds of civilians stranded behind, and evidently no railroad cars for St. John. But before April 2 a train left on the Richmond and Danville for Amelia loaded with artillery ammunition.

Lee's disappointment at finding no rations at Amelia was given a heartbreaking twist by his first seeing the line of railroad cars waiting for his army and then, on removing the tarpaulins, looking upon crates of dully glowing metal. Energetic St. John had collected — along with the stores at Richmond — 2,000,000 bread and meat rations at Danville, 1,500,000 at Greensboro, and 180,000 at Lynchburg. With subsistence waiting north, south and west of him, at Amelia Lee found only ammunition for guns when the horses were already breaking down from pulling the limbers over the muddy roads.

As Lee was seen then by one of his junior officers, George Cary Eggleston: "His face was still calm, as it always was, but his carriage was no longer erect, as his soldiers had been used to see it. The troubles of those last days had already plowed great furrows in his forehead. His eyes were red as if with weeping; his cheeks sunken and haggard; his face colorless. No one who looked upon him then, as he stood there in the full view of the disastrous end, can ever forget the intense agony written upon his features."

On that April 4 morning Lee, absorbing the enormity of the irreparable disaster, reached the turning point in his southward movement. Although he did not abandon the vaporous purpose of reaching Johnston, his succeeding decisions were directed primarily by the need of getting subsistence for men already on the point of starvation. Even Cooke admitted the effects that began to show among the soldiers following their failure to be fed at Amelia. "Their strength was slowly drained from them; and despondency, like a black and poisonous mist, began to invade the hearts before so tough and buoyant."

Outwardly Lee remained "self-possessed and deliberate," Eggleston recorded, "and his moral greatness was never more manifest than during those last terrible days." In his apparent calmness, Lee made the only two moves possible: he wired Danville for rations to be shipped up to Jetersville( eight miles south of Amelia) and sent his creaking wagons scouring the countryside for victuals. The weak men, who were to have pushed on southward along the Richmond and Danville Railroad as soon as they were restored by food, were permitted to rest.

During the afternoon while the men lay down in the fields outside the town, and the wagons lumbered toward farmhouses in all directions, Crook's Federal cavalry division reached Jetersville. This part of Sheridan's cavalry had moved west rapidly along the southern bank of the Appomattox, a shorter route than Lee's, followed by the V Corps. While Crook's troopers covered the front, the first units of the V Corps began to arrive and entrench themselves across the Richmond and Danville Railroad seven miles south of Lee at Amelia. As Lee's own diminishing cavalry forces were screened around Amelia, fighting off local forays, Lee was unaware that the Federals occupied Jetersville.

That night Lee's tent was pitched in the yard of a house in which Mrs. Francis P. Smith was refugeeing from Federal-occupied Alexandria. Her husband was a kinsman of Lee, whom Mrs. Smith had not seen since the war began, and they presumably talked of other days.

After a meager supper, Lee received a message from Ewell which indicated that his collection of troops and wagons from Richmond would have crossed Goode's Bridge by nine o'clock. At eleven Walter Taylor wrote out an order for Ewell's wagon train to follow the army's surplus wagons and weaker artillery batteries. Lindsay Walker, A. P. Hill's chief of artillery, had earlier been instructed to move this train on a route via Painesville — about ten miles west and a little north of Amelia. This route would parallel to the west the army's proposed march southwest to Jetersville. Lee's immediate objective was Burkeville, about twenty miles southwest of Amelia, where the Richmond and Danville crossed the Southside Railroad from Lynchburg.

When Lee went to sleep, his one assurance was that the convergence of his army had been completed, without serious damage inflicted by the enemy. As for the problems of food, he had done what could be done, and could only wait to see what tomorrow brought.

2

The next morning Lee saw that the wagons brought in almost nothing for the men. There were no provisions that early in the year in the lean farm countryside. The morale of the soldiers was not helped by a rumor that their ration train had been shipped to Richmond and the food squandered there. Many of the soldiers felt bitterly until their dying day about what they considered the government's betrayal of them at Amelia Court House.

What gave rise to the rumor was the fact that General St. John, unable to procure railroad cars, distributed the stored rations (including whiskey, real coffee and scarce tea, held for use in the hospitals) to the clamorous, hungry people of Richmond. From the poorer neighborhoods and the sporting section rioting mobs began to form during Sunday night of April 2. The news of the mob came with Dick Ewell, whose motley force arrived at Amelia during the morning of the 5th.

Ewell's collection of units had been the last troops to leave Richmond, passing over the bridge across the James at seven on Monday morning the 3rd. Ewell had foolishly issued an order for the burning of the arsenal and government warehouses. The mobs fanned the flames, spreading the fire to private warehouses — mostly tobacco — and flour mills. The fire spread to Main Street, where the old-line stores had given way to rows of auction houses jammed with the former belongings of private homes, and the hunger-crazed mob fought over food and whiskey and the treasures in the auction houses. Ruffians wearing newly acquired silk hats and opera cloaks lay in the gutter to sip the whiskey flowing from broken barrels, and harridans wearing ostrich feathers and lace shawls fought over a biscuit. No law existed.

From the south side of the James, Ewell's group — including the survivors of Kershaw's division, who had fought four years for that capital, and men whose homes were in Richmond — watched in sickened awe as the flames raged over the downtown section of the city and, beyond the island of Capitol Square, to residences on East Franklin and Grace streets. About an hour after these last defenders of the Confederate capital began their march southwest, General Weitzel, of the Army of the James, marched into the burning city with one division of the XXIV Corps and a colored division of the XXV Corps. The Negroes were singing "The Year of Jubilee." General Weitzel took headquarters in the recently vacated White House, his staff celebrating with wine left behind by Davis, and established military government in Richmond.

When Ewell, with his unhappy tidings, reached Lee at Amelia, only on paper did his force exist in "two divisions," approximating a total of six thousand. Kershaw's veterans had numbered less than two thousand when they left the lines. Custis Lee's division was listed at three thousand, with two so-called brigades formed of the artillerists from the abandoned stationary guns, government clerks in the local defense troops and a battalion of sailors. None of them accustomed to marching, they fell by the wayside in droves. Lee, however, formed them in the line of march that had already started for Burkeville.

In the lead went the troops then under Longstreet. Field's intact division of Longstreet's own corps marched in the van, followed by the reformed remnants of Heth's and Wilcox's divisions, and then the small, though still intact division of Billy Mahone — all formerly of Hill's corps. A line of wagons followed Longstreet's column.

In the next group came Pickett with his re-formed division "reduced to an inconsiderable number," and Johnson's re-formed division, in which Wise's brigade of less than one thousand was the only unit of any size. Wise, unengaged at Five Forks, had been withdrawn before the breakthrough. The Pickett-Johnson force was listed as the "corps" of dispirited Dick Anderson. Ewell's force followed Anderson, with another line of wagons behind Ewell.

Gordon, Lee's other dependable with Longstreet, fell in as rear guard. His division-sized corps included several hundred artillerists whose guns had been left spiked at Petersburg, and who received an issue of 225 rifles at Amelia.

Porter Alexander, who had commanded the artillery north of the James during the last months, came up with Ewell. He joined Lee and Longstreet when they left Amelia around one o'clock. As the three generals rode southwest, reports came that Rooney Lee was fighting Sheridan's cavalry across their path at Jetersville. Riding faster over the seven miles to Jetersville, Lee determined to attack with his infantry to clear the

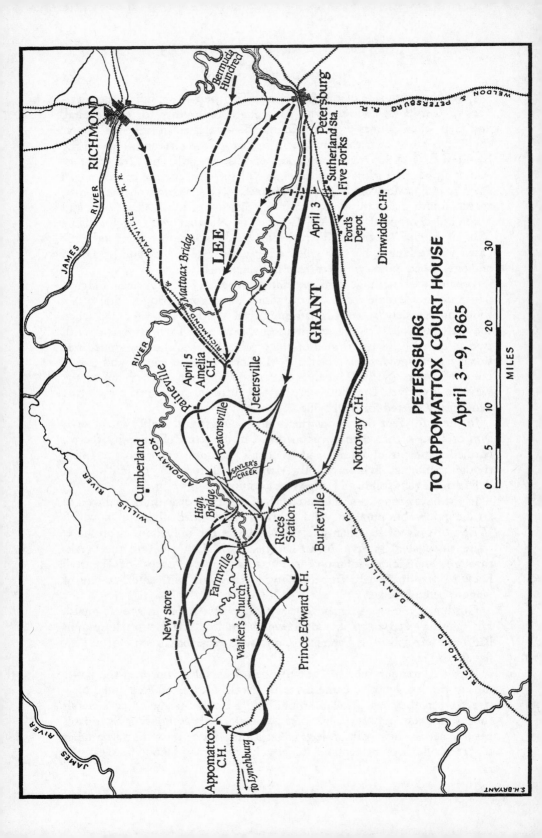

PETERSBURG
TO APPOMATTOX COURT HOUSE
April 3–9, 1865

RICHMOND

JAMES RIVER

Bermuda Hundred

Petersburg

Petersburg Sta.

WELDON & PETERSBURG R. R.

Sutherland Sta.
Five Forks
Ford's Depot
Dimwiddie C.H.

April 3

LEE

GRANT

DANVILLE R. R.

Mattoax Bridge

RICHMOND & DANVILLE R. R.

April 5
Amelia C.H.

Painesville

Jetersville

Deatonsville

SAYLER'S CREEK

Nottoway C.H.

Cumberland

APPOMATTOX RIVER

WILLIS RIVER

High Bridge

Rice's Station

Burkeville

RICHMOND & DANVILLE R. R.

New Store

Farmville

Walker's Church

Prince Edward C.H.

Appomattox C.H.

To Lynchburg

JAMES RIVER

0   5   10   20   30
MILES

S. H. BRYANT

railroad and his line of march to Danville. At that time he expected, or hoped, that the provisions ordered from Danville would be moving north by train. Nearing Jetersville, he heard his infantry skirmishers already engaged with the enemy, and then his son rode up. Big Rooney showed none of his sanguine nature.

The Federal V Corps had strongly entrenched during the afternoon of the day before and this morning, and at two-thirty Humphreys's II began to arrive and deploy in support. The VI Corps, which had followed Humphreys on the direct route south of the Appomattox, was also coming up. Lee sat silently on his horse as he absorbed the information which meant that his way to Danville, to provisions and Johnston, was blocked. This was the cost of the day lost at Amelia.

To attack was impossible, unless he wanted to bring a quick end, and this seems not to have occurred to Lee. With the instinct of preservation, he planned to turn west, across bad roads to Farmville. At this small city on the Southside Railroad, he could have rations sent from Lynchburg. As he later wrote Davis, Lee still clung to the plan of reaching Danville, by turning south from west of Farmville. But the immediate purpose was obtaining food for his men.

To avoid the enemy across his front and get to Farmville he must put his weakened men to the exertion of a forced night march, truly the last resort. With no show of emotion, he gave the orders for Field's lead division to make a short countermarch back up the railroad. The column would turn west into a road to Amelia Springs, the first placename on the winding course to Farmville. Beginning with this extemporized move late in the afternoon of April 5, the army as an organization began to fall apart.

As wolves nip at the flanks of an old animal staggering to his death, so Sheridan's cavalry struck at the unguarded sections of the miles of wagon train crawling through the muddy roads. Mackenzie's brigade got among the wagons in which Custis Lee had carefully packed twenty thousand rations before his Richmond defense forces left their lines on Sunday, the 2nd. All the food was burned. A brigade from Crook's division hit a stretch of Ewell's wagons at Painesville, and set fire to two hundred before driven off by Gary's cavalry brigade with help from the survivors of Rosser's and Fitz Lee's divisions. The wagon train was stalled for hours before the road was cleared of the charred, smoking wreckage. On both flanks the plodding foot soldiers caught flashes of the blue uniformed horsemen, sometimes lounging in their saddles out of rifle range and calling, "Come on in, Johnny, and get greenbacks."

When the van approached Amelia Springs at nightfall, the bridge collapsed over Flat Creek, an eighty-foot-wide tributary of the Appomattox. Lee was eating supper in the basement dining room of a hospitable family when the news reached him. Sending an order for the engineers, he rode at once to Flat Creek. He found the infantry wading across while the guns and wagons stood motionless on the dark road. There Lee was joined by his young friend, Colonel Talcott, with whom he had shared Christmas dinner.

Talcott recalled that "Lee did not leave until he was assured that material for a new bridge was at hand . . ." Lee "explained his anxiety by saying that General Gordon had captured a dispatch from General Grant to General Ord [commander of the Army of the James], who was at Jetersville, ordering an attack the next morning." Since Talcott's reference to the contents of the captured dispatch was accurate, he evidently learned later about the dispatch and confused the time sequence in his memory. Grant did not send the dispatch until 10:10 P.M.; some time elapsed before it was captured and more time before it was delivered to Lee.

The dispatch was carried by two "Jessie scouts," a group of Sheridan's troopers who rode ahead in Confederate uniforms and mingled with the army. Suspicion was attracted to these two spies, riding at the head of Gordon's rear guard, by the newness of their uniforms and the good condition of their horses. After the message was found in the coat lining of one of the fake Confederates, Gordon sent it to Lee by Major Hunter. Then on Gordon's staff, Hunter was the former staff officer of Allegheny Johnson, who had escaped in a black raincoat from the predawn breakthrough of the Mule Shoe at Spotsylvania and given Lee the first report. Major Hunter's report indicated that Lee wrote his reply to Gordon, three pages in pencil, immediately on receiving the captured dispatch. Lee's reply was dated 4 A.M.

Lee had obviously left the Flat Creek bridge before that. Fitz Lee was known to have conferred with him at Amelia Springs "during the night," and another soldier, who had talked with Major Hunter, stated that Hunter found General Lee "late that night at his headquarters near Amelia Springs." Actually Lee had been anxious at Flat Creek before he received the captured dispatch, and that was probably the basis of Talcott's confusion. In his pencil-written letter to Gordon, Lee wrote, "It was from my expectation of an attack being made from Jetersville that I was anxious that the rear of the column should reach Deatonsville as soon as possible." Deatonsville was the next town, southwest from Amelia Springs.

The importance of holding the enemy off until Deatonsville was reached was that at that point the creeping wagon train and the army, with its guns and wagons, would use the same road. The burden of Lee's message to Gordon was that it was necessary to tax the strength of the men and animals to keep them moving, and "keep everything ahead of you, wagons, stragglers, etc."

Before Hunter left with Lee's reply, he told the General that Gordon wished to know what disposition should be made of the spies. Lee asked Hunter to wait a minute and turned to give instructions to other officers. These "Jessie scouts" operated for Sheridan, the despoiler of homes and property, who in the Valley had hanged several men (one no more than a boy) on the grounds that they were "guerrillas" and not soldiers of a regular army. After Lee had spoken with the other officers, he hesitated before answering Hunter. Then he said, "Tell the general that the lives of so many of our own men are at stake that all my thoughts now must be given to disposing of them. Let him keep the prisoners until he hears further from me." It was his equivocal way of saying that the end was too near to take any lives not lost in actual engagements.

It was around the time of writing Gordon that he saw Fitz Lee and gave him orders for the next day. Since Amelia, the enemy cavalry had not been pushing against the army's rear but was beginning to move on a parallel route upon the left marching flank. Lee instructed his nephew to move out at daylight with most of his force to guard the left flank of the columns and wagons between Amelia Springs and Deatonsville. Rooney Lee would remain behind to see Gordon's rear guard on its way. By then, the cavalry was losing as many men from broken-down horses as from casualties. Though any estimate of remaining numbers would be only a guess, with Rooney left behind, Fitz Lee could not have drawn upon appreciably more than two thousand troopers.

Lee could have had little sleep on the night of April 5-6. At whatever late hour at night he left the Flat Creek bridge, he was receiving officers in his headquarters at Amelia Springs before four in the morning. Not too long afterwards, probably at full daylight, he mounted again. Before ten o'clock in the morning of the 6th he had ridden twelve miles from Amelia Springs to a Southside Railroad stop called Rice, or Rice's Station. On his way he rode to the head of the column that was diminishing with each mile. Even the bravest and most loyal, unable to keep up, steadily fell out of the ranks.

A man close to fainting from hunger, whose legs tremble and eyes keep closing as he tries to walk, will, as Cooke pointed out, " 'straggle' off to houses by the road for food and sleep. Desertion is not in his mind, but the result is the same. The man who lags or sleeps while his column is retreating, close pressed by the enemy, never rejoins it." On that night march, as the guns and wagons crowded the road, many groups under lax discipline moved by less congested byways — plantation roads and woods paths. When any of those men lay down to sleep, when morning came they did not even know where they were. They stumbled on westward in little bands, hunting for food, many too weak to carry their rifles.

3

Near Rice, Lee waited for the passage of the reasonably well closed up four divisions under Longstreet. At Rice, the road southwest from Amelia Springs cut back at a sharp angle northwest to Farmville, seven miles away. Between ten and eleven o'clock Lee received reports of three enemy threats. Cavalry attacks were hitting the wagon train two miles back, an enemy infantry force was approaching Rice from the southeast, and a raiding party was on the way to Farmville ahead of them. Some rations were accumulating at Farmville, where the raiders could burn the bridge on which Lee depended for crossing back to the north bank of the wandering Appomattox.

A group of stragglers was gathered under General Pendleton to beat off the cavalry attack, though not before some wagons were burned. Lee hurried the remnants of Rosser's and Munford's divisions ahead on their decrepit horses to drive the raiders away from Farmville. At Rice Longstreet formed his men in line of battle as the brigades came up. Ord's army of the James had to be held away from the sharp angle of the road leading to Farmville.

While Lee waited at Rice for Anderson's column, following on Longstreet, toward noon and again after noon, new attacks were made on the wagon trains. Anderson beat off Devin's cavalry division and the next attack, by Crook's cavalry division, was beaten off by the cannoneers acting as infantry with Ewell. During these halts, sometime after one o'clock Custer's cavalry division got across the road among wagons in a gap between Mahone, in the rear of Longstreet's column, and Pickett in the lead of the Anderson-Ewell force. Simultaneously, Humphreys's II Corps was pushing hard against Gordon's rear guard — separated from Ewell by miles of the wagon train. At this development, command in the army disintegrated through the breakdown of two lieutenant generals, Ewell and Anderson.

Ewell, whose decline began with the loss of his leg and the ascendancy of the Widow Brown, had little inner force left after the inactive months in nominal command of Richmond's defenses. When Lee had established Longstreet north of the James, Ewell's authority extended only to the personnel permanently attached to the fortifications, along with Custis Lee's Local Defense Troops, and their actual combat fell largely under Longstreet's direction. When Ewell fell in with the army at Amelia, his condition — evidently unsuspected by Lee — was close to demoralization.

Dick Anderson, having overcome an earlier drinking problem, had regressed under the prolonged stress to the need of an alcoholic stimulant to relieve the depression which by then possessed him.

When Anderson's halted column found the enemy in strength among wagons across its line of march, Dick Anderson rode back for a conference with Ewell. In view of the hard pressure being exerted on Gordon behind them, the two former commanders of great corps decided to attack the enemy's cavalry to clear the road and keep the columns moving. Though Ewell was senior in rank, he did not assume command of the combined force. Each general returned to his own small force. There each of them committed an act of negligence that would have been unthinkable in a trained soldier in command of himself.

In front Anderson, with his troops deployed to meet the enemy's cavalry, failed to notify Mahone ahead of him that he had halted to fight. With the wagons behind Mahone blocking any view of Anderson's column, the rear of Longstreet's column marched on, steadily widening the separation between the army's strongest remaining units and the small Anderson-Ewell force. In the rear Ewell, in order to combine with Gordon, ordered the wagon train following his column to turn off the road to another road running to the northwest. But he failed to notify Gordon that the wagons had been turned off the road the troops were using, and Gordon dutifully continued his march behind the wagon train. Thus, the Anderson-Ewell force isolated itself from the rest of the army, with Lee and everyone else unaware of it.

As Lee near Rice grew anxious for the approach of Anderson's column, the enemy's infantry began to mass on Ewell, about one mile and one-quarter behind Anderson. The two commands were themselves separated by a fork of Sayler's Creek. This stream followed a meandering course southeast from the Appomattox across a rolling, swampy country, sliced by small ravines, where thickets of pinewoods were broken by farms and a few plantations.

When Gordon had turned northwest after the wagon train, Humphreys's corps followed him, continuing to harass the rear guard. This cleared the road for Wright's VI Corps to form on the front and both flanks of Ewell's command of perhaps a little more than three thousand. About sixteen hundred veterans remained in Kershaw's division, with a like number in Custis Lee's groups of artillerists and sailors armed with rifles. Ewell's guns were in the wagon train and he had no artillery. So, instead of Ewell and Anderson combining to attack the cavalry across Anderson's front, Ewell arranged his forces to receive assault while Anderson — whose men were back with Ewell's — distractedly prepared his attack alone.

Before Anderson was ready, Wise threw his brigade at Custer's horsemen. The ex-governor of Virginia had lost none of his assertive independence since he had defied his rival Floyd in Lee's long-ago campaign in the mountains and, having a low opinion of Bushrod Johnson, he attacked without informing his superior officer. Custer's command was driven back by the isolated attack, but this resulted mainly in a hurry call for Devin to bring up his division in support. When the assault was later delivered against the two enemy cavalry divisions, Anderson gave little direction and no leadership. Bushrod Johnson himself — worn by the long strain in the trenches and perhaps disheartened by the wreckage of half his command at Five Forks — assumed a limp control of the remnants of his division. Some of his regiment-size brigades did not attack at all.

The disjointed assault briefly drove the enemy, before contact was lost between Pickett and Johnson. Then cavalry poured through the breech on the flank of the 350 survivors of Five Forks in Wallace's brigade. They fled the field. Whether their flight started or hastened the break, in minutes Anderson's force disintegrated. Except for Wise's brigade, and perhaps small parts of Pickett's division, the men simply took to the woods — with Anderson, Johnson and Pickett among the fugitives.

Behind them, in Ewell's battle, Kershaw's veterans made a brave stand. The naval battalion and the rifle-armed artillerists incredibly made a charge as reckless and, in its doomed way, as gallant as any in the army's history. Stapleton Crutchfield, who had been Jackson's chief of artillery before he lost a leg at Chancellorsville, fell dead among isolated groups that, surrounded and hopelessly outnumbered, fought on until the enemy killed them. Some were bayonetted to death. When Ewell saw the blue cavalry, fresh from routing Anderson, approaching the rear of Kershaw and Custis Lee, he surrendered.

The broken man was taken prisoner, along with stiffly dignified Custis Lee and Joe Kershaw, resolute to the end and proud of the last fight his skeletal division made against an army corps. Though Kershaw's survivors were totally enveloped, and he believed none escaped either death or capture, some individuals from his command and Custis Lee's made it into the woods.

The numbers that composed this wrecked segment of the army could be only rough estimates, as Confederate reports had entirely ceased and the Federal estimates were exaggerated. It was natural that Federal generals did not wish to dim the glory of defeating Lee's famed army by acknowledging they were fighting only a dying relic of what had once been an invincible enemy and that their victories were little more than shadow battles. General Wright, reporting the VI Corps defeat of the pitiful little band gathered without artillery under Ewell, wrote "the right of the rebel army was annihilated . . . and the corps . . . by its valor . . . nobly sustained its previous well-earned reputation."

Of the Johnson-Pickett force under Anderson, two of Johnson's four brigades and three of Pickett's had been mathematically eliminated by

Federal claims of prisoners taken at Five Forks. Yet, here at Sayler's Creek, the Federals listed Johnson's "division" at 3800 and "Pickett's division" at 2500. By all roster accounts, the combined remnants of Pickett's and Johnson's who were actually assembled with their regiments at Sayler's Creek could scarcely have totaled 3500 infantry in Anderson's "corps."

Whatever the numbers engaged, this connective force between the army's van and the rear — "the rebel right," as Wright termed it — was dissolved. Wise came out with the only unit resembling a brigade, about seven hundred men, with their organization intact and leader undaunted. Johnson's other three brigades combined numbered less than that as organized units, Ransom's having only eighty men present for duty. Pickett's command was totally shattered. Though one thousand were still unscathed and free of the enemy, the bulk of these continued their way westward, or fell out as stragglers, in separated and mostly unarmed groups. The numbers who rejoined Pickett and his staff were too few to be regarded by Lee as a military unit — even a regiment.

As in the breakthrough at Petersburg, Lee learned of this totally unexpected disaster only as a shocked observer of the aftermath.

4

After the rear of Mahone's column passed, and Lee had seen or heard nothing of Anderson's approach, he rode north to where he might get a cross-country view. Near where the single stream of Sayler's Creek — before it forked — flowed into the Appomattox, he encountered a cluster of somber cavalrymen. Listed as Roberts's brigade, the one regiment and one battalion of North Carolinians numbered little more than one hundred. Attached to Rooney Lee's division, when Rooney's two larger brigades were withdrawn from Gordon's rear, Roberts's troopers crossed Sayler's Creek in front of the wagons. What they were doing when Lee joined them was helplessly watching Gordon's rear guard on the other side of the creek trying to fight off engulfment by Humphreys's corps.

Lee dismounted and adjusted his field glasses to his eyes. At some distance from the fight, he observed a group of white objects. Turning to Captain Garnett, his young acquaintance from the Arlington area who had brought him the message of the Five Forks defeat, he asked, "Are those sheep or not?"

"No, General, they are Yankee wagons."

Looking again through his glasses, Lee said slowly, "You are right. But what are they doing here?"

Garnett had no answer. No one in Gordon's column knew that, in following the wagons, they had turned off from the army's line of march.

To find Gordon fighting alone, so closely pursued that the enemy's wagons were coming up, deepened the mystery of Anderson's whereabouts. Alarmed, Lee rode back toward Rice.

Near Rice he found Mahone, forming in line of battle behind Longstreet. While he was talking with Mahone, Colonel Venable rode up. He asked Lee if he had gotten his message. When Lee said, "No," Venable told him the enemy had captured the wagons at Sayler's Creek.

Lee exclaimed, "Where is Anderson? Where is Ewell? It is strange I can't hear from them."

No one made a reply. Then Lee ordered Mahone to pull his troops out of line and take his division back to Sayler's Creek. With Venable following, Lee and Mahone rode at the head of the column, climbing a low hill. On reaching the crest, they instinctively halted, as Lee gazed down at the flight of a mob that he had last seen as Anderson's corps. Teamsters without wagons were hurrying their horses, the traces dangling, and men without guns, some without hats, were following as fast as their weak legs could carry them. At the spectacle, Mahone recalled, "General Lee straightened himself in the saddle . . . looking more the soldier than ever . . ."

As if to himself, Lee cried out, "My God, has the army been dissolved?"

Mahone, as quickly as he could control his voice, answered, "No, General, here are troops ready to do their duty."

Lee then spoke in his more natural, mellowed tones. "Yes, General, there are some true men left. Will you please keep those people back."

Mahone formed his brigades as the pursuing cavalry of "those people" approached. From somewhere Lee had picked up a battle flag, which he held in his hand. At sight of the familiar composed figure, still on his gray horse, the fugitives began to converge toward Lee as their sanctuary. While "the retiring herd" — as Mahone referred to the fugitives — crowded around Lee, he received a five o'clock message from Gordon, fighting about three miles north of the Sayler's Creek mob scene.

In modest understatement, Gordon wrote, "I have been fighting heavily all day. My loss is considerable and I am still closely pressed. I fear that a portion of the train will be lost as my force is quite reduced and insufficient for its protection. So far I have been able to protect them, but without assistance can scarcely hope to do so much longer."

There was no assistance Lee could send, and Gordon probably expected none. As the opposite of Anderson and Ewell, he fought to get those wagons across Sayler's Creek as if the fate of his world depended upon it. An hour after he sent his report of the situation, while half his men were straining to get the wagons across the bogs of Sayler's Creek, the other half were engulfed by the II Corps. Along with the uncounted dead and wounded left on the field, hundreds more were gobbled up as prisoners. Humphreys's estimate of 1700 prisoners taken during the whole day's fighting was — by a comparison of Gordon's effectives on leaving Petersburg with those present after April 6 — demonstrably high.

Lee did not need to be informed of the later disastrous developments to recognize that Gordon, optimistic and understanding of the available forces, was in serious trouble when he wrote that he could not protect the wagons much longer "without assistance." But, such was his justified faith in Gordon's spirit that Lee assumed Gordon would keep his units intact, keep them moving, and save as much of the wagon train as possible. Assuming that Gordon would move westward after dark, Lee extemporized new plans while he talked with Mahone on the hill overlooking Sayler's Creek.

The enemy's pursuing cavalry halted before Mahone's deployed lines, with guns in position. Wright's VI Corps — overwhelmed with the "hard fight" of its triumph over Ewell — did not begin a pursuit until ordered out at seven the next morning. Mahone was to remain in line until after dark. Then he would move his division north to High Bridge, where a railroad bridge and a wagon bridge crossed the Appomattox to the north bank. Getting all guns and wagons across, he was then to wait until, or if, Gordon appeared and crossed over. Colonel Talcott's engineers were to burn both bridges.

Then Lee made preparations for Longstreet. His troops, not seriously engaged by Ord, had rested during the afternoon. He would leave Rice for Farmville during the night. The cavalry would form Longstreet's rear guard. Lee's hope was to issue rations to his men at Farmville and cross there to the north bank of the Appomattox, burning the bridges behind. With a river between him and the enemy, his victualed men could get some rest before moving westward again. Perhaps yet they might reach a point for a southward turn to Danville.

When Mahone moved off, and staff officers were dispatched to organize as far as possible into units the crowd that escaped from Sayler's Creek, Lee lay down on the ground, holding Traveler's bridle. A captain from army ordnance found him there "entirely alone" and looking "worn." After this brief rest, he rode on into Rice about sundown. At Rice there was at least one cheerful soul. Tom Rosser, in driving off the raiding party at Farmville, had captured 780 Federal prisoners and — more important to him — he had acquired the handsome black horse of Brigadier General Read, Ord's chief of staff, who was killed during the action.

At night Lee established headquarters in a field north of Rice. Longstreet's troops moved off, the thin rattle of their tin cups and canteens dying away in the darkness. Behind and to the north Mahone's troops remained in position, their campfires glowing against the sky. After midnight, from the direction of Mahone's camps, a strange visitor appeared at Lee's low burning fire of fence rails. This was Lieutenant John S. Wise, the general's son, who had left V.M.I. ten months before at the age of seventeen to enlist.

On April 2, young Wise had been attached to a small military detail at Clover Station, a telegraph office on the railroad. On April 4, Sheridan tapped the wires at Jetersville and sent messages which the operators recognized to be fake. By then Davis, in the temporary capital at Danville, was cut off from communication with Lee's army. The commanding officer at Clover Station, filling in Wise's name on a blank order signed by Jefferson Davis, gave him the mission of finding Lee and carrying information from the army to the President.

Wise set out on a railroad engine, with the engineer and fireman, and they made it almost into Burkeville at night before the glare of the headlights revealed Yankees all around them. The lieutenant took to the woods. Walking west through the night, early in the morning of the 6th he encountered a cavalry sergeant from the neighborhood who was just leaving for his regiment after a "horse furlough" — a leave to go home to replace a broken-down mount with a fresh horse. Wise, showing the sergeant Davis's order, talked him into surrendering a fresh and beautiful mare. Riding this well-conditioned horse, he picked his way to the edges of the field at Sayler's Creek where his father, bareheaded, had just led his brigade fighting its way out of encirclement. That night troops in Mahone's camps directed Wise to Lee.

As he rode up, Lee was standing beside an ambulance, one hand on the wheel and one foot on a log. He was staring into the fire as he dictated orders to Colonel Marshall, seated in the ambulance with a lantern beside a lap desk.

"General Lee?" the young lieutenant asked.

"Yes," Lee replied quietly.

Wise showed him his orders, bearing Davis's signature, and explained his mission. Lee gave a long sigh. "I hardly think it necessary to prepare written dispatches in reply. They may be captured. The enemy's cavalry is already flanking us to the south and west. You seem capable of bearing a verbal response. You may say to Mr. Davis that, as he knows, my original purpose was to adhere to the line of the Danville Railroad. I have been unable to do so, and I am now endeavoring to hold the Southside Road as I retire in the direction of Lynchburg."

With timid deference, the eighteen-year-old Wise asked, "Have you any objective point, General — any place where you contemplate making a stand?"

"No," Lee answered slowly and sadly. "No. I shall have to be governed by each day's development."

From this admission, Lee's governing plan of turning south to meet Johnston seemed to be fading even as a dim hope. After Wise left (making it through to Danville with the message to Davis), Lee rode on into Farmville and slept two or three hours in a bed in a private house.

5

On the morning of April 7, in the cheerful county trading center of Farmville, it looked as though Lee's men might get the day's rest he had worked toward. St. John was there with more than one hundred thousand rations of bread and meal brought on the Southside Railroad from Lynchburg. The food was distributed to Longstreet's soldiers as they crossed the bridge to the north bank of the Appomattox. Though Field's division, and the token divisions of Wilcox and Heth, showed marked thinning of their ranks from straggling, the units were intact, with all guns and wagons. Fitz Lee's cavalry was spread along the hills east of the town, guarding the enemy's approaches.

Lee was talking with some officers when he was surprised to see one of his young nephews, George Taylor Lee. This son of Lee's brother, Carter, was wearing his V.M.I. cadet uniform. Lee left the group of officers and, holding in his hand a leg of fried chicken on a slice of bread, rode up to the boy. Without any salutation, he said, "My son, why did you come here?"

The cadet said he thought it was his duty.

"You ought not to have come. You can't do any good here."

His nephew said he thought he would be taken prisoner if he went home — in nearby Powhatan County where his father, writing verse, was a local squire.

Lee gave him a kindly look. "No, I don't think they would do that."

Some officers began to approach then, and Lee asked the boy if he had eaten any breakfast. When his nephew shook his head, Lee thrust on him the chicken leg and bread, and told him to go away somewhere and eat it. Lee said he had to talk to some officers.

Lee learned that the troops which had escaped northward from Sayler's Creek, and crossed the Appomattox at High Bridge during the night, were approaching on the other side of the river. With no more breakfast than a cup of tea Lee then rode across to the north bank.

There Lee first met a demoralized Bushrod Johnson. He reported that his division was "cut to pieces and dispersed," with Brigadier General Wise among the dead. Johnson had hardly finished speaking when Lee saw Wise's brigade approaching in good order and in front, on foot, a weird figure who himself said he resembled a Comanche savage. It was Wise, wrapped in a gray blanket, wearing a Tyrolese affair with which he had replaced his own lost hat, and his face red from having washed in a muddy creek. It was one of the few times on the retreat Lee was reported to have smiled. For a moment he forgot the retreat in his amusement at the spectacle of the former governor.

"Good morning, General Wise," Lee said in his old tone of making a pleasantry. "I perceive that you, at any rate, have not given up the contest, as you are in your warpaint this morning."

After Wise joined in the laugh with the staff, Lee ordered him to obtain a horse and take command of the stragglers and disorganized men, forming them on his brigade. Wise did not relish the assignment. "It is not the men who are deserting the ranks, but the officers who are deserting the men who are disorganizing your army." Looking pointedly at the nearby Johnson, he asked, "Do you mean to say, General Lee, that I must take command *of all men of all ranks?*"

Lee, understanding the reference to Bushrod Johnson, turned his head to hide a smile. "Do your duty, sir," he replied.

(The next day Lee officially relieved Johnson of command, along with Anderson and Pickett. In the confusion, the order relieving Pickett was not delivered to him.)

Lee's lightened humor was short-lived. He was shaken by a report that the wagon bridge at the High Bridge crossing of the Appomattox had not been burned behind Mahone's troops. Talcott and his engineers had waited, with the materials for the burning, for Mahone's order. When it failed to come, Colonel W. W. Blackford had ridden four miles along the north bank to find Mahone. Even as aggressive a man as bantam "Billy" Mahone, whose determined defiance of the enemy was unshaken, showed the strain by having neglected to give a rudimentary order. By the time Blackford rode back with the order and Talcott's engineers started the fire, the advance brigade of Humphreys's II Corps rushed down to the bridge and put out the flames. When Lee heard this, Armistead Long said, "He spoke of the blunder with a warmth and impatience which served to show how great a repression he ordinarily exercised over his feelings."

With every detail falling into place for his men to gain a day's rest with the strategic advantage of the river between them and the enemy, one simple oversight destroyed the whole plan. By nine in the morning, the van of the II Corps crossed to the same side of the river with Lee. There would be no rest for his troops. Long spoke no more than the flat truth in saying that Lee "never appeared more grandly heroic" than when for the second successive day he gathered his inner energies to meet another emergency caused by the failures of men on whom he depended. With no repining after his outburst, he reacted by instinct to take the immediate measures to save his army.

He sent orders to Mahone to halt three miles north of the river crossing at Farmville to act as a rear guard in checking Humphreys's pursuit. Alexander was ordered to supply him with guns. Alexander sent off Poague's battalion, while he personally executed Lee's second order — to prepare the burning of the bridges at Farmville. Alexander, brilliant and hard, had lost none of his sharp-edged drive for perfectionism.

Lee waited on the north bank of the river, watching the engineers. They had the railroad bridge and wagon bridge blazing while the cavalry, partly dismounted, was fighting off Crook's division along the low hill just outside of town. When the bridges started burning, Fitz Lee withdrew his troopers around the town in the direction of a ford to the west. At the same time (and he was very reticent about this) he ordered Gary's attached brigade of a few hundred to cover *his* withdrawal by retiring through the long main street that comprised most of Farmville.

Shells from Crook's batteries were bursting over the street when Gary's troopers passed. The soldiers paused to assure the frightened citizens that the town would not be defended, and advised them to stay in their houses. The street ran into the bridge and Gary approached the bridge to see if it might be still passable. Finding it was not, his troopers took off west at a shaky gallop into a grove and on beyond along the railroad tracks. As the van of Crook's cavalry came thundering toward the bridge right behind them, and shells were bursting around the bridge, Lee on the north bank got the impression that his cavalry had been cut off from crossing the bridge.

With the calamity of the failure to burn the High Bridge fresh in his mind, Lee acted in the first excitement he had shown on the retreat. Previously he had not told Longstreet that the Federal II Corps was crossing at High Bridge, because he wanted Longstreet's troops to prepare their breakfast in peace of mind. Suddenly he galloped from the river to Longstreet's freshly built campfires. Saying that part of the cavalry was cut off and lost, with apparent agitation he ordered the troops to fall back into line and hurry out.

Everything was dumped back into the wagons except the food, some of which was uncooked and some still undistributed. The sudden hurry spread panic among the teamsters. As soon as the camp kettles were thrown over the tailboards of the wagons, the drivers lashed the feeble horses and went careening through the woods trying to find a road. Lee rode his gray horse toward the road that led to Cumberland Church, where Mahone had been ordered to stand.

Across from Farmville the line of the Appomattox turned northwest, forming a gap between the river and the road that ran north about three miles to Cumberland Church before cutting west. Longstreet's famished men, tormented by the lingering odors of cooking food which they had not gotten to eat, were forcing themselves into lines of march on the road to Cumberland Church. Poague's artillery, once the pride of A. P. Hill's corps, was already there and Mahone was presumably forming to receive attack from Humphreys's II Corps. Before Lee could start the ride to Cumberland Church, yells and the crackle of carbines warned him of a cavalry attack swooping down on the wagon train from the west. He turned Traveler across country and galloped toward the firing between the road and the river.

Crook's division had followed Fitz Lee across the ford northwest of Farmville. Seeking a repeat of the successful forays on the wagons at Sayler's Creek, Gregg's lead brigade galloped forward in a reckless charge. Gregg found there was still fight left in Lee's troops when, well led, they had a chance to stand. Lee saw Munford's troopers take the charge straight on while Tom Rosser, on the new black horse captured the day before, led his few hundred riders driving into Gregg's flanks. Gregg's brigade was routed, giving up several hundred prisoners, including Brigadier General Gregg himself.

Lee was momentarily cheered by this action. Impulsively he turned to Rooney and said, "Keep your command together, General. Don't let them think of surrender. I will get you out of this."

This unguarded reference to "surrender" revealed that Lee was aware that many of his soldiers, officers and men, were ready to end "the long agony." If he did not know directly of the officers who began to talk openly of giving up after Sayler's Creek, he could sense the attitude.

From the brief buoyance at the cavalry action, Lee again started the ride to Cumberland Church. When Lee reached the westward turn of the road, he found the passage west still open and Mahone's battle lines holding steadily against Humphreys.

As with Gregg, Humphreys had been influenced by his success the day before on Gordon's retiring column, encumbered by the wagon train. By the chance of battle, Mahone's division had not been seriously engaged since before the disastrous actions that began in late March, and his men in intact units were strongly dug in along the crest of a long open slope. Getting support from Poague's sixteen guns, Mahone had taken Humphreys's opening attacks around one o'clock with something of the spirit and fighting skill that formerly characterized the Army of Northern Virginia. When Lee reached the field in the afternoon, Humphreys was settling down to what had become a serious business.

By then Lee saw that one of Field's also intact brigades had come up and deployed in support of Mahone. Gordon, whose battered remnants had crossed High Bridge before Mahone and had been able to find some rest during the day, was also in supporting position. As Lee watched, a Federal flank attack at four-thirty was sharply repulsed "with considerable loss," Humphreys conceded. In fact, the II Corps's attack so lacked the élan of their ripping into Gordon's rear guard on the road the day before that Mahone attempted a counterattack of his own. As dusk came, Humphreys was content to let well enough alone.

From Lee's viewpoint, Humphreys had already done too much. He had held practically all of Lee's infantry in line of battle when, if he had not crossed at High Bridge, the troops, fed and rested, would have been well on their way west. For, on the morning of the 7th, Federal general headquarters had been unsure of Lee's movements, and during the day neither Ord nor Wright's VI Corps crossed the river from Farmville. Thus, the high cost of the failure to burn High Bridge reduced Lee's maneuvers to mere flight. Not only was the II Corps dogging his heels, but through Humphreys Grant was certain of his movements. The Federal cavalry, and other infantry, need only march south of the Appomattox by a shorter route west than Lee was following until the steadily narrowing river ceased to present a water barrier.

Since Grant recognized this as well as Lee, that night General Seth Williams, of Grant's staff, brought a note for Lee to Mahone's lines. It was delivered to Brigadier General Moxley Sorrel, Longstreet's former chief of staff, whom A. P. Hill had given a brigade late in 1864. Sorrel sent the note off by a courier who found Lee in a cottage. Longstreet was seated beside him. Putting on his spectacles, Lee read the note from Grant without change of expression.

"The results of the last week must convince you of the hopelessness of further resistance on the part of the Army of Northern Virginia in this struggle. I feel that it is so, and regard it my duty to shift from myself the responsibility of any effusion of blood, by asking of you the surrender of that part of the C. S. Army known as the Army of Northern Virginia."

Saying nothing, Lee handed the note to Longstreet. After reading it, laconic "Old Pete" summed up the shared attitude in two words: "Not yet."

The army was "not yet" *forced* to surrender. As long as the element of choice remained, the flicker of hope, as in expiring life, would not die. Now that the issue became narrowed to Lee's army, his thinking became more certain and he returned to the familiar ground of the concrete, the possible. For, while the element of choice remained, more favorable terms might be gained by negotiation — for his army. Saying nothing to Longstreet, Lee wrote a reply. In this, for the first time, he delimited peace discussion to the Army of Northern Virginia.

"Genl: I have read your note of this date. Though not entertaining the

opinion you express of the hopelessness of further resistance on the part
of the Army of N. Va. — I reciprocate your desire to avoid useless effusion of blood, and therefore before considering your proposition, ask the
terms you will offer on the condition of its surrender."

6

With little or no sleep on the night of April 7-8, Lee probably rode forward with Longstreet's troops. Shifted to rear guard, the men moved out
of their positions at midnight and started west on the Lynchburg Road
for Appomattox Station on the Southside Railroad. There rations were
expected from Lynchburg. Only the broken remnants of cavalry commands remained behind.

Gordon, whose motley command moved out ahead of Longstreet, then
constituted the van of the army. With the survivors of Anderson's Fourth
Corps, commanded by Wise, then a part of Gordon's Second Corps, there
was no middle between the van and Longstreet as rear guard. Longstreet's corps contained only one of his divisions, Field's, the other three
under his command still considering themselves as belonging to Hill's
Third Corps. The rest of the old First Corps had vanished for all military
purpose. George Pickett and his staff, without an organized command,
rode somewhere among the columns. During that night, while MacGowan's brigade was resting, a group of about 250 men approached them
from the woods. "What regiment are you?" one of MacGowan's officers
called. "Kershaw's *Division*," came the sad reply.

The dark morning hours of April 8 were most vividly remembered by
the men still loosely in line, or at least stumbling along with their units,
as the time when the army visibly disintegrated around them. At intervals
the road was blocked by teams whose horses or mules lay in the mud,
some panting and struggling to rise again, and some with their staring
eyes already glazed. At each block the men were forced to find rough
and sometimes swampy byways. There they passed clearings lit by fires,
where sorrowing artillerists chopped the spokes in the carriage wheels of
guns to be abandoned because their horses had broken down. Along the
roadsides and off the woods lanes, the men struggling to keep up with
their regiments — some no more than a dozen left — passed lines of individual soldiers. Overcome by exhaustion, these emaciated men were lying stretched out flat or sitting with their heads on their knees, waiting to
be gathered up by the enemy.

Most of the marching men carried in their pockets grains of corn from
an issue of two ears of hard corn intended for horses. Some would chew
on a few grains until the resulting toothache became too agonizing. Others at halts would build a quick fire and try to parch the corn. At every

fire ghostly, haggard men without arms appeared out of the shadowed woods looking for food. And every time a march was resumed after a halt, one or more men did not move again. Thousands of unarmed, disorganized men had fallen in on the wagon train. First they joined the trains in the fevered hope of finding food and then, mindlessly, by instinct they kept with their fellows around the wagons that represented a symbol of the army's organization.

These signs of disintegration affected Lee's general officers. The unvanquished soldiers in the ranks were cheered by the morning's bright sun and — as was said by Caldwell, in MacGowan's brigade — "by the soft airs, at once warm and invigorating, which blew to us along the high ridges we traversed." Also the enemy did not resume his attacks on the rear guard as the morning advanced, and the Federal cavalry's nipping at the flanks was insignificant. By noon not a cannon had been heard firing. But the generals, seeing the bleakness of the situation, did not share the troops' relief at the momentary lull in a pleasant spring morning.

A group of them came to talk with Pendleton. Evidently the whole group reached the conclusion that it would be well to represent to Lee their opinion that the cause was hopeless. To spare him the humiliation of surrender, the officers would, in Alexander's words, "allow the odium of making the first proposition to be placed upon them."

The part of Gordon and Longstreet in the decision was unclear. Both of them later denied that Pendleton represented their views. However, neither issued the denial until after Pendleton was dead, and Longstreet was demonstrably untruthful on many points in his recollections. Churchman Pendleton was, though often confused, an honest man. Including Gordon in the conference, he stated that Longstreet, after first indignantly rejecting the proposal, then permitted himself to be represented with the others. Pendleton was not necessarily wholly accurate, nor Gordon and Longstreet entirely wrong. The probability was that neither of the two remaining corps commanders tried to dissuade Pendleton.

Pendleton found his former classmate lying on the ground beside the road, taking a brief rest. Fumblingly he explained to Lee the proposition of the officers, whom he represented. The only certainty about Lee's answer was that he spoke very coldly. Pendleton was still embarrassed when he reported the interview to Alexander. The conflicting accounts of what Lee said were too verbose and high-flown to reflect his way of speaking. The gist was that he had too many brave men left to think of laying down their arms. Alexander's probably correct opinion was that Lee "preferred himself to take the whole responsibility of surrender, as he had always taken that of his battles, whatever the issue, entirely alone."

Lee never referred to the exchange with Pendleton. He resumed the march as if it never happened. Whatever their part in the conference,

Gordon and Longstreet also went on as before. Nor did Lee show any influence from the meeting when he received Grant's reply to his letter at the end of the day. At that time Gordon's dragging van had halted within a mile of Appomattox Court House, in turn two or more miles from Appomattox Station on the railroad. Lee was riding with Longstreet's column when Grant's note was delivered. He turned off the road to read it.

In the considerately worded note, Grant wrote, "Peace being my great desire, there is not but one condition I would insist upon [for the surrender of the Army of Northern Virginia], viz, that the men and officers surrendered should be disqualified for taking up arms again against the Government of the United States until properly exchanged. I will meet you, or will designate officers to meet any officers you may name for the same purpose, at any point agreeable to you . . ."

When Lee read this, he could still hope that it lay in the realm of possibility — though decidedly not probability — for his army to reach Appomattox Station, be victualed, and turn south to Danville before Grant crossed his line of march. As long as this hope was not extinguished, he would not voluntarily surrender. But, as this hope rested upon such recognizably faint possibilities, he was anxious to meet with Grant *before* surrender would no longer be voluntary. With the end at hand, he still clung to the purpose of the past two months of trying to obtain more favorable terms than total surrender.

He immediately wrote his answer to Grant. "I received at a late hour your note of today. In mine of yesterday I did not intend to propose the surrender of the Army of Northern Virginia, but to ask the terms of your proposition. To be frank, I do not think the emergency has arisen to call for the surrender of this army; but as the restoration of peace should be the sole object of all, I desired to know whether your proposals would lead to that end. I cannot, therefore, meet you with a view to surrender the Army of Northern Virginia; but as far as your proposal may affect the C. S. forces under my command, and tend to the restoration of peace, I should be pleased to meet you at 10 A.M. tomorrow, on the old stage road to Richmond, between the picket lines of the two armies."

On sending off this note, it was Lee's understanding that he had established a ten o'clock meeting with Grant the next morning. When night fell and Longstreet's column halted, Lee, Longstreet and their staffs pulled off the road. The rear guard was then not more than five miles from Gordon's van. No headquarters wagons could get up. Like a band of fugitives out of the ancient sagas, the men sat on the ground around a campfire built in an open woods on top of the first ridge north of the Appomattox. A large white oak towered above them, outlined against the moonlit sky.

Around nine o'clock or later, the night silence was broken by the roar of artillery pieces to the front, ahead of Gordon's van. No news came immediately to the startled group in the woods. None was necessary to inform Lee that some force of the enemy had crossed their line of march. He sent off couriers with orders for Fitz Lee, Gordon and Pendleton to come to his campfire headquarters. Later in the night Pendleton, disheveled and shaken, rode up to the campfire on a winded horse.

He had, he told Lee, been with the surplus artillery train under Lindsay Walker, camped off the road between Appomattox Court House and the railroad station. Out of nowhere enemy cavalry suddenly swooped down upon the unsuspecting camp. Walker, who had risen from volunteer in a Richmond militia battery to Hill's chief of artillery, was a gigantic man of cold resolution. More angry than shaken, he got several guns into action, armed two artillery companies with muskets and deployed them against the enemy's sharpshooters. Walker was managing to withdraw some of his batteries when Lee's note reached Pendleton and he left. He was riding along the road to Appomattox Court House when Yankee horsemen came rushing out of the woods shooting at everything in sight. Old Pendleton jumped his horse over a fence into the woods and kept him galloping for the two miles to Lee's campfire. He had, he reported, seen nothing except cavalry. But the horsemen were there in heavy strength.

Gordon came and Fitz Lee to join Lee and Longstreet at the campfire, and those four talked frankly together of what should be done. The atmosphere of the gathering was calm to the point of casualness. All emotion had been drained in the crises approaching the long-dreaded end. Gordon and Fitz Lee stretched themselves out on the ground. Longstreet sat on a log, smoking his pipe. Lee stood.

Their group decision held a classic simplicity: if only cavalry blocked their front and the way could be cleared for the army to move west along the Lynchburg Road, this would be done. If, however, heavy bodies of infantry supported the enemy cavalry, they would, as Fitz Lee put it, "accede to the only alternative left us." The decision would then be out of their hands.

The plans were equally simple. Fitz Lee would start moving all his cavalry to the front, while Gordon prepared his infantry and guns to join in an attack made as early as possible — preferably before daylight. Simultaneously Longstreet would move forward his column and form, facing the rear, to hold off the pursuers. For the attack Fitz Lee would have, including Gary's brigade, something over two thousand troopers, and Gordon would have about two thousand foot soldiers. In the rear guard, with the intact though diminished divisions of Field and Mahone, Longstreet would have about six thousand infantry. That, with sixty-one guns and two thousand artillerists (half of whose guns had been abandoned), comprised the Army of Northern Virginia when the awakened men started to drag along the road at one in the morning of April 9.

7

After sleeping perhaps a couple of hours, at three in the morning Lee began to dress in his finest uniform. Over a red silk sash he buckled on a sword with a beautifully carved hilt. Pendleton, who seems not to have taken any rest, could not conceal his surprise when he saw how Lee had turned himself out. Lee said, "I have probably to be Grant's prisoner and I thought I must make my best appearance."

Without breakfast, he mounted Traveler and rode toward Appomattox Court House. At about sunrise, around five o'clock, as he reached a low hill looking down upon the town, the firing opened to the west. A ground fog obscured the action developing beyond the cluster of red-brick buildings on either side of the stage road to Lynchburg. There were only a few houses — whose owners were burying iron pots filled with their silver — in addition to the court house, the jail, and an attractive country tavern with outbuildings. Other homes were scattered in the surrounding, rolling countryside, as was Sweeney's tavern, owned by the family of Jeb Stuart's former banjo player.

The volume of fire told Lee nothing. Though it would have made no significant difference, the breakthrough to the west came very close to succeeding. With Gordon attacking west along the Lynchburg Road and Fitz Lee to his right, the combined force drove Sheridan's dismounted cavalry from their temporary breastworks, overrunning two guns and gathering prisoners. The road west was open and Gordon shifted his troops to face south to protect the road for the passage of the greatly reduced wagon train.

At this point, before any message came to Lee, Federal infantry came on the field. Three divisions of Ord's two corps — after a march of twenty-four hours with only three hours' sleep — deployed in woods off Gordon's flank and in his rear. Then the V Corps came up across Fitz Lee's front and flank. Sheridan's driven troopers re-formed around their own infantry. Gordon was cut off from Fitz Lee and began fighting from three directions at once. At the deeper volume of fire, rapidly spreading, Lee sent Colonel Venable to discover the situation.

When Venable found Gordon, he was withdrawing his troops toward the town to avoid encirclement. Gordon said forthrightly, "Tell General Lee I have fought my troops to a frazzle, and I fear I can do nothing unless I am heavily supported by Longstreet."

When Venable delivered this message to Lee, Longstreet was formed to meet Humphreys about three miles back, with the II Corps moving up for attack. At last the decision was made for Lee.

"Then there is nothing left me but to go and see General Grant," Lee said, "and I would rather die a thousand deaths."

Lee's words quickly spread to the oddments of soldiers near him and the men, as Venable reported, were "convulsed with passionate grief." Some of them began to talk wildly. One voice was heard to cry, "Oh, General, what will history say if we surrender the army in the field?"

This was the cup that Lee had shrunk from taking. Lee answered the nameless questioner, speaking aloud his thoughts. "Yes, I know they will say hard things of us; they will not understand how we were overwhelmed by numbers. But that is not the question. The question is: is it right to surrender this army? If it is right, then *I* will take *all* the responsibility."

John Esten Cooke felt that at the thought of the actuality, Lee's "courage seemed to give way, and he was nearly unmanned." Lee's own words then showed that he meant literally he would rather die than surrender. "How easily I could get rid of all this and be at rest," he said with his deep voice heavy with sadness. "I have only to ride along the line and all will be over."

After a moment of silence, he sighed and said, "But it is our duty to live. What will become of the women and children of the South if we are not here to protect them?"

It was then perhaps eight-thirty and Lee had an hour and a half to wait for what he supposed was his meeting with Grant. He sent for Longstreet. To maintain his self-control, he talked first to Longstreet and then Mahone, asking them the rhetorical question of their views. Both said that unless he thought the sacrifice of his army would help in other quarters — which he did not — there was no question. Unable to remain silent while waiting, he then talked to Alexander. In his comparative youthfulness, Alexander envisioned a desperate measure as preferable to the ignominy of surrender. He suggested the men disperse and return to their states, reporting to their governors, to carry on the fight as isolated bodies.

Talking to him like a father, Lee explained that they could not consider how the act of surrender would affect them personally. They must consider how the country as a whole would be affected by what amounted to guerrilla warfare. Then Lee said he did not expect harsh terms from the general called "Unconditional Surrender" Grant.

Then the time arrived when he could start for the meeting. Accompanied by Marshall and Taylor and Sergeant Tucker, Hill's former courier, he rode to the rear along the lines of Longstreet's troops. Beyond the picket lines on nearing the meeting place, Sergeant Tucker moved out ahead with a flag of truce. When a line of Federal skirmishers was seen approaching, Marshall rode forward.

Instead of meeting any of Grant's staff, Marshall was given a note by good-looking young Lieutenant Colonel Whittier of Humphreys's staff. To Marshall's question, Whittier answered that he knew nothing about a meeting and was bringing a note for General Lee. Marshall took the note back to Lee.

Lee read that Grant declined to meet him, as he had no authority "to treat on the subject of peace." Grant repeated that the hostilities would end when "the South laid down their arms." It was, then, to be total surrender. Lee controlled any show of disappointment. Since he could only request another meeting — this one on Grant's terms — Lee told Marshall to write a brief note. Lee asked for "an interview in accordance with the offer contained in your letter of yesterday . . ."

Marshall rode with the note to Whittier and, telling him of its contents, asked that fighting be suspended until the message reached Grant.

Lee then sent a note to Longstreet saying that he had neglected to give notice of his meeting with Grant. He asked Longstreet to advise Gordon to seek a suspension of hostilities under a flag of truce.

It was not to be that simple. In the separated Federal forces an order from the distant Grant had set in motion the machinery for an attack.

Longstreet sent forward Captain Sims, formerly of Hill's staff, with the message for Gordon. Sims found Gordon's two thousand infantry scattered east of the court house town. The troops were facing, as Gordon said, "in nearly every direction," in awaiting the advance of more than forty thousand enemy infantry and cavalry. Sheridan's horsemen were poised to charge. Sims tied a new white crash towel to the tip of his sword to serve as flag of truce and galloped toward Sheridan's cavalry.

Behind him Colonel Peyton, of Gordon's staff, could find only a rag to carry as he rode off looking for Ord. Peyton could not find Ord and was led to Sheridan. Sims, looking for Sheridan, encountered bedazzling Custer with his flaxen curls falling to his shoulders. The twenty-five-year-old favorite of Sheridan was bellicose and reluctant to call off his charge. He agreed to wait until he received instructions from Sheridan and sent off a courier.

After the courier returned from Sheridan, Custer rode forward with an aide to Gordon. Flashing a saber salute, he said, "I am General Custer and bear a message to you from General Sheridan. The General desires me to present you with his compliments, and to demand the immediate and unconditional surrender of all troops under your command."

Courteous Gordon replied in a steady voice, "You will please, General, return my compliments to General Sheridan and say to him that I shall not surrender my command."

"He directs me to say, General," Custer said threateningly, "if there is any hesitation about your surrender, that he has you surrounded and can annihilate your command in an hour."

With the same polite firmness, Gordon said, in effect "annihilate away." General Lee had asked for a truce, Gordon went on, and any killing done under the flag of truce was Sheridan's responsibility and not his.

Baffled, Custer then had Major Hunter and Sims — who had identified himself as a staff officer of Longstreet's — take him directly to Longstreet. Coming up at a fast gallop, he shouted excitedly to Longstreet, "In the name of General Sheridan, I demand the unconditional surrender of this army."

"Old Pete" was not as polite as Gordon. All of his own frustrated aggression poured out a bellowing denunciation of Custer's impertinence in being in the enemy's lines without authority, in addressing a superior officer, and in showing disrespect to General Grant as well as to himself. "And," Longstreet finished, "if I was the commander of this army, I would not receive the message of General Sheridan."

A deflated Custer slunk off. About the same time of his interview with Longstreet, a little man (five feet two) on an enormous horse rode up to Gordon. Dismounted, Sheridan was a squat man with powerful shoulders, and he approached with a conqueror's swagger. Brusque in his manner, he exultantly reminded Gordon of having captured guns from the Second Corps in the Valley. Though Sheridan evidently had wanted to receive the surrender himself, he agreed to wait for the result of Lee's coming meeting with Grant on the condition that his own chief of staff could ride through Lee's army to reach General Meade. Sheridan said he felt he needed Meade's authority to recognize an armistice.

The armistice went differently with the infantry across Gordon's front. General Ord, who had actually saved Sheridan's cavalry that morning, immediately suspended operations on hearing of the flag of truce sent for the purpose of discussion of surrender. This was the general who back in February had tried through Longstreet to arrange a meeting between Grant and Lee by which peace might be arranged. On Gordon's flank and partly rear, Brigadier General Joshua Chamberlain, of the V Corps, in simple humanity on his own responsibility halted the assault his brigade was about to deliver.

Behind Longstreet, Humphreys — neither glory hunter, like Sheridan and Custer, nor using the humane initiative of Ord and Chamberlain — continued the inexorable advance of his II Corps as if he had been reduced to an automaton. His pleasant staff officer, Colonel Whittier, rode forward to announce to Marshall that the attack must proceed. Marshall asked him to show Humphreys Lee's letter to Grant. Back came Whittier, asking Lee to withdraw. Lee hurried off another note to Grant asking for "a suspension of hostilities" until the interview. Then a Federal skirmish line advanced, without Whittier. Under a flag of truce an officer warned Lee's party to withdraw or suffer the consequences.

Lee and his party rode back to within the lines of Longstreet's rear guard. There Whittier appeared again, this time saying that General Meade had agreed to a temporary cessation of the fighting. Lee sent off a third letter to Grant, repeating that he was requesting a meeting — and this time he stated it in unequivocal flatness — "to discuss the terms of the surrender of this army . . ."

With the temporary assurance that his men would not be needlessly killed, Lee gave in to his exhaustion. Under an apple tree Alexander had arranged a bed of fence rails covered with a blanket, and on this the "Old Man" (as his officers often referred to him) stretched out. The officers' talk around Lee showed their apprehension of harsher terms — even being sent to the deathtraps of Federal prisons. Lee himself seemed concerned that Grant's original offer might no longer obtain.

Shortly after the noon hour a gentle faced Federal officer with kindly eyes dismounted at the apple tree. Lee arose majestically and bowed when a Confederate staff officer introduced Lieutenant Colonel Babcock, of Grant's staff. Quickly Lee read the note brought by Babcock. He had only that moment, 11:50 A.M., received Lee's note, Grant wrote, and, then four miles west of Walker's Church, he would push forward to meet Lee. Courteous young Babcock then told Lee that he had been given the authority to arrange the meeting under any conditions preferred by him.

In the emotional turmoil of the moment at last at hand, Lee did not think of arranging a meeting place. With his set resolve of making the surrender personally, he thought only of advancing out of his own lines in the propriety of meeting Grant within Federal lines. He turned to Marshall and Taylor, who had been with him all morning. Taylor choked up and asked to be let off on the excuse that he had twice ridden through the lines that morning. Lee gravely nodded his understanding. With only Marshall and Sergeant Tucker, he rode beside Colonel Babcock down the incline toward the creek which was the Appomattox in that region.

Crossing the creek, he abstractedly halted and allowed Traveler to drink. Riding forward again, as he approached the court house town, Lee realized he had arranged no place of meeting. He sent Marshall forward to locate a suitable place in the town.

Marshall sent back Babcock's orderly with the report that they could use the house of a Mr. McLean. When the armies had gathered in Northern Virginia in 1861, McLean owned a farm on Bull Run and he had moved his family to Appomattox in southside Virginia to get away from the war.

Lee approached a substantial, unpretentious red-brick house of two stories and basement, with an inviting verandah across the front. Locust and elm trees shaded the lawn, on which there were some rosebushes. Lee, with Babcock and Marshall, entered a wide central hall that ran the length of the house. To their left was a comfortable family parlor, with a cold fireplace. In the dank silence, Lee seated himself to wait for the ultimate test of the tradition that produced him.

## 8

Outside, Sergeant Tucker removed Traveler's bit so he could nip at the spring grass, while Babcock's orderly waited mounted in the road for Grant. A half-hour later, around one o'clock, Grant came riding along the road with a large staff. Ord and Sheridan — who suspected that the truce was a ruse of Lee's — had gathered with other officers in the town, and exchanged greetings with Grant as he dismounted. Grant was a plain-looking man of five feet eight, with slouched shoulders, and his field boots and simple uniform — the single-breasted jacket unbuttoned over a matching waistcoat — were splattered with mud. In his early forties, his nut-brown hair and beard were untouched by gray. He climbed the porch steps and entered the house alone. In a different way, it was a test for Grant too.

As contrasted with Lee's aristocratic background and distinguished career, Grant came of plain people and his mediocre career before the war had been characterized chiefly by lethargy and a bottle problem. Now the army he commanded had defeated an almost legendary enemy and the country he represented had physically subjugated the proud society of the silver-haired older general who arose, handsome and patrician, to greet him. It would be too much to assume that unreflective Grant was aware of all the emergent historic forces he represented, far beyond the implement of the Army of the Potomac, and of the doomed civilization epitomized by Lee. But had he been profoundly aware of this symbolic crossroads in his country's destiny, and prepared himself carefully to play his part well, he could not have more perfectly met the occasion. It was perhaps in Grant's lifetime the most shining single hour.

With apparent unselfconsciousness and in simple dignity, Grant was motivated solely by the desire to make the ordeal as easy as possible for Lee. He wanted to end the fighting in a spirit of amity. On that April Sunday in the country parlor, Grant probably believed with all his heart that his victory reunited a nation and, by his own words, was deeply moved by the humiliation forced upon his opponent. "My own feelings, which had been quite jubilant on the receipt of his letter, were sad and depressed. I felt like anything rather than rejoicing at the downfall of a foe who had fought so long and valiantly, and suffered so much for a cause . . ."

He was unable to appraise Lee's feelings. "As he was a man of much dignity, with an impassible face, it was impossible to say whether he felt inwardly glad the end had come, or felt sad over the result, and was too manly to show it." Lee, then, had stood up to his own test of concealing his anguish.

After they shook hands, Lee seated himself beside a small table, on which lay his gray hat and buckskin gauntlets. Grant sat at a marble-topped table near the center of the room and spoke in an undertone to Babcock. Babcock left the room and returned followed by eight of Grant's staff officers and several generals, including Ord and Sheridan. Neither Grant nor Lee paid any attention as these officers formed in a group behind Grant and looked at Lee. Colonel Marshall remained motionless behind and to one side of Lee, leaning against the mantelpiece.

While the officers took their places, Grant opened the conversation by saying he had met Lee in Mexico when Lee, as Scott's chief of staff, had visited the brigade to which he belonged. "I have always remembered your appearance and I think I would have recognized you anywhere."

"Yes, I know I met you on that occasion, and I have often thought of it and tried to recollect how you looked. But," Lee went on, with an absence of his customary urbanity, "I have never been able to recall a single feature."

To conceal an embarrassment at introducing the subject of the meeting, Grant began some reminiscences about Mexico. Lee endured it as long as he could. Then he said, "I suppose, General Grant, that the object of our present meeting is fully understood. I asked to see you to ascertain upon what terms you would receive the surrender of my army."

Without change in his tone of voice, Grant answered the terms were those he had proposed in his letter — "that is, the officers and men surrender to be paroled and disqualified from taking up arms until properly exchanged, and all arms, ammunition and supplies to be delivered up as captured property."

Not showing his own relief that the conditions had grown no harsher, Lee said, "Those are the conditions I expected would be proposed."

Until this point, the two generals had talked of the surrender of the Army of Northern Virginia as if on the basis of any force surrendering in the field while a state of war continued between the two countries. Then Grant began to talk of the hope that cessation of hostilities between their two armies would lead to a general peace. It evidently never occurred to Lee that technically he possessed the authority to surrender the other armies, as by Act of Congress he had been designated "General-in-Chief, who shall be ranking officer of the Army, and as such shall have command of the military forces of the Confederate States." Still regarding Davis's "commander in chief" title as reposing all such authority in the President, Lee grew anxious to end the ordeal of surrendering his own army and suggested that Grant submit to writing the terms he had proposed.

Grant at once began to write rapidly in pencil in his order book, putting in simple language the terms of the verbal agreement. Brigadier General Horace Porter, of Grant's staff, recorded that Grant paused after he had finished writing and took a long look at Lee's sword. As Grant explained later, he then thought it would bring a needless humiliation on Lee's officers to give up their swords, baggage and horses. Grant had stopped his writing at: "The arms, artillery and public property to be stacked and turned over to the officer appointed by me to receive them." To this he added, "This will not embrace the side arms of the officers, nor their private horses or baggage. This done, each officer and man shall be allowed to return to their homes not to be disturbed by United States authority as long as they observe their paroles and the laws in force where they reside."

Grant then handed the paper to Lee.

Before Lee read the two pages, Porter observed the signs, though he did not interpret them, of Lee's struggle for self-control. "Lee took it [the paper] and laid it on the table beside him, while he drew from his pocket a pair of steel-rimmed spectacles and wiped the glasses carefully with his handkerchief. Then he crossed his legs, adjusted the spectacles very slowly and deliberately, took up the draft of the letter and proceeded to read it attentively."

After suggesting a slight change, Lee read on until he came to the added sentence about the officers retaining their side arms. "He showed for the first time during the reading of the letter a slight change of countenance, and was evidently touched by this act of generosity." In a warmer voice than his reserved tones until that time, Lee said, "This will have a very happy effect upon my army."

Grant then said he would have a copy of the letter made in ink to be signed.

Lee hesitated a moment, and then obviously forced himself to say, "There is one other thing I would like to mention. The cavalry and artillerists own their own horses in our army. Its organization in this respect differs from that of the United States. I would like to understand whether these men will be permitted to retain their horses."

Porter mentioned the impression made upon the officers by Lee's reference to the United States, "as showing how firmly the conviction was grounded in his mind that we were two distinct countries." It apparently gave Grant a turn too, for he answered flatly, "You will find that the terms as written do not allow this; only the officers are permitted to take their private property."

Lee picked up the paper and began to read over the second page. "No, I see the terms do not allow it," he said. "That is clear." For the second time his façade of composure failed to conceal his feelings, and they could all see from his expression his anxiety to have this concession made.

"Well," said Grant quickly, "the subject is quite new to me. Of course I did not know that any private soldiers owned their animals. But I think this will be the last battle of the war — I sincerely hope so — and that the surrender of this army will be followed soon by that of all the others." He went on about the need of the small farmers in the Confederate armies having their horses to put in a crop to get their families through the winter. Then he arranged terms for the men to keep their animals.

"This will have the best possible effect upon the men," Lee said appreciatively. "It will be very gratifying and will do much toward conciliating our people."

Here again he referred to "our people" as distinct from the United States, and revealed his inner thoughts on the need of conciliating the Southerners for the desolations they had suffered. Then, while the details of finding pen and ink, and writing out the documents, were being handled by Marshall and Colonel Parker, Grant introduced Lee to the officers there as spectators. Lee only bowed or silently shook hands until he reached General Seth Williams, who had been Lee's adjutant when he was superintendent of West Point. Their greeting was cordial. But when Williams, trying to relieve the tension in the atmosphere, referred jokingly to some event shared during their past service together, Lee's grief was too encompassing for him to rise to the social aspects of the occasion. He acknowledged his friend's pleasantry with only a slight inclination of his head.

After the papers were signed, and the surrender was completed, Lee mentioned that he had more than one thousand Federal prisoners whom he wished to return to Grant. They had been forced to share his men's rations of parched corn.

In replying that he should like to have his men returned as soon as possible, Grant said, "I will take steps at once to have your army supplied with rations. . . . Suppose I send over 25,000 rations, do you think that will be a sufficient supply?"

"I think it will be ample," Lee said, and added earnestly, "and it will be a great relief, I assure you."

After a few final details were discussed and disposed of, three hours had passed since Grant joined Lee in the McLean parlor. Lee shook hands with Grant, bowed to the others, and left the room with Marshall. Lee crossed the porch and walked down to the lowest step before Sergeant Tucker saw him. While Tucker bridled Traveler, Grant's party came silently to the porch behind Lee.

They saw him gazing across the valley in the direction where his army lay, absentmindedly striking one hand against the other. He seemed oblivious of the Federal soldiers in the McLean yard, who rose respectfully at his appearance. When Lee swung into the saddle, his dark eyes brushed Grant's group on the porch. Grant impulsively advanced and raised his hat. The other officers followed this courtesy. Lee formally lifted his gray hat and, followed by Marshall, walked his horse out of the yard to the road.

### 9

When Lee topped the hillside east of the town and rode into his picket lines, he seemed unprepared for the growing crowd of soldiers gathered to meet him. While he was with Grant, the news had spread through the army. However, many of the men — their minds numb from exhaustion, hunger and stress — failed to absorb the meaning of the meeting between the commanding generals. As Lee approached, some of the soldiers started to raise their customary cheer. The sight of his stricken face, stripped of the familiar expression of calmness, choked off the voices. The men swarmed around him, shouting questions.

Struggling against his emotions, Lee tried to speak. His voice lacked its deep resonance, and his words were indistinct. Ordnance Captain Colston climbed on the hub of a wagon wheel, where he could look into the General's face and hear him above the murmurings among the men. Colston thought he said, "Men, we have fought the war together and I have done the best I could for you. You will all be paroled and go to your homes until exchanged." Tears filled his eyes as he tried to say more, but could not go on. His lips moved and the words might have formed "Goodbye."

He pushed his horse forward. Men, with tears streaking through the dirt on their ravaged faces, pressed around the horse and rider. They touched Lee's person, his freshly polished spurs, Traveler's neck and flanks. Some began to throw themselves on the ground, sobbing loudly. Others cursed to God. Some just stood or sat on the ground, their eyes glazed and faces slack, unable to comprehend that Lee's army was no more. Sam MacGowan, weeping like a child, began to change from his muddy clothes into a dress uniform.

Lee finally got away from the terrible scene to the apple orchard where

Talcott's engineers had, like an honor guard, formed a cordon. Dismounting, Lee began to pace up and down, the long-held control at last completely broken. The tremendous power of the emotions he had always mastered — at the death of his mother and his daughter and his daughter-in-law Charlotte, of Stonewall Jackson and Jeb Stuart and Powell Hill — now took possession of him. At intervals, one of his staff officers brought forward small groups of Federal officers who wished to be presented to, or merely look at, their famous opponent. Though they were extremely deferential in their approach, each removing his hat, for once Lee held no control over his emotions and he lost his habitual courtesy. He glared at the men he regarded as intruders on his private grief at the death of his world, merely touching the brim of his hat in acknowledging them.

By the end of the day, the tumult of his passion was spent. Though looking weary and depressed, he was in command of himself. In the falling light, he rode toward the headquarters established in the open woods the night before. On this ride, he seemed prepared for the ordeal of passing though the press of the soldiers that lined the road. But he was not prepared for the wild cheers that greeted and followed him past regiment after regiment. Yelling through their sobs and with choked voices, the men sought to express the undying love and loyalty with which they wanted to support their leader. He did not try to speak. He rode with his silver head uncovered, the tears running down his cheeks.

At the clearing, where his wagon and ambulance had come up, his tent was erected and Lee dismounted to enter. There was a sudden rush of men to shake his hand, to cry out their devotion incoherently and — for some — to say they hoped to have the honor of serving under him again. For a while it looked as if he would not be able to enter his tent. Then, above the babble rang one loud, clear voice. "Farewell, General Lee, and I wish for your sake and mine that every damned Yankee on earth was sunk ten miles in hell."

Captain Potts, one of the soldiers present, recorded, "The General could say nothing to this, either in acquiescence or reproof . . . but taking advantage of the change caused by this honest outburst of sentiment, raised his hat in a general salute and retired into his tent."

That night, after quiet came, he emerged to join his staff around the fire. There he told Marshall to prepare an order — a farewell address — to his troops. The next morning, in a dismal rain, Marshall showed him a rough draft. Lee made a few changes, including the deletion of a paragraph which, Marshall recorded, he said, "would tend to keep alive the feeling existing between the North and South." Marshall returned to the ambulance, which served as office, copied the revised order and gave it to a clerk to write in ink. After Lee signed this copy, other copies were made for the corps commanders and the officers of the general staff.

When the order was seen, various officers hastily made copies for themselves and presented them to Lee for his autograph. (This practice continued for years afterwards.) As Marshall retained his own final draft, from which the clerks made copies, of the hundreds signed "R. E. Lee," none can claim to be the original of what became the famous General Order No. 9.

After four years of arduous service, marked by unsurpassed courage and fortitude, the Army of Northern Virginia has been compelled to yield to overwhelming numbers and resources.

I need not tell the brave survivors of so many hard fought battles, who have remained steadfast to the last, that I have consented to the result from no distrust of them.

But feeling that valor and devotion could accomplish nothing that would compensate for the loss that must have attended the continuance of the contest, I determined to avoid the useless sacrifice of those whose past services have endeared them to their countrymen.

By the terms of the agreement officers and men can return to their homes and remain until exchanged. You will take with you the satisfaction that proceeds from the consciousness of duty faithfully performed, and I earnestly pray that a Merciful God will extend to you His blessings and protection.

With an increasing admiration of your constancy and devotion to your country, and a grateful remembrance of your kind and generous considerations for myself, I bid you all an affectionate farewell.

Along with signing the first batch of General Order No. 9, Lee also sent orders to division commanders to file their reports and attended to various details incident to the physical surrender — such as the signing of paroles and the laying down of arms. He appointed Longstreet, Gordon and Pendleton to act with Grant's commissioners on arranging the physical details of the surrender.

Longstreet, a friend of Grant's since West Point, called personally on the Federal general. Grant greeted him warmly, offering a cigar. But Longstreet, supported by the petitions of Gordon and Pendleton, could not move Grant from his insistence upon an actual surrender of the arms of Lee's men to Federal soldiers. He would not permit Lee's men to leave their rifles and accouterments on the ground in their camps.

During the day of April 10 Lee was visited by friends from the Old Army, particularly Meade and the artillerist Hunt. By the time he talked with them, Lee had regained his composure and showed none of the strain of the day before. Though Lee looked "weary and careworn," Hunt said, he found him "the same self-possessed, dignified gentleman that I had always known him." Colonel Theodore Lyman, a staff officer of Meade's, meeting Lee for the first time, received the impression that he was "exceedingly grave and dignified — this, I believe, he always was; but there was evidently added an extreme depression, which gave him an air of a man who kept up his pride to the last, but who was entirely overwhelmed."

Also during the morning of the 10th, Lee rode out between the lines that still divided the armies to meet Grant. The purpose of Grant's friendly meeting was to try to persuade Lee to use his influence — the greatest wielded by any individual in the South, Grant said — in advising the surrender of the other Confederate forces in the field. Lee, while earnestly agreeing with the hope of ending the loss of lives and property, said that he could not take such a course without consulting Davis. Grant reported, "I knew there was no use to urge him to do anything against his ideas of what was right." Porter, repeating what Grant told him, added that Lee said "the authorities would doubtless soon arrive at the same conclusion" — that peace should be sought.

Lee, then cut off from contact with the President, was more removed from communication with Davis the man than he realized. In the temporary capital in Danville, the President declared that the relief "from the necessity of guarding particular points" opened a new phase of the war, in which the army would be free to strike the enemy far from his base. "Animated by that confidence in your spirit and in fortitude which has never yet failed me, I announce to you, my fellow countrymen, that it is my purpose to maintain your cause with my whole heart and soul."

The President was not shaken in this purpose to continue the hopeless struggle when young Lieutenant Wise made his report, based upon his visit with Lee after Sayler's Creek and on the way to Farmville. Wise explained that Lee had been forced to turn west from the railroad to Danville, and his impression was that the army was disintegrating. When Davis asked Wise if he thought the army could reach a place of safety, he answered, "From what I saw and heard, I am satisfied that General Lee must surrender . . ."

Thus, Davis was prepared when on Monday, April 10 — the day Lee talked informally with Grant about a general peace — the news of the surrender reached him. Davis's theoretical mind had never accepted the reality that Lee's army supported the government, nor that Lee symbolized Confederate resistance to the people of both sections. Withdrawn into the private world of his ultimate delusion, Davis — pathetically if psychotically — regarded Lee's surrender as merely one more disaster to the Cause which *he* sustained and would continue to sustain.

Lee himself, in the shock of surrender, seemed to assume a continuance in the government. At least, in his immediate reactions, he acted according to long habit in his relations with the President. On the next day, the 11th, when the reports from his division commanders came in, he began a report of the last days for Davis. Opening "It is with pain I announce to Your Excellency the surrender of the Army of Northern Virginia," and as flatly factual as any he submitted during any campaign, the report nowhere hinted of any effect on the government of the removal of his army from the field.

Judging from the advice he offered ten days later, after the immediate effects of Appomattox were behind him, when Lee wrote Davis the letter (posted April 12) it was not only that he felt the impropriety of advancing his views on peace to the authorities. Colonel Lyman said, he was "entirely overwhelmed" by the scene around him.

10

As Lee reported to Davis, 7892 "organized infantry with arms" were present for duty when he met Grant on April 9. Ten thousand more men, unarmed and unorganized, drifted into the lines during the next day. Yankee beef and hardtack had then been distributed to the famished Confederates. As this news spread, several thousand more trickled in, as individuals and in small groups, during the following two days — the 11th and 12th. Many of these were sick, some helped in by their fellows, and many more were in clinical stages of emaciation.

The Federal and Confederate surrender commission agreed to include in the surrender all troops within twenty miles of Appomattox and, with some specified exceptions, all operating with the army when truce negotiations opened on April 8. One of the exceptions applied to Fitz Lee's cavalry. Fitz Lee had held what he later called "the fond, though forlorn, hope that future operations were still in store for the cavalry," and had escaped with some units to the west when the flags of truce came out. Though he soon recognized the "impracticality" of his adventure, unknown numbers of his troopers came into the Federal lines either at other places or after the paroling of the Confederates was completed on April 12.

Of what had once been Jeb Stuart's 9700 troopers at the cavalry's peak strength, 676 officers and men, including Rooney Lee (who had not joined cousin Fitz), were paroled at Appomattox. In addition to these, Gary's attached brigade from the Richmond defenses numbered 833. Only a few staff officers followed General Gary when he personally rode off to join Johnston. Hundreds of his command — some without horses and some leading bony, sore-backed animals — were among those who drifted into camp after April 9.

When all the infantry had straggled in and had their names listed on regimental parole sheets, their total reached 22,349 officers and men. Richmond's famous First Virginia Regiment, dating back to Washington's day and heroic in Pickett's charge at Gettysburg, numbered seventeen. A. P. Hill's corps, despite the shattering of their lines in the Petersburg breakthrough, had the largest number of infantry present — 7937. Plain, sturdy Wilcox, inheriting the nucleus of Little Powell's original Light Division, paroled 2681, with MacGowan's South Carolinians the largest brigade at 867.

Longstreet's First Corps's total of 6805 was pulled down by the low numbers in the divisions of Pickett and Kershaw. Pickett paroled 1035, nearly all of whom drifted in as unarmed fragments, and Kershaw's survivors numbered only 805, hundreds of whom had straggled before the Sayler's Creek disaster. In Field's division were 617 survivors of the great Texas Brigade (including the 3rd Arkansas), first commanded by Hood and then at the Wilderness by Gregg, who was killed outside Richmond in the fall of '64.

Including artillery and troops listed as "miscellaneous" — such as engineers, the naval brigade, and oddments who had followed from Richmond — Lee's total number paroled by April 12 was 28,231 officers and men. All of these were not present with their units when the somber hour approached on which the men would perform their final duty under Lee — the act of laying down their arms before the enemy.

Neither Lee or Grant planned to attend the ceremony of formal surrender scheduled for the morning of April 12. Grant had already left Appomattox, and Lee was prepared to leave after his men had attended the funeral of their army. Lee, occupying himself in his headquarters tent, could not have borne to watch the men commit the physical act of submission.

Until that morning, Federal officers and soldiers had moved freely through the Confederate camps — some on business errands, some to look up old friends, some out of curiosity. All of Lee's men who commented on these gloomy, rainy days mentioned the "singular propriety" and the courtesy of the Federal visitors. South Carolinian E. M. Boykin said, "The Federal army officers and men bore themselves as brave men should. I do not recollect a single act . . . that could be called discourteous, nor did I hear of one." Except among old friends, however, there was little to no fraternization. Lieutenant J. F. J. Caldwell, of MacGowan's brigade, said, "Affiliation was out of the question: we were content with civility." But not a blue uniform was visible in the camps when the men in tattered uniforms, with set faces, fell in ranks at the call of "Assembly" for the last time as soldiers of the Army of Northern Virginia.

Though the rain of the past two days had let up, the sky was overcast and the air chilly. When the columns of fours were formed on the road, the officers mounted, and frayed red battle flags were lifted. All units did not have their battle flags. Some color-bearers hid their flags, wrapped around their bodies inside their shirts. In other units, like the Second Company of the Richmond Howitzers, the flag was cut up into pieces about four by six inches and distributed among the men.

The lines started over the hill and down into the valley according to their places when the fighting ended. In this way, without plan, the march was led by the five thousand survivors of what had been Jackson's Second Corps, led by John B. Gordon.

The road leading into the town was lined by Federal soldiers under the command of Brigadier General Joshua L. Chamberlain, the officer who had assumed the personal responsibility for withholding his attack on Gordon on April 9. Chamberlain had his own and the other two brigades of Griffin's division of Warren's V Corps. As no Confederate present wrote in detail of the surrender, and few even referred to it, Chamberlain was the chief recording witness of what he called "the passing of the armies."

At the impressive sight of the approaching soldiers, Chamberlain was so moved that he recorded, "I thought it eminently fitting to show some token of our feeling," and he instructed his officers to bring their troops to the position of the marching salute as each body of the Confederates passed. When General Gordon rode opposite him, Chamberlain had the bugle blown to bring the line to "attention," preparatory to executing the marching salute movement successively by regiments.

Before the bugle blew, Chamberlain wrote, "The General [Gordon] was riding in advance of his troops, his chin drooped to his breast, down-hearted and dejected in appearance almost beyond description. At the sound of that machine-like snap of arms, however, General Gordon started, caught on in a moment its significance, and instantly assumed the finest attitude of a soldier. He wheeled his horse facing me, touching him gently with the spur, so that the animal slightly reared, and as he wheeled, horse and rider made one motion, the horse's head swung down with a graceful bow, and General Gordon dropped his swordpoint to his toe in salutation."

Then Gordon sent back orders that his own troops take the same position in the manual of arms as they passed. When the Confederates reached the left of the Federal line, their column halted and swung to face the Federal line on the south side of the road. "Their lines were formed with the greatest care, with every officer in his appointed position . . . bayonets were fixed, arms stacked, and cartridge boxes unslung and hung upon the stacks. Then, slowly and with a reluctance that was appealingly pathetic, the torn and tattered battle flags were either leaned upon the stacks or laid upon the ground." At that, regardless of all discipline, some of the men rushed from the ranks and kissed their flag. This demonstration was the only item in the ceremony that Gordon mentioned. Many of the men were, he wrote, "weeping as they saw the old banners laid upon the stacked guns like trappings on the coffin of their dead hopes."

The Federal soldiers remained motionless and silent throughout the hours during which the other units followed Gordon in stacking their rifles. Chamberlain said, "Their battle-bronzed cheeks were not altogether dry . . . The emotion of the conquered soldier was really sad to witness."

Without their familiar weapons and accouterments, the men climbed back up the slope where only smoldering fires marked their bivouâc. The commands dissolved, some with short speeches from the officers. General Lee's Farewell Address had already been read by commanding officers to their troops.

Though many of the men were still in a state of shock, unable to absorb the reality of what had happened, the general talk on the breaking up of their camps was of the foreboding bleakness of what lay ahead. The planters and farmers particularly were aware of returning to the ashes of the homes they had left and the brush-covered land of what had been fenced fields. On the large-scale plantations there would be no labor and on the small farms no animals.

Some apprehension was expressed about their possible treatment from the United States. Mostly, in numbed acceptance of the fall of their own country, the men's thoughts were directed to the primary consideration of supporting their families in a region which some felt — as Gordon said — would be half a century in recovering from the ravages. And first the individual men would have to recover from the sense of defeat, from the ravages their own bodies had suffered to no purpose, in order to begin a new life under strange, unimaginable and frightening conditions among the debris of the communities in which they had grown up.

At the end of the day the men began to leave the area of Appomattox Court House. They left singly, in pairs and in small groups according to their destinations. For, before the new life was begun, first the men had to get home. They walked off in all directions except north, beginning foot journeys to South Carolina, to Mississippi and Louisiana, to Tennessee and Texas. The most painful journey was along the roads east to Richmond, retracing the steps of the retreat. Among those traveling the road that led through Buckingham Court House was the party of General Lee.

At some unspecified hour, presumably during the afternoon, he rode silently away from the woods in which he had made his last headquarters. Marshall and Taylor rode with him, and Major Giles Cooke, who was ill, rode in an ambulance provided by the U. S. Army. Lee's headquarters wagon and ambulance completed the cavalcade.

The party rode on until nightfall, halting at a clearing in a belt of woods. Just as on the night before, and all the other nights during the past four years, Lee's tent was pitched and covers laid on his cot. But that night, when he lay down, no campfires spread in the still darkness around him. He slept with only the ghosts of what had been an army, and they were never to leave his mind. Though he avoided discussing the war, when all control was gone in the last fevered sleep of his life, he talked to his men: in his last distinct sentence he called for A. P. Hill.

## CHAPTER XXII

## "I Would Recommend . . . the Restoration of Peace"

"APPOMATTOX" came into common usage as signifying the end of the war, though Lee surrendered only one army. To most people, North and South, this army by then had come to represent the only effective Confederate force, and as such its surrender symbolized the end of Confederate armed resistance. Jefferson Davis, however, still represented the Confederate government. When Lee reached Richmond on April 15, Davis, in inhospitable Greensboro, North Carolina, was saying to Beauregard and Joe Johnston, "I believe we can whip the enemy yet, if the people will turn out." Davis said this in a city whose citizens were so eager to be disassociated from the Confederate government that the Cabinet was forced to find quarters in a leaky boxcar on a railroad siding.

Also on the same day that Lee reached Richmond, Lincoln had died in the early morning hours from the gunshot wound inflicted the night before. This loss of strong leadership, accompanied by a factional power grab, threw the purposes of the national government into confusion at the time when Confederate armed forces remained scattered in the field and Davis, as a fugitive, moved southward with his mad dream of independence. The result was that the war never formally came to an end.

Lee, when the fighting ended at Appomattox, was under no illusions about the nature of peace, "reunion," under the best circumstances. However, the details of the return of the Southern states "to their proper relation" to the central government belonged in the realm of politics, and his one wish, his only wish, was to resume life as a private citizen. Prematurely aged and heavy with sorrow, he wanted of all things a personal peace, away from the echoes and the visions of what Mrs. Lee called "those dreadful battlefields." He wanted, as well as needed, to turn his attention to the security of his homeless family — as soon as he could recover physically and emotionally from the last months, and especially the last days.

On the Saturday afternoon when Lee arrived in Richmond, no one in the city knew that Lincoln had been assassinated. Brigadier General M. R.

Patrick, then stationed in Richmond as provost marshal for the Army of the Potomac, recorded that his office did not receive the news until five in the afternoon of the next day. Sunday night the people first heard "strange rumors" of Lincoln's murder. The general news of President Lincoln's death spread through Richmond on Monday, and the people, in their shock, felt a premonition that "restoration" would be harder for them. War clerk Jones, unrelenting Yankee hater, closed his diary with the entry: "It was a dastardly deed surely the act of a madman." From his flight in North Carolina, Davis issued a public statement in which, forthrightly admitting he had no love for Lincoln, he said, "I fear it will be disastrous to our people."

There was nothing of this then unrevealed calamity to affect the people in Richmond when they heard on the bright Saturday afternoon that Lee was coming. Undivided in their sympathy and reverence for him, men, women and children began gathering on the red-brick sidewalks to pay him homage.

His dilapidated little caravan crossed from the south side of the James over the pontoon which had replaced the vehicular bridge burned during the evacuation. Lee, on Traveler, rode past the blackened walls and charred rubble of the ruins where the evacuation fire had gutted the city's downtown section. He passed the site of the original capitol building in Richmond, where his father had argued so persuasively that Virginia would sacrifice none of her sovereignty by ratifying the Constitution of a federated republic. On the desolate street where his father had walked and talked with the giants of the Revolutionary generation, smartly uniformed Federal soldiers moved prominently among the pinch-faced civilians in their frayed clothes who stood silently, with their hats off, to watch their hero pass.

As Lee neared the Capitol Square, across from which he had begun his Confederate career in the offices in Mechanics' Hall, the crowds grew thicker where the fashionable residential area began. Cheering along the way was reported by some, but Thomas De Leon, a detail-minded chronicler of the wartime capital, recorded that "a deep, loving murmur rose from the very heart of the crowd." Lee acknowledged the homage by removing his hat and bowing his gray head.

Lee halted at the red-brick house on East Franklin where his family was staying, on the edge of the section of blackened shells of houses left by the fire. Dismounting, he climbed the steps of the small, columned portico, and his countrymen saw him for the last time in uniform when the white paneled door closed behind him. For a time few were to see him at all. Cutting off all communication with the public, he secluded himself to recuperate while meticulously observing his status as a paroled prisoner of war.

2

Because of his avoidance of public statements, and the weeks during which he conducted little correspondence, nothing is known of Lee's immediate reaction when he learned of Lincoln's assassination. His first and only known comment was in a September letter to Count Joannes of New York City, who had written Lee an offer of his legal services in defense against the charges of treason. In a noncommital statement, Lee wrote only, "In your letter to me you do the people of the South but simple justice in believing that they heartily concur with you in opinion in regard to the assassination of the late President Lincoln. It is a crime previously unknown to this country, and one that must be deprecated by every American."

In being extremely guarded on all statements concerning public affairs, Lee, on April 20, wrote Davis a letter that could have been read by anyone without exposing him to any possible charges of violation of parole. When he wrote this letter, the first to anyone after his return from Appomattox, he knew nothing of the condition or plans of the fugitive Confederate government. All news of Confederate officials and remaining military forces was suppressed by the Federal troops of occupation. The *Whig*, which accommodated itself to the military authorities, was the only paper permitted to be published.

In his letter to Davis, Lee did what he had told Grant, only ten days before, that he could not: at last, he advised the President to seek peace. "As far as I know the condition of affairs, the country east of the Mississippi is morally and physically unable to maintain the contest unaided with any hope of ultimate success. A partisan war may be continued, and hostilities protracted, causing individual suffering and the devastation of the country, but I see no prospect by that means of achieving a separate independence. It is for Your Excellency to decide, should you agree with me in opinion, what is proper to be done. To save useless effusion of blood, I would recommend measures be taken for suspension of hostilities and the restoration of peace."

When Lee wrote this last wartime communication, Davis and his Cabinet were in Charlotte, North Carolina, near the South Carolina border. After Appomattox, while the remnants of the government were taking cold shelter in Greensboro, Joe Johnston and Beauregard had left the fragments of a dissolving army in front of Sherman to confer with Davis about surrender negotiations. In an icy interview, they told Davis that the people were "tired of war," "our country is overrun," the soldiers regarded the war at an end since Lee's surrender and were leaving to go to their homes. The generals believed they should open negotiations with

Sherman, from whom, Johnston said, "We may, perhaps, obtain terms which we ought to accept."

Davis was skeptical about good terms from Sherman but, supported unanimously by the Cabinet, gave Johnston the authority to seek peace terms based upon the surrender of all armed forces. Davis's party then left for Charlotte where, on April 18, they received Johnston's report of surprisingly generous terms offered by Sherman.

For all the plague he had brought on his paths of march during the fighting, Sherman believed with a naive simplicity that with the war over the Union was restored. The terms he offered, as summarized by Judah P. Benjamin, Davis's Secretary of State, agreed that "the United States will receive the separate states back into the Union with their state governments unimpaired, with all their constitutional rights recognized, with protection for the persons and the property of the people and with a general amnesty."

The Cabinet unanimously voted to accept the terms. Forced to accept the inevitable, but anxious that history should know he had never advocated surrender, Davis instructed each of his Cabinet members to put in writing his recommendation for the acceptance of Sherman's terms. By April 24, when all the papers were in, Davis wrote out the agreement that would have ended the war and restored the Union.

Since restoration of the Union was not the purpose of the Radicals in Washington, Sherman was denounced as a traitor and accused of allowing Jefferson Davis to "escape." New President Andrew Johnson, for his own reasons, repudiated Sherman's terms. On April 24, before Davis could mail his signed agreement, Grant ordered Sherman to receive Johnston's surrender on the same terms he had Lee's. Sherman gave Johnston notice that the armed truce would terminate in forty-eight hours.

At this turn, Davis wired Johnston not to surrender on the terms Lee had accepted. Two days later Johnston, ignoring the order, surrendered the oddments of forces that were still called the Army of Tennessee. When this brought the end of armed resistance by the Confederacy's major forces — and, in effect, in the Confederacy east of the Mississippi — Davis then created a fantasy Confederacy of his own. He planned to make his way west of the Mississippi to Kirby Smith's separate domain in Texas, and there "carry on the war forever."

As his dwindling band made its way southward across South Carolina, accompanied by a few worn-out, unreliable mounted regiments of former raiders from Tennessee and Kentucky, other officers followed Johnston's example and acted independently. Naval Captain Parker personally disbanded the company of Naval Academy cadets, guarding the bullion remaining in the Treasury, and sent the boys on their way home. Davis's brother-in-law, Richard Taylor, on May 4 surrendered the Department of

Alabama and Mississippi, consisting of little more than a small infantry force under Maury and Forrest's attenuated survivors.

On the same day at Washington, Georgia, just south of the Savannah River, Breckinridge told the President that the broken-down cavalry regiments refused to reconnoiter the front where Federal troops were reported, and advised that the men be allowed to go to their homes and receive parole. By then Benjamin and other Cabinet members had dropped off — the portly, urbane Benjamin beginning an adventurous escape to England by way of Cuba. Soon Breckinridge followed Benjamin's course to Cuba.

From Washington, Georgia, Davis continued an aimless way southward with only Postmaster General John Reagan remaining of the Cabinet, and a handful of faithful followers. Along the way he joined the wagon party in which Mrs. Davis was riding. On the night of May 9-10, in a camp in the pine woods near Irwinsville, Georgia, sixty-five miles from Florida, he was run down by a Federal cavalry force and the Confederate government was brought to this undignified end. The news reached the subjugated citizens of Richmond through the shock of hearing newsboys call, "Extra! Jeff Davis captured!"

If Lee heard the news the same way, he made no public statement nor recorded his feelings in private correspondence. From later letters, it was known that he suffered when Davis was clapped into prison at Fort Monroe and suppressed his outrage at the treatment of the former Confederate President.

While Lee remained silent about Davis to avoid any expression that might be used controversially, he did seem to accept the practical end of the Confederacy with the disbanding of his own army, and appeared detached from its dying gasps. He made no recorded comment when, on May 26, Kirby Smith surrendered the last Confederate force in the field, the Trans-Mississippi. When this brought the land fighting to the end, Jo Shelby's cavalry refused to surrender and began the first mass emigration of Confederates out of the country. Joined by the still resplendent "Prince John" Magruder, Shelby rode across Texas into Mexico, and in Mexico City offered the services of his men to Emperor Maximilian.

Before any of the other armies surrendered, as early as April 21 Lee showed he was thinking of what lay ahead. General Patrick, the provost marshal, went to visit him and they talked more than an hour. "It has made me very sad, as I expected," warm-hearted Patrick recorded in his diary. "We had a very full and free interchange of opinions and views, after the restraint of our first conversation had passed away, and he seemed to me as much gratified at seeing me as any one I have met with. He is feeling sadly at the prospect before us . . . On the whole, I almost feel that our troubles are to come."

Though Lee's carefulness in all statements was a part of his meticulous observation of his parole, where he could express his personal views he made it evident that his mind had already turned to the future of the South. During the same period of his talk with Patrick, Lee had a surprise meeting with Channing Smith, a scout still active in the field with Mosby's Rangers. Lee sometimes took a stroll after dark, when he would not be recognized on the street, and one night, on dropping in at Colonel Chilton's shuttered house, he found the young scout a guest. Smith asked Lee if the Rangers should surrender.

To that Lee answered his parole made it impossible for him to give such advice. When Smith asked what he personally should do, Lee answered quickly and emphatically: "Go home, all you boys who fought with me, and help build up the shattered fortunes of our old state."

This was the advice Lee prepared himself to follow, before Davis was captured and long before Davis's last illusion died in the Trans-Mississippi. In his convalescence in the temporary sanctuary of the Franklin Street house, Lee was in no condition to make any plans for the future. First he needed, as Rob said, "the time and quiet to get back his strength of mind and heart." But, as when he commanded an army, Lee still retained his capacity of waiting for developments — immediately, in the clarification of his status as a paroled prisoner of war and the opening of roads of return to life as a private citizen.

# The Birth of the Symbol

## CHAPTER XXIII

## "I Have a Self-Imposed Task"

LEE'S official status as prisoner of war continued for nearly four years, until the general amnesty of Christmas, 1868, and the Southern people never permitted him to return to private life. Out of their needs, the people of the late Confederacy created a symbol of Lee. Like an exiled king, he served as the custodian of an ideal. With this unsought burden, he was forced to live the last five years remaining to him as a public example.

As this example, Lee reached the ultimate achievement of his life and waged his most taxing struggle — both against external elements and for self-control. The doctors in attendance at his terminal illness listed the cumulative strain of the postwar period, along with Lee's efforts at calmness, as "the real causes that slowly but steadily undermined his health and led to his death."

Yet, the most selfless struggle of Lee's life and his greatest contribution to the heritage of his country are the achievements by which he is least remembered. Historically, after Appomattox he seemed to vanish into some Valhalla as "the Rebel general." By no choice of his, in his lifetime he was cast forever as "General Lee." But the leadership of General Lee in his last years was in a fight for peace — for a union restored in the harmony and the mutuality of welfare of the republic into which he had been born.

For Lee and the South only the physical part of the war ended with the fighting. Then began the political subjugation and the financial exploitation of a people defeated by force of arms. This political-economic extension of the war, including occcupation of the conquered territory, lasted long beyond Lee's lifetime.

The physical defeat of the Southern states resolved the issue between those forces which during Lee's adult life had gradually emerged from subsurface conflict into a battle to the death of one of them. Lee was no less perceptive than most leaders, North and South, in not recognizing that the triumph of the northeastern industrial-financial combine meant a domination of the central government in a new kind of union. With the "checks and balances" intent of the Constitution supplanted by manipulation, the government of the new nation subordinated the common welfare to the advantages of special interests.

The Radical bloc of Republicans who seized control in Washington did not work consciously to serve the purpose of the monolithic interest that was to determine the character of the new union and shape its future. However, the Radicals, with their own program for establishing their party permanently in power, did share a commonality of sectional purpose in disposing of a region which had previously existed as a rival. While the rival was down, both the political and financial powers determined to fix him so he could never rise again. As early as April 24, H. Woodman of Boston wrote Stanton, "We have them now under a control which we must not lose, even if we hold them as military dependencies." The frenetic action of the Radicals indicated a fear of the South's resilience in alliance with the National Democratic Party.

Lee, typical of the moderate Southerner, was unprepared for a program aimed at the "reconstruction" of the whole region with the intent, as Benjamin Harrison had prophesied, of reducing the South to "an appendage" of the North. Though he had not expected a political restoration of the Union to be either simple or quick, he did expect Lincoln's nationalistic purpose to prevail. Even after the Radicals came into complete control of the national government, their manipulations of the Southern society so obviously exploited the fomentation of sectional prejudice that Lee viewed the measures against national unification as an unexpectedly harsh aftermath of war.

He thought that the armed victory had placed the government in the hands of evil men, supported by fanatics in the North, and he believed their reign represented a period which the Southerners must "endure" with "patience." It seems doubtful if he ever comprehended the reality that these Radicals, whose agents he observed working for immediate ends under the avowed goal of "human rights," were in fact imposing a "social engineering" that would lead to a new national structure alien to all his understanding of the republic.

To the extent that Lee hoped for a restoration to reestablish "the virtues" of the early republic, he was guided by a sentimental view of the past. It was understandable that he felt a personal reverence for the early republic in whose founding his father, kinspeople and father-in-law's foster father, George Washington, had been leaders. He accepted implicitly their eighteenth-century sentiment of rationality in which individual liberty would forever be secured through democratic processes by men guided by reason in acting for the general welfare.

With these convictions, Lee saw in retrospect the "golden age" as more golden than it had been in actuality. Perhaps because of his father's failure to achieve the ideal of "the good as well as the great" — with the consequent dislocation of Lee's immediate family — Lee overestimated the prevalence of the ideal that combined accomplishment with moral excellence to the suppression of self-centered interests. Whatever the idealization of the times of his childhood, Lee acted in total conviction that the quality of the early republic — where factionalism was subordinated to the common good — was the essential element in the re-forming of the nation.

In this ideal he was no more naive than was Lincoln in believing the existing Union could be restored by spreading death and ruin, misery and hatred, to which was added the moral divisiveness of stigmatizing Rebels with the odium of fighting to perpetuate human slavery. But, in physically unifying the entities of states, Lincoln acted in the nationalistic trend of the future. Lee's vision belonged to an old America of localities, of place attachment and community identification, of the dream of the individual's responsibility to himself under God.

It was not that Lee looked back to the physical past. He was the first to recognize that all represented by the plantation idyll was dead and to advocate that the Southern people turn their eyes to a newly conceived future. In the general neglect given his postwar life, little attention has been called to Lee's vanguard position in envisioning and working toward a New South. The vision was neither farseeing nor detailed but, characteristic of Lee, it was practical and directed at the immediate objective of rebuilding the devastated communities and restoring the ruined economy by the introduction of modern technological methods.

Most of all, he wished planters and farmers to break with the aspects of Negro labor where the workers existed in a dependent relationship extended from slavery. Lee stated that, though he deplored the way emancipation had come (and though he was baffled by the sociological problem erected between the races), he was relieved that slavery was gone. Going to the fundamental aspect of Negro labor, its effect on the sociey, Lee believed it was vital for the white man to do his own work. The small farmer and the artisan, who did not regard the downfall of planters with sorrow, had their own reasons for sharing Lee's view, and expressed it in their own way: "Now's the time when every tub has got to stand on its own bottom."

Lee practiced his advocation of rebuilding the South in a new direction in the most tangible way of all, through education. He wrote Rooney, "I accepted the presidency of the [Washington] College in the hopes that I might be of some service to the country and the rising generation, and not from any preference of my own. I should have selected a more quiet life and a more retired abode . . ." To Mr. A. M. Keiley, in battered Petersburg, he wrote, ". . . with a determination not to be turned aside by thoughts of the past and fears of the future, our country [here meaning the South] will not only be restored in material prosperity, but will be advanced in science, in virtue and in religion."

Lee's work in education, the tangible achievement of his postwar life, represented the practical aspects of his public example. As president of the small, bankrupt, provincial institution in the Shenandoah Valley, he introduced very advanced courses in technical studies, while inculcating the minds of youth with the forward-looking duty of assuming the obligations of citizenship in a republic restored on the virtues of the past. Committed to the belief that technological advances should come within a moral framework — the eighteenth-century "whole man" — Lee stressed the spiritual element as of paramount importance in turning to a future free of hostilities and resentments.

In transforming the little down-at-heels Valley college into a prosperous, progressive, expanding national institution, Lee prepared a college generation whose members fulfilled their community obligations in such capacities as judges, doctors, engineers, educators, ministers (including a bishop and the rector of St. Thomas's in New York City) and substantial men of business. David J. Wilson, of Maryland, wrote of his student life at Washington College: "I doubt if there ever lived a president of an institution of learning in our republic who during a space of time so short . . . used his influence in a greater degree, and with greater success, in the making of good citizens than did General Robert E. Lee." Dr. Chalmers Deadrick, of Tennessee, another student, wrote, "I doubt whether, in the world's history, a college president ever exercised as powerful an influence for good over his students and faculty as did General Lee."

Lee's constructive efforts in advancing toward his vision of a New South were largely obscured by the convulsive upheaval during the period called "Reconstruction." During "the Age of Hate," as it has been termed, Lee, by rising above all hostilities, was out of key with the times. His own spiritual force was historically overshadowed by the bitter clashes that formed the pattern of events. Yet, as an example, his outward serenity and steadfastly held policy of "conciliation" achieved effects no less significant because intangible.

2

As before the war Lee existed in a position between the battle lines of extremists on both sides. The Northern Radicals, justifying coercion by skillful propaganda about the South's "disloyalty" and resistance to the advancement of human rights, trampled over Southern institutions and community life to change the society immediately and totally. To the defeated people the changes seemed manifestly to the detriment if not the permanent ruin of the parts of their world that had survived the war. Along with a generalized sense of resistance to the cataclysmic changes, there were Southern extremists determined to change nothing. A combination of prewar Unionists turned hostile by the desolating invasion and some prewar secessionists — unchanged except for a new bitterness — would have remained irreconcilable separatists even if Lincoln had lived and been able to implement his sentiment of "charity to all and malice to none." Hating as vehemently as any Radical, they were bent on going their own way, in or out of the Union.

In the first sessions of state legislatures after Appomattox, such extremists in the legislatures of South Carolina and Mississippi passed vagrancy laws as measures of control of the freed Negroes. The laws were essentially concerned with preventing the gathering of large armed mobs and with getting the colored labor population back to work. Plantations desperately needed crops to be made and communities needed the subsistence. As vagrancy laws went, they were no harsher than those in force in New England. But as the laws were definitely aimed at the Negro and contained some stringent, gratuitous controls of the freedmen, in the current climate they were thoughtless or defiant, or both.

The Radical press, calling the laws "Black Codes," offered them as evidence of *The* South's intent to continue de facto slavery. Then, when Virginia and other states passed milder and reasonable laws of control, they were lumped together as more "Black Codes," and no state was allowed to enforce its vagrancy laws. By such examples, action and counteraction between the extremists began to spread combustible interaction.

At that time, the majority of Southerners were willing to accept, with whatever personal feelings, the arbitrament of arms. Grant, among objective Northern observers, stated his belief that the people were ready to return to the Union in "good faith." In the more ravaged regions, such as Sherman's swath through Georgia and South Carolina, doubtless some time would have to pass before kindly feelings developed toward the conquerors, but these were personal rather than political matters.

It was when the ravages of war were extended by the Radicals into the oppression of occupation rule that incalculable numbers from the majority drifted toward the irreconcilables — at least in sentiment. However small and scattered the blocs of irreconcilables might have remained had charity been extended to the people in national efforts toward restoration, the Radicals' invasion into private lives and individual liberties caused the spirit of resistance to expand around them.

It was not that the body of extremists was large, or that their leaders controlled all Southern states, but where they held influence, they were conspicuous by aggressiveness and frequently acted with the rashness of men either beyond reason or who have nothing more to lose. Though every reckless political action and every violent physical action fed the mills of Radical propaganda, solidifying their power to increase coercion, the extremists and their followers were driven by passion to a defiance that defied consequences.

Lee nowhere explicitly stated that the purpose of his example was to prevent the interaction of defiance and coercion from breaking out into anarchy and/or guerrilla warfare. However, his spoken and written advice urged Southerners to work for "the allayment of passion, the dissipation of prejudice . . . burying contention with the war." Not thinking in terms of retaliation, they should avoid controversies in which their arguments could be used against them. This, of course, was practical as well as Christian. On the principle of "least said, soonest mended," he wanted to avoid providing the Radicals with excuses.

In this inflammable area of interaction his influence could not be measured, not even approximated. Other prominent men spoke strongly for moderation — notably Wade Hampton in South Carolina, L. Q. C. Lamar in Mississippi, and Lee's former brigadier Francis T. Nicholls in Louisiana — and for years their voices seemed unheard. Yet, it is true that the states which had formed the Confederacy did not as a region follow the Southern extremists again. The prewar course was not repeated in insurrection, though toughened veterans, with everything gone, needed only the word to open guerrilla warfare.

In Lee's own state, the moderates held control and, though Virginia was the last state to be freed of the troops of occupation, it was the first state to return to the Union under its own representative government. Some states existed in a constant turmoil, and were held twelve years under bayonet rule, but in none was there anarchy. Nor was there ever any regional movement toward it. Regionally, the people as a whole acted according to Lee's appeals for "patience" and "fortitude" to "endure," and refused to be incited by the provocative humiliations of oppression.

After formal Reconstruction was over, a minority report of a United States committee investigating conditions in the South stated, "When the corruption, distortion and villainy of the governments which Congress has set up and maintained over the Southern states are thoroughly understood and made known, as we trust they will be some day, the world will be amazed at the long suffering and endurance of that people."

To whatever extent the people were influenced by Lee, this *was* the example he gave as a symbol. Yet, whatever the Southern people might have done — and segments of the irreconcilables repudiated his advice and excoriated him — Lee was guided by the perspectives of an eternal view that would have sustained his personal forbearance in enduring the acts and words of his contemporaries.

Refusing to identify principles with personalities, he never attributed to any governing body or region the character of its most uncharitable representatives. In years when ministers of God, high officials, reproachless idealists and crusading journalists daily denounced him and his fellow Southerners, urging that he be punished for "the sins of the South," Lee never passed judgment on a single person, living or dead.

With his own name defamed, his motives impugned, and living with a treason indictment over his head, he wrote Colonel Marshall: "My experience of men has neither disposed me to think worse of them nor indisposed me to serve them; nor, in spite of failures which I lament, of errors which I now see and acknowledge, or of the present aspect of affairs, do I despair of the future. The truth is this: The march of Providence is so slow and our desires so impatient; the work of progress is so immense and our means of aiding it so feeble; the life of humanity is so long, that of the individual so brief, that we often see only the ebb of the advancing wave and are thus discouraged. It is history that teaches us to hope."

### 3

The whole period loosely lumped as "Reconstruction" was actually four phases. The first lasted from the end of the fighting to December, 1865, when Congress convened. This period was characterized by President Andrew Johnson's honest if inept efforts to return the Southern states to the Union. The second phase, of fifteen months, was the period of the Radicals' seizure of power, with their preliminary plans and steps toward reducing the militarily occupied states to the vassalage status of "conquered provinces." The third phase, beginning in March, 1867, was the formal period of the enforcement of the Reconstruction Acts, during which ten Southern states, without representative state governments, were ruled as military districts. This lasted until 1870, the year of Lee's death. (Since, under these circumstances, Lee never attempted to exercise the rights of franchise after he was "pardoned" in the General Amnesty of Christmas, 1868, he died as a non-citizen.)

The fourth period, which lasted until 1877, was actually post-Reconstruction. When the Southern states had been readmitted to the Union in 1870, most were under synthetic Republican governments, formed of nonrepresentative state citizens during Reconstruction, and in several states Federal troops were frequently called in to support these synthetic governments in office.

Over the total period, embracing the four phases, the courses of action and attitude of the people were distinctly different in the separate Southern states. The Radical propaganda (establishing a future style) grouped the diverse states into the single entity of "The South," when actually the only unity was that which grew in reaction to the Radicals themselves. This was the unity of identity as ex-Confederates.

When the Confederates' own national government was dissolved and the conquered people were rejected by the government which presumably fought to reclaim them, Southerners were dispossessed of any nationalistic identity. During the war years the Confederate people had been hopelessly disunited, with large segmentts longing only for the end of invasion and the blessings of a restored Union. Among these, individuals repudiated the Confederacy and everything it stood for. Then, when all Southerners were dispossessed of any national identity, the defeated people came to view the Confederacy less as a fallen government than as a nation of the heart.

Most of those who had lost heart during the war defaulted in the belief that life back in the United States was preferable to continued suffering and loss of all economic security. They felt betrayed. Seeing all that had been swept away with the Confederacy, all the life as they and their ancestors had known it, the betrayed embraced the heritage represented by the vision of the Confederacy as they never embraced the actual nation.

Since none of the people ever conceded that the principles of the rights of secession had been invalidated by the force of might, the sense of injustice under oppression caused the ideal of independence to supersede all other elements involved in the seemingly endless struggle. The vision of the Confederacy rose as a purified ideal from the debris in which the people survived under enemy soldiers. As this ideal, the nation of the heart emerged as a "Cause" — a dream for which men and women had laid down their lives and for which they suffered into the unforeseeable future. Thus, the Lost Cause identified a nation of the mind, the only nationalism open to the people.

As the Lost Cause had no boundaries, no government, no leaders, it created a symbol to validate the justice of the Cause and exemplify the ideal. It was during the postwar years that the use the Radicals made of the victory transformed Lee from a beloved leader in a losing cause into the personification of *the* Lost Cause. Perhaps the historical foreshortening of Lee's career resulted partly from this identification with the Lost Cause in the meaning of the four years of the actual Confederacy. But Lee became a people's god in the meaning of the Lost Cause as an invisible nation that grew after the war.

Nothing in Lee's attitude changed during the changing conditions that created his symbolic status. Judging from what he did not say as Reconstruction continued, Lee evidently lost his conviction about the restoration of the Union on its original principles. Fundamentally, however, his view of the war and its results seemed completely formed during his recuperation in Richmond.

Definitely, he never said that he regarded the Confederate defeat as good. As with his fellow Southerners, he believed in the principles for which they had fought, even while he realistically accepted the arbitrament of arms. In the faith in Providence with which he made his acceptance to circumstances beyond his control, he brought the courage and wisdom to do (as always) the best he could with the conditions God gave him.

Lee clearly defined his attitude of acceptance in a letter written to wartime Governor Letcher in the summer after Appomattox. "The questions which for years were in dispute between the State and General Governments, and which unhappily were not decided by the dictates of reason, but referred to the decision of war, having been decided against us, it is the part of wisdom to acquiesce in the result, and of candor to recognize the fact. The interests of the State are therefore the same as those of the United States."

Lee's views of the principles were most fully developed in a letter written in late 1866 to Sir John Dalberg-Acton, later Lord Acton. Acton, acting as adviser for the editors of a projected English review, had written to request Lee to inform him "of the light in which you would wish the current politics of America to be understood." Acton wrote, "I saw in States' Rights the only availing check upon the absolutism of the sovereign will . . . The institutions of your Republic have not exercised on the old world the salutary and liberating influence which ought to have belonged to them, by reason of those excesses and abuses of principles which the Confederate Constitution was expressly and wisely calculated to remedy." Its example "would have blessed all the races of mankind by establishing the freedom purged of the native dangers and disorders of Republics."

Lee wrote Acton: "I have considered the preservation of the constitutional power of the General Government to be the foundation of our peace and safety at home and abroad." But he strongly believed that the mutuality of interests was based upon "the rights and authority reserved in the states," which constituted "the safeguard to the continuance of a free government. I consider . . . the consolidation of the states into one vast republic, sure to be aggressive abroad and despotic at home, to be the precursor of that ruin which has overwhelmed all those that have preceded it."

This was the ideal of Jefferson (who lived until Lee was a nineteen-year-old cadet at West Point) for a free society built upon a hierarchy of self-governing units, "forming a gradation of authorities." In the Constitution as the written pact for the union of states, nothing implied that any state or group of states was required to remain in the federated republic when their interests were no longer served. Certainly neither Virginia, Massachusetts nor New York would have ratified a Constitution which held the implication that, when the community of interests was lost, a majority of the states could impose their will physically upon a minority.

As late as 1848, this understanding was reaffirmed in the U.S. Congress. "Any people anywhere, so inclined and having the power, have the right to rise up and shake off the existing government and form a new one that suits them better. This is a most valuable and sacred right — a right which, we hope and believe, is to liberate the world." The congressman who made this statement was Abraham Lincoln.

When physical and political division came to an issue, over conflict of interests, the key to the decision lay in Lincoln's words — "any people anywhere, so inclined and *having the power . . .*" As Lee saw it, the South's lack of the power had made secession impractical rather than unconstitutional. But, since he had not approved of secession as a solution, it was important for him to point out to Acton Virginia's aversion to settlement by either secession or coercion. "Virginia to the last made great efforts to save the union, and urged harmony and compromise." He mentioned that Senator Douglas had stated in 1861 that "the only difficulty in the way of an amicable adjustment was with the Republican party."

In defining what he thought should be the result of the war, Lee was writing when the Southern states were excluded from representation in the national government. "If the result of the war is to be considered as having decided that the union of the states is inviolable and perpetual under the constitution, it naturally follows that it is as incompetent for the general government to impair its integrity by the exclusion of a state, as for a state to do so by secession; and that the existence and rights of a state by the constitution are as indestructible as the union itself."

When Lee wrote Acton, the U.S. Congress had passed the Thirteenth Amendment, making slavery illegal in the nation. Of this Lee wrote, "This is an event that has long been sought, though in a different way, and by none has it been more earnestly desired than by citizens of Virginia. In other respects, I trust the constitution may undergo no change, but be handed down to succeeding generations in the form we received it from our forefathers."

Lee made his personal feeling for the Constitution stronger in another letter written in 1866. "All that the South has ever desired was that the Union, as established by our forefathers, should be preserved; and that the government, as originally organized, should be administered in purity and truth." As for himself, "I was for the Constitution and the Union established by our forefathers. No one now is more in favor of that Constitution and that Union."

All this was in personal correspondence, which privately articulated his attitude. Since he wrote nothing for the public nor made any speeches, his attitude was reflected in the example of his life rather than by exhortations. But there was an emotional element in Lee's attitude which he suppressed in his carefully written answers to queries on his position, and which he tried to hide in his public appearances. This was revealed in an unguarded letter to his wife's cousin, Markie Williams, which he wrote in the Franklin Street house during the first days after Appomattox.

"We must be resigned to necessity, and submit ourselves in adversity to the will of a merciful God as cheerfully as in prosperity." In this one line he revealed the weight of defeat.

4

Aside from what his family and intimates saw during Lee's recuperative period, nothing in the man as symbol hinted at any sense of defeat — not from the very beginning of the first postwar phase under Lincoln's successor. Lee was uncertain about Andrew Johnson's intentions, but the maladroit fumblings of that unfortunate man bewildered all the Southern people.

Johnson's phase lasted about eight months, during which time, with Congress not in session, he tried to put into effect his policy — "My Policy," his detractors derisively called it. Lincoln had not left any machinery for the technical problems of readmitting the Southern states to the Union. With his confidence in improvising, Lincoln had worked pragmatically on the admission of several states separately through Federally created nonrepresentative state governments, but this was not a completed plan. When Johnson adopted Lincoln's general policy of reconciliation, he inherited a vast complex of problems with every conceivable disadvantage.

While Lincoln did not then loom as the mythical character of his apotheosis, he had the prestige of the President who "won the war," he controlled the party machinery and he was extraordinarily effective in handling people. Johnson, a Democrat in a Republican administration and a Southerner in an antisectional party, possessed none of Lincoln's skill in political maneuver and lacked any "crowd appeal." Indecisive and noncommittal, in debate the ex-tailor grew personal and allowed himself to be provoked into making intemperate and even foolish statements. With all else, he was distrusted by both Southerners and Radicals.

Before he succeeded to the presidency Johnson, as military governor of Tennessee and briefly as Vice President, had taken an extremely harsh position toward the South and advocated "punishment" for "treason." Since the Radicals had bitterly opposed Lincoln's sentiment of reconciliation, they looked upon his death as a Godsend and welcomed Johnson in the White House. When Johnson, sobered by the responsibilities of the President's office, reversed his position, the Radicals turned on him as an enemy — and not as an enemy they respected.

By the other side, Johnson was seen as a renegade who had gone against his own state of Tennessee and urged vindictive measures against the Confederates. Also, his humble beginnings had implanted in him an abiding hatred of the planter class, and he was the sort of self-made man who felt compelled to advertise his animosity. With this known background, he offered the Southerners no verbal reassurances of their reception back in a reunited republic. Though committed in his own mind to restoration and unwaveringly opposed to the Radicals' "conquered province" program, Johnson failed to articulate his policy with the warmth or clarity that would give Southerners understanding of his slow, groping, and occasionally inexplicable acts.

Anxious to begin his policy by first banishing the idea of secession, with very bad timing Johnson tried to create immediately a "loyal" population. He demanded oaths of allegiance from the numbed veterans, walking their barefooted miles to sites where homes had stood, and insisted that states at once ratify the Thirteenth Amendment, abolishing slavery. At this stage the Southern people were like weary, worn, hungry wayfarers who had returned from an unsuccessful quest to find their estates lost during their absence, but were grateful for shelter. With their minds on rest and bread, the people did not take kindly to signing papers Federal soldiers shoved at them on orders from a renegade Southerner in Washington. Before the echoes of the fighting had died, while Federal raiders were using the last opportunities to run off farm families' horses and to burn cotton bales that represented families' only tangible property, the germ of generalized resistance appeared in an atmosphere of uncertainty and apprehension.

From his provost marshal post in Richmond, Brigadier General Patrick wrote in the middle of May: "We are all in a muddle here, and Gen. George H. Sharp tells me we are in the muddle there — at Washington . . . He says that [General Benjamin F.] Butler is at work, taking advantage of the excitement in regard to the assassination of Lincoln."

While Johnson's cumbersome efforts to create a "loyal population" failed to give reassurance, the attitude of the Radicals in the background deepened the sense of apprehension. Senator Benjamin Wade, who had been one of the strongest opponents of Lincoln's program of readmission, wrote fellow Senator Charles Sumner in November that if the Negroes would stage "an insurrection" that "could contrive to slay one-half of their oppressors" the remaining whites would treat them with respect. With this sort of feeling in the air, returned soldiers began to question the possibility of personal futures under Federal domination.

Most of them needed to find new means of earning a livelihood, and the outlook was particularly bleak for professional soldiers in middle life with families to support. Men left the country to join expatriate colonies in Canada, Mexico, Brazil. Lee was appealed to for advice, and in two letters he revealed his recognition of the effect of the drift without the growth of a reconciliatory spirit.

In his August letter to former Governor Letcher, he advised Virginians to take the oath of allegiance in order to qualify themselves for suffrage. Since Virginia's "prosperity will rise or fall with the welfare of the country," he wrote, "the duty of the citizens, then, appears to me too plain to admit of any doubt. All should unite in honest efforts to obliterate the effects of war, and to restore the blessings of peace. They [ex-Confederates] should remain if possible in the country; promote harmony and good feeling; qualify themselves to vote, and elect to the State and general legislatures wise and patriotic men, who will devote their abilities to the interests of the country and the healing of all dissensions."

One month later Lee showed less certainty in the efficacy of good faith and honest effort. Matthew Fontaine Maury, formerly the United States' great oceanographer and later advanced experimenter with underwater torpedoes for the Confederate Navy, wrote Lee from the Confederate colony in Mexico. Lee's contemporary, from near Fredericksburg, asked him to join them. In September, 1865, Lee wrote:

"We have certainly not found our form of government all that was anticipated by its original founders; but that may be partly our fault in expecting too much and partly in the absence of virtue in the people. As long as virtue was dominant in the Republic so long was the happiness of the people secure. I cannot, however, despair of it yet. I . . . trust that time and experience, the great teachers of men under the guidance of an ever-merciful God, may save us from destruction and restore to us the right hopes and prospects of the past. The thought of abandoning the country and all that must be left in it is abhorrent to my feelings, and I prefer to struggle for its restoration and share its fate, rather than to give up all as lost . . ."

The concept of "struggle" had then entered his mind. Passions were being inflamed instead of "allayed." Lee, believing that a restoration of the old Union depended upon a true appraisal of the wartime events, began to recognize that the climate was then unfavorable for understanding. In the same month, he wrote Josiah Tatnall, former naval captain: "I have too exalted an opinion of the American people to believe they will consent to injustice. It is only necessary, in my opinion, that truth should be known, for the rights of every one to be secured." But in the atmosphere of dissension promoted by the Radicals — with support from Southern extremists — Lee felt the North was not ready to accept the truth.

Even with his strong feelings about the imprisonment of President Davis, Lee refused Mrs. Davis's appeal to defend her husband against one particularly vicious public attack. "I have thought, from the cessation of hostilities, that silence and patience on the part of the South was the true course, and I still think so. Controversy of all kinds will in my opinion only serve to continue excitement and passion, and will prevent the public mind from the acknowledgement and acceptance of the truth. These considerations have prevented me from replying to accusations made against myself, and induced me to recommend the same to others."

The amorphous Johnson phase, for all practical purposes, came to an end on December 4, when a Radical-dominated Congress convened. With the passing of the Johnson phase, all uncertainties ended, too. The Radicals made their intent clear on the first day of Congress. They refused seats in the House to the elected representatives from the Southern states. (Their state governments, however, were recognized for the ratification of the Thirteenth Amendment.) This sounded the opening gun for the war that was to be resumed on the political front.

Recognizing what lay ahead, Lee, ten days after Virginia's representatives were turned away at Washington, wrote Mrs. Fitzhugh, "Aunt Maria." In no letters to his immediate family, and in no words of his recorded by them, did Lee so simply, so completely, expose his inner feelings. "You are all that now binds me to the past, and my pleasurable thoughts come rather from the past than the future of this world."

## 5

What baffled Lee about the unconstitutional powers seized by the Radicals was the acquiescence of Congress and the American people to the manipulations of a small, avowedly vindictive group. The effective official power was in the Joint Committee on Reconstruction — usually referred to as "the Committee of Fifteen," or, by non-admirers, as "the Directory" — controlled by twelve Radically oriented Republicans. The hard core consisted of four: Thaddeus Stevens, of Pennsylvania, the Radical power in Congress; Secretary of War Stanton; and in the Senate, Charles Sumner, the abolitionist, of Massachusetts, and "Bluff Ben" Wade of Iowa. It was Stevens who made their objectives clear.

Dismissing all of Johnson's policy of readmitting the states, Stevens said, "The future condition of the conquered powers depends upon the will of the conquerors." One of his allies in the Senate, Zachariah Chandler, carried this further. The only rights left the Southerner were, he declared, "the constitutional right to be hanged and the divine right to be damned." For policy Stevens recommended indefinitely extended territorial governments in the Southern states until legislation had been passed, national and state, to "secure perpetual ascendancy to the party of the Union." The Radicals equated the Republicans with the party of the Union. The Southern states, Stevens announced, "will come in as new states or remain as conquered provinces."

By "new states" Stephens made it plain that he meant states in which suffrage rights had been changed to give the vote to the recently freed slaves while disfranchising non-Union whites — practically the total representative white population. "There will always be Union white men enough in the South, aided by the blacks, to . . . continue the Republican ascendancy." That is, the Negroes would be given the right to vote Republican. Beyond this shift in suffrage rights, Stevens's Radicals proposed to confiscate the land from white families and distribute it among the freedmen, destroy the institutions of the Southern society and, in brief, as Stevens said, "reduce the South to a mudhole."

General Lee, in his bafflement at the unimpeded growth of this policy during 1866, failed to perceive the ingenuity with which the Radicals had linked hatred and the political exploitation of the freed slaves in a single purpose under the ideal of "equality."

There was at the time a strain of genuine humanitarian interest in establishing the rights of the freed slaves, even though the humanitarianism often existed in abstractions, and some authentic abolitionists among the Radicals were committed to the "elevation" of the Negro, even though this purpose was often accompanied by hostility to the Southern white society and involved with the use of the Negroes for Party political ends. But to Lee and Southern moderates, clearly "equality" for all citizens could not be the guiding purpose in shifting voting rights away from the native white population to the recently freed Negroes and mostly imported Radical Republican ("Unionist") whites. Clearly no program existed for restoring the total society to health and a normal order in which both races would share citizenship and responsibility. Thus, while Radical propaganda established the belief that bad means were used for a good end, on the scene Lee and his fellow moderates saw the means as ends in themselves and regarded with distrust the agitations of Northern abolitionists who supported the Radicals.

In the absolute view these abolitionists could be seen as "fanatics for freedom." In the wreckage of a civilization they were also seen as fanatics for total war (in which they risked nothing) and, after the war, as fanatics for "retribution." In practical terms, the abolitionists' goal would seem to have been accomplished when slavery was abolished. However, the accomplished goal left them without a cause. Since these punitive abolitionists had always seemed to hate the Southern white at least as much as the institution of slavery, when the slaves were free, their hatred for the South shifted to retribution under the justification that slavery was associated with "treason." By linking the two, their postwar zeal could be directed toward the "punishment" of the South for its past guilt on one charge or the other. In resolving their own inner conflicts through this socially approved hostility, the abolitionists became extremely useful to the Radical Republicans in their program to prevent restoration and sectional harmony.

Though most abolitionists were probably not aware of being used — certainly not the sincere idealists who came into the Southern states — some of the abolitionist-Radicals deliberately combined "retributive justice" with the goal of "securing perpetual ascendancy" of the Republican Party. No abolitionist in Washington was as transcendentally self-righteous as Senator Sumner, and he accepted the cynical program as advanced by Jacob Howard, a fellow senator from Michigan. In a private letter, Howard wrote that the Negro vote was wanted to secure the South for the party, "whatever the Northern people may do to their own blacks."

With hatred and idealism joined by the cold ambition of men in power, the Radical program, quickly gathering momentum, naturally attracted opportunists to the movement. Johnson called these joiners "hypocritical fanatics," and Georgia's Ben Hill described them as those "invisible in war, invincible in peace." These bandwagon riders were anxious to make themselves useful — and also to make a profit — and they poured into the South like civilian armies.

The Radicals in Washington wanted unfavorable reports on the Southern states to show in the North that Southerners were not to be trusted and needed to be kept out of the Union under military rule. The propaganda campaign of 1866 was to prepare the Northern people for the use of force in states' internal affairs and for the use of force in granting freed Negroes rights that led to equality — an equality opposed by large proportions of the Northern people. The visiting observers dutifully reported back the conditions they were sent to find. Inevitable clashes between individuals and groups were reported in the North as "incidents" which supposedly represented the total condition.

When Lee was asked by a gentleman from Baltimore to contradict one persistent distortion, he wrote back, "It is so easy to make accusations against the people of the South upon similar testimony, that those so disposed, should one be refuted, will immediately create another."

Among the observers went some sincere men of idealism for a Union conceived in abstract. Unfortunately, these humanitarians took with them little human understanding and less compassion. They were constantly outraged at the lack of cordiality encountered in Southerners standing among the ruins left by Federal armies and surprised at the "touchiness" in the people. Most of all, the idealists were shocked at the absence of "repentance." Carl Schurz, the former German revolutionary and Federal brigadier, then touring the South as a journalist, wrote his wife, "I have found all my preconceived opinions verified." The general reports could only conclude that Southerners remained unconverted by the "lessons of the war" and showed a markedly rebellious attitude when it came to changing their ways — to becoming "Americanized," as James Russell Lowell advocated.

A fundamental misconception was held by the idealists who inadvertently or consciously furthered the purposes of the Radicals in government and, through them, the dominating purpose of the financial-industrial powers. Working in absolutes, they conceived their duty to be, as Wendell Phillips said, the "North making over the South in its own likeness." This Boston minister summarized the attitude by saying, "Reconstruction begins when the South yields up her idea of civilization, and allows the North to permeate her channels and to make her over, throughout the route that victory has given to the better and the dominant idea." In this sense, "repentance" meant the South's willingness to become a stereotype of the Northern society.

The deeper significance here lay in the concept of the obliteration of a minority, or diverse, society within the nation. It is doubtful if Phillips, and those for whom he spoke, recognized the ultimate implications of advocating a single stereotype for the national society. Their purpose was limited to remaking the South to conform to their *idea* of the North — the vision of the North as representing absolutism in virtue. Since neither the Federal soldiers nor the Radical emissaries in the South convinced the people of the superiority of Northern virtue, the very idea of being remade in the "likeness" of their despoilers — the presumption of moral superiority based upon conquest by might — made fiercer their attachment to their own nation of the heart, and promoted a blind rejection of anything Northern.

Out of this emotional reaction, which obviated either rational selectivity or the adaptiveness to make outward accommodations to the conquerors, the people did present a picture of such proud "unrepentance," accompanied by sufficient outbreaks into personal violence, as to provide the Radicals in Washington with all the support they needed. During 1866 they were to ram through Congress, over the President's veto, a succession of pre-Reconstruction bills.

First the Freedmen's Bureau, established near the end of the war, was indefinitely extended. The fundamental purpose of the Bureau's agencies, spread throughout the South, was to provide for the uprooted Negro population and guide the freed slaves in their bewildering new status. Instructions were given on the responsibilities of self-support, on the meaning of keeping a "contract" for work and on the duties of citizenship. For colored children nearly one thousand schools were established (with funds from the sale of Confederate property and confiscated private lands).

The purpose was sound and much good was accomplished. But, as the Bureau offered employment to thousands looking for easy work in an agency in an occupied country, among this personnel stealing ranged from petty thefts to grand-scale corruption, and inevitably some played Republican politics. Numbers of the Bureau agents advanced to positions of power in the Reconstruction state governments and many more worked to secure the hold of the Radical Republicans in the South. In general the Bureau reminded the Negroes that the material comforts came to them through the courtesy of the party of the Union.

In April the Civil Rights Bill was passed and, as the Radicals seemed to doubt that even their power could make this bill appear constitutional, it was largely incorporated in the Fourteenth Amendment. Passing both houses in June, 1866, the Fourteenth Amendment was a hodge-podge of separate clauses. The third clause denied the right of office to any former state or national office holders who had participated in or given aid to the rebellion, except with a two-thirds vote of each house. This removed from state or national office almost all the South's natural political leaders.

The fourth clause repudiated any claims for the losses incurred by the emancipation of slaves. Lincoln, following England's example on the abolition of slavery, had told the Confederate peace commissioners in February, 1865, that it was his intention to compensate slaveholders for their loss of property. Since slaves represented the single largest investment in the South, this financial loss was the most crippling handicap to the recovery of the agricultural region. Without slaves to work their land, the planters had no cash to hire labor, and the idle fields had a widespread effect on the region's total economy.

The key clause was the first. This established the citizenship of all persons born or naturalized in the United States, and declared that "no state shall make or enforce any law which shall abridge the privileges and immunities of citizens." Though no reference was made specifically to suffrage, the intent of the granting of citizenship was to give the vote to the Negroes *in the South*. The Fourteenth Amendment, however, was not immediately ratified by the states, and the Radicals simply gave the right to vote to seven hundred thousand Negroes in the South. (This was larger than the number of the whites permitted to register.)

During 1866 the Radical-dominated Congress extended its national power by passing bills to gain congressional control of the army and the Cabinet, and to control its own sessions. From the small core of vindictives, a centralized despotism had grown to establish the Radicals in absolute power in the nation as well as over the South. This power was not seized so much with the acquiescence of average Americans, as Lee believed, as with their indifference or ignorance.

The majority of Americans had turned to their personal affairs in regions that, untouched by the war, enjoyed a postwar boom. With the country expanding westward, enormous new industries, such as oil and steel, emerged to stimulate prosperity, and the financing of corporations created opportunities for a new style of adventurer. Unaware of the aftermath of war that spread like a plague over the Southern states, America was entering "the Gilded Age" — the conscienceless times that produced Fisk and Gould and Boss Tweed.

In this atmosphere the Radicals completed their program by passing, over Johnson's veto, the Reconstruction Act in March, 1867. Actually two acts (March 2 and March 23), with the second supplementing the first, the Reconstruction Act basically authorized the use of military force in reorganizing the Southern state governments according to the Radicals' purposes. Ten Southern states (Tennessee having been readmitted under a Reconstruction government) were divided into five military districts under Federal army commanders who exercised supreme authority.

Under their direction, elections were to be held for new state constitutional conventions, with the military seeing to it that the Negroes got out the vote, and various classes of ex-Confederates were disqualified. New state constitutions were to be written which established Negro suffrage, permanently disqualified Confederate leaders from office and included other proscriptive features according to the whims of the local Radicals. When the state legislatures then ratified the Fourteen Amendment and this was written into the Federal Constitution, the states would be eligible to apply for readmission.

President Johnson, stripped of power, made an accurate appraisal of the dynamics of Reconstruction rule and the inevitable consequences. "If a State is to be nursed until it again gets its strength, it must be nursed by its friends, not smothered by its enemies." The longer a plan of conciliation is delayed, "the more difficult will it be to bring the North and South into harmony." "The idea of legislating for one-third of the population of the country . . . passing constitutional amendments without allowing them any voice in the matter . . . is full of danger to the future peace and welfare of the nation. They cannot be treated as subjugated people or as vassal colonies without a germ of hatred being introduced, which will some day or other, though the time may be distant, develop mischief of the most serious character."

Anything Johnson said was answered only with epithets (Schurz likened him to Judas Iscariot and Benedict Arnold), and the imposition of Reconstruction rule began the third postwar phase.

6

When "extemporized citizens" — as a New Orleans newspaper called them — took over the local governments in the Southern states, reactions began to reach a climax in the interactive play between provocation and resentment. In Virginia, under the immediacy of Lee's influence and the fair-mindedness of the Federal military commander, Major General John M. Schofield, moderates controlled the population. In other Southern states the moderates could not control the reactions of the more violent where ruthless, tyrannical military commanders, such as Sheridan, incited even the most peaceably inclined. Mayors, judges, treasurers, all manner of local officials were ousted from their elected offices, to be supplanted by aliens. This happened in Virginia too, but where the Sheridans ruled, these upheavals in the communities were committed with a brutal joyousness in the use of force. In this formal phase of Reconstruction, it became futile for the moderates to urge the people to appeal to "law."

At the center of the interaction between coercion and resistance was the Negro. Immediate suffrage for the freed slaves was not part of Johnson's policy. On their release from servitude, the mostly ignorant people were not qualified to assume the responsibilities, as well as the privileges, of participating in government. Along with the unqualified condition of the Negroes, universal suffrage ran counter to the governing principles of Southern states.

Virginia, founded as an aristocratic republic, sincerely distrusted the mob, white or black, and a rule by "all the people" was antithetical to the political philosophy which produced the giants of the Revolutionary generation and the "Virginia dynasty" in Washington. Restrictions on voting and legislative representation had been a basic cause in the secession of the western counties to form a new state. In line with Virginia's property-owning qualifications, in South Carolina Wade Hampton advocated enfranchising property-owning Negroes. In Louisiana, Francis T. Nicholls advocated giving the franchise to educated Negoes and continuing to disfranchise the uneducated in both races. With this belief in restricting the electorate to "responsible" people, Southern leaders opposed *any* idea of forcibly granted suffrage — as well as the principle of the central government's usurping control of states' internal affairs.

Since the war determined only that the nation was indissoluble, Lee said that the state maintained "the exclusive right to regulate its internal affairs under rules established by the Constitution, and the right of each state to prescribe for itself the qualifications of suffrage."

In Reconstruction the Radicals got around this Constitutional block by a de facto control of the ballot box at the local level. Constitutional conventions were elected whose members would "prescribe . . . the qualifications for suffrage" in the state. This devious use of force in the voting franchise produced a more far-reaching effect on Southerners — especially in relation to the Negro — than all other acts of coercion, in war and Reconstruction, combined. A young Virginia woman on the scene, Myrta Lockett Avary, wrote forty years later, "The most lasting wrong Reconstruction inflicted upon the South was the inevitable political demoralization of the white man. No man could regard the ballot-box as the voice of the people, a sacred thing . . . It was the carpetbaggers' steppingstone to power. The votes of a multitude were for sale . . . to be had by trickery."

That the purpose of all the trickery (with whatever admixture of idealism) was to obtain the vote of the freed slaves for the Republican Party made inevitable the alignment of the races against one another. In the Negro's new status he was used as a pawn in a scheme to debase the society in which he must live and to corrupt its principles of government. Cajoled with promises, he became the ally of imported adventurers, "carpetbaggers," and native opportunists, "scalawags." In total indifference to the sociological problems of the two races, intertwined with the problems of economic and social reorganization in a destroyed civilization, some of the freedmen's allies actively sought to promote conflict between the Negroes and the native white population.

This alliance of the Negroes with the white population's avowed enemies did not arouse antagonism in the educated Southerners toward Negroes themselves. Lee was among the many Southerners who wrote of the misfortune brought on both races by the Radicals' exploitation of the Negroes. In fact, the Northern misrepresentation that he most regretted was the charge that Southerners fought the war to perpetuate slavery. Reverend John Leyburn, with whom Lee talked in Baltimore in 1869, recorded that "he seemed not only indignant but hurt" by these statements. Lee pointed out that the slaves he emancipated wrote him most affectionate letters during the war, and the Negroes he had known when stationed at Baltimore came up to his carriage during the 1869 trip to shake hands with him. Lee did not believe the Negroes would have received him so warmly if, Dr. Leyburn wrote, "they looked upon him as fresh from a war intended for their oppression and injury."

Aside from the personal feelings of moderates, politically the Negro was placed in the position of opposing the interests of the native white. This was not only the white's interest in recovering the government of his own state. There was the more frightening concern of saving all the people from the effects of the corruption in the carpetbagger governments. While breaking up the large holdings by taxation was part of the Radical system for "reconstructing" the Southern society, the exorbitant taxation imposed by some of the proconsuls for their own enrichment bled whole communities and loaded debts on the state governments to be paid by those then unknown.

In the poorer classes of Southerners the elevation of the Negroes by "foreigners," accompanied by the debasement of the white communities, did arouse a personal and immediate antagonism for Negroes. The non-slaveholding population had none of the paternalism of planter families and no experience in the affectionate relationships that developed through intimacies, especially those shared in childhood. To the unskilled, the poor farmer and the dispossessed farmer, freed Negroes were potential rivals at best — just as they were in the North. The conditions established by Reconstruction created active hostilities to the favored Negroes, which were fanned by clashes with Negro groups — who, themselves, could not always be characterized as peace-loving.

The strongest reaction in Southerners across all classes was aroused by the widespread web of the unofficial Union League. Its cells held secret meetings for Negroes, always at night, amid elaborate rituals. There the colored men, insulated against counterinfluence of native whites, were inculcated with Radical political doctrines and inflamed by promises that they were to be masters of the land. From incitement in the Union League night meetings, the more ignorant Negroes took to those swaggering assertivenesses in public — such as forcing white people off the sidewalk — that, small in detail, exacerbated the raw feelings. The more aggressive committed outrages against whites whom they had been taught to believe were to have no rights.

In the inevitable conflicts the Freedmen's Bureau, which represented Negroes in all legal matters, acted on the principle that the Negro was, by definition, always right. Two Federal generals, J. B. Steedman and J. S. Fullerton, reported after studying conditions that the effect of the Bureau was "to stimulate antagonism among the races."

Even the missionaries who came to spread the light in "Darkest Dixie" inadvertently did their part in fomenting hostilities between the races. Most of these humanitarians came with the loftiest purposes for educating the Negroes, but they concentrated on isolated aspects of enormous and complicated problems existing in a charged climate. As they isolated the Negroes from the total society and regarded the whites with pitiless superiority, it must be said that no aliens ever moved among a conquered people with more repellent tactlessness.

> *We go to plant the common schools*
> *On distant mountain swells*
> *And give the Sabbaths of the South*
> *The ring of Northern bells.*

No bells rung over the deserted plantation schoolhouses, whose owners had no money for tutors, and no system of compulsory public school education then existed in the South.

Miss Cornelia Hancock, of New Jersey, as a teacher in South Carolina, was an example of that zealous dedication to the Negroes' welfare which not only ignored the hardships of the Southern whites but sought to deprive them of their rights of property for the benefit of Negroes. After the early confiscation of private lands under various legal devices, President Johnson began to restore some of the property to families who had owned it for generations. Many Negro families had settled on these temporarily confiscated lands in good faith, and many others had settled on nonconfiscated land under the induced belief that all of it was going to be theirs. Restoring the land to its legal owners could, in many cases, bring further dislocation, poverty and bewilderment to freed slaves. Miss Hancock typified an attitude in seeing only their predicament, which she believed should be solved by illegal means that brought further dislocation and poverty to the whites.

Miss Hancock expressed the wish that "President Johnson could only feel it in his heart to help the loyal people, both black and white, instead of the aristocrats who, day by day, are receiving back their lands . . ." When the Southern whites took their claims to court, Miss Hancock wrote, "The Rebels, of course, have the sagacity to find some flaw in these [confiscatory] titles . . ." and the decision "depends much upon the person who interprets the titles . . . If desirous of Rebel favor, he will decide to restore the land. If desirous of helping struggling humanity, the lands will be kept for the blacks as long as possible."

Since Miss Hancock reflected an attitude that excluded Southern whites from "humanity" and recognized only the "struggle" of the Negroes, and since this attitude was implemented by militarily supported political force, all Southerners did not suffer this discrimination with Lee's forbearance. Nor could all be induced to submit indefinitely with nonviolence. In a hot country with long open seasons, where outdoor habits of shooting and hunting promoted a more primal and less reflective relationship with life, there had always been (as on a frontier) a strain of violence, of men acting directly for themselves. It was only a question of time when direct action would take the form of vigilantes, operating as secret organizations because the law was represented by a force of occupation.

The time came when Reconstruction settled upon the people into the unforeseeable future.

## 7

The most widespread and notorious of the secret vigilante groups was the Ku Klux Klan. Active only briefly, it represented a small segment of the Southern people, and never operated in Lee's home state. Though local Radicals reported large gatherings in Richmond, the most diligent studies of Congressional investigating committees never found and evidence of the existence of the Ku Klux Klan in Virginia.

In the states where the Ku Klux Klan operated, the moderates publicly denounced it as "the greatest blunder our people ever committed." The moderates felt the retaliatory violence hurt the South's position then, at the peak of the Clan's activities in 1868. Since the original, short-lived Ku Klux Klan became associated in the public mind with the organization that flourished under the same name in the twentieth century, more lasting harm was done the South than the moderates anticipated. The whole region paid heavily for the break-out of a few, even though the purpose of this few was to protect isolated families and did bring a measure of safety to terrorized rural districts.

"The instinct of self-protection prompted that organization," said General John B. Gordon to a Congressional committee. "Apprehension took possession of the entire public mind of the State [Georgia]. Men were in many cases afraid to go away from their homes and leave their wives and children, for fear of outrage . . . There was this general organization of the black race on one hand, and an entire disorganization of the white race on the other hand."

In developing his reactive theory, General Gordon listed the secret work of the Union League as the main reason for the counterorganizations. The Clan operated secretly because a public organization, he said, "would be construed . . . as antagonistic to the government of the United States."

General Gordon was borne out in the minority report of a committee sent in 1871 to investigate the Ku Klux Klan. Of the twenty-one committee members carefully selected to bring back the desired report condemning the South, eight refused to go along after a first-hand survey of Reconstruction at work. "Had there been no wanton oppression in the South, there would have been no Ku Kluxism. Had there been no rule of the tyrannical, corrupt carpetbagger, or scalawag rule, there would have been no secret organization."

In developing the conditions, the report stated, "When that [Southern] people saw they had no rights which were respected, no protection from insults, no security even for their wives and little children, and that what little they had saved from the war was being confiscated . . . when even the courts were closed and the Federal officers, who were made by Congress absolute rulers and dispensers of what they called justice . . . trampled upon the rights of the ostracized and disfranchised white man while the official pandered to the enfranchised negro on whose votes he relied . . . [when the people] saw that all their complaints and remonstrances, however honestly and humbly presented to Congress, were either wholly disregarded or regarded as evidence of a rebellious and unsubdued spirit, many of them took the law into their own hands."

This spontaneous movement did not begin with the purpose of violence nor with a plan to operate as a regional organization. When the first band of Clansmen met in Tennessee in 1866 it was a harmless local affair, termed "a hilarious social club." This band originated a name, Kuklos, from a Greek word which is the root of circle or cycle. By various minor changes, alliteration evolved Kuklos Clan into Ku Klux Klan, with the insignia, "KKK," which was to come for a time to hold the menace of the Black Hand.

During the early spread of the idea from the first club, the masks and regalia were regarded by members "as no more than a practical joke." There was no uniformity in the costumes, as "the bedsheets" of the twentieth-century organization. The costumes were designed to terrify ignorant Negroes as well as to provide disguises, and the various "dens" turned out in some grotesque arrays that in the relatively innocent days seemed ludicrous to the wearers. During this pre-violent period small groups rode out at night to frighten Negroes, especially those attending Union League meetings, mostly as a means of establishing protection for white families in isolated areas.

It was not that the masses of freedmen became lawless but that individual Negroes committed sufficient crimes in every criminal category to arouse fear of all Negroes. Chief of Staff Halleck wrote to Grant after Appomattox about one Negro unit: "A number of cases of atrocious rape by these men have already occurred. Their influence on the colored people is reported bad." To white families on isolated farms, any gang of roaming Negro men contained potential threat. The Negro militia — armed by the Radical governments while white men were forbidden to possess firearms — themselves suggested a force of menace.

When the Ku Klux Klan began to spread widely after Reconstruction came in 1867, violence was introduced as a method of reprisal and warning — and not only against Negroes. Occasionally alien agents were "run out of town." By 1868 the violence began to get out of hand. A rising generation of youth had grown up in the dislocations of war, amid the ravages of armies and raiders. Jobless and penniless in a land where aliens fattened themselves under the protection of troops of occupation, these dispossessed young men turned to the Clan with no purpose beyond the release of hostilities and frustrations. In the collapse of any respect for law, this personalized lawlessness gathered its own momentum, and in 1869 the leaders of the Ku Klux Klan ordered its units to disband.

During its brief period of intense activity, and afterwards, many acts of lawlessness were attributed to the Ku Klux, and the local Radicals exaggerated for Northern consumption the accounts of its alleged crimes. However, beyond lasting bad publicity for the whole South, the Clan's activities could not be exploited by the Radicals because of a national political shift.

Though the Republicans had praised themselves as "the party of the Union," and associated the Democrats with "rebellion," it became clear to the Radical leaders that presidential nominee Grant was by no means assured of winning the 1868 election. Suddenly the electoral votes of the Southern states were seen to be necessary in the Republican column. Measures were quickly taken to end the "territorial status" of "the conquered province" and to hurry the rejected states back into the Union under their synthetic Reconstruction governments.

Nine of the Southern states had chosen to remain temporarily outside the Union, under Reconstruction, rather than to be readmitted under new state constitutions which placed the states permanently in the control of carpetbaggers and Negroes. In a nonviolent method, the people refused to vote on the constitutions designed to disfranchise the representative white population. To get around this, the Radicals rushed through a bill on March 11, 1868, over the President's veto.

This bill removed the provision that required the majority of the total registration to ratify the new state constitutions and required only the majority of the votes cast to be necessary for ratification. To make doubly certain of the results, the bill also required only ten days' residence in a state necessary to qualify for voting (except to former Confederates). With this legislation, half a dozen Southern states were hurried back into the Union with their carpetbagger representatives during the summer of 1868. By election time in November only Virginia, Mississippi and Texas remained legally out of the Union.

Texas came in shortly afterwards. Mississippi had managed to muster a vote to defeat ratification of the new constitution, and Virginia was enabled to postpone the vote through the persuasions of its moderates and the fairness of Military Commander Schofield.

The presidential election showed the Radical leaders had estimated very accurately. The national vote gave war hero Grant a popular majority of little more than three hundred thousand, and this narrow margin was won by the approximately five hundred thousand Republican votes cast by Negroes in the Southern states — with Virginia, Mississippi and Texas not voting. The Radicals also showed their skill in propaganda by convincing history that the Negro needed them, despite their own demonstrable need of the Negro and the clarity with which the 1868 Republican platform delimited "equality" to the South. Declaring that Negro suffrage had been imposed upon the South in answer to demands of "every consideration of public safety . . . and justice," this plank assured Northerners that for them Negro suffrage "properly belongs to the people of those states."

After the votes of Southern states had been counted in a national election, the official phase of Reconstruction perforce began to come to its end. By 1870, the year of Lee's death, the last states were readmitted to the Union, mostly under the synthetic governments erected during Reconstruction. Virginia, through the patient maneuver and practical compromises of its controlling moderates, returned under its own representative government — though scarcely as the state that left the Union in 1861.

By record, Lee expressed no satisfaction at Virginia's readmission nor at the end of official Reconstruction. The physical unification of the political body manifestly represented no return to the original republic under the controlling direction of Providence. Lee had observed the techniques of mastery exerted in a moral vacuum covered by the myth of "equal rights." He had seen a new union founded on a myth that justified divisiveness and exploited sectional antagonisms. He had witnessed the death of a community of common interests which his father's generation had believed possible for rational men to maintain.

Near the end of his life he referred to himself as "an old Confederate" — as if he too was embraced in that invisible nation of the heart within a new nation which he had no desire to live to see. While devoting his waning energies to educating a new generation for a New South, Lee belonged in a time which had become "the past" during his own last years.

After his death, Mrs. Lee determined to see Arlington once more before she followed him. She wrote that she would not have recognized her childhood home except for a few oaks the Federals "had spared and trees planted on the lawn by the General and myself . . . My dear home was so changed it seemed but as a dream of the past."

8

The post-Reconstruction phase that continued for seven years in several Southern states after Lee's death tended to become confused historically with the Reconstruction period of occupation. During actual Reconstruction, new state constitutions were imposed which — though containing many enlightened and truly progressive elements (such as public school systems) — were primarily designed to assure state political control to a Republican party formed of nonrepresentative citizens. After 1870 the Republicans in Washington were primarily concerned with supporting the synthetic state governments in office and getting Republican majorities at the polls. The "equality" issue was officially ended in March, 1875, when a Civil Rights Bill was passed that eliminated the "mixed school" clause which Sumner had introduced for the new public school systems coming into being in the Southern states.

The leaders who had "reconstructed" the South, in order to "insure the perpetual ascendancy of their party in power," passed from the scene during the 1870-1877 period. Stevens, Stanton and Sumner went to their rewards, and Wade had retired from the Senate. The new leaders, for whom the Negro served no useful political purpose, concentrated on keeping alive the hatreds of the war in a campaign to identify all Democrats with "rebellion."

During the 1866-1870 period, when Federal agencies, such as the Freedmen's Bureau, and aid societies devoted to educating the freedmen, were active throughout the South, there was, in the amalgam of motives, genuine interest in the Negroes' rights of citizenship. Though the monovisual zeal of the most sincere was detrimental to racial relationships, many of the individuals and individual agencies worked effectively "for the Aid and Elevation of the Freemen." After formal Reconstruction ended with the readmission of the Southern states, this activity gradually ceased.

The passing of political interest in the Negro was accompanied by the waning of the humanitarian crusade that supplied private agencies with money. On the scene many of the "fanatics for freedom," after a couple of years of firsthand experience wtih the enormity and complexity of the problems created by sudden emancipation in a demolished civilization, abandoned the Negro in search of some more abstract cause — or simply abandoned him. Even the deeply dedicated, like Miss Cornelia Hancock, began to see that realistically the problem of the Negro belonged in the context of the problems created for the South.

"The depressed state of business in the South makes it very hard for them [Negroes] to get employment at remunerative rates; and the dense ignorance existing in the grown people's minds makes it extremely difficult for them to settle upon any business that requires forethought or calculation . . . anything that is to occur in two years is almost beyond their reckoning." She came to recognize, as the Southern emancipationists had for fifty years, that the freedman's central problem in an agricultural community was getting possession of land to work for himself. Where perhaps as high as 90 per cent of the colored working population had been employed in farming, or in unskilled labor, there was nowhere for them to turn without land. A circular problem had been created for which no simple solution existed, certainly not in a climate of discord.

Miss Hancock still hoped "for some liberal legislation" that would confiscate private land and apportion it among the Negroes, but, as the time for such measures passed, she wrote in her last letter from South Carolina, "I consider the schools have been the only systematic agency for permanent good."

Unfortunately, she was optimistic in thinking any permanent good had resulted from coercion applied to subjugated people, which such dissimilar men as Lee and Andrew Johnson saw could only produce future antagonisms. As the Congressional minority report pointed out in 1871, "corruption bred corruption." The post-Reconstruction phase was— with whatever concern for Negroes' rights persisting in individuals— fundamentally a power fight for control of state governments and the ballot box between the entrenched, self-interested Republicans and representative natives, including Negroes, as Democrats. Miss Myrta Lockett Avary, the Virginia lady who said that political "demoralization" had destroyed respect for the ballot box, wrote, "It was a poor patriot who would not save his state by pay or play."

In South Carolina, Mississippi and Louisiana, the Radical-appointed alien governors convinced Grant that the Democrats were practicing fraud, and constantly called on him to send in troops "to suppress insurrection." Though there was no question about the fraud on both sides, U. S. Army Colonel Henry A. Morrow, after a two months' inspection in Louisiana and Mississippi, reported that the people were not insurrecting against the Federal government. They were driven to extremes to overthrow the corrupt, manufactured governments that could not maintain themselves "in power a single hour without the protection of Federal troops." Grant, with his simple faith in the use of force, continued to dispatch the troops in such regular excursions that national Republican leaders warned him that continued armed intervention in states' internal governments would be harmful to the Party. Republican papers began to editorialize against bayonet ballots, and in 1875 the harsh measures suggested by Sheridan for disposing of Democrats in Louisiana produced a strongly unfavorable reaction in the North and in the Senate.

In three Southern states non-secret organizations, such as Wade Hampton's Red Shirts in South Carolina, began openly to apply counterintimidation measures, and Negroes in uncountable numbers, caught between the contending forces of natives and carpetbag-government troops, began to stay away from the polls. Aside from the element of fear at being caught in the middle, many freedmen had by then grown disenchanted with the Radicals' promises and rebellious under intimidations from members of their own race who enjoyed favor in the Radical rule. Educated Negroes and property owners perceived that the alien worked against the interests of the Southern communities, and many of these voted Democrat along with the native whites.

One of these men, Hiram Revels, former Methodist minister and educator, wrote to Grant after the 1876 elections in Mississippi voted the carpetbagger government out of office. Senator Revels, successor to Jefferson Davis's seat in the Senate, was the first Negro to serve in the U. S. Senate. He gave the President a firsthand view of the Mississippi election by saying that "men, irrespective of race, color, or party affiliation, united and voted together against men known to be incompetent and dishonest." Senator Revels went on to tell Grant that the bitterness created by the war "would have long since been entirely obliterated, were it not for some unprincipled men who would keep alive the bitterness of the past, and inculcate a hatred between the races, in order that they may aggrandize themselves by office and its emoluments . . ."

By 1876 the "hate the South" program had so lost its appeal (in a nation which, in its own giddy prosperity, had forgotten the South except as a remote appendage where the people had once fought to keep slaves) that the presidential election resulted in a disputed count between Republican Rutherford B. Hayes and Democrat Samuel Tilden. In a deal which awarded the election to Hayes, contested elections in South Carolina, Louisiana and Florida were decided in favor of the Democrats, representing the native population. (In South Carolina, Federal troops had changed into civilian clothes and voted repeatedly for the old Rebel, Wade Hampton, as governor.) When Grant left office in 1877, the alien rulers in those three states packed their bags and, after seventeen years, peace was restored in the last Southern states.

This last phase of bayonet-supported political manipulation in three states became, in a general impression, included in Reconstruction in *The* South because of a rationale that grew to unify the whole war period, 1860-1877, into the logical progression of a single humanitarian cause. For this unifying rationale, Lincoln's martyrdom was used for his apotheosis into the somewhat mythical figure of "Great Emancipator."

In this mythical father-figure of the new nation begun under the Radicals, it was necessary to ignore the facts that, before the admittedly expedient war measure of the Emancipation Proclamation, Lincoln never took any stand toward emancipation in the states where slavery existed; his solution for the problems created by sudden expedient emancipation was deportation of the freed slaves; he stated unequivocably his disbelief in any kind of equality between the races. To soften these stumbling blocks in the rationale of singleness of progression toward human rights, there has been a tendency to stress Lincoln's great humanity which would, in these times, place him in the vanguard of the fight for equality.

Yet, in these times, his humanity would hardly be praised for unleashing total war — especially if the other side possessed nuclear weapons for retaliation. It would seem that the use of Lincoln to personify the rationale of moral determinism in *The* Union required that he be placed in the context of his times where he might be judged by today's standards as a war maker and out of the context of his time where he is judged on his humanitarianism toward the Negro. By this deification the mythical Lincoln transcended all context of time to exist, supernally, as an Absolute of Wise Benevolence.

The dismissed contradiction in this mythical Lincoln validating the rationale of logical progression was that the Radicals violated his principles and policy of reconciliation. It seems generally agreed that had Lincoln lived there would have been no Reconstruction. There is also the possibility that had Lincoln lived he could not have controlled the Radicals, and the so-called "Vindictives" would have imposed Reconstruction over his opposition. Since, then, had Lincoln lived, either Reconstruction would never have happened or it would have been imposed over his protests, it follows that the rationale of a logical humanitarian progression from 1860 to 1877 was determined by the single bullet from the derringer of a mad actor.

None of this has anything to do with the living Lincoln, the mortal man with his gifts and limitations and broad humanity. But the mythical Lincoln of "the Great Emancipator" exists in curious contrast to the image of "Lee, the Rebel."

Lee *was* an active emancipationist, very advanced in his disbelief in war as a resolution and farsighted in anticipating its consequences. In his 1860 letter from Texas, about "a Union . . . in which strife and civil war are to take the place of brotherly love and kindness," he wrote, "I shall mourn for my country and for the welfare and progress of mankind. If the . . . Government is disrupted, I shall return to my native State, and share the miseries of my people . . ."

When, in sharing the miseries of his people, he felt it his duty to devote his remaining years to education for their future, he wrote his wife,

"Life is indeed gliding away and I have nothing good to show for mine that is past. I pray I may be spared to accomplish something for the good of mankind and the glory of God."

In pursuing this goal, Lee provided no material for myths that would serve either the Union or the South. There was nothing mythical about Lee at all. In living by an ideal under God, his being constituted a wholeness that permitted him to transcend all the hostilities and mutations of his time and circumstance. As Nietzsche said of Goethe: "He disciplined himself into a wholeness, he *created* himself . . . he stands amid the cosmos with a . . . trusting fatalism, in the *faith* that . . . in the whole all is redeemed and affirmed: he does not negate any more."

This was nothing conquerors wanted to see in the defeated military leader of a subjected territory, nor much that could provide practical impetus to his own people. In his service as a public example, the symbol Lee provided for their fallen civilization was of an ideal larger and purer than life — literally "the matchless Lee" — and he related as a god to the mythology that grew around the Lost Cause.

But even this deification made nothing mythical about Lee himself. In his own life he had simply realized his ideal of "the good as well as the great." It was through this self-realization that his spiritual force served to perpetuate the heroic quality of character, the nobility and grandeur of the individual concept, that existed in the republic from which the new nation derived. His example provided a personal distillation of the heritage of the idealism, inherent with a sense of personal honor, that characterized the American republic in its founding. Though his interpretation of the Constitution ran counter to the course of the future in practical application, his total commitment to principle was beyond the changes and mutations of practicalities in its timeless application. By this he perpetuated an essence from the past of the American people that transcended all transitory stages in the continuous evolution of a nation's self-identity.

Such considerations were not in Lee's consciousness when, at the end of the journey back from Appomattox, he began his postwar life secluded with his family in Richmond. Once, after the fighting was over, the Reverend J. William Jones, former army chaplain and Lee's friend, began to talk about certain turns in the war that had brought unhappy results. Suddenly interrupting him, Lee said, "Yes, all that is very sad, and might be a cause for self-reproach, but *that we are conscious that we have humbly tried to do our duty*. We may therefore, with calm satisfaction, trust in God and leave results to Him."

The perpetuation of the heritage was a result of Lee's humbly trying to do his duty, as God gave him to see it, beginning with his recuperation in the Franklin Street house in April, 1865.

*PART SIX*

# The Capstone of a Life

# CHAPTER XXIV

## "This Door and Not Another"

LEE'S house of sanctuary with his family in Richmond became more like a citadel. The fallen capital became a combination of tourist attraction, depot in the passage of troops from both armies, and refuge center for displaced farm families, white and colored. Out of the conglomerate mixture of crowds milling about the streets in the center of Richmond, streams branched off to the spacious red-brick house at 707 East Franklin. Most of the sightseers contented themselves with standing on the red-brick sidewalk, hoping for a view of "the Rebel chieftain," but a steady progression of visitors sought to gain admittance. Rob wrote, "All sorts and conditions of people came to see him."

To protect Lee from visitors, Rob, joined by Rooney and then Custis, along with various young Lee cousins temporarily camping at the house, took turns guarding the door. Lee would never turn away anyone, though his shaken condition was evident. Those who had not seen him during the last months of the war were shocked and grieved by his worn, wearied look of age and sorrow. While the entrance hall was guarded more rigidly than sentries had ever guarded Lee's headquarters tent, many more visitors than were good for the convalescent got past the cordon at the door.

Typical of Richmond's Greek revival houses of the eighteen-forties, Lee's residence was built close to the street, and its first floor, raised above an English basement, was reached by steps leading to a small, columned portico. Inside, to the right of a broad hall, a door opened into a front, or formal, parlor whose windows looked onto the street. As with most substantial, midtown homes during those first days of the city's occupation, the shuttered blinds were often closed to the front and always at night. Behind the formal parlor, entered by double sliding doors (which could be opened to make a single room for large parties) was the family parlor, or sitting room. Its windows looked across a columned balcony upon a walled garden. It was in this rear room that Lee sat, much alone, when he was not upstairs resting in bed.

Even considering his natural capacity for stillness, for some time he was noticeably quieter than usual. When he did talk, it was of anything except the war. Left to himself, he seemed to require only sleep and silence. There was probably, along with the rebuilding of body and spirit, an element of waiting on the clarification of his status as paroled prisoner of war. In this first period after Appomattox, it seems apparent that Lee expected soon to be released from his parole, as all fighting was coming to an end. He was also waiting, during this period of suspended time, for conditions to permit him to leave Richmond. While it was taxing enough to be a center of curiosity, the clamor in the neighborhood around him was a constant, noisy reminder of the upheaval in his known order and the turmoil to be faced.

His house was only one and one-half blocks from the Franklin Street entrance to Capitol Square, where the red-brick bell tower had only weeks before sounded the tocsin to call out the Local Defense Troops. The shaded and formerly tranquil hillsides sloping down from Jefferson's capitol, with the grass and foliage in freshly flowering green, had become the hurly-burly hub of the city's transient and dislocated population. Federal Army bands blared over the bustle around newly erected tents of American aid societies and agents of the Freedmen's Bureau.

Plantation Negroes from surrounding counties, and some servants from Richmond houses, found Capitol Square a haven of certainty in their purposeless wanderings through the charred ruins of the downtown streets and the silent residential streets with the shuttered façades of the houses. Partly joyous and partly bewildered, totally removed from the realities of their freedom, the former slaves drew daily rations from the bureaux and listened credulously to the agents' promises of a land of milk and honey that was to be theirs.

Coming in with the freed slaves, and also orienting themselves at Capitol Square, were those cold-faced, sharp-eyed, flashily dressed strangers who were to become known as "carpetbaggers." These men, and some women, were surveying the scene with an eye to making a quick dollar out of the distress of the people and the opportunities that would come with hard American cash in a prostrate society whose money was worthless. Fewer in number were the more plainly dressed men and women with expressions of fixed zeal — the missionaries coming to bring education to the freed Negroes and enlightenment to the whites.

Passing the streams of Negroes and "foreigners" went the melancholy trickle of men in the motley remnants of uniforms called "gray." Their cheeks hollowed and their eyes sunken, they shambled on their broken shoes through the streets, seeking food and former comrades, seeking transportation or shelter, and — as April passed — some seeking a horse or a mule with which they could make a crop. The martial order that took effect after Lincoln's murder bore hard on these uprooted men whose identity was still "Confederate." All Confederate insignia were forbidden on clothing. The benumbed veterans, removing the buttons from their jackets, held the holes together with string or pins, and, after removing their CSA belt buckles, tied their belts together with twine. Any more than two ex-Confederates gathering was prohibited as unlawful assembly. If two men met a friend, they had to keep walking.

Except among the inevitable type of officer with new authority, the attitude of the occupation forces was not harsh. General Godfrey Weitzel, whose troops first occupied the city, and then General Ord, personally were sympathetic to the people — civilians and returned veterans. Destitute natives were encouraged to draw bread and meat rations from the Federal bureaux, and some women of humble circumstances took their places in the lines.

The policies the military was ordered to enforce were harsh. Then, some of the soldiers, like any occupation troops, added to the gall by ostentatious high living, such as lolling in open carriages with imported prostitutes. Others, who seemed newly to have become acquainted with horsemanship, acted — as a native said — "as if a gallop was the only gait they knew." These mounted soldiers tore about the old streets in a hazardous fashion rarely before seen in a sober rider.

Also wandering about were a number of illustrators and correspondents for newspapers and magazines. Stories were hard to come by, as the people were not in a talkative mood, and the illustrators contented themselves with drawing pictures of buildings. Libby Prison, then containing ex-Confederates, was a favorite subject. The only artist or writer known to have been admitted to Lee was Mathew Brady, the photographer.

Brady had been an acquaintance of Lee's since the Mexican War, and for him the resting warrior dressed up once more in his battle regalia. Putting on the uniform evidently briefly revived in Lee the combative spirit of the war years, for there was nothing of premature aging or wearied sorrow in the gaze he turned on Brady's camera box. Patrician, self-composed, with perhaps a hint of defiance in the aggressive strength that characterized the often mentioned resolution in his face, the image of Lee, as captured in the Brady photograph, must have been the image his soldiers carried in their memories through all their enduring days.

An amazing number of Federal officers came on one pretext or another. Some came frankly out of curiosity, to look at, talk to, perhaps shake the hand of the famous soldier. Unless he was resting upstairs in bed, Lee usually appeared and suffered their presence. One blue-clad visitor, an Irishman, was unmistakably an old-line "regular," as distinguished from volunteer soldiers. Accompanied by a Negro bearing a large willow basket crammed to the brim with provisions, the Old Army trooper said that he had served with Lee in the 2nd Cavalry and had heard that the "colonel" and his family were in want of food. As long as he had a cent, the Irishman said, his old colonel should not suffer.

Hearing the conversation from the rear room, Lee walked into the hall. The old soldier drew himself up and saluted, with tears springing into his eyes. When Lee, deeply touched, assured the old cavalryman that he was not suffering for food, the soldier showed such disappointment that Lee accepted the basket to be distributed to the sick and wounded in the hospitals. Then the old trooper embraced his "colonel," and was only stopped from kissing him on the cheek by Rob and Dan Lee, Lee's nephew, recently of the Confederate Navy.

The hardest category of visitors the door guard had to contend with was Confederate veterans on their way home. If Lee had seen them all, he would have made no progress in his recuperation. Occasionally, as with the old trooper from the 2nd Cavalry, he would come out after overhearing their conversations. Once two emaciated soldiers appeared, saying they represented sixty more who were too ragged to come themselves. These men owned a good house and farm in the mountains and, hearing the General was going to be indicted for treason, they came to offer him a sanctuary in their hills where the Federals could be stood off forever. It was Lee who shed the tears when he came into the hall, and said, "You would not have your general run away and hide. He must stay and meet his fate."

On another occasion, Custis Lee was so stirred by a veteran of Hood's brigade that he went upstairs after his father. The tattered soldier, with his left arm in a sling, had said he just wanted to shake the General's hand before he started his walk to Texas. While Custis was gone, the soldier sat in the front parlor with Colonel Clement Sullivane, an aide of Custis Lee, and he was talking in a relaxed manner about his wound when they heard "the stately step" of Lee approaching.

They arose as Lee entered and advanced with outstretched hand toward the Texan. While the soldier was shaking Lee's hand, he struggled to speak but choked up. He burst into tears. Suddenly turning away, he covered his face with his arm and hurried from the room. Lee gazed after him without moving, as Colonel Sullivane wrote, "his fine, deep, dark eyes suffused and darkened with emotion." Then, bowing gravely to his son's aide, he returned to the stairs. What particularly impressed Sullivane was the absence of a single, spoken word during the meeting.

The wordless exchange was significant of far more than the emotional communication between the veteran and the General. In a broader sense, it indicated the needlessness of words in the bond between Lee and the Confederate people, as they began turning to him in unspoken allegiance to the personification of their lost nation.

2

Lee could not have been unmindful of the leadership thrust upon him by a people whose sharing of a common cause had led to the sharing of a common plight in a forbidding, uncertain future. Their turn to him for leadership was manifested by the variety of individuals who sought his advice and guidance.

Mostly Southerners were confused over the nature of the adaptation expected of them or possible to them. Though the primary — indeed, primal — concern of almost all of them was to find a means of subsistence, this basic problem of livelihood was involved with their future status as ex-Confederates and the future of the devastated land that had comprised the Confederacy. Their commitments were dependent upon the will of the conqueror, and the first indications of this will offered little assurance of a stabilized position for Southerners within the Union which showed no eagerness to reclaim them.

The flight of professional soldier Magruder to Mexico and of Benjamin, a lawyer, to England, only began an exodus from the conquered states. In addition to the colonies of expatriates formed in Canada and Brazil, individuals scattered in all directions. While Texas had been a Confederate state, countless ex-soldiers were drawn to the prairies, where Federal authority was thinly spread. For every one who went, countless more considered the advisability of seeking new lives in places removed from the power of the United States. And for every one who considered expatriation, countless more simply wondered in numbed apprehension which way to turn.

In Lee's immediate area, despite those who had no wish to live under the United States government, and despite the numbers who regarded the future with apprehension or despair, a heartening proportion of Virginians began — as the shock wore off — to put in crops where the obstacles were not insuperable. The area of nearly total blight (stretches of which were never reclaimed) lay between the Potomac and the Rappahannock. South of the Rappahannock to Richmond, westward toward the Valley, and south and east of Richmond, the devastation fell short of total blight. While many homes, barns and outbuildings were gone, and nearly all fences, the acute need for putting in a crop was for animals and farm implements. Many a horse that had been ridden with Jeb Stuart or pulled a gun carriage was put to the plow — where plows could be found and harness patched together. Borrowings were made from the plantations that survived in spared sections.

This was all at the level of subsistence farming and did not include the large money crops on which the plantation system was based. Planters were forced to make an even more formidable adjustment, for their operations had depended on the labor of slaves. In shifting themselves to subsistence farming, or trying to rework fields on a fair-sized scale, many tried making a "contract" with the colored people by which the hands would receive a share from the sale of the crop. Most of the recently freed slaves at first equated "freedom" with freedom from work, and when Negroes did sign on for a job they had no understanding of keeping a contract. Often the colored people gathered to laugh and jeer at some white man, wasted by four years in the army, struggling with a plough behind a gaunt mule or hoeing away weeds from a small field of corn.

With all their difficulties and the pitiful comparison with their prewar lives, these men — farmers or planters — worked with an uncomplaining resolution at the labor by which their families could be sustained for the present. Whatever the future might hold, they looked first to meeting the immediate needs as they were able to. This segement reflected the attitude Lee began to advocate as soon as he felt strong enough, mentally as well as physically, to take up correspondence.

In a letter to Colonel Walter Taylor, his recent assistant adjutant general, Lee advised him to tell the veterans "they must all set to work, and if they cannot do what they prefer, do what they can." Taylor had written that veterans in the Norfolk area were experiencing difficulty in finding desirable employment, and to that Lee wrote Virginia's future depended upon her sons applying themselves to what was at hand "to sustain and recuperate her." In his recognition of Virginia's need to rebuild in a new vision, Lee constantly urged that the character of her people must become independent of the familiar physical supports which had comprised their antebellum environment.

Lee personally, with his unshakable inner security, needed none of the tangible supports of the old society — its boundlessness, its gracious ease, its outward trappings of prestige. Having started life in the genteel poverty his mother maintained by character and scrimping, he saw no hazards to the spirit in being forced to make do with little. The hazard to the spirit was in looking backward, to repine over all that was gone and to feed on the bitter sense of injustice.

Two practical traits in Lee's character guided his early formation of this attitude. It was imbedded in his consciousness to hold an innate respect for, and adaptation to, constituted authority, and all his life — by predisposition and training — he had dealt in the tangibles of things as they were. His ready acceptance of the consequences of the arbitrament of arms, even though he personally regarded war as a poor way to resolve things, was an aspect of that intuitive wisdom in which he accepted all things he could not change. In that elemental wisdom he always recognized the difference between those things that could be changed and those that must be accepted.

Yet, in the living details of his personal future, total acceptance could not have come easily to Lee, though the consistency of his conciliatory advice and the composed façade could have made it appear so. In those first quiet weeks, of rebuilding (as Rob said) "strength of heart and mind," Lee must have known his own silent struggles. From his formative years in poor gentility, Lee had developed a hardy respect for the value of a dollar, and there was certainly nothing cavalier about his acceptance of the loss of Arlington. Two and one-half years of his own life had gone into rehabilitating that run-down showplace into a prosperous working farm, from whose profits would come part of the $40,000 of his daughters' inheritance. The legal term of "confiscation" could indicate nothing of the struggle of the heart and mind in accepting as a reality he could not change the finality that all this, the birthplace of his wife and children, was wiped out as if it had never existed for them.

No one knew by word of his the nature of the struggle he made in coming to terms with things as they were. However, even before the Confederacy's last forces had surrendered he had drafted a future totally different from the heritage into which he had been born and independent of the only profession he knew. In one of his earliest personal postwar letters, May 7, he wrote Armistead Long: "You young fellows must recollect that I am a very poor scribe. . . . You know how short-crabbed I am. . . . I am looking for some quiet little house in the woods where I can procure shelter, and my daily bread . . . and get Mrs. Lee out of the city as soon as possible."

Later in the month he wrote another friend, "My purpose is to procure some humble home for my family for the present until I can provide some means of providing it with subsistence."

During May, as his health returned and his mind began to project more definitely toward a future for his family, Lee was drawn to farming. Almost all men who had been exposed to the plantation society held a hankering to work the land, and Lee, with his long though abandoned dream of reclaiming Stratford Hall, had enjoyed the farming aspects of rehabilitating Arlington. He showed an interest when, with the return of Custis and the slackening of visitors, Rob and a cousin had gone with Rooney to rework the desolated land of the White House. There, after building a shanty, the three boys had already started putting in a crop. Late in May, Lee went to visit one of his cousins, Thomas Carter — recently 2nd Corps artillery colonel — to consult on the purchase of land for himself.

Carter's plantation, Pampatike, was on a section of the Pamunkey outside the paths of the armies and raiders. Lee saw there about ninety former slaves, who had stayed on the place, and he revealed at once the extent of his break with the past. Disbelieving in any practice that approximated the use of slave labor, he advised his cousin to rid himself of the colored working population. While they could find employment through the Federal agencies, Carter should pay wages to dispossessed white men. When Carter, who considered himself fortunate in not losing his people, protested that he must work with the labor available, Lee said, "I have always observed that wherever you find the Negro, everything is going down around him, and wherever you find the white man, you see everything around him improving."

Those families whose plantations had by chance been spared were disinclined to change, and Lee showed that he felt strongly the people's need to readjust their values to meet new conditions. While visiting his cousin, Lee was invited to dinner at the nearby plantation of Colonel Braxton's widow. Among her guests were Lee's sons, Rooney and Rob, from the White House, and tall, black-haired Tom Rosser, who had served the fateful shadbake at Five Forks. Mrs. Braxton's home, Chericoke, had long been famed for its lavish hospitality, and the widow provided a table that lived up to the reputation. The younger men, recalling all too vividly their years of starvation diet, ate heartily and "did not seem to think there was too much in sight." Lee, evidently recalling the ravaged faces that so recently had greeted him in the trenches, took — Rob said — "a different view of the abundance displayed."

When riding away from the Braxton house, he said to his cousin: "Thomas, there was enough dinner today for twenty people. All this now will have to be changed; you cannot afford it; we shall have to practice economy."

Even Lee would not be able to change the addiction to the table among Southerners who could manage it nor affect their hospitable habit of sharing — with a show of unlimited bounty — whatever they had with guests. (It was possible that Mrs. Braxton had served every particle of food on the place. Lee himself, during the war, had not blinked when Bryan had served to a distinguished guest the one chicken that had been attached to headquarters from Fredericksburg through Gettysburg and after.) But, as he had operated as a soldier, Lee considered every detail in envisioning a new concept for adaptation to the changed conditions of the future.

In that immediate post-Appomattox period, however, Lee exerted his most profound influence as an example of adjustment to defeat. His example was most significant in the area of the attitude to the United States — so recently to all, and still to many, "the enemy."

3

In April and May, the point at issue in the South was the oath of allegiance. In December, 1863, and later in 1864, Lincoln had offered a general amnesty to all Confederates — with the exception of six specified classes — who would sign a simple oath, in which they swore to "support, protect and defend the Constitution of the United States and the Union of states thereunder . . ." and to support the laws enacted during the rebellion for the emancipation of slaves. To Lincoln this amnesty, though it expressed his attitude to the South, was a war measure designed to weaken the will to resistance. Spreading copies of it had been part of the purpose of Dahlgren's raid on Richmond in February, 1864.

After Lincoln's death, the signing of this oath of allegiance as a condition of receiving amnesty remained tacitly in effect. This was not generally understood in the South. Where the oath was understood, there was some resistance to signing it, very strong among soldiers, who felt their paroles should suffice. At the same time other Southerners showed at least a willingness to sign the oath, and some in the excepted categories expressed interest in the procedure of applying for pardon.

Fundamentally, with their government collapsed (and the President in flight until mid-May), the people lacked direction. With United States President Johnson communicating no reassurance, and with the troops of occupation maintaining the atmosphere of war, there was nothing to draw, or lead, them toward acts of reconciliation. Grant, with more understanding of the actual Southern situation than the politicians in Washington and with an uncomplicated desire to complete the restoration of the Union won by arms, recognized the need of leadership from one of their own people. He believed Lee could provide the guidance they would follow.

On May 5 he wrote Major General Halleck: "Although it would meet with opposition in the North to allow Lee the benefit of amnesty, I think it would have the best possible effect toward restoring good feeling and peace in the South to have him come in. All the people except a few political leaders in the South will accept whatever he does as right, and will be guided to a great extent by his example."

On the same day that Grant wrote his letter, while the Army of the Potomac was parading through Richmond on its triumphal way to Washington, General Meade visited his old friend Lee to urge him to set an example for the Southern people by signing the oath. This was shortly before Davis's arrest, when President Johnson — either induced to believe or pretending to believe that Davis was implicated in Lincoln's assassination — had posted reward offers of $100,000 for his capture. Some civil officers had already been arrested, others were threatened with arrest, and Johnson's actions gave Southerners no indication that he had withdrawn from his earlier harsh position of demanding punishment for "treason."

In Virginia he continued Lincoln's expediency of recognizing Francis Pierpont's "restored government" as the legitimate government of the state. This was the state "government" created in 1861 in western Virginia, which the United States recognized for the purpose of observing the legal amenities in partitioning off Virginia's territory to form the new state of West Virginia. While the original purpose of this "restored government" ceased to exist when West Virginia was admitted to the Union (June 20, 1863), the puppet government was maintained in Alexandria under military protection during the war years and had figured in Lincoln's plans for restoration.

For Virginians the oath of allegiance included swearing loyalty to the "restored government," which came into being in Wheeling, West Virginia. Virginia's elected governor, "Extra Billy" Smith — one time brigadier in Jubal Early's division — had been quietly deposed by the military authorities, and Francis Pierpont and his bayonet-supported shadow government officially represented the state which Lee's father had governed.

With this background in the tenuous, undefined problems of "restoration," Lee told General Meade that he could not take a personal position that would serve as an example until the Federal government revealed its policy. Meade made the logical point that the Federal government was waiting for signs of allegiance from the Confederates. The argument grew circular around the question of what the Confederates were swearing allegiance to — beyond the authority of the United States. Lee, as a paroled prisoner, had already accepted this, he said. But, if his further actions were to serve as an example, he must be governed by what he thought best for the Southern people.

On this impasse Lee and Meade parted, and nothing changed during the following weeks except that the last Confederate forces in the field laid down their arms, and Jefferson Davis was captured. During that period also President Johnson discovered a way to vent his spleen on the planter class without including the whole Southern population. On May 29, three days after the surrender of the Confederates in the Trans-Mississippi, the President finally issued a proclamation.

Excluding specified classes of former Confederates, Johnson proclaimed that all persons who participated in "the existing rebellion" would, upon signing the oath of allegiance, be granted "amnesty and pardon, with restoration of all rights of property, except as to slaves." In the exceptions, Johnson raised Lincoln's six classes to fourteen, in one of which he got at the plantation aristocracy by excepting from the amnesty all participants whose property was evaluated at more than $20,000.

Lee came under any one of three of the excepted classes: he had held a rank above colonel in the Confederate armies; he had resigned from the U. S. Army to "evade duty in resisting the rebellion"; he had been "educated by the Government in the Military Academy at West Point."

All persons in the fourteen excepted classes (whose officially uncounted numbers approached the neighborhood of one hundred fifty thousand) could make special application to the President for pardon, "and such clemency will be liberally extended as may be consistent with the facts of the case and the peace and dignity of the United States."

With this declaration of policy from Washington, Lee did not hesitate in reaching a decision to apply for the pardon. Fully aware of the significance of his example, he was equally aware of the purposes he desired his example to achieve. Lee wanted the men of the South to regain the status of full United States citizenship with which they could best work to rebuild their states. As he wrote Walter Taylor about Virginia, the former soldiers must "put themselves in a position to take part in her government, and not be deterred by any obstacles [oaths] in their way. There is much to be done which they only can do."

Before Lee could write his application for a pardon, a complication was created by a demoniacal character named John C. Underwood. A Northern lawyer, Underwood had lived for a time in Virginia before the war until his radical abolitionism made it advisable for him to set up shop elsewhere. During the war Lincoln had appointed him district judge in Pierpont's puppet state government and, when the military occupation was established after Appomattox, this illy educated, venomous man became a Federal District Judge in Virginia. Using the powers of his court with no more sense of law, justice or even rationality than a Caligula, on June 7 Judge Underwood got from a Federal grand jury in occupied Norfolk an indictment against Lee, among others, for treason.

Though Lee had no fear of the trial, the indictment caused him to send his application for pardon to President Johnson indirectly through Grant. Stating to Grant that he had supposed the officers and men of the Army of Northern Virginia were protected by the United States under the terms of surrender, he wrote: "I am ready to meet any charges that may be preferred against me, and do not wish to avoid trial; but, if I am correct as to the protection granted by my parole, and am not to be prosecuted, I desire to comply with the President's proclamation. . . . Therefore [I] enclose the required application, which I request, in that event, may be acted upon."

In contrast to those applications which ran into pages of explanations and self-justifications, Lee's was notable for its brief, simple dignity.

His Excellency Andrew Johnson,
   President of the United States.

Sir: Being excluded from the provisions of the amnesty and pardon contained in the proclamation of the 29th ult., I hereby apply for the benefits and full restoration of all rights and privileges extended to those included in its terms. I graduated at the Military Academy at West Point in June, 1829; resigned from the United States Army, April, 1861; was a general in the Confederate Army, and included in the surrender of the Army of Northern Virginia, April 9, 1865. I have the honor to be, very respectfully,

Your obedient servant,
R. E. Lee

Grant immediately forwarded Lee's application to Johnson with the recommendation that amnesty and pardon be granted. In a long personal letter to Lee, Grant also wrote that he would ask that Underwood "be ordered to quash all indictments found against paroled prisoners of war, and to desist from the further prosecution of them."

Grant did not then possess the power that would accrue to him. Johnson ignored his recommendations. He neither acknowledged Lee's application for pardon nor ordered Judge Underwood to quash his indictment against Lee.

News of Lee's indictment immediately brought from Northern lawyers offers of their services in his defense. United States Senator Reverdy Johnson, a staunch Unionist from Maryland, said, "In saving him I would be saving the honor of my country." However, the case was never brought to trial.

Lee seemed to think the indictment would remain in the nature of a threat, similar to other threatening measures taken against other ex-Confederates, and he tried not to let it nag at him while he waited with his awesome patience for events to "take their course." Yet, for the practicalities of his status there was no escaping the reality that his application for a pardon resulted in leaving him personally in a nether world of noncitizenship, in which he was regarded as an apostate by some of his former Confederate associates.

4

Johnson's incomprehensible attitude in ignoring Lee's application was perhaps the most significant among several factors which prevented Lee's example from exerting as wide an influence among the classes excluded from the amnesty as was hoped for. Only sixteen thousand, scarcely 10 per cent, applied for personal pardons. Many who showed a tentative willingness to apply were repelled by the sordidness of the "pardon brokers" who set up shop in Washington to peddle influence for granting citizenship in the restored Union. Then, unestimated numbers were affected by the word-of-mouth news of the brutal treatment dealt out to Jefferson Davis, imprisoned at Fort Monroe. With handcuffs and leg irons, he was confined in a dank, stone-walled casemate, in which a light burned constantly and he was kept under a twenty-four-hour surveillance by armed guards. From the North came incessant demands for his trial for treason, many urging the death penalty for a "traitor."

To an undetermined extent, an amalgam of such factors undermined Lee's example for restoring "the good feeling and peace in the South," which Grant had hoped would follow Lee's "coming in." Also to an undetermined extent, these factors strengthened the influence of the segment of irreconcilables in the one hundred thirty thousand who never applied for pardon. Those die-hard Rebels felt that the application for a pardon admitted having done a wrong and cursed Lee for his act. Tempestuous Bob Toombs, at his home in Washington, Georgia, spoke for this group when he bellowed at a Northern questioner, "Pardon for what? I haven't pardoned youall yet."

However, the proscribed who refused to seek pardons (including Jefferson Davis) did not seriously affect the willingness of the majority of Southerners to submit to the authority of the United States. Where no seeking of pardon was necessary, the average ex-Confederate began to demonstrate his willingness to submit by signing the oath of allegiance. Following Lee's application for pardon — and before it became gradually known that his application was never to be acknowledged — there was an immediate general movement toward signing the oath.

By this act — to many mostly symbolic — the ex-Confederates committed themselves to resume the responsibilities and duties of citizenship in a common union of states. With whatever reservations individuals may have felt, they at least went on record as placing themselves under the authority of the Union in good faith in the Federal government's protection and restoration of their civil rights.

In their own commitments, the people seemed not to appraise the drift from north of the Potomac, as indicated by the pronounced lack of rejoicing which greeted Lee's application and the mass signings of the oath. Lee's fellow Virginians, in fact, expressed surprise at the published imputations of their lack of good faith in swearing allegiance. During the summer, citizens' meetings were held in various localities to protest against the questioning of their sworn loyalty, and a meeting in Richmond passed a resolution denouncing "the persistent and wicked efforts of a portion of the press and people of the Northern states to brand the people of the South with perfidy and insincerity . . . by questioning their fidelity and truth in the oaths of allegiance they have taken."

Despite resentments at misrepresentations in the Northern press, during the summer of 1865 the people expected their signing of the oath to be followed as a matter of course by the restoration of their position in the Union. In this understanding, as the physical and moral shock began to recede, the prevailing attitude around Lee was of hopefulness.

By the end of June, Lee, having done all he could at that time to promote reconciliation, was sufficiently recovered in body and mind to turn to a temporary solution for the affairs of his own family. The General had found his "quiet, little abode in the woods."

5

The sanctuary Lee accepted for his family was provided by Mrs. Elizabeth Randolph Preston Cocke, a stately widow of great elegance, whose plantation, Oakland, about fifty miles west of Richmond in Cumberland County, was among the showplaces on the south side of the James River. Whether or not Lee and Mrs. Cocke were aware of it, they were — as direct descendants of Robert (King) Carter — distantly related. Mrs. Cocke's great-grandmother, Elizabeth Burwell, whose brother Carter Burwell had owned Carter's Grove on the James, had been first cousin of Lee's grandfather Charles Carter of Shirley. It is also unknown to what extent they were acquainted, though Lee would certainly have known she was the granddaughter of Edmund Randolph. Before Randolph was Attorney General in Washington's Cabinet, he was the young governor with whom Lee's father had been allied when Randolph swung the balance of power to ratify the Constitution in the 1788 Virginia Convention. Mrs. Cocke, in passing through Richmond, had called on the Lees and first extended her invitation in person.

She offered them a small house, then unoccupied, on grounds adjoining the Oakland estate. After her visit Mrs. Cocke wrote them so graciously that Lee was, Rob said, "induced . . . to accept the invitation." There were other inducements, such as the seclusion of the vacant house, called Derwent, and its proximity to the James River and Kanawha Canal, which would spare Mrs. Lee the discomfort of stage travel. But there must have been a quality in Mrs. Cocke herself that gave Lee the assurance of being provided with protected privacy.

Three of Mrs. Cocke's four sons had served in Lee's army, and the oldest, William, had been left at Gettysburg. A lieutenant in the 18th Virginia, he was among those who went up the hill with Pickett and was never seen again. A graduate of the University of Virginia, of a quiet and scholarly nature, William Cocke had managed his mother's estate since the death of his father in 1855. While Mrs. Cocke had hoped against falling hope for news that her son would be listed among the captured wounded at

Gettysburg, her hair turned white before she resigned herself, after six months, to the reality that his body lay in an unmarked grave.

According to the Richmond *Daily Times* of Thursday, June 29, 1865, "General Lee . . . and his family left Richmond yesterday afternoon on the packet boat." Mrs. Lee, Agnes and Mildred took the night ride with the General on the canal. Mary was off visiting and Custis had ridden ahead. They left the packet boat shortly after sunrise the next morning, and were met by Custis and Mrs. Cocke's son, Captain Edmund Cocke. The party drove south from the river through the village of Cartersville to the overpowering approach to Oakland. Though the large and roomy house held none of the classic grandeur of Shirley, Stratford and Arlington, its eighteen-acre lawn was shaded by a park of trees dominated by fifty giant primeval oaks. Mrs. Cocke had breakfast waiting for them. Though most of her field hands had left and the house people were soon to go, the family butler still reigned in the dining room.

The Lees remained in the main house for a week while furniture was being moved into the small house they were to occupy. Derwent was on property, in Powhatan County, acquired by Mrs. Cocke's son Thomas before the war. Called a "cottage," Derwent was actually a two-story-and-basement frame house of four rooms, two on each floor, with a dining room in the basement. As Mrs. Lee, in her letters about Derwent, never referred to the basement dining room, presumably this was not used because of her difficulty in negotiating stairs. The low-ceilinged rooms opening off either side of a center hall were plain, though the room to the left, where the General and Mrs. Lee established the family room, was agreeable and of fair size (eighteen and a half feet by twenty-four). Windows to the north and south gave cross ventilation, and on one side of a large fireplace a cupboard (pent) closet, with bottom wooden doors and top glass doors, gave Lee a place for his papers, which he began to arrange in order.

Mrs. Lee gave her impressions of Derwent in a letter she wrote a friend in New York. "You would suppose from the title of this retreat that we are in sight of cool lakes and romantic scenery but it is a little retired place with a straight up house and the only beauty it possesses is a fine grove of oaks which surrounds it. Thro' the kindness of a friend who has given us the use of it, it has been rendered habitable, but all the outbuildings are dilapidated and the garden is a mass of weeds. As we shall probably not remain here longer than the season we shall not attempt to cultivate it and the kindness of our neighbors supplies us with vegetables, meat and ice, so that we want for nothing. Our future will be guided by circumstances. I dare not look into it, all seems so dark now, that we are almost tempted to think God has forsaken us. Yet we have many blessings."

Obviously Lee looked at once upon the "many blessings." As soon as he was away from the Franklin Street prison house and into the country, his spirits and energies took an immediate rise. During the two and one-half months from his arrival in Richmond to his settling at Derwent, Lee had completed not only the recuperation of mind, body and heart, but the period of serving passively as an example of reconciliation. He was ready for the activity of a new life in whatever future Providence would reveal to him.

On a rested Traveler he enjoyed riding along the shady roads, visiting his brother Carter and appraising the countryside — which he found "poor." Between his excursions, Lee began the correspondence which developed the reasoned purposeful attitudes (on which he had been acting instinctively) for the South's relations with the Federal government. From the Derwent cottage, he wrote his statements of position — as to naval captain Tatnall, Mr. Keiley, Governor Letcher and Commodore Maury — and a clear statement of his own feelings in a July 29 letter to Rooney.

"As to the [treason] indictments, I hope you at least may not be prosecuted. I see no more reason for it than for *all* who ever engaged in the war. I think however we may expect procrastination in measures of relief, and denunciatory threats . . . we must be patient and let them take their course. As soon as I can ascertain their intention towards me, if not prevented, I shall endeavor to procure some humble but quiet abode for your mother and sisters, where I hope they can be happy. As I before said, I want to get in some grass country, where the natural product of the land will do much for my subsistence."

He also recaptured his natural light vein, as reflected in a letter to Mrs. Caroline Benson, one of the countless ladies who wrote asking for a lock of his hair. Since she had known him twenty years before, he enclosed "the last photograph of the head from which it was cut," and told her she should have taken the lock "twenty years ago."

Most importantly, he found an outlet for his energies in a project which seemed to provide an objective for his future. This was a project that could be incorporated within his general goal of a secluded farm — a goal which, though diffused by time into the quality of a dream, he never relinquished. The new project was to write a history of the campaigns in Virginia.

While Lee never willingly talked of the war, evidently the memories had been awakened on those solitary rides across country similar to the ground his disintegrating army had stumbled over in its last retreat. In those last days of his army the one factor he expressed concern about was that history know the numbers against which his men had contended. At Derwent, one of the first letters he wrote about his planned campaign history was to Walter Taylor, on July 31.

"My dear Colonel: I am desirous that the loving devotion of the Army of Northern Virginia shall be correctly transmitted to posterity. This is the only tribute that can be paid to the worth of the officers and men. I am anxious to collect the necessary data for the history of the campaigns . . . I am particularly anxious that its actual strength in the different battles it has fought be correctly stated."

Lee sent copies of this letter (a "circular letter," he called it), with minor changes, to many of his former subordinates. In his letter to Wade Hampton, Lee wrote: "If you had been there with all our cavalry, the result at Five Forks would have been different. But how long the contest would have been prolonged, it is difficult to say. It is over, and though the present is depressing and disheartening, I trust the future may prove brighter. We must at least hope so, and each one can do his part to make it so."

Before Lee's first recorded commitment to his planned history, he apparently had been stimulated by a suggestion that he write of the war and by the interest of a publisher, C. B. Richardson, of the University Publishing Company, in New York. A July 28 letter from Richardson indicates that he had visited Lee in person earlier in the summer. Also sometime during July, Lee was given a letter which had been brought by hand from Canada, where it had been written on July 11 by Beverley Tucker.

Tucker belonged to the Colonial family that had been long distinguished for its learning and humanitarian enlightenment; one of his kinsmen had offered a plan to Virginia's General Assembly for the emancipation of slaves as early as 1796. Beverley Tucker performed valuable services as a Confederate agent during the war and, in July, was among the refugees in the Confederate colony in Canada. His words were colored by the bitterness whose expression Lee sought to silence, but, despite its tone, the letter appealed to Lee's susceptibility to calls to duty.

"It is true, you have filled to overflowing, the measure of a proud and enduring fame and a whole people's gratitude is your proud reward. But I conceive that God has in reserve for you a yet more noble and not less patriotic *role*. He has given you qualities moral and intellectual to fulfill a higher destiny. Next to the deliverance of a noble people from the thraldom of a wicked foe, and the establishment of the independence of our country, which through no fault of yours or your gallant armies you failed to accomplish, the most grateful and useful duty is to oppose your high character for truth, honor, and true Christian piety, to the thousand mendacious and hireling historians which will spring up in Yankeedom, and give to the world and posterity, a faithful history of the causes of the late terrible conflict, and the manner in which the war was conducted on either side."

The duty that Lee responded to was the vindication of his soldiers. "I shall write this history," Lee wrote one of his generals, because ". . . I want that the world shall know what my poor boys, with their small numbers and scant resources, succeeded in accomplishing."

In Lee's "circular letter" to his generals, the specific information he requested varied according to the general he was writing, but all the letters described the blank that existed from the winter operations of 1864-1865 to Appomattox: ". . . No report of the campaign in '64, and of the operations of the winter of 1864-65 to the 1st April '65, has been written; and the Corps and Division reports for that period, which had been sent to Hd. Qrs. before the abandonment of the lines before Petersburg, with all the records, returns, maps, plans, etc., were destroyed the day before the army reached Appomattox C.H. My letter books, public and confidential, were also destroyed; and the regular reports and returns transmitted to the Adjt. Genl. at Richmond, have been burned or lost."

As soon as the news of his project spread, he was encouraged by letters from all over the South ("that our fallen country's history be not left to . . . the lying tongues of Yankee Scribblers") and at least one from the North. The Honorable William B. Reed, of Philadelphia, was a prominent lawyer and diplomat who had suffered loss of esteem because of his strong opposition to the war, though, as he wrote Lee, he was a Northerner "by birth, education and association," and had never seen the South. The purpose of his letter was also to prevent the South's history's being presented by its enemies.

"I implore you, not so much for your own sake, as for the sake of your Southern country, and of us in the North who felt with you and for you — not to neglect the history of the war. By military reverses and the fall of the government you served, you have been prevented from making any reports of its closing scenes. But don't let the record fail. The prejudice and dark injustice which now obscures the public mind in this region will break before very long — but if New England is to have control of your history — alas! for truth and for you. It should be done while every thing is fresh."

Other publishers also approached Lee. Though he had signed no contract with Richardson on his campaign history, Richardson was active in helping him gather materials and also used a shrewd stroke in signing Lee to write a short biography of his father to serve as an introduction to a new edition of Light Horse Harry Lee's *Memoirs*. Richardson wrote that he wished to publish the new edition of the *Memoirs* simultaneously and "in uniform style" with Lee's campaign history. He believed that "in this connection it would meet with great success." For each of the books Lee would receive royalties of 10 per cent of the retail price.

In agreeing to write the introduction for the out-of-print *Memoirs*, Lee was probably motivated by the opportunity to vindicate his father and to bring his book back into circulation. He wrote his brother Carter, "All the profits on our father's memoirs you can take." In the same letter, August 18, he wrote, "I am fully alive to the propriety of making both works if possible a source of profit. For I have to labor for my living and I am ashamed to do nothing that will give me honest support."

6

At the time Lee wrote his brother, he had recently received an offer that would provide him with "honest support," and he was pondering its acceptance when he wrote Carter. The offer Lee had received was of the presidency of Washington College, a small provincial institution among the hills of Rockbridge County at the southern end of the Shenandoah Valley. When he eventually accepted this offer, his campaign history became an unadmitted casualty. He never began it and never abandoned it.

Although various reasons have been offered to explain why Lee did not write his history, on which he continued to collect material until the end of his life, his acceptance of the duties of a college president would itself offer almost sufficient explanation. Without any staff to help with the detested paperwork, he conducted a heavy correspondence — both as a college president and as the people's leader — along with the routine duties that filled his days and drained his declining energies. He was often ill. However, there was another fundamental element in addition to the lack of hours when his energies were fresh. Writing, after all, was paperwork, and Lee, in brief, disliked it.

Had he possessed an established income to support his family in his retirement, with uninterrupted time to work on his history, his sense of duty might have kept him plugging away at it. The result, as indicated by the flatness of the introduction he wrote for his father's *Memoirs*, would not have been happy and would have contributed little, if anything, to the understanding of the nature of the war. His abhorrence of controversy, with his fear of the use that could be made of words, would have kept him free from the very issues which Confederates wanted clarified. Except for generalized principles, he would not have met their desires for the presentation of the South's viewpoint. Nor, because of the controversial aspects involving Southern personalities and his own generals, would Lee have significantly illuminated his own campaigns.

Lee was two different people in his writings, one in intimate letters and another in words designed for the public eye. In the spontaneously written letters he wanted to write, as to his family and friends, Lee always reflected his own precise cast of mind, his turns of humor and the flavor of his personality. The letters were full of details on the minutiae of life, the relationships of people, descriptions of his surroundings and his reactions to them, and unguarded revelations of his feelings. Clear, informal, warm and sometimes very moving, Lee's personal letters perfectly mirrored the man.

In writing anything that might be published, he immediately became the "official Lee," and the man vanished behind a wall of words of bloodless formality. Though his actions made him a public figure, in self-expression Lee typified the old-line country gentlemen who instinctively guarded his privacy as a person. On a few occasions during the war when his emotions were aroused, as over the suffering of his men, his feelings broke through in official correspondence and he wrote with powerful force, even passion. But when he wrote contemplatively at leisure, his writing was so depersonalized that his battle reports might have been written by some time-removed recorder, remote from the action and unfamiliar with the ground and the participants. His longest reports and reports on the most controversial battles, as Gettysburg, written in impersonal reserve (never using the pronoun "I"), were restricted to generalities and aloofly detached from details, especially those of his generals' performances.

In some amalgam of "Christian forbearance," of natural "charity" of the mind, of the almost godlike acceptance of the limitations of mortals, Lee could not bring himself to expose in historic records the behavior of individuals that determined the course of battles. Behind each act of failure in performance — one general failed to attack and another lost control of his troops in action, one suffered loss of his own morale and another suffered paralysis of will — lay the deeper flaw in the character. Lee, understanding the man within the general, could not condemn in indelible records a patriot soldier who might have given all he had for the Cause, and whose "all" was not enough to help.

For him to understand was not to condone. He removed failures from his army, even as devoted and self-sacrificing a Confederate as Lieutenant General Richard Ewell. But he could not publicly judge them. On the contrary, he showed a strong tendency to avoid casting any reproach in written records.

Writing about the events he had directed was not a duty Lee was qualified to meet. His planned history served to give a sense of purpose to his energies in the restless period after his health returned, and perhaps stimulated some of his generals to prepare records which became useful to historians — as particularly the work done by Walter Taylor and Jubal Early in assembling data on the numbers present in the different campaigns of the army. But Lee was spared the fruitless drudgery of trying to write his history by discovering the true duty he was capable of fulfilling.

Essentially a man of action, Lee had made the history, and no words of his could (as Southerners hoped) have changed the interpretations that were to be made of it. As a man of action, Lee did possess the qualifications — far more than he realized — to provide a direction to the future of the South by the education of her sons.

When the offer came from Washington College, Lee's initial interest in his history had already pointed his mind toward a practical activity by which he could fulfill his duty of serving for the good of the South. It was not so much that the college presidency superseded his history as that the position offered him an active role in which he could produce more immediate and more definite results for the benefit of the Southern people. As he leaned toward seclusion, his campaign history might have served his personal preferences better except for the item of income. The $1500 yearly salary would remove the growing guilt about his failure to earn "an honorable support," as Mrs. Lee referred to her husband's anxiety on this subject.

Without an established income, his history would never have seemed a "job" to him. Lee had a little money coming due from investments that had survived the collapse of Confederate securities but, as this would not approximate enough for the support of his family, it in no way relieved him of his lifelong goad to the independence given by self-support. Of course, the $1500 income could not in itself have been a determining factor. He could have earned considerably more than that and, had he let it be known that his services as an educator were available, have obtained a position at a loftier seat of learning than the bankrupt little college in Lexington. It happened that the job he needed for his own self-esteem coincided with the job that needed him — according to the revelations of Providence.

That Lee regarded the specific offer from Washington College as a revelation of God's will was made clear by the Episcopal rector (later Bishop) J. P. B. Wilmer. While Lee was discussing the offer with his clerical friend, Mr. Wilmer expressed regret that Lee would consider such a humble position. He told Lee that "the institution was one of local interest and comparatively unknown to our people. I named others more conspicuous that would welcome him with ardor as their head." Then, Mr. Wilmer recorded, "I soon discovered that his mind towered above such earthly distinctions; that, in his mind, the *cause* gave dignity to the institution . . . that this door and not another was opened to him by Providence."

Lee's only concern was "of his competency to fulfill his trust and thus to make his few remaining years a comfort and blessing to his suffering country."

Immediately rising to the plane of Lee's thoughts, the clergyman congratulated him on the inclination of his heart and on being spared "to give to the world this august testimony to the importance of Christian education."

Never asking once if Washington College was important enough for him, Lee asked only assurance that he was qualified for the duty as he saw it. Mr. Wilmer's fervent assurances were joined by those of ex-Governor Letcher and Lee's recent chief of reserve artillery, the Reverend William Pendleton — then back at his small Episcopal church down the hill from the college in Lexington. It took Lee only a little more than two weeks to reach the decision that Washington College provided his one, true way to the future. He had not sought the way to serve; he had waited for the way to be revealed — and, as he believed, it had.

## 7

Lee being what he was, it was not so strange that he accepted the offer as that it was ever made. The temerity, the sheer presumption, of the impoverished provincials on the board asking the greatest figure in their land to serve their run-down, local institution could have been inspired only by the boldness of desperation. There was, however, literally a quality of inspiration in their recognition of the opportunity their college offered the revered Lee to serve his state and provide an example to his "admiring countrymen." The scope of this vision was eloquently expressed in a letter by Judge Brockenbrough, rector of the college, after his first interview with Lee.

The trustees of Washington College had decided in an August 4 board meeting to tender Lee the offer; and traveling funds, along with a suit of clothes, were borrowed to dispatch Judge John W. Brockenbrough on his mission to Derwent. Nothing is known of what passed between the General and the rector, though most likely Judge Brockenbrough let it be known that a new member of the board — a Washington College graduate who had studied law in the judge's private law school in Lexington — would be twenty-nine-year-old William Poague, recently colonel commanding an artillery battalion in A. P. Hill's corps.

On his way home on a canal packet, Judge Brockenbrough felt that he had not presented his case persuasively to Lee. On the boat, on the night of August 10, he wrote to Lee the appeal which — defining a concrete goal for Lee's then generalized purpose — probably provided the arguments that persuaded Lee to regard the college presidency as the path revealed by Providence.

"The desire I feel for the success of my mission is so absorbing that I trust you will pardon me for appearing somewhat importunate. It would be uncandid to deny that the advancement of the interest of our venerable college was the primary consideration with the Board of Trustees in inducing them to solicit your acceptance of its Presidency, yet it is but an act of simple justice to them to declare that your reputation is very dear to each of them and had they supposed that it could be imperiled by your acceptance of the position tendered to you, the tender never would have been made. But it is precisely because we feel assured that in discharging the comparatively humble functions of President of our College new luster would be added to your fame, and your character would be presented in a new and more attractive light to your admiring countrymen that we presume to urge the acceptance of the office upon you with an importunity that else might seem indelicate. You would thereby evince a mind superior to despair and by this exhibition of moderation and goodness establish new claims to the admiration and affection of your countrymen. To make yourself useful to the State, to dedicate your fine scientific attainments to the service of its youth, to guide that youth in the paths of virtue, knowledge, and religion, not more by precept than your great example — these, my dear General, are objects worthy of your ambition, and we desire to present to you the means of their accomplishment.

"The educational interests of Virginia, as of all her Southern Sisters, have suffered dreadfully by the war. The University [of Virginia], Va. Mil. Institute, Hampden Sidney, and William and Mary Colleges are all crushed and cannot be resuscitated, we fear, for years to come. Washington College alone possesses an independent endowment and you have only to stretch forth your powerful arm to rescue it, too, from impending destruction. You alone can fill its halls, by attracting to them not the youth of Virginia alone, but of all the Southern and some even of the Northern States. That all these desirable results would follow your acceptance of this trust, your friends feel the fullest assurance, though your genuine and unaffected modesty may have suggested doubt of their fulfillment to your own mind. We pray that the reflection you graciously promised to bestow upon the subject may lead you to the same conclusion."

Judge Brockenbrough's reference to "private endowment" gave Lee no illusions about the financial plight of the institution. Though Lee had no direct associations with Washington College, he knew the Valley town of Lexington — where the family silver from Arlington had been sent for safekeeping — and he held many associations with it from the army. Lee's son Rob had first served in the Rockbridge Artillery Battery, which was originally recruited entirely from Rockbridge County, with the Reverend Pendleton as its first captain and later Poague, before he advanced to battalion command. Stonewall Jackson, whose first wife was the daughter of the president of Washington College, had taught at the adjoining institution of V.M.I., which provided Lee with so many of his officers. Jackson was buried in a hillside cemetery, near the grave of Pendleton's son, "Sandie," former 2nd Corps chief of staff and a Washington College graduate. Lee had certainly heard enough indirectly to have some familiarity with Washington College.

Its origins lay in the middle of the eighteenth century, when a number of "classical academies" were established by the sober-minded Scotch-Irish Presbyterians who largely settled the Valley. Among them was Augusta Academy, twenty miles from Lexington, which Washington College claimed as its ancestor. After patriotically changing its name to Liberty Hall in 1776, in 1780 this school was moved near Lexington, on a ridge to the west of the town, and in 1782 the institution was formally incorporated by the Virginia General Assembly as Liberty Hall Academy and empowered to grant degrees. Its charter made it independent and self-perpetuating. At previous times the school had been under the care of the Presbyterian Church and, though individual Presbyterians continued to exert influence, after the charter there was not (as Lee was assured) any official church affiliation.

Hilly Rockbridge County was neither populous nor rich, and this school had struggled for existence until nearly the turn of the century. The citizens of the county were people of individual substance, characterized by a deep self-assurance of the dignity of mortals, and once before the trustees of the institution had aimed for help from the highest source possible in their state, George Washington.

After Washington had retired after his second term as President of the United States, Virginia's General Assembly voted him one hundred shares of stock in the James River Company. When it was learned that Washington planned to give his stock to some worthy cause, representatives of Liberty Hall waited upon the great and austere personage to present their school as the worthiest cause. Washington gave Liberty Hall his stock, the largest gift until that time ever bestowed upon a private educational institution in America. Not unnaturally, the name was changed to Washington Academy and, in 1813, it became Washington College when the institution was moved to Lexington on the site it continues to occupy.

As Washington College, its small student body was drawn almost entirely from Rockbridge County, or the adjoining area, and of the ninety-five students enrolled in 1860, only one came from outside the state. When war came, most of the students immediately enlisted in volunteer units. An infantry company, known as the Liberty Hall Volunteers, served in Jackson's Stonewall Brigade, and students volunteered in the Rockbridge Battery. With the students also departed the college president, Dr.

George Junkin, a Northerner who believed in slavery (he owned slaves) but hated secession. Jackson's former father-in-law took off in a huff, leaving a clergyman son who enlisted in the Confederate Army and an agitated daughter. Margaret Junkin, a poet and a sensitive observer of the times, was married to Colonel J. L. T. Preston, a Latin professor at V.M.I. and a brother of Lee's Derwent hostess, Mrs. Cocke. When war came, Colonel Preston went off on Jackson's staff.

During the war, the students dwindled away until in the last year there were none except in the preparatory department then attached to the college. Without a president, the faculty of four professors and one tutor kept the institution going, though by 1865 the buildings were little more than shells. In June, 1864, the war came to Lexington.

The twenty-odd-thousand raiding force under General David Hunter occupied the town, and Hunter decided to burn V.M.I. because treason was taught there and for the military reason that, as staff-officer D. H. Strother said, "the professors and cadets had taken the field against government troops as an organized corps." At two o'clock in the afternoon, all the Institute's buildings were put to the torch, including the homes from which professors' wives were evicted. Hunter, Colonel Strother recalled, "seemed to enjoy this scene and turning to me expressed his great satisfaction at having me with him."

Moving away from the fire, Strother reported, "the plunderers came running . . . their arms full of spoils." They brought such objects as "fine mathematical instruments," a human skeleton, "beautifully illustrated volumes of natural history," along with useless articles such as the high-topped hats of cadet officers. Others of Hunter's soldiers got caught up in the spirit and began sacking the buildings at adjoining Washington College. The library and laboratory were quickly stripped, the rioters destroying the books and equipment not carted off. The helplessly watching trustees, seeing the smoke rising from V.M.I., kept a discreet silence about the Liberty Hall Volunteers in the Stonewall Brigade. When Hunter moved on toward Lynchburg (from which he fled west into the mountains at Ewell's approach), the buildings were left in a sad state.

By 1865, lack of money and labor for repairs and upkeep made some of the buildings unfit for occupancy. During the summer, before Lee's acceptance of the presidency, trustees had borrowed money on their private credit for the repair of buildings and replacement of equipment, the payment of salaries and interest on the college's debts. As no reason exists to suspect Judge Brockenbrough of glossing over this forbidding picture, Lee was evidently aware of the general facts if not of the details. The college's poverty and physical dilapidation would never have affected Lee, except perhaps to stimulate an urge to help. He needed only to be assured of his own qualifications. Once he felt that assurance, he wrote his acceptance on August 24, two weeks after Judge Brockenbrough wrote him.

Gentlemen —

I have delayed for some days replying to your letter of the 5th inst., informing me of my election by the Board of Trustees to the Presidency of Washington College, from a desire to give the subject due consideration. Fully impressed with the responsibilities of the office, I have feared that I should be unable to discharge its duties to the satisfaction of the Trustees or to the benefit of the country. The proper education of youth requires not only great ability, but, I fear, more strength than I now possess, for I do not feel able to undergo the labour of conducting classes in regular courses of instruction. I could not, therefore, undertake more than the general administration and supervision of the institution. There is another subject which has caused me serious reflection, and is, I think, worthy of the consideration of the Board. Being excluded from the terms of amnesty in the proclamation of the President of the U.S. on the 29th day of May last, and an object of censure to a portion of the country, I have thought it probable that my occupation of the position of President might draw upon the College a feeling of hostility, and I should, therefore, cause injury to an institution which it would be my highest desire to advance. I think it the duty of every citizen to do all in his power to aid in the restoration of peace and harmony, and in no way to oppose the policy of the State or General Governments directed to that object. It is particularly incumbent on those charged with the instruction of the young to set them an example of submission to authority, and I could not consent to be the cause of animadversion upon the College.

Should you, however, take a different view, and think that my services in the position tendered me by the Board will be advantageous to the College and country, I will yield to your judgment and accept. Otherwise I must most respectfully decline the office.

Begging you to express to the Trustees of the College my heartfelt gratitude for the honour conferred upon me, and requesting you to accept my cordial thanks for the kind manner in which you have communicated its decision, I am, gentlemen, with great respect

Your most obedient servant,
R. E. Lee

About three weeks later, on September 15, he started alone, on Traveler, along the road to Lexington. The post-Appomattox hiatus had come to an end. At the age of fifty-eight, he was beginning a new life in a strange town.

## CHAPTER XXV

## "This Too Shall Pass"

LEE made his solitary journey "in four days' easy rides," as he wrote his wife. With a cavalryman's regularity, he rode out early in the morning and on the first two days reached his halting place at one, before the heat became unpleasant. On the third day he climbed the mountains and, in the cooler air, rode until three o'clock, when he reached the summit of the Blue Ridge. Below him opened the panorama of the Shenandoah Valley.

Narrower and hillier at the southern end, without the rolling, contoured fields of the more fertile sections, the Valley swept toward the Alleghenies in the tranquil majesty of nature to which Lee always responded. The next morning, September 18, he rode down the mountain, and around one o'clock reached the town across the fabled Valley Pike — famous as a thoroughfare to the West before it became associated with Jackson's marches.

In the undulating countryside, Lexington's main street ran along a low rise. Its red-brick post-Revolutionary buildings were mostly flush to the street, except the county court house. This was set back in a lawn, where the grass was wilting near the end of the long summer. Like any farmer coming to town, the aging man on the gray horse rode down the center of the dusty street, on his way to the hotel. His eyes were shaded by the wide brim of his slouch hat, weather-stained to brown, and he was wearing either white linen or a military gray coat from which all Confederate insignia had been removed. As the rider drew up at the inn, Professor White happened to pass. Greek professor at the college, James J. White had recently served as captain in the Army of Northern Virginia, and he hurried toward the rider.

Professor White — or Captain White, as Lee always addressed him — told Lee he was expected at the home of Captain White's father-in-law, Colonel S. McD. Reid, the oldest member of the college's board of trustees. Before Lee could turn his horse about, the loungers on the drowsy street came to life with yells that must have sent shivers down Lee's spine. The veterans came converging on him from all directions.

It was precisely the sort of demonstration Lee wanted to avoid, and he was to encounter them the rest of his life.

In Lexington Mrs. Margaret Junkin Preston, the former college president's daughter, described the deeper emotion the people felt for Lee after the war. "The affection of the people seemed more than ever a consecrated one." During the war soldiers and civilians had shown their veneration and trust, "but after defeat came, all this feeling was intensified by the added one of sympathy. Nowhere could he move abroad without being greeted with such demonstrations of love and interest as always touched his generous . . . heart."

When Lee first arrived in Lexington, the offer of affection was about all the people had for him. To bring in a little cash the college president's house had been rented, and Dr. R. L. Madison was in no hurry to move out. Carpenters were banging away in their repair work on the college buildings, "beautifully located" (Lee wrote Mrs. Lee) on an open rise paralleling Main Street west of the built-up part of town. Since the college would not be ready to receive students until October, after a few days Lee rode the eleven miles to Rockbridge Baths to "take the waters" in the charming, restful atmosphere of the springs. There he could avoid the crowds of the town, relieve Colonel Reid's family of the burden of hospitality and, independent of hosts, find his own needed privacy.

Lee was also suffering from what he called rheumatic pains, but which were probably caused by his heart condition. The relatively rapid aging of the previous two years, caused by the strain of the war on his heart, became accelerated by the prolonged stress of Reconstruction. Physically his deterioration began to progress far out of proportion to his years. Though the outward symptoms were not marked from day to day, four years after his arrival in Lexington, Lee, white bearded and white haired, looked an old, old man. During his stay at the Baths, however, he gave no indication of realizing the permanent seriousness of his condition and, enjoying old acquaintances, prepared himself for the routines of a new job.

2

On October 2, Lee went to work after a ceremony which was held to brief informality in accordance with his wishes. The graciously handsome red-brick buildings faced east along the rise, overlooking a field then under cultivation. In the building (now Payne Hall) north of the main building, an office on the second floor had been furnished by the ladies of the college — "very nicely," Lee wrote — with curtains up and a new carpet from Baltimore. From the day Lee began his duties in this office, promptly at eight o'clock six mornings a week, he dispelled any notion that some might have held that he was to serve as a "figurehead."

One of the professors, Edward S. Joynes, wrote: "He had from the beginning of his presidency a distinct policy and plan which he had fully conceived and to which he steadily adhered, so that all his particular measures of progress were but consistent steps in its development. His object was nothing less than to establish and perfect an institution which should meet the highest needs of education in every department. At once, and without waiting for the means to be provided in advance, he proceeded to develop this object."

Though office work was not to his taste, Lee was a natural executive, with broad experience in an army where infinite attention to detail was demanded, and with specific experience at West Point in supervising an educational institution. Beneath the talents his conviction — that Providence had shown his duty to be the training of young men for the South's future — was supported by the lifelong compulsion to make an accomplishment out of every task to which he set himself. By the end of the month, when he wrote Rooney that he had accepted the presidency in the hopes that he might "be of some service to the country and the rising generation," he repeated his preference for "a more quiet life and more retired abode than Lexington," and said, "If I find I can accomplish no good here, I will endeavor to pursue the course to which my inclinations point."

The results of his efforts showed almost immediately, and it was soon apparent that his accomplishments would be immeasurable. When college opened, about fifty students were in residence, and they kept coming. Soon their number reached one hundred, past the peak of prewar enrollment. Then this was doubled and doubled again, until more than four hundred students were registered by 1868. Where all except one student had come from Virginia in 1860, 68 per cent came from outside the state in 1868. These represented not only all the states that had comprised the Confederacy, but New York, New Jersey, Massachusetts, Ohio, Illinois, California, the District of Columbia, and one from Mexico. The Prussian Consul at New Orleans sent his two sons in 1867.

They all wanted to come where Lee was, though they did not know the name of the college. Letters came to "General Lee's College," "Lexington College," "Virginia University" and "Washington Institute." He was addressed "His Excellency," "Professor Lee," "Mr. Lee," "Principal," along with and most often "General Lee." Some students brought letters of social introduction to the Lees.

The student body soon overflowed the dormitories and boys were boarded in the town and neighborhood. Many of the students could barely scrape together the money for tuition and board. They dressed plainly and their pleasures consisted of the simple pastimes that cost nothing. They arrived in Lexington in all degrees of poverty. One boy, Harvey Butler Fergusson, had walked all the way from Alabama, carrying a gold watch and three hundred dollars in cash — all his family could provide for his four years. He boarded more than two miles from Lexington and in the summers stayed on, working as a field hand on county farms. (Later, Judge Fergusson became a United States congressman from New Mexico.)

In the first two years the students were divided between war veterans and boys just reaching sixteen and seventeen. A disparity naturally existing between the aims of the two groups could have presented a problem. The ex-soldiers were very serious minded about getting an education — actually the first volunteers in Lee's program of training through education to rebuild the South in a new direction — and these battle-seared men were anywhere from indifferent to scornful of the student activities that typified "bright college years." The younger boys, representing the average student, contained the normal component of the immature who were short on self-discipline and devoid of serious purpose.

In this more typical group was a segment of young men who had entered adolescence under unnatural conditions where the home environment was totally disrupted and they had grown up, without restraint, in the violent disorder on the edge of clashing armies and in the paths of raiding parties. A bitter strain ran through these undisciplined young men, and it was suspected their parents wanted them brought under control by General Lee's authority.

Completely free of any military touches, Lee assumed control of the faculty and student body with the same singleness of purpose and authority with which he had assumed command of the army, when Major Brent had said, "A new impulse was generated from general headquarters," and drew all its parts into a network under a single, guiding hand. As Professor Joynes wrote, "The utmost harmony and utmost energy pervaded all the departments of the college." Lee used the same technique with students that he had with subordinates: he placed them on their own responsibility; he placed them on their honor as gentlemen.

To Lee, education for the future depended as much on character as learning, and to him character was built upon the habits of self-control. He did not believe that intelligent self-government in men would be promoted by forcing students under compulsion, supported by penalties, to perform class assignments and conform to rules of personal behavior. He believed that by giving young men the opportunity to think and act for themselves, they would form the habit of making the proper choices. Strongly opposed to treating individuals as units in a system, he corrected a faculty member who appealed to precedent to support his own view that "we must not respect persons." Lee said, "In dealing with young men I always respect persons, and care little for precedent." With this attitude, he refused to encompass students with regulations and petty rules, nor would he have them watched over — "espionage," as it was called at the college — as if they were unable to govern themselves.

He was, of course, aware of the chances he took and was not surprised when some students abused the privilege of latitude. Each delinquent, either in studies or conduct, was called privately into Lee's office, to explain himself to the patriarchal presence. It was not his custom to reproach the boys. He advised them. One of his former students, who was himself never called to Lee's office, wrote, "I have heard the boys who were say his admonitions were as tender as a mother's and his warnings and instructions always fatherly and wise."

Lee tended by appeal to force a boy to look at himself as a man to whom the president had extended the courtesy of assuming he came of a good home in which he had been inculcated with honor, honesty, a conscience and self-respect. Had Lee misjudged him? Was it possible that his mother had not trained him so he could be placed on his own trust? The reference to the "mother" was the crusher to family-proud Southern boys, and rarely was a student called in more than once. The few incorrigibles were quietly removed from college.

In a very short time the response of the students to being placed on their own responsibility as gentlemen formed a voluntary code which might be considered an informal version of the "honor system." The men were proud of acting on their honor, and they obeyed Lee, one said, "not because they feared but loved him, and I don't think there was one of the boys . . . but would have died defending him if necessary." Chaplain Jones said the students were aware of the high standard of conduct and "tone of feeling," "and proud of themselves and of their college, as representative of the character and influence of Lee."

In the unifying spirit of the voluntary system of honor, the veterans exerted an influence on the purpose of the younger students, and the potential problem of the disparity in experience was resolved by emulation. It was a hard-working student body, characterized by the motivation that stimulated and gratified the faculty. "The highest powers of both professors and students were called forth, with the fullest responsibility," said Professor Joynes. Shiftlessness was the one sure way into Lee's disfavor. If there was one thing he could not abide it was a drone, and something about slothfulness made his gorge rise. Lee could grow angry at students, though often his shortness of manner would be displayed to the visitor following the one who had strained his self-control.

The natural exuberance of young men was not suppressed by their serious application to studies or their sense of responsibility for "gentle-manly" behavior. Periodically in town several students would hold wassail in the hotel, and occasionally one or more boys would have to confess to "taking on more than he could carry." Unless their frolics disturbed others Lee, while admonishing, was usually tolerant. The drinkers voluntarily took "the pledge" of abstinence. He refused to vote for the expulsion of one boy on hearsay evidence that he was "an habitual drunkard" and "frequenter of saloons." Evidently the student did hit the bottle but, with Lee's faith in him, he reformed.

The ages of Lee's own children, from nineteen upward when he came to Lexington, kept him close to the feelings of youth. He never talked to anyone as from across a span of generations — not even, or especially not, to the little children to whom he so freely gave his heart. With this tolerance, Lee showed his understanding of one group breach of "gentle-manly conduct" involving the rector of Grace Episcopal Church, former Brigadier General Pendleton.

The well-meaning bumbler of artillery was long winded, humorless and excessively pious. It was the good man's idea that the students would benefit from a weekly afternoon session in declamation. Probably not wanting to attend what they regarded as an unnecessary class in the afternoon in the first place, and doubtless having acquired at least hearsay knowledge of Pendleton's bombastic oratory, the students gathered in the classroom with a group determination to wreck the new course. After applauding Pendleton wildly before he started speaking, the students began throwing wads of paper at the volunteer lecturer as soon as he warmed up. Pendleton grimly persevered, making references to their ill-mannered behavior, and then reported the episode to Lee.

The next week Lee accompanied his rector to the classroom, and the boys listened to Pendleton with rapt and silent attention. The following week Pendleton returned alone. As he began his speech, bugles began blowing outside the windows and Rebel yells split the air. Flushed, Pendleton raised his voice and thundered on through the racket. Then a dog was let into the room and dashed madly about with a tin can tied to his tail. Again Pendleton scourged the students for their discourteous behavior, but he did not try to go on. One lesson he had learned in the army was: a good general knows when to retreat. That was his last lecture. Lee, having had four years of experience with the clergyman, made no reference whatsoever to the incident.

In a way, this indirect illustration of Lee's understanding convinced the students of his thoughtful knowledge of them as individuals. He gave each student the impression that he was interested in him personally, and he was. In speaking of his great executive ability, one of the students, later Judge Robert Ewing of Nashville, recalled that "he had the power to bring out, and did bring out, the very best there was in every student." Lee held a private talk with each student when he arrived, and after that conference Lee never forgot the student's name. Addressing them collectively as "my boys," he addressed them individually as "Mister," and called each one by name.

With the turnover of students in the constantly growing and changing student body, his memory of names was impressive to the faculty. "No one . . . who was ever associated with General Lee in the management of any enterprise could fail to observe the accuracy and tenacity of his memory. He never appeared to forget anything, however comparatively insignificant, which it was with him a matter of concern to remember." It was a matter of ultimate concern that each student was aware that the president knew him.

### 3

As it had been with soldiers in the army, students — and faculty as well — felt the pervasive influence of Lee's controlling direction without any display of official authority on his part. He actually appeared to exercise none. This was not the result only of his venerable position. The habit of command was instinctive in him. As his son Rob said, it had never occurred to him that he *could* disobey his father. Lee's total command of himself produced that kinglike quality which induced in others the impulse to follow. He did not have to act with official authority: he needed only to *be*.

In the first two months at Washington College, before his family joined him, Lee seemed not a happy man in beginning his new course of duty. Just separated from his wife and daughters after five months of home life, he lived like a transient in his third-floor room at the Lexington Hotel. In his letters he could not suppress lines that revealed his loneliness for his family, within the deeper unvoiced despair for all that was gone for them all.

In a different vein from his public attitude, Lee showed in a letter to Rob his disturbance at President Johnson's refusal to acknowledge his application for a pardon. "As soon as I am restored to civil rights, if I ever am, I will settle up your grandfather's estate, and put you in possession of your share." Twenty-two-year-old Rob, while uncertain about his inherited plantation, Romancoke, had come down with malarial chills working as a field hand on brother Rooney's White House land, and had joined his mother and sisters at Derwent to recuperate. His heart was set on farming, and Lee, doubtful about Rob's not completing his education, wrote, "I have thought very earnestly as to your future."

His inability to provide for his children made his absence from them more poignant, and he wrote his wife, "I wish you were all with me. I feel very solitary and miss you all dreadfully." In a letter to Mildred ("Precious Life"), he referred in his familiar joking tone to her pet chickens by name, indulged his unfailing interest in young people's romantic affairs by reporting two weddings, but wrote as a flat statement, "Traveler is my only companion; I may say my only pleasure."

On quitting his office at two o'clock, Lee rode the sharer of his war life on lonely journeys through the mountains, finding renewal for his spirit in the silence where nature remained untouched by man. Though Custis came up to Lexington, taking the chair of civil engineering at V.M.I., Lee never mentioned his sober son's having accompanied him on his afternoon rides. Beyond his trips and the drudgery of office work (which included answering the pitiful flow of applications for entrance to college from penniless, illiterate veterans), Lee found one absorbing interest. He began preparing the president's house for the occupancy of his family.

Dr. Morton's family did not leave until after mid-October, and the house was, Lee wrote, "in wretched condition." Their first house since Arlington, it was in a way a substitute for the home in which Mrs. Lee had grown up and for which she never ceased pining. Though comparatively modest when measured on the Arlington scale, the red-brick house was a charming example of the Greek Revival architecture of the early eighteen-forties. If not immense, its rooms were agreeably proportioned and by no means small. From the off-center entrance hall, doors opened on the left to the two main rooms, parlor and dining room, with kitchen adjoining. On the right was a fine, square room off which there was another smaller room. Lee selected these two rooms, something like a wing, for his wife.

Since Mrs. Lee could move about only in her wheelchair, except on crutches in her room (when she went out, two men were required to lift her into a carriage), it was essential that her rooms be located on the ground floor. As she would entertain much in her own rooms, her main room also needed to be given some of the comforts and atmosphere of a sitting room. Mrs. Cocke, their Derwent hostess, again played Lady Bountiful and assumed responsibility for Mrs. Lee's room, with the actual details handled by her artistic sister-in-law, Mrs. Margaret Junkin Preston. Mrs. Preston, who had lived in the house when her father was president, designed the furniture for the rooms and found a one-armed Confederate veteran to make it. General Lee had the painters working ahead of the furniture-maker.

Rarely making sentimental references to the past, Lee left no record of his feelings in moving about in that wing on the upper floor of which had lived his dear friend, "the great and good Jackson." Even after the death of his wife, Margaret Preston's sister, the then eccentric professor at V.M.I. had lived on in the house with the Junkins, and it would have required a colder man than Lee not to be aware of the spirit of the soldier whom he had seen last in the misty morning hours in a clearing in the Wilderness.

Outside Mrs. Lee's suite in the wing, the other rooms were more scantily furnished, largely with objects supplied by the ladies of Lexington. The curtains and handsome carpets had served at Arlington. When Federal soldiers were removing the Lees' personal belongings from Arlington — including the priceless heirlooms of Mrs. Lee's great-grandmother, Martha Washington — Mrs. Britannia Kennon, a cousin, had received permission to move the carpets and curtains. Storing these during the war, she sent them to the new house in Lexington.

Mrs. Fitzhugh at Ravensworth had kept the portraits of General and Mrs. Washington, and these were sent on. The Arlington silver, which had been stored in Lexington, was dug up from where a sergeant at V.M.I. had buried the chests when Hunter's raiders were looting the town. The most impressive object was a new "grandly carved" Stieff piano, sent by the Baltimore manufacturer as a token of admiration. With "something borrowed, something old and something new," the downstairs rooms and the upstairs bedrooms were made habitable by the end of November. Lee wrote his wife, "I think we should enjoy all the amenities of life which are within our reach, and which have been provided for us by our Heavenly Father."

Characteristically, Mrs. Lee did not leave on the canal boat the day of her scheduled departure, and a disappointed Lee, waiting at the packet landing, felt some anxiety. On the morning of December 2 she arrived in style, on the private boat of Colonel Ellis, president of the canal line. She was accompanied by Rob, still suffering from his chills, and Mary and Mildred, Agnes having gone to Richmond to attend a wedding.

The General was so happy at seeing his family that, Rob said, he "appeared bright and even gay." With his wife and children in a carriage, he led the way on Traveler, and proudly ushered them into the newly decorated house which he had supervised in every detail. The first things Mrs. Lee noticed were the rugs from Arlington on the parlor and dining-room floors, so large that the ends had been folded under. At the rush of memories, she appeared for a moment to be overcome. She quickly recovered herself. Mrs. Nelson, the wife of a professor, was there waiting to serve them all breakfast. Before they sat down to the table — the dining room contained no other furniture but the table and chairs — the General showed them the array of pickles, preserves and brandy peaches which neighbors had stacked in the storeroom.

With this homecoming, the former "heiress of Arlington" and the man who had been born in the grandeur of Stratford Hall resumed a family life which they were to share to the end of their days.

4

The arrival of his family opened Lee's life to the social activities he had been missing. Mrs. Lee entertained frequently and knew her husband liked having ladies in the house. "No one enjoyed the company of ladies as much as he," she said. "It seemed the greatest recreation in his toilsome life."

Soon after arriving, Mrs. Lee became active in the sewing society of the Grace Episcopal Church. The group's purpose was to raise money for the building fund of General Pendleton's small church down the hill from the college. As Lee told Mildred, "The Episcopalians are few in number and light in purse, and must be resigned to small returns." Mrs. Lee made a very practical contribution: she had the portraits of General and Mrs. Washington photographed, and used her considerable skill with the brush for coloring the pictures. The colored photographs sold all over the area.

The meetings of the sewing circle were usually held in Mrs. Lee's room, where she presided as a thoughtful hostess and delightful talker. Like her husband's, her hair was turned a silvery gray. Silver ringlets hung beside her forehead, and she often wore a lace-trimmed organdy cap. Never a beauty, her clearly defined features gave her aging face a certain sharpness, which was lightened by a cheerful expression and, when she talked, by a lively animation. She never complained about her invalidism, with its physical suffering — at times acute — nor about the loss in her fortunes. She turned her thoughts outward to the comfort of others and kept her hands busy with knitting and sewing; in the evenings she worked at mending and darning while the General read aloud to her.

With her practice of the virtues esteemed in her background — such as courage, courtesy, thoughtfulness — Mrs. Lee had not lost her usually suppressed imperiousness. While quietly heroic in her adjustment to circumstances, and a model of the patrician attitude of noblesse oblige, she was unmistakably the center around which the Lee home life revolved, and on occasions demonstrated to visitors her power over the South's Great Man. One afternoon when a group of visitors was leaving, one of Mrs. Preston's children could not find his hat. "Robert," Mrs. Lee said in tones of command, "go and find the Preston boy's hat." Without a word, General Lee fetched the child's hat.

Also, beneath the stoicism and outward cheerfulness, Mary Lee shared little of her husband's Christian tolerance toward their oppressors. In a letter to a friend, referring to "Uncle Sam," she wrote, "as I neither *feel* nor *owe* any allegiance to him, except what is exacted by force, my conscience does not trouble me. We are protected neither in person nor property by his laws; nor do I feel any respect for the military *satraps* who rule us." She also wrote in a letter, "When I say 'our country' I mean the South."

With passing time, too, Mrs. Lee began to miss the scenes and companions of her earlier life. While accepting dislocation with grace, her pleasingly mannered interest in the community came to form a façade for the inner longing for the "home" that was no longer there to return to. Yet this sense of being uprooted from plantation Virginia never lessened her gratitude to the considerate people of Rockbridge County. For them she formed a very real affection and adapted herself with an outward completeness that concealed the nostalgia she expressed in letters to the friends of the other times.

The three girls experienced a more difficult time in adjusting to Lexington. They were accustomed to the large parties in Tidewater and Northern Virginia, where their lifelong friends and kinspeople gave the plantation society something of the quality of a family. While Lexington became their home, one or more of the girls was frequently absent on long visits, and no trouble was too great for them to attend a wedding. Nothing said by any of the girls, or by their brothers and parents, indicated why they never married. The closest explanation came in a generality made in a light vein by Mrs. Lee. "The girls seem to be in the condition of 'poor Betty Martin,' who, you know, the song said, could never 'find a husband to suit her mind.' "

The girls were distinctly different — in looks, character and personality. Mary, thirty, with the finest features of the three, had become increasingly independent-minded and in time became something of an eccentric. When there, despite the unsettled conditions, she took long walks or rides alone in the country without any sense of fear, and seemed to assume that her arrogant pride protected her from any of the misfortunes or inconveniences that befell her fellow creatures. Mary was typical of her family only in her activities for the Church. She taught a Sunday school class, organized a Sunday school library, and assisted at fairs and bazaars run for money-raising. However, at home, she never helped with the housekeeping. In later years Mildred wrote of Mary that she "is not sympathetic with weakness and nervousness, and is always absorbed in self first and foremost . . . I try to steel myself against her sharp words by thinking she has always been the same with everybody."

Agnes, of the sweet expression, like her grandmother, Ann Carter Lee, made the best adjustment. From the time she came to Lexington, at twenty-four, Agnes never seemed to be in full health. She lived only to thirty-two. When Agnes first arrived in Lexington, her reserve caused the townspeople to think her haughty. Soon they discovered the thoughtfulness of a quiet, retiring nature, and when she died the Lexington *Gazette* referred to her as "a very gentle and gracious lady." Agnes was her mother's favorite.

Nineteen-year-old Mildred, her father's "pet," was the plainest of the girls and the most cheerful. When Lee came in at the end of the day, no matter who was present, he would call, "Where is my little Miss Mildred? She is my lightbearer; the house is never dark if she is in it." Very spoiled, Mildred remained rather immature, went on sprees of reading romantic novels (of which her father disapproved) and was given to self-dramatizing.

On her first arrival in Lexington, Mildred wrote a friend, "I believe it was you who told me Lexington was such a delightful place. I disagree with you in toto. I am often dreadfully lonely, know no one well in the whole town . . . The number of old maids here appalls me. My fate was decided the first moment I put my foot on the shore. Lucy, do you know what starvation of the *heart and mind* is? I suffer, and am dumb." She showed her flightiness by an abrupt change of the subject: "You ought to see the beautiful new black silk dress I've got, all trimmed with steely beads."

Mildred also seemed something of a busybody. Once when her sisters were away, Lee wrote, "She has consequently had her hands full, and considers herself now a great character. She rules her brother and nephews with an iron rod, and scatters her advice broadcast among the young men of the College. I hope that it may yield an abundant harvest. The young mothers of Lexington ought to be extremely grateful to her for her suggestions to them as to the proper mode of rearing their children, and though she finds many unable to appreciate her system, she is nothing daunted by their obtuseness of vision, but takes advantage of every opportunity to enlighten them as to its benefits."

All of the girls attracted young men who came to visit them and escort them to such pleasures as staid Lexington offered. They loved to dance and came home at two and three in the morning from cadet hops at V.M.I. When the girls were being visited by a beau, however, Lee kept a rigid curfew of ten o'clock, even though some of the dates were bearded war veterans far removed from adolescence. If they had not gone at ten o'clock, the father went around the rooms ostentatiously closing the shutters for the night. If the visitors did not take this hint, Lee said simply, "Good night, young gentlemen."

In their pleasures, the girls exceeded what had previously been regarded as "ladylike" behavior. They went ice-skating on the river with young men, students from the college and cadets from V.M.I. They also went on sleigh rides, and Mrs. Lee was amused at the shock given the Presbyterians. One night the bachelor professors of V.M.I. gave a dance for the reading society, of which the Lee girls were members, and the Virginia reel, the lancers and quadrilles were danced until three in the morning. The girls restrained themselves from asking for a "round dance," where the persons of the couples touched in a waltz, as they were certain that Brother Custis would have forbidden such goings-on.

Of the reading club, their father said, "As far as I can judge it, it is a great institution for the discussion of apples and chestnuts, but is quite innocent of the pleasures of literature. It however brings the young people together and promotes sociability and conversation." Anything they enjoyed seemed to give Lee pleasure. Perhaps because he had been so much separated from them and they were so dear to him, Lee may have been an indulgent parent, as Mrs. Lee was known to be. Rob said they could always "get around her."

Before the family settled in the (for them) small house in Lexington, the girls were comparatively useless at cooking and what their brother Rob called "the household arts." This was not typical of girls raised in the lavishness of plantation mansions with abundant servants. Usually they were trained to assume the direction of a huge domestic establishment, familiarizing themselves with the details. While most belles cultivated an appearance of appealing feminine helplessness, during the war the ladies showed themselves to be singularly self-reliant, resourceful and durable — and at least a dozen published memoirs of their experiences belong with literature. But when Mildred and Agnes tried to prepare meals, the efforts were so pitiful that their father teased them.

As servants were few in the house, and those neither permanent nor well trained, Lee constantly encouraged his daughters to try again. Without reproach, he would say, "You are all very helpless; I don't know what you will do when I am gone." Smilingly he advised, "If you want to be missed by your friends — be useful." Serious-minded Agnes evidently improved, for in 1867 Lee wrote that she "was becoming a very good housekeeper."

About the lack of any serious romances developing, Lee never made any references to the girls' marrying in his stream of letters to them. Nor did he joke about them in relation to courtship as he did about Rob, who he thought would be better off married. Once he wrote in a bantering letter to Agnes, "Your Uncle Smith says you girls ought to marry his sons, as you both find it so agreeable to be from home, and you could then live a Bohemian life and have a happy time generally . . . But I do not agree with him; I shall not give my consent, so you must choose elsewhere . . ."

All in all, it would appear that Lee was not anxious to lose his daughters in marriage. He expected the boys to go off, except bachelor Custis, who roomed nearby and took his meals with the family. But the girls formed a permanent part of the family life on which he grew increasingly dependent.

## 5

In November, 1865, before his family had arrived, Lee began the moves as college president that were to transform the curriculum. The traditional classical education was expanded in a broader liberal arts program — including modern languages and literature — to which were added scientific courses designed to train young men for a dual purpose: to earn their living and to develop techniques that would rebuild the South in the direction of contemporary technologies.

When Lee had first arrived, five professors were on hand for the standard courses in Latin, Greek, French, mathematics and physical science (chemistry and physics), with the chair of moral sciences vacant. This course, involving moral philosophy and political economy, had formerly been taught by the president. After Lee arrived the Board of Trustees, in an understanding with him, voted to establish five new chairs, three of them in scientific courses. The effect of Lee's positive attitude was reflected in the board's bravery in establishing these new chairs when the college was running mostly on credit on its operating expenses, while increasing its debts and finding no resources for new revenue.

Lee himself went right to the top in applying for help from Cyrus McCormick, the millionaire whose grain-reaper had helped enrich the Midwestern farmers while Southern farmers depended upon slave labor. McCormick was a natural choice. As a native of Rockbridge County, he had invented the reaper in a shed near Lexington. On November 28, Lee wrote him:

"At a late meeting of the Board of Trustees of Washington College, it was resolved with a view to a more thorough and extended course of scientific instruction; and to the liberal and practical education of the industrial classes; to establish five additional professorships without interfering with the regular classical and literary courses. The professorships proposed are those of 'Practical Chemistry,' 'Experimental Philosophy and Practical Chemistry' [one course], 'Applied Mathematics,' 'Modern Languages,' 'History and Literature.' Such a course of instruction is requisite to meet the present wants of the country; and to enable these young men who did not desire to devote themselves to special professions, requiring specific studies after graduating, to enter at once upon the active pursuits of life. To you who are so conversant with the necessities of the country, and its vast undeveloped resources, the benefit of applying scientific knowledge and research to agriculture, mining, architecture, construction of ordinary roads, Railroads, canals, bridges, etc., will be at once apparent."

Written with the constriction that often characterized Lee's official correspondence, this letter was particularly cumbersome because Lee was going strongly against the grain when he applied for charity, whatever the cause. He ended by appealing to McCormick "as one who has already done so much for the advance of agriculture and the relief of the husbandman." With all its stiffness, the letter got results. In January, McCormick announced that he was donating $10,000 (later increased to $15,000) to establish a chair in "Experimental Philosophy and Practical Mechanics." This went into the catalogue as the McCormick Chair of Natural Philosophy.

Later Mr. McCormick became a member of the board for the last twenty years of his life, and additional gifts by himself and his family (long after Lee was dead) amounted to more than $350,000. After McCormick's original donation for the chair, Northern admirers of Lee gave substantial gifts in sympathetic interest in helping the South rebuild through education. While Lee was president, George Peabody, the Massachusetts industrialist and patron of education, gave approximately a quarter of a million dollars; Thomas A. Scott, president of the Pennsylvania Railroad and Assistant Secretary of War in Lincoln's Cabinet, gave $60,000; W. W. Corcoran, the Washington philanthropist, gave valuable collections of books and $30,000; Rathwell Wilson, the Philadelphia scientist, sent several thousand books "to repair to some measure the effect produced by its [Hunter's force's] excessive destructiveness"; Henry Ward Beecher and Samuel J. Tilden, later (1876) Democratic nominee for President, in New York City raised sums to be sent early in Lee's administration.

Before these contributions came in, Lee, after his first letter to Mr. McCormick, the next month opened a correspondence with D. S. G. Cabell, a state senator from the district who had served in the Army of Northern Virginia. Lee wrote Cabell in December on the subject of getting for Washington College a portion of the land fund the U. S. Congress had donated to the states for educational purposes. (On that project Senator Cabell worked for more than a year, only to be informed by the United States Commissioner in 1867 that Virginia was not in the Union.) From this basis, Senator Cabell and Lee worked together in January, 1866, when Lee went to Richmond to appear before the House of Delegates' Committee on Schools and Colleges. The state had guaranteed the interest on the endowment of several colleges, including the $88,000 of Washington College, and during the war these interest payments had ceased. The purpose of Lee's appearance was actually to lend the weight of his presence to an appeal for the resumption of the interest payments.

At that time Virginia's government co-existed with the divided Federal authorities in the state in the period before President Johnson's restoration policies were sabotaged by the Radicals. Francis Pierpont, governor of the "restored government" recognized by Lincoln and Johnson, still remained the chief executive, but representative Virginians — excluding any prominent secessionists — had been elected to the General Assembly in the first postwar elections held in October. On December 4 the General Assembly met on the same day that its representatives to the U. S. Congress were refused seats in Washington.

In Richmond, the legislature's only action to attract Radical attention was the passage of a mild Vagrancy Act, designed both to control the uprooted masses of freed slaves and to get desperately needed labor. General W. R. Terry, then in command of the military occupation, forbade the execution of the vagrancy statutes. He was strongly supported by the anti-Southern press, which claimed Virginia's new law was one of the "Black Codes" aimed at continuing de facto slavery. On the scene, however, Governor Pierpont, an honest conservative sympathetic with the peoples' problems, worked sincerely to influence the General Assembly toward a course of action that would avoid conflict with the Radicals and lead to Virginia's readmittance to the Union. But, as Pierpont's efforts at restoration alienated the Radicals in the state, his position — like Johnson's — was weak, and the General Assembly's control of the state's internal affairs was uncertain.

None of the alien element made an issue of payments due the colleges on the interests on their endowments and, with Senator Cabell using a letter of Lee's in the Senate, the General Assembly voted to pay in installments the interest in arrears. From this modest beginning toward financial solvency, friends of the college where Lee was president worked in the East and the South to raise money, and the endowment fund — in addition to the gifts by the generous Northerners — began to increase sizeably.

With the financial burdens lightened so far as to allow the doubling of the president's salary (to $3000 a year), immediate progress was made on the establishment of the new chairs. Toward an emphasis on the new scientific studies Lee, the faculty and the board of trustees — after considerable discussion by the board members — introduced a new plan of an elective system of study for the 1866-1867 college year. In this the curriculum was somewhat grandly divided into nine departments or schools. Eighteen professors taught eleven courses, in which the scientific courses nearly balanced the "liberal arts" — combining the old classical subjects with departments of modern language, history, English language and literature. Eventually, the scientific courses would be grouped to form the studies for a bachelor of science degree, including pre-engineering and pre-medicine, while science and mathematics continued in the B.A. program. From the beginning rigorous mathematics was stressed and required hard work in the students. Also, Judge Brockenbrough's Lexington Law School became affiliated with the college, founding the basis of the later officially incorporated School of Law.

When chemistry became a separate department, the college was fortunate in already having on its staff Professor John L. Campbell, whose long interest in the chemistry of agriculture had been expressed in several pamphlets. For applied mathematics, which embraced civil engineering, Lee brought in Stonewall Jackson's former ordnance officer, Colonel William Allan. Allan, who had received his master's degree from the University of Virginia four years before the war, was a highly literate man who wrote a book on the Valley Campaign that became a standard. A fellow aide of Custis's on Jefferson Davis's staff, Colonel William Preston Johnston, came in as professor of history and political economy. Colonel Johnston had remained with President Davis to the end of his flight and was captured with him at the night camp in the Georgia pine woods.

Other men who had served the Confederacy were appointed to the staff, for, as little as Lee talked about the war, the four years had formed loyalties that superseded all others save those to his family. Reverend J. William Jones, a Baptist minister who had served as an army chaplain with A. P. Hill, was at that time a chaplain at Washington College and saw much of Lee. Of Lee's care for former soldiers, Jones wrote, "He said very little about it, but, whenever any place of honor or profit was to be filled by his voice or influence, he always gave the preference to one of his veterans, and would not unfrequently say very quietly, 'He was a good soldier.'"

On several unguarded occasions, Lee's flash of reaction revealed the intensity and depth of his feelings about the Army of Northern Virginia. One of the most brilliant students of Lee's time, M. W. Humphreys, later professor at the University of Virginia, had served in the army. Lee, once observing that Humphreys looked physically run-down, suggested that he might be working too hard. Humphreys replied, "I am so impatient to make up for the time I lost in the army —"

He got no further. Lee flushed, in the symptom of aroused feelings and, Humphreys recalled, answered in an almost angry voice. "Mr. Humphreys! However long you live and whatever you accomplish, you will find that the time you spent in the Confederate army was the most profitably spent portion of your life. Never again speak of having lost time in the army."

Humphreys reported, "And I never did again."

Lee gave standing invitations to graduates from the neighborhood to visit him when they returned home. One of his early graduates was Edward A. Moore, who had been in his junior year at the college before he went off to war with the Rockbridge Battery. After Appomattox, General Pendleton had thoughtfully given cannoneer Moore a staff parole which, under terms of the surrender, entitled him to one horse for his four years' service in the army. In drawing horses, Moore deferred to a genuine staff officer, who picked a handsome sorrel in exchange for his own bony young bay. Moore had observed the "CS" brand on the handsome sorrel and, as he had suspected, the horse was confiscated by the Yankees. Moore took some time to rest and fatten up the discarded bay, which he then sold for enough to return to college. As a returned veteran, in his senior year he averaged better than 98 in Latin, Greek, mathematics and physical science. After his graduation, the ex-gunner in Poague's battalion called on the Lees.

Mrs. Lee began talking about the well-clothed Federal soldiers she had seen coming into Richmond and, probably with some bitterness, began to contrast their fine uniforms with the ragged clothing worn by the Confederates. Lee had been pacing the floor, and suddenly his eyes lit up. Leaning toward his wife in a movement of grace that caught Moore's attention, he said, "But, ah, Mistress Lee, we gave them some awfully hard knocks with all of our rags!"

With the growth of faculty and students, courses and endowments, work went ahead continuously on the physical plant. The seedy-looking landscape that had greeted Lee on his arrival became so spruced up that a superintendent of building and grounds was appointed — thus relieving Lee of the unofficial capacity as grounds superintendent which he assumed after moving into the president's house. When he cleared the grounds immediately around his house, for the planting of a flower garden for Mrs. Lee and a vegetable garden for himself, the new president compulsively extended the area of his rehabilitation to include all the rolling land owned by the college. He gave personal directions to the janitor who doubled as yardman. When a lawn replaced the cultivated field sloping down to the chapel, Lee was very attentive to the care of the grass.

Colonel Preston, going from his home in Lexington to V.M.I., had formed the habit of riding across the lower hillside as a shortcut to the adjoining Institute, and occasionally he was greeted by Lee. One morning, after Lee's courteous salutation, Preston was puzzled when the General added solicitously, "I'm sorry your horse has sore feet." After he rode on a ways, Colonel Preston flushed when he realized that Lee was suggesting he keep his horse off the grass and ride by the road.

The most gratifying addition for Lee was the new chapel, opened in 1867, which he designed. The chapel to him was the center of the college. From his first days he had set an example for the students by appearing each morning at a quarter to eight for a brief service conducted by whichever minister in the neighborhood appeared. Lee himself was a traditional Episcopalian in the direct line from the Church of England in the earliest Colonial days, when his ancestors served on the powerful vestries that combined with the King's Council and House of Burgesses to rule Virginia. But the important thing to him was that students worship God and receive the guides of Christianity for their lives.

Built on the hillside, the chapel contained a lower floor in the rear, and in there Lee gave himself a new and larger office. It was a rectangular room, about thirty by twenty, that accommodated the heavy pieces of furniture with no effect of crowding. A secretary stood against one wall, his desk against another and across the room from the desk was a black horsehair sofa. At the end of the room away from the entrance a dropleaf table was placed under a window, and near it a stove stood in front of a fireplace. In the center a twelve-sided table was flanked by a black upholstered chair. The room was quite bare of ornamentation. Though not bright, it was comfortable for work, and the methodically industrious idol of a people occupied it until the end of his days.

In his more spacious office in the new chapel Lee received help in the burdensome correspondence that increased as the people's problems of adjustment were multiplied and their feelings confused by the tightening clamp of Radical rule. However, before formal Reconstruction in March, 1867, long before Lee opened his new office, he was drawn into the Radicals' first manipulations toward introducing Reconstruction when he had been at Washington College only five months.

6

On January 23, 1866, less than two months after the first postwar U. S. Congress convened, the Radicals began their groundwork for building a case to prove that the recently seceded states needed to remain under military occupation until they were "reconstructed" (i.e., voted Republican). A joint committee was formed to study conditions in the states "which formed the so-called Confederate States of America" to discover if any of them "are entitled to be represented" in Washington. The Southern states were divided into districts, from which representatives were to be examined by subcommittees, and Virginia was bracketed in the district with North Carolina and South Carolina.

Since the purpose of the committee was to prove that the Southern states were not entitled to representation, of the forty-nine witnesses called from Virginia nearly all were active Republicans, and the majority came from Northern states. When these men were examined in Washington, they declared that Virginians were disloyal to the Federal government, hostile to "good Union men" abiding in the state and, indeed, their lives would be endangered if United States troops were withdrawn.

After the parade of witnesses, the subcommittee for some reason called Lee in February. Perhaps the members thought his testimony would count little against the weight of evidence, and as a witness Lee would lend some air of legitimacy to the proceedings. Better than that, as the subcommittee was assured by its agents in Virginia that Lee was beyond all comparison the untitled leader of the state, it would be a great coup to trap him. Or perhaps the head examiner, Senator Jacob M. Howard of Michigan, simply wanted a go at the Rebel chieftain. Senator Howard was the man who had written his friend Sumner, the powerful abolitionist, that it made no difference what the North did with their Negroes just so the freed slaves in the South were given the suffrage to vote Republican.

Before Lee was called to Washington, in late January he began to perceive from the actions of the new Congress that a campaign was beginning for the purpose of blocking the restoration of the Union. As clumsy and inadequately defined as were President Johnson's measures toward restoration, he had convinced Lee and the Southern moderates of his good intentions and his responsible view of the tangle of problems — practical, legal and emotional. With the United States President working toward restoration, Lee was incredulous when the first move of the Radicals in Congress, the "test-oath," was taken seriously.

This "test-oath," requiring Southerners to swear they had not participated in a civil or military capacity with the Confederacy, could have no other object than disfranchising practically all representative white men over eighteen years old. When the legality of this new oath was taken in a test case to the Supreme Court, Lee wrote Senator Reverdy Johnson, the Maryland Unionist who had offered to defend him in the treason indictment.

The purpose of his letter, January 27, was to seek advice about reclaiming those sections of the Arlington property that had been bequeathed by their grandfather to Custis, for a plantation, and to Lee's daughters, to be sold as part of their legacy. The United States government had sold the property, Lee wrote, "in the belief, I presume, that it belonged to me . . ." and he could not act for himself because "I have been waiting the action of President Johnson upon my application to be embraced in his proclamation of May 29th, and for my restoration of civil rights." Then, referring to Senator Johnson's argument against the legality of the "test-oath," Lee mentioned the passage of the acts in Congress. "To pursue a policy which will continue the prostration of one-half the country, alienate the affections of its inhabitants from the Government, and which must eventually result in injury to the country and the American people, appears to me so manifestly injudicious that I do not see how those responsible can tolerate it."

By the time he entered the Capitol Building for his inquisition on February 17, Lee, having said he did not hope for a favorable decision on the "test-oath" in the Supreme Court, knew what to expect from Senator Howard. On the other hand, Senator Howard seemed not to expect from Lee the candid answers, without a shade of self-justification, delivered with dignified composure in an even, quiet voice.

After the senator had interrogated him along the line of Southern attitudes to the Union without getting anywhere, he persisted in seeking from Lee an opinion on a hypothetical situation. What would "secessionists" do if by joining an enemy at war with the United States the South could gain independence? Finally he asked the direct question, "Do you not think many of that class of persons whom I call secessionists would join the common enemy?"

"It is possible," Lee said, in surprising candor. "It depends upon the feelings of the individual."

Then Howard asked him what his choice would be.

"I have no disposition to do it now," Lee replied emotionlessly, "and I never have had."

Howard shifted to a sequence of questions about how Southerners regarded secession, if not as an act of treason. "In what light would they view it? What would be their excuse or justification? How would they escape in their own mind? I refer to the past."

Lee said, without change of tone, "I am referring to the past and as to the feelings they would have. So far as I know, they look upon the action of the state, in withdrawing itself from the government of the United States, as carrying the individuals of the state along with it; that the state was responsible for the act, not the individual."

"And," Howard asked, "that the ordinance of secession, so-called, or those acts of the state which recognized a condition of war between the state and the general government, stood as their justification for their bearing arms against the government of the United States?"

"Yes, sir, I think they considered the act of the state as legitimate; that they were merely using the reserved right which they had a right to do."

"State, if you please — and if you are disinclined to answer the question you need not do so — what your own personal views on that question were."

"That was my view," Lee said, "that the act of Virginia in withdrawing herself from the United States carried me along as a citizen of Virginia, and that her laws and her acts were binding to me."

Howard, giving up that line, then approached Lee on the feelings of

Southerners about freed Negroes. After Lee pointed out that he lived a retired life and was not conversant with the political aspects of Negro suffrage, Howard asked the direct question, "Do you not think that Virginia would be better off if the colored population would go to other Southern states?"

Ignoring part of the question, Lee answered the other part with simple honesty. "I think it would be better for Virginia if she could get rid of them. . . . I have always thought so."

As to their qualifications for voting, he said, "My own opinion is that, at this time, they cannot vote intelligently, and that giving them the right of suffrage would open the door to a great deal of demagogism, and lead to embarrassments in various ways. What the future may prove, how intelligent they may become, with what eyes they may look upon the interests of the state in which they may reside, I cannot say more than you can."

Finally Howard got around to the big question he had saved for the climax — Confederate treatment of Federal prisoners. Here the inquisitor was unaware that he was leading into an area about which Lee felt very strongly. It was one of the few accusatory distortions from the vindictive element in the North that rankled in him. Almost from the end of the fighting, the hatemongers had seized upon "Andersonville" as the Southern war crime and some Northerners had tried to associate Lee with the crime for which Wirz, the prison commandant, had already been hanged. There were three basic factors in the "Andersonville" hate campaign that Lee could stress.

The first, as Lee had mentioned in private correspondence, was that Northern prisoners shared the same inadequate rations and medical supplies as Confederate soldiers, and an extremely high mortality existed among Confederate sick as well in the last year. Based upon this, the second factor became more significant. While the Confederacy could not feed, clothe and care for its own people, fewer Federal prisoners died by number and by proportion than Confederate prisoners in the Federal prison camps of a prosperous, well-fed people in a land of plenty. The figures released by Stanton's War Department revealed that 13 per cent of Confederate prisoners died against only 8 per cent of Federal prisoners. Twenty-six thousand five hundred Confederates died among 200,000 prisoners; 22,526 Federals died among 260,526 prisoners.

Beyond the mortality statistics, in the damp, cold camps by the water, Fort Delaware and Camp Douglas, and in the freezing camp at Elmira, New York, where soldiers from the Lower South were given one blanket for sleeping on the ground in tents, men contracted upper respiratory and pulmonary diseases from which they never regained health and usefulness.

Lee did not develop these first two factors as they did not involve him directly. On the third point, which did directly concern him, he opened up. This was the factor that, against his often repeated requests to continue prisoner exchange, the Federals chose to expose their captured soldiers to the destitute conditions they themselves had created in the South. Grant himself had made this cold choice affecting Federal soldiers on the grounds that Confederate prisoners, when exchanged, returned to the army and reduced the proportion of numerical supremacy he needed in order to defeat Lee. Actually it was Grant who condemned the Federal soldiers to the Andersonvilles.

On replying to Howard, Lee said at first and then repeated that he knew nothing of the cruelties at Andersonville. Referring to Northern prisoners generally, he said, "I suppose they suffered from want of ability on the part of the Confederate States to supply them with their wants. At the very beginning of the war I knew there was suffering of prisoners on both sides, but as far as I could I did everything in my power . . . to establish the cartel [of prisoner exchange] as agreed upon."

Howard veered away, but Lee returned to this sore point of prisoner exchange and for the first time spoke at length. "I made several efforts to exchange the prisoners after the cartel was suspended. . . . I offered to General Grant, around Richmond, that we should ourselves exchange all the prisoners in our hands. There was a communication from the Christian Commission, I think, which reached me at Petersburg, and made application to me for a passport to visit all the prisoners South. My letter to them, I suppose, they have. I told them I had not that authority, that it could only be obtained from the War Department at Richmond, but that neither they nor I could relieve the sufferings of the prisoners; that the only thing to be done for them was to exchange them; and, to show that I would do whatever was in my power, I offered them to send to City Point all the prisoners in Virginia and North Carolina over which my command extended, provided they returned an equal number of mine, man for man. I reported this to the War Department, and received for answer that they would place at my command all the prisoners at the South if the proposition was accepted. I heard nothing more on the subject."

Nor did Senator Howard wish to hear any more on the subject. He withdrew and turned the questioning over to his assistant. The interrogation ran down then, a failure from the committee's viewpoint. Lee had said nothing that made copy for the Radical press and little notice was taken of his examination in the newspapers.

While Lee was in Washington, he was besieged by crowds composed of old friends, admirers and the curious. He was deeply pleased, he wrote, by the "kind reception" his friends gave him and suffered the attention of strangers. Among his acquaintances from the old days was Mrs. Clement Clay, wife of the former United States senator from Alabama, who had served as a Confederate diplomatic agent. Mrs. Clay was in Washington interceding with Johnson and Stanton for the release of her husband from Fort Monroe, where he had been imprisoned since May on a grotesque charge. Mrs. Clay said she saw General Lee "several times, surrounded by hosts of admirers, the ladies begging for mementoes, buttons — anything, in fact, he might be persuaded to give up, while he, modest and benevolent, yielded helplessly to their demands."

Whatever Lee might have told his family about the inquisition, his only written reference to it as an unpleasant experience was in a letter to his wife's cousin Markie Williams. "Knowing how our God mixes the sweet with the bitter, I had hoped I might find you" in Washington. Then, referring to friends, he wrote, "Yet, I am now considered such a monster that I hesitate to darken with my shadow the doors of those I love best lest I should bring upon them misfortune."

### 7

After his return from Washington, Lee grimly comprehended the reality that the Radicals were gaining control of the government and appeared bent on establishing a new Union with the South attached as a vassal state. What was incomprehensible to him was their ability to push forward their program that deprived the Southern states of their traditional representation and passed acts which "denied and abridged" the rights of one set of former citizens while conferring these rights on former noncitizens. At this revolutionary drift, with its incalculably harmful consequence to the future of the South directly and indirectly to that of the nation, Lee spoke more passionately and less guardedly than at any time after the fighting ceased.

While still extremely careful of any words he put in writing, Lee unburdened himself in a May interview with a visiting Englishman, the Marquis of Lorne — later Duke of Argyll and husband of Queen Victoria's daughter, Princess Louise. Since the British aristocracy had been sympathetic to the Confederacy throughout the war, and at Lexington Lee had received admiring tributes from educated Englishmen, perhaps he felt less need for restraint with a citizen of the land which Virginians still regarded as "the mother country."

He told the Marquis that none of the Americans who approved Johnson's reconciliation policy "seem to be courageous enough to oppose the Radicals . . . and no one stands fairly up to hinder them. Surely if the Union be worth preserving, they should try to conciliate the whole nation, and not do all they can against the Southern part of it."

The most grievous injury the Radicals were committing was to the future of race relationships. Unwilling to impute deliberate evil to another man, Lee said that the Radicals "do not seem to see that they are raising up feelings of race." Then, in evident sadness, he elaborated on the consequences of their policy.

"If a bad feeling is raised in consequence of unfair laws being passed against the weaker party it must yield. The blacks must always here be the weaker; the whites are so much stronger that there is no chance for the black, if the Radical party passes the laws it wants against us. They are working as though they wished to keep alive by their proposals in Congress the bad blood in the South against the North. If left alone the hostility which must be felt after such a war would rapidly decrease, but it may be continued by incessant provocation. The Southerners took up arms honestly: surely it is to be desired that the good-will of our people be encouraged, and that there should be no inciting them against the North. To the minds of the Southern men the idea of 'Union' was ridiculous when the states that made the Union did not desire it to continue; but the North fought for the Union, and now, if what appears to be the most powerful party among them is to have its own way, they are doing their best to destroy all real union. If they succeed, 'Union' can only be a mere name."

Realization of the Radicals' purposes against the South did not affect Lee's policy of reconciliation. Writing Rooney that one party could not remain in power forever, he continued to look toward a future which daily became more distant, while in Lexington he strove to prevent any "incidents" that would, by providing excuses, prolong the Radical reign. It was vital to prevent incidents involving Washington College students for more than the general reason of not supplying ammunition to the Radicals. "Lee's College" was a particular target of the Radical press. Unfavorable publicity there could affect all Southern colleges by halting the rise of sympathy in Northern individuals who were becoming interested in giving support to the South's efforts to rebuild its educational institutions.

As the Radicals grew more open in the frank campaign of hate, there was an increase in the number of prominent Northerners whose sentiments were expressed by Professor Rosewell Dwight Hitchcock of the Union Theological Seminary: "The cause of education in the South appeals not to prejudices of men but to the patriotism of the people." In nurturing these small, isolated roots of good will, Lee worked under the handicap of a war record which the partisan newspapers could use in discouraging support to Southern education by such statements as "Washington College is one of the most virulent rebel institutions in the land —

a school for the propagation of hatred to the government and its loyal people." One good "incident" was all they would need, and in March of the following year one was almost provided.

When the Reconstruction Act divided the states of the former Confederacy into military districts in March, 1867, the pride of Virginians was bitterly outraged by the suspension of the General Assembly, the oldest (1619) continuous legislative body of representative government in the New World. Mrs. Lee, with none of her husband's care of what she put on paper, wrote a temperate, well-bred expression of the general reaction.

"It is bad enough to be victims of tyranny, but when it is wielded by such cowards and base men as Butler [and] Thaddeus Stevens . . . it is indeed intolerable. The country that allows such scum to rule them must fast be going to destruction . . . They still desire to grind [the South] to dust and wish to effect this purpose by working on the feelings of the low and ignorant negoes, many of whom do not even comprehend what a *vote* means. My indignation cannot be controlled and I wonder how our people, helpless and disarmed as they are, can bear it."

Naturally such feelings were borne with less control among the students at Lee's college, where, as a chaplain said, "they were not likely to be as prudent in giving utterance to their sense of wrong as others of more experience and self-control." On the other hand, wrote the Reverend J. L. Kirkpatrick, "the late slaves, suddenly elevated to a position which they had scarcely ventured to dream would be possible to them, were, as may be supposed, greatly elated by the change; and they too were not always as prudent in giving expression to their feelings as a calmer judgment would have shown them was best. The two inflammable classes being inavoidably brought into proximity to each other, it was hardly possible to prevent occasional collisions. The danger engaged the most assiduous attentions of General Lee . . ."

Despite his attentions, after the Reconstruction Act was passed in March, a group of five of the younger students impulsively decided to attend a night meeting the agents of the Freedmen's Bureau were holding for Negroes in a Bureau schoolhouse. Incited by the violence of the times, an Alabama boy carried a loaded revolver, more in a spirit of bravado than with any intent of using it. However, as the five students first reconnoitered the meeting by peering in a window, they encountered a Negro man. He cursed them and moved in a way to suggest that he was reaching for a weapon. The Alabama boy pulled out his pistol and hit him. As this was more than they had bargained for, the other boys began to leave. The Alabaman followed them, and that ended the action.

Those not engaged in the altercation — three Texans and a Georgian — were caught, arrested, and placed under a peace bond. When, after their release, they were called into General Lee's office, the Alabamian voluntarily appeared and confessed that he alone had been engaged in the ruckus. There was nothing for Lee to do except expel him. After admonishing the other boys, he issued a public statement ordering the students to stay away from Negro assemblies and pointed out that any appearance of racial conflict was injurious to the reputation of the college and the community. The faculty clerk wrote a letter of apology to the Bureau school, with a copy for the Freedmen's Bureau.

The local military authority was Brevet Brigadier General Douglas Frazar, a volunteer soldier making a career in the army of occupation, and to him Lee had to write a personal letter to quiet his urge to blow up the incident. Some while later Lee indulged himself in the satisfaction of writing a tongue-in-cheek letter to Frazar over another of his protective measures of the Negroes' rights.

Frazar wrote Lee that a Washington College student named Lusk planned to leave town owing payment for his laundry to freedman Henry Johnson. As he, Frazar, believed Lee held "the authority to enforce payments for such debts," Frazar asked Lee to enforce the payment or "endorse so that legal action may be taken."

Then enjoying some help with his correspondence, Lee dictated a reply: "I have received your communication . . . requesting my interposition in the collection of a debt said to be due Henry Johnson (Freedman) by Mr. Lusk, a student of Washington College. Mr. Lusk has not yet received permission to withdraw from college [and] I presume he is amenable to the legal processes for the collection of debts. I am not aware of any authority vested in me, as President of the College, to enforce the collection of a debt of this character, but would be glad to have it pointed out to me. It is not the wish of the faculty that any student should evade a just debt."

After Frazar was quieted and the students, recognizing the potential seriousness of the episode at the Bureau school, obeyed Lee's order to avoid giving "any appearance of racial conflict," the first year of Reconstruction passed without Lee's or the college's becoming involved with the Military Government. Despite the unnatural conditions of living under occupation, Lexington appeared to recapture the atmosphere of leisurely casualness characteristic of the rural county seat. Lee himself, though sometimes sick, showed no outward strain when he rode along the main street, "his form erect and straight, looking like the great soldier that he was, and his bright dark eyes and kind sweet smile lighting up his face."

Lee had become a familiar figure in the town, and every child knew him. There was a sudden, intimate glimpse caught of him standing in a blacksmith shop watching the smithy put shoes on Traveler. When the hissing sparks flew up from the bellows, the big horse shied and the blacksmith looked questioningly at Lee. "He is just a little nervous," Lee explained gravely. "He has been through a lot."

Recollections of and about ladies in the town revealed the unchanging "image" the Southern people held of him, which, while in essence reflecting the inner man, did not represent the complete man — as known to his family and intimates. Mrs. Cornelia McDonald, who saw much of the public Lee, wrote, "Courteous and elegant in manner, there was still a sort of unapproachable majesty about him that made all feel his superiority." But Mrs. Susan P. Lee, a daughter of the Reverend Pendleton married to a cousin of Lee, was shocked to see the General in a playful mood when she came for an afternoon visit to his family.

Among the many presents sent by admirers, Lee received from Scotland an afghan and a teapot warmer shaped like an ancient helmet. Mildred was playing the piano in the parlor when, to Mrs. Susan Lee's horror, the Symbol of the South came dancing into the room with the teapot warmer on his head and the afghan swung rakishly about his shoulders. She could hardly wait to flee the house and spread the report of Lee's unlikely behavior.

Fortunately for the statuesque element in the image, no one saw Mrs. R. E. Lee cutting the General's hair. She was his only barber.

Intimacy, however, did not affect Mary Lee's perspective of her husband. She wrote in a letter, "I was ambitious enough to hope that the day might come when in a political sense at least he might again be its [the South's] deliverer from the thraldom that now oppresses it."

Lee strongly believed in political action at the local level as the means of restoring representative government in the Southern states. For himself, however, when Judge Robert Ould had asked him if he would accept the nomination for governor, Lee had stated his belief that his election "would be used by the dominant party to excite hostility toward the state, and to injure the people in the eyes of the country." At the same time, he was careful that his name not be used in any association to indicate approval of the "dominant party." In October of 1867, he made this very clear in reply to a letter from Longstreet.

Longstreet had prospered in New Orleans, accepting a post with an insurance company that paid him $5000 a year, and in June he announced his intention of working with the Radical Republicans to restore Louisiana to the Union through their power. "It is fair to assume that the strongest laws are those established by the sword," he wrote. "The decision was in favor of the North, so that her construction becomes the law and should be obeyed." When the Radicals made capital of this letter, giving it wide publication, former Confederates turned on Longstreet as an "apostate," and then he wrote Lee asking for an endorsement of his course.

In his answer, Lee revealed his own attitude about Reconstruction laws. "While I think we should act under the law and according to the law imposed upon us, I cannot think the course pursued by the dominant political party the best for the interests of the country, and therefore cannot say so, or give them my approval. This is the reason why I cannot comply with the request in your letter. I am of the opinion that all who can should vote for the most intelligent, honest and conscientious men eligible for office, irrespective of former party opinions, who will endeavor" to pass laws "as beneficial as possible to the true interests, prosperity, and liberty of all classes and conditions of the people."

When Lee wrote Longstreet, in Virginia a serious reverse had just come to the political movement designed precisely to get out the vote for the men "most eligible for office irrespective of former party opinions."

8

During the first year of Reconstruction in 1867, when the subsurface massing of outrage through the Southern states began to be expressed in the rise of the secret societies and the Ku Klux Klan going from threats to acts of violence, a Virginia girl wrote, "I . . . felt defrauded of my rights because I never saw a Ku Klux; my native Virginia seems not to have had any." She saw no organized violence in her own state because Virginia leaders were working on political action with a broad scope.

At basis, secessionists in Virginia had been an outvoted minority before Lincoln resorted to resolution by force of arms, and after the war a strong Unionist sentiment was resumed by another minority, which had on its side the influence of Lee's reconciliatory position. The whole state, though the scene of America's first revolution (Nathaniel Bacon's in 1676) and though supplying political and military leaders to the American Revolution, was proud of a traditional conservative order in its society.

Virginia's largely hereditary planters did not depend on the one money crop of the large (often absentee-operated) plantations of the newsprung bourbons in the Lower South, and there was a gradation between the baronial planters and the small, independent farmer — the self-reliant yeomanry upon whom Jefferson based his "democracy." This made for an essentially stable population, in which the sons of heraldic privilege, such as Rooney and Rob Lee, having land, were willing to work it themselves while living in a cabin. Then, while predominantly agricultural, there were cities and many towns to which the dislocated planters and farmers could migrate. There they were forced to adjust to the abandonment of all previously known standards of living and goals for their children, many eking out submarginal existences crowded together in cold rooms, but they became absorbed in functioning communities.

Also, the population of freed Negroes was less ignorant, and contained more skilled and semi-skilled workers, than those from the rice fields and cotton fields. From the proximity to white families in which they had lived there was less of the hostility (especially the hostility of strangeness) than in those Negroes who as slaves had related to the white population mostly through the debased men who worked as overseers. In addition, there was an existing core of freed Negroes: before the war more than half the freed Negroes in the United States lived in Virginia and Maryland.

Along with the character of both races and the traditional conservatism of the society (with its diversified economy), the honest efforts of harassed Governor Pierpont toward reunion and the fairmindedness of the military district commander, General Schofield, tended to prevent or minimize the conflicts, especially racial, that would provide the Radicals with excuses to tighten the screws. While where the Radical rule increased its oppression the reaction of people unprotected by law increased in violence, where this interaction was controlled, the Virginia moderates — who before the war held the balance between secessionists and Unionists — were neither drawn to the irreconcilables nor provoked into personal violence.

Out of this untypical background in the Southern states, the conservative leaders took a pragmatic, though long-range, view of their situation along the lines Lee expressed in his letter to Longstreet. Accepting the reality that the Republican *Party* (not only the Radicals) comprised the only power in the United States for the foreseeable future, the native Virginians began to work toward the formation of a coalition movement with conservative Republicans.

The first split among the Republicans came in April, 1867, when a Republican State Central Committee held a meeting in Richmond. This meeting was led by Virginia's most infamous "scalawag," James Hunnicutt, a South Carolinian and former slaveholder who had become a demagogic Negro leader. As in Hunnicutt's Radical Republican convention of 210, 160 were Negroes, conservative Republicans in the state began to break off from the Radicals in opposition to forming virtually a Negro party.

The native movement toward a coalition sought to combine not only all conservative Republicans but all freedmen not under the influence of the demagogues who promised every Negro "forty acres and a mule, and $100 in cash." Virginia's Negroes, however, many intimidated by their own fellows, rebuffed the native whites and formed a fateful alliance with the alien adventurers.

In the atmosphere created by Hunnicutt's convention, Jefferson Davis was brought to Richmond for trial after a two years' imprisonment. The trial was held in the Customs House, across from the foot of the hill of Capitol Square, where Davis and Cabinet members had their offices during the war. Presiding was Judge Underwood, who had indicted Lee for treason. Underwood opened his court with a tirade against Richmond and the Confederacy which the reporter of the New York *World* called "a disgrace to the American bench." The reporter of the New York *Herald* wrote, "The strangest mixture of drivel and nonsense that ever disgraced a bench . . . without a parallel with its foul-mouthed abuse of Richmond."

In his address, Underwood declaimed, "In this very room we now occupy dwelt the fiery soul of treason, rebellion and civil war, and issued that fell spirit which starved by wholesale prisoners for the crime of defending the flag . . . assassinated colored soldiers . . ." and, charging the Confederacy with actions of the invading Federal armies, "burned towns and cities with a barbarity unknown to Christian countries."

After Underwood's charge, the prosecution announced it was not its intention to ask for a trial at this time. Bail was set at $100,000, with twenty securities. The first signer of the bail was Horace Greeley, followed by other New Yorkers, Cornelius Vanderbilt, Augustus Schell, Horace Clark and D. J. Jackson. Philadelphian Aristides Walsh signed before Richmonders assumed the rest of the securities. After leaving the courtroom, Davis was free on bail.

While Davis was in Richmond, Hunnicutt gathered crowds of his Negroes in the deserted complex of buildings which had formed Dr. McCaw's great military hospital on Chimborazo Hill, on the eastern outskirts of the city. After being worked up there by orators who told them, "If the white men of the South carry the elections, they will put you back in slavery," the Negroes were packed into the Old African Church to hear a carpetbagger urge them to enjoy their "rights and privileges in whatever manner you see fit." As soon as Judge Underwood left town, the speaker told them, "You may have a high carnival in whatever way you please. It is not for me to advise you what to do, for great masses do generally what they have a mind to."

When General Schofield reprimanded this carpetbagger Radical for his inflammatory speech, petitions began to reach Washington asking for his removal. Long ago Provost Marshal General Patrick had been removed, on a suggestion from Grant, because of his "well known kindness of heart."

By October Hunnicutt's Radicals showed the reality of their power in the election to be held for members of a Constitutional convention. This was to write a new state constitution that would make Virginia acceptable to the Radical Republicans. With ex-Confederates disfranchised by the "test-oath," Hunnicutt's Radicals polled a two-to-one majority. Of the seventy Radicals who dominated the Constitutional convention, fourteen were native Republicans, twenty-five were Negroes, and thirty-one were carpetbaggers — two from England, one each from Ireland, Scotland, Canada and Nova Scotia. Such was the group that was to provide Virginians with an improvement on the 1829 Constitution.

Despite the conservative leaders' long-range plans, the triumphant power of Hunnicutt's Radicals made it inevitable that Virginians felt antagonism to Northern individuals in their communities who worked and associated closely with Negroes. This antagonism was particularly directed at the schoolteachers. Of these, Myrta Lockett Avary wrote, "Their spirit was often noble and high as far as the black man's elevation — or their idea of it — was concerned; but toward the white South it was bitter, judicial, and unrelenting. Some were saints seeking martyrdom, and finding it; some were fools; some incendiaries; some all three rolled into one; some straight-out business women seeking good paying jobs."

Collectively their fundamental unwisdom was coming with preconceived ideas into a country about which they knew nothing and, instead of gaining the cooperation of the dominant population, separating the Negro from the community in which he must live.

In a provincial, homogeneous community such as Lexington, the alien's identification with a separate colored society was particularly noticeable. Children and youths in their teens, overhearing conversations in their homes without understanding the political context in which they were framed, developed feelings of derisive hostility for the enemy strangers as individuals. One object for this youthful group hostility in Lexington was a former Federal soldier, E. C. Johnston, who had come with the American Missionary Association and operated a school for freedmen.

Johnston had given up his teaching and opened a store, but, as he had established himself originally with the Negroes, he continued to associate only with them. This may or may not have been his preference. Since every alien agent who consorted with Negroes was suspected of being an incendiary, he was a pariah to the white community. Johnston seems to have remained in Lexington out of paranoia, as he made a point of carrying a pistol (forbidden by occupation law for native whites) to protect himself against lawless rebels. No one had ever given him any cause to go armed, and the derisive attitude of Lexington's young people was only an attitude — until a February afternoon in 1868. That day Johnston decided to go skating on the river, and the wheels began to turn as in a Greek plot.

9

On the ice the ex-Federal soldier avoided the adult groups who ignored him and skated downriver. A mile or more away from the crowds, he came upon a group of young town boys, some no more than twelve, among whom were several of the younger college students. Away from the control of adults, the boys began to yell at Johnston in much the way any pack of boys will taunt an outsider who represents a hostile element. What seemed to rankle Johnston was that their yelling, he said, imitated the yell the Rebels used "when making a charge on the enemy." The crowd did no more than yell, however, and Johnston skated on beyond them.

When he returned, the boys took up their taunts again and some began making the insults very personal. Caught up in the persecution of the alien, a twelve-year-old boy skated close and called him an unforgivable name. Evidently having struggled to contain his temper until then, Johnston lost his self-control and grabbed the twelve-year-old. Pulling out his pistol, he threatened to shoot the boy if he repeated the epithet.

At this, the child's older brother and other boys started for Johnston. Turning loose the small boy, the harassed man bolted upriver as fast as he could skate. The whole crowd then took after him, nearly all of them shouting curses and threats, and some throwing loose pieces of ice. Beyond several minor bruises from the ice pellets, no damage was done, and when Johnston left the river he was not pursued. That ended the episode of Johnston and the boys, including three Washington College students.

That night several unknown adults, incensed over Johnston's drawing a revolver on a twelve-year-old boy, went to his store. Whatever they might have done, Johnston was not there, and by the next day passions had cooled. As far as Lexington was concerned, it was only another of the inevitable collisions from which, fortunately, no bloodshed had resulted.

But it was not over for Johnston. Claiming the group was composed of Washington College students, and denying that the boy he threatened to shoot was only twelve, he went to the mayor and demanded arrests. When the mayor told him he had no authority over college students, Johnston went to General Frazar. Apparently not wanting to become involved with Lee again, Frazar called on his superior, Major General O. B. Willcox. Located at nearby Lynchburg, Willcox commanded the subdepartment within Military District No. 1.

Unlike volunteer Frazar, General Willcox, a West Pointer with a Regular Army background, had commanded a division in the IX Corps of the Army of the Potomac, and fought against Lee all the way to Appomattox. Willcox came personally to Lexington to see Lee in the friendly spirit that — except with the Sheridans — was usual for conferences between old soldiers.

Lee and Willcox talked amicably with the honest purpose of reaching an understanding. If Lee had heard anything about the episode before, it was the first time he had heard that Washington College students were involved in the chase of Johnston on the river. When General Willcox gave him the names of three students who were said to have been present, Lee immediately sent home two of the boys who admitted they had bedeviled Johnston. The third boy, on the scene only as a spectator, asked for permission to withdraw, and this was granted.

Curiously, no names of the town boys came to light, and no action could be taken against the majority of Johnston's unidentified insulters. General Willcox, as might have been expected from his background, was convinced that no threat to the peace existed and — saying that Johnston himself was partly to blame for threatening to shoot a small boy — ordered the incident closed.

Johnston's desire for revenge remained unappeased. However, he turned his vengeance not on the town boys who had been the leaders in the verbal assault but on General Lee and the college. Almost immediately he was presented with an opportunity to injure both.

In early March the Reverend E. P. Walton, one of the college's most zealous and effective fund raisers, managed to arrange a meeting of a group of prominent New Yorkers at Cooper Institute, for the purpose of launching a fund-raising campaign in the North. Henry Ward Beecher led the meeting, at which were read letters of support from residents of New York State, including Governor R. E. Fenton and Gerrit Smith, the famous abolitionist. Since Smith had helped finance John Brown's raid, his letter — along with a check — was particularly impressive:

"I wish our wealthy men of the North could give that college a couple of hundred thousand. Sufficient cause why the North should give large help to the South is that one is rich and the other poor. 'But the South is a sinner,' say thousands. True, she is; but sinners should be helped as well as saints. What, however, is the North but her fellow-sinner? England cursed us both with Slavery. Then we cursed ourselves with it — the North as well as the South upholding it. And then came on the war. The South, no less brave than the North, yet being by far the weaker party, fell under. Now it only remains for us to forgive each other, to love each other, and to do all the good we can to each other. So shall we become a united people; and, profiting by our great mistakes in the past, we shall enter upon a new and happy national life."

Immediately the supposedly religious *Independent*, a powerful abolitionist organ published in Brooklyn, denounced the purposes of the meeting on the grounds that the money would go to an institution headed by a traitor who "imbrued his hands in the blood of tens of thousands of his country's noblest men for the purpose of perpetuating human slavery." Saying Lee was not "fitted to be a teacher of young men," the long personal attack called up all the stock lies, including the usual charge about his responsibility for Andersonville. The appearance of the paper in Lexington was what Johnston needed.

By then Johnston had moved his store to a town farther west, Covington, and a friend of his in Lexington wrote the *Independent* a highly colored account of the Johnston episode. He placed all the blame on students, to substantiate the periodical's claims that Washington College was a treasonable institution to which Northern philanthropists would be ill advised to contribute. The *Independent* printed the letter, signed "A Resident of Lexington," and added an editorial stating that any Northerner who had contributed to Lee's College could see "that his money was worse than thrown away."

Encouraged by these denouncements, a Miss Julia Anne Shearman wrote a letter to the *Independent* in which she recounted horrendous stories of her stay in Lexington while teaching at a Negro school. She reported that she had appealed vainly to General Lee for protection against the insults and threats of his students. Like-minded publications picked up the letters and editorials from the *Independent*, and the damage was done.

It made no difference that the New York *Tribune* published a letter in which a staff officer of General Willcox gave the facts of the Johnston incident. Evidently Willcox had been annoyed by the anonymous author of the "Resident of Lexington" letter for criticizing him for "consulting with Lee and other notable rebels" instead of making military arrests.

Johnston denied the facts in the *Tribune* in a long letter published in the *Independent*. In this, Johnston accused Lee of personally preventing him from identifying the students engaged in "the riot" — as he then called it, without once referring to the town boys or the twelve-year-old he had threatened to shoot. This attack of Johnston's was not answered by anyone, since the harm already done was irremediable.

After only $4300 had been contributed to the college, Reverend Walton's fund-raising campaign dwindled off in the North. Further contributions came only from those individuals uninfected by the poisons disseminated either by abolitionists or by expedient fanatics who appealed to that audience. The Lexington *Gazette* sadly commented that systematic misrepresentation "kept up and increased Northern prejudice against us."

Old Isaac Trimble, Lee's former brigadier who had lost a leg at Gettysburg, had written the General when he first went to Washington College, advising him to advertise in the North. Lee should invite "the young to come and learn what the South really is, an ignorance of which has been the source of all our troubles." After the results of Reverend Walton's efforts, Lee grew convinced of his original belief that the North was not ready for the truth. However, he felt even more strongly that the truth should some day be known, and began to collect items from the newspapers to save for future use.

10

Lee's hope that truth must ultimately prevail was an integral part of his ability to accept without reacting the infamy heaped upon him and his fellow Southerners. Lee held an abiding faith in the sense of justice in the American people. The very need to hate the South after it was conquered, along with the distorted uses of the "moral cause" of slavery and then "equality," indicated some uneasiness about the methods of force used in a nationalistic war — the same methods by which Bismarck was then unifying Germany.

In watching the progress of Bismarck's Franco-Prussian war, Lee revealed his own deepening belief in the folly and futility of war as a solution of political differences. He wrote of France and Germany, "I have regretted that they did not submit their differences to the arbitration of the other Powers, as provided in the articles of the treaty of Paris of 1856. It would have been a grand moral victory over the passions of men, and would have so elevated the contestants in the eyes of the present and future generations as to have produced a beneficial effect. It might have been expecting, however, too much from the present standard of civilization, and I fear we are destined to kill and slaughter each other for ages to come. . . . As far as I can read the accounts, the French have met with serious reverses, which seem to have demoralized the nation and are therefore alarming. Whatever may be the issue, I cannot help sympathizing with the struggles of a warlike people to drive invaders from their lands."

During this period, with all his hope for the eventual truth, Lee began to lose some of his certainty that the American people would return to the Republic as it had existed in his formative years. On Washington's Birthday in the following year, Lee wrote Markie Williams: "This day formerly brought great rejoicing to the country, and Americans took delight in its celebration. It is still to me one of thankfulness and grateful recollections, and I hope that it will always be reverenced by virtuous patriots. The memories and principles of the men of the earlier days of the Republic should be cherished and remembered, if we wish to transmit to our posterity the Government, in its purity, they handed down to us."

Here Lee shifted to the contingent *if*. With this contingency Lee revealed the personal nature of his attachment for the America of his youth with the line, "Who can ever rival Washington in our esteem and affection?" In this closeness to Washington as a person, Lee could conceive of a soundly restored republic only as a nation which perpetuated those political, moral and social values he revered from the past.

Perhaps because of his environmental influences, the value Lee placed on perpetuity strongly embraced a belief in history as a guide to the present and — most urgently while under Reconstruction — to the future. In his reading at Lexington, Lee followed the advice he gave Mildred: "Read history, works of truth, not novels and romances. Get correct views of life and learn to see the world in its true light."

The first book Lee took from the college library was Volume II of Goldsmith's *Roman History*. Its early chapters described the anarchy that followed Caesar's death, and Professor Franklin K. Riley called attention to a passage that must have held considerable meaning to Lee. "The most sacred rights of nature were violated; three hundred senators and above two thousand knights were included in this terrible proscription; their fortunes were confiscated and their murderers enriched with their spoils." By reading the settlements of earlier convulsions, Lee wrote Colonel Marshall, "It is history that teaches us to hope."

A British admirer sent him a copy of Marcus Aurelius, which he read with especial interest, as he remembered passages he had long ago read in the *Meditations*. He read aloud to his family Philip Stanhope Worseley's translation of the *Iliad*, a copy of which the English poet had sent him. He read everything at hand on George Washington — Marshall, Sparks, Irving — and studies of the Constitution and the Revolution. In literary studies he read a *Life of Goethe*, and his favorite book of escape in the college library was *Calculus*. Typical of Southerners of his background he regularly took out issues of *Blackwood's Magazine*, and in that he followed the installments of "Historical Sketches of the Reign of George II."

Most of all he read the Bible, particularly the New Testament, in which he marked many passages. Nothing of a Bible-quoter, very occasionally Lee would use a quotation where it seemed called for. Once a minister was harshly denouncing the entire North over Lee's indictment for treason, and the General quietly interrupted him. "Doctor, there is a good book, which I read and you preach from, which says: 'Love your enemies, bless them that curse you, do good to them that hate you and pray for them that despitefully use you.'"

Lee actually tried to live by that, though, in his humility before God, he never assumed that he had always acted acceptably in the eyes of God. It was his ceaseless *effort* to live his life according to the divine design that sustained him and supported his long perspective. As to him Providence was an assumed reality, as the air he breathed and the mountains he gazed upon, his faith in Providence gave him the assurance that the reign by men of ill will must end — "this too shall pass."

He had come to realize that it would not pass in his time. He would not live to see its end, nor to know again his familiar world. As for the future, when these social convulsions were over, he believed that a general faith in Providence was the essential element needed for the new nation that would emerge.

His personal belief in the necessity of the spiritual element grew into Lee's strongest conviction about the future of the South within the nation. The Reverend Dr. J. L. Kirkpatrick, Professor of Moral Philosophy at the college, once told Lee a visiting minister was enjoying success in developing the religious welfare of the students. With one of his rare displays of emotion, Lee exclaimed, "If I could only know that all the young men in the college were good Christians, I should have nothing more to desire."

## CHAPTER XXVI

## "It's Time . . . to Rest"

IN GENERAL LEE'S sixtieth year, the summer of 1867, he suffered his first postwar siege of illness, and his mind began to turn toward acceptance of a decline leading to the end. In time he was only five years past the vigor of his magnificent manhood of the summer when he assumed command of the army. However, less than a year later had come the illness before Chancellorsville — diagnosed as "inflammation of the heart sac" — and the unremitting stresses that followed began the weakening of his damaged heart.

Lee's sickness in the summer of 1867, not medically diagnosed, may or may not have been related to his general cardiac condition. Lee did not write of the symptoms in detail, and the symptoms of the deterioration caused by his heart condition did not appear until 1869. As Lee's references to the encroachment of age began in 1867 before his late summer illness, it would seem he felt that in the duty God assigned him he was drawing near the point where he could say, "I have finished my course."

Whether he was aware of the strain on his heart physically, Lee acknowledged the drain on his inner forces in supporting the exertions of actual leadership during the war and the demands to maintain his self-control during Reconstruction. With intimates Lee began to make more frequent casual references to the war years, and several times mentioned the strain on his body and mind, especially during the last months. He continued to eschew talk of battles, the enemy, and controversial aspects such as strategy and personalities — though at the mention of Jeb Stuart his face lit up and he talked with warm enthusiasm of the cavalryman as his "ideal of a soldier." Of himself, he said to George Taylor Lee, the son of his brother Carter, "I do not see how I could have stood what I had to go through" without solitary rides on Traveler. "No matter what my cares or troubles were, I put all such things out of my mind, and thought only of my ride, of the scenery around me, or of other pleasant things, and so returned to my work refreshed . . . and in a better and stronger condition."

Indicating that a similar strain existed at Lexington, in his dual role as college president and people's leader, he told his nephew that his afternoon rides were essential to him. That summer he was able to enjoy the companionship of Mildred on his rides, through the acquisition of a second horse. Lucy Long, the mare given him by Stuart in 1862, had experienced considerable adventures since Lee last saw her in the spring of '64.

At that time, as the sorrel mare was "much reduced," he had sent her to a western county for rebuilding, and she had been returning to Lee with a stable of horses under Major Paxton when Petersburg was evacuated. Unable to reach the army, Major Paxton had moved his stable of horses south to North Carolina. When the fighting ceased Major Paxton, evidently not knowing Lucy Long belonged to Lee, gave her to a Virginia soldier, Mr. Deniux, for the ride back home. Back home Mr. Deniux sold her to a Mr. William Campbell for $125, who in turn sold her to a Dr. Fauntleroy, who seemed interested in breeding the mare. After an involved four-way correspondence, including Dr. Clarence Garnett — who first recognized the ten-year-old mare, with her blazed forehead and white hind legs — and the payment of $125, the lost friend was claimed by Rob for his father.

In riding with Mildred during the early summer, Lee began to talk of retiring. He liked to learn the name of every farmer in the county, and often, when looking at some simple homestead, he would say, "I wish I had a little farm of my own, where we could live in peace to the end of our days. You girls could attend to the dairy and the cattle and the sheep, and wait on your mother and me, for it is time now for us old people to rest."

Also in the early summer, on June 8, he wrote Rooney, "I think after next year I will have done all the good I can for the college, and I should like then, if peace is restored to the country, to retire to some quiet spot, east of the mountains [Blue Ridge], where I might prepare a home for your mother and sisters after my death."

In early August, before his illness, he wrote Rob how much he missed him since his youngest son had started farming on his own at Romancoke. "I feel sensibly, in my old age, the absence of my children."

This imminence of retiring from active life grew stronger after the undefined attack that struck him in August. With Mrs. Lee, Custis, Agnes, and her friend Mary Pendleton, the General had gone in July to White Sulphur Springs, the prewar resort of fashion which by a drunken loop in the surveyor's line was embraced in the new state of West Virginia. Until his illness, Lee enjoyed himself as he always did in a gentle society where pretty young girls were present. As at many of the watering places, families resided in cottages and the guests gathered in a main building for meals and at evenings in the parlor. Though the people showed him the usual honors (they stood when he entered the parlor), there was none of the crowding around that embarrassed him, and visits to the Lee cottage in "Baltimore Row" were informal. In the midst of this pleasant relaxation, Lee began to feel sick.

When the family moved on to Old Sweet Springs, Lee could barely make the ride on Traveler. At Old Sweet, whose red-brick buildings nestled in a beautiful, tranquil spot, Lee became so ill that he was put to bed. Without describing the nature of his suffering, he wrote that all the sickness in his life put together "would not equal the attack I experienced." In early September, when it was time for the family to begin the torturous journey by stagecoach and railroad back to Lexington, Lee was forced to go by easy stages, stopping at Hot Springs, Healing and Rockbridge. On September 12 from Healing Springs he wrote Mrs. Lee, already home, that he had expected to resume his journey that morning but "did not feel able." Back in Lexington, he wrote Rooney on the 20th that he was too feeble to attend to the "pressing business connected with the college." More than one month later, October 25, he wrote Rooney he had been prevented answering a letter "by business and sickness," and that was a very important letter from Rooney. He was getting married again.

Rooney's fiancée was Mary Tabb Bolling, of Petersburg. Lee remembered the attractive young lady pleasantly from the days of the siege, when her father, G. M. Bolling, had shown him many kindnesses, but he did not feel up to attending the wedding. "I do not think that I could add to the enjoyment of any one." Instead, he suggested that the couple come to Lexington for a visit after the wedding.

At that, Rooney took a trip to Lexington to persuade his father to come to the wedding in Petersburg. Evidently Lee's illness had passed gradually, leaving him weakened, and his strength had returned with a slowness that produced an uncertainty about his physical powers and a withdrawal from demanding social situations. While he agreed to attend the wedding, in mid-November, on writing Rooney about plans, he said, "I do not think I shall be able to go to the White House at all [before the wedding]. I would not be able to aid you or Rob, my only object, and would put you to much trouble."

From the social schedule Lee was able to maintain when he did go to Petersburg and Richmond at the end of November, manifestly the physical effects of the summer's attack had passed. His fatigue came, with declining power, from the burden of being "General Lee."

2

General Lee's trip to the wedding was coincident with his appearance in Richmond as a witness in the trial of Jefferson Davis. Since his release on bond, the former President had been wandering around restlessly awaiting his trial on the charge of treason: spending the summer in Canada, in the fall he had tried Havana and New Orleans before returning to the desolate wreckage of Brierfield, his home in Mississippi. In Richmond, he was staying at the home of Judge Robert Ould, wartime commissioner of prisoner exchange. Whether or not Lee knew Davis was staying at Judge Ould's, after his supper at the Exchange Hotel Lee went to visit the judge on Monday night, November 25.

For the first time since before the evacuation of Petersburg, Lee and Davis met — in the same neighborhood as in the bitterly cold months of the last winter of the war. Though Davis had aged since his imprisonment, Lee was surprised at how well he looked, and wrote Mrs. Lee that he seemed cheerful. Following his capture, Davis had accepted the martyr's role thrust upon him, and in this his courage and innate dignity — free of the stiffness that sometimes marked his period of authority — revealed the man at his very best. "The consolation that I derived from the intense malignity shown to me by the enemy was in the hope that their hate would, by concentrating on me, be the means of relieving my fellow countrymen."

Yet, in this letter to Lee's former chief of staff, General Chilton, Davis revealed that nothing had changed the delusions he held during the last year of the fighting. "That hope has been disappointed, and the worst fears which I entertained as the consequence of the surrender of the armies without terms . . . have been fully realized. Each concession has been but the means of securing further progress in the destruction of the South." He would never accept the reality that the military leaders in the fields had no choice except surrender without terms or that the postwar "destruction of the South" was not the consequence of concessions following surrender without terms but the application of force by those who possessed it.

In Judge Ould's parlor the night before the trial it was not likely that the former associates in war talked of the past. From a reference in Lee's next morning letter to his wife, the conversation at the Oulds' generally was about the trial. Of anything Davis might have said, Lee wrote only that "he inquired particularly after you all." Lee did not mention that he and the ex-President posed together for a photograph taken of their meeting.

For the next two days Lee went to Judge Underwood's court, where he was questioned as a witness, and Davis's trial was again postponed. On Thursday morning, the 28th, Lee boarded a special car of wedding guests for the twenty-mile trip from Richmond to Petersburg over the railroad tracks he had defended with his starving army those long months. It was the first time since the fighting that he was visibly and admittedly affected by memories of the ordeal.

Rob said that his father "did not enter into the gay conversation of the young people, but appeared sad and depressed." Of the trip Lee himself wrote, "When our armies were in front of Petersburg I suffered so much in body and mind on account of the good townspeople . . . that I have always reverted to them in sadness and sorrow. My old feelings returned to me as I passed well-remembered spots and recalled the ravages of the hostile shells."

After the wooden coaches shook to a halt in the Washington Street Station, Lee heard a band playing the "Marseillaise." The people were forbidden to play "Dixie," or to show the Confederate flag or any insignia, but the occupation forces were apparently unaware that a Southern version of the "Marseillaise" had been very popular.

> *Sons of the South, awake to glory,*
> *A thousand voices bid you rise . . .*
> *Your country every strong arm calling,*
> *To meet the hireling Northern band*
> *That comes to desolate the land . . .*
> *To arms! . . .*

With the strains rolling through him, Lee climbed down the coach steps to face a crowd that, jamming the station, broke into cheers at the sight of him.

This was one demonstration that seemed to please the General. He had carried in his mind that remembrance of a battered city, its freezing citizens emaciated and fearful, and he was greeted by a cheerful people who looked, at least outwardly, healthy and prosperous. He wrote, "A load of sorrow which has been pressing upon me for years was lifted from my heart." From the moment he greeted old friends in the throng, Lee entered into the spirit of the festivities and seemed to give himself to the traditional ceremonies that gave a sense of perpetuity from the past. No longer ago than the life span of man Ann Carter had been married in the ceremony at Shirley plantation, and for the wedding of her grandson the notables and the simple of their world turned out to do homage to her son, who far surpassed the glory of his colorful father.

General Mahone was among those who had prospered well. A successful young railroad executive before the war, Mahone found quick opportunity in the physical rebuilding of the railroads, whose tracks, rolling stock and depots were mostly destroyed. With great enterprise, he manipulated the depleted bonds to form three short-line roads into a new system (which became the Norfolk and Western) and was on his way to becoming a new power in the state. Mahone provided a carriage with four white horses to convey Lee to his home. The crowd followed Lee to the doors of the Mahone house, where Lee was to stay.

That afternoon, wearing a new suit acquired for the occasion, he went to the overflow church for the wedding. A radiant Mildred was the only daughter present, but both of Rooney's brothers were there — "Custis very composed," Lee wrote his wife, "and Rob suffering from chills." Among the groomsmen was Cousin Fitz, so recently a fellow division commander in the cavalry. "The bride looked lovely," Lee wrote, "and was in every way captivating."

After the wedding Lee remained for two days at the Mahones, where the lavish servings at breakfasts and dinners were a contrast not without melancholy to the sparse diet of the last winter of the war. In all his relief, and in his pleasure in the marriage, Lee did not forget those last days. He made a sentimental journey west of the city to the site of the Turnbull house, which he had left under the fire of Federal guns on April 1, 1865.

His ostensible reason for the trip was to visit an old woman who had served him eggs and butter during those last months. But he looked long at the charred remnants of the house and the lines of earthworks that remained almost as he had left them in the area of those last established headquarters, which he evacuated on the way to certain defeat.

It was at the Turnbull house he had received the news of Powell Hill's death and said, "He is at rest now, and we who are left are the ones to suffer." A week later at Appomattox he had said how easy it would be to ride out in front of the lines and "it would be all over." He had meant it quite literally when he said, "I would rather die a thousand deaths" than to meet General Grant. Then a year and a half after Appomattox, in the fall of 1866, Lee wrote Rooney that he had missed visiting the grave of his daughter Annie, "whose quiet and innocent repose I much covet." As Lee was not one to speak in hyperbole, obviously some element of the will to life went out of him at the defeat of his army and all it implied.

Though the missing element did not affect his relations to his family, his state and country, nor his task at the college, the encompassing sense of duty to God and the work God assigned him became a sustaining force without the hope of rewards on earth. At the bleak site of the Turnbull house, Lee returned to the hours when all his energies had been gathered in a concentrated intensity that would not come again. The postwar period was in no sense an anticlimax to Lee. In the way he lived, giving each day that day's value, it would have been blasphemous to minimize a day of life which God gave. But with the passing of the army with which he identified himself, and the cause of independence it represented, the burden of carrying his duty grew heavier, and his thoughts turned to relief from it.

Lee was not depressed by the journey to the past; if anything, the contemplation renewed his energies for a continuation of the socializing he had dreaded before coming. On Saturday he returned to Richmond, and spent an evening dropping in on old friends.

He was staying at the Exchange Hotel, where East Franklin sloped downhill from Capitol Square, on the fringes of the area gutted by the evacuation fire. Almost nothing remained of the night life that had flourished in the "sporting section" during the war, but the hotel, convenient to the commercial section being rebuilt on Main Street, was a favorite place for Northern commercial travelers and the country people — still called "planters" — who could afford to come to town. Local beaux and belles, without the cash to patronize its once famous dining room, used its parlors for meeting places.

Here all the guests swarmed around Lee when he crossed the lobby, Northerners vying to shake hands with him, and as at Petersburg, the General seemed pleased rather than embarrassed. Perhaps he was relieved to find a cheerful humor also in Richmond. In the Capitol Square neighborhood he was seeing only a limited section of the city, remote from the neighborhoods where displaced farm families were suffering at the beginning of cold weather, but in this center of Richmond nothing in the purposeful attitude of the citizens suggested that they were defeated people living under an occupation government.

In the remote area of Lexington, in thinking of the cities as he had seen them last (he had seen nothing of Richmond on his brief trip in January, 1866), Lee had probably imagined that the humiliations of Reconstruction rule had prevented any emotional recovery in the people or physical recovery of the former Confederate capital. On the contrary, the citizens of Richmond had displayed during 1867 an incredible determination even while Reconstruction measures multiplied the occupation force's areas of authority.

Considerate General Schofield, under pressure from the Radicals, constantly replaced native officials in city offices with military appointees. When Judge W. H. Lyons died, the people were angrily hurt when Colonel H. B. Burnham, of New York, was placed in the court long presided over by a greatly loved Richmonder. These steady encroachments into local government seemed to goad the citizens rather than to induce despair. The Corn and Flour Exchange was opened, the Board of Trade reorganized with its name changed to the Chamber of Commerce, eleven banks were doing business, and two months before Lee came to Richmond the people had shown their resolution and faith by voting in a local election to subscribe $2 million to a new railroad. This railroad, the Chesapeake and Ohio, was the consolidation of the Covington and Ohio with the line that Lee had devoted years of his life to protecting — the Virginia Central.

Though the growing prosperity of some individuals was by no means reflected in the general population, the prosperity of the few promised work for the many, along with bringing cash — United States dollars — into their city again. During the weeks before Lee's visit, the citizens could even be diverted by a murder trial. Two days before Lee arrived, the jury disagreed over the conviction of Jeter Phillips, a former Confederate soldier, for the slaying of his wife, and papers sold on the downtown streets almost as in the old times.

(There was a curious sidelight on Reconstruction in Phillips's later conviction in 1868. Around the same time Caesar Griffin, a Negro in Lexington, was sentenced to two years in prison for the nonfatal shooting of Judge Brockenbrough's young son. In the U. S. District Court, Judge Underwood ordered Griffin released on the grounds that the Rockbridge County judge had no authority, since Virginia's courts were not legal. When Phillips's appeal for a new trial was denied by Virginia's Court of Appeals, his attorneys immediately petitioned Judge Underwood for a writ of habeas corpus on the same grounds that he had freed Griffin: the Virginia courts were not legal. Underwood was saved from the dilemma of emptying the penitentiary by Chief Justice Salmon P. Chase, of the U. S. Supreme Court, who reversed Underwood's ruling in the Griffin case and established the legality of Virginia's state courts — even though Virginia was not a state.)

Lee apparently took no interest in the trial, one of the most sensational in Richmond's history. Monday, a cold December 2, he went by boat down the James River on a promised visit to Harrison kinspeople at Brandon. He sailed past the earthworks at Drewry's Bluff on the south side and Chaffin's Bluff on the north side, where his weary ragamuffins had crossed the pontoon, panting from one line of works to another. Brandon plantation was on the south side of the river, in the neighborhood where Wade Hampton had run off 2500 Federal beeves in the fall of '64 to provide meat for the army. Brandon, with its handsome gardens high on a bluff, was a place of serene beauty, but Lee's mind returned to the past. He thought of Shirley, across the river, where he had spent so many happy times in his "earlier life," and he longed to see the paneled rooms associated in his memory with his mother.

Relieved by the signs of recovery beginning in Richmond and Petersburg, Lee had also reestablished the flow with the past, and he returned to Lexington in stronger spirits — though there was no change in his acceptance of the approaching end of his life.

### 3

During 1868 Lee was provided with the interest of building a new house. The growth of the faculty at the college required more housing, and the board voted $15,000 for a new house for the president. General Lee never intended it to be his own home; he guarded a fund put aside for a home for Mrs. Lee after his death. However, he designed "the President's House" according to his own preferences and the convenience of his family, without introducing any features that would either set the building apart from its fellows or leave architectural eccentricities for future occupants to deal with.

Custis worked with his father on the plans, and the two engineers designed a traditional house with the wide central hall and large rooms on either side. It was of two stories, with attic and basement. Mrs. Lee's room was in the southwest corner on the first floor, with General Lee's above, and both commanded a fine view of the Alleghenies to the west. Downstairs there would be a formal parlor (in which Mildred's piano would not dominate the room) as well as a family sitting room. The dining room, as in many plantation houses, was very large, to accommodate family gatherings. A side entrance was built into this room for the passage of children. In the backyard a brick stable was built for Traveler, who then looked something like a plucked chicken from the damages his mane and tail had suffered from souvenir-hunters.

As locally made bricks were cheap, the General and his son built the walls with a thickness of four bricks, with an air space in the center. The cluster of chimneys at Stratford Hall was reproduced in one central cluster, in which one of the chimneys was actually a ventilating shaft. In experimenting with air conditioning, over the door of each main room the Lees built grilles about 12 inches by 24 inches which were connected with the central ventilating chimney. When a trigger opened these grilles, cool air was brought into the house in summer and fresh air could ventilate the closed rooms in the winter.

General Lee came regularly to watch the progress of the carpenters, and one of them recalled that Lee said, "This is the only house I've ever built and it must be right." The work on the house progressed steadily during the year, but for some reason it was not ready for occupancy until after the end of the college year the following June, 1869. Money may have been a factor, as a rear brick-floored basement was never completed.

The Lees' personal finances had improved considerably since the end of the fighting. Although many of his securities were rendered worthless by the fall of the Confederacy, his remaining stocks began to pay an interest of around $3500 a year. His percentage of the tuitions raised his pay to something over $4500 a year, bringing his income to above $8000 a year. This was relative affluence in a period when the large commercial companies that sought his services dangled a $10,000 salary as a bait. Lee continued to act poor — talk "poor-mouth," as the country people said —

in his preoccupying anxiety for the future of his daughters and his then "helpless wife."

Of the three major properties in the Arlington estate that were confiscated, the Virginia courts were able to reclaim only Smith's Island, an abandoned stretch of four thousand acres on the Atlantic Ocean. Rob and Rooney, who diverted much of the flood of his energy to working with his father, appraised the property and bought it jointly for $9000 advanced them by the General. Along with lending his sons this money without interest, Lee invested $9000 (by the sale of some securities) to form a fund that would constitute at least a part of the cash inheritance left his daughters by their grandfather's will.

Washington Custis had not foreseen the loss of profits from the total Arlington property, along with most of the property itself, and Lee had struggled since 1861 with the problem of adhering to the intent, if not the letter, of his father-in-law's will. In a family less unified any one of the heirs could have made trouble. As it was, Custis Lee, the big loser (Arlington itself), cared only about his parents' welfare, and the girls continued as dependents without worrying about their cash inheritance.

The girls, with their constant traveling around and clothes necessary for the formal occasions they liked, were a steady drain on Lee's income. New furniture had to be acquired. Aside from transient cooks, Mrs. Lee always had a personal maid. Though Lee wore his clothes beyond the point where a less established person would be unwilling to appear in them, he did need new suits and linen for making appearances as the college president. Most of all, the trips to the springs were costly in cash.

Through the frugality instilled by his mother, ceaseless concentration on small economies constituted a lifelong habit, but never before in his married life had he pinched on such a modest scale. When Arlington was the base, with its abundance of house servants, Lee had kept good horses and fine carriages, turned himself out well (even during the war his uniforms were handsome), and he liked the cash on hand for the trips his wife and daughters took.

With the loss of income after the war, his horror of debt — also instilled by his mother and a sort of reverse heritage from his father — goaded him to sacrifice the good physical things of life in order that his wife and children would never be left as Light-Horse Harry Lee had left his mother and her children. As Lee advised his children, he strongly believed that a person lost his independence when he lost solvency. The one point on which he would indulge his family and himself was in the vacations to the springs. There was no way to economize on the set rate charged by the spas that catered to the rich and the very rich from the North.

The expenses of the springs were justified on the grounds of health, for Mrs. Lee and for the General's "rheumatic" pains. But there were less costly resorts in Virginia than "the White" and "the Sweet," "the Hot" and "the Warm," as the most fashionable places were referred to by their habitués. At those long-established resorts, Lee was assured of his family's meeting old friends, of fellow guests who would not make a to-do over him, and of an understanding care of his wife. Unable to go to the main building, Mrs. Lee was served her meals in her cottage.

There was also the factor of mental health for Mrs. Lee in the summer of 1868. Imprisoned in the house, forced to remain there alone on such occasions as when the rest of the family went off to her son's wedding, she had begun to brood over their troubles and had grown nervous. Lee believed her agitation increased her suffering, and he was "anxious to give her new scenes and new thoughts."

In mid-July the General and Mrs. Lee, accompanied by Mildred, left for Warm Springs for a stay before Lee went on to the White. The Warm Springs buildings, at the foot of a hill, looked north up the lush valley that led to Monterey — the scene of Lee's miserable Western Virginia Campaign in 1861. The baths at Warm Springs, supposedly of great therapeutic value, were two circular pools (one for men and one for ladies) of sulphurous water enclosed in wooden buildings. The body tended to float in the heavy water and, if nothing else, an hour in the "baths" was very relaxing. Mrs. Lee seemed to improve, as did Agnes, who joined them at the springs after having been detained by sickness in Baltimore. But Lee's pet, Mildred, came down with a cold, which took a turn for the worse. She was confined to bed with a low, pertinacious fever thought to be typhoid.

Since Mildred's room was on the second floor, and Mrs. Lee could not get up the stairs, the nursing fell upon Agnes and the General. Soon the patient dismissed Agnes and would allow only her father to nurse her. At night she could not go to sleep unless he sat beside her, with his hand in hers. With illimitable patience and gentleness, he catered to Mildred's whims, writing Rooney, "You know she is very fanciful, and as she seems to be more accessible to reason from me, I have come to be her chief nurse, and am now writing in her room, while she is sleeping."

Could Lee have remembered, as the hours passed in the sickroom, that a quarter of a century before at Fort Hamilton, New York, the grown son to whom he was writing the letter had been a sick little boy who improved only under his father's ministrations? Lee had written then about Rooney to Mrs. Fitzhugh, as he now wrote about Mildred to Rooney. Possibly his early experiences in looking after his sick mother had developed the tender patience that served in healing.

Mildred was not well until late August. Then, leaving Mrs. Lee and Agnes at the Hot, no more than five miles from the Warm, Lee and Mildred went on to White Sulphur as he had originally planned. There Lee did not recapture the pleasure of the summer before, for he was circuitously drawn into the area of politics.

4

A number of prominent Southerners gathered at the White that summer, and to see them came General William S. Rosecrans, recently of the U. S. Army. Old Army men warmly remembered "Rosy," a genial and friendly man, and Lee remembered him particularly as his opponent in the second part of the Western Virginia campaign in the region of the springs. Fortune had not treated Rosecrans kindly.

Graduating in the West Point class of 1842, Rosecrans served in the engineers until a few years before the war, when slow promotion forced him to leave the service for mining engineering in the Western Virginia mountains. Returning with volunteers, he rose to army commander in the West and fought Bragg and Longstreet at Chickamauga. Not a lucky general, and a Democrat, Rosecrans came under the disfavor of the Radicals and resigned from the army shortly after the war. In the postwar years success had eluded him in civilian life and, as a new venture, he was managing the election campaign of Governor Horatio Seymour, running against Grant for President. (Andrew Johnson, who had narrowly escaped conviction after he was impeached by the Radicals, would not stand for reelection.)

Rosecrans, in neat clothes that were rusty with wear, had come to White Sulphur to gain the support of the ex-Confederates in the Democratic campaign. The Democrats would have to counter the claims that the Republicans represented the "Union" party and that their defeat would put the Negroes back in slavery. At Rosecrans's request, Lee gathered the Southerners in his cottage. They all assured the ex-Federal general of the people's desire for restoration of the Union, with acceptance of the Negroes' status, but nothing positive was accomplished. Then Rosecrans wrote Lee and asked if he personally would get the signatures of the members of the gathering on a formal statement that could be used in the campaign.

Though Lee believed this was the kind of gesture to be made, whether or not it elected Seymour, his position was, as he later wrote, "[I] did not intend to connect myself with the political questions of the Country." It happened that among the guests was Alexander H. H. Stuart, Virginia's elected congressman who had been refused his seat in Washington in 1866. Lee turned to him. At the time Lee approached him, Stuart, a staunch Virginia Unionist from the Valley town of Staunton, was engaged in a personal campaign to bring Virginians to ratify the new state constitution, which the Radical-controlled convention had introduced in April.

This was at the time when the Radical powers in Washington had suddenly changed their minds about keeping the Southern states indefinitely out of the Union and, to get the Negro votes in those states for the presidential election, were hurrying their readmission as soon as their new Reconstruction constitutions were ratified. Except for a "scalawag" in North Carolina, the states were returned with carpetbagger governors — South Carolina had one from Ohio, Florida one from Wisconsin, Louisiana one from Illinois — and mostly carpetbaggers in the state governments and as representatives to Congress. As an example, Alabama had a dubious native as nominal head, but other state officials were from New York, Maine, Wisconsin and Ohio; one of its senators was an Ohioan and one was a New England sutler (army peddler) who, by way of Iowa, had come into the state following the Federal troops. Four of its six congressmen had come to Alabama as agents of the Freedmen's Bureau.

The Reconstruction constitutions were ratified in six states partly because the representative citizens had grown apathetic about using a ballot box controlled by Radicals, and Negroes and Republicans polled a majority. Also, the new constitutions in those states were less proscriptive than those in Mississippi and Virginia. In Mississippi the Ku Klux Klan (then at its peak) out-intimated the Union League and scared the Negroes away from the polls, so that the native whites could vote against ratifying the new state constitution.

Alexander Stuart's purpose was to prevent Virginia's making the same choice. Two major provisions in the new constitution aroused resistance — the Fourteenth Amendment and the inclusion of the "test-oath." The Fourteenth Amendment, with its inferential enfranchisement of the Negroes, did not alone present an insurmountable obstacle. While a sincere belief existed that the recently freed slaves were unqualified for the responsibilities of suffrage and office-holding, the people's major opposition came from having a change in their internal affairs forced upon them. On that point Stuart believed the natives could be convinced that it was more realistic to be in the Union with the Negroes voting than out of the Union with the Negroes voting.

But the "test-oath" — which disfranchised and excluded from office all ex-Confederates, military and civil — placed the majority of the native white population, including their natural leaders, in the dilemma of being "damned if they did and damned if they didn't." If they refused to ratify the constitution, the state would remain under military occupation outside the Union; if they did ratify the constitution, the people would be turning the state over to the rule of Radical aliens and Negroes. Any uncertainty about the nature of the future under the new constitution was removed when Major General Schofield, presumably on orders, replaced conservative Governor Pierpont with H. H. Wells, a Radical from Detroit. Wells, a brevet brigadier general of volunteers, had first come to Virginia as a provost marshal, and his ambition was to become the elected governor when the state returned to the Union under Radical control.

To persuade native conservatives to accept the enfranchisement of the Negroes for the larger practicality of returning Virginia to the Union under the government of her own people, Stuart would first have to obtain support in Washington for removing the "test-oath" from the constitution. If this were accomplished, Stuart could form the desired coalition government with the conservative Republicans in the state, who disassociated themselves from the Negro party as formed by Wells's Radicals.

These Republicans had as a candidate Gilbert Walker, then in Norfolk. Not a native himself, Walker could be called "a nice carpetbagger." Nothing of a demagogue, he possessed a pleasing manner and personal charm, he was sympathetic to the native population and, if his interest in the state's future did not go very deep, his financial adventures were on a relatively modest scale. With Walker, Virginia could return to the Union under a Republican governor, though with all Radical domination removed. But everything was blocked by the "test-oath."

Manifestly, Stuart could do nothing about eliminating this from the state constitution during Johnson's collapsed administration. If, however, Grant were elected, Grant would be in a stronger position than Johnson, and up until that time appeared sympathetic to the South in his desire for a restoration of the Union. Stuart believed he could approach Grant about having the "test-oath" voted on separately.

On the other hand, if Democrat Seymour were elected, the problems of the South would be over. Thus, when Lee approached Stuart at White Sulphur, he gave this farsighted realist an opportunity to express conservative Southern views to a national audience — whether Democrat or (non-Radical) Republican.

Stuart's paper, based on the point of "the re-establishment . . . of the right of self-government . . . justly regarded as the birthright of every American," denied the charges that the South felt hostility to the Negroes, and developed the conviction that adjustments between the white population and the former slaves would be solved when demagogues ceased agitating the total society by pitting the races against one another.

Stuart expressed the realistic humanism of those actually involved in the solution of a sociological problem without precedent or program. The great need of both races was the opportunity to begin making adjustments. Since the former slaves could not be absorbed as citizens in the society without the willingness and cooperation of the dominant white population, the imperative measure was to end the use of force — the bayonet — which kept the native whites on the defensive. Stuart expressed Lee's fundamental point, the need to end the contentious spirit of the war, in order that the South might adjust to its new condition in peace.

On the point of representative government, Stuart was candid in stating that he did not believe the country as a whole felt the recently freed slaves were capable of operating governments. "It is true that the people of the South, in common with a large majority of the people of the North and West, are, for obvious reasons, inflexibly opposed to any system of laws which would place the political power of the country in the hands of the Negro race . . . This opposition springs from no feeling of enmity, but from a deep-seated conviction that, at present, the Negroes have neither the intelligence nor the other qualifications which are necessary to make them safe depositories of political power. They would inevitably become the victims of demagogues who, for selfish purposes, would mislead them to the serious injury of the public."

But his conviction that it was not practical — nor, frankly, desirable — to place Virginia's government in the hands of Negroes should not imply any desire to treat the Negro unfairly. On the contrary, he could promise that Virginians, with representative government restored, would "treat the Negro population with kindness and humanity and fulfill every duty incumbent upon peaceful citizens." In this, Stuart expressed the view of his generation. In the context of the relationship of their time to the Negro, neither Stuart nor Lee (any more than had Lincoln) extended this kindly feeling into a concept of "equality." Stuart felt no need to mention the idea in addressing a Northern audience, nor did the majority of Northerners expect it.

At that time the interest on the $2 million George Peabody Fund was being used to help found the public school system in Southern states. The executive director of the Fund was Dr. Barnas Sears, of Massachusetts, who was serving as president of Brown University when appointed. Dr. Sears, working on the scene in various Southern states, was supported by board chairman Robert C. Winthrop, also from Massachusetts, in his strong stand against forming "mixed schools" in the new system. As his purpose was to "encourage universal education," and not to become involved "with any party questions," the Fund's general agent in the Southern states worked actively in the development of separate schools and in opposition to Sumner's "mixed schools" clause in the 1875 Civil Rights bill.

Even the Radicals themselves (except for some individuals) in Southern state governments made no practical application of the "equality" abstraction. When Virginia's new state constitution established public schools, the Northern whites who dominated the convention flatly refused to consider the Negro members' proposal to establish "mixed schools." One of the leading Northern advocates of the Fourteenth Amendment put himself on record in Congress with the statement that separate schools did not constitute an abridgment of "the privileges and immunities of citizens," and stated specifically that "mixed schools" were not included in the purposes of the amendment. Within the national attitudes of his day, Stuart's paper was a well-reasoned and dispassionate appeal for the end of Reconstruction rule — as he said, for "peace."

It was a letter that could be useful to the Democrats, with nothing in it to antagonize a non-Radical Republican, as Grant was assumed to be. Actually, the appeal of the letter was to the Northern population in general.

Since Stuart's paper essentially expressed Lee's consistently held viewpoint, the General, after deleting a word he felt might be too strong, signed it. Thirty-one other Southerners, many with nationally known names, followed with their signatures. At Democratic headquarters "the White Sulphur Letter" was so successful that Rosecrans, after conference with some of Seymour's campaign advisers, sent Lee a proposed program of its use and urged him to have public meetings held in the Southern states to ratify the paper.

Lee received the communications when, in mid-September, he was back in Lexington after his unrestful vacation. Through General John Echols he sent the correspondence to Stuart, stating that he had gone as far as he could. So had Stuart. Avoiding any alliances, he took no part in Seymour's campaign.

When Grant was elected with the slim popular margin of the Negro votes in the Southern states, it appeared that the Radical program did not enjoy the support of the majority of the Northern population. Assuming that Grant himself would not support Reconstruction rule, Alexander Stuart, then heading a "Committee of Nine," called on the President-elect. Grant unhesitatingly assured Stuart that, as soon as he could after his inauguration, he would move to eliminate the "test-oath" from the constitutions of Virginia and Mississippi, and have this provision voted upon separately.

Grant kept his word. Though Governor Wells and Radical committees from Virginia warned Grant of the necessity of retaining the "test-oath" in the state constitution (that is, it was necessary to their tenure in office), in his first message to Congress the new President recommended an act which would permit a separate vote on the provision disqualifying ex-Confederates from voting or holding office.

Lee appeared remote from these political activities affecting his own state. After his brief involvement, through Stuart and Rosecrans, with the famous "White Sulphur Letter," he withdrew from the political area as though withdrawing his hand from fire. As far as he showed the world, his interest was centered at Washington College during the period — from the fall after his return from the springs in 1868 to the fall of 1869 — when Virginia was struggling for readmission to the Union. Lee's effect was in the cumulative influence of his example, in which moderation made it possible for Virginia leaders to reclaim their own state government by legal and orderly processes.

5

In July, 1869, when Virginians were given the opportunity to vote on the new constitution and the "test-oath" separately, the people naturally repudiated the "test-oath" while ratifying the constitution which presumably qualified the state for readmission. But the Radicals were not done.

Congress had then passed the Fifteenth Amendment. Dismissing the confusing clauses of discrimination against ex-Confederates and the vague implications of suffrage in the Fourteenth Amendment, the Fifteenth Amendment stated simply that the rights of citizens "to vote shall not be denied or abridged . . . on account of race, color, or previous condition of servitude." The Radical Congress then ruled that Virginia could not be readmitted until its General Assembly ratified this amendment. When this new provision was introduced, the blocks to Virginia's readmission took a farcical turn.

General Schofield had by then been succeeded as military commander by General George Stoneman, and after he had also displayed the undesirable qualities of fairmindedness, General E. R. S. Canby became — as the locals referred to him — "the monarch." Canby, a fifty-one-year-old Regular Army man from Kentucky, seems to have been a fool. Though the citizens had voted to abolish the "test-oath" as a requirement for office, the state was not yet readmitted to the Union, and Canby ruled that the "test-oath" was thus still in effect. However, the state could not be readmitted to the Union until the General Assembly ratified the Fifteenth Amendment, and Canby forbade the General Assembly to meet because of its ex-Confederate members who could not take the "test-oath."

This impasse was broken by the United States Attorney General, who ruled that the General Assembly could meet for the single and specific purpose of ratifying the Fifteenth Amendment. Hence, in October, while Virginia was not a state, its legislature ratified the Fourteenth and Fifteenth Amendments. After this ratification by a non-state and over the last-ditch stand of the die-hard Vindictives like Charles Sumner — who shouted in the Senate, "Virginia is smoking with rebellion" — Virginia was accepted as a state of the Union on January 26, 1870.

While among the last of the former Confederate states to be readmitted, Virginia was among the first to be readmitted under a government without significant vestiges of the Reconstruction rulers. With Conservative Republican Walker replacing Wells as governor, the new General Assembly, containing a bloc of Radicals and Negroes, was dominated by white conservatives. Some Federal troops remained in the state but not in official occupation, and Canby exercised no authority in civil affairs (though once, out of habit, he moved soldiers into Richmond).

A new era did not dawn overnight. Walker, the most attractive of the carpetbaggers, was at the helm when the legislature passed a controversial Funding Act. In this the state disposed of its railroad stocks at a sacrifice in response to lobbyists' appeals to Virginia's "honor and integrity" in paying its prewar debts to the last dollar. Then, with Virginia's holdings gone and the state in debt for current operations, Walker went his debonair way. James Kemper, the sole surviving brigadier of Pickett's charge at Gettysburg, became the first of a line of Confederate governors.

Lee never commented on the state's political activities and the political leaders did not try to involve him. Having fulfilled his duty as he saw it, he had neither need nor heart for position, and his time was running out.

## 6

Before Virginia's readmission to the Union, Lee's personal status was changed on Christmas Day, 1868, by President Johnson's proclamation of a general amnesty to former Confederates. This at last lifted the treason indictment from General Lee, his sons and nephew Fitz, along with Jefferson Davis and other Confederates. By this delayed "pardon," and because he had earlier taken the oath of allegiance, Lee was restored to his civil rights, including suffrage. (Unless he sought the approving vote of two-thirds of Congress, he was forbidden by the Fourteenth Amendment from holding office.)

By the time Lee's reenfranchisement came, ending his nearly four years' status as "a paroled prisoner of war," he showed interest only in the possibility that his restored civil rights might lead to the recovery of some of Mrs. Lee's personal property which had been taken from Arlington.

Mrs. Lee, pining more deeply for the days that were gone, sentimentally wanted the Washington relics from Mount Vernon of which her father had been the custodian. Some of these had been looted by individuals and were, Lee wrote, "scattered over the land." Showing a flash of his old humor, he added a tongue-in-cheek comment: "I hope the possessors appreciate them and may imitate the example of their original owners, whose conduct must at times be brought to their recollection by these silent monitors. In this way they will accomplish good to the country."

Other relics had been collected by the Patent Office, where they were exhibited under the label "Captured from Arlington." In February, 1869, upon the suggestion of a friend in Washington, Lee advised his wife to write personally to President Johnson — in the last month of his administration — and appeal for the return of her personal property.

Johnson and his Cabinet agreed that the relics should be returned to Mrs. Lee, but the Radicals in Congress heard of the impending transfer of property. John A. Logan, a politician from Illinois who had risen to major general of volunteers in Sherman's army, was not among the ex-soldiers with kindly feelings toward the old opponents. Having changed from Democrat to Radical Republican, he was one of the organizers of the G.A.R. and three times president of this veterans' organization. As congressman from Illinois, Logan introduced a resolution calling on the committee on public buildings and grounds to discover the authority by which "the Secretary of the Interior surrenders these articles so cherished as once the property of the Father of his Country to the rebel general-in-chief."

That was on March 1, 1869, only two days before Congress adjourned at the end of Johnson's administration. Acting with urgency, the Radicals in Congress pushed through a resolution, late on March 3, declaring that the relics belonged to the United States. The Patent Office was forbidden to return Mrs. Lee's family heirlooms to her.

At this spiteful persecution, Lee remained outwardly philosophical. To George W. Jones, in Iowa, he wrote, "I hope their presence in the capitol will keep in the remembrance of all Americans the principles and virtues of Washington." He never made any reference to the effect of the disappointment on his wife, who had been led to believe the relics would be returned. This episode concluded Lee's dealings with the authorities of the United States.

In early May he did call on Grant, newly in the White House, on a purely social visit. Lee had been in Baltimore, acting for a group of Valley businessmen who were trying to raise financial backing for a railroad to Lexington. In passing through Washington on his way back to Virginia, Lee made what amounted to a courtesy call on his fellow general. The meeting was brief and a little constrained, though the men greeted each other and parted cordially, shaking hands each time.

At that period Grant had revealed none of the tendencies that were to make his second administration a succession of national scandals and a curse upon those Southern states which, legally readmitted to the Union, were being despoiled by the leftover Reconstruction governments supported by Federal troops. The limited man, originally a nonpolitical-minded Democrat, was not only unfitted by nature for high office. Personally honest and not too bright, he permitted his loyalty to friends to blind him to the corruption they participated in and to the outrages perpetrated in South Carolina, Mississippi and Louisiana by the remnants of Radicals still in control. Grant's private secretary, General Orville Babcock, was doubtless saved from conviction in a trial for complicity in the odorous Whiskey Ring by a deposition from the President: this was the kind-eyed, courteous Colonel Babcock of the Appomattox surrender negotiations.

Grant probably knew no more of what was going on when Lee visited him than he did later. But in those first months in office, his friends had not yet gotten their fingers in the pies, and his generalized sympathies for the Southern people (neither deep nor motivating, though certainly free of vindictiveness) had not yet been changed by the pressures brought from those around him for the protection of the Radical interests remaining in Southern states. Grant's later change was caused mostly by his believing what was told him by those he trusted. In policy Grant developed no more calculation than he displayed to Lee, who evidently accepted him on the good intentions he showed at Appomattox.

Neither Grant nor Lee thought to comment on the visit. Lee wrote his wife, "I have bought you a little carriage, the best I could find, which I hope will enable you to take some pleasant rides." He did not mention that he had visited the President of the United States.

On leaving Washington, Lee gave himself the luxury of a sentimental visit to Alexandria, the nearest thing he had to a home town. Living there in his mother's house from the age of five until he entered West Point, he had later resumed associations there when he was at Arlington in the last years before the war. Then he had worshipped at Christ Church, come to town for newspapers and, in the spring of 1861, to board the train for Richmond and his Confederate life. He had not visited the city since.

Lee stayed at the town house of his wife's aunt, Mrs. Fitzhugh, of Ravensworth. The attachment between "Robert" and "Aunt Maria" had grown deeper across the years, and he was her adviser on the management of her estate. Mrs. Lee was her heir, and ultimately Ravensworth would go to Rooney. At Mrs. Fitzhugh's, Lee found nephew Fitz and his mother, "Nannie" Lee, wife of Smith Lee. On hearing that his brother was in Alexandria, Smith came up from his home on the Potomac, and the General and the admiral met for the first time since having parted in Richmond after the war.

Soon "Aunt Maria's" house overflowed with visitors — kinspeople, old friends, acquaintances of Lee since childhood — and hundreds more wanted to speak to or be presented to Alexandria's most famous living citizen. Finally a reception was given in the evening in the parlor of the

Mansion House, where strangers were introduced by Montgomery Corse, a brigadier with Pickett who had been captured in the debacle at Sayler's Creek. For more than two hours a line of admirers filed past the white-haired man with the calm expression.

Lee had then lost the magnificent carriage which so many observers had formerly commented upon. Though he stood straight, his shoulders sagged in a settling of his body, and all suggestion of vitality was gone. But he was still "Lee." Nothing changed the structure of his patrician face, the clear, warm gaze of his brown eyes, and the resolute mouth, revealing his long-contained sadness by a faint downward pull at the edges.

After three days among the old scenes he returned to Lexington on May 8, apparently none the worse for the trip. He told his family that the people made "too much fuss over an old rebel" and he wrote Rooney he would have preferred to see his old friends and neighbors "in a more quiet way," but he said it was "upon the whole, a pleasant trip."

Lee was home no more than two weeks — preparing for examinations and the move into the new house — when he was called upon for activities that placed a new strain on his laboring heart. Lee seemed to have reached a certain fatalism: while taking every precaution for his health in his normal routine, he no longer avoided the stresses of special occasions. As a vestryman of Grace Church, he accepted the responsibility of attending the diocesan council at Fredericksburg when, as he wrote Rooney, he must be prepared for the approaching commencement, "a busy time with me."

It was not that Lee participated in the meetings. Church politics were as alien to him as civil politics. He only lent his presence, and at Fredericksburg this subjected him to the revival of those emotional memories he sought to avoid. Referring to the war, he said, "I do not wish to awaken memories of the past."

Since the citizens of Fredericksburg knew of his public appearances in other Virginia cities, they also turned out in mass. When the band of the 30th Virginia serenaded him and voices split the air with the Rebel yell, he could not halt the rollback of time — to the day he watched the beautiful houses burning from Burnside's cannonade, the December night when the women, children and old people made their exodus in the sleet, to the cold day of battle when Stonewall Jackson stood beside him and Jeb Stuart came up with his golden laugh, making a joke at Jackson's expense that drew an embarrassed smile from the grim lips.

From that ordeal Lee returned to the rush of commencement, and immediately from that to moving into the new house. When the family was settled, he wanted to visit the White House, to see the grandson who had been born in February. Instead, he wrote Rooney on the last of June that the doctors thought the springs would be beneficial, "and I am obliged now to consider my health." As it turned out, he went to the White House anyway.

While he and his wife were at Rockbridge Baths, news reached him that his brother Smith had died suddenly. Lee had never lost the closeness he had felt since childhood for the brother so outwardly different from himself. Smith had been as good looking as the General in a less classical way, warm and vivacious where his brother had been characterized by stateliness, and Rob said, "No one could be near my Uncle Smith without feeling his joyful influence."

With this glow unexpectedly extinguished from his life, Lee journeyed back to Alexandria, arriving July 24, the day after the funeral. Lee felt the inadequacy of his efforts to give comfort to Nannie Lee, his sister-in-law. "The attempt to give consolation is very hard," he wrote, "when you have no words to express it and your own heart requires it."

Resting a few days before his return trip, he visited Ravensworth, where Mrs. Fitzhugh had gone from her house in town. There, giving in completely to memories of the distant past, the golden years before the war, he went to the room in which his mother had died while he nursed her. To Rob he said, "Forty years ago I stood in this room by my mother's deathbed. It seems now but yesterday."

Having broken into his health routine by the trip, Lee decided after all to go with Rob to the White House. Rooney had built a new house on the site of Martha Washington's home, and crops spread across the flatland above the Pamunkey where McClellan's huge base had been destroyed. After a brief visit there, Lee wrote his wife he was bringing "our daughter Tabb" and her baby, Robert Edward Lee III, back with him to the Baths. He wrote that his new daughter-in-law showed the effects of not having been "altogether well," and the baby "would also be improved by mountain air." Probably he wanted the young mother and his grandchild to visit Mrs. Lee and himself.

The trip from the White House, by way of Richmond, was very taxing. While staying overnight at the Exchange Hotel in Richmond, Lee was besieged by so many visitors that he was compelled to hold a reception in the parlors. His grandson had not fully recuperated from a long attack of whooping cough, and the baby could only have increased the strain of the tiring train rides.

After Tabb Lee and her baby were settled at the Rockbridge Baths with Mrs. Lee in early August, the General then returned to his original June plan of going, according to his doctor's advice, to White Sulphur. Mildred and Agnes went with him. Mary never went with her family to the springs. The girls had a fine time. With White Sulphur so crowded that visitors were turned away, parties were continuous. The crowds and the gaiety were too much for Lee. "I should prefer more quiet," he wrote Mrs. Lee, and said, "No change in myself as yet." By that he evidently meant the waters had given no relief from the "rheumatic" pains. Before the end of August, he went back to Lexington, to wait for the return of his family to the new house.

While Lee prepared for a new college year — in which he would introduce a course of study approximating a school of commerce — he showed no immediate ill effects from the strain of the traveling and public appearances that had begun in April. However, with the first chills of the fall, he came down with a heavy cold that hung on into December. From this debilitating siege, he never recovered his strength. In October and November, while in Richmond, Virginians were making the moves to effect the state's readmission to the United States, Lee took the physical turn that marked for him the beginning of the end. He knew it, with acceptance.

# CHAPTER XXVII

## "Strike the Tent"

THE WEAKENED condition in which the fall cold left Lee was not immediately recognized by the college community as the beginning of a general decline. Nothing changed in his outward attitudes and habits. Lee had designed a wide porch for three sides of the new house, so that Mrs. Lee could sit in the sun, and regularly the General could be seen pushing his wife's wheelchair around the porches. He kept to his routine at the college and showed interest in the expanding social life.

In the 1869-1870 college years, student "hops" were inaugurated as a climax to the social activities which developed under Lee's lightening of the former restraints. Dancing had become accepted, and social clubs — which promoted the hops — grew along with the flourishing literary societies. Students continued to visit the Lee home, along with townspeople and strangers, and Lee remained accessible to all.

It was alone with his family, when not required to maintain the presence of the symbol, that he often showed, as Rob said, "great weariness and depression." The two local doctors, even with their limited methods of diagnosis, recognized a serious trouble about his heart, as did Lee. He began to speak of himself as an invalid, as he felt his life energies diminishing.

Any rapid movement, either in walking or riding, caused pain and difficulty in his breathing. The consolation of his afternoon trips on Traveler was often denied him and when he did ride out, "Traveler's trot," he wrote Rooney, "is harder on me than it used to be and fatigues me." Traveler, a strong horse, needed lots of work, and his trot had always been disagreeable, a fretful chafing, when he was not ridden regularly and hard. Occasionally Lee felt strong enough to let the horse out. On one mellow autumn afternoon his friend Captain White, the Greek professor, came upon him on the road when he had his gray horse going at a full run.

When the last of the mild days passed and winter settled bleakly over the mountainous countryside, the rides became less frequent and Lee could hardly walk farther than from his house to the college buildings. Pain was constant then. Seldom complaining, he admitted his suffering to his family. When he began to need care, it was quiet Agnes, herself not well, who became his "kind and uncomplaining nurse." She rubbed prescribed medical preparations on the parts of his body afflicted with pain.

Mildred, the pet at whose bedside he had held the long vigils at the cottage in Warm Springs, was away on an extended visit to Richmond. She took off before Christmas and did not return the whole winter. Mary was at home but Lee made practically no mention of his oldest daughter in his letters. In closing a letter to Rooney, he wrote, "Mary as usual" — apparently her usual independent self.

In the early part of the new year, 1870, Lee's friends and members of the faculty became aware of the steady decline in his health and grew alarmed. Professors and intimates began privately to urge him to take a vacation in a warmer climate, simultaneously with the doctors' advice that he should avoid the effects of the cold weather. For some time Lee, as Chaplain Jones said, "with his wonted gentleness of manner . . . declined to adopt their advice." With a sound instinct, Lee wrote in a letter to Mildred, "I think I should do better here, and am very reluctant to leave home in my present condition." In late March, however, he allowed himself to be persuaded to go South, for fear of appearing "obstinate, if not perverse," if he continued to resist the persuasions of those that "seem so interested in my recovery."

Lee's rather sudden decision to make the trip looked as though he was doing what was expected of the symbol rather than following the preferences of a dying man to cling to the familiar comforts of his home. But once he made the decision to travel, Lee also decided to make the trip a pilgrimage to places he wanted to see before he died. He wanted to visit the graves of his father and his daughter Annie, to see once more the home of his mother and the face of his cousin Hill Carter. While he made no announcement of this intention to anyone, it was obvious that he planned to make the trip a farewell journey in his mortal life.

In his condition, Lee could not have expected to benefit physically from the taxing fatigue of travel and the inevitable crowds. A student who had graduated the year before, D. Gardiner Tyler, later a judge, returned for a visit to Lexington and saw Lee just before he left. "I was painfully struck with the change in his appearance since I had left Lexington the year before, and I think he had little hope of recuperation. His face showed the deep lines made more, I think, by grief for his people than by disease, and he seemed weary and broken."

2

Lee boarded the canal boat with Agnes on the afternoon of March 24, writing, "I . . . will take Agnes to Savannah . . . or, perhaps, she will take me." He arrived at the Exchange Hotel in Richmond the following afternoon, feeling "a little feverish." He had found the night aboard the packet "very trying" and the railroad trip the next day was dusty, but, he wrote his wife, he "had a more comfortable journey than I expected."

Staying in Richmond Saturday and Sunday, Lee did not stir about to see old friends. He left the hotel only for an extensive medical examination by three doctors, including James McCaw. He had been director of the wartime Chimborazo Hospital, the world's largest military hospital and probably the most progressive hospital of its era. With Lee the combined medical experience produced no conclusions.

On Monday he and Agnes began the train trip to Savannah, stopping first at Warrenton, North Carolina, for the visit to Annie's grave. It "was mournful," Lee wrote his wife, "yet soothing to my feelings." This was almost the last soothing hour the General would enjoy for the next six weeks. Lee wrote his wife very little during the trip and recorded none of his inner feelings or his reactions to the trip that turned into a public tour. To a man suffering acutely from angina and longing for privacy, the constant acclaim of crowds could have been saved from being an ordeal only by the sense that, once again, he was doing his "duty to the end." He said as much when he wrote his wife on arriving in Savannah. "I have had a tedious journey upon the whole, and have more than ever regretted that I undertook it."

His hectic period of living as a public personage began on the night of March 29 when Lee, with Agnes, took his first trip on the new Pullman sleeping cars. During the night he was awakened when the train stopped at Raleigh, and a crowd was gathered in the station to cheer him. "Lee, Lee," they chanted, while the General lay as quiet as a mouse in his berth. The next day he was required to appear at train stops — Salisbury, Charlotte, Columbia, South Carolina — to acknowledge by a bow the clamor of gathered crowds. As Columbia, the state capital which Sherman had burned, stores were closed and people had stood in a driving rain waiting for his train. "Why should they care to see me?" he protested to Agnes. "I am only a poor old Confederate."

That night they reached Augusta, Georgia, and in his fatigue Lee readily consented to spend the next day there, though this meant one long reception. He and Agnes reached Savannah on April 1, and passage through the dense crowd had to be forced for the open barouche carrying them from the station. They were staying at the home of Andrew

Lowe, who lived alone in a partly dismantled house. There Lee and his daughter, who herself took sick, enjoyed comparative quiet. They stayed until April 25, with a four-day interlude for a boat trip to Lee's father's grave on Cumberland Island.

After a week in Savannah, Lee wrote his wife, "I seem to be stronger and to walk with less difficulty, but it may be owing to the better [less hilly] streets of Savannah." Writing that he "hoped" he was a little better, Lee at least felt like going out to see old friends. From Columbia on southward, Lee had been greeted by former generals, and he was cheered by their prosperous condition. These were the men who, putting the war behind them, had overcome the obstacles of Reconstruction and achieved successes comparable to their army records.

Porter Alexander, then president of the Columbia Oil Company, was just beginning the rise that would take him to financial prominence as railroad president — coupled with the lasting contribution of writing probably the best critical narrative of the Virginia campaign. Rans Wright, Powell Hill's former brigadier, published a newspaper in Augusta, where Lafayette McLaws, a division commander with "Prince John" Magruder when Lee assumed command, was selling insurance. In Savannah Alexander Lawton, whose untried brigade in new uniforms had helped turn the tide at Gaines' Mill, was successfully practicing law and entering state politics: in the first postwar Democratic administration, Cleveland's, he would become minister to Austria. J. F. Gilmer, who as chief engineer of the War Department had worked with Lee on the Richmond defenses, was president of the Savannah Gas Light Company.

On the trip to his father's grave Lee found Colonel R. G. Cole, lately the army's chief commissary, able to do better for his old commander than at Petersburg: he was living in comfort on a plantation, on which the General enjoyed the novelty of picking oranges from a tree. Another recent member of the general staff, chief quartermaster Colonel J. L. Corley, was in circumstances that permitted him to perform a very real service. Meeting Lee in Richmond, Corley had gone ahead to Charlotte, from where he handled the details of arranging Lee's trip to Savannah, and accompanied the General and Agnes from Charlotte on.

In Savannah, Lee also saw his old friend Joe Johnston, the one Rebel still fighting — not the Yankees but his true enemy, Jefferson Davis. He was working on memoirs to justify himself in his private war. In the "for the last time" atmosphere of the whole trip, Lee submitted to the photographer for a picture of his last meeting with Johnston. Though they both looked withered old men, Johnston was to live on for twenty years.

Neither the pleasant reunions nor the warm fragrant weather (both he and Agnes mentioned the yellow jasmine perfuming the air) brought any significant change to his health. After ten days in Savannah, Lee wrote,

"The warm weather has . . . dispelled some of the rheumatic pains in my back, but I perceive no change in the stricture in my chest. If I attempt to walk beyond a very slow gait, the pain is always there."

A week later he returned from the visit to his father's grave, and this boat journey along the St. Johns River — even though it included another crowd demonstration at Jacksonville — was "a very pleasant trip." He felt stronger then, he wrote Mrs. Lee, but the chest pain came whenever he walked. Then he added ominously, "I have felt it also occasionally of late when quiescent . . . which is new." Two more doctors examined him, increasing his confusion about his heart ailment. Significantly, he asked his wife to pass his letter along to any of the children she wrote to, as he had been unable to write any of them. Even when the lines had been about to break at Petersburg, he had written letters to his daughters.

From Savannah Lee returned to Richmond by a different route, visiting at Charleston, Wilmington and Norfolk, where his escort through the crowd was Colonel Walter Taylor. This former intimate of his headquarters was also prospering, in business, and he too would soon produce a book on the war. Taylor's book, self-effacing and written to produce the "truth" Lee wanted, would make an invaluable contribution to the knowledge of the numerical strength of the army. In all three cities Lee allowed himself to be entertained at large and elaborate dinners, as well as greeting the throngs, and these exertions brought the need for immediate rest.

This he found the first week in May in the quiet among his kinspeople at Brandon, and then on Tuesday, May 10, he crossed the James on a steamer for another last visit — to Shirley. Though Lee had not visited Hill Carter since the war, the cousins were close to one another in their affections. Except for the absence of slaves, Lee found no significant change from the picture he held in his memory of his mother's birthplace. Some of the old trees had gone (to McClellan's campfires), some of the buildings were gone from the great forecourt and others damaged, but the house reposed serenely on the banks of the tidal river, and there was no suggestion of ravages in the area of the lawn and garden. Cousin Hill's large family looked cheerful and well fed, as indeed they were.

Along with Shirley's having been spared the total devastation that struck other plantations, Hill Carter's continuous management had protected the estate against the dislocations of Reconstruction, such as confiscations for taxes accrued during the war years. Absorbing the loss of slaves, writing off the ruined crops and loss of animals in McClellan's 1862 passage, Carter, always a practical farmer, managed by going shares with an overseer and found various means of bringing in cash. He rented out part of his farmland, installed a new sawmill, and from prewar savings invested in state stocks — accumulated in the same careful husbandry Lee's Carter grandfather had instilled in his mother — lent money to neighboring planters in need of cash. While the income did not run into the above $20,000 volume of the antebellum years, his meticulous bookkeeping still showed a cash balance in his favor after all expenses were paid in maintaining the baronial style of the tradition.

The day after Lee arrived, a hard rain was falling when he awakened in an upstairs bedroom overlooking the river. After the rain ceased around noon, the weather remained sharp with a wind out of the northwest. The weary visitor evidently spent the day indoors, in the large parlor in which his parents were married, for one of the young ladies present mentioned cousin Hill's grandchildren clustering around him.

"I can only remember the great dignity and kindness of General Lee's bearing, how lovely he was to all of us girls, that he gave us his photographs and wrote his name on them. He liked to have us tickle his hands, but when Cousin Agnes came to sit by him that seemed to be her privilege. We regarded him with the greatest veneration. We had heard of God, but here was General Lee!"

From his father's grave to his mother's childhood home, Lee had completed the cycle of communication with the past. Though the peaceful visits at Brandon and Shirley had halted the dangerous drain on his energy, Lee needed to recuperate from his trip before returning to Lexington. Mrs. Lee, after many threats, had finally made the trip to White House for a visit with her son's family, and the General and Agnes joined her there on May 12.

Mrs. Lee, looking for the effects of the trip on her husband, found that he had put on a little weight, but still seemed stiff in his movements. Referring to the flush of his skin, she wrote Mary, "I do not like his complexion." She also thought Agnes looked thin, though that might have been "partly owing to the *immense chignon* which seemed to wear her down."

Mrs. Lee revealed in little flashes her constant awareness of the changes in their life. She wrote her daughter of the blossoming countryside — "the woods lovely with wild flowers and dogwood blossoms and all the fragrance of early spring, the dark holly and pine intermingling with the delicate leaves just brought out . . . daisies, wild violets and heart's ease . . ." Then, referring to Rooney's first wife, who died while he was in prison, she added, "The locust trees are in full bloom, and the polonia, the only tree left of all planted by poor Charlotte and myself. How all our labors have come to naught . . ."

Lee found a restorative in another child, his namesake grandson, who at fifteen months was beginning to call people by their names. He was riding on the General's knee, Mrs. Lee wrote, "sitting as grave as a judge." After a few days' rest, Lee felt strong enough to make a trip with Rob, mostly by boat, to his plantation, Romancoke. Rob was living with a bachelor's rough simplicity in the former overseer's house, and his father, for once startled out of his urbane self-control, was momentarily unable to conceal his shock at the primitive conditions.

From there, again mostly by boat, the General and his son went to visit Dr. Prosser Tabb's family at White Marsh, a plantation on the north side of the York River in Gloucester County. Mrs. Tabb was another of Lee's innumerable cousins. As was customary in eastern Virginia, the house was full of visitors when they arrived, and father and son shared a bed for the first time in many years. Lee, recurring to the past, told Rob he remembered the days when, "as a little fellow," he had begged for the privilege of climbing into bed with his father.

This completed his journey, except for a four-day stop in Richmond for more medical examinations. "I am having a great medical talk tomorrow," Lee wrote grimly to Mildred. While in Richmond, Lee bought a full set of plated forks and spoons to send Rob, who used them the rest of his life. The General looked at the old streets around Capitol Square, the red-brick sidewalks shaded by the budding trees, for the last time. As when he had come to Richmond another May nine years before, to offer his services to his state, the city looked quiet and peaceful.

Less than a month before, the last vestiges of Reconstruction had passed during a tragic disaster. After Virginia's readmission to the Union in January, Richmond elected its own mayor, H. K. Ellyson. George Chahoon, the mayor appointed by the military during the occupation, refused to leave office and was supported by the U. S. District Court, presided over by Judge Underwood. The case was carried to the Virginia Court of Appeals, which met in a room in the Capitol used by the state senate during the war. Before the trial opened, the overcrowded gallery collapsed, and more than fifty people were killed in the crash. Hours were required for the wounded, including Mayors Ellyson and Chahoon, to be carried out of the debris. A relief fund was established, and Richmonders, in their grief and shock, were deeply moved by the contributions that came, along with expressions of sympathy, from New York, Philadelphia and other Northern cities.

It was almost an anticlimax when the Court of Appeals ruled that Ellyson, as elected by qualified voters, was the city's mayor. (Chahoon soon went to the penitentiary, after the U. S. Supreme Court ruled on his trial, for complicity in a forgery case.) What the people remembered about the capitol tragedy was the spontaneous sympathy shown in the North; as Richmond's chronicler, Dr. W. A. Christian, said, "sorrow breaks down every barrier." When Lee left the city in whose defense he had suffered such anguish and heart strain, he could have felt that the years of his postwar life had made some contribution to restoration of peace.

However, nothing in his letters or recorded conversation indicated that Lee experienced any sense of personal accomplishment by his example. The painful struggle for readmission to the United States had gone on so long, covering the period in which the last of his energies were consumed, that he was worn out and probably felt no more than relief at knowing peace had been legally restored before he died. He was less sanguine about a future of true reconciliation than in the first year after Appomattox.

He had not been unaffected by the continuing slurs on the Southern people, both the denunciations and the indirect judgments, such as the one Harvard's president delivered that year. "The duty of the North," said President Thomas Hill, "is to spread knowledge and culture over the regions that sit in darkness." By the time Lee took his last departure from Richmond, he had suffered for the people across such a span that, looking down the long road which stretched ahead of them, sorrow for those who had been Confederates mingled inseparably with the shadowy prescience of his own end.

### 3

Back in the new house in Lexington, on May 28, Lee apparently felt better generally than before his trip. "I am improving, I think, in general health," he had written Mildred before leaving Richmond. Rob thought his general condition had benefited by the rest and change, the meeting with old friends, "the great love and kindness shown him by all." It was soon obvious that no improvement had been made in his basic trouble, though it was, Rob wrote, "for a while held in check."

Lee felt well enough to sit for a bust for Edward Valentine, a thirty-two-year-old Richmond sculptor. He had been measured by Valentine during his visit in Richmond. When, at that time, Valentine said he would come to Lexington either immediately or in the fall, Lee had replied the sitting had better be at once. Valentine received the impression that Lee felt no certainty about his future. In Lexington, where Valentine set up a studio in a vacant store under the hotel, Lee showed no signs of illness except to place his hand on his chest occasionally as if in pain. Informally composed himself, Lee chatted reminiscently and sought with quiet humor to put the young sculptor at his ease.

Valentine recorded his own awe at approaching "this grand idol of the South. I had been told of his noble simplicity, of his gentle and kindly bearing, but I confess I could never appreciate how these qualities could ever neutralize the inquietude which I felt until I was once in his company. He who poses for a bust or a portrait may be expected to look his best, or what at least may appear to him his best. I could observe no difference in General Lee's manner when he was sitting for me from that which was his ordinary bearing . . . An artist, above all other men, is quick to observe the faintest suggestion of posing; the slightest indication of a movement or expression that smacks of vanity he is sure to detect. Such weaknesses (which, as far as I know, are shared by many who are called the 'great ones' of the world) were totally lacking in General Lee."

During the pleasant association that developed, Valentine wanted some photographs taken, and he called on Michael Miley. Three years younger than the sculptor, Miley had lived on a farm near Lexington until he enlisted in a volunteer company that became absorbed in the Stonewall Brigade. Captured, he nearly died in damp Fort Delaware ("this Northern bastille," a fellow prisoner called it) and, on coming home, turned from farming to photography in Lexington. Miley was not only the one photographer for whom Lee sat willingly, but he took the only picture Lee ever requested of himself in Confederate uniform.

It was a side view of Lee mounted on Traveler, and Miley caught, as Lee wanted, a perfect likeness of the General's most constant companion. That was in 1868, when Lee felt premonitions of the future, and told Miley he wanted one picture of Traveler and himself "just as we went through the four years of war together." By such small revelations Lee showed that, for all his avoidance of talk on the war and refusal to read books about it, the four years were deep inside him.

When final examinations had been held at the college, Lee left on the last day of June to be examined by yet another doctor in Baltimore. Dr. T. H. Buckler, the most internationally prominent of those who had yet probed him, diagnosed Lee's trouble as arising "from rheumatic excitement" and treated him symptomatically. He was, Lee wrote his wife, to follow the same directions as the other physicians had given — "guard against cold, keep out in the air, exercise, etc.," with the added item of trying lemon juice and watching the effect.

Though Buckler evidently missed the cardiac damage, he made a highly favorable impression on Lee, and the two took a liking to one another. The doctor was only in Baltimore on a visit from Paris, where he lived with his family, and he later invited Lee to visit them in Europe. In declining, Lee asked Buckler to bring his wife to the mountains. Showing his awareness of the presentations of the South in print, he wrote in gentle humor, "We are all peaceable here now and she will find that we are not as bad as we have been reported to be."

On the Baltimore trip Lee was almost equally impressed by a depth of fatigue that kept him late in bed one morning. Having suffered from the heat more severely than he ever remembered, he wanted Mrs. Lee to tell the girls, "I could not get up this morning until 8:00 A.M." Everyone who had ever visited the Lee household knew that the one inflexible ritual to be observed was the appearance at the breakfast table at seven o'clock, when the General said morning prayers.

From Baltimore, he went — also for the last time — to Alexandria, to see his lawyer, Francis L. Smith. This was his final effort to reclaim the confiscated Arlington property for his family. The inability to supply his daughters with their grandfather's inheritance continued to weigh on his mind, and he wrote if he could only fulfill that, "I shall be content." Lawyer Smith gave him no encouragement: the General wrote Mrs. Lee, "the prospect is not promising." That was where the matter ended.

While in Alexandria, he made what turned out to be a farewell round of visits to kinspeople in that area, including his first cousin and child-hood intimate, Cassius Lee. It was to Cousin Cassius that Lee gave the only recorded statements of unguarded, personal opinions about battles and leaders during the war. In the privacy of his cousin's home, as if making a final testament, Lee forgot about the possibilities of creating controversies.

Asked which of the Federal generals he considered the greatest, Lee replied emphatically, "McClellan by all odds."

About Gettysburg, Lee believed he would have won if Jackson had commanded the Second Corps instead of Ewell. Jackson would have held the heights which Ewell failed to attack on the first day; with Cemetery Hill taken, Meade could not have occupied the formidable ridge as a defensive position.

As to why he crossed the Potomac in the Sharpsburg campaign, he said, "Because my men had nothing to eat. I went to Maryland to feed my army."

Most of all, he unburdened himself on the failures of the Commissary Department. While commanding the army, Lee wrote more words on the need of victualing his men than on all other subjects put together. He diverted more energy to feeding his men than to strategy and tactics and suffered more anguish at the failure than over any battle — except perhaps the collapsing action from the breakthrough at Petersburg to Appomattox, and even that disintegration was determined by food. In permitting himself that afternoon to relive the war, Lee revealed that his strongest feeling was not against the enemy he had fought but the enemy within.

Returning to Lexington from the trip in July, Lee applied himself to the treatment of symptoms under the new impetus from Dr. Buckler, and included the springs' cures urged by his local doctors, H. T. Barton and R. L. Madison. In this he seemed to be following his sense of duty. In his letters he tried to appear hopeful but, while reporting his dutiful execution of instructions, he knew the fundamental and fatal disease was unaffected.

Before leaving for the springs, he wrote Dr. Buckler, "I am pursuing your directions and hope that I am deriving benefit from them." He went to Hot Springs with his professor friend, Captain White, and upon his arrival wrote Mrs. Lee on August 10, "I hope I may be benefited."

The therapeutic baths were of two kinds, Hot Spout and Boiler. The water from the spout he received, he wrote his wife, "on my shoulder, back, and chest. The sensation is pleasant . . . but it is too soon yet to look for results." After taking the Spout for five days, he shifted to the Boiler for four days, and wrote his wife on the 19th, "I do not perceive any benefit yet, though some little change in the seat of my pains."

On the 23rd, he wrote the most revealing letter. "I hope that I am getting better, but am aware of no material change, except that I am weaker. I am very anxious to get back. It is very wearying at these public places and the benefit hardly worth the cost." The gatherings of gentle people at the resort had lost the pleasure they gave him in the previous years. Conscious chiefly of his health, he was aware that his dutiful application to the advised treatments served no purpose. Significantly he added, "I do not think I can even stand Lexington long."

While he was at the Hot, his wife wrote him of the death of their cow, which was pastured on the farm of Andrew Cameron. Lee commented, "Our good cow will be a loss to us, but her troubles are all over now."

Just before Lee left the springs, his attitude took a curious turn. On August 27 he wrote Mrs. Lee that he would like to remain a week longer, "as I have felt in the last few days better than I have yet." He had to leave to be in Staunton on Monday, the 30th, for a meeting of the stockholders of the Valley Railroad company. At this meeting, the stockholders agreed that the prestige of Lee's name was necessary for the railroad company's success and chose him as president. At first he declined. Not mentioning his physical unfitness, he said only, "It seems to me that I have already led enough forlorn hopes." Under persuasion he accepted the office (which carried a salary of $5000), though he did not live to become active in this new responsibility and probably did not expect to.

On returning to Lexington, the "little improvement" he mentioned before leaving Hot Springs evidently continued during the mild September weather. After the college session opened on the 15th, he resumed his regular duties, and on the morning of the 28th wrote S. H. Tagart, a Baltimore friend, "I am much better. I do not know whether it is owing to having seen you and Doctor Buckler last summer, or my visit to the Hot Springs. Perhaps both. But my pains are less and my strength greater. In fact, I am as well as I shall be. I am still following Doctor Buckler's directions and in time I may improve still more."

Except for the mention of possibly further improvement, Lee gave an accurate, realistic appraisal of the local effects of symptomatic treatment and of the mental stimulant given by a new doctor. The hot-water cure had decreased the pain, and the lessening of the drain of pain on his energies would make him feel stronger. Also he had rested, in warm weather, a large part of the time during the past three months.

The reference to further improvement must have been only a reflection of the hopeful attitude he assumed. For, when he collapsed later during the day after writing the letter, his family mentioned the "sublime resignation" that came over his face as he realized that "the hour had come when all the cares and anxieties of his crowded life were at an end." While the doctors were treating him, one of them said, "He neither expected nor desired to recover."

His letter to Tagart would seem to have been, in presenting a cheerful attitude, his final act in doing his duty to the end. These words were the last he ever wrote.

4

At the very end Lee was granted his long wish for privacy. In his terminal illness, he was secluded with his family and family physicians, Dr. Barton and Dr. Madison. The one person in attendance not a member of the family was Professor, recently Colonel, William Preston Johnston, a friend of Custis's. No mention was made of the presence of any of the ministers of the community who served as college chaplains. Only Colonel Johnston and Mrs. Lee, in two letters to friends, recorded the details of Lee's last days.

On Wednesday, September 28, after completing his duties for the day in his office under the chapel, Lee came home for his midday meal — dinner in the South since earliest plantation days. After the meal, he dozed in a chair until it was time to leave for a four o'clock vestry meeting at the Grace Episcopal Church. This was a short walk down the hill from the President's house, but the day had turned chilly and rainy. In the damp cold of the unheated church, Lee kept his military cape thrown about his shoulders as he took his seat in a pew.

The meeting was long, going on until seven o'clock. Despite Lee's generous contributions to the church, the treasurer announced they were still $55 short of the fund required for Dr. Pendleton's salary. Lee ended the meeting by saying quietly, "I will give that sum." He seemed a little tired then, and his flush was unusually high, but no one at the vestry meeting was alarmed.

When Lee left the church, the rain was coming down hard, and in the wet darkness he climbed the hill along the edge of the grassy slope leading up to the row of college buildings. Entering the house, he found his wife and daughters in the dining room waiting for him before having tea. Since he was the soul of punctuality, Mrs. Lee said, "You have kept us waiting a long time. Where have you been?"

Instead of replying, he took his place at the head of the table, standing to say grace. No words came. He looked neither puzzled nor agitated. He sat down quietly in his chair, and his expression changed into the sublime resignation — the look which, Mrs. Lee said, "was never to be forgotten." From that moment on, "his whole demeanor," she said, "showed one who had already taken leave of earth."

As he had faithfully followed the doctors' directions during the summer at the springs, he submitted to their ministrations without protest, suffering the medicines poured down his throat. However, it was clear he acted purely out of his lifelong habits of doing what was indicated.

Doctors Barton and Madison had not reached their homes from the vestry meeting when the urgent call came for them to hurry to Lee's house. They applied, Colonel Johnston said, "the usual remedies," partly undressed the General and placed him on the couch beside the windows. Later his bed was brought down, the dinner table moved out, and the pleasant room he had designed for family gatherings became the sickroom.

The doctors placed stress upon mental and physical strain — "moral causes," as Colonel Johnston interpreted it — which induced "venous congestion of the brain." It would seem something like a stroke except for the absence of apoplexy or paralysis. The doctors reported that the congestion in the brain "gradually caused cerebral exhaustion and death." Lee lingered for exactly two weeks.

Until next to the last day, Lee maintained control of his mind in the self-composure that characterized him. Colonel Johnston said, "Never did the habits and qualities of a lifetime, solemnly gathered into a few last sad hours, more grandly maintain themselves amid the gloom and shadow of approaching death."

During the whole illness he never smiled and rarely spoke, except to answer questions in monosyllables. When Custis made some reference to his recovery, Lee shook his head and pointed his finger upward, to heaven. Once when Agnes brought his medicine he said, "It is no use." Under a little urging, to please her he patiently swallowed it.

Most of the time he slept or dozed. He did not seem in any great discomfort, and could move himself in bed. He showed he wanted his wife and children around him and greeted them "with a kindly pressure of the hand." Rob and Rooney were unable to reach Lexington before he died. Though Lee seemed aware of everything about him, nothing indicated any sense of unfulfillment at the absence of his sons. It was truly as if he felt the completion of his life at the moment he was struck (as St. Paul: "I have fought a good fight, I have finished my course"), and only waited for the final sleep.

The fatal illness had come to him when his affairs were in good order, with no unsolved anxieties for his family's future. In fact, conditions for his wife — in her remaining three years of life — were better than he realized. The board of trustees had passed a resolution giving Mrs. Lee lifetime occupancy of the house and a continuation of Lee's salary. Lee had refused to accept this, but the trustees intended to do it anyway. Then, after Lee's death, when Mrs. Lee also refused the offer, the trustees found a simple solution. Custis was appointed president and moved into the house with his mother and sisters. Though this was not the kind of perpetuity of position which the Lees and Custises had traditionally been born to, it was fitting for the family of R. E. Lee, since it represented a perpetuity earned by his own efforts.

On the Monday morning of October 10, Dr. Madison seemed to think the patient looked better and tried to cheer him. "How do you feel today, General?"

Lee answered slowly and distinctly, "I feel better."

"You must make haste and get well," the doctor said. "Traveler has been standing in the stable so long he needs exercise."

Lee slowly shook his head without replying and closed his eyes. During the afternoon there was a sudden change for the worse. His pulse became feeble and rapid, his breathing hurried, and he showed other signs of exhaustion. At midnight he was seized with a shivering from the debility. Dr. Barton felt obliged to advise the family of the danger.

The next morning it was evident that he was sinking. For the first time he seemed insensible of his family's presence. By the muttering of broken words Lee revealed he was dreaming of the war. He was in battle again, and one sentence came clearly from his lips. "Tell Hill he must come up." (Seven years before, Stonewall Jackson, in his dying delirium, had also called the name of Powell Hill: "Tell A. P. Hill to prepare for action.")

That night, the 11th, Lee went into his final sleep. Colonel Johnston sat in the darkened room where a fire was lit in the hearth. When the hearth fire cast shadows "upon his calm, noble front," Johnston wrote, "all the massive grandeur of his form, his face, and brow remained; and death seemed to lose its terrors, and to borrow a grace and dignity in sublime keeping with the life that was ebbing away."

Lee never regained consciousness. The next morning, lying still with his eyes closed, he continued to mutter words that grew unintelligible.

During this delirium he spoke his last clear sentence, and that open to two meanings. Was he back with the army and breaking camp to move out? Or, in one flash of prescience, did he speak symbolically?

"Strike the tent," he said.

Around nine-thirty on Wednesday morning, October 12, he gave one deep sigh and, his wife wrote, "at last sank to rest."

In writing her cousin, Mary Meade, the widowed Mrs. Lee epitomized her husband's life in the one quality whose emphasis would have meant the most to Ann Carter Lee's son: "I have never so truly felt the purity of his character as now, when I have nothing left me but its memory, a memory which I know will be cherished in many hearts besides mine."

# Acknowledgments

I T IS NOT customary in bibliographies to list places where "visual history" can be studied but, as I started in history as a novelist, the physical environment is of extreme importance to me. I like to walk in the rooms where those who went before laughed and wept and exchanged their dreams, where mothers brought life into the world and families watched at deathbeds. I find it helpful to walk the streets of Alexandria, Old Washington, the Battery section of New York; to see the plains of Texas and the mountains of Mexico; to see the countryside as they saw it — the views from a country road and from bedroom windows, and an individual's constricted views of the ground where armies clashed. (No battlefield looks as one imagines it.) For this reason, I wish first to acknowledge those who have helped in "researching" the physical sites.

To the late Dr. Beverly Randolph Wellford, Mr. MacDonald Wellford, and Mr. Joseph Heistand, rector of St. Paul's Church, Richmond, I am most grateful for companionship that across the years amounted to a cooperative group effort in working battlefields from Gettysburg to the James and in probing the back country.

At Shirley plantation I received, also across the years, the most constant and interested support from Mr. and Mrs. Hill Carter. I am particularly grateful to Mr. Carter, the great-grandson of Lee's Cousin Hill, for his extremely generous help in providing copies of scattered letters of Ann Hill Carter Lee, for the loan of Shirley's Farm Journals and Account Book, and, in the course of answering interminable questions, for producing obscure Carter family records.

For Stratford Hall, I am grateful to Admiral Irving Duke, to Miss Edith Healy and Mrs. George P. Keller. At Stratford Hall, as at Shirley, one feels the grandeur of which Lee was dispossessed. Miss Healy and Mrs. Keller were also helpful in providing copies of letters.

At Washington and Lee, I was most fortunate on several visits in receiving the charming, solicitous guidance of Dr. William Gleason Bean, professor emeritus of history. His encyclopedic knowledge of nineteenth-century life at Washington College and in Lexington, of Rockbridge County soldiers in Lee's army (as well as of the Army of Northern Virginia itself), is as intimate and casual as of the minutiae in the lives of his family. I can never properly acknowledge the help of Dr. Bean in making real Lee's postwar life at Lexington and, by making the time there so pleasant, transforming work into the nature of a visit into the past.

Also at Washington and Lee, I am indebted to Mrs. Charles P. Light, who now lives in the first, or "old," president's house, and to Mrs. Fred C. Cole, who occupies what has been the president's house since the Lees moved in in 1869, for their kindness and interest in describing the details of the houses during the occupancy of the Lees. Mrs. Cole also gave me a copy of a paper written on the house.

On other aspects of research at Lexington, I am grateful to Dr. Ollinger Crenshaw for giving me the use of his unfinished history of the college, with chapters on Lee's presidency. Dr. Crenshaw and Dr. Allen W. Moger gave valuable assistance in reconstructing the life of Washington College in Lee's time and his effect upon it, and guidance on sources.

To Mr. Jay W. Johns, president of the Stonewall Jackson Memorial Institute, I am deeply indebted for his generous efforts in providing copies of the letters Lee wrote from Derwent.

At the major source of research, the Virginia Historical Society, I am deeply grateful to Mr. John Melville Jennings, the director; to Mr. William M. E. Rachal, for his invaluable guidance on the period of the founding of the Republic and for his corrections on the section of the manuscript covering the period of Light-Horse Harry Lee's life; to Mr. Howson Cole, for his inexhaustible patience and generous cooperation in my work with the illimitable unpublished material in the Society's collection; and to Mr. James A. Fleming and Mr. Virginius Cornick Hall, Jr.

Of the many individuals to whom I am indebted for contributions, I wish to make grateful acknowledgment to Miss India Thomas, former regent of the Confederate Museum, and to the assistant regent, Miss Eleanor Brockenbrough; to the staff of the Virginia State Library, particularly Mr. Milton C. Russell, Mrs. Pinkney Smith, Mrs. Lewis Causbey, and Miss Eudora Elizabeth Thomas; to Mr. Francis L. Berkeley, Jr., and Mr. Robert Stocking, of the Alderman Library, University of Virginia; to Mr. Robert Waitt, of the Richmond Civil War Commission; to Mrs. Virginia Catterall, of the Valentine Museum, Richmond; to Dr. W. H. Stauffer, of the Richmond Civil War Round Table; to Mrs. Jackson L. Fray, Jr., of Culpeper, Virginia; to Dr. Chester Bradley, curator of the Jefferson Davis Casemate at Fort Monroe, Virginia; to Mr. N. E. Warinner, of Richmond, for guidance on ordnance and consultations on details of the Seven Days battlefields; to the late Dr. Douglas Southall Freeman, of Richmond; to Dr. Frederic Tilberg, historian of the Gettysburg National Battlefield, and Mr. Ralph Happel of the Fredericksburg National Battlefield Park (which includes Chancellorsville and the Wilderness); to Lieutenant General Louis W. Truman, deputy commanding general of the Continental Army Command, for illumination on the comparison of Lee's staff with modern procedures; to Sir John Wheeler-Bennett, of Oxford, England, for the privilege of drawing upon his background on the history of staffs; to Mr. Stuart Rose, of Cheyney, Pennsylvania; to Dr. Harry Warthen and the late Dr. Beverly Randolph Wellford, of Richmond, for advice on medical aspects of the armies; to Mr. Bruce Catton and to Mr. E. P. Long; to Dr. Meriwether Stuart, of New

York City, for making available his pioneer studies in the numbers actually "present for duty" in Lee's army; to Mr. W. E. Pullen, of Baltimore; to Mr. H. R. Preston, of Baltimore, for his interested cooperation in answering queries and supplying material on his grandmother, Mrs. Margaret Junkin Preston, and for sending me a copy of the out-of-print book *The Life and Letters of Mrs. Margaret Junkin Preston;* to Mr. Monroe F. Cockrell, of Chicago, for his unfailing thoughtfulness over many years in supplying interesting material, especially a pamphlet on Wilmer McLean, on the surrender house at Appomattox. For the factor of stress fatigue in Jackson's performance, I am indebted to Dr. David Markham and Dr. Dupont Guerry III, of Richmond; to Dr. Theodore Sanders, of St. Louis; and to Mrs. June Huntley, medical librarian of the Medical College of Virginia, for her invaluable interest in supplying a bibliography on the study of stress.

Just as I cannot list (or even remember) every book and article on the general subject I have read over the past decades, so I can not list every person with whom I have corresponded or talked with profit. In thanking them all, I would like to express my gratitude to several who were not directly involved in this book: my former editor at Little, Brown, Mr. John A. S. Cushman; Mr. Samuel Neal, of Chatham, Virginia; Colonel Geoffrey Galwey, of New York; Mr. Malcolm Jamieson, of Berkeley Plantation, Virginia; Mr. Francis L. Berkley, Jr., of the Alderman Library, University of Virginia; Colonel Herbert W. K. Fitzroy, of Richmond, Virginia, and the late Mr. David L. Cohn.

I wish especially to express grateful acknowledgment to Miss Louisa Pastors, for her work in typing the manuscripts (the many versions) and for assistance in research, particularly in reading through a magnifying glass the weatherstained, almost undecipherable letters written by Lee from Mexico.

It is by no means a courtesy acknowledgment I make to my wife: beyond the customary "encouragement," I am deeply grateful to her for the very real contributions made from her studies in clinical psychology in discussions of character motivations, personal relationships and the effects of illness on behavior.

I cannot sufficiently thank my publishers, Little, Brown, for their supportive cooperation on this book, as well as on *The Wartime Papers of R. E. Lee* and books on Lee's army, and particularly my editor, Mr. Alan D. Williams, for his constant and thoughtful encouragement and advice. As it is not my habit to consult other writers on my books, nor to have the manuscript read for suggestions, my dependence for consultation and suggestions is almost entirely placed upon my editor and publishers, who become quite literally for me the "without whom, etc."

Finally, I wish to acknowledge my long-dead grandmothers, who survived the war around Richmond in their teens and told me of wartime life in my formative years. My paternal grandmother, Ann Blount (who had four brothers with Lee), lived on a plantation between Richmond and Petersburg which was overrun in Butler's breakout in 1864, and which lay in the pathway of deserters from both armies during the winter of 1864-1865. She recalled vividly the hunger of the emaciated Confederate soldiers and the disbelief of all soldiers, of both sides, that her family had no food either.

# Principal Unpublished Sources

Virginia Historical Society.

This vast repository of material on Lee and the Lee family (fortunately situated three blocks from my house) provided the major source of unpublished papers.

*George Bolling Lee Collection.* New acquisition. Mss. 1. L5114. c and d. The subdepartment c contains 78 Lee letters, mostly unpublished, and mostly written before the war. The subdepartment d contains 247 letters, some from Lee, but mostly from members of the Lee-Custis families.

*Robert E. Lee Headquarters Papers.* Mss. 3. L515. a. (785). (1) General and Special Order Books from February 9 to April 10, 1865, unpublished. (2) Reports of operations of various commanders during last of March and up to April 9, 1865, unpublished: these reports by Longstreet, Gordon, Ewell, R. H. Anderson, Fitz Lee, Rooney Lee, Pendleton, Quartermaster General Corley, among others, provide almost the only firsthand official military accounts of the campaign from Petersburg to Appomattox. (3) Official letters and reports, published and unpublished. (4) Letter Books and Telegraph Books for periods of the war, many of which have been published in *Official Records.* (5) Miscellany.

This collection, a primary source for the Appomattox campaign, was assembled by Lee and in his possession at Washington College. At his death, the papers passed to Custis Lee. Custis made them available to Colonel Marshall, for his projected book. When Colonel Marshall died before his book was completed, Custis then turned the collection over to the Confederate Veterans of Virginia. Captain Gordon McCabe, of Richmond (who had served on the staff of Willie Pegram), as a committee member of the veterans' organization, prepared a handwritten guide of the papers. On his death, the surviving members of the committee in 1922 deposited the papers in a vault in the First and Merchants National Bank. From thence the collection passed to the Confederate Memorial Association, and when this merged with the Virginia Historical Society in 1946, the extremely valuable and little-used papers finally found a repository. (Captain McCabe's listings are entirely factual except for his comment on Pickett's report. On this he wrote, "contains a highly fanciful and inaccurate account of 'Five Forks.'")

*Robert E. Lee Papers.* New acquisition. Mss. 3. L515. b. 557 items, letters written in 1861.

*Miscellaneous Lee Letters.* Fifty separate Lee letters, unrelated, from the constant acquisition from individuals. (The number of Lee letters in private possession is unknown, though, judging from those that continue to appear, the amount is evidently considerable.)

*Collection of Lee Family Letters.* This extensive collection, formed in subdepartments, is not listed in detail, since its references to R. E. Lee and his immediate family are slight. The bulk of the material relates to collateral Lee lines and the Colonial period.

*Andrew Talcott Papers.* Contains prewar letters from Lee to his friend from the Fort Monroe days.

*The 1964 acquisition of two collections.* More than 600 items of Lee personal letters and papers owned by Mrs. Hunter De Butts and Mrs. Hanson Ely, daughters of Captain Robert E. Lee, Jr., and more than 100 items of Lee-Custis family personal papers, owned by Mrs. Hunter De Butts. Most of the letters were published in Captain Lee's *Recollections and Letters* and in Jones's *Life and Letters* and *Personal Reminiscences.* As minor changes were sometimes made in the published versions, the originals are useful for comparison. These papers were formerly a part of the collection at the Library of Congress, as listed below.

LIBRARY OF CONGRESS.

*Personal correspondence and private papers of Lee.*

*Papers of Richard Bland Lee.* Some of these concern Lee's parents.

NATIONAL ARCHIVES.

*Letterbook copies, signed letters, etc.* of Lee's wartime papers.

DUKE UNIVERSITY.

*Lee correspondence and papers.* A growing collection that numbers more than 100 items.

UNIVERSITY OF NORTH CAROLINA.

*Robert Edward Lee Papers.* Among collections of papers of Confederate leaders.

MCCORMICK LIBRARY, WASHINGTON AND LEE UNIVERSITY.

A storehouse containing Lee letters, copies of Lee letters, letters received by Lee, the Letter Books (incomplete) of Lee's presidency, minutes of the trustees, early college catalogues and various oddments. The famous letter of Dr. Brockenbrough, rector of the Board, which probably persuaded Lee to accept the presidency, is kept in a safe in the treasurer's office; it was recently brought to light by Dr. Moger. Also recently discovered were private papers of Colonel William Preston Johnston, including memoranda of conversations with General Lee.

VIRGINIA STATE LIBRARY.

Papers relating to the organization of the Virginia state troops during Lee's command in 1861.

SHIRLEY COLLECTION.

*Farm Journals of Hill Carter, 1816-1875.*

*Account Book of Hill Carter, 1816-1875.*

*Copies of Ann Carter Lee's letters,* the originals of which are scattered and largely owned by individuals.

*Several postwar letters of Lee to his Cousin Hill.*

*Carter family records.*

STONEWALL JACKSON MEMORIAL, LEXINGTON.

Mr. Jay W. Johns, president, made available copies of the twenty-odd letters Lee wrote from Derwent, in July, August, September, 1865. These extremely valuable letters, written by Lee in the first quietude of four years, form the basis of his postwar attitudes and guidance. The originals are widely scattered.

ALDERMAN LIBRARY, UNIVERSITY OF VIRGINIA.

*Dabney Papers: copy.* University of North Carolina is the depository. The papers of the Reverend R. L. Dabney, Jackson's onetime chief of staff, were used for the Seven Days campaign.

*Diaries of individual soldiers in the Army of Northern Virginia.*

*Miscellaneous papers.*

CONFEDERATE MUSEUM.

*Chilton Papers.* Collected by Brigadier General R. H. Chilton, Lee's chief of staff.

*Wartime letters of individuals.*

*Miscellaneous papers.*

ROBERT E. LEE MEMORIAL FOUNDATION, STRATFORD HALL.

*Records, letters, miscellaneous papers* relating to the Lees.

MISS JANET FAUNTLEROY TAYLOR, NORFOLK, VIRGINIA.

*The priceless collection of Colonel Walter H. Taylor's correspondence* from Lee's headquarters and after the war. The most valuable items are the letters Lee's assistant adjutant general wrote to his fiancée and kinspeople, though the postwar letters are also very useful.

*Several Lee letters.*

*Much miscellany.*

JOHN WARREN COOKE, MATTHEWS, VIRGINIA.

Unpublished diary of his father, Major Giles Cooke, the last surviving officer of Lee's staff.

OLLINGER CRENSHAW, WASHINGTON AND LEE.

Chapters on Lee's presidency of Washington College from Dr. Crenshaw's unfinished manuscript on the history of the college.

MRS. MARY COULLING, OF LEXINGTON, VIRGINIA.

Unpublished manuscript, "The Lee Girls," based entirely upon letters — mostly unpublished and many at Washington and Lee.

Single Lee letters in the possession of individuals are not listed. There was one enigmatic note placed at my disposal by Mrs. Jackson L. Fray, Jr., of Culpeper, Virginia. Written to Stonewall Jackson on April 25, 1862, during their collaboration on what became Jackson's Valley campaign, Lee's full note reads: "Gen'l: I have just rec'd your note. It is too late for me to get to the artist by the hour designated."

(The letters of Lee to Henry Kayser, his former assistant engineer on the Mississippi River work at St. Louis, and five letters written to Mrs. Lee from Fort Monroe are listed in published sources, as they appeared in a magazine and a pamphlet, but these valuable letters should also be included as collections of the Missouri Historical Society and the Huntington Library, San Marino, California.)

# Selected Bibliography of Published Sources

It was not easy or simple to divide the published sources into books related directly to Lee and those which formed the general background. Many of the items listed as general background contain considerable material on Lee. However, since many others of these items, containing little or nothing about Lee, were used to develop the environment of the events through which he lived, all items not concerned with Lee *as the subject* were somewhat arbitrarily grouped as background.

Of the period from 1790 to 1861, except for one book on the Constitution, no books of general history have been listed. Of the books that deal with specific aspects of this period, the few listings are limited mostly to standards. On the war period, 1861-1865, there are no books of general narratives; no books on leaders and campaigns not directly associated with Lee; nor any on specialized aspects outside of his province — such as currency, post office, secret agents, etc. The majority of personal narratives are by participants in Lee's operations.

On the period 1865-1870, except for a few current reappraisals, the small list on Reconstruction is composed entirely of standards. No attempt was made to cover thoroughly the large and growing amount of material on the Reconstruction era, which in itself can be divided into about a dozen major aspects of study. The items here cited were used to provide only the general background of the period in which Lee lived his last five years.

### Items Relating Specifically to Lee and His Family

Adams, Charles F. *Lee at Appomattox and other Papers*, pp. 1-19. Boston, 1902.

Alexander, E. P. "Lee at Appomattox." *Century*. April, 1901.

Anderson, Charles. *Texas . . . on the Eve of the Rebellion*. Cincinnati, 1884.

Armes, Ethel. *Stratford Hall*. Richmond, 1936. (Based on documents, letters, records, etc.)

Bond, Christiana. *Memories of General Robert E. Lee*. Baltimore, 1926.

Boyd, Thomas. *Light-Horse Harry Lee*. New York, 1931.

Bradford, Gamaliel. *Lee the American*. Boston, 1912.

Cabell, D. S. G. "Lee As an Educator." *Southern Historical Society Papers*. Vol. 17. Jan.-Dec., 1889, pp. 351-362. (Contains the account of Lee's collaboration with Senator Cabell in obtaining funds for Washington College from the General Assembly of Virginia.)

Carter, Robert Randolph (compiler) and Robert Isham Randolph. *The Carter Tree*. Santa Barbara, California, 1951.

Cooke, John Esten. *A Life of General Robert E. Lee*. New York, 1871.

Craven, Avery, editor. *To Markie*. Letters of Robert E. Lee to Martha Custis Williams. Cambridge, Massachusetts, 1933.

Cuthbert, Norma B. "To Molly: Five Early Letters from Robert E. Lee to his Wife, 1832-1835." *Huntington Library Quarterly*. May, 1952, pp. 257-276.

Darrow, Mrs. Caroline Baldwin. "Recollections of the Twiggs Surrender." Vol. 1 of *Battles and Leaders* . . . (Johnson and Buel), p. 33. (Contains glimpses of Lee during secession action in Texas.)

Davis, Jefferson. "Robert E. Lee." *North American Review.* January, 1890, pp. 55-66.

Dodd, William E. "Lee and Reconstruction." *South Atlantic Quarterly.* January, 1905, pp. 63-70.

Dorsey, Florence L. *Master of the Mississippi.* Boston, 1941. (Biography of Henry Shreve, with whom Lee worked during his assignment at St. Louis: pp. 191-193 specifically on Lee.)

Dowdey, Clifford (editor) with Louis Manarin. *The Wartime Papers of R. E. Lee.* Boston, 1961.

Drum, Ella. "Robert E. Lee and the Improvement of the Mississippi River." *Missouri Historical Society Collections.* February, 1929, pp. 157-171. (Article contains flashes of Lee as well as details on his work.)

Fishwick, Marshall. *General Lee's Photographer: Life and Work of Michael Miley.* Chapel Hill, N.C., 1954.

Freeman, Douglas Southall. *R. E. Lee: A Biography.* New York, 1935, 4 vol.

Gaines, Dr. Francis Pendleton. *Lee: The Final Achievement (1865-1870).* Pamphlet, n.d.

Garnett, T. S. "Glowing Tribute to General Lee." *SHSP.* Vol. 28. Jan.-Dec., 1900, pp. 106-114. (Contains firsthand account of Lee in crises of Five Forks and Sayler's Creek by a cavalry staff officer who had known him before the war.)

Hendricks, Burton J. *The Lees of Virginia.* Boston, 1935.

Henry, Robert Selph. *The Story of the Mexican War.* Indianapolis, 1950. (Not specifically on Lee but used as a guide for the campaigns in which Lee participated, and contains a significant little-known item which authenticates Scott's request for Lee's services on his staff. A newly discovered Lee letter in the George Bolling Lee collection also confirms this.)

Hoyt, William D., Jr., editor. "Some Personal Letters to Robert E. Lee, 1850-1857." *Journal of Southern History.* November, 1946, pp. 557-570. (Letters to Jerome Napoleon Bonaparte, of Baltimore, written when Lee was in Baltimore and mostly when he was superintendent at West Point. This correspondence shows a genial Lee, with flashes of lightheartedness.)

Johnston, Col. William Preston. "Death and Funeral of General Lee." (One of the two firsthand accounts of Lee's death, the sketch appeared first in Jones's *Personal Reminiscences*, pp. 446-459. Professor Johnston wrote the sketch for a memorial volume projected by Washington and Lee and, when this was abandoned, made it available to Chaplain Jones. The sketch was reprinted in Riley's *General Lee after Appomattox*, pp. 206-218.)

Johnstone, W. J. *Robert E. Lee the Christian.* New York, 1933.

Jones, William J. *Personal Reminiscences of General Robert E. Lee.* New York, 1874.
———. *Life and Letters of Robert Edward Lee* . . . Washington, 1906.

Krantz, John C., Jr. "The Implications of the Medical History of General Lee." *Virginia Medical Monthly.* October, 1961, pp. 25-31.

Lee, Cazenove Gardner, Jr. *Lee Chronicle.* New York, 1957.

Lee, Edmund Jennings. *Lees of Virginia, 1642-1892.* Philadelphia, 1895. (A standard.)

Lee, Fitzhugh. *General Lee.* (New edition.) New York, 1961.

Lee, George T. "Reminiscences of Robert E. Lee." *South Atlantic Quarterly.* July, 1927, pp. 236-237.

Lee, Henry. *Memoirs of the War in the Southern Department.* Edited, with a biography of the author, by Robert E. Lee. New York, 1869.

Lee, Mrs. Robert E. Letter to Miss Mary Meade, October 12, 1870. *Virginia Magazine of History and Biography* (Hereafter *Virginia Magazine*). January, 1927, pp. 23-26. (One of the two firsthand accounts of Lee's death.)

Lee, Robert E. Letters of —— to Henry Kayser, 1838-1846. "Glimpses of the Past":
Supplement of the *Missouri Historical Society*. January-February, 1936, pp. 1-43.
(These letters to Lee's former assistant engineer at St. Louis, who carried on the
work as city engineer, comprise a valuable collection. Beginning with discussions
of the work on the Mississippi, the letters grow increasingly intimate and reveal
many of Lee's attitudes to life and personal details of the period at Fort Hamilton.
They also show the businesslike side of Lee in money matters.)

Long, A. L. *Memoirs of Robert E. Lee* . . . New York, 1886. (A standard by General
Long, member of Lee's early staff and later chief of Second Corps artillery.)

MacDonald, Rose Mortimer. Mrs. Robert E. Lee. Boston, 1939.

McDonald, Hunter. "General Lee after Appomattox." *Tennessee Historical Magazine.*
July, 1925, pp. 87-101. (Issued May, 1927.)

Mason, Emily V. *Popular Life of General Robert Edward Lee*. Baltimore, 1872.

Maurice, Sir Frederick. *Robert E. Lee, the Soldier*. Boston, 1925.

——, editor. *An Aide-de-Camp of Lee: The Papers of Colonel Charles Marshall* . . .
Boston, 1927.

Meredith, Roy. *The Face of Robert E. Lee.* New York, 1947.

Moger, Allen W. "General Lee's Unwritten 'History of the Army of Northern Virginia.'" *Virginia Magazine.* July, 1963, pp. 341-363.

——. "Letters to General Lee after the War." *Virginia Magazine.* January, 1956, pp.
30-69.

Montague, Ludwell Lee. "Richard Lee, the Emigrant: 1613(?)-1664." *Virginia Magazine.* January, 1954, pp. 3-49.

Page, Thomas Nelson. *Robert E. Lee, Man and Soldier*. New York, 1911.

Powell, Mary G. *History of Old Alexandria*. Richmond, 1928.

Preston, Mrs. Margaret J. "Lee after the War." *Century.* June, 1889, pp. 271-273.

Riley, Franklin P. *General Robert E. Lee after Appomattox*. New York, 1922.

Rister, Carl C. *Robert E. Lee in Texas*. Norman, Oklahoma, 1946.

Robert, Joseph C. "Lee the Farmer." *Journal of Southern History.* November, 1937,
pp. 7-25. (Mainly concerns Lee's rehabilitation of Arlington.)

Taylor, Walter H. *Four Years With General Lee*. New York, 1877.

——. *General Lee: His Campaigns in Virginia* . . . Norfolk, 1906.

United States 39th Congress, 1st Session 1866. Committee of Inquiry on Reconstruction. (Contains the interrogation of Lee in Washington, March, 1866.)

Valentine, Elizabeth Gray. *Dawn to Twilight: Work of Edward V. Valentine*. Richmond, 1929. (Pages 107-114 contain the narrative and personal observations of
the sculptor who did a bust of Lee in 1870.)

Venable, C. S. "The Campaign from the Wilderness to Petersburg." *SHSP*. Vol. 14,
pp. 522-542.

Wayland, John B. *Robert E. Lee and His Family*. Staunton, Virginia, 1951.

Wilmer, Rt. Rev. Joseph P. *General Robert E. Lee*. Nashville, 1872.

Winston, Robert W. *Robert E. Lee* . . . New York, 1934.

BASIC SOURCES ON THE WAR

*The War of the Rebellion: A Compilation of the Official Records of the Union and
Confederate Armies*. Washington, 1880-1902. The 128 volumes plus atlas of the *Official
Records* (OR), which comprise the literally indispensable source, contain thousands
of items of Lee's official correspondence, orders, reports, etc.

*Southern Historical Society Papers*. Richmond, 1876-1819. 50 volumes. For the Confederacy this rich collection is as indispensable as the *Official Records*. Contains personal narratives of ex-Confederate soldiers on every conceivable aspect of the war,
including the full course of the Longstreet "Gettysburg controversy." There are
countless references to Lee — general impressions, observations on and descriptions of
him during specific actions, episodes of individual soldiers with Lee (as the cavalry

courier after Five Forks), narratives of actions involving Lee and sketches on personal details of aspects of his army life. A few listings have been made of specific references, where they constituted part of the primary sources.

*The Rebellion Record.* Frank Moore, editor. New York, 1862-1871, 12 vols.

*Photographic History of the Civil War.* Francis Trevelyan Miller, editor. New York, 1911, 10 vols.

### GENERAL BACKGROUND

Adams, Henry. *The Great Secession Winter, 1860-1861, and Other Papers.* New York, 1958.

Agassiz, George R., editor. *Meade's Headquarters, 1863-1865: Letters of Col. Theodore Lyman from the Wilderness to Appomattox.* Boston, 1922.

Alexander, E. P. *Military Memoirs of a Confederate.* (A standard.)

Allan, Elizabeth Preston. *Life and Letters of Margaret Junkin Preston.* Boston, 1903.

Allan, Elizabeth Randolph Preston. *A March Past.* Richmond, 1938. (Evocative for postwar life in Lexington.)

Andrews, Eliza Frances. *Wartime Diary of a Georgia Girl.* New York, 1908.

*Annals of the War.* By Participants, North and South. Philadelphia, 1879.

Avary, Myrta Lockett. *Dixie after the War.* New York, 1906.

Barringer, Dr. Paul B. *The Natural Bent.* Chapel Hill, 1949.

Beale, G. W. *A Lieutenant of Cavalry in Lee's Army.* Boston, 1918. (Good for cavalry in Gettysburg Campaign.)

Beale, Howard K. *The Critical Year: A Study of Andrew Johnson and Reconstruction.* New York, 1930.

Beale, R. L. T. *History of the Ninth Virginia Cavalry.* Richmond, 1899.

Bean, W. G. *Stonewall's Man: Sandie Pendleton.* Chapel Hill, 1959.

———. "The Ruffner Pamphlet of 1847: An Antislavery Aspect of Virginia Sectionalism." *Virginia Magazine.* July, 1953, pp. 260-282.

Berkeley, Major William N. War Letters to His Wife, 1861-1865. Unpublished ms. (Courtesy of Francis L. Berkeley, Jr., of Charlottesville, Virginia.)

Bigelow, John, Jr. *The Campaign of Chancellorsville.* New Haven, 1910. (A standard.)

Black, Robert C., III. *The Railroads of the Confederacy.* Chapel Hill, 1952.

Blackford, Launcelot M. *Mine Eyes Have Seen the Glory.* Cambridge, Massachusetts, 1954. (The story of a prewar Virginia emancipationist, Mrs. Mary Berkeley Minor Blackford.)

Blackford, Mrs. Susan Lee, compiler. *Memoirs of Life in and out of the Army in Virginia* . . . 2 vols. Lynchburg, Virginia, 1894-1896. (Mostly letters from Lee's army.)

Blackford, Lt. Col. W. W. *War Years With Jeb Stuart.* New York, 1945.

Blair, Lewis H. *A Southern Prophecy: The Prosperity of the South Dependent Upon the Elevation of the Negro.* 1889. New Edition: Edited by C. Vann Woodward, Boston, 1964.

Boatner, Lt. Col. Mark Mayo. *The Civil War Dictionary.* New York, 1959.

Borcke, Heros von. *Memoirs of the Confederate War for Independence.* New York, 1938, 2 vols.

Bowers, Claude. *The Tragic Era.* New York, 1929.

Boykin, E. M. *The Falling Flag: Evacuation of Richmond, Retreat and Surrender* . . . New York, 1874.

Bradford, Gamaliel. *Confederate Portraits.* Boston, 1917.

Brent, Joseph L. *Memoirs of the War* . . . New Orleans, 1940.

Bridges, Hal. *Lee's Maverick General: D. H. Hill.* New York, 1961.

Brock, Miss Sally. *Richmond During the War.* New York, 1867.

Brooks, U. R. *Butler and His Cavalry* . . . Columbia, S.C., 1909.

Brydon, George M. *Virginia's Mother Church.* Richmond, 1947, 2 vols. (This story of the Anglican Church in Virginia, 1607-1814, develops the political-social background from records.)

Buck, Paul H. *The Road to Reunion*. Boston, 1937.

Burge, Mrs. Thomas. *A Woman's Wartime Journal* . . . Edited by Julian Street. Macon, 1947.

Caldwell, J. F. J. *The History of a Brigade of South Carolinians*. New Edition: Marietta, Ga., 1951. (A classic among brigade histories: the Gregg-MacGowan brigade, with A. P. Hill.)

Campbell, John A. *Reminiscences and Documents Relating to the Civil War During the Year 1865*. Baltimore, 1887. (Former Supreme Court Justice Campbell, as a member of the Confederate "Peace Commission," met with Lincoln in February, 1865, and again, after Appomattox, during Lincoln's visit to the evacuated Confederate capital.)

Carpenter, Jesse T. *The South as a Conscious Minority, 1789-1861*. New York, 1930.

Carson, Jane. *Colonial Virginia at Play*. Williamsburg, 1957.

Catton, Bruce. *A Stillness at Appomattox*. Garden City, 1953.

———. *Glory Road*. Garden City, 1952.

———. *Mr. Lincoln's Army*. Garden City, 1951.

Carter, Hodding. *The Angry Scar: The Story of Reconstruction*. Garden City: 1959.

Casler, John O. *Four Years in the Stonewall Brigade*. New Edition: Marietta, Ga., 1951.

Chamberlain, Joshua L. *Passing of the Armies*. New York, 1915. (The fullest account of the surrender of the Army of Northern Virginia, written by the generous Federal general who commanded at the laying down of arms.)

Chamberlaine, William W. *Memoirs of the Civil War*. Washington, 1912.

Chamberlayne, C. G., editor. *Ham Chamberlayne — Virginian: Letters and Papers of an Artillery Officer* . . . Richmond, 1932.

Chesnut, Mary Boykin. *A Diary from Dixie*. New York, 1905. (A standard for social life in the Confederacy.)

Christian, W. Asbury. *Richmond, Her Past and Present*. Richmond, 1912. (A standard year-by-year chronicle of factual events.)

Claiborne, J. F. H. *Life and Correspondence of John A. Quitman*. New York, 1860.

Clark, Walter, editor. *Histories of . . . Regiments . . . from North Carolina*. Raleigh and Goldsboro, N.C., 1901. (A standard.)

Clay, Mrs. Clement C. *A Belle of the Fifties*. New York, 1904.

Cleaves, Freeman. *Meade of Gettysburg*. Norman, Oklahoma, 1960.

Cockrell, Monroe F. *Gunner with Stonewall: Reminiscences of William Thomas Poague*. Jackson, Tenn., 1957.

Cook, Joel. *The Siege of Richmond* . . . Philadelphia, 1862.

Cooke, John Esten. *Life of Stonewall Jackson*. New York, n.d.

———. *The Wearing of the Gray*. New Edition: Bloomington, Ind., 1959.

Coulter, E. Merton. *The Confederate States of America, 1861-1865*. Vol. 7, *A History of the South*. Baton Rouge, 1950.

———. *The South During Reconstruction*. Baton Rouge, 1947.

Couper, William. *One Hundred Years at V.M.I.* Richmond, 1939, 2 vols.

Craven, Avery O. *The Coming of the Civil War*. New York, 1942.

———. *The Growth of Southern Nationalism: 1840-1861*. Vol. 6, *A History of the South*. Baton Rouge, 1953.

Cumming, Kate. *A Journal of Hospital Life*. Louisville, 1866.

Curry, J. L. M. *Civil History of the Government of the Confederate States*. Richmond, 1901.

Dabney, R. L. *Life and Campaigns of . . . Jackson*. New York, 1866.

Dame, William M. *From the Rapidan to the James*. Baltimore, 1920.

Daniel, Frederick S. *Richmond Howitzers in the War* . . . Richmond, 1891.

Daniels, Jonathan. *Prince of Carpetbaggers*. Philadelphia and New York, 1958.

Davis, Jefferson. *The Rise and Fall of the Confederate Government*. New York, 1881, 2 vols.

Davis, Rev. Nicholas A. *The Campaign From Texas to Maryland*. A facsimile reproduction of the 1863 Richmond edition: Austin, Texas, 1961. (Written by the chaplain of the 4th Texas, it contains an account of Hood's Texans at Battle of Gaines' Mill.)

Davis, Mrs. Varina Howell. *Jefferson Davis: A Memoir by His Wife.* New York, 1890, 2 vols.

Dawson, Francis W. *Reminiscences of Confederate Service.* Charleston, 1882.

Dawson, Sarah Morgan. *A Confederate Girl's Diary.* New York, 1913.

DeLeon, T. C. *Belles, Beaux and Brains of the 60's* . . . New York, 1909.

——. *Four Years in Rebel Capitals.* Mobile, 1890.

Dickert, D. Augustus. *History of Kershaw's Brigade.* Newberry, S.C., 1899.

Dodd, William E. *Jefferson Davis.* Philadelphia, 1951.

——. *Statesmen of the Old South.* New York, 1911.

——. *The Cotton Kingdom.* New Haven, 1919.

——. *Lincoln Reconsidered.* New York, 1959.

Douglas, Henry Kyd. *I Rode with Stonewall.* Chapel Hill, 1940.

Dowdey, Clifford. *Death of a Nation.* New York, 1958.

——. *Experiment in Rebellion.* Garden City, 1946.

——. *Lee's Last Campaign.* Boston, 1960.

——. "The History of the Virginia General Assembly." *Virginia Record.* January, 1964.

——. *The Land They Fought For.* Garden City, 1956.

——. *The Seven Days.* Boston, 1964.

Dunaway, Wayland F. *Reminiscences of a Rebel* . . . New York, 1875.

Durden, Robert F. *James Shepherd Pike: Republicanism and the American Negro, 1850-1882.* Durham, N.C., 1957.

Early, Jubal. *A Memoir of the Last Year of the War for Independence.* Lynchburg, Virginia, 1867.

——. *Autobiographical Sketches* . . . Philadelphia, 1912.

Eckenrode, H. J. *Political History of Virginia During Reconstruction. Johns Hopkins University Studies in Historical and Political Science,* Vol. 22. Baltimore, 1904. (The only complete study of Reconstruction in Virginia.)

Eckenrode, H. J. and Bryan Conrad. *James Longstreet, Lee's Warhorse.* Chapel Hill, 1936.

Eggleston, George Cary. *A Rebel's Recollections.* New York, 1875. (A standard: sketches of leaders in Lee's army.)

Elliott, Charles W. *Winfield Scott, the Soldier and the Man.* New York, 1937.

Farrar, Emmie Ferguson. *Old Houses Along the James.* New York, 1957.

Fleet, Betsy, editor, and John D. P. Fuller. *Green Mount: A Virginia Plantation Family During the Civil War.* Lexington, Kentucky, 1962.

Fletcher, W. A. *Rebel Private, Front and Rear* . . . New Edition: Austin, Texas, 1954.

Franklin, John Pope. *Reconstruction: After the Civil War.* Chicago, 1961. (Contains comprehensive bibliography.)

——. *The Emancipation Proclamation.* Garden City, 1963.

Freeman, Douglas Southall. *Lee's Lieutenants.* New York, 1944, 3 vols.

Fremantle, Lt. Col. A. J. L. *Three Months in the Southern States.* April-June, 1863. New Edition: Boston, 1954.

Gills, Mary Louise. *It Happened at Appomattox.* Richmond, 1948. Pamphlet. (The story of the court house village.)

Gordon, John B. *Reminiscences of the Civil War.* New York, 1903.

Gorgas, Josiah. *Civil War Diary.* Edited by Frank E. Vandiver. Tuscaloosa, Alabama, 1947.

Govan, Gilbert E., and James W. Livingood. *A Different Valor: The Story of General Joseph E. Johnston* . . . Indianapolis, 1956.

Grant, Ulysses S. *Personal Memoirs.* New York, 1885, 2 vols.

Grigsby, Hugh Blair. *The History of the Virginia Federal Convention of 1788.*

Edited by R. A. Brock. *Virginia Historical Society Collection*, New Series, Vol. 9. Richmond, 1890.

Hamlin, Percy G. *Old Baldhead*. Strasburg, Virginia, 1940. (General R. S. Ewell.)

Hancock, Cornelia. *South after Gettysburg: Letters 1863-1868*. New York, 1956. (A Northern schoolteacher's views of postwar South Carolina.)

Hanna, A. J. *Flight into Oblivion*. Richmond, 1938. (A narrative of the movements of Jefferson Davis and his Cabinet from the evacuation of Richmond to the dissolution of the party.)

Happel, Ralph. "The Chancellors of Chancellorsville." *Virginia Magazine*. July, 1963, pp. 259-277.

Harrison, Mrs. Burton. *Recollections Grave and Gay*. Richmond, 1911. (A standard on the social life in wartime Richmond.)

Harrison, Walter. *Pickett's Men*. New York, 1870. (Division history.)

Haskell, John Cheeves. *Memoirs*. Edited by Gilbert E. Govan and James W. Livingood. New York, 1960. (A number of observations on Lee, and other generals, by one of the army's top artillerists.)

Hassler, Warren W., Jr. *General George B. McClellan*. Baton Rouge, 1957.

Hassler, William Woods. *A. P. Hill*. Richmond, 1957.

Helper, Hinton Rowan. *The Impending Crisis of the South: How to Meet It*. New York: 1857. (A standard: a North Carolinian's unwelcome advice to the South on slavery.)

Henderson, C. F. R. *Stonewall Jackson* . . . New York, 1936.

Hendrick, Burton J. *Bulwark of the Republic: A Biography of the Constitution*. Boston, 1941.

———. *Lincoln's War Cabinet*. Boston, 1946.

———. *Statesmen of the Lost Cause*. Boston, 1939.

Henry, Robert Selph. *The Story of Reconstruction*. Indianapolis, 1938.

Hoke, Jacob. *The Great Invasion of 1863*. New Edition: New York, 1959. (Written by a native of Chambersburg, Pa., this is the standard account of a Northern view of Lee's army on the way to Gettysburg.)

Hood, John B. *Advance and Retreat*. New Orleans, 1880.

Hoole, William S. *Lawley Covers the Confederacy*. Tuscaloosa, 1964.

Hopley, Catherine C. *Life in the South from the Commencement of the War*. London, 1863.

Horn, Stanley F. *Invisible Empire: The Story of the Ku Klux Klan, 1866-1871*. Boston, 1939.

Howard, McHenry. *Recollections of a Confederate Soldier and Staff-Officer*. Baltimore, 1914.

Humphreys, A. A. *The Virginia Campaign of 1864 and 1865*. New York, 1883. (A standard on Federal operations, written by a Federal corps commander and onetime chief of staff.)

Hunton, Eppa. *Autobiography*. Richmond, 1933. (Privately printed.)

Hyman, Harold. *The Era of the Oath: Northern Loyalty Tests During the Civil War and Reconstruction*. New York, 1954.

Jackson, Mrs. Mary Anna. *Memories of Stonewall Jackson*. Louisville, 1895.

Jacobs, M. *Notes on the Invasion* . . . Philadelphia, 1863. (A Pennsylvanian's view of Lee's army at Gettysburg.)

Jefferson, Thomas. *Notes on the State of Virginia*. London, 1787. New Edition: Chapel Hill, N.C., 1955.

Johnson, Robert Underwood, and Buel, Clarence Clough, editors. *Battles and Leaders of the Civil War*. New York, 1887-1888, 4 vols.

Johnston, David E. *The Story of a Confederate Boy in the Civil War*. Boston, 1904.

Johnston, Joseph E. *Narrative of Military Operations* . . . New York, 1872.

Jones, J. B. *A Rebel War Clerk's Diary*. New York, 1935, 2 vols. (A standard by the War Department's Pepys, on the minutiae, gossip and rumors, weather and food prices, of Richmond during the war.)

*Journal of the Congress of the Confederate States of America.* Washington, 1904-1905, 7 vols.

Kane, Harnett T. *The Lady of Arlington.* Garden City, 1953.

Kean, R. G. H. *Inside the Confederate Government.* Diary. Edited by Edward Younger. New York, 1957. (Kean served in the War Department.)

Kern, M. Ethel Kelley. *The Trail of the Three-Notched Road.* Richmond, 1929.

Kocher, A. Lawrence, and Howard Dearstyne. *Shadows and Silver: A Pictorial Review of Virginia 1850-1900.* New York, 1954.

Lasswell, Mary, editor. *Rags and Hope: The Memoirs of Val C. Giles, Four Years With Hood's Brigade* . . . New York, 1961.

Leech, Margaret. *Reveille in Washington, 1860-1865.* New York, 1941.

Little, John P. *History of Richmond.* Richmond, 1933.

Loehr, Charles T. *War History of the Old First Virginia Regiment.* Richmond, 1884.

Longstreet, James. *From Manassas to Appomattox.* New Edition: Bloomington, Ind., 1960.

Lonn, Ella. *Desertion During the Civil War.* New York, 1928.

McCarthy, Carlton, editor. *Contributions to a History of the Richmond Howitzer Battalion.* 4 pamphlets. Richmond, 1883-1886.

———. *Detailed Minutiae of Soldier Life in the Army of Northern Virginia.* Richmond, 1882. (A standard.)

McClellan, George B. *McClellan's Own Story.* New York, 1887.

McClellan, H. B. *The Life and Campaigns of Major General J. E. B. Stuart.* New Edition: Bloomington, Indiana, 1958.

McElroy, Robert. *Jefferson Davis: The Real and the Unreal.* New York, 1937, 2 vols.

McGuire, Judith W. *Diary of a Southern Refugee.* Richmond, 1889. (A standard on life in wartime Richmond.)

McKim, Randolph H. *A Soldier's Recollections.* New York, 1910.

———. *The Soul of Lee.* New York, 1918.

Malet, Rev. William W. *An Errand to the South in the Summer of 1862.* London, 1863.

Malone, Bartlett Y. *Diary.* Edited by W. W. Pierson, Jr. New Edition: Jackson, Tenn., 1960.

Marshall, Charles. *Appomattox: An Address* . . . Baltimore, 1894. (A standard on details of Lee's surrender.)

Maury, Major General Dabney H. *Recollections of a Virginian.* New York, 1894.

Maussion de la Bastie, Gaston Marie Léonard, and Maussion, Mme. Hélène. *They Knew the Washingtons: Letters from a French . . . family in Virginia.* Indianapolis, 1926.

Meade, George Gordon. *Life and Letters of* . . . New York, 1913, 2 vols.

Meade, Robert Douthat. *Judah P. Benjamin* . . . New York, 1943.

Meade, William. *Old Churches, Ministers and Families of Virginia.* Philadelphia, 1889.

Milton, George Fort. *The Age of Hate.* New York, 1941.

Mixson, Frank M. *Reminiscences of a Private* . . . Columbia, S.C., 1910.

Moore, Albert Burton. *Conscription and Conflict in the Confederacy.* New York, 1924.

Moore, Edward A. *The Story of a Cannoneer Under Stonewall Jackson.* New York, 1907. (A Washington College student, before and after the war, in the Rockbridge artillery battery.)

Mosby, John S. *Memoirs.* Edited by C. W. Russell. New Edition: Bloomington, Ind., 1959.

———. *War Reminiscences and Stuart's Cavalry Campaigns.* New Edition: New York, 1958.

Munford, Beverley B. *Virginia's Attitude to Secession and Slavery.* New York, 1911.

Munford, Robert Beverley. *Richmond Homes and Memories.* Richmond, 1936.

Myers, Frank M. *The Comanches: A History of White's Battalion, Virginia Cavalry,*

*Laurel Brigade, Hampton's Division*. Baltimore, 1871. (A source for the cavalry on retreat to Appomattox.)

Napier, Bartlett. *A Soldier's Story of the War*. New Orleans, 1874.

Nevins, Allan. *The Emergence of Lincoln*. New York, 1950, 2 vols.

———. *The War for the Union*. New York, 1960, 2 vols.

Nichols, James L. "Confederate Map Supply." *The Military Engineer*. Jan.-Feb., 1954, pp. 28-32.

Nisbett, James Cooper. *Four Years on the Firing Line*. Chattanooga, 1914.

Norman, W. M. *A Portion of My Life*. Winston-Salem, N.C., 1959. (Memoirs of a North Carolinian, prewar attorney, imprisoned at Johnson's Island, Lake Erie.)

Oates, William C. *The War Between the Union and the Confederacy*. New York and Washington, 1907.

Olmstead, Frederick Law. *Journey in the Back Country*. New York, 1860.

———. *Journey in the Seaboard Slave States*. New York, 1858.

Owen, William M. *In Camp and Battle with the Washington Artillery of New Orleans*. 1885. (A standard.)

Owsley, Frank L. *King Cotton Diplomacy*. Chicago, 1936.

———. *States' Rights in the Confederacy*. Chicago, 1925.

Parker, William H. *Recollections of a Naval Officer, 1841-1865*. New York, 1883.

Patch, Major Gen. Joseph D. *The Battle of Ball's Bluff*. Leesburg, Virginia, 1958.

Pember, Phoebe Yates. *A Southern Woman's Story*. New Edition: Jackson, Tenn., 1959. (A classic of wartime Richmond written by the matron of the great military hospital Chimborazo.)

Peterson, Harold L. *Notes on Ordnance of the American Civil War*. Washington, 1959. Pamphlet. (A concise basic handbook.)

Phillips, Ulrich D. *Life and Labor in the Old South*. Boston, 1929. (A standard.)

———. *The Life of Robert Toombs*. New York, 1913.

Pickett, George E. *Soldier of the South . . . War Letters to His Wife*. Boston, 1928.

Pike, James S. *The Prostrate State: South Carolina under Negro Government*. New York, 1874. (A standard from the rabid anti-Negro view, written by a Republican abolitionist from Maine.)

Poindexter, James E. *Address on . . . General Lewis A. Armistead*. Richmond, n.d. (Almost all of the slim material on the brigadier killed at the crest of the charge at Gettysburg.)

Pollay, J. B. *Hood's Texas Brigade*. New York, 1910. (A standard brigade history.)

Potts, Frank. *The Death of the Confederacy*. Edited by D. S. Freeman. Richmond, 1928. (A brief firsthand account of the evacuation of Richmond and retreat to Appomattox.)

Pryor, Mrs. Roger A. *Reminiscences of War and Peace*. New York, 1906.

Quarles, Benjamin. *The Negro in the Civil War*. Boston, 1953.

Ramsdell, Charles W. *Behind the Lines in the Southern Confederacy*. Baton Rouge, 1944.

———. "Lincoln and Fort Sumter." *Journal of Southern History*. Vol. 3, 1937, pp. 259-288.

Randall, J. G. *Civil War and Reconstruction*. New York, 1937.

———. *Lincoln, the President*. New York, 1945, 2 vols.

Reagan, John H. *Memoirs . . .* New York, 1906.

Richardson, James D., editor. *Messages and Papers of the Confederacy*. Nashville, 1906, 2 vols.

Roberts, Joseph C. *The Road from Monticello: A Study of the Virginia Slave Debates of 1832*. Durham, 1941.

Robertson, Alexander F. *Alexander Hugh Holmes Stuart, 1807-1890*. Richmond, 1925. (The Virginia Unionist, and leader in achieving the state's readmission, who collaborated with Lee on the "White Sulphur Letter.")

Robertson, W. G. "A Biography of A. P. Hill." *Richmond Times Dispatch Sunday Magazine*. Oct. 14-Nov. 11, 1934.

Roman, Alfred. *The Military Operations of General Beauregard.* New York, 1884, 2 vols.

Ross, Fitzgerald. *Cities and Camps of the Confederate States.* New Edition: Urbana, Ill., 1958.

Royall, William L. *Some Reminiscences.* New York and Washington, 1909.

Runge, William H., editor. *Four Years in the Confederate Artillery.* Chapel Hill, N.C., 1961. (The diary of Private Berkeley, who ended in Fort Delaware.)

Russell, William H. *My Diary North and South.* New Edition: New York, 1954.

Sanger, David Bridgman: *James Longstreet, Soldier,* and Hay, Thomas Robson: *James Longstreet, Politician, Office Holder, Writer.* Baton Rouge, 1952.

Schaff, Morris. *The Battle of the Wilderness.* Boston, 1910.

——. *The Sunset of the Confederacy.* Boston, 1912. (Details of Appomattox, by a Federal officer.)

Schenck, Martin. *Up Came Hill* . . . Harrisburg, Pa., 1958.

Schwab, John C. *The Confederate States of America.* New York, 1901.

Scott, Mary Wingfield. *Houses of Old Richmond.* Richmond, 1941.

Scott, W. W., editor. *Two Confederate Items.* Pamphlet. Richmond, 1927. (Judge Moncure in his reminiscences writes of when, as a young trooper in the 9th Virginia, he served as Lee's guide on the night ride from Spotsylvania to the North Anna.)

Shanks, H. T. *The Secession Movement in Virginia, 1847-1861.* Richmond, 1934.

Simkins, Francis B., and James Welch Patton. *Women of the Confederacy.* Richmond, 1936.

Simms, Henry. *Life of Robert M. T. Hunter.* Richmond, 1935.

Smith, Gustavus. *The Battle of Seven Pines.* New York, 1891. (The major source for the collusion of Johnston and Longstreet.)

Smith, Justin H. *The War with Mexico.* New York, 1919, 2 vols.

Sorrel, G. Moxley. Recollections of a Confederate Staff Officer. New York, 1917.

Sparks, David S., editor. *Inside Lincoln's Army: The Diary of General Marsena Rudolph Patrick, Provost Marshal General, Army of the Potomac.* New York, 1964. (Contains fresh observations of Lee and Richmond after Appomattox.)

Stark, Richard Boies, M.D. "Surgeons and Surgical Care of the Confederate States Army." *Virginia Medical Monthly.* May, 1960, pp. 230-241.

Starr, Louis M. *Bohemian Brigade: Civil War Newsmen in Action.* New York, 1954.

Steele, M. F. *American Campaigns.* Washington, 1909, 2 vols. (A standard on maps. Maps have grown more elaborate and more detailed since Steele, as styles changed, but his rather small, accurate maps, with all their limitations, remain basic.)

Stephens, Alexander H. *A Constitutional View of the Late War Between the States.* Philadelphia, 1868, 2 vols.

Stephenson, Nathaniel W. "A Theory of Jefferson Davis." *American Historical Review.* October, 1915, pp. 73-90.

——. *The Day of the Confederacy.* New Haven, 1919.

Stewart, William H. *A Pair of Blankets.* New York, 1911.

Stiles, Robert. *Four Years under Marse Robert.* Washington, 1903.

Stone, Kate. *Brockenburn: Journal 1861-1868.* Edited by John Q. Anderson. Baton Rouge, La., 1955. (Intimate account of the impact of war on a Louisiana plantation, written by a sensitive young woman.)

*Stranger's Guide and Official Directions of the City of Richmond, The.* Richmond, 1863.

Strother, David Hunter. *Diaries.* Edited by Cecil D. Eby, Jr. Chapel Hill, N.C., 1961. (Strother served on General Hunter's staff during his occupany of Lexington.)

Stuart, Meriwether. "Samuel Ruth and General Lee." *Virginia Magazine.* January, 1963, pp. 35-109. (New findings on Unionist activities in Virginia during the war, particularly by the superintendent of the R.F.&P. Railroad — whom Lee vainly sought to have removed from his supply line.)

——. "The Military Orders of Daniel Ruggles." *Virginia Magazine.* April, 1961, pp. 149-180. (Concerns mustering of state troops while Lee was in command of Virginia's defenses.)

Sydnor, C. S. *Gentlemen Freeholders*. Chapel Hill, N.C., 1952. (Fine brief study of Virginia's ruling class in government.)

Tankersley, Allen P. *John B. Gordon*. Atlanta, 1955.

Tatum, Georgia Lee. *Disloyalty in the Confederacy*. Chapel Hill, 1934.

Taylor, Richard. *Destruction and Reconstruction* . . . New York, 1879.

Thomas, Henry W. *History of the Doles Cooke Brigade*. Atlanta, 1903. (A standard brigade history.)

Thomason, John W. *Jeb Stuart*. New York, 1930.

Tilley, John S. *Lincoln Takes Command*. Chapel Hill, N.C., 1941.

Trowbridge, John T. The South: *A Tour of Its* . . . *Ruined Cities, a Journey Through the Desolated States* . . . Hartford, Conn., 1866. (One of the standards among the published accounts of observations by Northern visitors to the post-war South.)

Vaughn, William P. "Partners in Segregation." *Civil War History*. September, 1964, pp. 260-274.

Voegeli, Jacque. The Northwest and the Race Issue, 1861-1862, *Mississippi Valley Historical Review*. September, 1963, pp. 235-251.

Wainwright, Col. Charles S. *A Diary of Battle*. Edited by Allan Nevins. New York, 1962. (Highly literate observations of Lee's army and wartime Virginia by a volunteer colonel in the 1st New York Light Infantry — from the Peninsula through Appomattox.)

Wallace, David Duncan. *South Carolina: A Short History, 1520-1948*. Chapel Hill, 1951.

Walthall, Ernest Taylor. *Hidden Things Brought to Light*. Richmond, 1933. (Facets of Richmond's history.)

Warner, Ezra. *Generals in Gray*. Baton Rouge, 1959. (Biographical sketches of general officers.)

Warthen, Harry J., M.D. "Confederate Medicine." *Virginia Medical Monthly*. October, 1961, pp. 573-575.

*Washington and Lee University Bulletin*. 1963-1964.

Waterman, Thomas T. *The Mansions of Virginia, 1706-1776*. Chapel Hill, N.C., 1945.

Webb, Alexander S. *The Peninsula*. New York, 1885. (Standard account, by a Federal general.)

Weddell, Alexander W. *Richmond, Virginia, in Old Prints (1737-1857)*. Richmond, 1932.

Welch, Spencer G. *A Confederate Surgeon's Letters to His Wife*. New Edition: Marietta, Ga., 1954.

Wellman, Manly Wade. *Rebel Boast*. New York, 1956.

Wertenbaker, Thomas J. *The Planters of Colonial Virginia*. Princeton, 1922.

Wesley, Charles H. *The Collapse of the Confederacy*. Washington, 1937.

Wiley, Bell Irwin. *The Life of Johnny Reb*. Indianapolis, 1943.

———. *The Plain People of the Confederacy*. Baton Rouge, 1944.

———. *Southern Negroes 1861-1865*. New Haven, 1938.

Williams, Kenneth P. *Lincoln Finds a General*. New York, 1949, 2 vols.

Williams, T. Harry. "An Analysis of Some Reconstruction Attitudes." *Journal of Southern History*. November, 1946, pp. 469-486. (Succinct tracing of the various historical viewpoints on Reconstruction.)

———. *Beauregard: Napoleon in Gray*. Baton Rouge, 1954.

———. *Lincoln and the Radicals*. Wisconsin, 1941.

Wise, Jennings C. *The Long Arm of Lee*. New Edition: New York, 1959. (Standard on the artillery of Lee's army.)

Wise, John S. *The End of an Era*. Boston, 1927.

Wolseley, Field Marshal Viscount. The American Civil War: an English View. Edited with an Introduction by James A. Rawley. Charlottesville, Virginia, 1964.

(This collection of Wolseley's first-hand observations contains his well-known description and estimate of Lee.)

Wood, William Nathaniel. *Reminiscences of Big I.* Edited by Bell Irwin Wiley. New Edition: Jackson, Tenn., 1956.

Woodward, C. Vann. *Reunion and Reaction.* Boston, 1951.

Worsham, John H. *One of Jackson's Foot Cavalry.* New York, 1912. (A standard unit history — Richmond's Company F, a corps d'élite.)

*Wright, General A. R., Tribute to.* Privately printed pamphlet. (Through the courtesy of Miss Nell Wright Wise, the granddaughter of one of the few heroes of Malvern Hill.)

Wright, Mrs. D. Girand. *A Southern Girl in '61.* New York, 1905.

Wright, Louis B. *First Gentlemen of Virginia.* San Marino, Calif., 1940.

PERIODICALS

*Harper's Illustrated Weekly.* New York.
*Magnolia Weekly.* Richmond.
*Record.* Richmond.
Richmond *Dispatch.*
Richmond *Enquirer.*
Richmond *Examiner.*
*Southern Illustrated News.* Richmond.
*Southern Literary Messenger.* Richmond.

# Index